The Market is not Random

(Unabridged)

First Edition

by,
Anthony J. Klatch II

For the investors who trusted and for the traders who believe.

Thank you.

My Work and My Life have not been in Vain.

&

The Pursuit of Knowledge is Never Complete.

"To punish me for my contempt for authority, fate made me an authority myself."
- Albert Einstein

© 2012, 2013, 2014 by Anthony Joseph ("A.J.") Klatch II c/o Artlu Media Net Corporation.

All Rights Reserved.

Library of Congress Cataloguing Data Pending

Right Holder: Artlu Media Net Corporation

Registered With: The Writers Guild of America, West, Inc. / Registration #: 1718686

Klatch II, Anthony J. (A.J.)

The Market is not Random (Unabridged, First Edition)
/by Anthony Joseph Klatch II –

ISBN-13: 978-1499508727
ISBN-10: 1499508727

BISAC: Business & Economics / Finance / General – United States

anthonyklatch@gmail.com

Table of Contents

Forward	7
Introduction	9
Chapter 1: Trading versus Investing	17
Chapter 2: The Truth about Investing (i.e. Fundamental Analysis)	27
Chapter 3: Trading Styles and Capitalization	41
Chapter 4: Risk Management and Money Management	57
Chapter 5: Art, Science, Ego	69
Chapter 6: Price Structure	83
Chapter 7: Range Retracements	103
Chapter 8: Swings, Projections, Double Tops and Double Bottoms	123
Chapter 9: The trend (is your friend)	145
Chapter 10: Trendlines, Fans, and Triangles	157
Chapter 11: Common Patterns	169
Chapter 12: Wave Analysis and Corrective Phases	175
Chapter 13: Mathematical Clusters	187
Chapter 14: Technical Indicators	193
Chapter 15: Tape Reading	199
Chapter 16: Market Tendencies	213
Chapter 17: Time Structure	227
Chapter 18: Repetitions of Time	235
Chapter 19: Time Cycles	251
Chapter 20: Trading in Time	267
Chapter 21: Klatch's Contradiction to the Efficient Market Hypothesis	293
Afterward	299
Appendices	305
Appendix: How to Always Beat the Market	309

Forward

It was never the money. People always think it was the money. It was the pursuit. It was doing what humankind has never been able to do. It was a feeling – a necessity – instilled in me since I had conscious, memorable thought. It was a drive and a magnetic attraction. It bordered on love, and it became a true obsession. It was an all-encompassing mindset that led to irrationality because of a belief in a purpose; a purpose to quantify and define what no man has yet to do. That is the why.

The market is. It exists. It is never-ending. It can be personified. It is an organism that man created, which unknowingly became a palpable connection to our Creator, and it is a report card for our efficient use of balancing the resources given to us. In some ways, it is alive. It has taken lives. It has destroyed lives. It has led to riches beyond compare, and it has led to inefficiencies that were exploitable. It changes the course of humanity. It changes what drugs come to market. It changes what diseases are cured. It changes who eats what, where, and when. The market is its own dynamic, and everything links back to it. There is nothing else that can compare, and aside from prayer, there is no other object on earth that commands as much attention; not law, not medicine. Only God and the market exist in a realm of cumulative intelligence affirmation. It is in those two realms of thought that one can understand the power of the financial markets. It is in those two realms of thought where we can visualize and connect with the future, which allows man to unite his mentality in the present moment with true divinity.

With this line of thought, dear reader, you can see that the market means more to me than money. Money is the eventual output; that is all. My obsession with the market reached addiction level in 2004. Everything else except for love became meaningless in my life. As such, I give myself the title of Financial Scientist. Just like a genetic scientists spent decades decoding the human genome, I have spent my entire life decoding the market; taking in other people's thoughts and ideas, and making them quantifiable; making them understandable and teachable. Although there is no branch of collegiate learning that can grant a doctorate of Financial Science, it is my belief that this book is the start-point of uncovering this new field of quantitative study that I define as the **Marketome**, and this book is my "On the Origin of Species" or my "Wealth of Nations."

Thomas Edison used to say, "Ideas are in the air, and you just have to pick them out." Amazingly, there is truth to that statement, and this line of thinking has even been classified as parapsychology. Interestingly, many universities, including some as prestigious as Duke, have research departments focused on this theory. In essence, parapsychology is the belief that we, as humans, have access to a subconscious network of information outside of our mind, and psychiatrists have acknowledged this throughout the years as well. Hence, in a way, I have come to realize that my construction of this book was borne from this unquantifiable ethos while still being based on a learned, but incomplete, skill. Ironically, I now believe that this book has led to the completion of that skill, and in order for me to now effectively build a respectable money management track record, I have realized that I had to reach the point in my life where I was given the time and the distance from the market in order to place the knowledge of this book into a learned, practical realm. For this reason, I have come to believe that I had to write this book in order to connect the missing mental links in my brain between trade theory and actual trade execution. Therefore, I gravitate towards the realm of parapsychology disbelief because, although many of the concepts in this book were taught to me, many more conclusions, ideas, and assertions that I achieved by writing this book just seemed to come "out of the air."

Fascinatingly, I say this because upon rereading portions of this book, even I find some ideas hard to comprehend. Sure, in my mind, I knew all of these concepts to some degree, but only by writing this book and taking a break from the markets, did I finally reach a complete understanding of the true market structure. As such, the interesting observation that not everything constructed herein was part of my learning and that some of the ideas and derived conclusions were not part of my apprenticing relationships, with the three trading mentors I have had in my life, has been mysteriously mind-bending. In a way, the definitions, the formulas, and the connectivity that I found while writing this book seemed to exist, and I just had to avail my mind to linking that information from an untapped resource – be it external or internal remains the parapsychology mystery.

For all of these reasons, I believe that I succeeded in defining the Marketome by writing this book, and I believe that this book is full and complete. ***Technically***, this is the end; the culmination, but at the same time, it is the beginning; the genesis of moving technical analysis into the ***correct*** path of study.

Amazingly, over the past 10 years, I have come to learn that I do not have an inventive or a creative mind. No, I believe that my mind and my intellect is that of efficiency. I have the ability to take in, comprehend, and reiterate anything. I have the ability to make it better, and to make it understandable. Subconsciously, I pursued an educational path that focuses on efficiency: Industrial Engineering and Project Management. In a way, a mind like mine was necessary in order to be able to refine the thoughts that have existed since the markets began, and I have been able to bring this book to the masses by applying rational efficiency to these concepts. Therefore, I have no doubt that this book is the start of a new technical collegiate, teaching revolution, which I believe is necessary due to the imminent death of traditional investment banking. I say this because, as humanity becomes more globalized and as technology allows for greater pricing efficiency, the past methods of market approach will become obsolete. Instead, we will find and define a new era of money management that has to deal with the true structure of the market, and building computational algorithms that make pricing efficient will be the next wave of financial market philosophy. Thus, this book is the start of these future algorithmic implementations, and this book lays the groundwork for the future quants. Ironically, this is done by relying on the concepts that were defined in the past before computers even existed. Furthermore, the importance of using the Marketome in order to increase the efficient use of resources, which ultimately ties back to the efficient pricing of markets, cannot be understated because I believe that the world needs to embrace this new era of computational, quantitative efficiency. If the world chooses not to, humanity will reach a point of inefficiency that causes a continuous depletion of resources. Should that happen, we will cease to exist, and the fiat money system will implode. The only question is, "Are we already too late?"

Lastly, this book is not a typical book. Upon my edits, I realized that I have written this book as three books in one. This was done because I believe that I must give the reader an adequate, collegiate-level, technical discussion about the learned material presented herein, but at the same time, I need to explain to the reader the method in which this technical material was learned. I believe this is necessary because the sacrifice and the life story that I gave to the market is something that I believe is worth presenting in order for the masses to understand my market awareness. Thus, the first parts of this book also palpably illustrate the psychological component that exists in the trader's mind, and I believe this component broke down in my head because of the obsession to define the indefinable, which led to my federal incarceration. Therefore, the first part of this book is a presentation of this technical knowledge, but at the same time, the first part of this book is also the psychological extrapolation of what I learned through trading execution-based discovery. Further, I believe that the insights presented by that personal, intrinsic discovery process are valid to the reader. Contrarily, the second part of this book, which I have dubbed, "The Campaign," is a focused autobiography of sorts, and it shows the reader the pursuit of this knowledge. I believe this autobiography is necessary because of my age and my unorthodox approach to an atypical Wall Street career, and the autobiography serves as a testament to the reader of my own brilliance and my own love/obsession for the market. Hence, my age and my incarceration must be mitigated because my purpose was to quantify and to define the markets as an inherent structure, which has never been done before. Therefore, with my level of knowledge and my life sacrifice to attain this knowledge presented to the reader, I must say that I feel that I have done something for humanity that can never be done again, because, by writing this book, I have defined a methodology in order to quantify any market in any time frame, which means that I have proven, "The Market is not Random."

Introduction

As I write this book, I acknowledge that the reader has the right to know the truth regarding the author because of the claims that will be stated in this book regarding the superiority of the *Time and Price Symmetry* method to portfolio management. What you will learn by understanding the implementation of *Time and Price Symmetry* is a quantitative ability to reach a deterministic value for time and for price that the market will respect in the future. However, despite my obsession in deducing this methodology, the truth is that I have lived the life of a failed trader on my pursuit of attaining this knowledge. I have failed and bankrupted five investment companies / hedge funds since I began trading in 1999, and even more amazing, I did this all before my 27th birthday. However, for me, the pursuit of knowledge was the goal because, ever since I can remember, I believed that there had to exist a true market structure that would work forever; hence the definition as Marketome as given in the *Forward*. This belief was necessary because my love for the market told me that I needed to find a method that could work until my dying day. In a way, this knowledge was the pursuit of finding a lifelong skill that could not be effaced as humanity advances, and after 12 years of study, I found and I have defined that structure to the masses.

In the beginning of my career, my failures were due to not having an understanding of the Marketome, but once I learned of *Time and Price Symmetry,* my confidence became an enemy. When I found the knowledge that I sought for nearly 12 years, I became disillusioned with my own abilities; I forgot to remain humble and in the present moment. I was acting under the belief that I was always running out of time, and by writing this book and by analyzing my life story, I have come to realize that I have never been properly capitalized at any point in my trading career. Eventually, my obsessions with the knowledge that I am putting into this book led to a severe addiction to the market, and I have come to realize that I sleep deprived myself for 8 years, which lead to an irrational mentality with respect to my physical health, my mental health, and to the law. Once my obsession caused my mind to break, I wantonly broke the law in order to keep my lifestyle growing while simultaneously allowing me to continue my education and my validation-seeking outlook with respect to *Time and Price Symmetry*. That irrational mentality ultimately led to a Federal Indictment through actions that I believe never had criminal intent. No, my actions had a higher goal of holistic market attainment, but the representatives of the United States were not intelligent enough in order to understand nor believe that statement. However, my mental disablement was stabilized by my incarceration, and I have been given the break I needed in order to finish defining the knowledge that I acquired, quite literally, over my entire conscious lifetime.

Further, *Time and Price Symmetry* execution and understanding is not a passive approach to portfolio management, and in a way, I define it as a market-based *artistic* approach. This artistic implementation of *Time and Price Symmetry* is not akin to other technical analysis-like techniques whereby the analyst waits for a stock to reach a moving average, and then, enter the position. No, *Time and Price Symmetry* is a continuous updating and a continuous labeling of the inherent market structure in order to correctly understand the future, possible market inflection points. The *Time and Price Symmetry* trader will always be engaged in this process in order to accurately define these inflection points in terms of price clusters and in terms of time windows. Therefore, the ease that initially seems apparent from this text becomes arduous once properly implemented. Thus, *Time and Price Symmetry* is an interactive trading style that becomes very hard if one was to trade multiple instruments at one time, which is why I will recommend that the reader becomes a specialist in one market-trading instrument.

Moving on, I must state that upon first read, this book may seem simplistic to some, but that simplicity will only exist in those who have found success in this industry or those who believe that technical analysis is fake. Both of those biases are derived from pride and from ego. The power and the worth of this book are both extreme, and I ask the biased reader to understand that this book has a hidden level to it that I call **Quantitative Synchronicity**, which will be defined within this text. However, essentially, Quantitative Synchronicity is the understanding of how every subject in this book exists in multiple time period simultaneously, and one's brain must synchronize the summation of these market-based objectives in order to form the complete market picture. Reaching that level, by using the concepts of this book, is far from easy, and maybe, it too relies on some type of parapsychology. Therefore, the depth of the teachings of this book is multidimensional because Quantitative Synchronicity is the third, unseen dimension to the markets, and in order to explain this dimension of market depth, I must use visualization.

If one is an Apple OS X Operating System user, there is an application called Time Machine, which is used for backups. When you engage the Time Machine application while viewing a folder, you see an infinite collection of images that represent what is in that folder over various time frames, which go back in time in an orderly fashion. This time-stacked display appears three-dimensional from a two-dimensional view of a simple folder. In a way, Quantitative Synchronicity is the same thing because we begin with a static two-dimensional image of Time versus Price, but then, we take more images of that relationship in varying time frames (one minute chart, 60 minute chart, daily chart, etc.). Once we take those images, we form a cube that is created by stacking those charts together (a composite of synchronizing market objectives), *which gives the market its depth*. Hence, Quantitative Synchronicity is the depth of the market, and as any graphic designer will tell you, two-dimensional animation production is simplistic compared to three-dimensional image constructions. Hence, we must understand that although the two-dimensional study presented in this book as *Time and Price Symmetry* may seem elementary to begin with, ultimately, the cumulative understandings derived from watching the market adhere to the structure defined in this book, in multiple time frames (via Quantitative Synchronicity), is what is needed for the market participant to achieve extreme success. What's more, that level of cumulative understanding must be built in one's mind, and getting to that point will require a total commitment to the market while surrendering oneself to the present moment. Only then, will another dimension of higher thought processes emerge, and only then, will *Time and Price Symmetry* fall into a realm of profitability and comprehension.

Therefore, like Dr. Nash's Game Theory, I believe that the theories and the conclusions stated in this book will take many years to be fully comprehended by the masses. For instance, W.D. Gann's books have been around for nearly 100 years now, and so far, no one has been able to understand the conclusive thought paths that he had with respect to the market (until now). Only within this information-age has it been possible to take his teachings to the next level, and therefore, I have been able to build off that knowledge in order to define what he could not. What is more, I believe that it has been my life purpose to write this book as an appeal to the educated masses in order to shift their focus. By doing so, the theories and ideas herein can be deduced into logical conclusions that can be quantified and taught to others.

As such, I must tell the reader one last thing before we begin down this path of understanding the true market structure. Unequivocally, please understand that I believe attaining the knowledge in this book was my life purpose since I was 12 years old; a purpose that I had to keep hidden and denied from others. However, what remains undeniable is that now, I believe that my purpose is now complete, and in a way, I believe that there is absolutely nothing left for me to learn with respect to the financial markets.

Now, in some ways, I feel that I need to discuss the timeline that was used for me to attain the knowledge in this book. Thus, I would say that by March of 2009, I had a Bachelor's Degree in *Time and Price Symmetry*. Concurrently, I would say that I had obtained a Master's Degree equivalent by the first quarter of 2010, which was when I lived with my mentor, and lastly, I feel that this first edition of *The Market is not Random,* is my doctoral thesis, which would justify an equivalent degree conference. Therefore, this book serves as my thesis as well as my life story.

Throughout this book, I will take the reader through the learning process of quantifying every relevant high and low that is made in the markets in regards to the price level of that high or low and the anticipated time that the high or low occurs. This approach will fundamentally look at the X-Y relationship that exists, simply, because it has to, based on how price structure and time structure work. Furthermore, this book is an existential extrapolation in regards to my own trading psychology because the psychology of trading is one of the hardest mental battles that we, as humans, can undertake. This inherent understanding is also helpful for the reader because, as market participants, our careers and our lives are constantly at risk. As such, throughout this book, you will see me refer to several psychological-based definitions that I have had to research in order to properly quantify my own psyche. Interestingly, I have always had a proclivity towards Psychiatry, and amazingly, it is my belief that the markets themselves are an extrapolation of every human mind's contribution at any given present moment. Thus, it is my belief that *an individual's psychology in relation to trading is more important than the person's trading strategy.* As such, without me realizing it, over the past few years, my love of the markets has also satisfied my mind's curiosity with psychiatry/psychology. Simultaneously and contrarily, I do not claim to the reader to be any type of psychological expert, but I have no doubt that my level of study in understanding how to accomplish extreme goals via psychological mind management with respect to the markets has been just as much of a goal as defining the market itself. Further, I believe that a trader needs to always understand and be in control of his or her psyche in order to be successful in the markets, and this, too, is part of the learning process that every trader must go through. Unfortunately, it is not the job of this book to make the reader aware of how to embark on his or her internal learning process, but the complete trading picture would be missing without a heavy focus on psychology.

Although my ego is palpable throughout these writings, I believe that my story of attaining the knowledge herein is quite interesting because I believe that if I went the traditional Wall Street way, I never would have learned the skill that I always sought. Therefore, in a separate book, which I have dubbed "The Campaign," I will simply explain the story of my life through this extrapolated life-story based *curriculum vitae*. More important, because of my failures, I feel that I need to discuss the psychological traumas I was under that led to an aversion of profit, and why I believe I am now free of that trauma. Therefore, the purpose to writing this book functions on two levels in higher cognitive thinking processes. First, this book teaches the ability to learn a strategy that will never fail you, and second, this book illustrates the amount of time and the amount of energy that we, as traders, must exert in order to properly understand how to make our psyche aligned to success. Again, learning to train our ego will be just as important as any trading strategy. Quite simply, I believe my life story needs to be told and needs to be understood if I am to get another chance in this industry because I need to show that I accept responsibility for my actions by making the masses comprehend the power of the kind of knowledge and conviction one gains by learning *Time and Price Symmetry*. Essentially, I feel that true egoism becomes paramount when one knows exactly what will happen in the market, on an hourly basis, and this edification can lead to such a feeling of certainty that nothing else will matter. But reaching that level of attainment came at an irrational price because it cost me the person I loved the most.

Now with that preamble being stated, I must be clear to the reader, and say that I do not believe that *Time and Price Symmetry* is a market strategy. I do not believe it is some magic formula. No, it is a way to anticipate and calculate future, *possible* points where the markets will find support and resistance, and trading strategies can be built around that knowledge. Further, this knowledge must be coupled with understanding and comprehending the overall trend, which requires an ethereal qualitative argument with quantitative time and price structured components. Therefore, the level of intellect needed in order to properly define every single movement that any market makes is only the first step of *Time and Price Symmetry*, and the true task comes from being able to profit from that knowledge. That is why I have no fear in putting this knowledge into the public realm. It takes years and it takes commitment to become profitable. But I must caution, no book can teach you how to properly train your psyche in order to profit from the market, and I do not know if good traders are born or made. However, there are hundreds of books in regards to trading psychology, and all of them, at their true basis, are some form of psycho-cybernetics. As such, the trader must learn to live within the mind of one's self in order to visualize the necessary components that must be aligned in order to generate profits, and it takes years of observation and years of ridding the mind of emotion with respect to trading decisions in order to become successful. As such, even through incarceration, the knowledge that I have regarding the market is not completely put to waste. In fact, the mind does not differentiate between an actively lived experience or an experience created within the mind itself. Therefore, in a way, my incarceration has been able to free me from my stresses by making my worst fears come true, and instead of targeting a $6mm trading objective, I am spending every, single day visualizing the path to managing $1T.

The power of living within the mind is something that people of this current generation are losing very quickly. The ability to connect every human impulse fiber optically to whatever that human wants is becoming part of our actual mechanical structure. Our devices – our smart-phones – are constantly available to us in order to feed our desires. Sadly, these devices also cause us to engage in continual distraction. The human mind was built in order to allow the subconscious to have freedom to solve problems, and in fact, many people believe the subconscious derives its ideas/conclusions from a superior Creator. In a way, human society is losing the ability to have one individual be able to change the world for the better; instead, it is the combined efforts of the masses that now causes the thought revolution that changes the world. Therefore, I must ask, "Where is this generation's Archimedes, Pascal, Newton, DaVinci, or Einstein?" I would argue that using a group mentality to accomplish significant goals is a step backwards because every single person should be allowed to have their subconscious needs be satisfied. Without that fulfillment, every human will feel a longing with respect to his or her existence. In fact, I believe that the level of psychological depression that is now being felt by the masses is derived from the fact that most humans are never able to execute in a fashion that allows their subconscious directive to be fulfilled. Who knows, but maybe the fact that I have found my own subconscious mind's purpose will make me one of the great "thinkers" of this generation. This line of thinking is why in some ways; my arrest has been healthy for me. It allowed my mind to finally digest the past 15 years of my life; my Marketome education. It allowed me to use the autonomic mechanisms of my subconscious in order to properly interconnect my knowledge to my goals by making my goals a certainty instead of a mere possibility. Henceforward, incarceration is a very peaceful experience that allows a person to become healthy in mind and in body once a person removes the fear from the equation. However, it is quite sad that most human beings have no clue of the potential they have in being able to live within the mind. The mind is incredible, and the fact that I was mentally preparing myself to live in a consciousness that can affect my subconscious through the books I have gravitated to over the past fifteen years is now being put to use by refining my thought processes in a peaceful way. I can now take a break for a few years in order to set my mind and my sights on much larger goals through this incarceration. With those goals redefined, I have no doubt that I can quickly rejoin myself to being a member of the "Superclass" (as dubbed by Peter Rothkopf), which I see as a main objective for my life, because my incarceration took me from being in the top 1% to the bottom 1% overnight (talk about social mobility).

Hence, the ability to interface with members of the "Superclass" is just as much a motive for me as monetary attainment because I want to resume the path that my life was on before my arrest, which will become apparent by anyone who has followed my life. In fact, one of my endearing hopes that I have with respect to writing this book is that a member of the said "Superclass" values my market knowledge to the point whereby I will be immediately welcomed back to the Financial Industry because I believe that my level of knowledge is equitable to the select few money managers that make centi-million dollar salaries every year from their own trading or their own hedge funds. Thus, I feel that my level of knowledge is equitable to that pay level because of the value I could provide to a multi-billion-dollar hedge fund through *Time and Price Symmetry*, and I do not say this for edification but with pure conviction in my level of knowledge, which is why I have written and included the autobiographical section in this one book. In addition, I believe that the push to more and more transparency is going to be required by even the members of the "Superclass," as technology evolves, which means that Fu Chenguy's (a member of the "Superclass") comments about transparency are valid, when he said, "Transparency makes shareholders love you." Thus, that transparency is what I want to have for anyone I engage in business with again because it is a necessary reality due to my incarceration because there exists the idiotic, biased conclusions in the general masses that were echoed in the Wall St. Journal (September 22/23rd editions) by Gerri Walsh, the Vice President of FINRA, that has validity towards mass populous perception whereby her comment, "There is a fair amount of recidivism when it comes to fraud," gains validity. Her comment is not only biased, but totally lacking judgment because fraud exists in many ways. Thus, it is the intent behind the fraud, which is *supposed to matter*. That is why I wish to publish my autobiography in order for the reader or for a member of the "Superclass" to understand that my intent was never criminal; nor was it premeditated.

Going back to the mind, these mass perceptions of convicts and criminals has to be changed, and that is why I have needed to focus on my mind. Further, in order to illustrate the power that one needs from their subconscious mind with respect to trading is apparent in my trading logs over the 16 months prior to my arrest. During that time, I was cooperating with the government on their civil investigation because I never believed I did anything criminal. However, during those 16 months, my trading showed a series of consistent profits, and then, one day of dramatic losses, which coincided with more requests from the government. Eventually, in late April of 2011, the government seemed to "stop" their investigation, and once I finally felt free from the baggage I carried for the last 7 years, I was able to logically and methodically trade for the first time since 2007! Therefore, I beg the reader to use my life and the knowledge of the first five chapters of this book in order to truly prepare you for the life of a trader. Please, learn from my mistakes, and please remember how important a healthy mind is with respect to trading.

Thankfully, as I write this book, I am only 27 years old, and the fact that I am writing this book at such a young age should testify to my brilliance. What is more, I will get another chance at my life by my 30th birthday, which will finally be baggage free and lifestyle free. However, the saddest thing I now have to face is the fact that the CFTC has achieved a permanent injunction to prohibit me from trading futures for the rest of my life. However, I am optimistic that I can fight the permanence of that injunction, and if I cannot, well I will be relegated to being an equities trader or a fund of funds manager, as stated. I feel that this is the saddest thing of all because it prohibits me from repaying my debt to those I have harmed, and furthermore, I have no doubt that I would be a billionaire trader within ten years of re-entering the market after my release from Federal prison, but that path becomes much harder with my injunction. Moving on, I pray that my story, my life, and my sacrifices are not what it takes to become successful in this industry, but it may be what is necessary in order to be regarded as one of the best traders of all time. Every person has a story, and the story of one's life is more important than the money that person has made. As a word of caution, the power of *Time and Price Symmetry* is so life changing that from the instant the trader grasps these concepts and these understandings, there will be a sense of egotistical empowerment that can lead to irrational decision-making based on unjustified prior results and/or risk management techniques. Therefore, it must further be cautioned that it will take years of observation in order to gain the intrinsically learned knowledge base that will justify the trader's confidence. Ultimately, the subconscious thought processes is where trade inceptions must occur via the mind's recognition of past experiences. As such, this book is not a magic formula or some-type of easy theory to be practiced. It is the actual market structure that exists in front of our eyes by divinity. In fact, I will provide the necessary logic that one could use to define every relevant price level that serves as a major high or a major low. This is a structure that goes back to the beginning of markets, and it is a structure that allows a trader to look at a chart from 1892, 1992, or eventually 2092 and see the same structure. Just like God, this market structure *has always existed and will always exist.*

As part of that same logic, I must also alert the reader to something important regarding this ever-present Marketome, with respect to this book, and that important subject is the relevant audience for this book coupled with the examples listed herein. Since this book has been hybridized in order to push the gist of these concepts into the reader's mind, this book has been simultaneously been written for those of a collegiate level. No doubt, I envision this book becoming further collegiatized in the future, but as for now, I have tried to write this book for all educated, audiences, which will be discussed momentarily within this *Introduction*. That being said, I must also state that I have tried to use as many examples from the 2007-2012 market time period because it is my belief that this latest market crash has been widely disseminated and understood by the masses. However, as another word of clarification, *I am not* using these examples in order to confirm the writings of this book. No, instead, I ask the reader to be aware of the fact that I have tried my best in order to use the latest time relevancy for examples discussed herein, but the simultaneous reality that must be understood by the reader is that I could have just as easily pulled up 10-year charts from, let us say, the 1970s. Had I decided to use those charts, I would have been able to just as easily write this book and convey the Marketome examples to the reader. What is more, I am writing this first version of this book while being incarcerated, which means my materials used to construct this book are highly limited because I do not have internet access in order to pull up chart examples. However, I see that limitation as a positive thing because I have recreated over 60 charts by hand for this book, which does not have any "market noise," and I believe that lack of *noise* will help the reader understand the concepts in this book.

    Another thing that I have learned about this federal incarceration period of my life is that had I not been incarcerated, the theorems and the conclusions that I have been able to come to would never have happened, and maybe this was all a part of God's predestination plan for me because I learned many things by writing this book. In fact, even though I had all of the mechanics taught to me before being incarcerated, I had no idea of how powerful some of those mechanics are in the market. Therefore, by writing this book, I have completely changed my thought path regarding the market's underlying objectives. In a way, I feel like this incarceration process was necessary for me to finally understand everything that I have learned over the last 15 years. As Leonardo DaVinci once said, "It is the moment they are working the least that higher minds achieve the most." By finally returning to a normal sleep cycle and properly taking myself away from 14-hour workdays, I have been able to understand *Time and Price Symmetry* on an entirely new plane. As such, I am extremely excited to enter the trading world again upon my release from Federal Custody on January 2015 because I believe my entire trading strategy has now matured and changed. I have been forced to grow up in many ways. Conclusively, I believe that I can now state that my past performances were not indicative of my forthcoming, future results.

PERCEPTIONS

Chapter 1

Trading versus Investing

Like everyone, when I first started to look at the Stock Market, I was intrigued by the idea of buying a part of a company in order to take ownership in that company. I was unaware of the trading nature that existed as an underlying profit generator for many individuals. However, my mathematical inclinations soon became satiated with the fact that there must be some type of logical reason behind what the market is doing. I could not simply believe the common affirmation that the market is random; that every day is a "crap shoot." As such, I spent the first 7 years of my relationship with the markets spending every extra-minute I had reading countless books about technical and fundamental analysis. Simply put, I was too egotistical to drink the same Kool-Aid as everyone else. However, there was never any common theme in my aimless readings except in regards to trading psychology, which I now deem as paramount to working in this industry. Hence, my belief focused on the fact that the Law of Attraction is at play within our universe, and invoking its attributes is necessary for any trader or for any investor to be psychologically honed for this career choice. Only by visualizing goals can one understand how to use the market in order to attain those goals. Without that visualization, the market participant is as aimless as a lemming. As such, we must first describe what a market truly is if we are to profit from it.

The **market** (any single market) is simply a way of discovering price clusters and time windows that allow for trade inception points, and unarguably, the reactive price cluster can be derived from supply and demand laws, whereas, the time component remains an educational mystery. However, I encourage the reader to understand how powerful the market is. I encourage the reader to view the market as I do; as The Great Equation that serves as humanities efforts to utilize its resources. With that level of respect given to a market, the trader will already elevate their subconscious seriousness. Similarly, it is interesting to note that as humanity begins to consume more than it produced, there has always been a need to create money that was no longer backed by material goods. This, in effect, became the fiat money system that now exists in today's world. Fortunately, because of the illusory nature of this money system, there exists the potential for irrationality to emerge through volatility or governmental action. I deem this as fortunate because this is where profits can be made; this is where *Time and Price Symmetry* gains validity along with the vocation of trading itself.

All of this being said, I forewarn the reader that history has shown us that every fiat money system has eventually failed, and I have no doubt that our own system will one day collapse. The market participant must be aware of this because the reality of monetary illusory is the second introductory component that I wish to emphasize to the reader. Hence, the level of fear can be removed once the trader realizes that this system is fake and is fragile. What is more, I believe that only by eradicating the fiat money system, will we ever be able to reach a solution to The Great Equation, which would balance supply and demand harmoniously, but this fiat monetary system abandonment would be disastrous to us traders because thankfully, with *Time and Price Symmetry* acting as our guide, we have the ability to view the market as a machine that can provide consistent profits regardless of trading style or goals. Even more thankful, we can use *Time and Price Symmetry* on any asset that trades as well. As such, if the fiat money system does fail, we will still have a working methodology regardless of monetary policy.

So, the reader may ask, "What exactly is *Time and Price Symmetry?*" Well, in the *Introduction*, I acknowledged that it is a method of navigation for the markets, and it is a way to approach the markets with respect to any trading instrument in any time frame. However, the pure definition that I will give for this book with respect to *Time and Price Symmetry* is that it is a structural approach to any trading market that has enough liquidity in that market in order for historic data to record a visual, rhythmic pulse, similar to a heartbeat, which is repeated and echoed through future price levels and at future times. The key to *Time and Price Symmetry* is that the underlying market instrument must be liquid and tradable.

Market Morality

Since the beginning of capitalism, there has been a perspective of mystery and anger towards those that have achieved extreme wealth through the markets. Often, this is because that wealth may have come at the expense of others. For example, a private equity company that buys a corporation, fires its employees, and then, sells the underlying assets for a profit is considered an evil thing that must be tolerated within capitalism. However, markets and capitalism have also attracted many other negative connotations over the past several years with scandals like Enron, Bernie Madoff, or me. Unfortunately, in several ways, the future progress of society acquiesces to the needs of society without respect to morality or to religion; just as the money manager acquiesces to the needs of the market. One of the most famous arguments to support this conclusion was done by Phillip Yancey in his essay entitled *Immediate Gratification in American Society,* which is self-explanatory. Sorrowfully, unknown to many is that there are actually people who stand up to this moral debasement to society, and the most famous example, which illustrates the power of divinity within one human mind is when Pope Paul VI decided that contraception was against Roman Catholicism even though the Cardinals voted 52-4 to accept contraception. Therefore, actions like that (and I am in no way saying I am against contraception) show that sometimes the needs of society can be wrong, which I feel is important because sometimes the money manager acquiesces to the needs of himself, and within that mindset there is the death of personal morality. Not only is this selfish compulsion of money managers misguided, but it is also a breach of fiduciary duty on behalf of the money manager's clients. However, current income structure of the market is tailored to this bonus-like approach, and this too will require a discussion in later chapters.

Over the years, there have been several people to illustrate and to question this debasement approach to morality by comparing God to money or capitalism. These famous minds such as Freidrich Hayek, Reinhold Neibuhr, G.K. Chesterton, Charles McDaniel, John Maynard Keyes, Milton Friedman, and Pope John Paul II, have always challenged the conventional thinking of the various economic theories. Regardless of their amazing contributions to this subject matter, I have to state that I believe, unarguably, that capitalism pushes forward regardless of ethics because of the inherent, sin/evil of man (or more precisely Man's Will versus God's Will). Now, that being said, there is something important to realize about money management, and this book is not a book to trounce capitalism because only if governments become capitalistic themselves will they survive within the capitalist inevitability constructed by the fiat money system, as I alluded to in the *Introduction*. However, there is a moral responsibility that is tied to money and to intelligence, and this responsible, relevant conduct will be a constant theme in these Perception-oriented beginning chapters because profitable traders hold higher responsibilities within the constructs of society, due to their inherent power gained by the vocation of money management. Thankfully, Freidrich Hayek said this best in that "every human being is led by the growth of civilization into a path that is not of his [or her] own choosing." But, what is not stated or realized by Hayek is that wealth becomes a predominant factor that changes the plan of civilization, and obviously, money managers are the group of people that end up with the most influential power whether they realize it or not. Therefore, in order to understand this morality obligation with respect to money managers, I need to refer to a very important characteristic regarding opportunity costs with respect to the markets because this is not an obvious conclusion, and it requires a change in one's perceptions as well, which ironically, is to the benefit of the market participant.

Gloria Zuniga postulated this argument quite succinctly in her 1998 commentary entitled *Truth in Economic Subjectivism.* In that text, she discussed the moral component of money based on the opportunity cost between purchasing different examples of hats. Let me summarizes her example by saying to the reader, "What happens if you are faced with the decision to buy two hats, one red and one blue.? Is this a moral decision?" In the beginning, if both hats cost the same amount of money, $20, then, No. However, what happens if the red hat is $40 and the blue hat is $20? Now, is there a moral decision? Not only will there be a mental, preferential shift to the cheaper item for the average person, but also there will be a moral component to the cheaper item, which is very important to understand with respect to morality and the markets because undoubtedly, people in capitalistic societies never think about this moral component because the truth is that, in a way, if someone chooses to buy the $40 hat, that person is deciding to make a morally degrading decision. However, that conclusion is not readily palpable and it is not easily connected in one's mind when one clicks the buy or sell button with respect to trading. Granted, there is also a personal preference to the hats, which could be a factor, but let us assume that for us money managers we have a proclivity towards everything more expensive because money is more abundant for people in this career path. Therefore, regardless of personal preference, we have an egotistical desire towards the more expensive hat even if we don't like the color red! This is why the morality of the money manager is different then the average person in capitalism. We have disregard to others and we have that disregard because of our superior intellect that is edified by profits. However, this selfish tendency needs to change, and the money manager needs to be cognizant and aware of his or her decisions whether it is buying Apple Stock or buying the "red hat" because, as Ms. Zuniga points out, the $20 opportunity cost that was used to buy the more expensive hat could have been used to feed the poor or help the homeless. As such, I begin to form my logic for this discussion, which holds relevance to the importance of our jobs as market participants.

As traders, investors, or money managers, we are faced with opportunity costs all of the time, but often, we do not think of the opportunity cost with respect to morality; there is a hidden component that exists within the trade itself, and that moral existence must be acknowledged if we are to benefit our fellow man from trading. Herein we come to a third way that I am asking the reader to realize the importance of the reader's job as being a market participant because the respect given to these market-based vocations must be emphasized within the subconscious framework of one's mind if success is to exist. In fact, the only reason I choose to acknowledge this morality is not because of God or because of ethics, but because these postulates can change the seriousness of one's trades or one's investments. By being morally conscious, we can selfishly benefit ourselves, which leads to a direct correlation on negatively affecting others! As such, the reader needs to realize that a decision to place a trade could be at a cost to doing human benefit, – doing something good – and this *type of thought is powerful*. This type of thought allows the inception of seriousness that will continue to be elaborated on in these first five chapters with respect to the market. In fact, famed economist Michael Novak says this best when he implies that "the existence of markets is evidence of their virtuosity for the market's dependence upon [social virtues] is very high." Further, Novak has stated "a business [or market-oriented (for the sake of this book)] career is not only a morally serious vocation but a morally noble one."

This begs the question, "Have you ever considered trading and the markets noble?" Undoubtedly, the answer is no, and that is because of how the image of capitalism is currently being portrayed through protestation events such as the "Occupy Movement." Thus, it is a sorry sight to see the American populous become lazy and not only bow-down to socialist-like implementations. No, the average American is encouraging them! Ergo, instead of striving to be the best, the average American, who is disillusioned by such idiocy as the "Occupy Movement," is stating that he/she has lost his or her desire to strive for excellence. Now, the average American would rather be comfortable and lazy because technology has afforded a level of comfort that has eliminated the "survival of the fittest instinct," and this inherent belief in governmental assistance is not capitalism. What is more, a government that is supposedly capitalistic has acquiesced to this new directive in an alarmingly short amount of time. Thus, it is a sorry sight to see capitalistic practices bow down to regulation and socialist implementations in American life, and even sadder is that this is done without mass recognition or understanding. Regardless, my hope with this morality discussion to the reader is simply a continuation of my *Forward* that started this book because of the seriousness and respect that one must have and maintain in order to enjoy a career of longevity, and more important, *meaning* in the markets.

Often, money managers find *meaning* difficult in their job as their age in this current day. In fact, that lack of meaning is why the average money manager tends to change their vocation in later life, but if you morally approach the markets with a sense of responsibility, I assert that you can find meaning every day. In essence, proper, serious money management is noble because it can lead to one's own impact on society, and unarguably, society is now delusional by no longer understanding what the correct definition of capitalism is for this current (my) generation. Because, unfortunately for today's world, American society has no idea what capitalism used to be like, and frankly, neither do I. Hence, my understanding of individualized capitalism is that because of my intellectual faculties, I have a responsibility to my heirs, which is to attract as many assets (capital) as possible, in order for me and me alone to fit the definition of acting as a true capitalist. Unfortunately, in this generation, that outlook is now seen as evil! What's more the average American now comes to the first conclusion that capitalism takes its root in evil practices such as insider trading or insider information. The new age capitalist is currently seeing capitalism as a bad thing, which in turn means that immense wealth is a bad thing. Concurrently, us capitalists are to blame for this evil understanding because most true capitalists have done wrongful and hurtful things to others in order to make themselves satiated. However, that is simply Darwinism at its finest! Thus, the new age capitalist needs to understand that these old, evil capitalistic ways are dying because as technology and government have continued to expand, that inefficient application of a market-based vocation is slowly reaching cessation, which is directly correlated to my own experience as a now, imprisoned money manager. Hence, we are reaching a level of new capitalism, which requires a true capitalist to attract capital via some superior mental or physical faculty, which should be great news. Thereby, I think it is funny to conclude this section of this book by a famous paragraph from G.K. Chesterton's essay "On a Sense of Proportion" dealing with self-delusions of the traditional capitalist from 1986:

> He [the capitalist] puts on his curious and creative hat, built on some bold plan entirely made up out of his own curious and creative head. He walks outside his unique and unparalleled house, also built with his own well-won wealth according to his own well-conceived architectural design, and seemingly by its very outline against the sky to express his own passionate personality. He strides down the street, making his own way over hill and dale towards the place of his own chosen and favourite labour, the workshop of his imaginative craft. He lingers on the way now to pluck a flower, now to compose a poem, for his time is his own; he is an individual and free man and not as these Communists. He can work at his own craft when he will, and labour far into the night to make up for an idle morning.

I believe that quotation's irony is necessary concerning market-morality because we must not be disillusioned that we are masters of our own destiny in the markets despite capitalistic infrastructure. We, as market participants, cannot decide when we can "linger to pluck a flower," and if we do decide to linger too long, the markets (the true capitalists) can and will destroy us. No, unfortunately, we as market participants are controlled by the market, and we have to be subjugated to that role in life if we are to take advantage of opportunities that avail themselves through *Time and Price Symmetry*. Therefore, never forget the subordination that comes with working in the markets, and never be disillusioned that you can treat the market as another capitalistic pursuit because although the market is the epitome of capitalism, the market is also the epitome of slavery to the higher intellect because of the need to quantify the unknown, which has always been my drive and my purpose. Simultaneously, do not allow yourself to see this personal suppression to the markets as a negative because if you are able to correctly navigate the markets, you will find yourself elevated to that of the noble man that can better the lives of more people than any one medical doctor could over a lifetime career. Therefore, take comfort in this obsession, and enjoy your belief that your resultant decisions may lead to moral good at the end of a successful market-based career.

Market Purpose & Definitions

Another thing that must be discussed with respect to understanding the nature of traders or investors is to define goals to your endeavor in the first place. In no way should my personal goals be correlated with that of the reader. In fact, I encourage the reader to find a goal that will do two things: (1) make that person feel successful and invigorated each day in order to enjoy their work and (2) define a goal either monetarily or performance-based that leads to gratification upon accomplishment. Defining those two parameters can come from the dualistic nature of the markets based on one's own time and abilities, and that duality that exists in the market can now be defined properly as trading and investing, which is this Chapter's title.

To begin, I realize that there are many successful people in this industry, and I hope some of those people acknowledge how much luck has played in their success. However, those successful without luck; those who devised strategies and models should be applauded because I know and I understand that there is more than one-way to skin the proverbial market cat. As a corollary to that statement, I also know that any strategy that is not in this book will cause the cat to eventually run out of skin. Therefore, I encourage all traders with valid strategies to acknowledge the finite time they have with their strategy (Richard Dennis's large blow-up in the late 80s is a prime example), and to use the profit from that strategy in order to become investors. Unfortunately, most successful traders are plagued by their mind and their ego. They do not recognize the finite life cycle they will face one day, and without proper risk management, the market will humble any and every trader. In fact, the market will humble everyone, and in a blink of an eye, a lifetime of work can be wiped out with one wrong click of the mouse.

Again, you can tell that I am already confirming a duality of the mindsets that exists in finance: traders and investors. I would further affirm that most investors (even amateurs) would make money, as the market's nature is to move higher due to inflationary theory and Price Theory, as we will learn. On the other hand, I am confident in saying that 99.999% of all traders will lose and fail.

I will define an **Investor** as someone who purchases an asset in the belief that over a long period, the asset will be worth more. As an example, Warren Buffett is commonly referred to as the most successful investor of all time. The psyche of an investor is kept in check by low volatility, which is a period of slowly rising prices with quick retracements that lead to new higher price levels defined as Price Objectives.

Concurrently, I will define a **Trader** as someone who has no care about the underlying asset that they trade. The trader cares about **Liquidity** (the ease of entering and exiting a position) and the amount of movement the underlying asset makes on a daily basis either up or down, which we will define as a **Trading Range**, which is different than the term Range defined in Chapter 6. In addition, the actual degree (size) of movement of creating these ranges can be defined as **Volatility Implied Trading Ranges**.

Amazingly, to this day, no one knows who the most successful trader of all time is. W.D. Gann, who I will credit with being the first one to establish the pathways that led to the knowledge in this book, was rumored to die bankrupt, but other sources claimed he used his own airplane to fly large sums of cash to islands in the Caribbean. Also like Gann from the early 1900s, Jesse Livermore was famous for crashing and burning repeatedly in his career, but his intellect was far more rational then to let that happen, and rumors have always stated he kept his money in a Scrooge McDuck-like vault in another country where no one knew of the actual value. Every New Year's Eve, he was rumored to spend the New Year alone in that vault counting his money, and none of these market fables are without merit.

In today's world, the most famous traders, who most common pundits regard as being the best, are simply lucky. For example, George Soros made a good currency call once in his life, and it fueled 20 years of investment success. T. Boone Pickens threw a big dart at oil once every quarter until it worked and finally reached billionaire status in old age. However, I must acknowledge Steve Cohen, Eddie Lambert, and David Tepper as three great traders in today's world, but the best ever? Hardly. What makes them great is that they took their trading strategies and then, became investors. They knew when to flip the switch in their mind in order to preserve their capital. They did not keep the trading-mentality going once reaching a certain level of success because the mentality necessary to trade properly takes immense concentration that eventually causes health problems (mentally and physically). More important then the aversion to mental stress is the aversion to the actual dollars and cents. As their capital under management grew, their trader's worth (their balls) was tested. At some point, all of the traders that have reached longevity have caved under that pressure. Then, these great traders went from being people that lived and died by volatility to people who lived and died by warm and cozy feelings of safe returns with the hope of low volatility. In essence, they had enough, and their preservation of capital kicked-in, which meant they hit their limit. They became investors. They forgot that the dollars and cents were fake.

This career-shift is not uncommon, and this thought yields to understanding the goals that one needs as a trader or as an investor. For example, my goal, which is to eventually reach trillionaire status, would mean that I have a very long time to go in order to flip the trading switch off and the investor switch on. What is more is that my goal is irrational. In life, we live with the law of diminishing returns. For example, what is the difference between making $100mm a year and making $200mm a year? Not much. I remember, one time, when I was working for a hedge fund manger in Philadelphia, I asked him, "Why do you play the powerball?" His answer, "If I win, I can add a zero to the end of my orders." Again, at some point, the money reaches a level that is meaningless, but only if you let it. Therefore, the number, the goal is only somewhat necessary, and many movies have emphasized the fact that most billionaires have some set number in there head. However, for me, that goal is not about the number it is about proving intellect, which is directly correlated to that number, but proving intellect is much different then proving, who the best trader is. And that definition – that reverence – is greater than knighthood.

Limitless Power & Value of: *"Time and Price Symmetry"*

Summarily, what you will learn in this book is not a trading strategy that has a limit. What you will learn will not be "arbed-out" (arbitrage occurs when many traders learn a method that works and piggy-back onto it until it no longer works, which was common with the high frequency traders of the last 10 years). With what is presented in this book, the market cat will never run out of skin. This is a structure that exists; a structure that always existed, and it has existed in every time frame and in every market forever. I can look at a Japanese rice charts from the 1400s and see the structure. I can look at the Tulip charts from the 1600s and see the structure. I can look at a Dow Chart from 1929 and see the structure before the crash. I can look at the oil chart from 2008, and see the structure, and I can look at Apple Stock yesterday and see the structure. It is right in front of your eyes, but no one notices. It has been there waiting for all eternity, but no one has put it into simplistic words. It is a level of comprehension and understanding that comes from a sixth sense derived not only from the instruction in this book but from thousands of hours of watching and witnessing. It is a structure that requires discipline and focus, and the only question is, can you handle it? Physically? Mentally? Emotionally? Can you sacrifice to attain a level of mastery? Can you give up your entire life to something, which (for me) caused such irrationality in other areas of my life that I ended up in Federal Prison? Few are called, and I believe that only two are alive on the planet right now that are chosen; my mentor and me.

However, you, the reader, have the power to learn this structure and become the best trader in the world. In a way, I am self-sabotaging my own goal by writing this book, but please believe that I will never measure the best in terms of dollars and cents, which is meaningless anyway. No, I will measure a trader's success in the percentage of time you are in the market and the percentage of times that you are on the correct side of the market; long or short. What's more, I will also measure a trader's success in terms of his giveback to humankind. For me it has always been the pursuit of this knowledge along with the ability to have the highest percentages of accuracy (not money), and what's more, because of how difficult the third dimension of the market is to grasp (I.e. Quantitative Synchronicity), I feel a necessity within my conscience to share this knowledge with my fellow man because I know the sacrifices it takes in order to achieve what I have by writing this book. Hence, it is my duty to establish this knowledge for humanity, and I believe that *the three-dimensional Marketome should be taught to all business students* because I know that the knowledge presented herein will appear priceless in many job vocations. Should that happen, regardless of my incarceration, the fact that I have literally created a new form of business sciences – vis a vis the Marketome – will warrant Nobel Prize recognition. . In addition to that delusional gradiosity claim, I must state that my decision to give this knowledge to humankind is done out of humility and humbleness, and that thought is also relevant to the Royal Academy of Sciences in Stockholm, Sweden. Thus, aside from trading, my personal goal is to share my sacrifice with the world; the sacrifice that allowed this book to be written. What's more, I have no fear in sharing this knowledge because reaching the level of profitability that I believe I am at with my own trading skills takes several years, if not a decade, and do not be disillusioned that you can jump right into this career choice.

That being said, let us take this discussion outside of the collegiate / Nobel Prize realm because concurrently, for those who would be come true disciples of *Time and Price Symmetry*, you must remember that as your Marketome understanding matures, which in turn, causes your accuracy to increase – your trading percentages rise – the money will take care of itself. Hence, to conclude this discussion, my motive does not equate to a number-based goal of being the best, and I would consider a person who buys 1 share of stock, remains in the market 90% of the time, and is profiting from the market 90% of the time as a better trader then me. In fact, with those statistics and without fiat money procurement or selfless act demonstrations, that person would receive my label – my recognition – of being the best trader in the world.

Expert Execution

The last discussion that I wish to have in this chapter is a discussion on expertise. We must understand that true experts, in any vocation, are only effectively working a marginal amount of time compared to the amount time that they spend preparing and keeping themselves relevant, and this conversation will bleed into my favorite comparison regarding doctors and traders. However, in order to explain the difference between execution and preparation, let us start with an easier visualization. For example, let us take a professional football player, and I will be speaking in terms of averages.

In a given year, a professional football player spends close to 2,000 training, exercising, reviewing tapes, studying, etc. However, I must ask the reader, "How much time does that football player actually spend doing his job?" Well, think about it. In a given season, there are 16 football games, and aside from the Quarterback, most of the players are rotating in and out of positions. So, in a given Football Game that has a total of 60 minutes of play time, an actual expert probably is not doing his job more than 5 minutes per game! In fact, that number is high if one was to research it. Therefore, in a given year, a professional athlete may spend 2 out of 2,000 hours doing his or her actual job. The same is true for trading.

With *Time and Price Symmetry*, we will learn that it is a constantly interactive process that requires surrendering and abandonment to the present moment, which is a trading concept as well as a religious concept as defined by Father Caussade's *Sacrament of the Present Moment* from the 1600s. However, because of that abandonment to the present moment, the actual time that the trader is engaged in trading is very low. I mean, how long does it take to click the darn mouse a few times? Hence, we understand that a trader is like a professional athlete, or like any other professional. Even a brain surgeon doesn't spend many hours actually slicing the brain. In a given operation, the surgeon may spend only a few minutes making expert incisions, and the rest of the time, the surgeon is calculating, maneuvering, and trying to figure out what is wrong. Hell, let us debase the conversation for hyperbole, and let me ask the reader, "How much time does a professional porn star even spend on his or her one scene per movie?" Think about it. Experts are everywhere, and there is no reason that a professional trader must always be trading, which is the point of this complex metaphor.

As such, it always amazes me about the lack of respect people choose to have when they begin trading, and I am guilty of this on many, many levels. Trading is by far the hardest mental activity a human can engage in (not medicine, not rocket science, and not the law). Trading is a continual battle of the mind to stay alert, focused, and unemotional to your actions; it requires the ability to not forecast while simultaneously reaching a meditative state of living in the present moment that is free from past experiences or future predictions. Trading is a job where one mistake can lead to the death of a lifelong career. *Everything is always at risk*. Therefore, I encourage anyone who reads this book to get more than 10,000 hours of observation before ever taking a real, live trade. Let my life be a testament as to why you need this level of observation. I could not adhere to this rule myself, and it put me in jail; pure and simple. Ironically, I was put in jail when I was having the best success (percentage wise) in my career, and with a few more months, I was on the verge of paying all my debts back. However, I accrued those debts by external forces that made me trade when I should have been getting experience instead.

On the other hand, if I lived a monkish lifestyle with minimal cost and minimal human interaction, I would not have had the pressures to perform in the first place. I caused my own failure because of my desire for material objects. I also had pressures from my investors, pressures from my past, and predominantly, pressures from myself to keep trading through an addiction borne from the market. However, the truth was, even I, was not ready. To put it in perspective, my mentor in *Time and Price Symmetry* waited 19 years before doing his first *trading campaign*. I waited 2 months.

Unfortunately, there are no teachers and no college classes (not yet anyway) that will teach you the knowledge in this book. So getting your four years of study (4 years = 250 trading days per year * 10 hours a day * 4 years = 10,000 hours) is a sacrifice for most people in society. People need food, clothing, and shelter to survive and people need the internet, computers, and charting software to learn how to trade. It simply costs money (price) and time. Moreover, there are no student loans or financial aid offered to people who want to learn how to become a trader, and most traders are mentored in a style when they are hired to a trading firm after college. These styles often have limited life cycles, and what is unfortunate for the trainee is that he or she is unaware that his or her new career may be short lived, but thankfully, this is not true of *Time and Price Symmetry*. Hence, even though a trainee may be facing unknown, early termination, the mater-trainee relationship emphasizes the fact that the markets are one of the few areas of our society that still requires masters and apprentices in order to be competent. The problem is that the masters are not competent in understanding the true market structure, which becomes the future problem of the apprentice. Therefore, I hope the scholastic respect for trading changes, and that students can explore the logic of my writing while under a university's umbrella, but even if my dream of having people research the "why" behind *Time and Price Symmetry* is fulfilled, I doubt that furthered study will ever yield conclusive proofs. Because of the lack of help to enter the realm of trading, college education currently leave students unprepared for careers as traders, and more important then education is the mentality learned by attending the school of hard knocks, which requires learning in how to deal with successes and failures. Until you feel what it is like to lose a million dollars in a few hours, you are not ready, and unfortunately, I have had that experience twice. Then again, the trick is to remember that the dollars and cents are imaginary anyway, but still, there is a growth that must occur from the pain of loss.

Often, I have referred to myself as a "Brain Surgeon of the S&P." My mother hates this comparison as her life has revolved around medicine, and her personal feeling is that the market is pure gambling. However, I believe that having the knowledge to make billions of dollars in one's life can not only help a specific group of people, but that level of monetary attainment can actually be used to help entire societies. Moreover, this comparison yields two more revelations for the trading community. One, it acknowledges the need to practice for several years. I ask the reader, "Does a brain surgeon perform surgery on his first day of medical school on a live patient? " No. Then, why should trading be any different? Two, doesn't a doctor decide to specialize in some field? Yes. Then, why wouldn't you do that for even a harder intellectual exercise? This second point is of most importance, and I encourage any trader to specialize in one field (one instrument) just like a doctor. For me, I gravitated towards the Futures market due to their liquidity, leverage, and 24-hour trading schedule. In a way, they are the riskiest investments but also the safest due to their 24-hour nature. Furthermore, I specialized in the U.S. Index futures with the S&P being of primary focus due to its liquidity. Most comparisons in this book will look at the S&P E-Mini Futures Contract for examples of charts, etc. My concluding thoughts on my edification metaphor between a brain surgeon and myself are this: I hope that the importance of the concepts in this book is treated as seriously as any other area of study be it engineering, medicine, or law. I state this with utmost sadness because my past trading losses have affected the lives of nearly 100 people in a negative way. My actions can almost be equated to being a civil engineer, who built a bridge that collapsed. Thankfully though, my failure did not result in death, which should be an important distinction (but the government didn't agree to this comparison either). Therefore, I can say that my actions that led to my current life outcome are the same as a doctor, who performed surgery while drunk. Or, my actions were the same as an incompetent lawyer, which caused an innocent man to go to jail. Thus, the trader / the market participant must remember that actions derived from the markets have consequences, and those consequences need to be remembered. I hope that others can realize that as well, but we have to remember that these consequences are only borne from a belief in a synthetic instrument; the dollar itself.

Closing Thoughts

Now that I have stressed how important the market is at changing people's lives, I must add a corollary. This book is not "Trading for Dummies." As such, I expect the reader to know most standard definitions and market concepts. I expect the reader to have some basic skill set with respect to the market, and hopefully, the reader is not completely biased to availing his or her mind to the concepts herein. Therefore, I must be clear that this is a higher-level book and the reader should know common investing vocabulary such as: futures, stocks, options, derivatives, long, short, margin, etc. Essentially, throughout this book, I will be writing and explaining examples with the assumption that the reader has more than a basic level of education regarding how the market works. However, there may be terms that I decide to re-define for my own purposes throughout this book, and this is only done to ensure that we are all speaking the same market language.

As I close this chapter, let me be clear once more; trading is hard. Investing is not. Trading requires thousands of hours of observation and simulation-based testing, and even then, it takes an ego that can disassociate itself from risk and the love of money. Remember, no one is better than the market, and my hope is that this book will open the eyes from the average investor to the PhD quant so that we can move forward in understanding the why behind the markets movements. In fact, I dream of a day that those millions of minds that produce countless hours of research will be able to understand the future of the market's pricing. By understanding that future, market participants will be able to forecasts world events and catastrophes beforehand, and that will cause another insurance-based layer to develop that will lead to saving human lives. These last few sentences should not be taken lightly, and I encourage the reader to understand how important *Time and Price Symmetry* can be with respect to understanding the future. In essence, we can use future pricing objectives in order to predefine the future, which should emphasize how powerful the knowledge and this book can be, when it is properly understood.

Chapter 2

The Truth about Investing (I.e. Fundamental Analysis)

There is no doubt in my mind with respect to the necessity of fundamental analysis in the financial industry, which may seem contrary to every claim read thus far. Ultimately, trading becomes constrained by size limitations, which can be usurped by trading multiple assets at once. However, there will always be an asymptotic trading limit, and as discussed in the last chapter, this limit can just as easily exist based on one's own risk aversion as well as from the size limitation that exists in the market. Therefore, eventually, it is my belief that keeping one's wealth will come by placing trading profits into investments that will appreciate over time. Every famous trader that has managed to maintain his or her wealth has gravitated to this investment-like approach later in life once the emotion of preservation of profits became the primary goal instead of making more profits. This fear can be derived from one's family, one's upbringing, or most likely, from setting subconscious goals on how much is enough; again, the law of diminishing monetary returns. However, the most famous traders (not necessarily the best) were never able to achieve "enough" in order to stop trading, which either led to a catastrophic collapse or immense volatility once they became mentally fatigued.

Restating from last chapter, trading is often equated to that of a high-performance athlete because of the mental fatigue that is required day-in and day-out. Fortunately, for athletes, they only need to operate at this peak performance for very short intervals of time. Unfortunately, for traders, we have to act at peak performance for 80 hours per week, but one of the things we will learn in regards to *Time Structure* is that we can use Time Windows in order to define periods that will require us to focus our peak mental energy into very few minutes during a trading day, which again is just like an athlete. However, also like an athlete, our careers exist in a finite time-line, and in a way "investing" can be metaphorically compared to a retired athlete who becomes a sports commentator. Investing is a way to remain engaged in the market, but to do so in a way that allows longevity. The most glaring example of this is Jim Cramer. Undoubtedly, he was a great trader, but now, in a way, he is kind of like a market commentator. He has kept his career going in the markets just like a retired athlete would, and that comparison is fascinating to me. Therefore, at some point, investing becomes a necessity for a trader. That being said, I believe everything one needs to know about investing / fundamental analysis can fit in one Chapter. One *logical* Chapter.

During my undergraduate education, I had the fortune of working with a fundamental hedge fund manager in the Philadelphia area for several months. Although we would butt heads, I had to acknowledge that out of the $100mm+ firm he ran, a majority of the capital was his own. I learned everything I could from him, and I coupled that knowledge with the knowledge I learned in the initial stages of my career. As such, I believe this chapter will contain all that one needs in order to be a successful investor; not trader. However, what makes a successful investor? We are no longer dealing with percentages, per-trade risk management, liquidity, or volatility as we would in regards to trading statistics. Instead, we are dealing with an actual product or service that exists and is being offered by a company; an actual investment. We want this company to be a success, which will be reflected in our yearly profit and loss statement as owners of this company. The root derivatives of the purpose of the market must always be remembered, and the market does serve the same purpose as it did a hundred years ago. Good companies will thrive, pay dividends, split, and continue on an upward path over time, but just like a trader, every company hits an asymptotic limit and becomes "lazy." That being stated, you must not forget that the Stock Market is still a market of companies' stock.

People have always asked me, "If I have $50,000 ($5,000, $10,000, $100,000, etc.) what would you do with it?" Unfortunately, what I would do with it is not the answer that person is looking for. I cannot make someone a trader like myself because it requires lifelong devotion that I have discussed in the last chapter. Therefore, my inquisitive reply to that question has typically been, "How much are you willing to lose?" That number is the monetary number that is important when someone asks me about what I would do with his or her money. Let me explain...

Modern Portfolio Theory

Society has been brainwashed in a Modern Portfolio Theory that advocated diversification for the past fifty years or so, and let us not forget that this methodology justified a Nobel Prize. However, diversification is an evil, evil thing, and I ask the masses to please explain to me how they allowed themselves to be hoodwinked into believing in diversified portfolio theory! Please, I must ask the reader, "Tell me why?"

In order to understand the fallacy of diversification, let us start with Mutual Funds. Mutual Funds are diversified so that they do not fail. Please. Stop. Understand that statement. Mutual Funds are diversified so that they do not fail. Ergo, the goal of a Mutual Fund is to continue to exist, and ***not to*** make the investors in that Mutual Fund wealthy. (Notice I used the word wealthy instead of just making money, which is the purpose of a mutual fund because it is aligned to the manger's income.) That being said, even the best Mutual Funds eventually (and always have) under performed the market given enough time because the manager himself or herself has gotten "lazy." Hence, we must understand the power of diminishing returns in this industry, and good hedge fund seeders understand this concept implicitly, which is why they like investing in a new fund's first 3-5 years. Those 3-5 years are typically when the manager has the energy and the drive to stay aggressive because he is "money hungry," which can be a bad thing.

Getting back to thee more common understanding of mutual funds, it must be stated that, ironically, when people invest in Mutual Funds, they simply are happy when they do not lose money. This thinking is a common ideology that most of the world adheres to with respect to investing. In fact, very few people expect large gains from investing in general, and eventually, the laziness that is required to run a Mutual Fund leads to the manager seeking diversification in order to continue receiving his or her management fee. So, diversification and modern portfolio theory does serve a purpose! It allows for an allocation of risk in order to ensure continued existence, but this, dear reader, is not the purpose of the market. Continuing to exist instead of striving for superior profits is the purpose of the weak and the lazy. It is the purpose of the socialist and not the Darwinian capitalist. Therefore, the investor must realize that by simply ensuring existence, the Mutual Fund investor is being cheated out of the positive irrational exuberance that also comes from the market; the white-swan if you will. It is therein that we understand that a Mutual Fund Manager and a Mutual Fund Investor's goals/objectives are not symmetrical.

As we see in any market crash, the black swan of human irrationality will level the playing field, and the good managers become recognized while the bad manager's recede into the shadows with the hope of maintaining their existence. During bear markets, nearly all assets will depreciate, which causes much fear in the mentality of the average Mutual Fund manager. The Mutual Fund manager's existence thrives on the hope of never having bear market scenarios, which we know is a somewhat impossible ideology. During market corrections, the Mutual Fund manager becomes at risk of losing his or her job because the truth behind their overall laziness becomes evidenced in their performance. Therefore, diversification, which is required for the continued existence of the Mutual Fund Manager, fails the Mutual Fund Investor by not allowing the investor to reap the benefits from the positive, statistical "white" swans while only exposing them to the negative (and far reaching), "black" swans, which compounds the losses for the individual because the mutual fund manager will still get paid! In effect, during a crash, all assets will depreciate, but when a stock or an industry bubbles, only a select few assets will bubble at the same time.

The bubble nature of the market is quite important to understand for investors, and I ask the investor reading this book to please read Chapter 9 and this Chapter over and over again.

Now, obviously, the astute mutual fund investor must realize that he/she has made the subconscious or conscious determination that he/she is admitting that investing is a hard job, which must be left "to the professionals." However, it is amazingly interesting to see the herd mentality of the masses that continuously ply Mutual Funds with money when the reality is staring the investor in the face that every mutual fund managers has failed to beat the market indices over time, and the reason for this is quantified in Klatch's Marketome Theory in Chapter 19. Thus, the investor must realize that with that reality, which is *common knowledge,* there is absolutely no purpose to mutual funds. What's more, there has been proven studies that people are investing in mutual fund managers that have been beaten by monkeys that have randomly picked stocks (seriously). In order to further elaborate on the sheer laziness and fear of maintained employment on behalf of most money managers, the Wall St. Journal published an article on September 24, 2012 that stated, "Some money managers who caught the year's stock rally are sitting on percentage gains well into the double digits and are considering watching the rest of the year from the sidelines." This decision to just "stop working" was echoed by several money managers mentioned in the article, and effectively, this is how the average mutual fund manager thinks! It is utter lunacy! Thus, in order to put this in comparison, my trading mentor in *Time and Price Symmetry* told me, "I don't care if my mother is dead. I don't want to know about it during the trading day because it serves me or my clients no good if I knew that during the day." Although that is extreme, that statement is meant to convey the level of importance that someone like me has with respect to the markets versus the common mutual fund manager, who wants to just "protect" his good numbers for the year, which again is not market-oriented thinking as we will continue to discuss. In essence, please rethink your assumptions.

The True Costs of Investing

Next on the chopping block, I will examine the so-called *Savvy Investor,* who feels that he or she can build a portfolio better than the pros. I applaud your misguided ambition, but I have one question for you. At the end of the year, I ask, "Are you are happy to simply break-even?" Seriously, look inside yourself, and undoubtedly, you will admit that you are happier with not losing any money instead of focusing on how much you did or did not make. This thinking is an inherent human flaw, and nearly every gambler experiences this feeling as well. In fact, I guarantee that your subconscious goal has always been to "not lose money on your investments" instead of saying to your subconscious, "I am investing to make money." Thus, we find that the Law of Attraction must be shifted into proper focus if we are to avail it to our subconscious. Furthermore, you must understand the true costs of investing for one's self. Therefore, I now ask the *Savvy Investor,* "Did you factor in the hundreds of hours you spent researching stocks, watching the ticker on CNBC, purchasing magazines and newspapers, and stressing over your portfolio? Did you still break even?" That is the question, and undoubtedly, if you were to answer truthfully, the answer is "No," which is how we start to redefine the true costs of trading or investing.

Now, let me explain how you can define these true costs. If you have a $100,000 portfolio, and you do 10% per year (much better than the average Mutual Fund, by the way), do you feel successful? Victorious? I bet you will feel superior to every market pundit and ever market analyst you hear. In fact, the reality is that you would have done better than 99% of all professional investors that year based on two standard deviations. Good for you! But, what did that 10% cost you? 10 hours a week? 20? Total it up. If you made $20 per hour at your regular job, and you spent those same 10 hours a week working would you not have made the same 10%; the same $10,000? Think about it. Not only would you have made more money working your regular job, but you would have done it risk free. No stress. Now, here is where my mother's comments regarding the gambling nature of the stock market get validation. The average person will undoubtedly say, "Trading is fun and exciting!" Uhh-ohh, let us get back to seriousness now. Trading is not fun and exciting. It is not gambling. No, trading is a serious commitment that requires 12 hours a day, 6 days a week until your dying day. There are no days off. There is no retirement. There is no sick leave or maternity leave. Don't believe me? Again, look at Jim Cramer. He is retired after an amazing run with Gotham Capital Partners, and does he not still spend 12+ hours a day on the market. Yes. If you want fun and excitement, go play craps. Hell, you will probably do better than 10%.

So, you may be thinking to yourself, "Why bother?" Do not fear, there is a reason, and there is a way. First, you must accept that large percentage returns are possible from the market. The veil of perception that has been deployed by the mutual fund managers of the world has to be negated; preconceived notions regarding return must be disregarded. You have to realize that large percentage returns are possible; not 10%, not 100%, but 1000% plus returns. More revealing is that you do not have to wait for the next Microsoft, Google, Apple, etc. There are opportunities in the market *every day* for investors. In fact, as you will learn in this book, nearly every stock will undergo an amazing life cycle that will yield oversized returns. Second, you need to acknowledge that outsized returns take a long time to achieve as an investor but not for a trader. You will need patience, and you will need to have a continual belief in the company you invest in; we can classify this as discipline. Third, (like Einstein) you must believe in the power of the concept of compounding returns. You need to ignore the dollars and cents, and you need to keep building your account on every trade as if it was the first. For example, the fundamental hedge fund manager I worked for bought Nutristystem at $2 and sold it at $74. That is the conviction it takes to make money in the market. He did not sell at $20, $30, or even $50, no, he didn't care about the money. He knew the proverbial saying of "when to hold'em and when to fold'em." He knew about individual stock life cycles. More important, I will quickly teach you a way to quantify the price level for that stock in order to have a quick heuristic of when to exit your fundamental position! Remember, no part of this market machine is random regardless of trading or investing.

However, before understanding when it could be time to exit a position, we need to realize that this Nutrisystem example is an example of the good "white" swan as I alluded to. This is important because unless you were fully invested into Nutrisystem, you would not have benefited from this singular white swan. In fact, if you were diversified, you would have left yourself open to a global "black" swan. That is the differentiating factor. "White" swans are centralized and focus, and "black" swans are not. Therefore, the trick is to understand that every stock will have a "white" swan period as long as the company continues to grow. However, the odds of having two "white" swan periods are quite low, which again, will be expanded upon in Chapter 9. Therefore, the most important thing for you to remember is that both the black and the white swans exist in the market daily and consistently because we are not dealing with a normal distribution of risk in the market. In fact, I believe that market statisticians serve no true purpose in the end because we are dealing with irrational human behavior and emotion. Concurrently, we can also be dealing with our Creator's predestined plan if one were to believe as much, but thankfully, this plan is visible through *Time and Price Symmetry,* as the trader will learn in Chapters 6-21.

This brings us to the question from the beginning of this chapter, which was my corresponding inquiry in understanding how much a person is willing to lose instead of how much a person is willing to commit to the market. With leverage, trade capital is mostly irrelevant (not completely). As I stated, the value of a person's tolerance for loss is truly the monetary number that has importance for me because it tells me what approach I must utilize in achieving outsized returns from the white swans of the investing world. Thus, deciding how much capital that one has available to use via investing or trading will be defined as **risk capital.** Quite simply, this means that *you must risk all of this capital in order to beat the market.* So if you have $50,000, what can you afford to lose? That is the real question.

Furthermore, time is the most precious commodity that we, as human beings, have. This is what us MBA project managers would call **human capital**. Therefore, if you are going to risk your time, it had better not be for the goal of breaking even at the end of the year or even making a 10% return! No, your precious time should be sacrificed for much loftier gains. Don't you think? Once again, even when discussing investing, we are going to look at time and price in a new relationship, which is the purpose of this entire book (along with Quantitative Synchronicity). Moving on, with a few mental tweaks, we can measure our personal time as being much more valuable (price) just by a slight change in your thinking. The personal risk of taking time from your life will forever forthwith have the possibility of a much bigger return if you think in terms of higher percentages. I will effectively be increasing the value of yourself in a few quick statements.

Since this chapter is geared towards investors, I must apologize, but in order to illustrate this example, I need to use math, which may be something a casual investor is scared of. Alas, I hope that you can follow these examples through because their importance is immense for understanding the true costs of investing (not to mention being able to increase your worth as a human being looking to define yourself in terms of monetary attainment, which is my assumption as to why you would buy a book like this in the first place).

To begin, if you have $100,000 currently in the market, but you tell me that you can lose 20% ($20,000) then you really have $20,000 to put to work; this is your risk capital allocation. Before a mentality shift and without you realizing it, the black swan of the market actually put your total $100,000 at risk. I bet you never even realized that! However, the human capital or the time component is much scarier. If you put 10 hours per week into your $100,000 portfolio, you literally were risking 500 hours out of your life per year -- nearly an entire month! However, let us shift the mentality to focus on your risk capital ($20,000) and your newfound skepticism of 1000% return possibilities, which on $20,000 would equate to a $200,000 profit. If your 500 hours of market research per year remained the same, essentially your human capital, then, I have just shifted your mentality to making your life worth 20 times more with 80% less risk. Understand the logic for yourself. It just took some enlightenment in your thinking and your expectations. Your *perception* on what is possible had to change. Now, I must shift your analysis in order to prove to you that you can find the 1000% plus opportunities, which will be the meat of the second half of this chapter.

Before going forward, I want to address the sophisticated investor/trader whose mind is undoubtedly being tempted by the options market. Yes, options will allow for more high-percentage returns, but one must focus on safety of principal despite using risk capital. Moreover, it is a common statistic that 90% of all options expire worthless, which should be a major fear of any option trader's existence. However, I am trying to outline the fact an investor needs to treat a $20,000 investment the same as if it was a $10,000,000 investment in both the commitment (risk capital and human capital) and conviction. Remember, money is meaningless, and we must focus on the fundamental nature of investing, which is to believe in the underlying investment itself. Remember, with proper execution, the money will always take care of itself.

Compounding Returns on Investments

Next, I want to acknowledge the 1000% return statement, which is unarguably an arbitrary number. However, a complete commitment to investing with the principal of risk capital only, and specifically, the reinvestment of that risk capital in subsequent investments will lead to percentage returns far higher than that 1000% figure. Let us use another mathematical example before we move on, which will focus on three trades over three years. Let us use an imaginary three stocks: VWX, WXY, and XYZ. Our first stock, VWX is trading at $5 per share, and for 1000% returns we would need the stock to break the $50 mark. However, we purchase VWX, and once it reaches $10, we decide that WXY is more attractive at $5. We sell our VWX position, and buy twice as much WXY. Now, WXY reaches $20 in the next year (which is actually $40 on our basis (5 x 2 x 4=40)). Yet again, we decide to sell WXY at this $20 and focus on buying XYZ, which is trading at $7. Again, we ignore the value of the money in the account (aside from if we had to pay taxes), and we move the account into XYZ at $7. Now, XYZ does not triple on us, but it does reach the $10.50 level, which means our basis has reached $60 or 1200% return (5 x 2 x 4 x 1.5=60), and we have eclipsed that 1000% mark. It took three trades in committed investing over a three-year period in order to produce staggering results, and if it took 10 trades over 10 years to get the same result, we would still be doing much better than any manager adhering to the idiotic notion of diversification via Modern Portfolio Theory. Of course, finding stocks that will move in these percentages is the true battle, but never fear, our discovery process is actually quite easy to define as well!

Fundamental Analysis Defined

Fundamental analysis of stocks breaks down into two areas for achieving consistent results: **revenue growth** and **corporate management.** Unfortunately, for most small investors, dealing with the analysis of management is not possible, but its importance cannot be understated. As such, since it is an intangible qualitative argument, I will quickly discuss corporate management before expanding upon revenue growth.

When you invest in a company, not only is the product or service important, but your investment is actually in the people who work for the company. For example, people buy Berkshire Hathaway because they are buying Warren Buffett. This is true of every company, and why the late Steve Jobs' health had such an influence on Apple's stock price. In fact, most small companies will gladly accept meetings from stock market investors if they know your investment is substantial. Regardless of your investment size, it never hurts to call a company. In person or even over the phone, you will learn more about the company then any tangible market statistic. Recognizing the future beliefs that the management team holds for their company must be palpable in this humanistic type of analysis. Essentially, if the people working there believe in what they are doing then you can get greater conviction in your investment. Doesn't it make sense to meet the people you are investing your money in anyway? But, have you ever even thought about it before, or have you just bought a stock because it "looked good?" Amazingly, even if you did think about the management company, have you ever thought about calling the company on the phone? Undoubtedly, that answer is also "no." However, again I must reference Jim Cramer one last time in this book. How many times has Jim Cramer said on "Mad Money," "I know the CEO and he's a good guy." *The management team matters*. The qualitative humanistic approach is real with respect to investing.

That being said, there is only one true, definable characteristic that foreshadows investment growth regardless of one's capability of analyzing a management team. That criterion is simply revenue growth and understanding revenue growth. Many companies (especially, pharmaceuticals) actually trade without having any revenue. Eliminate these from your criteria. We are not seed or angel investors taking a chance. We are looking for a product or service that is already in the market, and we are making a determination on our own belief that the company's product or service has growth potential. If we combine this with a palpable excitement that comes from the corporate management qualitative component, we have found our potential investment. Thankfully, the analysis of revenue growth is a viable statistic for creating a summation of the underlying company's performance. Notice I am talking about revenue; not profit, sales, EPS, or costs. If a company has revenue growth, the logical conclusion is that economies of scale will prevail, and profit will eventually take care of itself. Nutrisystem, as I referenced earlier, is a prime example, and once a product reaches the masses, a stock will have its own bubble regardless of market conditions (again, further elaborated on in Chapter 9).

Analyzing revenue growth in percentage terms is important in knowing when to buy or sell as well. Not only do we want to see revenue growth growing per quarter in terms of dollars and cents but also in terms of percentages. For example, let us say a company has a new product, and we are observing 2% revenue growth per quarter in terms of the actual dollars and cents. In the next year, we observe 3~5% quarterly growth. This is important in terms of identifying when the benefits of economies of scale are occurring, and also, this is important in determining if the management of the company starts taking this extra revenue for themselves, which is actually a positive heuristic (in most cases) because it means that profit expectations are healthy. In a way, revenue tells us all we need to know about the management team's performance and society's adoption to this new product or service. We can learn to determine stocks that are on the cusp of bubbling when we turn to the simplistic analysis of just viewing percentage growth quarter over quarter. At the first sign of the percentage of revenue growth decline (even if the quarterly growth in terms of the dollar amount is still positive), there should be a red flag in the investor's mind. It will be helpful to use swing trade analysis in understanding trends in order to determine if the stock is now poised to move lower, which will also be discussed in Chapter 9. However, a good company can also have a repetitive, bad quarter based on a cyclical market tendency. Because of this tendency, not only do we have to examine quarterly revenue growth quarter over quarter, but we also must compare the prior year's quarter over quarter growth. For example, let us say we have a company that in year 1 has quarterly growth as follows: 2%, 2%, 3%, 1%. Next year, 3%, 4%, 4%, 2%. In this example, we notice that the year-over-year fourth quarter seems to be a declining factor for our phantom company's product or service, but the percentage growth is still upward sloping. As such, seasonal/cyclic tendencies must be recognized and scrutinized in order to determine if the underlying growth is still there in order to validate the continued holding of the investment. As those percentages increase, we find a greater chance of the stock being on the cusp of bubbling, and more often than not, we will be looking for companies that are generating revenue growth in excess of 25% year over year. Contrarily, this same logic can assist is in determining when to exit this stock position. The negative case holds that when all of the percentages decrease across the entire year, we can see a negative downturn in the stock, which usually is foreshadowed by a quantitative price structure component known as a "downswing." That being said, even if a company's revenue growth is slowing, as long as revenue continues to increase, eventually, the stock should reach new highs because of the revenue multiplier effect, which I will redefine for the masses within this Chapter.

So, with that, we can end the discussion of investing. Honestly and truly, it is that simple. There is no magic formula, and there is no big secret. Investing boils down to pure logic. Is the company generating more revenue? Does the management team believe in the product? Do I, as the investor, believe in the product? And the last question that must be asked, which has not been discussed thus far, is, "Has the stock price bubbled yet?" When those questions are appropriately answered, we can conclude that this simplistic but logical approach to investing has always existed, and when it couples with trend and swing analysis, it becomes quite powerful. Don't believe me? Ask Mr. Buffett. He's been doing it for nearly 70 years.

Calculating Share Price / Market Capitalization

As mentioned, we have to understand what the value of a company can be in order to know when it is an attractive "buy." (It should be noted that, as investors, we are not looking to discuss short positions because that removes the 100%+ return possibilities.) Aside from understanding the proper valuation that indicates a stock is a potential buy, we also need to understand how revenue is utilized in order to discern the seemingly linear relationship between revenue growth and stock price appreciation.

Sometimes, we can use market capitalization in determining the fair price for a stock (usually after an IPO), and sometimes we can use market capitalization to predict the high-end of the bubble-price of a stock in order to tell us when we should exit the company (this is the situation I alluded to earlier in this chapter). In order to do this, we need to understand that revenue is also the most useful determining factor of market capitalization, which is another reason that I refuse to look at revenue-less companies because we can never get an adequate picture of their valuation.

Now, I must be a bit hotheaded because the current, market-pricing models are simply stupid, and many idiotic fundamental investors come up with complex ways to define criterion that calculates a share price. Commonly, this is known as the "P/E Ratio." For example, if the P/E Ratio for an industry is 12 and there is a company trading at a P/E Ratio of 10, then, the conclusion is that the company with the P/E ratio of 10 is not properly valued. As such, the idiotic fundamental analyst is quick to quote on the various news networks that there is a 20% discrepancy between the current price and the actual worth based on their P/E ratio analysis. This is pure lunacy!

What's more, these people that think they are so intellectually insightful in understanding a 20% differential do decide to factor in revenue growth into some arbitrary, moronic fashion. For instance, a firm may say that if a company has a P/E Ratio of 10 relative to an industry P/E Ratio of 12 along with having a 25% year over year revenue growth, then they create some type of multiplier effect, which is made up of some obscure formula that has no valid historic basis over any given length of time. They may say, well the stock is 20% undervalues, and we can factor in a 25% growth rate, and compare it to the industry, and blah blah blah blah…. Now, instead of completely bashing 99% of all market participants who engage in this exact same analysis, I must say that, thankfully, these people are at least recognizing the importance of revenue, but all of these approaches to fundamental valuation are utter nonsense. The only, O-N-L-Y, point I would concede to these people is that the P/E ratio of the entire S&P does matter to some degree. Historically, that P/E ratio has been used in determining overbought/oversold conditions, but even then, for an individual stock, it is irrelevant. It is more relevant to understanding potential trend, but I am terminating this discussion here because we start dealing with self-fulfilling prophecies, which I do not like. So, obviously, I must prove what is relevant if I am going to make such cocky assertions and put down the work of so many people, and of course, I will.

In order to understand Market Capitalization also known as a company's valuation, you need to understand the relationship between revenue and earnings. Earnings are another word for profit. First, profit is always the wrong number to work with. Always. Sometimes companies have acquisitions, and their profit dramatically shifts. Sometimes companies write off assets, and their profit dramatically shifts. Sometimes companies account for fines and legal costs for breaking the law, and their profit dramatically shifts. Sometimes companies account for Good Will type expenses in a given quarter, and their profit dramatically shifts. Sometimes a major drug is taken off the market, and their profit dramatically shifts. Do you get the point? Profit is inconsistent. Thus, we need to go back to revenue, because although revenue can also shift substantially, it remains more constant than profit, but in order for revenue to be useful, we need to put revenue into a relationship with the profit. This is difficult, and this relationship is not linear nor is it quantifiable.

Now, in order to define this causal relationship, we have to understand that profit comes from revenue. They are intrinsically linked. Obviously, revenue is all the money coming in, and profit is the amount of money that is left over after the bills are paid (simplistically speaking of course). As such, we find that we need to use the percentage of profit with respect to revenue. This is also a common statistic for fundamental analysts. However, we need to define a **revenue multiplication factor** based on this percentage. The revenue multiplication factor is a number that we will use in order to determine a company's valuation / market capitalization.

To begin the process of moving revenue into the capitalization equation, we need to understand something quite obvious. There is an asymptotic limit as the percentage of profit increases with respect to revenue. This means that profit can never be 100% of revenue unless there is absolutely no expenses of the underlying company, which is not possible. As such, this percentage of profit needs to be defined, and we can picture a graph that reaches an asymptotic limit as profit divided by revenue approaches 1. Obviously, this graph is simplistic to picture in the X-Y plane, and I have produced an *example* graph below.

Figure 2.1: Revenue Capitalization Factor

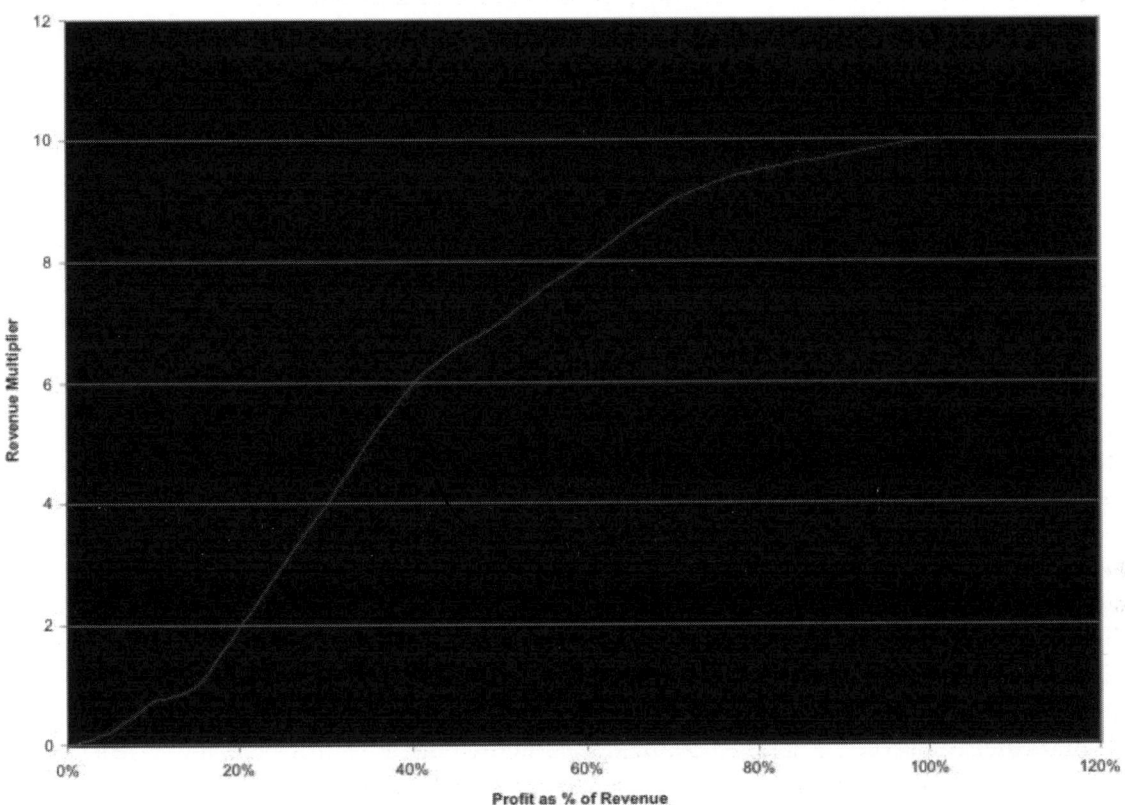

In Figure 2.1, I ask the reader to not take this graph literally. These are made up numbers, but they are fictitious in order to illustrate a point; the point that they do not really matter. Mostly, when we start to rely on the profit percentage, we will be focusing on a simple multiplicative factor of 10. In a way, this factor verifies the logical thought pattern that all we truly need is a heuristic; a quick and dirty way to determine capitalization. What should be obvious to any reader of this book is that the true, current, price of a stock is never defined adequately by fundamentals. As such, there is absolutely no need to come up with a complex system of defining the value of a share price based on non-technical numbers. Instead, we only need something quick and efficient in order to give us a concept of capitalization and of future growth potential, which gives us a **fundamental valuation range**.

This calculative process is necessary to discuss because many people do not understand what happens when a company goes public. Many people do not understand how people become millionaires overnight when a company goes public, but it is in the multiplier effect as stated herein. Therefore, we need to understand how important revenue can be in defining the value of a company. In order to do so, just like with everything else, we must be logical. In order to be logical, we need to look at the fundamentals of the company, which makes sense if we are fundamental analysts, right? As an example, let us look at Amazon Inc. Amazon makes 1.7 cents profit per every $1 of revenue. Obviously, that makes sense because Amazon is simply a retailer. They sell other's products, and they make a very small portion on each sale. Over time, that adds up to a lot of money. Now, let us look at a company like Berkshire Hathaway. They are mostly a profit-generating machine. Everything from insurance to NetJets provides substantial profit. In fact, the only time losses occur is from major catastrophes, which again makes the P/E ratio irrelevant. However, when we look at Berkshire Hathaway, we can see that they make much more than 1.7 cents profit per every $1 of revenue. I believe they make close to 80 cents profit per dollar of revenue. Thus, we now yield to the profit percentage in the graph above. We have AMZN at 1.7% and Berkshire at 80%. This is important to some degree, but it is not the secret sauce to a magic formula because no magic formula exists.

If we look at our chart in Figure 2.1, once we define our profit to revenue percentage, we can go and grab our revenue multiplier. This multiplier is a value between 0-10, but there is a much higher weighting to the 10 multiplier than to the 0-1 multiplier range. In this example, using AMZN's multiplier, we would get a value of 1 or less but for a company like Berkshire Hathaway would be around a 9.5. I also feel that the reason I chose to focus on Amazon is that it is an example where the correct multiplier may be less than 1, but I assert that this is a rarity that is mostly relevant to retailer-type situations. However, one of the hidden items that must be accounted for with respect to retailers (like Staples for example) is that they may own a tremendous amount of commercial real estate, which must be factored into their valuation as well. On the other side of the spectrum, if we are to look at a company that had 100% profit from revenue, which cannot exist, that company would have a perfect 10. Therefore, we create a new asymptotic picture of this revenue multiplier via the percentage profit. I believe that any company that generates more than 50% profit from revenue would warrant an 8x multiplier or greater. Again, I do not want to try to come up with some elaborate equation to put these companies into this multiplier effect, and if you want to, go ahead, just use 10. Why? Because we are relying on common sense and logic. A company like AMZN would be a 0.5, 1, or 2 and a company like Berkshire could be an 8 or a 9 (or 10). A company like Apple may be a 4 or a 5 (or 10). You, dear reader, must evaluate how much revenue affects the company, and how that company benefits from economies of scale. Unfortunately, that analysis requires human thought, which is a rare and priceless commodity in today's world.

Okay, so the reader should now understand the picture. We have revenue, and we have a positive profit flow. With those two factors, we are basically taking are value of the revenue, and we are multiplying it by 10, which should be easy enough. But before we move on, I must state that this approach is a great heuristic in order to *quickly* visualize market capitalization and share price valuation; especially, for new companies trying to go public. In order to implement these simplistic calculations, we can define **market capitalization** as the revenue multiplier based on the percentage of profit times the total revenue. Lastly, we must add in the value of any tangible assets for correct market capitalization, and in order to balance the balance sheet, we must subtract liabilities. Therefore, we can define the **market capitalization equation** as yearly revenue times the revenue multiplier plus tangible assets minus liabilities. (For mathematicians we can say $C = R \times \%P + A - L$ (Capitalization = Revenue times Percentage Profit of Revenue + Assets - Liabilities.) Finally, in order to get **market capitalization-based share price**, we can divide the market capitalization by the number of outstanding shares ($P = C / \#S$ or, using words, Share Price = Capitalization divided by Number of Shares). Therefore, now that all of the formulas have been discussed, let us do a quick and dirty example.

The Open Capital Corporation has 1,000,000 outstanding shares. The company has $5mm in cash or tangible investments (assets) and no liabilities. The company generates $1mm per year in revenue, and the company is making 80% profit off that revenue. This would be similar to a hedge fund of funds. Now, we can see that the company has a current valuation of $5mm from the balance sheet, and every share of stock would be worth $5 ($5,000,000/1,000,000) before we factor in revenue. However, The Open Capital Corporation is going to go public. The fancy investment bankers come in, and they decide that they will need to value the company as part of the underwriting process. Now, because these are smart bankers, instead of using the P/E ratio, the bankers decide to use revenue. They notice that the high percentage of profit is enough to warrant a multiplier greater than 9. They choose 10 because they are optimists, and they recognize the inefficiency of valuation calculations. Therefore, the company now has a

10*$1mm (current revenue) and becomes worth $10mm once we apply the revenue multiplier. Next, all we have to do is add in the tangible assets. Thus, we get a value of $15mm. Therefore, the reader can now easily understand why companies go public; we see that by going public, the company is now worth three times as much than its book value alone, and we would expect that the share price would be $15, which is the appropriate assumption because it has valid analysis.

The next thing that we have to factor in is **revenue growth**. Obviously, revenue growth is important to me, and it is important for fundamental analysis. It was already discussed, but now, it requires an elaboration based on my simplistic market capitalization equation(s). Again, I find it amazing how ignorant and how incorrect people are when they try to come up with fancy equations for factoring revenue growth into a stock's price, and more likely than not, these equations are never sustainable in the real world. However, if someone does find one that works, then, they too, will prove that the market is not random from a fundamental standpoint (good luck).

Moving on to the example let us logically assume that The Open Capital Corporation has a revenue growth of 50% per year. This means that next year, after going public, the company expects to make $1.5mm of revenue ($1mm * 1.5). The company expects this revenue to remain at 80% profit to revenue, and again, we rely on the simple 10x multiplier. Now, we see that we have $15mm ($1.5mm * 10) of multiplied-revenue and $5mm of tangible assets (for those people who look to this example with scrutiny, yes, we can add in $800,000 from the prior year's $1mm of profit, but let us leave it at $5mm for simplicity's sake). Now, we see that we get a total market capitalization of $20mm. We divide this valuation by the outstanding shares in order to get our market-capitalization-based share price, and we see that we get a market capitalization-based share price of $20 per share. Therefore, we reach something important; something related to market inefficiency (see *Chapter 21*). We see that we have a current price of $15 per share and we see that we have a future price of $20 per share based on revenue growth projections. As such, we have two simultaneously linked prices, and therefore, we do not know which one is correct. However, we do now see the inception of understanding the inefficiency of the market, which becomes the reason to be an investor or a trader in the first place. Hence, we see that we have a range of possible prices between $15 and $20 that a fundamental analyst can adequately quote as being fair value based on current pricing or based on future expectations, and I will elaborate on this price range momentarily.

There are two last issues that I want to discuss regarding market capitalization before we move on. First, and most important, I need to discuss to the reader how important understanding revenue and market-capitalization can be. These exercises are not done in vain even for the person reading this book with an objective of understanding *Time and Price Symmetry* only. I say this because of how quick these simple calculations can be in doing a quick analysis of stock selection criteria (remember, traders will reach an asymptotic limit). Thus, the power of understanding the causality between revenue, assets, and share price is necessary for *all* market participants in terms of making a tremendous amount of money off human irrationality, which leads to incorrect valuations. Therefore, I want to discuss Facebook's' IPO, and the Lord could not have supplied me with a better example to utilize for the reader than this stock.

When Facebook went public, they went public at an IPO share price that would yield a $100bn valuation, which, to me, seems to be a number chosen out of thin air by using non-fancy investment bankers. The investment community was thereby told by the investment bankers that the initial share price was $38 in order to reflect that valuation. However, Facebook has stated, that at the time they went public, their revenue was $3.9bn. If we apply the simple 10x multiplier, we get $39bn. Arguably, Facebook does not have a ton of tangible assets since they are a tech company, so let us assume we have a $40bn market capitalization based on my simplistic formula. This would imply that Facebook's $38 IPO stock price is absurd. My calculation would yield a price of $15.25 (60% less than $38). Amazingly, if one was to go back and look at what happened after the IPO, one would see that Facebook's stock came almost straight down to this market capitalization-based share price, but it did not hit it exactly, which is where we start to build the concept of revenue ranges. However, any person that has just read this section of this book should be able to see how powerful and how simple the understanding of revenue can be with respect to understanding a stock's true, inherent, market capitalization-based share price. Had a reader of this book observed Facebook's IPO, he/she never would have even considered buying the stock at those levels! Now, let me explain the power of revenue ranges.

If we are to assume a 50% growth in Facebook's revenue, we can plug $39bn * 1.5 into our equation, and we can again add in $1bn of tangible assets, which was also an assumption. With this 50%revenue growth forecast applied to Facebook, we can find a price value of $22.8 simply by multiplying our market capitalization-based share price by 1.50. As such, we define a price range of $15.25-$22.80 for a current, accurate market valuation-based share price, and what the reader must understand is that any price within that range is fair.

Another thing that is necessary to mention with this discussion of capitalization is the difference between basic share number versus diluted share number, and this is where the fundamental mathematicians (oxymoronic I know) will be satiated. What may people do not know is that when companies go public, the company itself may have the authorization to dilute more shares into the market place either via employee stock options, corporate takeovers, etc. For obvious reasons, these details are buried. Therefore, the diluted share number value is much higher, and it is most important if one is to truly understand and calculate the low of Facebook's stock price that held two in early September of 2012. In order to understand this difference, we again must turn to realistic numbers and calculations in order to understand the diluted market capitalization-based share price.

The **diluted market capitalization-based share price** is the market capitalization divided by the total numeric value of the outstanding possible shares once factoring in for maximum dilution. Again, using Facebook, let us use there revenue, $39bn, and based on Factset.com, we can use their diluted share number 2.8bn versus their basic share allotment of 2.2bn, which the reader should note as a gigantic discrepancy that is often not known. Hence, when we recalculate the capitalization based on these numbers, we see that the value is equal to a much lower price of 13.92 than our standard market-capitalization-based share price of 15.25. However, when we start getting intricate with the mathematics, we have to realize one last concept, which is relevant in understanding the power of accurately calculated share prices just off the value of revenue, the amount of revenue growth, the revenue multiplier, and the proper number of possible outstanding shares. This concept will be defined momentarily as present moment revenue.

Obviously, when a company reports revenue, they are reporting the revenue for a period of time that has *elapsed*. However, in the present moment, we have to realize that if a company is growing their revenue, the previously reported revenue is not the most valid number to use. Therefore, we have to make assumptions, and those assumptions have to be done in the present moment. For example, let us assume that we are dealing with a company that has projected 50% year over year revenue growth. Well, in the present moment, we can see that obviously that 50% growth is a completed, future value of revenue. Thus, we now know the past reported revenue, and we now have an assumption about the future revenue. However, we can now ask, "What is the present moment revenue?" Well, the **present moment revenue** is defined as being approximately equal to the last reported revenue plus 25% of the value of the one-year projected future revenue from the last reported revenue number. For instance, if we were to say that company XYZ released revenue of $10mm for the quarter ending March 31, 2011; well we would look to see what they are projecting for the quarter ending March 21, 2012. If that value is $20mm, we would be able to define our present moment revenue as $20mm x 25% + $10mm or $15mm. (In order for this calculation to work, we must be reliant on the 12-month forecast, which is why we use a ¼ multiplier.) Now, let us tie this back into Facebook in order to conclude the mathematics of fundamental analysis.

With Facebook, we know that they reported $3.9bn of revenue when they went public. They also claimed that they were expecting 50% year over year revenue growth. That means that their future revenue would be equal to $5.85bn. Therefore, we can find our present moment revenue by taking $3.9bn + 0.25 x

$5.85bn, which is equal to $5.3625bn (we are using large numbers so please do not round off). At this instant, we can go through our standard calculations for market capitalization, and we can also factor in the correctly diluted share values. Thus, we can come up with an accurate diluted market capitalization-based share price, which again, is the value derived from the calculations that I have personally set forth in this chapter. The mathematics for calculating Facebook's true diluted market capitalization-based share price is defined as $5.3625bn x 9.5 (a more accurate revenue multiplier), which yields a market capitalization value equal to $50.95bn. Then, we take $50.95bn and divide by the diluted share number of 2.8bn, which yields a price per share of $18.19, which was approximately 50 cents from the September 2012 low that led to Facebook's rebound! Therefore, with the proper mathematics and using simple numbers, we find a share value that has the potential to be much strong and more accurate, and we can use this example to lead us into our final discussion regarding revenue and market capitalization: market bubbles.

As we will discuss in Chapter 9 regarding individual stock lifecycles, a stock will tend to enter a bubble period where it will have irrational growth. It is my assertion that the price range derived from properly understanding market capitalization can actually serve as an indicator of when a stock becomes irrational; when a stock leaves its valuation behind. (Later, this will be clarified symmetrically through Price Structure as swings.) When a stock leaves its rational valuation behind, we must remember that it will only do so when supply and demand laws have been satiated at its proper valuation values. This concept is another reason I decided to focus on the Facebook example. Since after Facebook's IPO the stock came down to its correct valuation levels based on revenue, the stock can now indicate a potential bubbling period of irrationality should it exceed its fundamental valuation range. It was not possible for this to happen until supply and demand laws were adhered to, and the laws of supply and demand must be fulfilled before bubbling. Again, this is a far from perfect indicator, but I feel it is essential to mention. They key, of course, is patience and logic. Logically, the smarter market participants will start buying at the correct valuation, and they, too, will help start the bubble. If you don't believe me, try and do calculations for Netflix of Research in Motion over the past few years similar to what I have done with Facebook, and you will find that this type of logical thinking works extremely well. Google is probably the most prime candidate for this analysis because, like Facebook, it sold off after its initial IPO price, but quickly, it began a tremendous ascent. Thus, we must understand that once supply and demand has been met and once the stock exceeds its proper valuations, we are alerted to the possibility of massive profits! Along with logic, I must again reiterate that we are not angel investors. My formula is not possible if revenue *or profit* is non-existent for a company. Therefore, in order to summarize, we need to focus on stocks with revenue, and with growing revenue. If profit is negative, obviously, the formula falls apart because I built them in that fashion as a fail safe. I built them to fall apart to always remind the investor to focus on a company with a tangible product/service along with actual profits and actual revenue growth. This is logically done as a check on our mentality in order for us to make sure we are buying a company that is growing. Thus, these equations serve as a reminder in order to prevent a fundamental investor from making a mere market gamble.

Fundamental Investment Logic

The last topic for discussion regarding fundamental stock selection criteria is that you need to *be logical*, and I think I may have mentioned this once or twice thus far. In fact, I have stressed the word logic throughout this entire chapter, and sometimes, this thinking can be called common sense. Logic or common sense is necessary with fundamental analysis because fundamental analysis is easy compared to the technical analysis that we will be embarking on immediately after this chapter. The math will get tougher, and the theories will get more esoteric. However, even with what I have discussed thus far, if a person was to simply remain logical, focus on revenue growth, and focus on correct corporate valuations, then, we have already defined a successful investment strategy that will never fail. However, we need to utilize concepts in this book in order to define periods of rationality.

Thus far, I have a simple indicator defined in order to indicate the possibility of a forthcoming bubble, and I have defined this indicator by stating that after a stock breaks out of its correct market capitalization-based price range, then, we can get a hint of a bubble. However, this too relies on logic. If you see people start flocking to an industry, a service, or a product, the price of the company offering that service or product in that industry will start to go up. It's that simple. It doesn't take advanced degrees, but it does require "*Wall Street-smarts*" and observation. Therefore, please, if you want to remain fundamentally based, I encourage you to not underestimate the power of knowing your own industry because, if you do, you will have an advantage on knowing whether a product or service is truly good. Therefore, if you stay fundamentally based, please pick an industry you know. If you are a computer consultant, stick to tech. If you are a petroleum engineer, stick to new oil companies and products. Don't try to be a master of all trades (literally). You have no one to impress. You can only be impressive to yourself if you are seeing *consistent,* positive results. The other thing I recommend for investing, but should never be a concrete deciding factor, is finding stocks that are under the $10 mark. Since we want to get a multiplier effect on our return, the lower the price, the greater the multiple effect each $1 has. Granted, we could have a high share price based on a low float (amount of stock available), but again, this is only a suggestion. Obviously, the revenue growth and the power of the product or the service being offered is much more important. For instance, the people who believed Apple's stock was too high at $200 still achieved a triple return when it went to $600! Furthermore, when dealing with fundamental analysis, please stick to a stock on major exchanges as well, but do *not be afraid of overseas markets*. If a stock is lifted properly on an overseas exchange, then, try to remove your perception bias regarding risk of investing in overseas companies. Many times, another country's underlying market may be in bull market scenarios that actually facilitate revenue growth and bubbling type tendencies for your investment. I must stress that there is a major difference between companies listed on valid, overseas exchanges versus over the counter (OTC) stocks, pink sheet(.PK) stocks, or bulletin board stocks (commonly known as penny stocks). These risky penny stocks are all, frankly, worthless until they achieve sufficient listing requirements by a major exchange. If your tendency is to target these markets for insane returns, I suggest that you go play the lottery instead.

In order to summarize this chapter, investing is logical, but it requires conviction, discipline, and commitment in order to see the big picture. More importantly, you have to remain focused on the investment in order to stay with it until revenue growth declines, or it reaches its bubble stage. Furthermore, contrary to Modern Portfolio Theory, which has a main component as risk, you have to remove the perception that has been ingrained in your mind over the past 50 years with regards to investing. Sure, investing requires risk, but with simple shifts in your mentality, you can define your risk by defining how much capital you want to risk in terms of your money (risk capital) and your time (human capital). Even if you decide to allocate more of your money to your risk capital account over time, I encourage you to not begin diversifying. Instead, if your investment position is working favorably for you, buy more of it! Remember, the simple act of purchasing more of something that you believe in is how the market was designed to work in the first place, and conversely, you invoke the Law of Attraction. Hence, your commitment of more capital to your investment is the logical approach to have if you are seeing the investment perform; in effect, if you are investing $10,000 or $10,000,000 your monetary commitment drives the price higher. That being said, if you learn one thing from this chapter with respect to believing in your investments, learn never to add to a losing position, which is commonly known as. dollar cost averaging. If things are working, keep adding to it. If they are not, either wait until your investment has started to perform, or get out now. Concurrently, remember the old axiom, "scared money doesn't make money."

Chapter 3

Trading Styles and Capitalization

Many traders fail due to being under capitalized for their objectives and/or their lifestyles. Objectives come from external forces more than anything else in this industry such as: investors, bosses, peers, advisers, board holders, and benchmarks. However, sometimes our internal requirements (greed and lifestyle) can hinder ourselves as well, and my internal requirement was one of my primary reasons for failure. However, proper capitalization will fix anyone's internal requirements, and therefore, capitalization is correlated to internal and external human forces/emotions.

The **pressure to perform** (defined as make a certain amount of money in a specific period of time) is mentally taxing and prohibitive to a trader. It causes a trader to have emotion, which we will learn is counter-productive to trading success. Most people make the market 50% technical and 50% emotional, but the market is 100% technical and never emotional. A good example of how the outside world affects our emotions with results is that of monthly reporting requirements for any type of Fund. In effect, these requirements, which give investors the warm fuzzy feeling, will cause a trader to become goal-oriented; not market-oriented. Having a goal-oriented nature is necessary in this industry, but the goal should not be based on making a certain amount of money by a certain date. For example, my new goal is to make $1bn, and I hope to do this over ten years. Nevertheless, I am not using 10 years as the defining criteria for the goal. I am letting the market define the time that it takes to reach it, which means that I may reach the goal in five years or maybe in fifteen. The trading opportunities that avail themselves through *Time and Price Symmetry,* are how a trader learns to become **market-oriented** with respect to his or her decisions. In effect, the proper level of trading execution is directly linked to how many trade opportunities the market is availing itself. Ultimately, this will be up to volatility and the number of *Time and Price Symmetry-based* market inflection points, which cannot be forced, and the mindset of the trader should always be focused in the present moment in order to avail the mind to the **Moment of Recognition.**

Trading in the present moment (a Law of Attraction concept) will be a constant theme in this book, which will be elaborated on in Chapter 5. Focusing in the present moment is necessary in order to remove one's focus on the dollars and cents that financial traders deal with. Focusing on the present moment allows the trader to see the market structure, the Marketome, and the market opportunities that may be presenting themselves in the here and now. When true opportunities are recognized via *Time and Price Symmetry*, there will exist moments in a trader's life that warrant going "all-in" on a trade. For me, my recognition of the March 6, 2009 low at 3:34pm was an "all-in" moment, and I circulated an email 10 minutes after this to over 50 people that I knew. These fleeting moments, where the market hits a *time and Price Symmetry-based* market inflection point that the trader has predefined, require extreme focus in order to properly read the market's reaction to that predetermined time and price level. If the market does react/begin to reverse, the trader needs to make sure that he/she remains in the present moment in order to capture this moment as the recognition of a new trade possibility; hence, the Moment of Recognition. The faster one's intellect can learn to grasp this Moment of Recognition, the tighter the trader can trade; meaning more, employable leverage or smaller potential losses via tighter, more effective stop placement. Being market-oriented and not focusing on monthly reporting requirements or the capital itself, will be necessary in the trader's mind in order to properly shift mentality to present moment, market-oriented thinking. In fact, it is in the best interest of the client even if it makes the client (including yourself) uncomfortable. *The moral is, it is good to have a monthly trading goal, but do not let the goal become the objective.* Let yourself focus on all the trade opportunities, and I guarantee your results will exceed even the loftiest goal with the proper implementation of leverage.

In terms of my personal career and my analytical observations, the monthly performance goal was always a nail biting experience for me regardless of profit or loss. It made me feel like the end of the month number is what will stick with me for my entire lifetime, which festers irrationality. Therefore, my suggestion to any Fund manager is to allow for daily reporting of performance, or at worst, weekly reporting. Moreover, the manager's psyche should never be stressed because of performance. Remember, performance comes from the market and your ability to recognize *Time and Price Symmetry* levels. The best way to free yourself from your performance is to distance yourself from it. I suggest that you actually employ a person for a Fund that intercepts and reads the manager's emails/phone calls during a trading week. It is my belief that Risk Management Officers need to serve dual purposes in the financial industry. First, obviously, they should force the adherence of risk management strategies, but they should also serve as risk managers for the actual lifestyle of the manager him or herself. This lifestyle awareness is in relation to not only physical health but also mental health, which is why a staff Psychiatrist/PhD Psychologist is the defined criterion for a Risk Management Officer. Hence, the Risk Management Officer needs to ensure that the portfolio manager's awareness remains calm and focused, and as we are discussing, there are many things that can hinder that required mentality. As such, Risk Management Officers need to expand in their job function in order to help managers decide when to, quite literally, take a break. Furthermore, I believe that dealing with investors is time consuming and counterproductive. As such, money managers should set aside a specific time period, be it at the end of the quarter, or at the end of the year, in order to then, confront and answer all of these questions that cannot easily be answered by an assistant or a Risk Management Officer.

Distraction

Clientele/investors are their own worst enemy. They cause managers to fail due to unnecessary pressure. The client is paying the manager to deal with this pressure already, and as such, they need to step back and trust the manager in the first place. When people are locked-up in a fund for 2 years, they cannot change their investment outcome anyway. Moreover, the belief that performance justifies a bonus, which is an approach that most of Wall Street has used for the past two centuries, is idiotic. Performance-based bonuses create needless risk by an individuals' greed-oriented nature to achieve returns in order to satiate their own lifestyle. Likewise, paying manager's only at the end of a year also encourages seasonality that unnecessarily influences irrationality. Again, these are only logical conclusions, and it seems obvious that a manger that finally has a break out year will tend to go a little crazy in the first few months of receiving his or her first large paycheck, which directly impacts future performance! Thus, only if a manager has reached extreme wealth whereby the increase of his or her personal net worth has a diminishing effect on his or her lifestyle can a manager that is incentivized by performance-based income truly be profitable to his or her clients. I believe this concept is very important to stress because there is also an ethereal, unquantifiable, holistic oneness to be found between the money manager and the market itself, and taking steps in order to ensure a stress-free external environment from trading is crucial, in my eyes, to a money manager's longevity. Summarily, the markets are stressful enough; let the manager do his/her work, and if the results do not reflect the investor's intention after the monetary lock-up time-period is over, then, simply, tell your investor to redeem his or her investment. Remove that investor's stress from your life as quickly as possible.

In order to further expound on this statement, I ask the reader to research the lives of the top CEO's and of the top traders. If you do that research, you will learn an interesting correlation. In addition, I feel that I must also describe one of my mentor's own approach to ridding himself from external stresses. If you were to read biographies or intertwine yourself into the opportunity to avail your life to the true masters of any profession, you will find that those masters have eliminated any level of distraction completely from their work life. In order to go back to the comparison of the doctoral relationship in regards to trading, I must simply appeal to the reader's preexisting perception of doctors. Does a doctor use his cell phone during surgery? Does he tolerate any type of distractions when his patient's life on the line? No. Of course not. Going back to football as well, does the kicker bring a cell phone on the field? Again, No. Of course not. In trading, when I spent time with my mentor in *Time and Price Symmetry,* he literally told me, "I don't care if my mother is dead, I don't want to know about it during my trading hours. What difference does it make to me if I know this at 1pm or at 430pm. I cannot change the outcome, and all it can do is serve as a distraction." The best traders, the best CEO's, the best doctors, the best whatever, learn to live in a life that is free of distraction while they are working in the present moment. This seriousness is seldom done for casual market participants, and even mutual fund managers/fundamental managers are rarely without distraction. It is simply disturbing about the prevalent lack of respect that is given to the markets, and when the reader understands that 99% of industry participants never respect the power of the market in the first place, the ability of ascertaining tremendous profits becomes near certainty if one remains humble and acquiesces to the humility quickly inflected by incorrect market assessments.

Furthermore, because trading is often done at "home" and is often treated without its deserved respect, many people do not correctly free themselves from distraction. Being at home often means that your wife or your children can come into your office at any time. In addition, being at home has its own psychological issues that appear over time in relation to overall laziness, which also reinforces the need to have a Risk Management Officer that is a Psychologist. As such, I must make emphasis of how important our jobs are as traders. Sit your family down, and tell them that even if you are home, they need to make an appointment to see you. In addition, psychological research has shown that people who work at home (like writers) need to do similar routines to those employed in offices in order to ratchet up the level of professionalism and respect for their jobs. For example, make yourself drive every morning to get a cup of coffee in order to simulate being in the work/commuting environment. Dress yourself well and professionally in order to allow the subconscious realization that is gained by psychosomatically aligning your external life to that of a "real" job. Proper, professional mindset alignment is necessary in order to work at your peak utilization. If you cannot find this work balance at home, then, I suggest renting an office space, waking up at 2am, and getting to work by 3am. Do whatever you can to prepare yourself mentally for your job. You need to avail your mind to the present moment in order to recognize the Moment of Recognition. More uncomprehending is that the overall attitude that most people have for the markets must be changed. Most people treat the markets it like is a casino, and the level of seriousness required for trading is never emphasized in a University-like setting. As such, I believe that university-based educational institutions need to add into their curriculums some type of fellowship or training program like it has in other education derivatives (again akin to residency for doctors). Conclusively, it is my sincerest hope that the seriousness of trading or of money management is recognized and respected properly by the masses. Elevating the role of the financial market participant to that of a surgical doctor is necessary if we are to evolve to the next level in understanding the true structure of the market. It is not a game.

Capitalization

The concept of capitalization is the antithesis of the statement that I made in the *Introduction* that "money is meaningless." Unfortunately, we are in the business of money, and it is a necessary evil. More important, money has to be treated properly in order to ensure that there is money available day in and day out in order for us to perform our jobs. However, making money is not the goal, and money is simply the manufacturing input for the production of our product, which are more moneys defined as percentage returns. However, while money remains necessary for our job, the thought process regarding "what money is" must be forgotten. The trader must remember that the dollars will always take care of themselves if the trading strategy and the trader's mind are properly aligned, but everyone's level of aptitude for performance will be different, which is why, you, as the reader, have the ability to become the best trader in the world. Your aptitude for trading may dictate that type of output, but that aptitude can be quantified based on trading statistics only if money is removed from the thought process. For example, I do not know how many times I have stated to people that I wish I could just call trades instead of thinking about the size I am trading or thinking about whether or not I was properly filled or not. If it was possible to just call it as I saw it, I have no doubts that my level of performance would exponentially increase, but unfortunately, we as humans are not wired that way. As an aside, even the bible talks about money on a consistent basis, and it would not surprise me that, in the hereafter, there is a spiritual currency that is also tradable.

What is more, our lives and our companies (hedge funds in particular) have their own monetary requirements. Employees, houses, cars, offices, computing, lawyers, accountants, food, clothing, etc. are all components that exist in order to take our minds off the present moment. These lifestyle and corporate needs are also unavoidable requirements that exist in order to take our minds out of the market and back onto the dollars and cents. The requirements of life will lead to goal-oriented thinking, and that is why new traders must minimize their living requirements when they decide to become traders.

Using my life as an example, I needed to make $65,000.00 per month in order to pay for my lifestyle, my Fund, and my employees. This figure, of approximately $800,000.00 per year, was the basis of my capitalization requirement. As a hedge fund manager, my fees were 2% of the base capital per year and 20% of the profit per quarter. Therefore, in order to trade without emotion, my capitalization requirement was $40,000,000.00, but my fund had less than $10mm in it. I was 75%+ under-capitalized, which meant danger to the trading psyche. In fact, in my entire career, I have never once been properly capitalized! It is my belief that with regard to making my psyche feel calm, I would have needed the management fee (2%) to cover the external, monetary requirements regarding myself, my employees, and my Fund in order to be free of the burden of goal-oriented trading. Thus, the trader must ascertain the proper level of capitalization that is necessary in order to stay market-oriented, and sometimes, this is done by building a personal monetary surplus. For instance, an alternative solution to freeing yourself of monetary burdens is to set aside corporate and lifestyle expenses for a three-year period, and with that accomplished, the size of the fund's assets under management would dramatically decrease.

However, the most obvious solution you may be thinking is: **REDUCE YOUR REQUIREMENTS**! This is one of the hardest things for us to do as humans: take a step-back in lifestyle. As we age, we are faced with the "more-monster." More houses. More cars. More Vacations. More of everything, and usually, more expensive every-things. Unfortunately, it took my incarceration to reset my lifestyle that already had high-requirements from success in other endeavors. I expect that when I get the opportunity to rebuild my life, my new yearly requirements will be less than my previous monthly requirements, and my capitalization needs will drop by 90% (assuming I am only trading for myself without the costs of added employees or fund operations). I pray that it does not take a nearly life-ending event like the one it did me for you to realize that sacrificing lifestyle (dropping the capitalization requirement now) will provide a path to a much greater lifestyle later.

As you may have noticed in our discussion of capitalization thus far, I did not factor trading profits into the equation for an individual trader or for a Fund Manager. The purpose in removing profits from the equation is to remove the goal-oriented and greed-oriented thought processes that exist for a trader when he or she is under the pressure to perform. Specifically, the current implementation plan that most hedge fund seeders or even angel investors use when building a company that has a relation to the markets is absolutely upside down in my eyes. During the first year of formation, a new trading-based/investing-based company is at most risk of failure. There are already enough external pressures in the first-year of a start up that, by pressuring the manager(s) to meet a certain asset appreciation goal in order to continue subsequent existence, is idiotic. Seed investors should ply managers with the most money they can from day one in order to ensure safety of the manager's psyche in relation to the market. If necessary, those seeders should then reduce the monetary allocation at the end of the year if the performance-based income is enough to fuel operations for a year or more (as I referenced earlier, I believe 3 years is ideal).

Being a "clutch-trader" or a "crisis-trader" is a well-proven disastrous mentality. Sure, it can be done in limited bursts that lead to outperforming intervals, like in the case of relief pitchers in baseball, but even a relief pitcher can only maintain that level of performance for so long. With respect to my own career, I spent the 16-months of the CFTC investigation that lead to my arrest as a "crisis-trader" with the feeling that I had to make $6mm back in order to get out of the problem I had. That constant, agonizing mentality led to more and more loss. Granted, I do acquiesce that trading in "crisis-mode" should be learned to some extent because during extreme volatility, the trader or money manager needs to be able to handle the added pressure in order to perform at our best, but again, being a "relief trader" does not foreshadow recurrent success. Amazingly, when I learned *Time and Price Symmetry*, it was during the financial collapse of 2008, and in a way, I was able to achieve a much greater intrinsically learned knowledge base because of the volatility of that time. However, since I learned *Time and Price Symmetry*, I have never been able to implement trading calmly and methodically, but finally, upon the termination of my incarceration, I will be free from burden.

Unfortunately, the mental fatigue that I worked myself into allowed for large percentage returns that often times happened but never lasted. This type of market gambling became my goal, which was wrong. Instead, my goal and all traders' goals should be to allow consistent profits to occur, which will yield the required performance metrics that allow for more leverage implementation over time. Summarily, the ironic nature of when the trader has the least amount of capital available is usually when the trader is also confronted with the most pressure to perform, and that is why the smartest fund seeders are those that supply large amounts of capital in the beginning in order to allow the trader to stay focused in the present moment. It pains me to think about how many successful Fund Managers have never been able to reach their potential because their first year of operations were so difficult, and I feel that I am one of these managers. In a way, all five of my Funds failed due to the feeling of being under-capitalized, and in the last two, I was also in a crisis mindset. Therefore, I encourage the start-up facilitators in this industry to remember this paragraph in relation to their future endeavors. This type of knowledge recognition concerning manager mentality may actually cause a fund seeder to execute new start-ups that have a higher probability of longevity!

Trading Styles

In the last Chapter, I discussed Mutual Fund Managers and savvy individual investors. However, the recurrent theme in this book thus far has been aligned to a private fund manager (a hedge fund manager), which is probably the smallest audience for this book. Nevertheless, the concept of performance requirements and monetary requirements are found in every trading style. Thankfully, $50mm is not the base requirement for every type of endeavor in this industry. There are many different approaches to the market, and in Chapter 2, we discussed that the investing approach could be accomplished with as little as $5,000-$10,000. Therefore, the trading styles that are found in this Chapter will outline the objective of trading each style along with what is required in order to function in that type of trading style; these requirements will be in terms of mental aptitude and capitalization. **Trading Styles** will be methods of operation in terms of asset appreciation and statistical performance in terms of winning/losing, which includes individual trade metrics. We will begin the discussion of trading styles with the hardest style, which is defined by the highest percentage of failure. This type of trading style comes coupled with the lowest capital requirement necessary. I am speaking of course of **campaign trading**, which has been my primary, life goal since May of 2005.

The purpose of a trading campaign is to turn a small amount of money into a vast sum over a small time period using high leverage afforded by the derivatives market and high volatility market conditions. In order to accomplish a **trading campaign,** a trader must build a project plan that is based on intervals. In the beginning of my understanding with respect to what a trading campaign was, I used time as a component for defining these intervals, but in May of 2011, I rationally analyzed all of my campaign failures. I realized that once I hit my daily loss, I kept trading because of a mentally traumatized psyche borne from the CFTC investigation that was going on in my life. The investigation led me to feel that I had a set amount of time in order to reach my goal, and I always felt like I had to keep pushing it or my time would run out. Of course, I did end up running out of time, and that pressure that I was under was not illogical or imaginary. Hence, that investigation is correctly correlated to the pressure caused by time, which led to failure. Ironically, in my personal psychoanalysis that I embarked upon since my incarceration, I have learned that this stress is common for people, who have never been in trouble with the law before (like me). In fact, this mental trauma (not illness) is defined as **Critogenic Stress**. People who go through divorces or paternity disputes often feel this as well, but for me, I feel that it is just as applicable, and I ask any other traders that may ever encounter a probe from any of the oversight agencies to cutback on trade size and be proactive about trying to reach a conclusion. Had I done this, I believe I would never had been incarcerated (for one), and I also believe that I would have had success with running a trading campaign.

However, that May 2011, I switched to performance-based intervals instead of time-based intervals in order to define these compounding levels. Immediately, I found success. More relevant, performance-based intervals allowed my intervals to be connected to one another based on their performance up versus performance down. For example, each interval had a 50% profit target and a 33% loss so that if you failed in reaching the next interval, you simply went back to the previous interval. (i.e. a $100,000 interval 1 that reaches a 50% goal, $150,000, interval 2 returns to interval 1 by a 33% loss back to $100,000). This led to immediate success, and that is why I believe that I was on the verge of making all the money back that would have made things right in my life. Therefore, in order to understand the power of these intervals, I ask the reader to look at the spreadsheets attached in the *Resources* section of this book. In that section, a 2-month and a 15-interval campaign can be constructed in order for you to visualize the power of compounding on profits with the use of high-leverage.

The risk associated with running a trading campaign is huge with typically 25% to 50% of the campaign trading account at risk every day/interval of the campaign. A trader must be in control of his or her mind and emotions for an extended period of time. The trader must literally live in the present moment for 1-2 months, which is extraordinarily hard to accomplish because the ego will intervene when large losses occur or when large amounts of money are put at risk. Basically, in order to handle the stress of the risk at the higher levels of the campaign, when every click of the mouse has hundreds of thousands of dollars at risk, a trader must truly rely on the subconscious processes in order to accomplish the goal. Again, athleticism is an important correlation here. Does Tiger Woods fret over every swing? Obviously, there is some degree of apprehension, but, at the moment of execution, it is my belief that people like Mr. Woods acquiesce to the subconscious autonomic processes. The *campaign trader* must effectively do the same thing.

Now, in order to emphasize the profit potential of campaign trading, the 15-interval campaign that I was in the process of accomplishing at the time of my arrest had a goal of taking $22,000 to $6,000,000 in 15 intervals using a high-leverage brokerage firm in the S&P Futures. In order to clarify my introspective analysis of my trading campaign failures, which may be relevant to future **campaigners**, I feel that I must mention that my biggest emotional struggle was when I found myself reaching a daily stop-loss level early on in the day or even an interval profit objective early on in the day. On these days, when a trader is either properly executing or quick to fail, the trading mentality of trying to make more money later in the day (if failure) or trying to keep your profits going (if properly executing) is a hard mental demon to fight off.

Often, I could not just walk away for the rest of the day because I would be forced watching all of the perfect trade setups that I was not taking. The psychological impact of missing trades is just as strong as unrealized profit because the *imagination of our minds sees both of these emotions as equal*. Therefore, we have to rely on the baseball analogy from earlier concerning trading; we have to realize that we have finite mental energy when executing under stress (or duress in my case), which comes from losses or volatility (or governmental investigations). We also have to realize that every human mentality has limits that can be reached, and we need to utilize other parts of our life in order to successfully continue the act of trading. Again, would a surgeon perform two 14-hour surgeries in two days? No. Again, that is why I believe Risk Management Officers need in order to effectively manage a manager's mind and lifestyle just as much as the portfolio.

For me, the transition to performance intervals instead of time intervals allowed me to do two things. First, when reaching the next interval (through profits) or the prior interval (through losses) I learned to take an exercise break for at least an hour in order to get my mind off the market and allow me to get back into the next interval. In fact, any connection to the market had to be severed or the reset mechanism required of the intervals would not occur. Second, moving to performance-based intervals allowed me to reset my interval profit/loss targets in order to allow me to properly rethink the trading size I was using. This is a critical note because overuse of leverage under mental fatigue is disastrous. Therefore, I find it essential that a trader must forget what he or she did earlier in the day, good or bad, and the trader must always learn to refocus on the present moment. The trader must "forget the last pitch."

Okay, with this discussion on campaign trading, we see the apparent overemphasis on sports analogies that I have consistently and consciously derived herein, but we are approaching the diminishment of these comparisons because campaign trading is not possible as a daily endeavor. Therefore, in order for me to conclude these streaming metaphors, I must yield to one of today's best coaches in order to elaborate on having the correct mindset with respect to staying market-oriented. In a recent Fortune Magazine interview with Nick Saban (Fortune Magazine, September 24, 2012, p. 158), coach Saban goes on to describe how in his fourth year at Michigan State he was a true underdog against number one ranked Ohio State, and when I read his statement, the correlation to the trading mentality necessary to remain market-oriented was truly palpable. Further, this quote is the pinnacle of summing up the goals for a successful trading mentality, and that is why I feel I must quote Brian O'Keefe's article in its entirety to the reader (bold/italicizes and bracketed additions done by me):

> Saban points to a game in November 1998 as a key moment in his evolution. He was in his fourth year as the head coach at Michigan State, and his unranked Spartans were scheduled to face the undefeated No. 1 team, Ohio State, on the road. During practice that week, Saban told his team that they weren't going to worry about winning the game. ***They would treat every play [or trade] in the game as if it had a history and a life of its own. And regardless of what happened in the play before [or trade before], they were going to focus only on the next play.*** [With this approach] He found that his players were looser and more confident. In a huge upset, Michigan State came from behind to win 28-24. Saban decided to stop talking about the importance of winning and double down on his process-oriented approach. "I'm not naïve enough to think winning isn't important," says Saban. "But what that game made me realize is how much better it is for people not to worry about the opposition but ***to focus on executing and know if they do their job correctly they're going to be successful,*** rather than thinking the other guy's going to determine the outcome."

The problem that many traders have is that they feel the market is against them, or they feel that their trading strategy is not working. The market is totally indifferent. Yes, the market does sometimes screw you, but the market itself is impersonal. The market engages in these battles because it is the collective consciousness of mankind; a collective search to exploit the weak. Hence, Coach Saban's comments completely reflect the counterargument to those thoughts. Therefore, aside from Coach Saban's comments, the trader must realize that because the markets are continuous, especially in our day and age, that there will always be future trading outcomes. There is no rush, and the trader does not need to constantly be immersed in the market. Thus, we can terminate the sports metaphors because unlike a sports game, the markets are eternally present.

If the trader's line of thinking is properly aligned to active market-oriented analysis, instead of time-focused pressure, the trader or the manager basks in the reduction of unneeded and undeserved pressure, which causes an aversion to proper execution, and again, I must emphasize that I envisioned this was the direct causation of my campaign failures. Only by removing this type of incorrect thinking can we realize that trading is not something we do for a few years and quit. No, traders just like doctors (or even like Coach Saban), should be traders for life, which yields to Freud's basic principal of mental health, which is "to love" and "to work." Therefore, please try to obliterate the thought that since "the markets are theoretically continuous anyway, why shouldn't my trading?" The answer is that you are not a computer nor are you God. Instead, the trader needs to modify that ever-obnoxious question. In fact, the question must be converted to a declarative statement such as, "Since the markets are 24-hours, I can trade whenever I am mentally ready to trade." This thought is a much better, logical conclusion, and I wish I had arrived at it many years ago. However, I had an aversion to going backwards in trade size after drawing down to the previous interval, and I ended up employing more leverage when my mentality was now fatigued. It was an ass-backwards approach, and I needed a way to take a break in order to refresh my psyche. For me, this was a major breakthrough for my personal mentality, and it will be up to every trader in order to determine what mental demons are preventing his or her success in a trading campaign. In a campaign, the trader must realize that they will fail; often, but *you*, as the trader, have the power to analyze your own failures, and *you* have the power to fix them. Unfortunately, I had my analysis-derived revelation approximately 2 months prior to my incarceration, and for the first time, I was finally having consistent, positive performance being in campaign mode, which is why I felt that I was on the verge of righting all the wrongs that finally caught up to me. Sadly, for my investors, I ran out of time.

Getting back to intervals with respect to training campaigns, although I chose $22,000.00 as my starting point, this number is arbitrary. My trading mentor, who took 19 years before doing his first campaign started with $2,500.00, which turned into $21mm+ over 38 trading days. Therefore, capitalization requirements for this trading style are relatively low, but your experience reaching this level of trading is immense in terms of time and money. In a way, I have come to see that I have had a $14,000,000 education over the last 7 years, and now, I am using my 3 years of incarceration in order to pay off that debt akin to the old Solomon Brothers associates in the 70s and 80s. However, once you feel that your trading acumen and your Moment of Recognition have become honed to a point of implementing a campaign, you will need to define how much capital to commit to each campaign, how many campaigns you plan to attempt before giving up, and how much money you need to satisfy your lifestyle while you are trading in campaign mode. Once defining these numbers, a trader should be able to focus purely on trading in order to allow the results to take care of themselves. It is also very important to a successful campaign to take no profit out of the account while working in campaign mode because this will make the dollars and cents more relevant again. I cannot stress this enough, especially with respect to trading campaigns, you, dear trader, need to disassociate yourself from the money, and instead, the numbers need to be thought of as simply being linked to your intervals on your spreadsheets. Often, I have found that using numbers instead of dollar signs in spreadsheets is another subconscious disassociating technique that is useful in allowing your mind to think in terms of simply being in the interval you are in with respect to maintaining a market-oriented performance objective. Forget the actual "$."

A trading campaign takes years of market experience in order to gain the intrinsic knowledge necessary and the mental fortitude necessary in order to be successful. In fact, a trader may decide never to embark on a campaign in his or her career. Moreover, the conditions necessary to run a successful campaign will only present themselves a few times per year when the volatility of your trading instrument is high. As such, one cannot expect to be a campaign trader every day of his or her trading career. It is not sustainable from the market or from you as a human being. However, it only takes getting rich once to catapult your trading to new levels (See *Reflections: The Path to a Billion*). With that, I have finally been able to define a *trading campaign* to the audience of this book, and undoubtedly, there was a purpose in doing so in order to explain to those people that trusted me what I was trying to do wit their capital, and I hope that with the proper definition of a *trading campaign* now extrapolated, those previous investors (and my family and friends) can understand and comprehend, what the hell I was trying to do.

I will group the next two sets of traders into the same pile: proprietary ("prop") traders and personal traders. **Proprietary Traders** are essentially daytraders with more leverage offered to them from their brokerage house; essentially, they are "propped" up with more firm capital. However, the capitalization requirements are quite similar for prop traders and personal traders. The capitalization is simply whatever the trader needs in order to reach his or her performance goals based on his or her aptitude to execute. However, for longevity as either type of trader, I highly recommend losing the goal-oriented nature that is derived from personal expenses. As a personal trader, you are literally trading as your main job with your own (or your firm's) money. Therefore, your personal living expenses are often the number one goal to reach, when they should be forgotten. Subsequently, larger profits become less important to your psyche when you focus on your cost of living as well, as palpably referenced via the Wall St. Journal article discussing the lackadaisical attitude that becomes emergent once objectives are reached. Therefore, you need to stop placing a higher weighting on your personal expenses versus your subsequent profits. In fact, both should be forgotten, and the only thing that should be maintained is a constant awareness of the mind to the present moment in order to be availed to the Moment of Recognition. No matter the style, the goal should always be to remain market-oriented.

The largest problem with prop traders and personal traders is that if they are still trading, they have undoubtedly found a method that works for them, but these traders do not recognize the finite time they may have until catastrophic failure (unless they become investors). Moreover, luck also becomes a huge crutch to these traders because often, a trade that may completely eradicate their account is not taken. As such, the belief in the longevity of their strategy becomes further engrained in the ego. Therefore, the problem that a personal trader has, when reading a book like this, occurs when the trader comes to the factual conclusion that they need to adjust their trading strategy to be aligned with *Time and Price Symmetry*, while still being able to meet applicable expenses with their own strategy. The fact is that over time, your current method of trading will work against you, and by shifting your subconscious earlier, you can digest this new information now instead of later. Only by witnessing thousands of examples over several years will you burn *Time and Price Symmetry* into your mind. You will need to become a believer, and furthermore, hone your grasp of the Moment of Recognition so that you are fast enough in order to compete (putting more favorable reward to risk skewed in your favor). As such, the capitalization requirement for current traders, who are dealing with strategy conflict, is more arduous because you also have to give up the opportunity cost of live trading. There is no other viable solution in my mind. You cannot trade two strategies at once unless one of them is automated in some fashion, and unfortunately, you do need to spend at least 10,000 hours on *Time and Price Symmetry* before being at the point of preparedness for executing in time and in price. Conclusively, the egotistical mentality of already successful traders is a big perception that must be changed. The fact is ***successful traders are not humble people.*** They are egotistically edified, and often, rude. They do not tend to avail their minds to anything else because they believe they are market gods, but thankfully, there will come a day that all traders will be humbled. These traders do not know when that day will come, and I encourage those traders who are egotistically edified to learn to become humble and thankful to the market. The reason I say this is that the *successful trader* will feel that because of his or her attainment of material-success already, the trader will not invest the time/years into *Time and Price Symmetry*. They will feel that after only a few months, they are ready to start trading again. Unfortunately, I did this, and it led to disastrous results. *I was not humble, and I destroyed my life.*

Thankfully, despite my disparaging remarks in the last paragraph, I must state that successful traders have one major advantage! Typically, they have plenty of money to take a step back. Therefore, the capitalization requirement for these traders usually already exists, but these traders face something much harder than the monetary commitment as I already mentioned. These traders not only give up the opportunity cost of trading, but they have to give up their beliefs in their currently, working systems, which may have been engrained in themselves for several years if not decades. In fact, these traders may have spent twenty years developing a system or a strategy, and here, I am coming along and positing the reality that their work was meaningless. Although that statement is the utter reality and the utter truth that the edified intellect must learn to accept that does not mean their work was meaningless if they have been profitable with their strategy up to that point. However, I am trying to let the accomplished party know that their method of trading is finite whereas *Time and Price Symmetry* is not. Mentally, understanding the reality that I am now stating as fact will be a hard transition, but if a lifelong trading career is your goal, then you must decide to make the transition and live with it. The first step will be to evaluate your lifestyle expenses for at least four years in order to learn how to trade in *Time and Price Symmetry*. You will also need a base amount of capital to trade with at some point, and finally, you will need to give yourself time to become profitable with a new method. Consequently, your time may stretch to five or six years of banked expenses in order to prevent yourself from becoming goal-oriented. So, the harsh reality is that the requirement to embark on trading as a career will basically be five years worth of living expenses along with a starting account size. It is hard. Again, I could not do it myself. I tried learning on the job, and it led to disastrous results. Regardless of your intellect, I further encourage that you use five years as a conservative estimate. You are not better then the market, and if you are a genius (pompous/egotistical and not humble) the market will humble you. Quickly. Some day. "Like a thief in the night."

The last groups of traders are institutional traders that are already managing hedge funds, mutual funds, or family offices. When I first began to learn *Time and Price Symmetry*, I grouped myself into this category more than the last category. At that time, I was managing a quantitative hedge fund with a strategy I spent several years developing. My backtests were good. My drawdowns were low, and when the time came to go live, the live results were in-line with all of my testing. However, 2008 came, and all those years of work became irrelevant within one month of trading. In the face of my model's failure, I found myself learning *Time and Price Symmetry*, which is the true market structure that I believed existed from the first day I entered the markets. However, my ego and my lack of exposure to *Time and Price Symmetry* prevented me from giving up on my quantitative model, which only made matters worse. Furthermore, I wanted the prestige that once existed as being known as a "hedge fund manager." I suspect that for the institutional trader reading this, your job title (your career path) will be the hardest sacrifice in order for you to become a disciple of *Time and Price Symmetry*. It will be another test of your ego, and I must recall a famous quotation from the movie *Fightclub*, "You are not your job. You are not how much money you have in the bank."

That said, this egotistical test was another error of mine because I too could not get rid of having the exclusive title of "hedge fund manager," and as you will learn in my selective autobiography at the end of this book, I ended up using the capital in my subsequent hedge funds in order to pay for my four years of experience with live trading instead of observing and testing. I also had to give up over 15,000 hours of experience and studying that I had done in quantitative models and other trading methods. More important than the ignored necessity of getting the proper experience is the fact that while running a Fund, there are several other pressures. Therefore, be aware and acknowledge all of the pressures you will have with remaining institutional, and do not deviate from your current company's profitable trading method. Instead, be aware of the strategy shift, and make the transition when confident and when necessary.

Although my life is an extreme example of what can go wrong when an institutional trader encounters strategy shift, I do believe that one can embark on this learning process while still being a profitable portfolio manager. In fact, had my quant model not failed in 2008, I would have done the same thing – left the model run while I studied and practiced my knowledge in *Time and Price Symmetry*. It's not like the implementation of a profitable quantitative model takes much time anyway, and I am sure that most portfolio managers take a passive approach to the markets until certain conditions are met based on their investment strategy. However, do not forget about the law of 10,000 hours. Once you have achieved the requisite time in order to trade in time and price for your Firm/Fund, do so slowly, by slowly allocating capital to this new Tactical Strategy Pool after, of course, making the relevant adjustments to your prospectus/memorandum; allow your Fund to make *Time and Price Symmetry* a part of the plan. Over time, as your original strategy reaches its finite time of existence (unless you are a pure fundamental fund) in the market, you can fully transition over to *Time and Price Symmetry* for the benefit of your firm and your investors. By no means am I stating to give up on what is working for you now, but be mindful that unless you embrace what is in this book, your strategy will fail or you will become an investor once your asset level reaches a certain valuation. Summarily, an institutional trading mentality is much different then a private/prop trader because you can still maintain your base salary from your Firm. You are not trading to pay your bills for the most part, and you can maintain two disciplinary focuses at the same time because you do not have to weight one more than the other. It will purely be at your sole discretion on how you reach 10,000 hours of observation, and how you decide to implement *Time and Price Symmetry* for the benefit of your firm. However, successful Fund Managers have to deal with many more problems than just the markets; most specifically, employees.

Employees are a large detriment to many managers because managers feel the pressure to work in order to ensure the livelihood of other individuals, which can sometimes skew results in unforeseen ways. In fact, because of the other aspects required when managing a Firm, I decided to pursue my MBA in Project Management instead of Finance. More important, my own personal feelings regarding the closeness of my employees in my last fund, led to irrational behavior, which ultimately, became criminal. In fact, instead of protecting them from emotional stress, I put them at criminal risk. Therefore, be aware of the employee-factor, and do not underestimate it. As such, my desire for running a future fund is highly weighted against doing so because of the emotional component that emerges through the workplace. However, at the same time, there is a tremendous benefit to having employees, and especially, the necessity for Risk Management Officers. Hence, I hope to find a balance that will work for me one day, and I plan to do so by minimizing the personal, emotional risk between myself and my employees except for the employees that must be placed into trustworthy positions, like Risk Management Officers.

There is another corollary to this "Law of 10,000 Hours" discussion, which I feel is relevant. This corollary is something that I describe as sure certainty in reaching centi-million dollar status (if not billion dollar status) within 20 years of entering the market. Notice, that I am using a realistic timeline by stating 20 years, and I am not a proponent of something implausible or impossible. This understanding is something that I feel has to do with the mental conditioning necessary in order for one to exponentially increase position size in the market, and I add the term "elastic" because I believe that even if you are to take a break from the market for some time, the mental conditioning to risk is something that can snap easily back in to place (i.e. meaning that if you were a 20 lot trader, and you took a break for a year or two, you can easily become a 20 lot trader again). That said, let me explain the causality that it takes to reach proper conditioning.

I will use the S&P 500 E-Mini Futures contract for this example. So far, I stated that you need 10,000 hours before placing your first live trade, which takes approximately 4 years to achieve. From that point forward, I posit (since I have no statistical backing it must be philosophical) that one can increase the basis (see Reflections: Understanding the Basis Position) position size by a magnitude of 10 with ever increase in 10,000 hours of experience. Ergo, at the start of year 5 someone can start trading 2 lots in the S&P 500 E-Mini (again for example purposes only). If we are to assume that the trader is able to take 10 points per day out of the market over a 250 trading day year, then, we see that the trader should net $250,000 in their first trading year ($250,000=250*10*2*$50). After another four years, the trader can then up their basis position to 20 lots, which means an annual salary of $2.5mm. After another four years, 200 lots, which means $25mm a year. At 200 lots, the trader should be able to reach whatever monetary goal they had ever dreamed of, and with the continual expansion of volume/liquidity in the derivatives market, after another four years, there is nothing stating that 2,000 lots would not be possible as a basis position size yielding $250mm per year in income. Therefore, after only 20 years of market trading, we find a guaranteed path to multi-billion dollar status. What other area of employment can have such certainty, but the ever-present problem is that people never decide to apply this type of project managment skills to the market, which leads to failure. The market is not a game, and this level of thought and position sizing control is necessary if one is to understand the need to mentally condition oneself through progressively building one's own wealth.

Of final discussion regarding trading styles and the commitment necessary in order to learn the methods in this book, I have been consistently reflecting on the importance of 10,000 hours of experience in order to begin having success in *Time and Price Symmetry*. Although this is a psychological necessity that should be placed in Chapter 5, I believe it has more relevance in relation to Trading Styles because a person needs to spend this amount of time learning whatever style that they may choose when commencing trading. More specifically, using 10,000 hours is not arbitrary, and many books have been written regarding the psychological impact of attaining expertise by this time-based figure. In fact, I encourage you to read several books on the subject, which will lead you through several examples of how important getting 10,000 hours is, for us humans, to excel in any one field. In a way, it is a race to meet that level of exposure in order to be able to compete in a profitable manner, but unfortunately, you cannot rush the race; you need to let it come to completion itself. You cannot control the market's trade inceptions, and the market should not control you. However, you must relinquish your goal-oriented methodology, and you must acquiesce to taking what the market gives you.

Defining Expertise, a Personal Perspective

I feel it is important to stress my qualifications to the reader at this point because I have now defined the ambitious task of trading campaigns and interval segregation. Thus, the reality must now kick-in for the reader that these concepts and these implementations are extraordinarily innovative. I ask the reader, "Have you ever heard of these concepts before?" Undoubtedly, the answer is no, and almost every definition in this book his stated with the purpose of redefining a completely new industry; hence the Marketome. Therefore, I ask the reader to share in the enlightenment process that it is happening through this writing because I find it fascinating. You and I, as reader and author, are razing conventional financial analysis and implementation as it has been known for millennia. We are engaging in original human thought, which is extraordinarily rare in this point in history. Hence, I feel a responsibility to the reader to emphatically define my level of expertise before we get to the nitty gritty of *Time and Price Symmetry*, and I must begin this discussion by stating that although I never went the traditional path of money management in order to get a trading education from an investment bank, *I am educated*.

In fact, I hold the egotistical belief in my trading acumen that I contain within me a level of market understanding and market appreciation that fewer than 5 (if that many) individuals on this planet share. That said, I must emphatically refer to the old Wall Street idioms that tended to rely on quotations such as, "Ohh, you can trust him, he was educated at Goldman Sachs." That slavery of investment banking training is dying, and with that death, there are fewer and fewer true traders being educated. So, I must now possess inherent, complete belief in the fact that I envision this book as the focal point for an entirely new realm of University education, and as the father of "The Marketome" I feel that I must equate my knowledge base in terms of university-like comparisons for understanding my commitment and my lifelong purpose of defining and teaching the true market structure.

Thankfully, we have mathematics in order to help us in understanding typical college requirements for attaining conference of a degree. Thus, we can define the level experience necessary for one to become a professional in understanding the Marketome! If one was to think of a typical four-credit college course, one can easily say that this course typically has a requirement of 4 hours of teaching and 8 hours of study per week. At some point, the course requires 2-3 tests, which requires (say) 10 hours of study each. There are about 13 weeks in a semester of college, which means that a four-credit course is equal to 186 hours of human capital or 46.5 hours per credit. In order to equate this in terms of spending 10,000 hours to understanding *Time and Price Symmetry, Quantitative Synchronicity, and The Marketome,* then, that means that a degree in professional trading would equate to 215 credit hours. Using current university requirements, this 10,000 hour level of knowledge is essentially equal to a Bachelor's Degree, a Master's Degree, and nearly all the class work required for a PhD. For me, I have estimated that over the last 12-15 years, I have amassed close to 30,000 hours of study and market observation, which would be equivalent to nearly 600 credit hours of collegiate education, or 4-5 PhDs, but out of those 30,000 hours, I believe I have only attained 12,000-15,000 hours of experience in the three derivatives referenced above. Therefore, although I was not educated at Goldman Sachs, *I am educated*.

Aside from justifying my obsession and my education to the reader, I feel like this personal, egotistical metaphor of collegiate learning is important for me to stress at this point in the text because of two important (although ancillary) factors: my age and the lack of a positive track record because I know I am young and I know that I am stating things throughout this text that have no track record of success (at least with respect to me). However, I need to explain my qualifications because the informational conclusions herein are something that I believe are extraordinary. Not only extraordinary, but I believe this text was part of my life purpose; my one true original mastery. Therefore, dear reader, I hope that you will find a way to seek you own validation from the ideas and thoughts throughout this book, and if those ideas and those thoughts lead to a net benefit for your life, then, in someway, I can feel that my life was not lived in vain. In a way, that is why I am also bringing this information to the public. Although it does me no good to essentially put my trading/investing strategy in the public realm, it is my belief that since this is a legitimized inherent, market structure, the people who read this book can only benefit from these thought processes. Hence, my life is justified by the number of *Time and Price Symmetry* disciples that this book generates. Since I am hopeful that this text will be published while I am incarcerated, the weekly email report that my friend will send me, with regards to how many sales of this book have occurred over that time span, will help me find a way to continue to justify my existence as the father of the Marketome. However, if this book sells 1 copy a week or 1,000 copies a week, it does not matter. Either way, I will know that the knowledge I have amassed and quantified herein is spreading. Therefore, I get a reinforced psyche by sales of this book, and I hope that you, dear reader, can see that it is not about the money with respect to this book; just as it was never about money with respect to my "market education." No my need to see recurring book sales is because I need to feel useful and purposeful with my life. I need to see this knowledge conveyance occur. Therefore, I will find legitimate positive outcomes for my life by seeing this book spread to the masses, and I hope, dear reader, that you can appreciate that fact because in a way, I am writing this book for you. This knowledge is personal. This knowledge cost me everything to attain, and please know that I sacrificed my health and my old life to attain this knowledge *for you*. It cost me everything, and I am giving it to you.

Trading for Life

On another personal note, one of the primary reasons that I love trading is because of the mental edification that is instantly palpable by being correct in making a decision. Deriving profits from the market over a consistent period of time is not luck or gambling. No, it is a true validation of one's mental acuity with relation to the millions or even billions of other minds (meaning machine or human) at work at any given present moment. Thereby the act of deriving profit from the markets, on a consistent basis, allows one to feel superior to his fellow man or machine. However, this takes us out of our humble outlook, which is required to maintain longevity in this industry. Furthermore, many traders may choose to act in different Trading Styles throughout their career. A Fund Manager may become an independent trader. Then, he will engage in a trading campaign. Then, he may disregard all trading, and he will become an investor in his old age when he no longer has the mental fortitude or mental energy in order to properly account for the time requirements of trading. Undoubtedly, the individual who has chosen the market as his or her area of expertise will need to learn how to exercise his or her career via any one of these styles.

The concept of **Trading for Life** is very important to me. When I was 17, I was diagnosed with a heart condition, which may cause me to have a limited lifespan. Thankfully, it is only a possibility and not an actuality, but regardless, I became equally obsessed with understanding the power of the human mind concerning longevity of life just as I was obsessed with the markets. The never-ending pursuit of understanding the human mind and the human imagination has been an undying mental necessity for me because the imagination is our most God-like trait.

At first, I turned to books like "The Secret," which discussed the Law of Attraction. Then, I expounded into the root of "The Secret," which was defined as "Psycho-Cybernetics" by Dr. Maltz, who was a plastic surgeon who often witnessed remarkable changes in his patients due to some feeling of inadequacy. At the end of the day, it is my opinion, that "Psycho-Cybernetics" is the scientific quantification of prayer, which took 6000 years to define. Prayer is the root cause of directing our psyche to wish or to hope for some outcome, which is exactly what the Law of Attraction states. Now, this concept is not abstract or hidden from the masses. If you were to survey any of the top performers in the world, you would find that they have some knowledge of Psycho-Cybernetics. In fact, again I must yield to the genius of Alabama Head Coach, Nick Saban. In a recent interview in Fortune Magazine, he said that he paid a Seattle based group to help his football team understand "mental conditioning." When I read the article, I realized that this Seattle group was not doing something novel or something new as part of their approach to this "mental conditioning." No, that group was simply using something that was already derived in Dr. Maltz's 50-year-old book. I came to this realization because in the interview, Mr. Saban indicated that the players were told that Imagination x Vividness = Reality (I x V = R). For me, truer words cannot be stated in such mathematical beauty as that equation because if we are to be profitable and humble traders, we have to have our imagination grasp the concept of account valuations of multi-billion dollars, and we have to create that mental picture with such vividness that we have the feeling it has already been attained. Once that mental conditioning is done to our subconscious, the subconscious will cause that imaginative dream to become reality. In essence, your brain has the power to make that dream come true, and if you are a person who is already picturing yourself as a wealthy individual, then, I further deduce that the Law of Attraction has brought this book to you. **You** did not find it. No, your subconscious put the Law of Attraction to work, and it attracted you to this book in order for you to learn and to understand the true market structure that can be utilized for limitless wealth. Interestingly, the fact that *you* are reading this sentence quite possibly became reality only because it was your subconscious wish!

As an aside, I must get somewhat philosophical regarding this discussion, and if we are to believe that we are intelligently designed and if we are to believe that we are made in the image of God, then, it seems logical that we are being creatively evolved towards some pure goal by a superior consciousness. In a way, if that is true, then our evolutionary goal may be spiritual to the point that we are capable of manifesting our realities, which again, echoes Law of Attraction-like soundings. In any event, it is an interesting outlook that we all have to have with respect to our own life's purpose, and the purpose of this discussion is relevant to trading and to death because I believe it is the responsibility of intelligence to live as long as possible because making millions or billions of dollars from the market can impact millions of lives. It is a fact that money matters in people's lives while remaining meaningless in the grandeur scheme of things. In a way, it is my belief that those who have goodness as part of their psyche need to strive towards attaining financial, physical, and holistic health while giving them a reason to continue existing. It is quite common for an elderly person that retires to quickly fall-ill and pass away. It is quite common for a marriage partner to pass away shortly after the other because of the loss. Our minds and our bodies possess an incredible creative force within us through our imagination, and the abilities of controlling our subconscious mind to provide healing or longevity is something that I hope I see quantified in my lifetime. Because of the frailty of time that my own life may have, I have tirelessly searched for the way to increase my longevity, but once I became imprisoned, I felt that I was "evil" and I should just cease to exist. Aside from the personal struggle that I am dealing with in my current present moment, the fact is that I LOVE TO TRADE. I want to do it every day for the rest of my life. Getting up at 2am was fun for me because I loved my job, but it became an unhealthy obsession that could have actually taken my life. By being compulsively addicted to the market, I was inadvertently causing other parts of me to lose rationality, and it wasn't until I had the ability of spending 2-3 hours per day with an incarcerated doctor that I realized that there must be balance to life. Again, I must marvel at God's predestined plan for my incarceration because what other way would I ever have had to spend week after week with an M.D. Psychiatrist? Therefore, the learning availabilities in the Federal Incarceration Process do not necessarily yield more criminality unless you want it to, and because of this superior collegiate-like attention I have had throughout my incarceration, I unequivocally state that I now understand how the market obsession can grab hold of someone, but the truth is that you must have balance in life in order to be a successful trader. However, I understand how hard this is for traders, but you must learn the power of Quantitative Synchronicity in order to realize that you can apply *Time and Price Symmetry* in a fashion that allows for a balanced lifestyle.

By learning this methodology, you can rest comfortably in the fact that you know that before the market has a major crash-like move, the market will tell you beforehand through time and through price. Therefore, you can use *Time and Price Symmetry* in order to tell you when you should do this job as an 8-4 trader or to tell you when you should do this job as 3am-4pm trader. Thus, *Time and Price Symmetry* exists in order to help us in our lives as well as in our trades, but it will only do so *if we let it*. Because of this realization, I now truly understand that if one is to remain a trader for life, then he or she must learn to find this unique blend of life balancing, and only by consciously understanding how much the market's drug like effect can take hold, will you be able to fight it. In fact, we have the best example of this type of thinking in Warren Buffett. If you were to look at Buffett, who is now in his 80s, doesn't he always seem calm? That is not by accident, and it is done because he has a complete and balanced life. He knew this at a young age, and he realized that if he was going to be an 80-year-old market participant, he needed to find a balance. Hence, he became an investor as soon as he could because he knew the toll of the markets, and he realized, he didn't need anymore money then he already had. He could afford to slack off in some way, and by no reason is that an insult because by slacking off, I think he unconsciously attracted more gain by focusing on higher cash yielding like business vis a vis, insurance. All of these things are something that I do not think I would have consciously realized or thought about had I not been arrested or had I not written this book, and I hope that the reader takes these comments seriously because if the market is something you plan on being around for the rest of your days, you must find a balance.

Hence, the foreshadowing can now be concluded by stating that because I had such a strong desire for the market, I have found that it is an industry that can be done for life, and that is why I always believed that my pursuit of the knowledge in this book existed; my prayer or my Law of Attraction request was answered. I say this because you can literally use *Time and Price Symmetry* and Quantitative

Synchronicity in order to trade or invest until your dying day unless you suffer some type of mental malady that takes you out of the market such as Alzheimer's Disease. Therefore, finding something that I loved to do every single day, which can be done, every single day, has been important to my rational mentality. By finding the true structure to the market, I believed that I could increase my longevity. Quite literally, I truly believed that I could fight off death and increase my own life by having my desire to wake up in the morning keep my subconscious mind aware of a need to continue existing. Using *Time and Price Symmetry*, I believe that I can even work into my 90s. It is a proven fact that having a reason for living for post-retired people increases their lifespan, and the same was true of prisoners during World War II at Auschwitz. Therefore, why should finding a reason to remain excited every day be any different? I assert that if you find a job that you love to do and that you can do until your dying day, then, you will increase your lifespan, and this conversation directly echoes Dr. Freud's analysis that we have a need "to work" and "to love." However, that logic must stay rational, and my 14-hour workdays were not rational. Apropos, those days were necessary to understand the Marketome, but they are no longer necessary in terms of execution. Hence, I have learned from my incarceration experience that a balance must be found with the financial markets for the sake of my physical and mental health. You, dear reader, must also realize this. The markets or any job that keeps you exhilarated is still not a supplement for health (mental or physical), but if properly utilized as part of a healthy lifestyle, a job that can be done for one's entire life will give you a reason to keep going. Quite literally, the stock market matters so much to me that I believe it can literally extend my life. As such, it should be thought of as a life saving drug, but if that drug is taken in too large of a dose, like with anything else, it can lead to an overdose.

    In summary of this Chapter, **Capitalization** is directly linked to **Trading Styles** because each style of trading has its own capital requirements, but more importantly, each style of trading has living capital requirements in order to be learned. Therefore, the primary objective of capitalization is to ensure adequate time in order to learn how to trade in *Time and Price Symmetry*. Essentially, the goal is to amass enough capital in order to allow you to forget about the need of money, which will allow the trader to become focused on being market-oriented via the mind availing itself to ***moments of recognition***. The inception of new trade ideas must occur at the subconscious level, and that will only occur with enough exposure to the market. Moreover, I believe that goal-oriented trading/reporting is in its final stages of its existence in the Financial Industry, as more and more clients will simply want to see real-time performance and allocation of their capital, which the Information Technology Industry can now provide. Further, the old adage of "only performance matters," will become irrelevant as more people understand the use of leverage. My vision of the future is that a trader's statistics that are correlated to their accuracy will outweigh performance figures because the higher the percentages of being on the right side and being in the market will allow for more leverage, which makes performance irrelevant because it then becomes simply a matter of dialing up the risk tolerance in order to achieve additional profits. (*See Resources: The irrelevance of performance numbers due to leverage*). This type of perception-shift will ultimately make all Trading Styles equated because the statistical conveyance can be transplanted in any trading style if certain performance metrics are attained by an individualized trader. Lastly, I am personally advocating trading because I believe it can help people extend their life even into post-retirement by giving the retiree a reason to wake up in the morning; to stay involved with the outside world. It is a truly amazing industry that one can spend their entire life working in.

Chapter 4

Risk Management and Money Management

My hope, in writing this introductory chapter, is to outline to the reader that, despite having a trading strategy with a high probability of success, there are many ways a trader can fail because of a lack of appreciation or a lack of implementation regarding money management and regarding risk management. Thus, these rules of money management and of risk management maintain paramount influence throughout a trader's day, career, and life because in order for the market participant to do his or her job, the market participant must have capital to trade with at the next day (or interval).

The most prominent source of failure with respect to money management and risk management is the ego because the ego will cause a trader to stop adhering to the rules of money management and risk management out of emotions such as fear, pride, greed, or the feeling that the market participant can *do no wrong* (*See Reflections: Trading Ideologues to Live By*). As we saw in the last chapter, our ego will cause us to trade under conditions of under-capitalization based on various differentiating factors. In this chapter, we will explore the importance of managing the capital directly, and we will observe how our ego will try to prevent us from adhering to rules that the market participant should have peremptorily outlined before commencing trade execution. These rules must be explicitly stated and understood by the market participant in order to allow the market participant to understand his or her per trade risk and overall capital base (money) management. Thus, I ask the reader to emphatically remember that *capital preservation must supersede any trading strategy because, again, we, as traders, must have capital to trade with the next trading day.*

For our purposes, I will define **money management** in relation to the dollars and cents that exist in our trading account at the end of a defined interval of trading (day, week, month, quarter, year, or as I personally defined in my trading campaigns, a fixed percentage of profit or of loss). As for a definition of **risk management**, we will be focusing on our per trade and per strategy capital that is placed at possible loss in the market. This book will only outline two strategies: fundamental investing and of course, *Time and Price Symmetry*-based trading with Quantitative Synchronicity.

The most commonly used term in risk management is that of using **stop losses** in trading. The purpose to a stop loss is to have a broker execute an exit order for a trade after hitting a certain loss level. This loss level can be defined as a value that our asset hits in order to trigger our exit order, or it can be defined as a percentage of capital committed to the trade, that when hit, our broker will execute our exit order. This latter point is more important for investors than for active traders.

Stop losses are necessary at all times in trading, and sometimes these stop losses can only be set mentally because the trader may be trading in an illiquid market or a market that would target that stop. Regardless to whether or not the stop loss is mentally set in the trader's mind or tactically set at the brokerage itself, the stop must be adhered to. Every position (not trade because trades can be additive to positions) must have a stop loss associated with it, and I encourage traders to predefine this value prior to taking any position. Simply put, allowing dynamics in stop placement/management will cause emotional interference. Similarly related to that last comment, stop losses are also the cause of failure to even the highest intellects because *higher intellects cannot accept being wrong*, which is a prideful, an anti-humble, and dangerous monetary ailment that the brilliant market participant must correct. Quickly.

The primary sources of failure from stop losses occur by **incorrect stop placement**. Incorrect stop placement can come from trading too tight due to emotion, fear, or a delayed reaction to the Moment of Recognition. (At this point, I hope the reader is understanding that risk and money management fails because of emotion, because in reality, money/risk management is the simplest thing to define while remaining the hardest thing (mentally) to execute!) Additionally, trading too tight can be caused secondarily from misunderstanding the trend of the market as well. However, the primary reason that people trade too tight is emotion. As a position works favorably for a trader, the ego takes over and **preservation of profits** kicks in. Preservation of profit is the fear of giving back gains to the market, and it is an emotionally tied concept. One of the greatest idioms in trading has always been, "Don't let a winner turn into a loser." But, when is a position defined as a winner? As we will learn, a position will be deemed as a winner when it reaches its Price Pattern Objective/Price Objective or when a new technical *Time and Price Symmetry* price structure component takes over from a preexisting one, and all of this nomenclature will be described in the forthcoming sections of this book. Only then, can we reduce our position risk to break-even using stop losses if the new stop requirement allows us to place that break-even stop. It should be noted that there is nothing wrong with making your position risk zero in order to preserve capital, but if it is done at inopportune times, this type of mentality will lead to more stop-outs, which test our emotions even further. Hence, a trader that likes to reduce position risk to zero is justified in doing so *only if* that trader can accept and can understand the higher frequency of stop outs, which is extraordinarily difficult to the mind because the feeling of being stopped-out is a constant battle for the ego, and it leads to the second reason that stop losses can cause failure.

When being stopped on a position, the mind has to cope with two things: being wrong and being taken out of the market. Unfortunately, the nature of the market is to take you out; to test your conviction. But remember, the market is not treating you as a target. The market is indifferent towards you, and although I personify the market consistently in this book, you must remember that the market is not "happy" when you lose nor is the market "happy" when you win. No, the market is oscillating through its price discovery process, and the hope is that you, as the *Time and Price Symmetry* trader are aware of the exactness where the market will reverse its oscillating process. Therefore, we have to remember as market participants that sometimes, we can take a position that has perfect analysis, but due to our Moment of Recognition occurring too late or our rules of risk management being used properly, we are forced to place a stop in an arbitrary area instead of at the *technical* place it should have been placed at. That is a very important statement; *risk management can actually cause us to be stopped incorrectly from a technical/Time and Price Symmetry viewpoint.* When risk management interferes with *Time and Price Symmetry,* the market will proceed to take us out of that trade for a loss, and then, follow-thru leaving our opportunity to not only be missed but to have now become a loser instead of a winner. Quite frankly, this will screw you up for the rest of the trading day; it can cause you to keep trading with the thought that you need to get back in the market when you should have still been in the market in the first place. Amazingly, these are all difficult things for our ego to handle, but in actuality, these understandings are impersonal and trite. Furthermore, a trader that is stopped based on his or her risk management must learn to realize that the trader did the right thing by taking the loss because the trader did not break his or her rules. Again, adhering to the rules of risk management and money management is more important than the trading strategy even if that trading strategy is *Time and Price Symmetry.* Therefore, in order to find an over the counter remedy in mitigating the fallacy that can be borne from *proper* risk management, we must introduce a new concept called **risk-based trading size,** which will allow us to adjust our trading size in order to place our stop loss where it should be in order to adhere to our defined risk management while simultaneously allowing us to technically implement our trades based on our trading strategy.

Essentially, risk-based trading size is necessary in order to allow us to trade even if the market has moved away from our optimum entry price. As an example, let us say we are a 10-lot trader of the S&P E-Mini Futures Contract. We have defined our position risk to be $1,000.00 or 2-points ($1,000 = $50 x 10 x 2). However, we are looking at a trade in which the market has already moved away from the *Time and Price Symmetry* defined market inflection point, and in order to place our stop-loss at the appropriate location, we would need to risk 4-points instead of 2-points, which would break our risk management rules. Do we not take the trade? Maybe. But, we could trade 5 lots instead of 10 with the 4 point stop, which gives us the same $1000 risk (5 x $50 x $4 = $1000). Even though our profit potential is cut in half for the position, it would allow us to get back into the market with our stop placement in the logical place in order to give us a higher probability of a profitable outcome. Thus, we allow the ego to be calmed by staying in the market, staying within our risk management rules, and (hopefully) seeing the position work out favorably. Simultaneously, the trader must obliterate the feeling of smaller gains because of trading half of the trader's typical trading size. Again, those are feelings and emotion, and (for the tenth time) the proper application of risk management and money management is primary.

The concept of reducing base position size is very important to money management as well (especially for investors). It is a natural human instinct to buy more of something if the price decreases, and this instinct is another inherent human flaw from our Creator. Earlier, I stated this concept as dollar-cost averaging at the end of Chapter 2. This is the *opposite* mentality than what is required to be in the market. By definition, if your position has decreased, you are currently wrong. Therefore, the only reason to add more to a losing position is typically from the unnecessary emotion of "hope." The trader may think, "Well, I *hope* I can double down and get out at the midpoint between the two prices." Thus, we see the Law of Attraction emergent in that line of thinking, which is that the trader is now trying to get out without a *loss* instead of focusing on making a *gain*. Please. Please, understand this concept. The Law of Attraction running through the universe is invoked in a negative way by doubling down and focusing on the loss because the trader is observing visually, in real time, the current loss in his or her account because the trade is a loser. In fact, that is why I advocate that the trader use a very tight stop tolerance because when the trader is wrong, he or she must get out quickly. The visualistic, subconscious cue understood by the psyche is impaired by viewing a loss. It is seeing loss, which means it attracts more loss. Likewise, the point of trying to get into favorable trades that are held for long periods of time is to encourage the gain to become a greater gain!

Hence, even if after that cautionary explanation the trader should choose to defy the statements in the prior paragraph, then, the trader must target profits instead of "not getting out at a loss." What's more, the reason dollar-cost averaging is a failure aside from the Law of Attraction is that when someone commits double their money to a trade, their emotional connectivity to that trade increases exponentially because the new trade size may be an unknown to the trader's psyche. In fact, more money is at risk, and that money is now summed together into a total loser! To our mind's imagination, our loss has now increased. Therefore, we see a multiplicative negative effect of dollar cost averaging in the realm of the trading mentality with respect to the Law of Attraction. Ergo, just as we needed a slight shift in perception about investing, we will do the same thing with risk management and with money management.

No matter what trading mode you are in, you will need to define your money management rules based on the interval you established for your goals. Let us take a person with a $100,000.00 trading account. This person decides to remain non-goal-oriented, and they use 1-week (five trading days) to elapse before analyzing their account. The question then becomes, "How much to risk per week [interval] (money management) and how much to risk per trade (risk management)?" The reader should note that we are no longer thinking in terms of how much profit we make per week by staying market-oriented, and we are focusing on each trade itself just as quoted from Coach Nick Saban's commentary in the previous chapter.

Next, let us say that our trader decides on 10% risk per week or $10,000.00, which is money management. Now, using the blind squirrel analogy, how many trades per week does our trader have to find his or her nut? Let us say our trader has allocated 50 trades for the week, which is calculated via risk management. (Although slight, I encourage the reader to delineate between the concepts of risk management and money management via this example.) With 50 trades defined through risk management available before exhausting our money management allocation, we must understand that this means we have 50 trades at our maximum per position risk before we stop ourselves out for the interval based on our rules of money management. Once stopped out, we either wait for the next interval (if it's based on time) or go to the previous interval (if it's based on some type of return figure). Next, we divide our risk by the number of trades we want to take, which yields $200 risk per trade in our example ($10,000.00 Risk / 50 Trades = $200 Risk / Trade). Moreover, if we look at the entire account ($100,000.00), we can see that we are giving our trading endeavor 10 weeks and 500 trades before hitting zero. Therefore, we have 500 trades to find our "nut," and if we had a trading strategy of throwing darts at a board to pick when to place trades, we can see that with effective money management, undoubtedly some portion of those 500 trades will be profitable, and it will be hard for us to deplete our account to zero if we are working with favorable reward to risk parameters. In order to further illustrate the power of reward to risk ratios, if we use strict price targets for profits that are twice as much ($400.00) as our loss ($200.00), we see that only one third of all our trades need to be accurate in order to break-even based on an expected value probability calculation. Therefore, it is perfectly fine to have a trading strategy that wins less than 50% of the time if your reward is greater than your risk so that the statistics of your strategy yield a positive expected value. A visual example can be utilized by again referring to the spreadsheet in the *Resources* section in regards to the relevance of performance numbers based on returns. This is a common concept in trading books, and that is why I have created a spreadsheet that links numbers to performance, which is a perception shift that is uncommon when discussing trade statistics.

Compounding & Contracting

So far, you may have noticed that I have made a clear distinction between per trade and per position risk. The importance of this is paramount to building positions in the market; especially, for an investor who wants to allocate more capital to an investment as his or her risk capital increases. Secondarily, for traders, as your confidence (ego) grows due to consecutive successes, you will want to grow larger in your base position size, but in this sense, it is still not okay to allow the ego (emotion) come into play if it causes a breach of the rules of money management. That said, we must accept that it is "okay" to add to our winning positions because it is a proper application of the Law of Attraction. Thus, we get to the concept of **compounding on profits**. Compounding on profits is critical to trading campaigns, but it also serves importance for normal trading condition in order to take advantage of more volatile environments without increasing risk. Let me illustrate a new example of an aggressive S&P Futures trader with a $25,000.00 account. I'll call him Jim.

Jim will risk 20% ($5,000.00) per day on 10 positions. This means that Jim risk $500.00 per position, and depending on his stop placement he uses a varied position size in order to keep the stops where they should be technically. However, his average stop is 2 points ($100 in S&P E-Mini Futures per contract) so his average position size is 5 contracts ($500 risk per position / $100 risk per stop = 5). Jim is having a great day and he has made 10 points in the S&P E-Mini in the early A.M. market action on his average position size. He has made $2,500.00 (10 points x $50 per point x 5 contracts). Jim is a trader that compounds on profits, and he realized that this $2,500.00 has now increased his risk account from $5,000.00 to $7,500.00 because Jim is not recognizing this as account profit until his interval has completed (one day). The beauty of this is how exponential Jim can grow his position size without taking on more daily risk. I want to follow this example through to completion in order to emphasize the potential of compounding on profits. At 9:30, Jim starts trading 8 lots in the S&P E-mini, which is approximately 50% more since his risk allocation has grown by 50%. Again, he makes another 10 points profit by lunch, which is $4000 (10 points x $50 per point x 8 contracts). Going into the afternoon, Jim once again adjusts his risk account, but now he has $11,500 of risk capital. Jim follows his formula in order to properly calculate his new position size, and he now trades with 12 contracts in the afternoon, which is a 140% increase over his initial trading size! Upon this third recalculation, he still is allowing for 10 position losses before exhausting his total risk allocation of $11,500 even though he has less than 3 hours of trading time left for the day [interval]. Therefore, the reader should start to be amazed at the ability of proper compounding on profits because now Jim is truly able to reach extreme profits in these last through hours. In fact, he can make up 2 to 3 days of profits in just one good trading afternoon that was built up from prior trading. This is an important concept and I ask the reader to also review the *Reflection* entitled *Understanding the Basis Position.* There is one more extraordinary takeaway from this example that must be emphasized, and this takeaway requires common sense otherwise defined as logic.

Logically, I emphasized that there were only three hours left in Jim's interval. However, now that he is trading at 12 contracts, he has increased his profit potential on the day by over 100%, and if he decided that, due to the short window of time left in the trading day, he wanted to give himself only 5 more trades, he could then trade with 24 lots, which is nearly 5 times his starting position! Alternatively, Jim may decide that he wants to move his money management interval's risk to zero, which is an extremely important concept. As stated, Jim began the day with a $5,000.00 risk allocation, and as he approaches the end of the day, he has built $6,500.00 of profit, which has allowed his total money management risk allocation to grow to $11,500.00. However, Jim may decide to (mentally) move his money management interval risk to zero, which means he is only focusing on the $6,500.00 of profit he made for the day, and likewise, he is being logical and only assuming that he has to account for the *possibility* of five more losses. This means that Jim can calculate his trading size as being equivalent to 13 contracts ($6,500 / 5 Trades = $1300 risk per trade / $100 risk per average stop = 13 contracts), which is still 160% greater than his starting trade size! Again, all we needed is to shift our perception in terms of when we recognize profit or loss (at the end of intervals) instead of instantly.

Now, let us use an example on one of Jim's bad days based on the same formula. This is where most traders fail, and this is where our egos fight us in a very harmful way. On bad days, we often feel pressured to trade so that we can make our losses back. I was forced to live every day living with this type of mentality for the three years leading to my arrest. The pressure of taking large risks in order to make money back is our perception of how the market wants us to feel, but remember, the market is not emotional. Therefore, we have to recognize this *feeling*, and we have to obliterate this type of emotional thinking in order to stay successful under periods of loss (drawdown). In order to do so, I recommend turning to many books regarding psychological conditioning such as "Psycho-Cybernetics" as already mentioned or books by Dr. Ari Kiev and Dr. Van Tharpe, who are Psychiatrists for traders. Incorrect thinking and defiance to the adherence of rules of money management and risk management will force us to trade larger positions under drawdown because it is an inherent, human, flaw, and we simply have to recognize this internal human ineptitude. By growing positions under drawdown, we will be destined to fail and fail faster. Moreover, the Law of Attraction (and the Bible) always teaches us that loss attracts loss and gains attract gains. So, we need to take our losses away as much as possible, which is difficult because often times with trading systems, we have more losses than wins, but our wins are greater than our losses. Therefore, preservation of capital must exist in order to minimize losses as much as possible while still maintaining adherence to price patterns that are defined through *Time and Price Symmetry*. We need to have our minds stay focused on the gains only, and we must learn forget immediately about losses. Remember what we have just learned from these examples: if we focus on gains, even if the gains are much smaller then the losses, we can utilize the subconscious mind's ability to conform to the Law of Attraction that tells us that consistent gains turn into bigger gains with correctly implemented compounding rules. "To who is given much, more is given."

Sometimes, people contain an inherent mental flaw (possibly by genetically linked inclinations to gambling) that prohibits them from adhering to risk management, and I humbly admit that it is quite possible that I am one of those people. However, every problem has a solution, and since I have defined risk management as my only problem, I have now found a solution. What's more (and as I stated), risk management is extraordinarily easy compared to the actual act of understanding the market and/or trades. In fact, all it requires is a consistent use of a darn simplistic spreadsheet, which is also included in the *Resources/Appendices* section of this book. Therefore, I have no doubts in my ability to recognize trades and to avail my mind to the Moment of Recognition, which is the true difficulty of market participation. In fact, once more for my pride, I have no doubt that I am one of the best trading analysts in the world, and I have no doubt that I have the potential to be the best trader in the world. Simultaneously, I need to honestly state that I am the most awful risk adhering person in the world. I always felt too empowered in my abilities, and even if I had 99 out of 100 trades right, that 1 out of 100 – that black swan if you will – will destroy me. It is my confession to you as the reader, and I hope the reader sees that I am honestly portraying my belief in my intellectual aptitude. This is not a facetious or egotistical claim, and it is the honest derivation that every market participant must make of himself or herself. Therefore, I have found a solution to my problem, which is actually external to trading! I have now realized that I need a risk-nanny; a person to dictate trading size for me; a person who allows me to focus purely on the market and a person who allows me to forget about the dollars and cents. With this partner-like corrective process implemented, I have no doubt that I will achieve my loftiest dreams. Gratefully, this "mental fix" for my defined flaw may be possible through technology. The reason I belabor this point is because of how important risk management is with respect to trading. No matter who the trader, what the strategy, or how long of a track record, even one deviation from stated and implemented risk metrics can destroy the longest career. Don't believe me? Look at 2008. Look at how many people neglected their documentation.

Thankfully, our fictitious trader, Jim, does not suffer from my malady. In fact, he has recognized his internal failure of how he is instinctively conditioned, and in our example, he used a pragmatic way to determine his position size under drawdown by a quick spreadsheet heuristic, which is again provided in the *Resources* section of this book. Let us move through this next example, which will discuss and elaborate the concept of **contracting on losses**...

Jim has been trading the S&P Futures since 3 am, and he has taken 5 losing trades using his average trade size (5 lots) and his average stop of 2 points ($100). He has exhausted 50% of his daily risk (-$2,500), and if he were to continue, he has 5 trades left before exhausting his risk capital for his interval of one day. However, it is only 8 am, and there is a lot of time left in the day (interval). He has acknowledged his poor trades, and he wants to not walk away with a failed day. Notice, I did not say he wants a profitable day, but I said he wants to not have a failed day. This is extremely important for our trading mentalities. It is okay to have a negative interval if that negative interval closed on a series of consecutive positive trades, which gives us confidence going into our next interval. Further, Jim has recognized that his failures have come from a delayed reaction to the Moment of Recognition, and he wants to use an average stop size of 3 points for the rest of the day. How much should Jim now trade if he wants to take 10 more trades before exhausting his risk capital? He has $2,500.00 left in his risk allocation for the interval; he wants 10 more trades at $150 risk per contract (3 points instead of 2). We then take 10 x $150 and divide by $2,500.00. Since we cannot trade the S&P E-mini futures in fractions of a contract, Jim's analysis tells him he can trade between 1 or 2 contracts and still stay in the market. With reduced size, Jim has a much higher hill to climb in order to get positive for his interval, but as profits build, we saw that position size increase fast (especially when factoring time in to the equation in order to make an educated guess as to how many trade opportunities will be left for the defined interval). *The importance of trading under a drawdown is not to get profitable, but to get back to making right decisions.* As Jim's ego becomes profitable, his account will take care of itself. The key thing is to forget about the losses that knocked his trading size backwards, and instead, focus on moving forward to start building gains. The losses have already happened, and they must be forgotten.

Now, we have to understand what can happen to Jim once he contracts his trading size after readjusting his risk management parameters for the remainder of his interval. Part of this thinking also has importance to Jim's subsequent trading days, which requires elaboration as well, and now, we need to ask the question, "So, did Jim succeed in not having a failed day?" I propose that if he traded well since his risk adjustment (his contraction), but still had a negative day, that he, in fact, had a winning conclusion to his interval (or trading day). He adhered to his risk management rules. He regained harmony with the market, and although, unquantifiable, he has mentally prepared himself for his next interval (day). However, here is where the power of this redefined thinking comes in. At the end of Jim's interval (because it is defined by time), he has closed out negative, but he has closed out negative while properly trading for the rest of the day on a smaller position size. Furthermore, when he sits down to trade at 3am the next day, Jim is now resetting his parameters for this new interval. Hence, Jim may have closed out the prior trading day by trading 1 or 2 contracts, but at 3am on the next day, he may once again be trading 4 or 5 contracts. This understanding is extreme because, by finishing his last trading day on a successful note, based on the Law of Attraction, he is giving his next interval a higher probability for success, and since his position size has returned to normal, and for this reason, the Law of Attraction is relevant and extraordinarily important with respect to Jim's mentality at the end of the prior interval's terminal point. What's more, by staying engaged in the market during the previous time-based interval, he allowed himself to stay in the market for the rest of the day in order to give him further clarity on possible *time and price components* he may have missed by walking away. By walking away, he is cheating himself out of more subconscious learning, which arguably, is just as important as missing good trades. Similarly, if Jim did not recalculate his risk management earlier in the day and if he was stopped out for the day, he would have been forced the mental anguish of not being allowed to take subsequent trades that may have setup perfectly based on *Time and Price Symmetry,* and for me, this was the hardest mental demon that I have ever had to encounter in the markets.

The last concept in money management and risk management that I want to share at this time is that of **Infinite Downward Departure** ("IDD"). As we noticed in Jim's losing example, he was able to take his position size from 5 to 2 contracts in order to stay in the market. He was downwardly departing from his basis in order to keep trading. However, his interval is based on time, so, based on Jim's money management rules, every day he is starting at his base position size of 5 (if his account dictates). This is why I defined my personal trading intervals in terms of percentages instead of time. By defining intervals by percentages, I am taking advantage of IDD to infinitely prevent a drawdown to a previous interval (if it was possible to trade in fraction sizes of course). I must use one more example in order to illustrate the power of this concept and the reason that more money makes trading easier, which resonates with our prior chapter's discussion of proper capitalization.

Mary has been on an ambitious trading path towards a goal of $10mm so that she can start investing. However, she has decided to use the S&P Futures as her trading specialty until she gets to that high level of capital. Her intervals thus far have been defined as 25% profit versus 20% loss. For example, if she currently has a $1mm trading account, she needs to reach $1.25mm before hitting her next interval. Once at that interval, if she loses 20%, it will bring her back to $1mm; her previous interval, and this is how I have chosen to define intervals for my own trading. Now, in order to follow through on demonstrating IDD, let us take this $1mm account as an example because IDD is more relevant for larger account sizes, and is one of the reasons that the more money you have the easier it is to trade.

Mary has just reached the $1mm interval, and her readjusted spreadsheet shows us that she has $200,000.00 (20%) of risk capital based on her money management rules. After analyzing her trading history, Mary uses 2 point as her average stop ($100), and she gives herself 20 trades per interval. Therefore, she is trading 100 lot positions ($200,000 / (20 trades x $100 risk / trade)). However, Mary has decided that the mental pain her ego feels when drawing down must be subdued in a way such that *she never reaches her prior interval*. What Mary does is implement IDD so that after every 10 losses (50% of her risk capital) she readjusts her spreadsheet in order to allocate another 20 trades. In effect, Mary is creating an interval inside an interval, but she is doing so without further risk to her **master interval**, which was defined from her money management rules. Therefore, her master interval was simply her original profit and loss definitions based off her $1mm starting point. What's more, Mary is smart. She knows that sticking to her master interval will keep her on the path towards $10mm, and the only question is how much time it will take to get there, which further emphasizes the fact that Mary appreciates and understand the concept of being market-oriented. Thus, she is just like me, and she is focused on the market, she is focused on her master interval, and she is focused on positive implementations of the Law of Attraction. Also like me, she is not focused on some arbitrary time-based goal such as performance statistics or money to live. She is comfortable, and she is in the present moment. Now, let us move through this example for Mary's drawdown period because it is important.

To begin, she is trading 100 lots, and she has a disaster on her hands. She has lost $100,000 almost immediately from 10 straight losses, which was half of her risk capital allocation and half of her trade allowances. However, she remains unemotional, and she readjusts her trade allowance to account for 20 more possible losing trades, which means her trading size has now reduced to 50 lots (contracts). Once again, she loses 10 more trades and she readjusts. She is now trading 25. Then, 12, 6, 3, 1... As we can see, the concept of IDD will approach an asymptotic limit, but that limit will always be 1. This further emphasizes how important it is to be properly capitalized because you can see that more capital will allow for many more opportunities by evoking IDD as part of your interval/drawdown parameters. More capital gives you more chances to recalculate down to 1 lot.

At this point, I feel I need to make something obvious to stock traders, which is actually not an obvious assumption. If you are a stock trader, your leverage is limited to 4x your capital via day trading margin requirements, unless you have an arrangement like a prop trader. However, as a stock trader, we must realize how hard it is to drawdown to prior intervals. For example, if you trade the SPY ETF as your main trading vehicle, your equivalent loss of 20 trades or 20% of your capital, like Mary, would require a huge amount of capital implemented per trade, which may not be practical based on the size of the market you are trading! Hence, we find that stock traders that use the concept of IDD *properly* have an inherent failsafe. In fact, it would actually be hard to lose the amount of money necessary to drawdown to prior intervals as a stock trader. In addition, a stock trader would be trading 50,000 shares or so even with Mary's capital base if the stock trader was risking an equivalent sum as Mary per trade, and with a starting point of 50,000 shares, the stock trader has several more recalculations before reaching 1 share of stock! Therefore, we understand how easy stock trading is compared to derivatives trading.

Unfortunately, the fact is that most traders (stock or derivative) cannot do what Mary did because of our goal-oriented nature along with a feeling that we are in some sort of race to some imaginary finish line. The mentality it takes to go from trading 100 lots to 12 or 5 is mentally hard for our ego to deal with, and in fact, it causes us to lose respect for our trades, which is probably one of the most important phrases in this entire book. ***Every trade, regardless of money must be treated with the same level of seriousness and the same level of respect.*** In a way, I also stated this in Chapter 2 with respect to investing in a company the same way with $10,000 as if it was $10,000,000. Please, dear reader, I ask you to understand that: ***there is no trade more important than the current one in the present moment.*** However, because of this lack of respect that occurs when money or trading size becomes smaller, we have to be aware of the ego because the ego will tell us that the seriousness of trading 100 lots is not necessary when trading 12 or 5. In fact, the *opposite* is the truth. When we are trading under drawdown, our psyches are impaired. We are in a losing mental pathway that is battling the Law of Attraction, and we need to remove losing from our minds. Therefore, the level of seriousness with respect to trading must increase when trading size decreases because gain will attract gain. I cannot stress this thought path enough to the reader of this text because it is not an easily understandable conclusion, but it is an extraordinarily important one. You, as a trader, have to realize that this readjustment to a new perception of seriousness, *as trading size is decreasing*, is something that has to be reconditioned into your mind, and it has to be confirmed and it has to be acknowledged for you to have consistent success.

Contrarily, the astute reader may recognize the fact that seriousness and that respect are emotionally tied concepts, which makes them invalid in the first place, but alas, we are human. We are emotional, and therefore, the only way to otherwise understand this reeducation process is that the trader can work on maintaining a consistent present moment mentality whereby the size of the trades does not matter at all. The trades are simply "called out," and an application or another human being implements them, which should allow a eurhythmic plan for execution because what matters is our adherence to our rules of money and risk management above all else. I will call this entire realm of thinking position-bias, and you need to free yourself from position-bias. If I was able to accomplish this goal for myself, I have no doubt of my imminent success.

Position Bias is defined as having a bias to higher trading size based on previously reached trading size goals (based on intervals), and it is essential to condition your ego to obliterate these thought processes because the most important thing about a correctly implemented approach to trading size is that if you remember, just as losses knock us back in position sizes, our gains will allow our trade size to grow. For example, if Mary makes $100,000 instead of losing it giving her risk account $300,000 instead of $200,000 she can trade in 150 lot sizes as well, which is a tremendous monetary increase. Therefore, I ask you to please bear in mind that it is all about being right instead of being wrong, and as long as that is the correctly implemented approach to trading, then, the percentages of winning trades and the percentages of being on the right side of the market will increase, which will allow profits to take care of themselves.

There is also another form of Position Bias that can creep into the trader's mind, which can cause a trader to react irrationality, and we must be aware of this second form of Position Bias. This second form of Position Bias, I will modify to be called Position Fear. **Position Fear** is defined as an emotional trade barrier that causes a trader to react in a different manner had the trader simply neglected the size of the position. Hence, Position Fear occurs when a trader is trading outside of his mentally accepted trade size, and again, this is typical when we are talking about a trader that is incorrectly adding to losses through dollar-cost averaging. Now, let me explain an example of Position Fear, and this example will help the reader understand why this fear must be understood and removed from the trader's decisions.

Let us say that Bill is a consistently profitable trader when he trades his default trade size in the S&P E-Mini Futures, which is 20 contracts. On 20 contracts, Bill is making $1,000 of profit per S&P Point that he makes from trading. However, on Bill's good trading days, he decided to leverage up in the last hour of trade, and he starts to trade 100 contracts instead of 20 contracts. Because of this new size, Bill experiences Position Fear in many different ways. First, Bill decided to use a tighter stop loss than if he just traded his normal 20 contracts. Second, Bill decides to take 20 or 40 contracts off after just a few ticks profit, which he does out of fear that the market will come back, and this is something that Bill normally would not have done on 20 contracts. Third, Bill completely stops being in an analytical mind frame, and he *falls in love* with his expected outcome for this 100-lot trade. Thus, this means that Bill experiences Position Fear because he is once again focusing on money (goal-oriented) instead of on trading (market-oriented), and this is a very profound and common occurrence that exists within traders; big or small. *In fact, it is a form of Position Fear that causes even the greatest of traders to become investors*. Quite simply, every money manager that has lost their "edge" and has become an investor has reached a level of emotional comfort whereby they cannot execute their old trading plan effectively with the new trading size that is required of them. Therefore, we see another asymptotic limit that is correlated to emotion, which helps the reader understand why there are no trillionaires on this planet. That said, once you are aware of this emotional fear, which is linked to the position size, you can overcome it by conditioning your mind to trade fluidly, and I assert that the best traders that became relegated investors have never even stopped to understand why they have become happy with 10% per year instead of striving for 100%. Hence, by recognizing fear, you can overcome fear. However, regardless of emotion, regardless of fear, these larger trades *must only* be taken if they adhere to your money/risk management techniques and/or your compounding on profits spreadsheet, which are all parts of a market participant's trading plan.

This entire chapter can be summarized in one sentence: *I am attempting to shift your mentality into a new way of thinking about money that obliterates emotion from trade implementation*. I have discussed the importance of money management with respect to preservation of capital along with the importance of sticking to predefined intervals, and although intervals can be seen as a goal, with proper structure, intervals will help to free us from goal-oriented thinking. Further, we discussed how risk management comes into play on a position basis so that we can have flexible position sizes in order to prevent us from missing opportunities. This led to examining the use of stop losses, and how they are always necessary. Lastly, I have explained a new way to compound on profits while contracting on losses. All of these concepts will be vital to any trading plan, and the adherence to these rules will be the most difficult battle our minds will be faced with because we are always dealing with a continuous updating process to our position size unless we have reached a contract maximum that is either defined by our psychological monetary trading limit or by the actual market that we are trading in.

In my career, I have defined that this adherence to compounding on profits / contracting on losses is the *only* failing part I have to trading, and I do not say this for edification because this mental failure has cost me my life, as I knew it. Amazingly, I must reiterate that upon my own, introspective analysis, I have surmised that 99 out of 100 times, I can correctly implement my spreadsheet calculations for my trading size in the present moment, but that one time that I fail, nearly all of my gains are wiped out (if not more). As such, I have awoken from self-denial, and I have admitted to the reader that my personal failures can either come from a hereditary gambling inclination that manifests itself in seeking large risk (i.e. getting the mind to chemically react in a way that enjoys the volatility of dealing with losses in order to satisfy some hereditary urge) or, from the pressure I was placed under the last few years because of the government's investigation. My failure to adhere to these rules has also affected the lives of other people in a negative way through my companies, which was never my intent. Upon further inspection, I realized that my major failures came from not adhering to my daily or interval stop-loss rules (i.e. money management). No, I was prideful and I was egotistical because of fear from the unknown of the investigation. Thus, I would break my rule, and despite my superior intellect, I would keep going! In essence, I was engaged in the actual definition of insanity because no matter how many times I realized and witnessed this failure by not stopping when I should, I kept doing trading under interval drawdown and with incorrect size. More egregious, I kept doing this over and over again (which should have validity the insanity plea for my crime)! Logically, as a person of higher intelligence, this incorrect implementation of money management and risk management made no sense, but in hindsight, I can finally look back and I can finally understand what happened to my brain. I can now see that because of the time pressure I was under, I was forced to trade. I was forced to keep going on my bad days. I was sleep deprived to the point of irrationality, and I was not acting logically. I was diminished, and I believe that it is quite possible that the stress from the governmental pressure caused me to go insane. Ergo, understanding what happened to me along with explaining that understanding is part of the reason I am writing this book, but the reader should be aware that after we move to Chapter 6, the introspective analysis mostly terminates here.

Thankfully, this personal analysis and personal admission of irrationality is not all bad news. Because I have decided that I want to continue to surround myself in the markets, only by analyzing the problem can I allow the potential for a cure. Thus, the *diagnostic recognition of my failures has a cure*, and I believe that I can either be "cured" by having a trading assistant to govern me with my risk management at all times, or, hopefully, creating a method of trade execution via a trading platform where I just have to set the interval limits, and then, the trading size will be appropriately allocated; all I will have to do is call out the trades. Therefore, the reader needs to understand the realization that *I can be fixed*, and I can obliterate any gambling like addiction that my genetics may carry. What is more, if you are finding yourself in a continuous cycle of destruction, do not despair because I believe that if I can be fixed, then, so can you! Hence, it remains my eternal hope that when I reenter the markets, this failure of mine will now be fixed by the removal of the fear I carried around for the last few years. For me, since I begun the process of truthfully admitting and accepting my inherent, *possible* flaws, I started to focus on reconditioning my mind. For example, some days I try to visualize a chalkboard with the phrase "trading

= gambling," and I then visualize me erasing that text from the chalkboard or putting a slash through the equals sign in order to create an unequal sign! In a way, I am mentally telling my subconscious to rid itself of the only trading demon that I believe that I have, and with proper research into your own mind, I hope that you too can find the root cause of any trading failure so that you can find a solution; however, ethereal the solution may be.

Lastly, although this book is meant to educate and I am contradicting that goal by these personal, introspective commentaries, I ask the reader not to take this chapter summary lightly, because this in-depth analysis that I have had to do is demonstrative for the reader. Every trader must do this analysis for him or herself if they are to be honest with themselves in order to break free from their trading failures, and part of that analysis is for even the best traders to humble themselves by waking up from self-denial about their trading methodology and being able to admit their pride and egoism. Just like an alcoholic, who admits to being an alcoholic at an AA meeting, so too must the trader admit his wrongdoings with respect to his or her trading strategy. With that openness and oneness between the trader's recognition with his or her inherent abilities, the mind can advance forward in developing a proper way to overcome the recognition of the trader's human flaws. Then, the subconscious autonomic servomechanisms can begin the process of creating corrective action, which will allow trade execution to evolve from the Law of Attraction's invocation through the desire to fix one's flaws.

Chapter 5

Art, Science, Ego

This last introductory chapter will focus on an introduction to price and time. Also in this chapter, I will also elaborate more on the chapter summary from Chapter 4 with respect to how our human minds are naturally conditioned for failure, as traders, because of our perceptions of reality derived from our ego. In a way, this egocentric focus is due to free will, and when we, as humans, choose to walk within our own free will, we are taken out of the present moment because in the present moment, God exists.

Now, I can literally write an entire book on the psychology of trading or investing, but there are already several books on the subject by very prominent doctors. As such, I have kept a consistent psychological theme of Law of Attraction type concepts throughout this book because the Law of Attraction is something that I believe is the true paradigm of reaching the internal mechanisms of our subconscious in order to make us good traders or good investors. Therefore, our discussion on psychologically analyzing our ego will take us into the realization of the human fallacies of the ego coupled with allowing us to remain engaged in the present moment. Furthermore, the introductory principles of this Chapter will begin the comprehension of understanding how Price Structure is like science because it is exact. Whereas, Time Structure is like art, and we ***all can*** see something different. Lastly, we will address the concept of understanding that a single trade is not equated to a single position, but that multiple positions in one market are derived from single trades that are implemented based on *Time and Price Windows*. By understanding this additive benefit of positions, we can begin to comprehend the faith in letting go, which is very important. A trader must have such faith in his or her trading strategy that, at some point, that trader decides to take his conscious mind away from the market. Jesse Livermore was famous for saying, "he made more money while he was asleep then while he was awake." He was able to state this ironic conclusion because he finally learned to let go; he learned to have faith in the market; he learned to have confidence in his conviction, which will only occur with the mind's recognition of repetition. Unfortunately, we are inherently wired to get ego-edified as our account size and our accuracy increases, which takes us out of the present moment because, in a way, the present moment (where God exists) is inversely correlated to money. It says so in the bible! Therefore, realize this ego-edification, and learn to let go at all times. Learn to have faith in the present moment, faith in your trading strategy, which I hope will be come *Time and Price Symmetry,* and learn to have faith in yourself.

Often, I am asked, "Why do you trade in price and time only?" To many, it seems like a step backward in technical analysis. In essence, Time (x-axis) and Price (y-axis) have existed from the beginning of the markets, and because of their simplistic nature, people feel that humanity has reached some new, higher echelon of quantitative reasoning that makes the fundamental derivatives of a price chart irrelevant, which is the largest, inaccurate perception that exists in the trading community today! The two components of price and of time have appeared as a two-dimensional representation in either linear or logarithmic relationship based on the rate of growth since man has been capable of charting the market. Doesn't it make sense that it should still matter today? If there is truly "nothing new under the sun," then, we should be able to turn back the technological clock in order to understand our current future with respect to the underlying market structure. However, as humanity has technologically moved forward, technical analysis became a tool (or crutch) in order to analyze these relationships, and in that process, people forgot about the basic X-Y chart, which means that only a select few people even understand that price structure and time structure existed and, more important, that they still exist. I believe that prior to writing this book; there have been fewer than 20 price and time traders over the recorded history of the markets! When I read a book by Charles McDaniel called *God & Money,* I came across a quotation regarding morality that I believe also is valid with respect to the market. In Mr. McDaniel's book he states, "We are arriving at a point in history where we may be required to deny ourselves some of the benefits of our economic and technological prowess for the sake of our moral survival." I believe this quote is extremely important because in order to ensure our trading survival, we need to deny ourselves some of the benefits of technology's impact on technical analysis. Just as morality needs to revert to earlier years, so does our thinking with respect to technology and with respect to the market/technical analysis.

Now, in order to elaborate on what the collectivist technical analysis theory is with respect to today's society, I find myself tending to ask a person a simple question in order to gauge their technical acumen. That question is typically something along the lines of, "when you think of a technical indicator, what do you think of?"

The most common answer is usually a blank stare, but more often then not, I hear, "Moving averages." But, this begs the follow-up rebuttal, "What is a moving average?" Interestingly, but upon my second question I come to realize that most people never even stop to think about it. They never realize that a simple moving average is simply an average of price over time. Price and time are staring us right in the face. Even in a June 2012 edition of the Wall Street Journal, I saw the Journal overly the Dow Jones Industrial chart from the year 2010, 2011, and 2012. Amazingly, the late April/Early May time period was perfectly lined up on the chart, which showed Time Symmetry, but again, people never even realize it. Price and Time are right there for us to grasp, and with respect to moving averages, price and time are right there in the calculation. Bollinger bands, stochastics, MACD, RSI, etc. are all based on price and time (and occasionally volume). Price and time are the inputs, and everything else is a derivative. Therefore, technical indicators are delayed. Learning to trade in price and in time increases your speed of trading. It places you in the present moment of the market whereas technical indicators are putting you in the past. In effect, technical indicators are **lagging indicators** because they lag *Time and Price Symmetry*. Therefore, doesn't it make sense to learn the intricacies of the price/time relationship, first, before anything else? We learn algebra before calculus. Right?

Science

So, now we can start the reason of this books existence. We can ask, "What is price?" **Price** is the value of an asset based on the current **asking price** of that asset. Price is not the last traded value of the asset because that is in the past. Therefore, we have to learn to trade at the asking price for an asset in order to prevent missed trades; we cannot trade in the past, and incorrectly, implementing positions based on previous prices have caused traders to miss market moves consistently throughout history. In order to elaborate, many traders will place a trade at the bid price or last sales price, and this incorrect understanding of the true price results in the trader missing a fill (or a complete fill) on his trade. This occurs because people tend to gravitate towards what they can see, and what they can see on their chart is the last known matched price, which means that in the present moment, that price exists in the past. This discussion on understanding true price based on asking price is important because just as stop losses can take us out of the market when they are incorrectly placed, which takes us out of the trade flow, missing fills will do the same thing. As you will learn in this book, there is never any reason to ever be out of the market. *Time and Price Windows* will form in order to tell us if we should be long or short; there will always be a reason to be on one side of the market or the other, and the only remaining question on entering the market will be based on reward to risk criteria. Therefore, I encourage traders to go at the market when they recognize a *Time and Price Symmetry* inflection point based on the Moment of Recognition. Of course, I must caution that trading size does matter, and yes, it is justified to enter positions as limit orders once your trade size has an impact on the underlying price. Even then, going at limits above the current market's asking price cannot guarantee complete order fills.

As we continue this scientific metaphor, with respect to what price truly is, we also have to understand that *Price is also where our profit and loss come from*. Price is the reason we are in the market in the first place, and the reason we place trades is for asset appreciation (longs) or asset depreciation (shorts). Again, we see that this number is quantifiable, as we would expect in a scientific comparison with respect to price. As we will see in the following chapters, price patterns or price ratios will also be quantifiable as well. As traders, our jobs will be to interpret these patterns and ratios in order to determine future asset valuations, which correspondingly dictates to how we implement our trades. We will also explore the macro and micro relationships between markets in order to determine trend, which I foreshadowed in the *Introduction* of this book with respect to Quantitative Synchronicity. This will allow us to quantify many trends that co-exist in many different time periods. Correctly determining the trend in the present moment gets exhausting and difficult, but it is possible. Further, it becomes easier as our understanding increases. Conclusively, I must state that as we move to shorter and shorter time frames, the level of trading difficulty increases. For instance, it is much easier to see the trend on the daily chart then on the 1-minute chart. It is much easier to implement one or two trades per month instead of one or two trades an hour. Therefore, the synchronicity that must be developed between all trading timeframes is a learned skill that is learned in our subconscious minds. It is the reason that I overstressed the 10,000 hour trading requirement in earlier chapters, and as discussed in the *Introduction,* Quantitative Synchronicity is what is required in order to have extreme success in an endeavor such as a trading campaign. Thus, Quantitative Synchronicity is having the complete knowledge of understanding the full market picture with respect to: knowing the trend, price objectives, and price pattern objectives in every time frame and in every present moment (all of these terms will be defined in Price Structure), which gives the third-dimension of the market via Quantitative Synchronicity its Depth.

Thankfully, we can start implementing trades early on in our *Time and Price Symmetry* careers if we start with trades that occur in longer time windows, and we can build our confidence and understanding between the synchronizing of trends as we move to shorter time periods. Let me state this clearly, *a trader must learn to ignore his or her ego with respect to trading frequency*, and a trader may decide to never move to a shorter time period. A trader may decide to remain a trader that takes 1 or 2 trades per month, and that is okay. Please remember, you have no one to impress but yourself, and please do not feel like you should ever work outside of your God-given abilities. That being said, the reason I try to exhaustively discuss trend is because we, as traders, can be profitable across all time periods if we know the overall trend. This means that we can profit from knowing the trend without knowing total synchronicity, and thus, the trend becomes one of the most esoteric and difficult parts for a trader with respect to that trader knowing the trend in the time period that they are trading in. That last sentence is critical to trading, and as traders, we need to determine how much are mental acuity is refined with respect to how often we can trade. Trend analysis thereby becomes one of the most important parts of understanding Price Structure, and I emphasize the fact that a trader should never trade if they do not know the primary trend. Moreover, the esoteric nature of trend analysis (with respect to total synchronicity) is a concept that I believe will remain unquantifiable with respect to Price Structure because of Time Structure's impact on the trend. As such, the necessity of witnessing thousands of hours of the market will lead to an ethereal understanding of this unquantifiable concept for the subconscious servo-mechanisms in our brain. What is more, trend analysis will be crucial in understanding what price patterns and ratios will be relevant in finding tangible highs and lows that are availing themselves through *Time and Price Windows* but exist as counter-trend indicators. Thankfully, we have a natural filter to stop us from over-trading counter-trend, and it exists on the x-axis as Time.

Art

Time is more important then anything else in trading because time will act as a predestined trade quantifier. Further, time windows will exist in order to show us when price patterns or price ratios should be analyzed for a trade opportunity. A time window is simply an interval of time that opens up for us to focus our energy on determining if the market is going to react or not. Or, a time window can exist as a pre-determined point in time for taking a trade in the first place, which completely invalidates the underlying price. In order to understand and quantify these time windows, we must realize that **Time Structure** will be based on repetitions of time or cycles of time that have been defined by humans. For an example of a time repetition, we observe that at 10:01 am our underlying asset made a high. Well, for the remainder of the day, we will observe if highs or lows are made at one-minute after each subsequent hour. In a way, we see that this window opens up right at 10:01 and it closes at 10:02. Consecutive repetitions will reinforce the time window, and in order to define that reinforcement, we will record how often this time window has validity. Most important and as alluded to earlier, time windows will help us conserve our mental energy by telling us when we need to focus on price. This dualistic benefit of time leads to higher probability trades because it allows us to save our mental energy for doing the reactive analysis to understand if the market is starting to reverse/react. Therefore, Time Structure will act as our divinely guided hand in helping us to define the success of a trade based on underlying Price Structure risk to reward ratios. Time can also be used as a filter that will slow our trades down, which is a clandestine conclusion that the masses do not easily understand. I believe the benefit of time, with respect to slowing trading down, is very important because over-trading is a big problem for most traders.

The problem with Time Structure is the trend. This understanding is important because, at some point, both Time Cycles and Time Repetitions can become quite numerous, which may be counterproductive to over-trading. In fact, Time Structure definition can sometimes reach the illogical point that we start to visualize that every day or every minute has a Time Window kicking in. We can become disillusioned with what we think is happening, and this will lead us to irrational thinking by being too inundated with time. For example, a trader may start to illogically picture that at 10:01 Am, every fourth day of the month that falls on a Tuesday, will yield a successful trade. It becomes idiotic, and I will discuss proper ways to filter our thinking in order to use Time as the most important trading edge that exists, while simultaneously being aware that we can abandon time, and instead, we can abandon our trade to the trend. Remember, the power of time is immense for focusing mental energy or being aware of the Moment of Recognition, but overall, the trend will dictate the resultant performance of the trade.

When I first started understanding Time Structure, I started a deep analysis in order to find different patterns in time. In fact, I expect higher intellects will follow down that same path of thinking. Our logical minds will try to find validity by finding a quantifiable formulation that will ultimately be able to define as to when Time can be a trading factor. Sorry, but this will not work. Time is art; not science. We have to learn the KISS method ("<u>K</u>eep <u>i</u>t <u>s</u>imple <u>s</u>tupid"). It will do no good to create something out of nothing, and I will illustrate how to keep it simple for those of us who are ***intelligently acting stupid***, or as St. Paul said, "Sometimes I do what I do not want to do, and I do not know why." Please note, I do not mean to insinuate that time should not be further analyzed, and as I said in the *Introduction,* the analysis of Price Structure and Time Structure by the PhD audience is something that I hope will occur after publishing this book. That being said, we must remember that we will all see things (time windows) differently that may or may not be valid, and our challenge will be to understand what the artist (God or collective human thought) is trying to portray in the present moment.

Although, repetitions will be our primary concept of time, time cycles will be a big area of discussion. The problem with time cycles is that people seem to invent them arbitrarily. Sometimes they work, and then, they just fail. Our focus on time cycles will be to analyze a few of them, but more importantly, to analyze when they are or are not working. True trading acumen will avail itself by our abandonment to understanding the time cycle coupled with the price objectives of the trend. Further, I need to discuss the fact that sometimes the basis for a time cycle is quite right, but the cycle itself has experienced a time shift based on when markets made important highs or lows during respective bull or bear markets. Therefore, we will have to be aware of this time shift so that the time cycle can still offer us value in the future. I would like to give one more interesting example in order to illustrate this point. In the late 90s, A Princeton researcher came up with something called the *8.6-year global economic confidence model*. (As an aside, after publishing his paper on this model, he went to Federal prison; like me, and I will let the conspiracy theorists have at that coincidence.) Anyway, this cycle is of extreme importance to us as traders, but it requires interpretation. It requires to be split into four chunks of 2.15-year intervals in order to have success for our needs. For now, I will illustrate one example using the 2008 market crash in order for the reader to comprehend how powerful time can truly be.

After the crash low on March 9, 2009, (which I called by 4 minutes, as my emails would prove) I defined this low to be relevant for a time shift. After that low, the market staged a large rally for almost 2 years with only one decent correction in 2010. However, beginning in late April of 2011, the market stopped going higher, and it had an even larger correction, but why? The 8.6-year cycle was the primary reason. Almost exactly 2.15 years from the crash low, we had a relevant high. Go calculate it for yourself. As you will see, the basic time cycle required analysis to be effective. I suspect many people will have their own artistic view on many of the time cycles that I discuss, and I hope you help and not hurt yourself in your analysis.

The biggest problem with time cycles (not repetitions) is how large of a time window we have to look at. As time gets larger, we need higher tolerances in order to validate effectiveness. A completely arbitrary example that uses the 8.6-year cycle could be that when looking at 8.6 years we look at 8.6 years +/- 0.5 years, but at 2.15 years we may look at +/- 0.05 years. The fact is that no matter how much statistical analysis you perform, you will never find the right values for the deviations because many time cycles co-exist at any given present moment. As an aside, smoothing these together is a useless exercise as well. I know. I tried. Therefore, my purpose in discussing Time will be to explain what works, and more important, I will describe how Time is part of the true market structure/Marketome.

Hence, as a conclusion to our introduction to time, I ask the reader to take a step back from the numbers when looking at time. Find something that works for you and your mentality, and use it to increase your conviction in your trades. Please don't look for things that simply aren't there. I guarantee that any financial engineer/scientist/quant will start measuring the time between events as a first step. I've gone down many of these roads as well, and it is a useless waste of life. Please, dear reader, understand that the relationships between time and price, as an inherent certainty, is due to the underlying structure of the market. Also emphasized, I encourage you to use Time in order to slow down your trades as well, and to get you back with the proper trend because getting back to the trend is the ultimate goal, and making money with the trend is the easiest part of trading. Therefore, use time to give you windows of focusing your mental energy at crucial moments so you can think clearer. Do not think you are above the concepts in this book, and I know that statements such as these are my ego seeking edification, but it is the truth; everything you will need is written in these pages. As such, the most important thing that I ask the reader to realize about learning *Time and Price Symmetry* is that *Time and Price Symmetry* will ALWAYS tell you what side of the market to be on. It may not be clear, but there is always a reason to be long or short a given market based on *Time and Price Symmetry* defined inflection points. However, it will be your lack of conviction, your lack of clarity, or your lack of intelligence that keeps you out of the market. It will never be *Time and Price Symmetry*

Ego

So far, I have referred to the ego several times throughout this book, but why, you may ask, "Is it such a big deal?" The ego prevents us from living in the present moment, and that is why it is a big deal. It causes us to feel pain of loss. It causes us to fall in love with our positions, which leads to forecasting about that position's future profitability. The ego uses our past memories to hold us back, and it uses our future hopes to prevent us from seeing the present, which is the reality of our situation. The ego also makes us feel omniscient as our confidence grows, and it tells us we can do no wrong, which leads to breaking our rules of money/risk management. Our ego makes us feel that we cannot cope with a reduction of our trade size under drawdown because we are too good to go backwards. Wouldn't it be nice to do this job without having an ego?

Unfortunately, we cannot, but God gave us a person, not only a person, a neuroscientist, who experienced the beauty of living without an ego for a few hours; the beauty of living without our past emotional pains that knock us down every day of our lives.

Dr. Jill Bolte Taylor recounted this experience in front of the illustrious crowds of TED. She gave a talk entitled, "Jill Bolte Taylor's Stroke of Insight." To date, she is one of a handful of people known to feel the beauty of living in the present moment. Sadly, in order to have this experience, she had a stroke that came on gradually, which allowed her to analyze her mind using her education as her ego diminished from her conscious thought. Her account is quite remarkable in regards to how beautiful the world became, and how she felt peace within herself and everything around her. Her presentation is a powerful, palpable, emotionally driven recount of living without the ego. Thankfully, she survived this experience in order to convey the message to us, and it serves as a reminder to us, as traders, how we can become harmonized to the market by living in the present moment. Often, I have engaged in religious counter-thought of what happens to us when we "ascend to the hereafter." For years, I felt that our body and our brains are an area that allows us to maintain memories that make us who we are over our lifetime here on Earth, but I could never conclude that thought and memory transcends the body. Similarly, I could never fully believe that when we die, our memories and mental faculties will come with us, because logically, we know that the brain is a network of neurons that forms clusters of memory based-thought, and with diseases such as Alzheimer's, we can see the destruction of those memories. Therefore, I could never scientifically or religiously comprehend how, in death, we could retain certain faculties. Hence, it has been my belief, after studying Dr. Taylor's presentation, religion, and my own mind that I have reached the conclusion that Heaven may simply be the soul's freedom to exist in the present moment.

This existence as pure energy is not to be understood lightly, and as we are learning from science, the matter that is attached to energy (as determined from the Higg's particle) may imply some type of thought that exists as energy. This thought-based power may lead to some type of memorial imprinting on the soul, and this imprinting may cause our soul to carry forward inherent abilities or memories, which yield proclivities for our life purpose here on Earth (for instance, if we are reincarnated, I believe my proclivity to trading may still exist). Granted, this imprinting process is undeniably neither unknown nor quantifiable, and only God knows what we take with us.

Biologically, scientifically, and religiously, this makes sense to me. Without the flesh (or matter) of the brain, we no longer have memories or the ability to imagine the future, we only have the present moment in all its beauty, which may be how God sees the world. This also serves as a valid explanation for those of you who believe in reincarnation; this dialogue explains why we do not keep our previous memories when we move between lives. Before moving on, I must make one revelation that is more on the personal-side regarding these thoughts as well. In life, I have often found that being with a partner has lead to my happiest moments, and in many ways, I found it very sad when I read in the Bible that Jesus says, "there is no marriage in heaven." I believed that if I was in love with my partner on Earth, then, Heaven would be spending eternity with that person if she was my "soul-mate." However, if you lose the ability to recall memories, I surmise that you would lose the feeling of love with respect to another person because ultimately, love is borne from the memories and attachments that are built as a necessity in our physical lives. Therefore, coming to the deterministic point of view that human beings are meant to live in the present moment in order to have heaven on earth has been my ultimate conclusion to my religious study, and in particular, if we are to believe that the markets/humanity are following a predestined plan, then becoming "one" with the present moment of the market is how we can execute in the perfect manner. In a way, we need to have oneness with the market as well as with ourselves in order to surrender to God's Will, which is, essentially, our human purpose. By abandoning ourselves to the present moment, as Father Jean-Pierre de Caussade wrote many centuries ago, we can be at peace with everything in life. However, I take this much further. I believe that this peace from the present moment is only one aspect of understanding the benefits of present moment surrendering. By surrendering ourselves unconditionally to the here, we are capable of applying instant, conscious thought to our decisions, which occur as a summation of our collected subconscious and conscious mind output, which may also grasp onto parapsychology at some unknown, unseen level. This is a fantastic area of mental study that I encourage the reader to embark on because, it is my belief, that only extraordinary results in any part of life can come from pure abandonment to the divine Will, which exists in the present moment. For instance, does an athlete not abandon him or herself to the present moment while reacting in sports? Trading must be thought of in the same way, and only then, will the power of abandonment unleash results that we humans have never even contemplated.

Obviously since we are still alive, we cannot remove our ego, but we need to train ourselves to be humble and to be grateful to the market for the opportunities that are availed to us everyday; we have to strive to become more God-like by living in the present moment. We cannot forecast. We cannot feel pain from prior losses. We cannot have fear. So, we have to let go of our cognitive thinking capacities by utilizing the subconscious mechanism that is built by thousands of hours of study in order to allow us to live in the present moment, which helps us to avail the mind to the Moment of Recognition. Analytical thinking about failed trading will get you nowhere, and as Al Pacino said in *The Devil's Advocate,* "Guilt is a pound of fucking bricks." We cannot relive past traumas, and we must realize that no matter what our intellect is, we are no better or smarter than the markets. In fact, no one is except for God.

Investing and the Ego

Investors will have a much harder time coping with ego since they are not actively trading, which means they are not training their subconscious to do the analysis portion of their trades. Investors are forced to use their cognitive, higher-level, conscious thinking patterns, and if we cannot rely on the subconscious as a heuristic for trade decision, it is good to define the trade/position parameters that the investor is looking for. Obviously, this is not a present moment approach, which is quite obvious if we look back on history. In today's world, people forget that it was only 25 years ago that a majority of investors/traders were able to see the value of their position in the following day's newspaper. There was no internet. There was no wireless data. No, investors or traders tended to make decisions that were after the fact. It is my belief that proper trading was not even possible until the proper connectivity was implemented, and that is why, historically, investing has done quite well. People we forced to abandon their position to the will of the markets, but today, unconditioned investors are more prone to irrationality. The ease of seeing their position rise and fall on a shorter, time basis is counterproductive to anyone that has not conditioned themselves to present moment thinking, and instead, investors need to go back to the way it was if they are going to have success. Investors need to remain believers in their investments, and they need to minimize trade frequency. I will not belabor this topic because known or unknown to the reader, I have already discussed this in Chapter 2, so now, I need to move forward to recognizing the passive versus active role that some market participants have.

Conclusively, investors need to be passive. Hence, passive investors, in comparison to active traders, do not get the training to become emotion-less humans that disregard the money amount of their account. Investors have to deal with the fear of loss and the fear of giving back profits since their exposure is purely minimized to money. I ask you to think about that last sentence for a minute because it is not an easy, obvious realization. Furthermore, the love of money in an investor's account will cause an investor to feel pangs of pain due to the ego not being properly conditioned for the market. The ego will prevent the investor from allocating 100% of their risk capital on subsequent trades because of these types of fears brought to the surface by the ego. However, please do not be discouraged. Instead, investors need to be mindful of their ego at all times. They need to stay calculated, and refer back to their rules. Further, they need to keep the concept of risk capital in mind. In fact, even traders that are well conditioned (like the large hedge fund managers that are now more investor-like than trader-like) will be faced with this aversion to risk as their account sizes grow, but amazingly, it has been my observation that traders sometimes have the opposite reaction.

Size and the Ego

As account sizes grow, the confidence of any human being's mind is stroked by a different part of the ego. The person will commit more money to subsequent trades due to some egotistical feeling of invincibility: The "I can do no wrong" complex. When that occurs, we can get too far away from the benefits that the ego contains (yes, it's not all bad). Traders and investors always need some level of fear, or we will end up just clicking the mouse in order to buy/sell more and more and more until our broker becomes the limiting factor (or account size). Due to the amount of capital I lost in the beginning phases of my career, I became too far emotionally detached from the market. I was trading by the seat of my pants (so to speak) through massive leverage and unwarranted conviction. I never thought about the consequences of the trades because I knew more capital was available to me. This detachment from the ego is a disaster, and we must learn to use our ego in order to help us rationalize our trading, which will allow us to stay in line with our risk management and money management rules. This is why I have defined a difference between trades and positions in the last chapter.

There is nothing wrong with a trader or investor having a double or triple position in one market; especially, if you are specialized in one market. However, the reason for the increase in position size must not come from the ego. You have to learn to differentiate between when you are trading logically or emotionally. Ironically, becoming devoid of emotions regarding fear allows our ego to manifest new emotions, which leads to unwarranted actions. Logically, we have to remember that multiple positions are okay if each position still adheres to our risk management rules, but more important, additive positions should come from new *Time and Price Windows* that are made in the same direction of our previous trade (i.e. a long indication and then another long indication). For further clarification, you can also have two positions in one market with two ***different*** corresponding stop losses (both of which adhere to your risk management criteria), and one position may be stopped out where the other may not. However, the greatest thing we need to remember is that we are trading in the underlying market structure of *Time and Price Symmetry*. As such, every additive position must have a logical reason behind it. For example, a new *Time and Price Symmetry* inflection point availing itself in line with our first position/the underlying trend. Another way that we may logically justify additive positions is through profits on the day as we saw in our example with Jim in the last chapter. However, as we saw with Jim, he had a logical formula to increase his trade size, and he did not do so in a seemingly random fashion. I think this is an important statement because it deduces the fact that traders need quantifiable rules just as much if not more than investors. As traders, we must remember to not get cocky, which is contrary to the lifestyle that is borne from wealth. Therefore, you can understand, dear reader, why I stress the fact that market participants must remain humble, logical, and have a defined set of criteria that will eventually become part of our subconscious thought processes. If we don't, the market will take the wind out of our sails in the blink of an eye.

NLP

Part of understanding how to condition the ego is something referred to as **neuro-linguistic programming** ("NLP"). NLP has been made popular by Tony Robbins in the past decade or so, and I have actually taken part in one of Mr. Robbins's "Unleash the Power Within" seminars as part of my ego conditioning. NLP is an extremely powerful tool for us to use as traders. When we are stopped out of a trade or if we are taken out of the market, traders and investors have a hard time coping with what to do next. If we are taken out with a loss, this allows new, subconscious servomechanisms to engage. We have to learn quickly to recognize these negative feelings, and we need to do something physically to obliterate those feelings. That physical action that causes a biochemical change in our mental state is what NLP is. Therefore, NLP is the easiest way to get us back in the market.

Once we realize the pang of anxiety, which is what some people call a "Gambler's High," we need to become alarmed and aware. The Gambler's High is a powerful, negative reaction that links our brain to losses instead of gains. Essentially, that is how a Gambler's High manifests itself anyway, through losses, and any market participant needs to learn how to correct this proven, human flaw; fast. Moreover, this human flaw is strengthened based on genetics. Aside from hereditary proclivity to this chemical brain imbalance, neuroscience has found that in almost all individuals, losses trigger many more neurotransmitter releases in our brain because of the anxiety of making money back, which is actually *a fear of the future*. This means that not only that gambling mentalities are aligned to losses (not gains), but all of humanity is aligned to loss more than gain. In order to understand this, I have to use an example.

Let us discuss what happens if someone has $700 and they make $1000 through gambling activities. In this scenario, the gambler does not really feel anything. Their thought is simply, "Gee, I made $300, now what?" However, if the gambler loses the whole $700 and it was all he or she had, the mind starts kicking in with thoughts like: "Now what am I going to do?" "How do I make this money back?" "What will my wife or husband say?" These thoughts will cause neurotransmitter release that quantifies as a <u>mental high</u>. As such, we have to use NLP to do two things: First, when we take a loss that starts triggering negative thoughts, we have to immediately focus our mind on something different. For example, the simple act of making yourself smile can literally change the chemical reactions of your mind. When you lose, look away, and smile. When you lose, look at some art work in your office. When you lose, go do some pushups. Find a way to condition your mind to happiness instantly, and as your NLP learning matures, you will be able to instantly rekindle a memory of happiness in order to drive the Gambler's High away. Second, we have to use NLP in order to condition our minds to have the same level of neurotransmitter release with profits as the mind has with losses. In a way, I do not know if this is even possible, but I surmise that if you were able to psychologically analyze the brain of the best traders via a S.P.E.C.T scan, you would find that their brains' feel some type of elation in regards to making profits. The best traders or investors probably have some type of chemical release when they take profits that are <u>stronger</u> than when they take losses. These hereditary outliers may be thinking of a material object when they make profits, or they may bask in the instant mental gratification of being right. Whatever it may be, market participants need to learn how to reprogram their subconscious to be just as reinforced with neurotransmitter releases as the best traders do. Thankfully, it is my belief that we can use NLP to accomplish this goal. Again, it is unfortunate, but how to accomplish this mental reprogramming is out of the scope of this book, but it is extremely important to understand this idea. As such, I hope you find what works for you, and I hope I have now found what works for me.

External Ego Distracters

Moving towards our concluding thoughts regarding the ego, we have to address something that happens to many traders: "the criticism of losses." The best traders have the ability to forget about their losses. Just like the "Gambler's High" in the last paragraph, humans are designed to remember their losses and not their wins. Take a second and think back to your own trading, do you find yourself thinking about the days that you had your biggest losses or your biggest gains? Undoubtedly, your mind will remember the losses because there is more of an emotional attachment to it. This too is incorrect thought patterns and recordings, and we again have to utilize some sporting-based psychology in order to understand that we can reprogram the way the computer in our brain records its data just as we can reprogram the brain for when it chemically releases neurotransmitters when we take gains.

For example, when someone starts learning a new sport, they make many more mistakes. Say, for instance, when a young person learns how to swing a bat towards a baseball, undoubtedly, they miss most of the time. However, as they get experience in making contact with the ball, their brain records the correct mechanics that led to this action; we can apply this metaphor to many other sports, and golf is also a good comparison. Yet, the same must be true about trading. The monetary aspect of trading does not exist for most people in regards to sports. When you learn to swing a baseball bat, you are not taking a monetary loss by it, so you are not recording the missed swing with an emotional tie to money, but I surmise that if an individual was to lose money with every swing of the bat, those with gambling mentalities would never get better where as those with out a gambling tendency would tend to get better. I have never seen a study done like this, but it is simply my metaphorical relation to trading that when we swing a bat and hit the ball, our mind records and remembers this positive act, and we have to do the same thing with trading whether or not money is there or not.

Something that I believe is relevant to discuss is the concept of the "Painbody" as defined by Ekkard Tolle (spelling?). His concept of a painbody can be external or internal, and we have to learn to understand this painbody. We have to separate it from ourselves, and we can do that through NLP techniques. In a way, in order to successful understand how to recognize and defeat the painbody we have to recondition our neurological-thought processes. For instance, when we make a successful trade, we have to emotionally ingrain this success in our mind so that we can duplicate it repeatedly. We need to have a much greater emotional affinity for being right than for being wrong in order to obliterate the losses from our mind, and it will be up to you in order to figure out how you can accomplish this task; in order to destroy your own painbody.

Another major distracter for the ego comes from investors, benchmarks, and peers. I touched on this heavily in our discussion of market-oriented versus goal-oriented thinking, but it is more important here in this discussion of ego. Outside influences exist purely to take us out of the present moment, and as money managers, we need to be aware of those influences. There is not much more that can be said about these influences except that the manager must be aware of them, and again, it is my hope that the role of the risk manager in your life is more than just there for the portfolio's risk. Only by minimizing stress is it my belief that true traders can execute their job, and we must not forget the power of NLP in righting the mentality back to the present moment.

The ego is a marvelous thing. It allows us to derive feelings from our past actions, and neuroscience has proved that we can utilize our conscious ego to speak to our subconscious self. Therefore, we need to learn to use the ego to help us to choose and to help us to imagine successful trades instead of emotionally linking our past failures. In a way, the ego needs to learn how to live in the future by visualizing our trading growth in the present. As traders or investors, we need to learn how to do this from the inception of our careers in the market. We have to program our imagination for success. Functionally, the ability to reprogram the subconscious in methods of recognition that are chemically tied to gains is the true key in understanding the psychological aspect of trading, and arguably, this is also the key to correctly implementing the Law of Attraction / prayer as part of our trading plan. I encourage the reader to embark on their own, honest analysis of what their current flaws are with their trading psychology, and even without getting to *Time and Price Symmetry*, I guarantee that the correct reprogramming of the subconscious mind through conscious, positive repetition reinforcement, will have an immediate impact on your trading abilities.

Divination and the Ego

In order to understand the quest that we are going to embark on, I feel that I must refer to something relevant to trading and to our own human abilities. Obviously, these introductory chapters that have discussed one's psyche can be summarized in one word, "humility." Humility and humbleness are necessary for market longevity, and the reason for this non-egotistical approach is that we, as humans, cannot achieve godliness; holiness, yes; godliness, no. As such, I must make a clear distinction between the understandings of *Time and Price Symmetry* versus divination, with respect to the Catholic Church. St. Thomas Aquinas (1225-1274), a Doctor of the Roman Catholic Church, tells us in his *Summa Theologica* (Chicago: Encyclopedia Britannica, Inc., 1952) that, "Future events are known to God alone and that every created intellect falls far short of God's eternity; hence the future as it is in itself cannot be known by any created intellect." However, this Saint further elaborates in his doctrine that a created intellect could understand and have knowledge of the future defined as "by the cause." For instance, if a person jumps into a pool, the short-term rational mentality is able to understand that he or she will become wet in the future. Thus, we need to think of *Time and Price Symmetry* in the exact same way because the reality of trading is that we need to elevate our mentalities (our Wills) to have oneness with God in order to understand His future; not our future. Therefore, a clear distinction is made, which negates the claim of divination. In essence, I am saying that the reason the market reacts is through divinity, but we are not engaging in sacrilegious practices of divining the future.

From a scientific perspective, I also must reflect back on Chaos Theory mathematics as mentioned in the *Introduction* of this book. Renowned physicist Mitchell Feigenbaum was notorious fur understanding that there was rationale to chaos; there was order in turbulence. He observed that there was a sequential spectrum that appeared random to the unlearned observer by studying varying frequencies. As such, when the realization that he made was that there was an inherent structure to this turbulence, he posited that it means there must be a divine creator to turbulence. In a way, Fibonacci, who will be mentioned throughout this book, did the exact same thing. Like Feigenbaum, Fibonacci observed that there was rationale in nature. He saw that there was also mathematical harmony to the human body, which was also elaborated on by Da Vinci. Hence, I am doing the same thing in my writing; I am revealing God within the markets, but in no way am I saying that we are ever our own God because that would make us the devil.

Further, I must emphasize this fact, which is that we are not trying to become like God, no, we are trying to understand God's plans through His Divine Will, which is observable through the chaos of the markets because, in reality, that chaos is structured, as the reader will learn by reading this book, and we can only do this structural decomposition through humbleness. Summarily, this understanding can be accomplished for us by St. Thomas Aquinas, when he tells us that, "Man Cannot know future things, except in their causes or by God's revelation." Thereby we can relate this to our internal ego and to *Time and Price Symmetry* by understanding that we are analyzing the "cause" in the market, and we are able to see the result, and this discussion is concluded in Chapter 20.

In summary, I am excited to move past these Chapters that deal with preconceived industry notions / perceptions, and now, we can focus on *Time and Price Symmetry*. We will be dealing with the fundamental, technical (ironically, true) basis of how the market gyrates purely based on how price action must work, and how time avails itself to us, which makes time our best ally when properly implemented. However, please, I cannot emphasize enough how important it is to control your ego. It is a forever time consuming task that requires meditative thought. The ego must be conditioned to get past fear, while at the same time, being conditioned to not becoming overconfident in one's abilities. It is a fine line that can be honed by setting rules for all aspects of trading. In fact, my ego cost me my life as I knew it, and it cost me the life and the family I thought I was going to have. Therefore, never let your beliefs become forecasts for the results of what you are doing because you never know when you will run out of time or be destroyed by the market. Therefore, all market participants need to remember to live in the present moment, and we must all focus on the decisions regarding trades and our trading accounts in order to stay grounded to our end goal. Whatever that may be.

PRICE STRUCTURE

Chapter 6

Price Structure

In order to understand Price Structure, we need to understand the power of the human mind, and specifically, we need to understand the power of the subconscious human mind, which we talked about in the last five chapters. I say this because we are embarking on a journey to quantify the intangible, and the reader's belief has to become aligned with my belief that, although the conscious mind cannot define an esoteric theorem, the power of the subconscious mind can. Therefore, this learning process will begin by understanding the great power of the subconscious mechanisms that will grasp a level of understanding that we cannot consciously avail to our rational mentality. Thus, the reader must contemplate that, by understanding the conscious concepts listed here forward, he or she will fuel the subconscious learning mechanisms, and this understanding is necessary because we need to understand the future market objectives at the gray line between subconscious trade inceptions and conscious trade implementations. What should be obvious is that we need to have this internal interfacing occur instantaneously if we are to yield profit from the mind's recognition of underlying market objectives. This concept of subconscious utilization is not new, but I am probably the first to write about this understanding with relation to trading. However, because this concept is not new, we need to observe the power of the subconscious mind for profit, which does not always have to be defined in terms of dollars and cents.

In 1760, Thomas Bayes came up with the theorem of "Subjective Probability," which can crudely be called "the method of quantifying a hunch." Basically, Bayes believed that a group of humans that were able to place calculated odds-like bets, would be able to unlock the collective intelligence that exists at the subconscious level, and Bayes' Theorem is not without practical merit. As such, the first thing we learn from Bayes is that the usefulness of a theorem should not rely on its provability, which is also crucial for understanding *Time and Price Symmetry*. As a result, the power of correctly stated and correctly propagated theorems cannot be diminished because, if President Lyndon Johnson did not call on a group of scientist to use Bayes' Theorem, the United States may have never recovered a nuclear bomb that was lost at sea after a B-52 bomber collided with an in-air refueling tanker. It was the power of Bayes' Theorem that was able to calculate within 500 yards the location of that "lost at sea bomb," and had the mathematicians not invoked an improvable theorem, who knows how many lives could have been lost had that bomb fallen into the wrong hands. Therefore, we have to understand the powers of the subconscious servomechanisms, and we must not be afraid to rely on improvable methods in order to accomplish a great task. Concurrently, if we were to equate this usage of an improvable theorem to profit, I could say, in other words, that the United States' profit from this intangible theorem was truly priceless because that profit was measured in human life.

Bayes' Theorem is a fantastic lead in to *Time and Price Symmetry* and my own conjecture of quantifying the intangible through *Time and Price Symmetry,* and the first intangible exists as my own Price Theory that is based on underlying Price Structure. Hence, we need to understand that, as with Bayes' Theorem, we are yielding to the mass subconscious of the market that is made tangible and conscious through the visual two-axis representation of the market. What is more, through the markets movements, we see that the conscious mind has a direct link to the subconscious through the market's price discovery process, and through that visual representation, we get a glimpse at the mass combined subconscious of humanity. However, we need to recognize this mass subconscious, and we need to allow our personal subconscious to be awakened. Only then, can the trader use *Time and Price Symmetry* in order to profit from outstanding market objectives. Further, the goal of the trader from here forward will be to train the internal subconscious to understand the future outcome of every trade (once properly conditioned), and I must be clear that this understanding is not the same as mass-market psychology or self-fulfilling prophecies. Therefore, the technical discussions in this book are an extrapolation of trying to define the intangible but learnable market structure through conscious explanation that will allow the subconscious to recognize the ultimate, *future* market objectives. With that being said, we can now begin this discussion by understanding that, although unquantifiable, Price Structure must exist because it is the way that markets must gyrate through time and through price.

In order to begin our understanding of conscious concept recognition, we need to realize that Price Structure is based on the logical definition of how price must work since it deals with prices of trading instruments that are moving up or moving down over a given period of time, which establishes ranges of price. The movement of price is the fundamental basis of all Price Structure because that is what markets are designed to do: move up or move down. Obviously, the printing of a price is derived from the exchange of a buyer and of a seller at a specified time in history, which links the two components of time and of price. However, as we move to the future, we need to understand and recognize that prices can go higher or lower. Therefore, the basis of **Price Structure** will focus on conscious components that help the trader understand whether a market will make a new high or a new low outside of a defined range, which is formed as prices move inside of that range as the market moves forward in time. A **Range** can simply be thought of as a diagonal line that links a low/high to a high/low on a chart, and we will further clarify range types within this chapter. What's more, a Range is created from these two links that are dubbed as market inflection points, which will be defined shortly. However, in essence, we must understand that a range must exist for Klatch's Price Theory to hold, which means we can only acquiesce to Price Rheory once a range is formed. That said, a range can be formed on a micro basis by looking at a tick chart or it may be formed over an immense period of time (i.e. the range formed between the yearly low and the yearly high discreet points.)

Klatch's Price Theory

In order to establish the thesis-like assertion of this book, which also serves as my basis for invalidating the *Efficient Market Hypothesis*, I will now define **Klatch's Price Theory** ("Price Theory" or "Klatch's Range Theory" or "Range Theory") as: *if a market fails to take out a new high, of a previously established range, that market must make a new low of the said range, and conversely, if a market fails to make a new low, of a previously established range, that market must make a new high of the said range*. This conjecture will serve as the underlying basis for all trading, and we will learn in later chapters how to quantify the direction that the market is going to break based on subsequent chart pattern formations or windows of time. Hence, the sole purpose of this book is to avail our minds to the structure of *Time and Price Symmetry* that causes the market to break any given range. However, regardless of the knowledge that exists in further chapters of this book, the dominant fact is that at some point, price action must adhere to Price Theory because it has no other choice (unless the markets were to shutdown/close). As a corollary to Price Theory, I feel like I must mention to the reader that the concept of ranges and ranges being broken was never taught to me by any of my trading mentors, and understanding the market's objective to expand a given range is the first conscious concept that must be driven into the subconscious. Further, the concept of range expansion is the logical conclusion to understanding the true market structure that exists, but the true power that exists from range expansion based on Klatch's Price Theory is done through Quantitative Synchronicity because one must be aware that there may be simultaneous range expansion objectives that are being targeted at any given present moment. That being said, this concept is now claimed by me, but this concept remains mathematically unquantified. (However, a mathematical quantification of the theory is proposed and used for contradicting *The Efficient Market Hypothesis* in Chapter 21.)

Moving forward, the first thing the reader should be contemplating from the introduction of

Klatch's Price Theory is that of range expansion. Range expansion simply means that a preexisting range is somehow expanded once a prior range is broken. Therefore, we can now define this range expansion in logical wording, and we will call the concept of market objectives based on Price Theory's range expansion goals as **Price Objectives**. The Price Objective for an underlying market instrument is to determine if the high or the low of a given range is going to be broken based on Price Theory (I.e. the range is expanded). Further, Price Objectives will exist for helping us stay committed to our trades, and it is another way to prevent over-trading. In effect, the concept that the trader must understand is that by using Price Theory, we can wait until Price Objectives are fulfilled before taking profits or realizing losses because for every established range, we will have to decide, in the present moment, if the market is going to take out the high or the low of the targeted range, and we can use the knowledge of Price Objectives in determining profit or loss rules for every given trade. Furthermore, Price Objectives help us in stop loss placement, trend definitions, additive positions, and reduction of trade frequency. This is all a very simple conclusion from a simple observation, but that simplicity does not negate the realism or the profitability of understanding outstanding Price Objectives based on Price Theory. Thus, like most of the other concepts in this book, thinking in terms of a Price Objective will require a shift in conventional thinking because Price Objectives allow us to take the psychological fear out of trading, which cannot be understated. For an example of fear eradiation, the trader must understand that, when he or she is placing a trade, he or she is deciding if the market will take out a new high or a new low of a given range. Therein lies the peace garnered by Price Theory because we are no longer have to be afraid that the market is going to make some random move because, at this point, price action that is based on Price Objectives validates Price Theory. As such, one can now simply approach the market with calmness by remembering that for every given trade, the market is either going higher or lower in order to satisfy an outstanding Price Objective. In later chapters, we will also expand this definition in order to include Price Pattern Objectives that exist when standard Price Objectives do not, which only occurs during the range expansion process. For now, however, I ask the reader to understand the fact that the market must take out a new high or a new low of an established range as time moves forward. In this way, Klatch's Price Theory gets validation, but due to the possibility of infinitesimal movements that may exist as contraction of ranges, I cannot validate a proof. Concurrently, if time were to cease, Price Theory would also fail. Now, let us look at some figures in order to elaborate on the definition of Price Theory and Price Objectives.

    Although I root myself in the belief that if you are able to have a complete understanding of time, Price Structure becomes irrelevant, there remains a realistic recognition that the trader must be aware of. Simply, we cannot become perfect Time Structure market participants, which is a shame, and maybe someday with the help of computers, Time Structure will be perfectly quantified. However, we live in the real world, and in this last discussion on Time Structure, I must acquiesce back to the power of Klatch's Price Theory.

    At its core, the market will ALWAYS adhere to Price Theory. Therefore, to me, Price Theory remains as the penultimate understanding that the mind must have. For example, the concept of Range Expansion/Range Invalidation is so important that we must never forget the current Price Objectives based on the last market inflection point. By always keeping the Price Objectives as the focal point for our analysis, we can weed out as much noise as possible, and when we are in a conflict about whether or not to reverse based on Time Structure, we have Price Objectives and the trend to keep us grounded on the actuality of where the market is going. Remember, the inflection point invokes causality to determine for us where the next Price Objective target is, and we must minimize subjectivity as much as possible. Hence, we draw one final conclusion about Time Structure.

    Time is most powerful at terminal points (discreets). Obviously, when I called the March 2009 market low, we were at a terminal point, and it gave Time such an extreme weighting in that decision that it is not quantifiable. Likewise, the same can be true of many of the yearly highs/lows that have formed along the way. However, I have defined for the reader a simple heuristic of outlining discreets even in the short term, and when we are at new discreets (meaning we can think that we are in a new and in a continuously expanding positive/negative range), we can give Time much more of a weight in our trade decisions. However, when Price Theory is valid for a current range (again, the current range is based on your trading time frame), we must always acquiesce to Price Theory. To me, it is the most powerful market understanding that exists, which is why I feel it must be taught to all market participants.

Figure 6.1: Visual Representation of Klatch's Price Theory With Equal Price Objectives

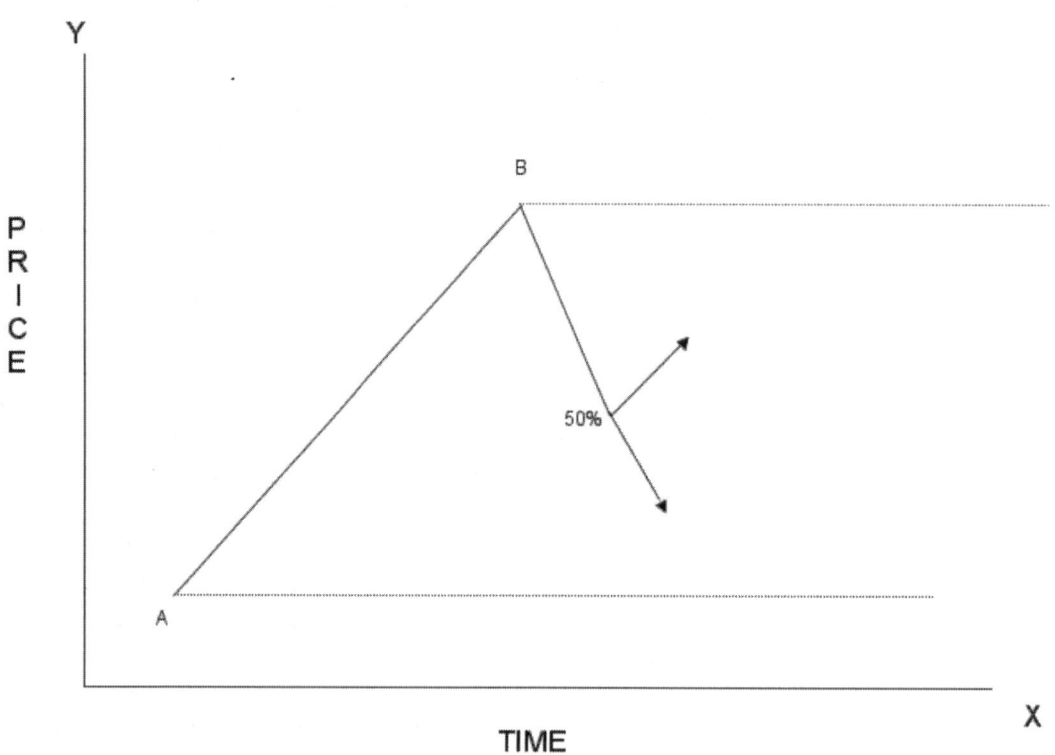

In Figure 6.1, we see that there is a range established with a low at point A to a high at point B. Further, we see that the middle of the range is highlighted by the value of 50%. At the 50% point, we can observe that the market would be at the midpoint of the range, which means that without any further knowledge a trade can be taken long or short at the point with equal probability. Now, Price Theory tells us that the Price Objective of the market is to challenge either the high or the low of the range, which can be seen as either a break of point A or a break of point B. This is the basis of Klatch's Price Theory because we see the range, and we see the two possible Price Objectives that exist.

Unfortunately, with the knowledge presented thus far, the reader must comprehend that Price Theory can be challenged many times as markets move into numerous, new but contracting ranges as time expands. Because of the possibility of infinite range expansions that yield infinite Price Theory Price Objectives, we need to understand that time becomes the counterbalancing deciding factor, and the reader now needs to understand that price and time exist in a symmetrical way in order for us to invoke Bayes' Theorem of Subjective Probability. By using Subjective Probability, we are using the belief of our intrinsic knowledge base to quantify our subconscious *hunch* that Time Structure indicates a probabilistic edge that filters out extraneous Price Objectives, and even more unfortunate, by using that time based process, we exist in a circuitous route of unquantifiability, which we will learn in the later chapters that deal with Time Structure. Therefore, because of the unquantifiability of *Time and Price Symmetry,* we must rely on the visual understanding and the conscious, visual picture that exists as the X-Y market, which shows valid ranges that may be broken. Further, we can then understand, quite literally, see that although the possibility for infinite Price Objectives exists, that outcome is very improbable, which allows us to use Klatch's Price Theory as the basis for all trading. In essence, we can see that even if the markets develop ranges inside of ranges, the ranges will break quickly. Therefore, the unquantifiability required for Price Theory like Bayes' Theory lies in the logic of the human mind that can be expressed as the "Qualitative Eye." What this means is that we have to keep a "qualitative eye" on understanding the process that yields a range contraction or a range expansion, and a **Qualitative Eye** is an important concept, which is now defined for us traders as a non-quantifiable assertion that requires one to use his or her logical, rational mentality, along with his or her intrinsically learned knowledge base of the market in understanding the true Price Objective of the market in the present moment.

What is also garnered from this qualitative eye-based approach is that when we are observing range expansions based on Price Objectives being fulfilled, we get an inclination of the market's underlying trend. Therefore, one's qualitative eye and one's concept of Klatch's Price Theory yield insight to understanding the trend, and unfortunately for readers of this book, trend analysis will focus on this type of esoteric (but practical) thinking. However, trend analysis will require conscious thought instead of subconscious recognition, which is why I indicated to Investors that they should also read about trend determination because it can be approached from an educated perspective instead of from an ethereal, inherent recognition. In order to clarify, an example of how Price Theory is challenged is a common chart pattern known as a contracting triangle formation, which in effect becomes ranges inside of ranges (See Chapter 10).

Another possibility that exists for us traders to deal with is when Price Theory get validated on the break to a new range, but simultaneously, after that break, the markets will fail to follow through in providing subsequent profits outside of the range. This will challenge traders and investors because we may have invalid signals as to what the underlying trend is. Thankfully, failures of the market to follow-through after a range has been breached will yield **price patterns** (or price structure components) that can also be quantified. A Price Pattern is a pattern based on the market's movements that conform to some type of range-based objective, and these price patterns will have corresponding price pattern objectives. The primary price patterns based on Klatch's Price Theory that will be focused on and redefined in this book are: retracements, double bottoms, double tops, swings. Further, there will be numerous discussions and recognitions to other trading patterns that are not a part of Price Theory. However, all of these topics can be defined under the same umbrella known as price structure. As such, we, as traders, can become confused by the underlying market action, and we will need to remember that our charts are constantly moving forward in time, which means that we can always find the relevant range if we are able to understand the range that the market is currently targeting to break. More important than anything, as I reach the conclusion of Time Structure towards the end of this book, I will pose a validation as to why indices have ever present, unending price objectives to reach new highs, and this is the irrefutable bull market scenario becomes the most powerful assertion in this book. Hence, this is the assertion that I foreshadowed in the *Introduction* of this book that holds the power to change conventional market psychology someday when the full effect of this conclusion is properly digested and properly understood by the masses.

Opponents to my Price Theory are undoubtedly going to claim that I am simply stating the economic laws of Supply and Demand that were proven by Debreu in achieving his Nobel Prize, but along with that acknowledgement, I must highlight the differences between what I am saying along with acknowledging when economic supply and when economic demand gain substantiation. As such, I agree that, when a market finds a high or a low, and then, the market challenges that high or low, at the point where the market defends the high or the low (the secondary inflection point inside of the range), the laws of supply and demand have kicked-in in order to bring demand in at that price level (for a low) or bring in excess supply at that level (for a high). However, the laws of supply and demand *fail* to tell us that after we have successfully established a low/high and then have that low/high retested, that the Price Objective is to now create a new high/low (the inverse of the retest point) outside of the base/original range. That is where Klatch's Price Theory comes in. Price Theory tells us conclusively that the market's Price Objective (in fact, *any* market's Price Objective) is now to yield to those two co-existing Price Objectives, which gives us two *quantified* possibilities as to where the market is going to go next because the market *must* expand its base range. **Hence, by that statement we disprove efficient market theory, and simultaneously prove that "The Market is not Random"** (again see: *Chapter 21* for the mathematical contradiction to the *Efficient Market Hypothesis*). Furthermore, if the reader were to jump ahead to Chapter 19, he or she can view the ultimate, priceless conclusion yielded from this extrapolation of Price Theory, and it is my belief that once recognized, this priceless Price Theory may lead to a Nobel laureate-type of recognition due to its conclusive power with respect to fundamental investors as well as traders, which has never before been attempted because when all is said an done, an investor is a trader that is focusing on yearly price bars.

Unfortunately, my mind is limited as to the "why" behind the logical conclusion of Price Theory except if I were to simply defer to the expectations theory of inflation, which is the highest correlated theory to Klatch's Price Theory that is commonly grouped under all inflationary theory, which again, I admit undoubtedly echoes Price Theory as well. However, that inflationary theory or all inflationary theories fail to explain why the market has these Price Objectives on a second-by-second basis, minute-by-minute basis, hour-by-hour basis, or month-by-month basis. No, inflationary theories only explains Klatch's Price Theory on a year-by-year basis, which has made inflationary theories valid for investors, but even inflationary theories are not conclusive on a year-by-year basis *at all times*. That being said, the reason as to "why" the market has this outstanding need to satisfy a Price Objective at every given present moment (unless the market is making a new all-time high or a new all-time low, which only occurs on a fractional-second basis *that already exists in the past*), remains a currently undefined answer in my mind, (at least) as to the "why." Thus, I come full circle in my human humility because I must rely on the intangible, like Bayes, and because of this intangibility, we find correlation with this book's *Introduction*. Hence, it is my belief that this future movement (this outstanding Price Objective that must be fulfilled) is predestined, and we must yield our humanity to divine intervention as an explanation. As such, it is my eternal hope (also as stated in the *Introduction*) that the university audience for this book is able to refocus their mental energies in helping to define the "why" behind the reason as to "why" Price Objectives *must* be fulfilled once a high/low is successfully defended by the market participants. However, the corollary to that last statement is that my Price Theory expands upon all inflationary theories by saying that this Price Objective *holds* for *every* time frame that is traded.

Trade Theory

In essence, we have already established all of the logic that exists in trading! I will define this logic as **trade theory.** Now, it is my belief that trade theory is simply the unending purpose of a market to create new ranges and break old ranges, which yield observations that can be interpreted for use in understanding what range will break next. More relevant, these observations can be turned into profits by correctly predicting the range break. Hence, therein lies the purpose of trading: to determine if the range will be broken to the upside or to the downside. Therefore, our job as traders, investors, and money managers is correlated because we should all have the same objectives based on Price Theory. The job of the market participant is simply to determine which way the market is going to break out of a given range, and if we are correct about that prediction, we profit. If not, we lose. We can further define trade exit and trade entry criteria simply by the knowledge of a range, which is our first expansion of trade theory, which avails to us the mentality shift of thinking in terms of reward to risk ratio.

Figure 6.2: KPT With Favorable Risk/Reward

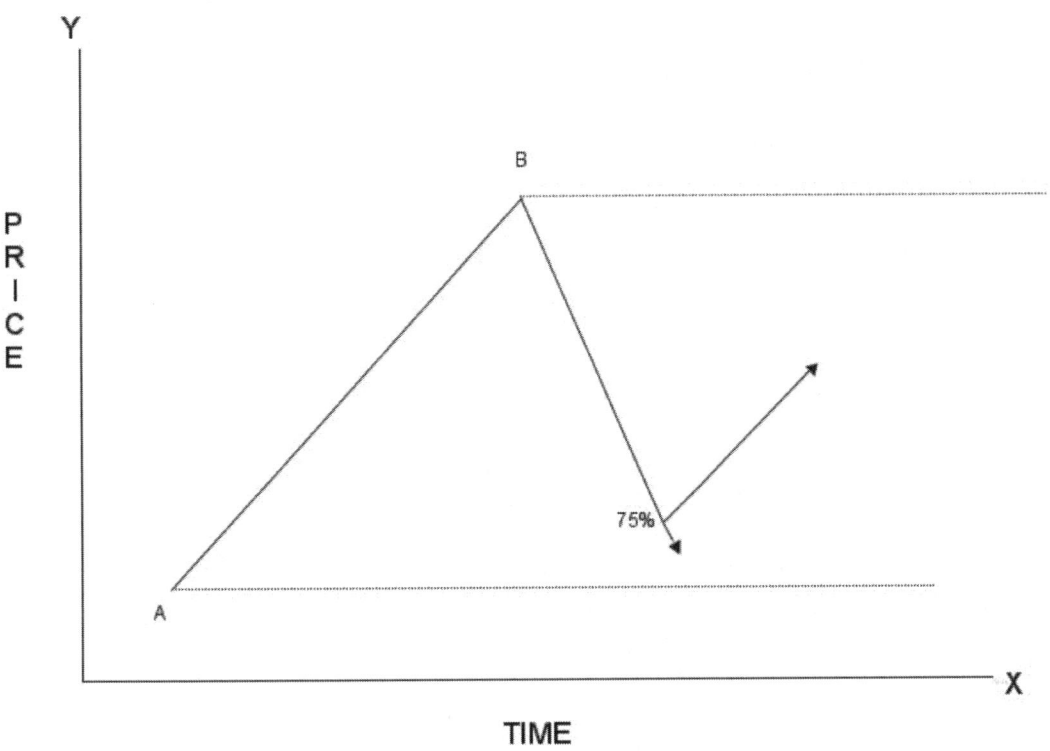

In Figure 6.2, we have now slightly changed the last figure, which stopped at the midpoint of our range, which was labeled 50%. However, now, we see that the market has continued lower, and it has now moved 75% of the way back through the range. However, the same two Price Objectives still exist based on Price Theory, but the difference is that each Price Objective now has different criteria for reward and for risk. Using the example, we can see that if a trader decides to go long the market at the 75% range, which is indicated by the up arrow, the trader will achieve a greater amount of profit should Price Theory's Price Objective be fulfilled by a breakage of point B (new highs). However, if the trader decides to sell short at that 75% value, we can see that the profit potential achieved once point A is breached (new lows) is much less profit. Therefore, we see that going long gives us three times more profit potential then going short, and now, the trick is understanding which way the market will break. Therefore, I have now completed the entry thought-tree, and now, we need to discuss the criteria for exiting trades at losses in order to quantify risk.

As discussed in regards to risk management, we will have two bases for exiting a position with a loss. First, either we can adhere to some arbitrary risk management rule that we have pre-established for our trading plan, or we can utilize the knowledge of the range in order to define where to place a stop loss order based on the range itself. Concurrently, the knowledge of Price Objectives based on Price Theory will be our quantitative criteria for defining the success of a trade/the profit potential of a trade, which can be determined in advance by limit orders. Not only has this short introduction in price structure and Trade Theory already told us all that we need to know in regards to how we can now think about trading with respect to trade initiation, but we have also learned how to determine and place applicable profit/loss orders based on a given range. This simplistic understanding is critical. Further, it should not be taken lightly because this is the ongoing process of price discovery that the market embarks upon with respect to continuous changes in supply and demand for any given market-based trading instrument! Moreover, because of the inspection of a range coupled with the forecasted break of that range, we are given a quick heuristic to establish risk/reward by the visual analysis of our range that yields our trade, and unarguably, the decision to take the trade and determine the range break that will lead to profit will come from and be defined by Klatch's Price Theory.

Going back to Figure 6.2, we can now elaborate on the exit criteria that exists for each trade inceptions. If we were to go long at the point labeled 75%, we stated that our personal belief is that the Price Objective at Point B will be fulfilled instead of the Price Objective at Point A. Therefore, we see that the market itself tells us our risk and our reward. For going long at the 75% point, our reward is new highs over point B. However, our risk is that we are wrong, which means that Point A will be breached. Thus, we see the correlation between two Price Objectives. One is always our risk and the other is always our reward; again, assuming we are not using any other components of *Time and Price Symmetry*.

Since this correlation must always exist because a given range will always have a high or low (unless we are moving in a straight line higher or lower), we see that Price Objectives serve as our heuristic for risk, reward criteria. Using the long example, we see that our reward is that the market will give us three fourths of the range as profit if not more should the market decide to move higher. However, our risk is only one fourth of the range because if the range is broken to the downside we will be taking the loss on that 25% range, which makes easy enough sense to any astute observer. Hence, just using Price Objectives we can see that our reward is three times our risk. What is also transparent is that our risk is now quantified, but our reward is potentially limitless, which is the power of understanding the trend and the markets. Thus, we see the validity in my definition of Trade Theory because we see that we can trade calmly by knowing our predefined stop while availing every trade for limitless profit!

Because of the Price Objectives that the market always has because of Price Theory, it is my belief that the market cannot be efficient. Over time, the market must eventually breach a relevant range on the upside or on the downside. Due to the necessity for the market to breach a relevant range, the knowledge in this book will allow the trader to combine trading edges in price and in time that will help us decide the probability of an upside or downside break of the relevant range. Therefore, due to the inherent certainty that prices must eventually be higher or lower than they are now based on Price Theory, we can conclude that the market is not efficient because the efficient price resides in the future with a degree of profit potential between the present moment and the expected upside or downside break. Deterministically, this tells us that the efficient price of the market does not exist in the present moment, but the efficient price exists in the future, which also disproves the *Efficient Market Hypothesis*.

As we move forward through all of price structure, the unfortunate thing is that many of the definitions for defining price structure rely on the knowledge that is interwoven through all parts of this book. Therefore, we must introduce concepts early on in some places in order to properly define parts of price structure. In fact, I have used nomenclature in the introductory chapters of this book that is only defined in these two sections. Therefore, I encourage the reader to re-read the chapters dealing with price structure and time structure once all appropriate concepts are taught because not only does this book serve as testimony for the genesis of how the populous needs to understand market action, but this book needs to consistently define concepts, formulae, nomenclature, notation, and terminology that have been previously undefined for the trading community! Hence, it is truly my palpable belief that this book will spawn an entire new field of academic study once the value of the knowledge is confirmed by the masses.

Highs and Lows

So far, we have defined a Price Theory with corresponding Price Objectives, and our minds are now shifting so that we are now thinking in terms of highs and lows of a given range. But, what exactly is a high and a low? More important, how do we know what high and low to use for establishing a range?

On a chart, we see many highs and many lows, and we will group these into <u>discreet</u> highs/lows or <u>secondary</u> highs/lows. Unfortunately, as we will learn, we will still have many discreets and/or secondary highs/lows on a given chart. Secondary highs/lows are where we will have a quantified retracement or a corrective projection that occurs between two discreets. Before I define what a discreet high/low is, I must first discuss the concept of **conjoined-discreets**. For example, every discreet low/high will be connected to a new discreet high/low, which occurs as we more forward in time. As we will learn, this is where a primary retracement will come from. For those of us mathematically inclined, I will define **Range Notation** as "D/S: $(T_1, L_1/H_1)$ → $(T_2, H_2/L_2)$". As one can see by the definition, the X-Axis is represented by Time whereas the Y-Axis is represented by prices. Now, for a real-world example, we can look to the discreet low in the S&P Futures on March 9, 2009 can be linked to the discreet high on April 27, 2011 by the following Range Notation: D: (030909, 666.75) → (042711, 1347.00). In all of our Range Notations, we need to define that $T_2 > T_1$ and D/S define discreet/secondary ranges. Therefore, every discreet high/low must be linked to another discreet's low/high, which will be our conjoined-discreet pair that defines our range. Also, once we have properly defined what exact ranges and discreets are, I will use a shorthand of range notation that simply links two points together moving forward in time as simply A → B, and using our prior example, the shorthand would simply be 666.75 → 1347.00, which we see as a **positive range** since it would be linked by a diagonal line resembling a backslash. (Also, in Figure 6.1 and 6.2, we saw that we were dealing with a positive rang.) Conversely, if we were linking a high to a low, we would have a **negative range**, linked by a diagonal line resembling a forward slash. For mathematicians, a positive range has a positive slope, and a negative range has a negative slope; this is in respect to the diagonal line that connects the two anchor points of the two conjoined-discreets. Now, we can define exactly how to find these discreets along with the disparate discussion necessary in order to define secondary highs/lows.

As we visualize a chart, we will see the market moving forward in time with prints of price being recorded because of buyers and sellers matching orders. Like everything, the time period we are looking at will have a different set of criteria for the discreet discovery process. This time value-based criteria cannot be quantified easily (as I learned through hundreds of hours of computer programming analysis), and instead, it is much easier for the human eye to see and understand the relevant points on a given chart. Therefore, there is some realm of logic that must be applied to this discussion of finding and defining highs and lows. In a way, it is easy to see discreets from a visual perspective as just recognizing them as the absolute low/high to the absolute high/low on a chart over a given time interval. Our own intelligent design is more useful in properly observing the discreet highs/lows that exist in the historic database of a chart. However, in order to understand this concept with some degree of formality, let us use 180 **bars** (a bar is the open/high/low/close of a market defined in a period of time such as 1-minute bars, 60-minute bars, etc.) as the starting point for our discreet discovery. The simplest explanatory definition of a **discreet** is the highest high and lowest low that completes a given range over a period of time with the market not penetrating either the high or the low. In order to define this "look back" criteria for defining a high/low as a true discreet or a secondary, we will rely on the formal definition of looking back 180 bars. If the high/low has not been breached, then, our current high/low becomes discreet. However, it is important to note that we may have multiple discreets. For example, the March 9, 2009 low is a discreet low just like the September 2011 low is a discreet low with regards to the stock market indices.

Now, that I have probably inundated the reader's mind with many innovative definitions, I will yield to a figurative example that may look simplistic, but when Price Objectives get to be formed simultaneously, we will find that the Quantitative Synchronicity concept will eradicate that simplicity. Let us look at Figure 6.3.

Figure 6.3: Range and Discreet Discovery

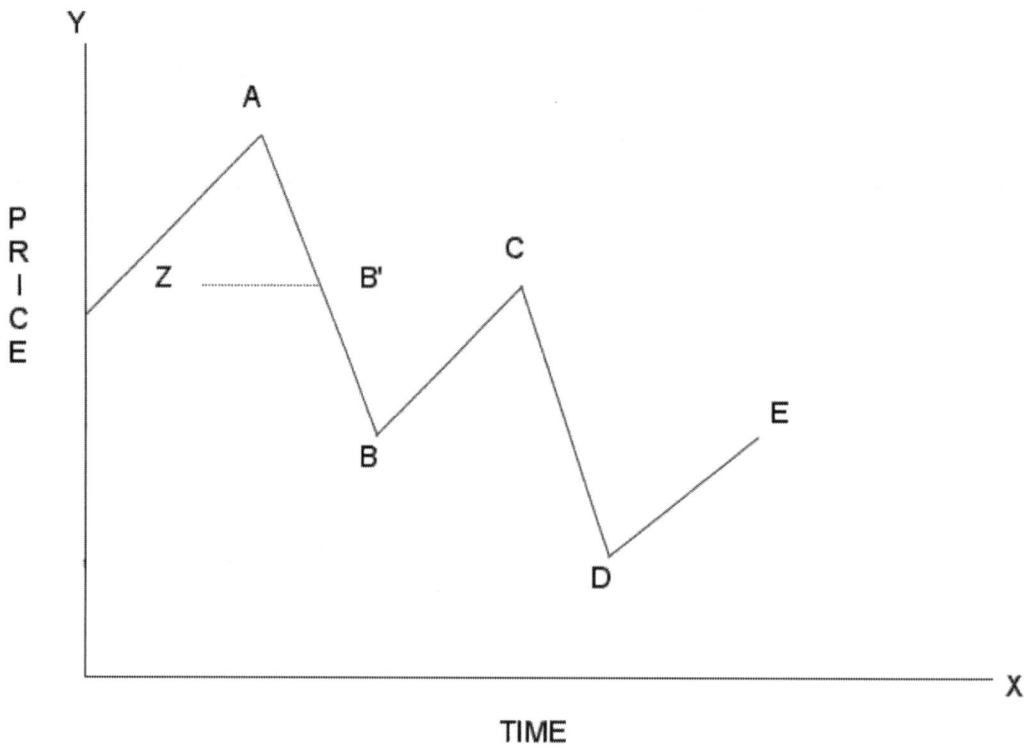

Moving from left to right on our chart in Figure 6.3, which means we are moving forward in time, we begin at point A. Point A is the highest point on the chart, and it becomes a discreet high. It also starts our range. From A, the market comes down to point B, which is the lowest low at that time. This establishes our new range, and it is a discreet, negative range. In fact, all points along the A → B range are discreet ranges as represented by B'. We can visualize that as the market reaches point B, our range is simply expanding, and in fact, we have an infinite number of points along the A → B range, which we can call points Z that are also definable ranges until we establish point B as our discreet terminal point. In other words, if we visualize that our A → B range is truncated at point Z, this would still be a discreet range that gets invalidated with every print of price that is lower than point Z. However, in this example, we do create a terminal point B, which finalizes our negative range and is defined as D: $(T_A, P_A) \rightarrow (T_B, P_B)$.

Next, from our discreet B, the market retraces to a point C. Since we are moving forward in time, point C becomes another discreet in the newly formed positive range B → C. However, C is a secondary high in respect to point A because point C is not higher than point A. Therefore, C yields a discreet range in positive ranges, but since it is not higher than point A, it yields secondary ranges if those ranges are negative. (If C was higher than point A, then point A would become irrelevant and point C would be the new discreet high. In addition, if we go back to the 180-bar example for discreet discovery, we could say that point C WOULD BE a discreet high <u>if point C occurred 180-bars further out in time then a point along the A → B range that corresponds to the same price value as C.</u>) However, for this example, let us assume that point C occurs less than 180-bars away from that point along the A → B range, and point C is simply a secondary high. Based on Price Theory, we visualize that point C failed to take out a new high above point A, so we can see the market takes out point B and forms point D. At point D, we now have four ranges. Let us use range notation in order to link all of these points: D: (T_A, P_A) → (T_B, P_B), D: (T_A, P_A) → (T_D, P_D), D: (T_B, P_B) → (T_C, P_C), and S: (T_C, P_C) → (T_D, P_D). Now, you may be wondering what happens to our A → B range since point B has been exceeded. This brings up the concept that I will define as **discreet replacement.** As we saw with point C, it was not higher than point A so it becomes secondary once a new low was formed with respect to negative ranges. On the other hand, point D exceeded point B. In fact, D can be any value less than or equal to point B, and it would replace the B discreet. Once B loses its classification as a discreet, it then is replaced by a new discreet such as point D. Therefore, any range that used point B can be deleted from the list of ranges because point B has been replaced with a new, lower discreet. Therefore, from our list of four ranges above, we can delete two of those ranges, and these ranges then become irrelevant except for historical analysis or price projections, as we will discuss in later chapters.

Once arriving at point D, we are left with the two ranges: D: (T_A, P_A) → (T_D, P_D) and S: (T_C, P_C) → (T_D, P_D). However, once we start to retrace (moving in the opposite direction) either of these two ranges by forming point E on our Figure 1 chart, we will be given a positive range of D: (T_D, P_D) → (T_E, P_E). Therefore, if we ignore point B after it is exceeded by point D, and if we assume point E is the closing point for our chart, we are left with the two negative ranges and the one positive range. (In range notation, it is not necessary to define a positive or negative range because when we use numbers for points A-E we will be able to visualize quickly a positive range or a negative range based on which of the two numbers is greater in either normal or shorthand notation.)

Price Theory Visualization

Now that we have graphically illustrated a way to represent highs and lows along with a simple way to classify them, I want to elaborate more on Klatch's Price theory and Price Objectives by Figure 6.4.

Figure 6.4: Price Theory and Price Objectives

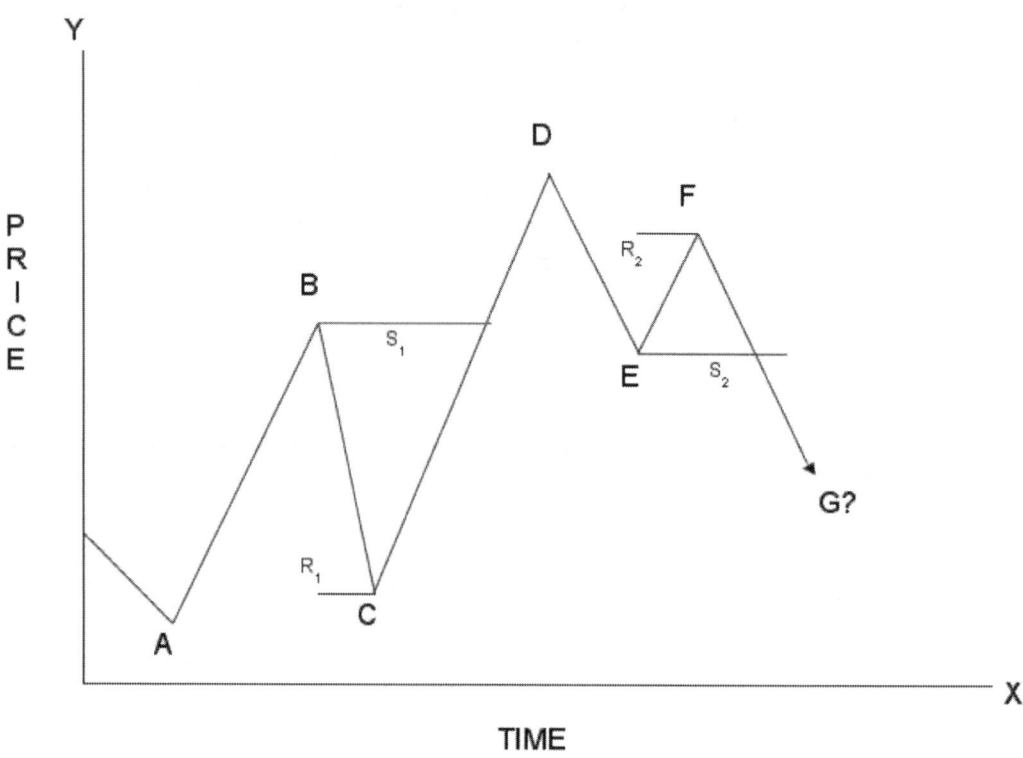

As always, we will start from left to right, which again, is forward in time. We find, D: (T_A, P_A) → (T_B, P_B), then, D: (T_B, P_B) → (T_C, P_C). Once point B is exceeded, we defer to the rules of discreet replacement, and we are left with two positive ranges D: (T_A, P_A) → (T_D, P_D) and S: (T_C, P_C) → (T_D, P_D). Let us now look what happens to this market as we move from point A to D with respect to Price Theory and its corresponding Price Objectives.

I ask the reader to imagine that this chart is an actively moving market. This market instrument representation comes down to form our discreet low at point A. The market rallies higher to point B, and then, retraces to point C defined as a percentage of the A → B range as R_1. At point C, we observe that C > A so we have failed to take out a new low of the A → B range, and also, we observe that C is now a secondary low with respect to A (assuming it is less than 180 bars with respect to time). Therefore, the market failed to take out a new low, and it must take out a new high based on Klatch's Price Theory. This occurs at point D, and point D invalidates point B so all relevant ranges that use point B become irrelevant (except for price projections). In fact (and as we will discuss in depth in later chapters), point B is actually defined as a **Swing Point.** We can define point B also as S_1 in order to indicate this swing point, and this too is shown on Figure 6.4. Once B is exceeded, we can see that we are left with the two ranges that are linked to the terminal discreet D. Therefore, we can introduce the union symbol for our discreets as "U," and we can say that any union pair of two discreet ranges where the second discreet is equal in both ranges will be defined as **paired ranges**. Therefore, D: (T_A, P_A) → (T_D, P_D) U S: (T_C, P_C) → (T_D, P_D) is our paired range, and this concept will be further elaborated on in Chapter 8. For now, let us visualize what happens as the market moves from point D to point G.

To begin, we define all of the ranges illustrated in the chart as we move to point G, and I will now use the union symbol in the appropriate place in order to yield more to a mathematical nature of range notation. These ranges are: D: (T_D, P_D) → (T_E, P_E), D: (T_E, P_E) → (T_F, P_F), D: (T_D, P_E) → (T_G, P_G) U S: (T_F, P_F) → (T_G, P_G). Putting the market's movement into words, we can say that first we create our range D to E, which as a negative range. Then, the market has a retracement of this range (R_2) to the point F. However, F<D (since we are now dealing with negative ranges we use less than instead of greater than), and based on Price Theory and Price Objectives our objective is to take out a new low under point E. In essence, we say that the market has to test point E in order to probe price as part of the price discovery process. This is an extraordinarily important quotation in order for the reader to understand. There is a need, which I again acquiesce to supply and demand theory that must be fulfilled by the market or even the market participants. Hence, it is this belief that is necessary to understand because this is where the conventional logic of supply and demand falls apart. Coincidentally, the market's ability to probe supply (at lows) and demand (at highs) is a necessary part of the market, and in fact, the closer the market comes to probing a given high/low the stronger the conviction will be in the validity of that high/low. The importance of this is extremely relevant because when Klatch's Price Theory gets fulfilled at a later time after the relevant high/low is successfully probed and challenged, we will have executed a swing based on a given swing point. Therefore, it is very important for the reader to learn at this stage that point E is that Swing Point, S_2, which again is important in later chapters. As point E is penetrated, which activates our swing point, we get a new point, G, which leaves us with the following two negative ranges because of discreet replacement: D: (T_E, P_E) → (T_G, P_G) U S: (T_F, P_F) → (T_G, P_G). However, since A is still the lowest discreet on the chart, we still have the positive range of D: (T_A, P_A) → (T_D, P_D), and since point G does not appear lower than point C, the secondary range of S: (T_C, P_C) → (T_D, P_D) is also valid. Moreover, these two positive ranges are unionized so we can see that A → D U C → D, and in fact, we are left with two paired ranges at the current, visual representation of point G.

Understanding Future Objectives based on Price Theory

The last analytical observation that we can derive from Figure 6.4 is to outline the future possibilities of our market, which are not shown in Figure 6.4. This is how we must start living in the present moment while at the same time, availing ourselves to all possibilities. What is more, I will outline how we must shift our thinking by using Price Theory in order to profit from this theoretical concept shift. I must be clear, that these are not forecasts, but they are simply possibilities that are presented due to the proper application of Price Theory. We, as traders, must always be aware of *all* possible market opportunities, and we must not fall in love with one possibility more than the other, which makes present moment thinking important. Summarily, by making ourselves aware of all possible outcomes without having any underlying market bias, we can live in the present moment as to what can happen with the future of any market. We must be aware of future possibilities, but we must learn to control our bias as to which possibility will be the outcome.

Mentally, this is quite exhausting because our objective, as money managers, is to be involved in the market, and our objective is to be in the market to make money and not lose it. This means that we will have a position open on the long side or on the short side, at any given time we choose. Therefore, our ego will surface in order to cause us to think of how wonderful it will be for our trade analysis to be accurate; our ego will cause us to fall in love with our position. This type of thought processes will cause hesitation on the part of the trader's mind, and this hesitation causes us to not be aware of the present moment/the present scenario we are faced with. We become biased, which means that we have to learn to disassociate ourselves with our hopes and dreams of any one trade, and instead, we must allow our mind to forget about the underlying position's current price objective so that we can reverse to a new price objective if the conditions are warranted. Obviously, this reversal of price objectives would correspond to a reversal of our position, and reversal trading is the hardest skill to grasp. Many people cannot take their entire analysis, which lead them to put a position on in the market in the first place, and then, simply shift their mind the opposite way. Granted, fundamentally oriented market participants have a much harder time with this concept because, often their position decisions are done by committee and not by just one portfolio manager. This, by definition of time, is also counterproductive to the proper market-oriented thinking that is needed for success, but I rely on this fundamental comparison in order to note how hard it can be in certain situations for a trader to just click the reverse button. For example, let us say an analyst spends 3 months researching a stock, and then, that analysis presents this research to the portfolio manager. The manger puts the trade on because he agrees with the analysts work, but the manager is properly trained in *Time and Price Symmetry*. As such, the manager holds the position for 2 or 3 days, and then, decides to click the reversal button, which makes the analyst's work meaningless. Therefore, the open-mindedness of the manager to the true market structure can be more powerful than hundreds of hours of external work. The manager did not fall in love with the analyst's recommendation, but undoubtedly, the analyst was still be in love with his or her position regardless of what the market is doing in the present moment.

What is more challenging is what happens as *Time and Price Symmetry* traders evolve to the ability of maneuvering the market on an hourly basis. When that occurs, the present moment thinking becomes crucial because the trader may be clicking the reversal button 1-4 times per hour in order to capitalize on every market's movement. Furthermore, this is not an impossibility with *Time and Price Symmetry*. As a trader's intrinsically learned knowledge base grows, he or she will find that every market move is tradable and quantifiable, but at the same time, this trading leads to a mental tax that can cause a trader to incorrectly reverse one, two, three, or four times because of being mentally tricked by the market. It can be counterproductive, and as stated in the introductory chapters, sometimes, the trader just needs to let go of the market, and give in to the underlying trend, which is the more powerful focus of any type of non-present moment trading. Understanding how and when to correctly reverse will always be a battle of the subconscious analysis in determining which range will be broken, but it will be a conscious process to limit ourselves from becoming literally, flippant in regards to our trading.

Going back to understanding the future possibilities of Figure 6.4, we see that point G has an arrow drawn on it in order to indicate further price movement. I will now list the possibilities that can happen in our market by this further price movement. As we interpret the point G of Figure 6.4, we can guess that the market will have further downward momentum based on our activated negative swing/negative ranges along with inferring this from the arrow representation on the chart. So, the question becomes, will G exceed point A to the downside? If yes, then we could delete our remaining positive ranges A $\rightarrow$ D U C $\rightarrow$ D from our list because they become invalidated since these ranges were unionized by Point A, and point A has now been replaced by a lower low, which means there are no more positive ranges on the chart. Therefore, if G < A, A becomes replaced, which means all A ranges are invalidated, and we are left with D: (T_D, P_D) $\rightarrow$ (T_G, P_G) U S: (T_F, P_F) $\rightarrow$ (T_G, P_G). If this scenario occurs, we are left with assuming further declines in price until G has bottomed out and reached a terminal point, which will render subsequent secondary, negative ranges and subsequent discreet, positive ranges. However, Figure 6.4 does not give us enough information to discern what those new ranges may be if G < A.

Secondarily, we can look to see what happens if G > A. If this happens, we can garner some new information. If G > A we can look at our chart and say once again that our market has failed to take out a new low (below A), and it must take out a new high over D, which is of course derived from Price theory. Therefore, price objectives would become validated at point D, and point D would actually become a new swing point if G > A, which is not represented on the chart. Furthermore, we can conclude two separate observations if G > A, again concerning point C. The remaining questions are: is G > C or is A < G < C. If G < C and G > A then all ranges with point C become invalid since C is now meaningless. However, if G > C, then our A and C ranges remain valid, and we have in effect just widened our trading range, which widens our price objectives based on Price Theory, and it should be noted, point D is now an **additive swing point** that will be discussed and defined in subsequent chapters.

Price Theory and Quantitative Synchronicity

The last subject of immense importance linked to Price Theory goes back to our original discussion on ranges, which allow us to implement basic Trade Theory, and this leads us to our first understanding of trading edges. For now, I simply ask the reader to understand that an edge is something that gives us a higher probability of success (i.e. skews the odds in our favor), but we will discuss a more proper definition of trading edges at a later point.

Now, in order to understand the power of Quantitative Synchronicity (and also the difficulty of the mind's proper comprehension of it), we must look at two charts in order to explain how we can use Price Theory and Quantitative Synchronicity in a harmonious relationship. In order to do so in this section, I am renaming figures 6.1 and 6.2, and I am also changing the order that they appeared earlier along with what they represent, but nevertheless, they are the same chart diagrams. Hence, these diagrams are renamed as Figures 6.5 and 6.6.

Figure 6.5: XYZ Stock on a Daily Basis

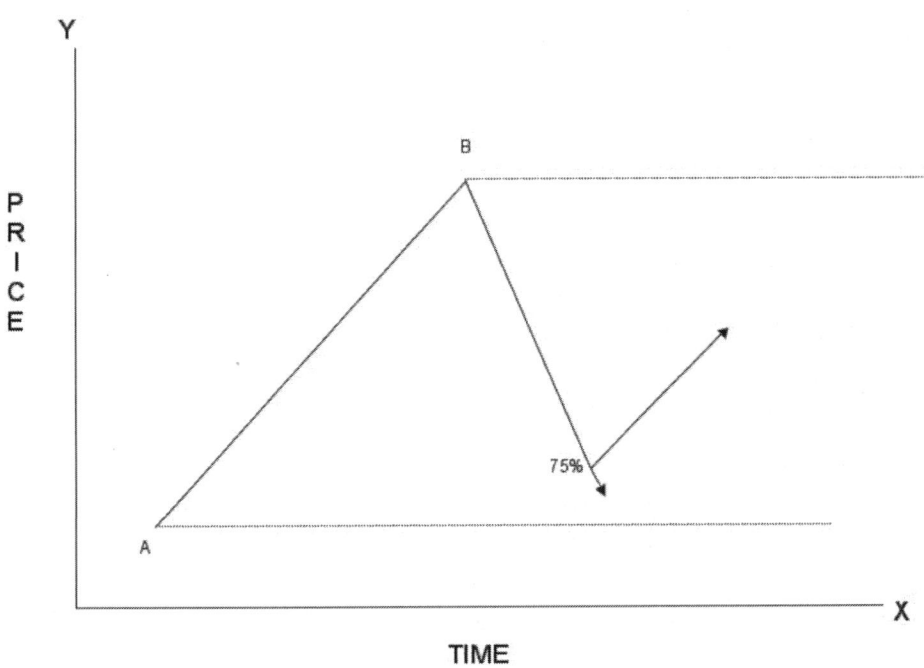

Figure 6.6: XYZ Stock on an intra-day Basis

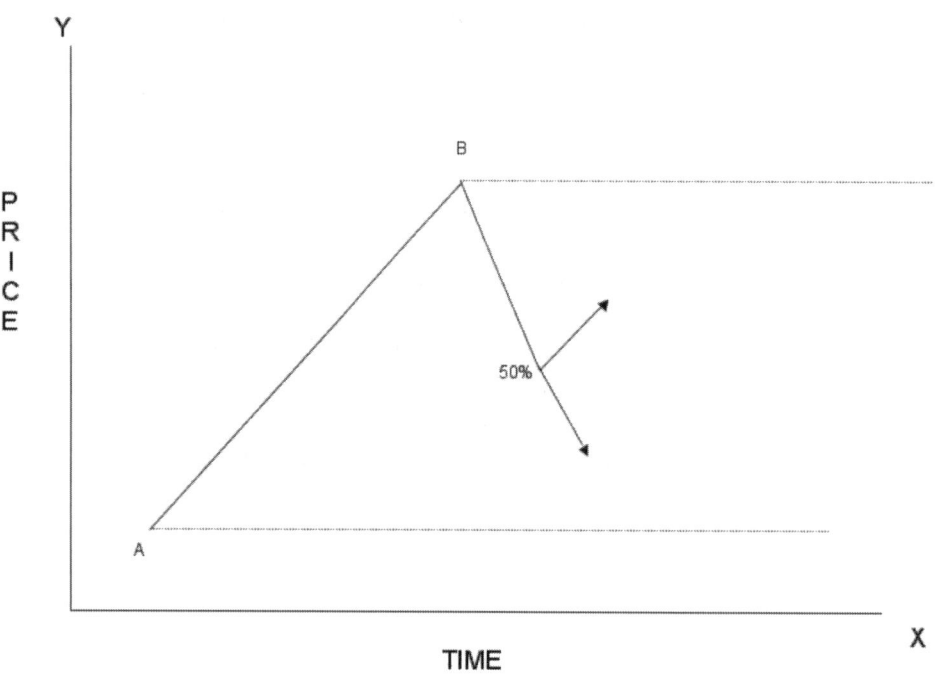

    The first thing that I ask the reader to do with these two Figures is imagine in the reader's head that these two images are stacked on top of each other in a way that they are both visible. For example, imagine drawing a cube on a piece of paper by using two squares that are offset to some degree, and then connecting the supposed visible lines to each other in order to form the visualization. Once done, we see that we have a three-dimensional representation from two two-dimensional X-Y graphs. Hence, this example starts to portray the depth that makes the third dimension of the Marketome referred throughout this entire text as the elusive concept of Quantitative Synchronicity.

    Moving on, what we also can see in these similar charts is that they now represent two different time periods of the same market instrument, which causes us to invoke the concept of Quantitative Synchronicity instead of just the depth-like illustration. What the concept of Quantitative Synchronicity tells us is that we have to be aware of *both* Price Objectives that exist in *both* time frames, and what is not as obvious is that we also have to be aware of the reward to risk criteria that exists in *both* time frames. Hence, we see the multiplier effect of required knowledge for the third-Marketome-dimension. For example, Figure 6.5 can be thought of as a yearly chart for the stock that I have named "XYZ." Because this is a yearly chart, we see that we are sitting within 25% of a new yearly low. However, as a trader, we must understand that our job is to define our belief on whether we are going to fulfill the Price Objective to the downside or the upside on this chart, and once we have conviction in that belief, we can use Quantitative Synchronicity in order to discuss a possible trade implementation utilizing the shorter term Figure 6.6 chart. Therefore, on the Figure 6.5 chart we can make a logical thought such as, "I believe the trend is up for all markets, and that this is simply a deep retracement of the yearly low. Therefore, I believe the Price Objective will be to reach new highs above point B at some future point longer out in time."

    Okay, with that line of thinking, we can see that there exists favorable reward to risk if we were to approach our trade implementation on the longer term chart, but how do we handle this if we are a daytrader? Well, let us discuss the edge that we ascertain by zooming into this micro time frame (the intraday chart in Figure 6.6) in order to understand our first example of Quantitative Synchronicity that helps us understand basic Trade Theory.

As we defined in the earlier chapters, there are many different ways that a person can trade, and furthermore, I stated that often these methodologies bleed into one another. For example, a person can trade intraday, multi-day, or even longer periods, but a multi-day trader can decide to hold the trade as a longer term investment. Therefore, we see that we are redefining the standard "bottom-up approach" that is often discussed by the talking heads on television. However, because we know how moronic those people are, we must understand how we are using time as a criteria to help us change our thoughts of this approach. Thus, we do this by using Quantitative Synchronicity by combining multiple Price Objectives and multiple time frames *in our heads* in order to determine the trade inception. Thus, by using the longer-term chart, Figure 6.5, we are making a bold decision that says the low at Point A in *that* chart will hold, which means Price Theory tells us to expect new highs over Point B. However, this is fine and good if we are investors, but now you may wish to understand the question, "How does this help us as a daytrader?" Well, we must discuss the intraday chart shown in Figure 6.6, which is also for "XYZ" stock, and this discussion will give us to new trade constructs that also *bleed* into each other.

Figure 6.6: XYZ Stock on an intra-day Basis

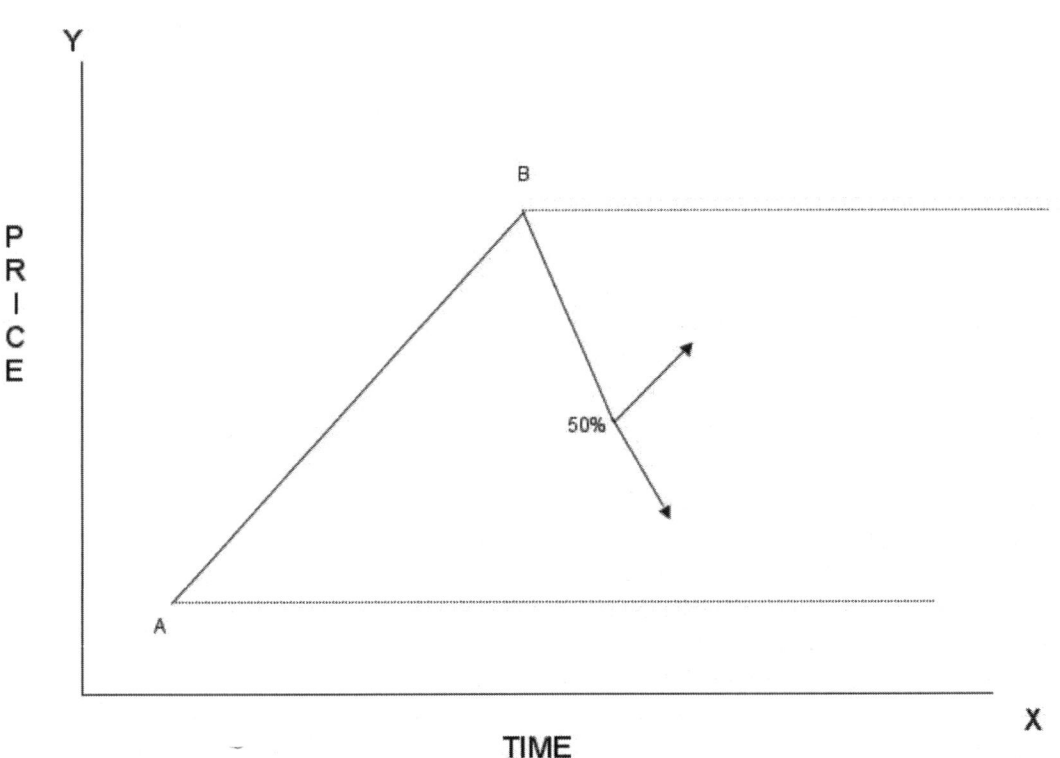

Okay, so we see in Figure 6.6 that we are sitting at the mid-point of a range during a normal intraday daytrading session, and this midpoint level tells us (at least at this point in the book) that we do not have any type of reward to risk criteria that is favorable. No, we have even reward to risk criteria, and I must also state that for the reward to risk criteria of a trading instrument to be even, we have to assume transaction costs are zero, which was not discussed earlier. That said, we could now invoke the concept of Quantitative Synchronicity, which means that we have two insights, as I foreshadowed. First, if we are wrong on our intraday trade, which means we went long based on the longer term Price Objective but on the intraday chart we took out point A, well, we can hold the position overnight until the larger stop-loss would be invoked instead of taking the stop loss intraday, or second, we can make a judgment call that says, "Based on my belief that XYZ stock is not going to take out its longer term low, I believe it is ready to inflect and move higher." Hence, we are using the longer term chart to transition an edge into our shorter term time window's trade criteria. Basically, we are simply saying that, "I believe the Price Objective will be reached to the upside on the intraday chart because the Price Objective is to take out the high on the daily chart, but should this not happen, I will still hold this position because I believe the Price Objective will be reached to the upside on the longer term chart." Therein, we find an edge using the concept of Quantitative Synchronicity, but we must further discuss the fact that we may need to hold the position overnight, which changes our basic trading methodology.

If we are wrong intraday because the market is moving down on that day, and we reach our stop-loss point for the intraday trade, we have two decisions that must have been decided *before* reaching this level. First, do we exit the trade at the stop loss point based on simple Trade Theory that has already been defined in this chapter, or second, do we hold onto this trade, which means we have to now set the stop loss to the low below Point A in Figure 6.5. If we decided on the latter scenario, we must now understand that we may have taken a position trade instead of a daytrade because we do not know how long it will take for either of the Price Objectives to be reached. As such, we must understand that if we acquiesced to holding this trade, we must not take profits on the trade until w have favorable reward to risk, which does not mean a Price Objective has to be fulfilled at all. No, it simply means that when the held position reaches the 50% retracement level (or less) of Figure 6.6, we now have an even reward to risk ratio based on our expanded holding. That *must* be our new profit target if we transition from daytrading to position trading. What's more, we see that if we decide to hold this trade until the Price Objective is reached above Point B, we see that our original reward to risk of 1:1 (on the intraday chart), has now increased to 3:1 by acquiescing to the longer term chart, which means that we have invoked Quantitative Synchronicity in order to find our *cumulative* trading edge. To conclude this complicated circuitous discussion, I must show this last outcome as Figure 6.7.

Figure 6.7: XYZ Stock Reward/Risk Criteria

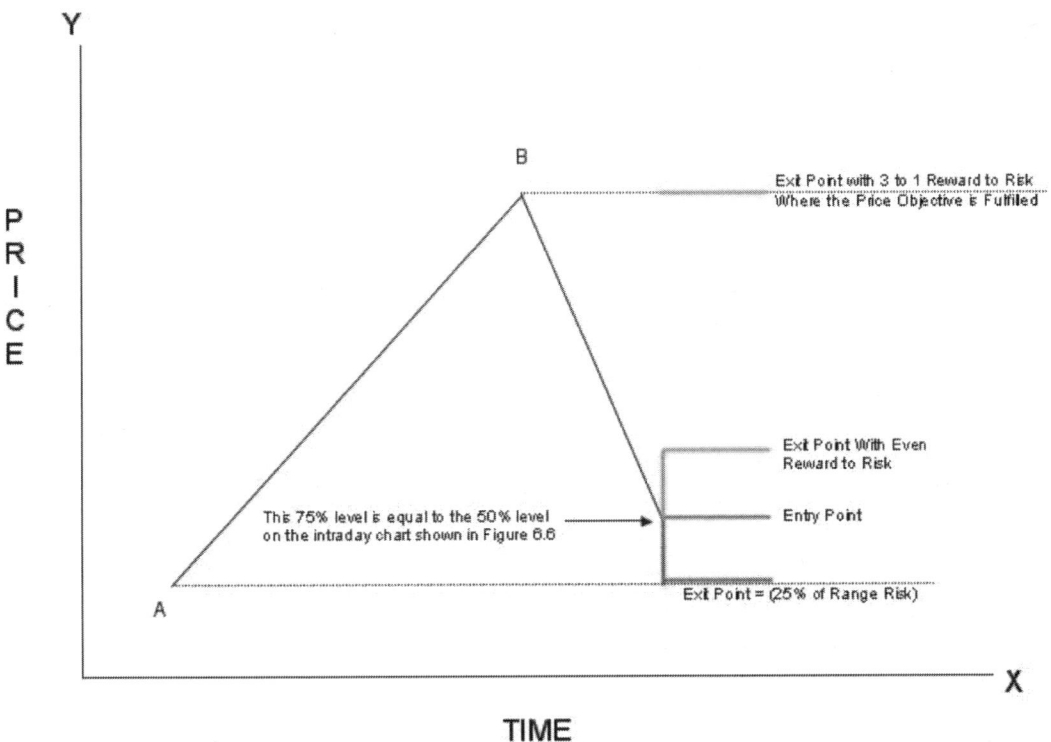

In Figure 6.7, we see what happens when we take the daytrade and make it a position trade. We see the entry point defined by the horizontal blue line, and we see our three exit points now defined as two profitable exits(our reward) and our one loss exit (our risk). Hence, we must understand that in order to maintain proper trading protocol, we must always adhere to reward to risk ratios that our favorable to us. Therefore, we can see that our risk remains fixed in this example shown as the horizontal red line that is activated upon the fulfillment of the downward Price Objective based on Price Theory, and we have our two exit points defined by (a) our reward to risk criteria and (b) the Price Objective based on Price Theory that tells us the range must be expanded, and in this case, that expansion would be to the upside. Consequently, we see the power of Quantitative Synchronicity by allowing us to take an intraday loss to a multi-day profit simply by understanding the cumulative Price Objectives that must be synchronized within our minds, and we can now move on.

In summary, this first chapter in price structure indicates that we are learning how markets have objectives of forming new highs and new lows outside of their respective ranges based on Klatch's Price Theory. We have also learned a way to write these highs and lows as discreets and secondary high/lows along with when to replace these discreets when they are penetrated (a.k.a a swing gets activated). However, I ask the reader to remain diligent in study on the logic of ranges. All subsequent chapters will build off this process, and even at the conclusion of this first chapter of the book, a person can formulate a trading strategy simply off Price Theory, which is why Price Theory is the basis of all market action. Lastly in this chapter, I had to allude to the mentality that is going to become challenging to our psyche with respect to properly accepting and recognizing future possible outcomes. These outcomes will undoubtedly have a bias with respect to our current position being held in the market, but we must learn to erase that type of thinking from our mentality in order to truly live in the present moment so that we can always make the correct decision. From this point forward, things just become more complex, and as such, I encourage the reader to review several charts in order to gain the understanding necessary of properly seeing and understanding range breaks based on Price Theory.

Closing Notes on Chapter 6 / Price Theory Corollary

The concept of Klatch's Price Theory must be expanded via a corollary-like argument, which I feel is necessary in order to complete the understanding of Price Objective thinking, which will be elaborated on in Chapter 20. That said, we must realize that the purpose of Price Theory is first and foremost range expansion based on the definitions defined within the theory itself. However, the corollary posits that there is also the secondary objective of Range Invalidation. Range Invalidation occurs when we take out the discreet low/high of the base range. For example, if we are in a positive range, the range will be expanded via Discreet Replacement at point B, or it will be Invalidated when point A is breached. In any event, we are widening Price Theory to allow for the potential of invalidation, but what is this invalidation?

Well, let us take for example a positive base range, which is in line with the figurative examples in this chapter. When the market moves down off a given high, then, the market is now forming a NEW NEGATIVE base range, is it not? Then, there is a positive retracement range, and if that retracement range fails to achieve Discreet Replacement of the basic range, then, we see that the Price Objective is to now target Range Expansion via discreet replacement of the new negative range's low. Therefore, when the market is heading lower during its retracement move of a base range, it is simply creating a new range. The market is moving in newer and newer ranges at all times. However, the purpose of defining the corollary is immense. What is indefinable/unquantifiable at this point in my career is to understand that once the negative range begins to expand, there is an invocation cause Range Invalidation. Thus, we can visualize this by realizing that if we fail to take out a new high of the base range (i.e. discreet replacement), we now invoke a Price Objective to take out the new low. This target first has the objective of Range Expansion of the new negative range, while secondarily having the objective of Range Invalidation of the original base range. Thus, if we assume infinite movements, and because price does not allow infinite dissections, we see that over time, if we fail to take out the high of the base range, the low becomes the target.

This corollary is immensely important for our trading because once we observe that the trend has changed via a swing down (see Chapters 8 and 9), which means that the positive base range has yielded a negative range that has invoked price theory to the downside, we find a new terminal objective which acts as a gravitational pull. The market has an objective to take out the discreet. Therefore, with the Corollary, Price Theory gives us two terminal objectives "Omega-0" (Range Expansion) and "Omega-1" (Range Invalidation).

Chapter 7

Range Retracements

This chapter will build on the concept of ranges and Klatch's Price Theory by discussing the characteristics that a market makes when it moves back inside of a given range. The concept of a retracement begins at the termination of a given range. When a range is defined, which means it has created a discreet high/low with a corresponding low/high, the movement of price derived from buyers and sellers ultimately causes the market to move back inside that terminated range. We can see this from an economic viewpoint by understanding that supply or demand has been exhausted at these points. That exhaustion is noted by time as well, and hence, becomes the building block of understanding the relation to price retracements inside of given range.

Now, the distance that the market moves back inside of that given range is defined as a **retracement**, which will be indicated via a percentage of the **reference**(d) **range**. Let us refer again to Figure 6.4, which is shown here as Figure 7.1. This chart, which was already introduced, will help us in order to define a retracement visually.

Figure 7.1: Price Theory and Price Objectives

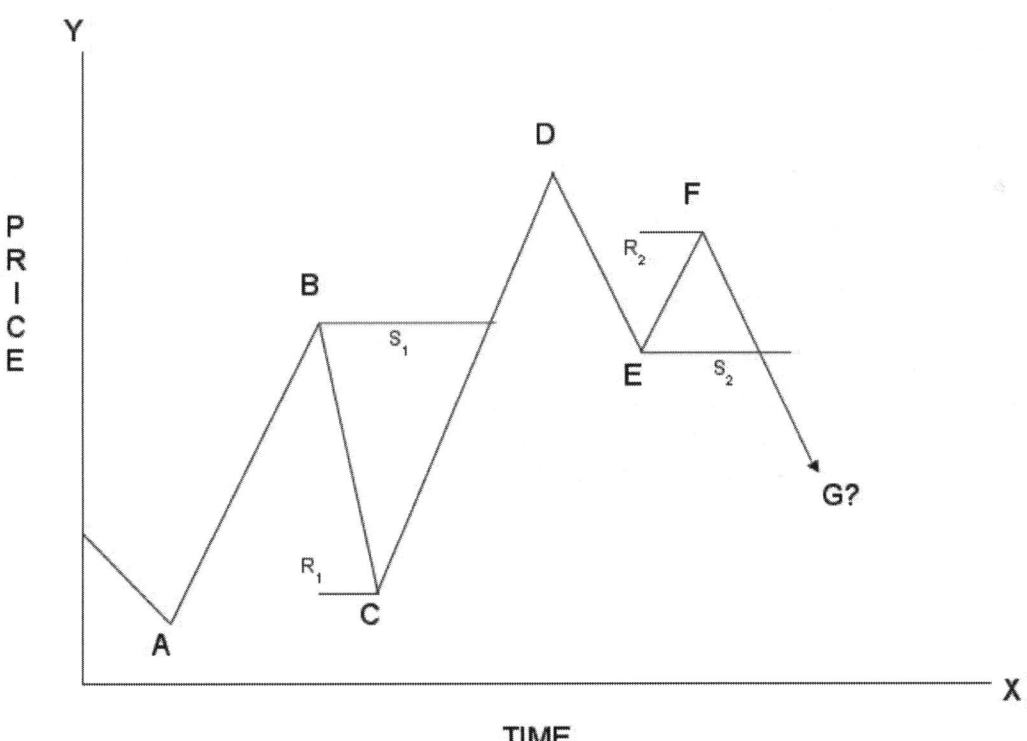

103

For the given discreet range, D: $(T_A, P_A) \rightarrow (T_B, P_B)$ the market will create that range, and terminate at the value of point B, which becomes the point of exhaustion After that termination, the market will retrace some level of the A $\rightarrow$ B range to a point defined in this example as point C. We can say "the market has retraced the A $\rightarrow$ B range to point C as a price value coupled with a corresponding percentage known as R_1." In order to clarify further, let us use numeric values for A, B, and R_1. We will set A = 100, B = 110 and R_1 as 50% or 0.50. We can now ask the question, "What is the 50% retracement of the A $\rightarrow$ B range?" (This is defined as point C). Since A $\rightarrow$ B is a positive range, we take (110 – 100) * 0.50 + 100 to define point C as $(T_C, 105)$, and the mathematics of this will be properly illustrated herein. However, although this is a simple example, if we forget the valuations of A, B, and R_1, we can state that point C can exist in any place along price levels (not time periods) of the A $\rightarrow$ B range. Thankfully, these possible values for C are not arbitrary, and in our first example, we saw that C = 105 meaning a 50% retracement. Thankfully, because these values can be predefined, we start to find the first clue to an inherent market structure. Thus, the purpose of this chapter will be to define those relevant points ("C") that occur in the retracement of the A $\rightarrow$ B range (or any given range) for us to use as possible trade signals.

Due to the predetermined nature that we can find for retracements, we can create a list of possible values for point ("C"), which will be known as retracement levels. Therefore, each one of these retracement levels will give us values for C, which can yield possible **market inflection points**, as a market moves back inside of a given range. A market inflection point is simply a level at which the market finds support/resistance and reverses off that value (commonly, these are also known as pivot points). These points of inflection become the basis for new trade inceptions, and I must differentiate that a market inflection point and a pivot point are not synonymous. Further, since market inflection points along any given range are not be arbitrarily defined, we see that this becomes the first mathematical concept that exists for us in defining how "The Market is not Random."

Due to mathematical definitions, we will be able to define relevant retracement levels of any given range by the knowledge in this chapter. This will be an important concept to furthering our understanding of how valuable Klatch's Price Theory becomes. By defining market inflection points in advance that are calculated as range retracements, we can visually use price action patterns (and later time repetitions/cycles) in predicting the low/high for a given range that will lead to a new high/low outside of that range based on the price objectives of Price Theory. In essence, we are mathematically calculating future points in order to determine if the market will hold that point (retracement) to break the high/low of the range, and later, we will learn how to calculate these points not only in price but also at a specific time, which becomes mind blowing.

Like many things in this book, the concept of retracements is far from innovative. However, my purpose is to shift the reader's perception on how to utilize retracements, and by simplistic tweaks to normal convention, the reader will garner a lot more use out of the concept of retracements. In turn, these newfound usability and understanding of retracements should equate to profound trading results by the combined mentality understanding of retracements and Price Theory. Thankfully, because retracements are so common in the area of technical analysis, most charting software programs have a "retracement tool," and this inherent functionality makes our job infinitely easier. Despite the common knowledge of retracements, nearly every trader I have ever encountered thinks of retracements in the wrong way. They do not couple the market's adherence to a retracement with Price Theory in order to align with underlying price objectives. Furthermore, retracements are an essential definition as part of the underlying market structure because markets reach exhaustive periods where they are forced to make a retracement simply due to the way in which price action works.

Now that I have defined what a retracement is along with explaining their importance for underlying market structure, let us learn how we can use these retracement value calculations to trade. To begin with, we will define the **retracement levels**. A retracement level is a quantified percentage that a market retraces a defined range (long or short / positive range or negative range). For the purpose of proving the non-randomness of the market, we will predefine ten retracement levels that have possible usability of determining terminal points of a retracement range. More important, each level will have characteristics and tendencies that yield their own discussions.

Amazingly, despite the advances in technology and trading efficiency, the retracement levels that work as market inflection points are derived from two age-old principles. Remember, since I have made the claim that this structure has always existed, it should be of no surprise that we are going back over 100 years in order to determine the values of our retracement levels. The retracement levels that will withstand the test of time come from (1) Fibonacci and (2) the concept of 1/8 intervals. For those readers who do not believe in Fibonacci, you are more than welcome to use the 1/8 intervals for all relevant retracement levels because they will yield close approximations to the Fibonacci calculations. However, I encourage all traders to free themselves from preconceived notions and embrace this new knowledge. In a way, we need to remember that God is palpable in the markets and in nature; hence, Fibonacci. Essentially, Fibonacci uncovered the mathematics of nature when he defined the Fibonacci Sequence, the Golden Ratio/Number (phi), and the value of Pi. The interconnectedness of mathematics in nature and the market should come as a natural realization if one is to believe in the inherent cycles that exist in the market and humanity. That being said, I will explain the ways that Fibonacci gains validity in trading, and to begin, let us now take a look at a visual representation of these 10 retracement levels (9 if you use 1/8 intervals instead).

Figure 7.2: Retracement Levels

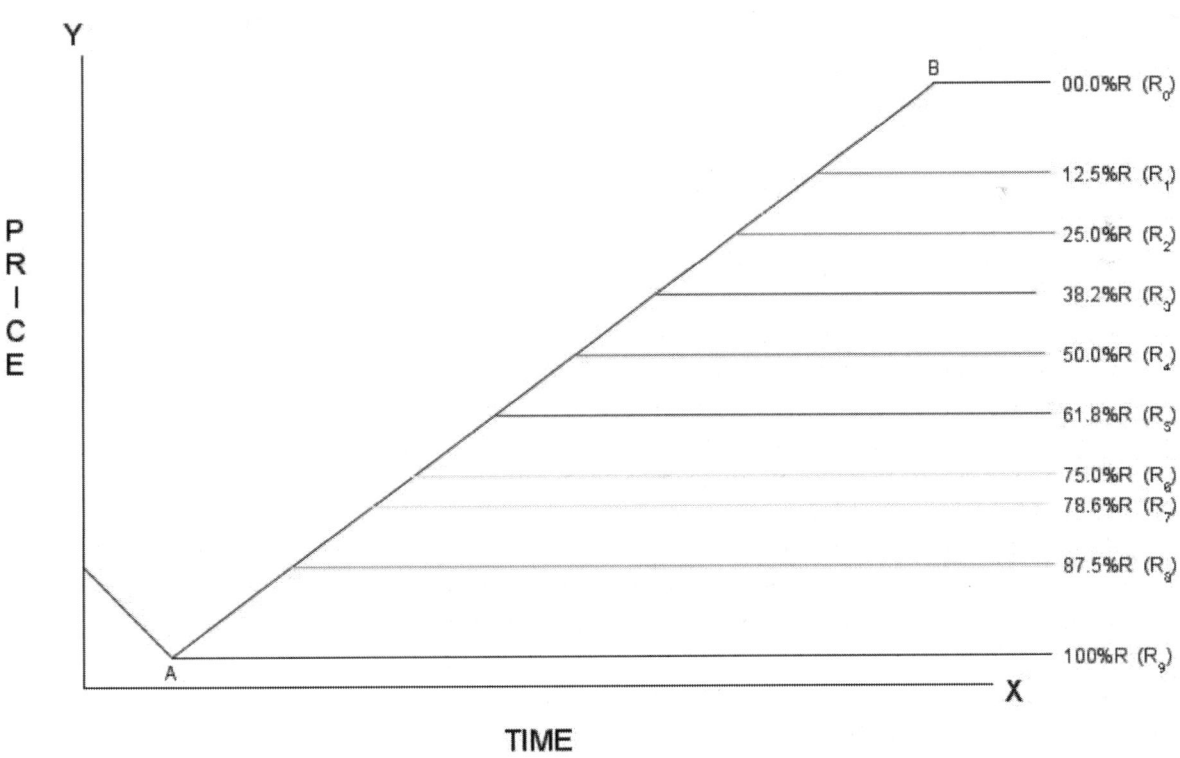

Using Figure 7.2 for a positive range representation, we can see the retracement levels we will define for this positive range as: 0% (R_0), 12.5% (R_1), 25% (R_2), 38.2% (R_3), 50% (R_4), 61.8% (R_5), 75% (R_6), 78.6% (R_7), 87.5% (R_8), and 100% (R_9). Of note, the Fibonacci levels are R_3, R_5, and R_7, which can be approximated to 1/8 intervals as $R_3 = 37.5\%$, $R_5 = 62.5\%$, and $R_7 = R_6$, but I will be utilizing the combined Fibonacci and 1/8 interval levels for all future discussions, which I encourage the reader to do as well.

Before we learn what these levels mean and how to use them, I must define a mathematical notation in order to correctly write the range/retracement relationship. From there, I will also define a mathematical calculation, which will be based on the notation for calculating retracement values like I did in the example that introduced this chapter.

Retracement Notation will be written as $P_{Rn(A, B)} = R_n R : [\ D/S: (T_A, P_A) \rightarrow (T_B, P_B)\ ]$. Putting retracement notation into words, we are simply asking for the price of the retracement of the A → B range ($P_{R(A, B)}$) defined by a percentage (R_n). For example, let us say we want to a 25% retracement of the A → B range from Figure 3. We would write this as $P_{Rn(A, B)} = P_{25\%(A,B)} = 25\%R : [D: (T_A, P_A) \rightarrow (T_B, P_B)]$. Now, we can define our **Retracement Calculation** mathematically. For positive or negative ranges, this calculation will be the same. Retracement Calculation will be defined as $P_{Rn(A, B)} = R_n R : [\ D/S: (T_A, P_A) \rightarrow (T_B, P_B)\ ] = (P_B - P_A)(1-R_N) + P_A = P_B - P_B R_N + P_A R_N$ for any given range (A → B) and retracement (R_N). Just like we had shorthand range notation, we will also have shorthand retracement notation, which is already defined in Retracement Notation by the first part of the notation: $P_{Rn(A, B)}$. Now that I have adequately defined our retracement notations and calculations, I want to do two examples in reference to Figure 7.1 again.

To begin our example calculations, we will define interpretive values that are based on the visual illustration as A = 100, B = 110, R_1 = 75% (example 1) and D = 115, E = 107.5, and R_2 = 50% (example 2). For our first example question, I will ask "What is the 75% retracement of the A → B Range?" For our second example question, I will ask, "What is the 50% retracement of the D → E Range?"

Example 1: $P_{75\%R(A,B)} = 110-110*(0.75)+100*(0.75) = 102.50$ = Point C on Figure 2
Example 2: $P_{50\%R(D,E)} = 107.5-107.5*(0.50)+115*(0.50) = 111.25$ = Point F on Figure 2

To conclude and properly state the answers to these examples, I will put these calculations into words in order to not confuse the reader with language representation in subsequent chapters. Therefore, we can say the 75% retracement of the A → B range is 102.5, and the 50% retracement of the D → E range is 111.25.

Just as we had discreet and secondary ranges, we will also have two classifications for retracements. These will be defined as **primary retracements** and **secondary retracements**. Primary retracements will be linked to discreet ranges and secondary retracements will be linked to secondary ranges. In addition, *secondary retracements need to be defined only at prior, primary retracement levels or mathematical clusters*, which will be discussed thoroughly in Chapter 14. Visually, let us refer to a quick example using Figure 7.3.

Figure 7.3: Primary and Secondary Retracements

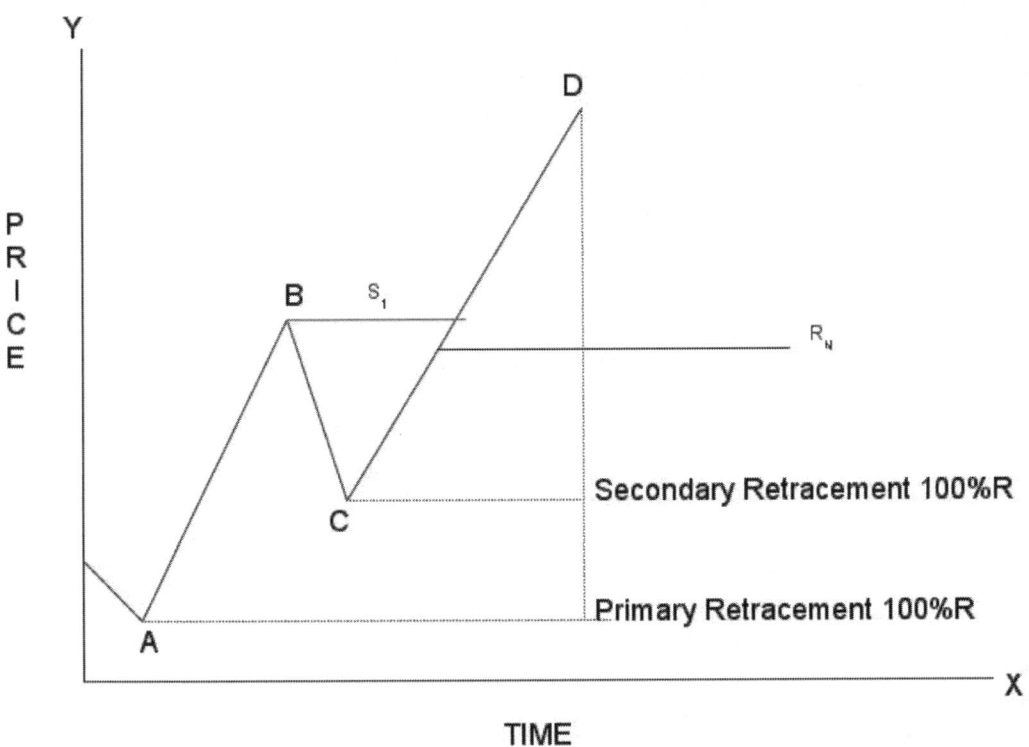

To begin this quick example using Figure 7.3, let us begin with a positive range A → B, which has a retracement to point C. Point C is one of our 10 predefined retracement levels. From there, the market adheres to Price Theory and takes out new highs over point B, which becomes point D. We now draw a primary retracement of the A → D range, and we draw a secondary retracement using the range C → D. In order to understand the reason to the secondary range's validity, I must state that it was <u>because C was one of our quantified retracement levels</u>. This is a very important topic of discussion, which requires an elaborate, wordy clarification.

As trader's, when we start to determine the underlying market structure for a specific trading instrument, we will often start with the lowest low or the highest high depending on the orientation of the chart moving forward in time. If we assume that we are using the lowest low for quantifying prior retracements in an up-trending market, which has a positive range that first links the discreet low (lowest low) and second, links the discreet high (highest high), we can understand the difference between the price objective based on Price Theory because of the primary range's dominance over a secondary range.

Now, in order to begin our market structure definition using retracements alone, we would start at our lowest low and gradually tag relevant highs as we move forward in time by observing all visual, possible retracements on the chart. Now, we must determine what lows occurred after each relevant high that are quantifiable based on primary retracement calculations. For those lows that match a given, primary retracement value, we will find our usable lows for secondary retracements. These lows will be tagged as well and linked to the highest high on the chart. Thus, we begin to observe that we may have one or two primary retracement (again, we have the 180 bar rule as a qualifier as well), but we could have many secondary retracements. However, it will be typically that the terminal points for secondary retracements have the same terminal point as the primary retracement <u>if they are in the same direction as the primary retracement</u>.

In order to further clarify, let us say that we have a stock that moves from a low to a high over a period of one year. Over that one year, the stock has four corrective retracements in its up move. In that up move, there were undoubtedly many more than just four retracements of relevant highs. However, for our purposes, we will only look at the four corrective retracements that were quantified by our defined, primary retracement levels. The values for the primary retracement levels are recalculated each time we look at a new range that links the lowest low to new, subsequent highs until we reach the terminal/discreet high. In this example, we have four such lows that were quantified by our primary retracement moving forward in time. As such, those four retracements would be annotated on the chart, and we would draw secondary retracements to the absolute high from those four retracement lows. Therefore, our final chart would have five total retracements over the one-year period to the current relevant high. These five retracements would consist of one primary retracement from the lowest low to highest high and four secondary retracement from the subsequently made retracements over that one-year period to the highest high. All retracements that are in the same direction will have the same terminal ending point; for positive ranges, this means the terminal point is the highest high but for negative ranges, these would only be formed after finding our terminal high. However, as the market created its four previous retracements over the course of the year, there were four previous negative ranges, but once a new high was achieved outside of the primary range, the negative ranges were removed from our list. Of interest and for the quantitatively anal audience, I must note that there may be other relevant lows that can be defined by other mathematical price structured components, and those too will be relevant for our future discussion on mathematical cluster averages. In essence, we may have more than 4 secondary retracements on a stock because of other lows that occurred within the stock's up move. For now, **the main purpose of these five retracement is to form mathematical clusters that are made up of more than just one retracement.**

Visually, let us go back to Figure 7.3 in order to illustrate a quick example of the concept of mathematical retracement clusters. (Mathematical clusters of support/resistance will be a constant theme throughout price structure, and we will have more clarification in Chapter 13.) In Figure 7.3, we observe that there is an R_N for the primary retracement and an R_N for the secondary retracement so that $P_{25\%R(A,D)} = P_{50\%R(C,D)}$. To put this into specific valuations to prove the concept of clusters of mathematical support/resistance, let us say that A = 100 D = 120 and C = 110. In this case, $P_{25\%R(A,D)} = 115 = P_{50\%R(C,D)}$.

Let us now properly define the introduction of all of these new terms. A **<u>mathematical cluster</u>** is the average of multiple mathematical support/resistance numbers occurring around the same approximate value. **<u>Mathematical support</u>** is a value calculated using price structure that may serve as a possible low. Concurrently, **<u>mathematical resistance</u>** is a value calculated using price structure that may serve as a possible high. Therefore, in order to finish our example in Figure 7.3, we can define our mathematical support as $((P_{25\%R(A,D)} + P_{50\%R(C,D)})/2)$, which is equal to our cluster average defined using the variables above as 115. We would call this a two-number cluster, and in theory, the more numbers that form the cluster, the more powerful it should be in holding the market.

One last high-verbiage discussion needs to be mentioned before moving on, and this discussion needs to clarify a common occurrence. If we go back to our one-year stock example that has four secondary retracements, I need to clarify what happens when we have a secondary range that has a lower low (or higher high) then a previous secondary range within a market move. We will call this concept, **<u>secondary range replacement</u>**. Secondary range replacement occurs when a proceeding inverted range (negative range if the base range is positive) reaches a low/high that is lower/higher then any of the previous lows/highs that were part of past secondary ranges. For example, let us say that in our one-year up move, there were four secondary retracements, which led to new highs. Well, if the second of the four secondary retracements was lower than the first secondary retracement (when the second, secondary retracement is being made obviously the third and fourth secondary retracements are not existent), then, the first secondary retracement is also validated, and we would be left with three secondary retracements on the chart.

Figure 7.4: Secondary Range Retracement Bounces and Swings

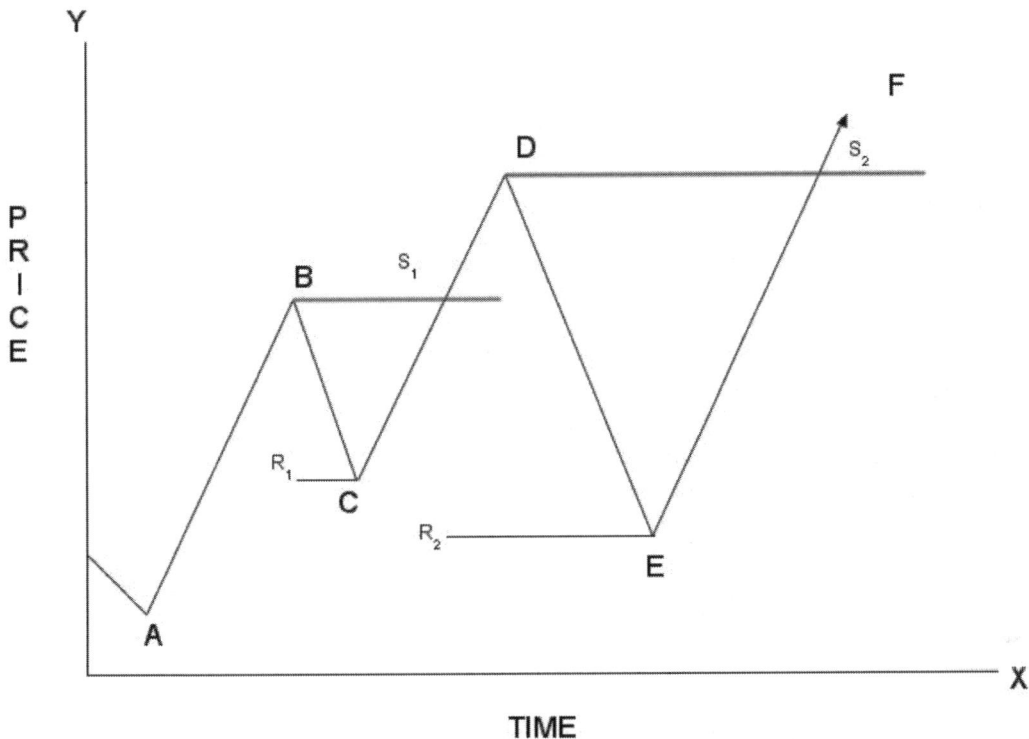

In order to describe secondary range retracement visually, I have to introduce Figure 7.4 at this time. Figure 7.4 is important for many principles relating to swings and range replacements, but I will speak of it now as a clear example of a secondary range retracement. If we look at the figure, we can see that B → C is a secondary range, which foreshadows a break to new highs based on Price Theory that was confirmed by the activation of S_1, which created a new terminal discreet range A → D. However, we notice that a new secondary range forms with a terminal point at E, but E < C. Hence, point C now becomes invalidated/replaced, and we are left with a replaced secondary range of D → E, which also foreshadows a break to new highs based on Price Theory over point D. If this were a yearly chart, the invalidation of point C would mean that our resultant ranges are A → D, D → E, and E → F because points B and C have been completely replaced.

Retracement Levels

Now that I have covered most of the definitions necessary in order to properly discuss retracements, we will look at each relevant, retracement level. Each retracement level will have its own nuances and tendencies as mentioned earlier. For the ease of discussion, we will be focusing on a positive range market. This market will have some type of retracement back into this positive range, and we will use the knowledge of Price Theory to determine that our objective will always be to take out the discreet high of this positive range. Conversely, all the commentary regarding the market to target new highs of our positive range should be inverted for negative ranges. Again, an example and an illustration of what these retracements look like for a positive range can be viewed in Figure 3.

0%R

The 0% retracement is not a retracement since it is the discreet high of the range, or our demand exhaustion point (demand because we are using a positive range). However, there are two things to note about the 0%R-value. First, it will always be a discreet high at the current time that we are analyzing a range. This means that for historical analysis, we will be looking at the time this discreet high occurs, and what happens prior to that high being exceeded in the future. Second, since it serves as the top of the range, the line that our retracement tool draws off that point will not be removed unless the discreet low was violated. In effect, the line drawn off the 0%R will exist to remind us of the current price objective based on Price Theory once we have determined whether another retracement has held the market. In a way, we can determine that if R_1-R_9 holds the market, then R_0 becomes the target until R_9 is breached.

Another important characteristic of the 0%R is that while the market has moved inside the range, the 0%R is equal to the 100%R for the negative range that is conversely drawn from the discreet high to the low that the market makes while inside of that range.

12.5%R

It still amazes me how such a seemingly small retracement as the 12.5%R can have so much power in calling relevant, secondary lows in long-term trends. The 12.5%R and the 87.5%R are the two least known, and therefore, least recognized of all the retracements. However, their power cannot be understated.

The 12.5%R is considered a **shallow retracement,** which is any retracement less than the 50%R.

In small ranges concerning price or time, the 12.5%R is also of little use because the 12.5%R is easily violated on any pullback from a relevant high in any corrective move down from that relevant high. However, in longer-term trending markets, the 12.5%R will work magnificently. For example, using the prior, real range from the S&P Futures of 666.75 → 1347, we can see how the 12.5%R held the market numerous times on the way to that discreet high of 1347. We can anchor our retracement tool at 666.75 and we can observe the 12.5%R holding several times by placing the terminal point at various highs as we move forward in time. Nearly every 12.5%R that held has led to subsequent higher highs until we reached our terminal discreet at 1347, which became taken out in early 2012.

Another observation is how large this retracement can be in longer-term observations. Using the same range example, the 12.5% retracement came in all the way down at 1262 in the S&P Futures, which is nearly 100 points off the high. Therefore, we can further view that since this is the first relevant level of support in any major correction, we can look to this area to have a magnetizing effect for the market and/or potential mathematical cluster averages.

Along this same line of thinking, in longer term trading strategies, we can view this 1262 support area as a major inflection point that the market will make, which will result in a new relevant high based on Price Theory (should it hold). As such, if the market simply corrects to the 12.5%R (or any other retracement), we can simply use this example to predict nearly a 100-point positive move based on the new price objective to take out the relevant high. By observing a 12.5%R holding on a longer-term chart, we can discern and visualize vast profit potential with very minimal loss by buying this retracement level because as we will learn, a retracement either holds or it doesn't.

The last observation about the 12.5%R level is that it often clusters with secondary retracements or corrective swing patterns. It is quite common to see a 12.5% primary retracement level couple with a 25% secondary retracement level as an example, and these two levels may be 10~15 points apart (on the S&P Futures), which means their cluster average is somewhere in the middle. Therefore, we must be aware that the 12.5%R may be a likely magnetizing target for a major correction in a longer term trend, but that the 12.5%R may be missed on the upside or downside by +/- 0.5% based on possible cluster averages occurring higher or lower than the exact value.

25%R

The 25%R is the second shallow retracement, and once the 12.5%R is penetrated, it will serve as the next likely area of mathematical support (again, since we are looking at a positive range example). Like all retracements, once it holds, we again look at Price Theory in order to determine the objective of the market to take out the relevant discreet high outside of the current range.

The 25%R is large enough that we can now add it back into our arsenal when we trade in shorter time frames or smaller price ranges. Therefore, if we witness a fast moving market that is having retracements to the 25%R, we can observe that we have a very strong trend underway because there is a lack of sellers pushing the market back down any further than 25% of its current range. More important, is that after we see a 25%R start to hold the market, we often observe the market's tendency to have a memory of this value, and it will allow us to think in terms of future 25%R that may hold the market.

Another observation about the 25%R is that when it is holding in strong markets, we can generate swing trades off this value, which will be discussed in the next chapter. It is the first retracement that we can look at for swing trades projections (next chapter).

In order to show the power of shallow retracements, we can discuss the major bear market low that occurred in March of 2009, and then, we can look at the first noticeable correction, which occurred in July of 2009. This correction was approximately a 25%R from the March low to the early July high, and once we saw Price Theory analysis yield a new high over the early July 2009 high, we generated a swing that is still in effect today (April of 2012). If we think about this for a moment, the knowledge of simply witnessing the 25%R hold off of the major bear market low of March 2009 became enough of a trade signal to warrant almost a 100% projected move in the underlying indices once the swing activated, because the conclusion of this swing activation was enough to warrant a new bull market that now has targets above the November 2007 high. Remember, there is still another available range that has its own available Price Objectives base don Price Theory. Therefore, the reader can now start to view the power of Price Theory and retracements because this is an example of how Price Theory can expand to one range, and then, another. Now, the only remaining question to the masses is, "How long it will take to get there?"

38.2%R

Out of all the retracements, the 38.2%R is the second most magnetizing; meaning that markets will often find some type of price action occurring at this level regardless of whether or not the level holds or not. For the first time in the discussion of retracements, questions will start to formulate in our mind as we go deeper through the primary range as to if Price Theory is still predicting new highs above our discreet high. Hence, we find the inception of doubt come into effect based on whether or not Price Theory will hold for this range. An example question that we now must ask ourselves is, "will the 38.2% retracement hold or will it simply be a probably area of support?" This is a question of significant importance as we get to double tops and double bottoms in Chapter 8. However, for now, the magnetizing effect of the 38.2%R will be our first challenge to Price Theory.

Since markets will tend to have some type of reaction off a 38.2%R, we have to start thinking about the inverted negative range that is formed from our current discreet high to our bounce off the 38.2%R. At first, this bounce will have us thinking that Price Theory will hold, but if we see a bounce, which is followed by a breach of the 38.2%R, we now must be aware that the market has satisfied the price theory of the new negative range instead of the positive range, and we may be in for a further correction deeper of the primary range, which also means *that we may be targeting the low of the primary range* that formed the 38.2%R in the first place; hence, doubt.

This is how Price Theory becomes interesting because we have two ranges that have different price objectives – one higher and one lower. Sometimes, our smaller, negative range price objective is filled instead of the primary range's price objective based on Price Theory, which means that the Primary Range's 38.2%R is breached, but then, another one of the retracement levels will hold in the primary, positive range, which then adheres to Price Theory. The concept of time along with understanding qualified swings in subsequent chapters will help us to filter these scenarios as we move through later chapters. However, because of how important it is at this point for the reader to understand the power of the 38.2%R coupled with understanding the possibility that a future retracement can still be used to validate Price Theory, I need to portray this modus operandi visually. Therefore, let us look to Figure 7.5.

Figure 7.5: Retracement Bounces and Swings

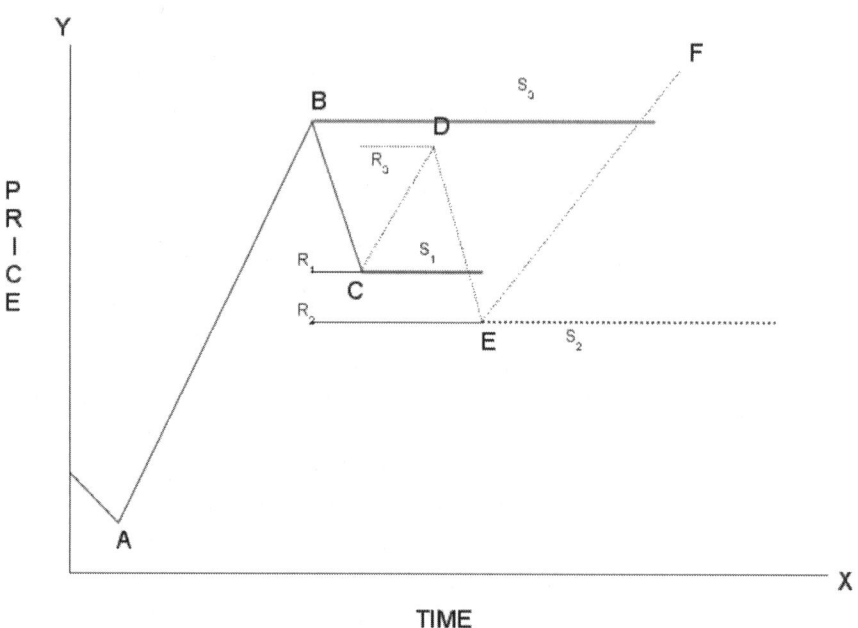

In Figure 7.5, we have an illustration of the possibilities that we must openly recognize as traders. In Figure 7.5, we have a market that rallies to form the A → B range. From there, we form a retracement shown as R_1, which is also point C. Now, using the dashed lines we can visualize the 38.2%R bounce if we set R_1 = 38.2%R = 0.382. We observe that the market bounces off point C, and Price Theory kicks in. Price Theory tells us to target new highs over B, which is our discreet high of our primary, positive range. However, what happens instead? Instead, we fail to take out point B, and in fact, we form a deep retracement of the negative B → C range; valued as a percentage (R_3) and a price D. So, again, Price Theory kicks in by telling us that we failed to go to new highs, so we must target new lows below point C. Since point C is our 38.2%R, we can now visualize two resultant scenarios for which only one is illustrated due to our limited knowledge of other concepts at this point in the book. However, in order to properly reflect the two possibilities, I will tell the reader to acknowledge that once point C is penetrated, the market may be targeting new lows below point A (the 100%R) since point C becomes a swing point, S_1. This swing point may have turned the trend down, and this conclusion is not observed from the chart, but is inline with the preceding revelations of possible occurrences based on **Intra-range Price Theory**, which can now be defined. Intra-range price theory is the conflicting parameters of two or more simultaneously linked price objectives based on Price Theory that are diametrically opposed to each other. It is our job, as traders, to understand which one of the price objectives based on Price Theory will be fulfilled, but the more important answer to determine is, *"Which one of these Price Theory price objectives will be fulfilled first?"* At this point, let us simply keep these questions in mind, and let us move forward.

Therefore, let us look at what actually happens based on the possibility that does exist in Figure 5. What is shown was the second scenario that was discussed. In this visually conclusive scenario, the market takes out the 38.2%R-value after having some type of bounce that seems to initially validate Price Theory in relation to the negative B → C range being the terminal point of the retracement. However, the market decides to not adhere to Price Theory and after violating the 38.2%R, the market finds support at another of the retracement levels indicated as R_2. The price value of this R2 percentage is labeled as point E, and once again, once the market has probed support, Price Theory kicks in, which tells us to look for new highs over point B for the primary, positive A → B range. Visually, we can see that this does indeed happen in Figure 7.5.

The important take away from this example is that these two scenarios exist for any value of R_N and R_{N+X} when dealing with retracement. Therefore, we have to be aware that not every retracement bounce will lead to successful trades that take out new discreets of our primary range. However, that does not mean that we cannot use these retracement levels with tight stop-losses in order to validate large reward to risk ratios by using Price Theory in order to properly determine the profit objective, which is outside of the current primary range.

Moreover, although our Figure 7.5 example alone applies to every retracement, I must emphasize that even in fast moving markets, the 38.2%R will lead to some type of price action, possibly observable as a pause in time. Therefore, it is a powerful retracement in every time frame, and as such, I encourage the reader to personally visualize the 38.2%R in historic analysis in order to see how often the market has some type of reaction to the 38.2%R level. It will be important to understand that markets will have some type of reaction at retracement levels, and our job will be to quantify if that retracement and, more importantly, the primary range will hold or not. The final words to properly link this discussion to Price Theory is that if we believe that the market's goal is to find support at one of the retracements along the primary range, then it would be a suitable idea to place stop losses at any value less then the base point for our range, and as such, we could then place a limit trade at every retracement level anticipating new highs outside of the range. Future retracement level discussions will not belabor this example again, but be aware of the intra-range Price Theory price objectives that occur at any and every retracement level.

Lastly, I have to turn to the 2012 market in order to show the reality that these types of patterns are continuously working in the market. Just as we went through the example of the 25%R that occurred in the summer of 2009, we can look at the 38.2%R that called the 2011 fall low, which foreshadowed a break to new highs over the April 2011 high. This retracement was extremely valid (as it was in 2010), and it activated a swing that takes the S&P Cash Index all the way up to 2050 as the end of this bull market cycle, which will be elaborated on in later chapters.

50%R

The 50% retracement has two main areas of discussion: (1) change of trend confirmation signals and (2) corrective swing patterns (both of which will be expanded upon in later chapters). In addition, the 50%R is no longer considered a shallow retracement, but it is not a deep retracement either since it is the midpoint of the range. Logically, after the 38.2%R fails, the 50%R is the next mathematical support, and if we assume that Figure 7.5 is drawn to scale, we can see this retracement in the Figure by assuming that the 50%R is shown as R_2.

Interestingly, the two areas of discussion for the 50%R are diametrically opposed. First, a market that has retraced at least 50% of its range has retraced enough such that a swing to new highs out of the range has satisfied one of the requirements of trend change confirmation. On the contrary, a corrective swing pattern that is activated after a 50% retracement, then, reaches a given projection level, and starts to reverse from that level may invalidate the change of trend confirmation. As such, (since we are dealing with positive ranges for all of our retracement discussion), we can witness that if that projection levels holds, the market will actually reverse back below the initial discreet low of the original retracement range. Let us look at Figure 7.6 for a reminder of how mentally anguishing the market can be.

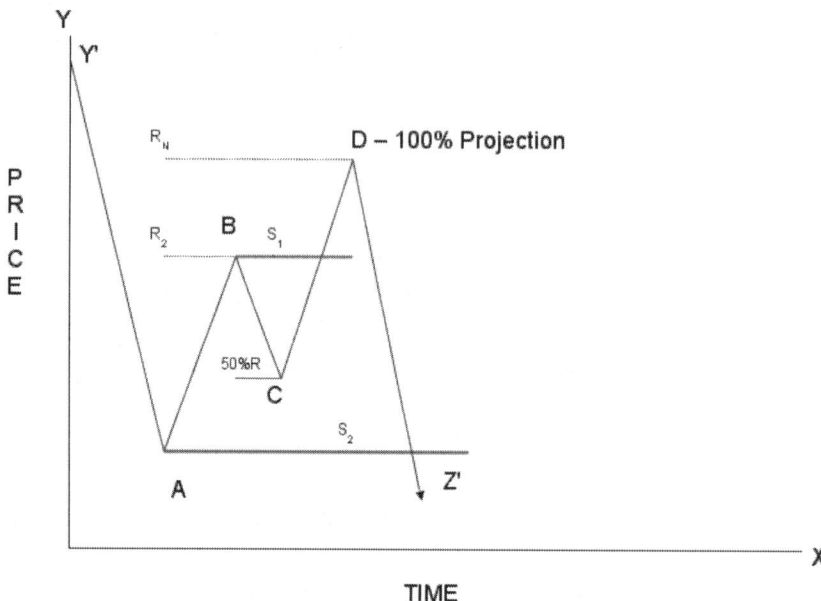

Figure 7.6: 50% Corrective Swings

In Figure 7.6, the market is coming from some unknown high (y'). It forms a discreet low, A, and then, retraces the y' → A range some percentage R_N to form point B. Point C then forms from a 50%R of the A → B range, which creates the Swing, S_1. This is known as an ABC corrective swing. Now, our example market finds a value of D, which we will discuss in depth next chapter, but for now, we see that D comes from the price distance of $(P_B - P_A)$ added to point C. This is a 100% projection. We can observe that D is less than y'. At point D, our market stops and reverses to new lows below A based on the original range's Price Theory. This is an example of how we can be tricked into misinterpreting the trend, but when we realize that this corrective retracement was simply a positive corrective swing, we can use that knowledge for tremendous profit.

In the next chapter, we will also define that a 50% or greater swing is what we would like to see in order to have a qualified swing. As such, this retracement level is seen as a part of future qualification criteria, but it is not an absolute requirement.

61.8%R

The 61.8% retracement is the most powerful of all retracements. It is also our first **deep retracement** back through the range. Like the 38.2%R, regardless of the market trend, the 61.8%R will frequently lead to some type bounce that is derived from price action around this level of any given range. Like all concepts in this book, we can go back in time in order to see the 61.8%R in action. Over the years, it has been one of the most prevalent topics for discussion, and even most fundamental investors have known or have heard of the 61.8% Retracement. Historically, every major new bull market has had a 61.8%R or greater after putting in the bear market low except for our current bull market of 2009-.

The accuracy and the power of the 61.8%R is extremely important, and when we learn more about mathematical clusters, it will be essential to properly calculate cluster averages that appear close to this retracement. In addition, the more powerful we go out in time, the greater the chance of the 61.8%R leading to some large profit potential. For instance, if we draw a 61.8%R of the negative range formed by the bear market high in Late 2007 to the bear market low in March of 2009, we can see how powerful the market danced around this retracement before breaking above it. We also have our intra-day ranges as well, and the power of the 61.8%R is going to be in front of our eyes numerous times. When the market reaches a 61.8%R that also combines with Time Symmetry, we reach moments that will justify large uses of leverage!

Lastly, for new traders, it is a good idea to look at this retracement as a basis of automated trading setups. The reason behind this is because, if you expect markets to break out of the range simply by buying this retracement, you will have a positive reward to risk ratio. If you couple that with the knowledge that his level is often used by the masses, you can find yourself making scalp trades around this area as well. *The 61.8%R cannot be ignored in any time frame be it minute by minute or year over year.*

75%R/78.6%R

Due to their proximity in the range, I will group the 75%R and the 78.6%R into one heading for discussion. Along these same lines, when we continue are discussions of mathematical clusters later in Chapter 14, we will see that we can often times average these two retracements together in calculating a more powerful number for the mathematical support that exists near these retracements.

Just as I discussed the magnetizing effect of retracements, we also have the concept of **retracement memory** that was mentioned earlier on regarding the 25%R, but it can now be defined. Retracement memory is simply the markets tendency to continue having retracements of future ranges equal to retracements of prior ranges that have been expanded. I touched on this topic briefly with the

12.5%R and 25%R, but this concept is of most importance as we discuss these two deep retracements due to their tendency to foreshadow **reciprocal retracement memory.** Reciprocal retracement memory is that once we have a 75%R on a positive range, when we create a new, negative range off the positive range's discreet terminal high point, we will observe the negative range to have a 75%R as well, and this discussion will be important for discussing triangles within Price Structure.

As we are learning, aside from taking out new highs/lows, the market objective is to take people out of the market; to test the conviction of the masses at all times. Since the 61.8%R is well known to most good traders, the market will test their conviction of their trades. As such, we will often see the 61.8%R fail in order to take out the traders who bought/sold at that level. Essentially, these traders are stopped out of their positions. So, what happens next? Usually, not only will those traders be stopped out, but also they will start thinking that the market is going to a new low outside of the current positive range. The trader may then go short, but then, to continue the mental anguish, the market finds support at the 75%R/78.6%R, which leads to a reversal back up through the range, and possibly, to new highs based on Price Theory!

Therefore, this ability to be mentally taxed is something that we, as Time and Price Symmetry traders, must be cognizant of at all times. Therefore, we have to remember the validity of all possibilities by staying in the present moment, and thankfully, because of retracement memory, the future adherence to one of these deeper, retracement levels can tip us off about further retracement levels during our current trading day. These types of deep retracement trading days exist to ruin 61.8%R traders, or to ruin automated trading robots built around this commonly known value. It is an observation that these deeper retracements will continue to hold several times through the day, and when reciprocal retracement memory happens, we form a common trading pattern known as a contracting triangle. This pattern is the trend trader's enemy, and we must be on alert that 75%/78.6%R retracement holds may foreshadow tight trading ranges in our given time period, which leads to our lost topic of relevant discussion.

Although 75%R/78.6%R often cause triangle formations, their depth in the trading range coupled with taking the 61.8%R traders out of the market is a good signal of a major low once we activate a swing by achieving new highs over our positive trading range. As such, we are deep enough in the range to say that we have successfully retested a relevant low. At these retracements, we can visualize that the conviction of most traders has been shaken, and we are in a period of lower willingness of the market participants to buy so close to the prior low. Essentially, the "scared-money" has been shaken out. That is why there is significant retracement memory at these values. Each time we have a deep retracement coupled with a break to new highs with a subsequent deep retracement, the market is shaking more traders out with each deep retracement retest.

Figure 7.7: Deep Retracements and Three Higher Bottoms / Triple Swings

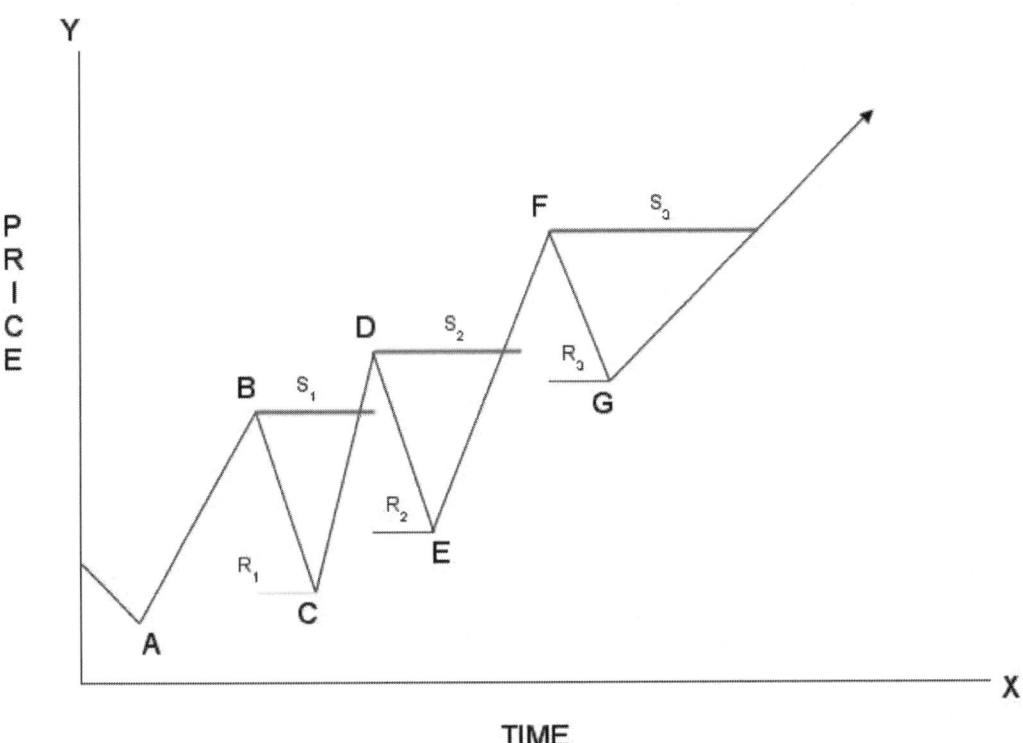

We can refer to Figure 7.7 for a graphical illustration of a market defending a new low with continued deep retracements, and if we set $R_1 = R_2$, we could say that one was a 78.6%R and the other a 75%R, which validates this discussion. However, since the market is filled with countless examples, let us look at the two subsequent days that occurred after the S&P Futures made the March 2009 bear market low.

In the two days after that low, the market had two deep retraces that were both of similar magnitude. In effect, at that low, the most people were shaken out and had their conviction tested twice before cementing a large rally that led to continuous new highs. This is not uncommon because once most of the market participants are shaken out, the activation of the major swings leads people to have to get back in. Therefore, the magnitude of the move gets bigger depending on how many times the market tries to shake people out of it. This is an important knowledge to use when holding onto positions in order to determine the possible strength of the trend move out of the given range, and we can look to deep retracements to clue us in on how powerful the new trend may be.

87.5%R

The deepest retracement for mathematical support calculations is found at the 87.5% retracement. Like the 12.5%R, it is also little known to the trading community. In a way, you can think of it as the last line of defense for a given range to hold. Characteristically, when markets are making major highs they do so in low volatility and we will see more 87.5%R occur at highs than at lows. Logically, during low volatility, markets are lackadaisical and they may drift higher as traders keep expecting subsequent new highs, but then, an 87.5%R holds the market. At that instant, a trade-able high emerges with minimal recognition from the overall market participants since they were easily expecting a new high. Thereby, the 87.5%R catches traders by surprise. Moreover, since we are deep into the range, trading an 87.5%R provides excellent reward to risk opportunities. Price Theory tells us that if we fail to take out a low/high, we must target the high/low for the current range as our objective. Therefore, since the 87.5%R is all the way through the range, our reward is a break of the corresponding high/low!

Next, we can again look at Figure 7.7. It is unusual for an 87.5%R to have retracement memory, which means we will often see it hold once, but it's not unusual to see subsequent deep retracements after an 87.5%R holds to create a new range. We can visualize this in Figure 7.7 by saying $R_1 = 87.5\%$ and $R_2 = 75\%$ and $R_3 = 38.2\%$. These would all be primary retracements of their relevant ranges. As such, we can anticipate at least one or two deep retracements after observing an 87.5%R in order to clue us in to when we should start looking for new trade opportunities on the subsequent pullbacks.

The importance of the 87.5%R cannot be understated, because when it holds, we are witnessing the least amount of market participation, and the 87.5%R is often an essential component to a major high or low that is formed in the markets.

100%R

Like the 0%R, the 100%R will be special. In fact, a 100%R will be considered a double bottom or a double top, which Chapter 8 will focus on in depth. By definition, a 100%R is a market that has fully retraced its range. Since these are double bottoms/tops, a whole set of new rules will apply. For now, we can just visualize these 100%R using Figure 7.8.

Figure 7.8: Double Bottom/Top Objectives

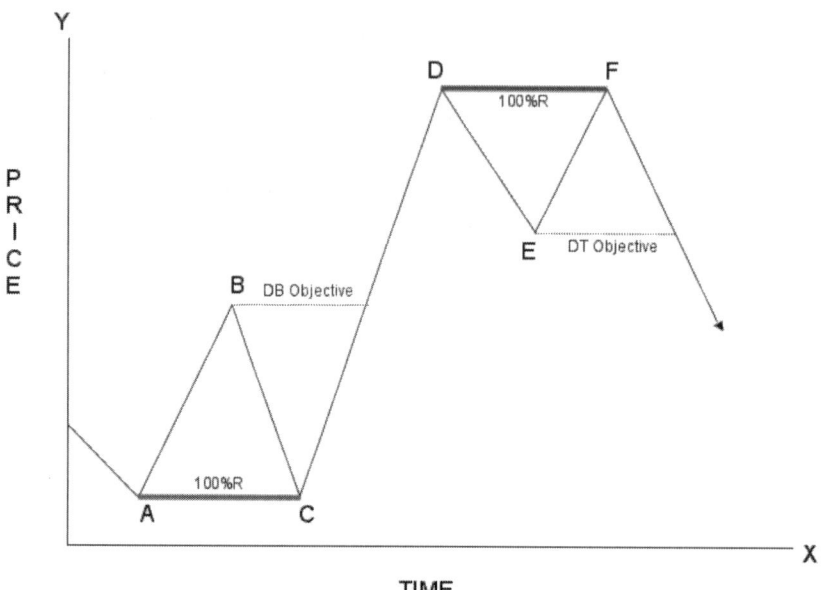

In Figure 7.8, we have a range A → C with a double bottom/100%R at price C = A. Then, we have a range D → E with a double top/100%R at price F = D. These are both 100%R, but the problem here is Klatch's Price Theory.

Since Price Theory gives us price objectives of new highs/lows outside of a range, we will often see that the 100%R are penetrated by a very shallow margin, and then, form our double top/bottom formation. In fact, it is rare to see a 100%R hold cleanly in terms of being breached or not. Contrarily, it is also true and frustrating that sometimes, we get so close to a high/low being breached, but we fail to take it out. Therefore, at these points, I have to yield to supply and demand as causes for this in general because, if there is a lot of support under the market, it will be common for that support to not be filled under that low. No, it will be more probable that the 100%R becomes more like a 99%R. However, because of Price Theory, the probability of breaching the 100%R is higher than not breaching it and this is true of the 7-year double top on the S&P 500, which foreshadowed the 2008 financial catastrophe. In November of 2007, the S&P took out its previous high, which was as predicted by Price Theory once there was an upswing off the October 2002 low. However the market did not get much higher than its previous high in November of 2007, and as such, it became a double top.

Therefore, these 100%R points provide us with major reward to risk opportunities, but it is also the market's way of suckering people in by taking a breather before violating the 100%R. Extreme highs and lows are very tricky areas that require much mental focus and subconscious observation in order for a trader to fully understand what the market is going to decide to do at these levels, and these levels will be left for further discussion in later chapters. Thankfully, Time Symmetry will be there for us as well in order to make things more palatable.

Retracement Remarks

With our conclusion of the discussion concerning the predefined retracement levels, we can focus on a few more areas of discussion in order to use retracements for our benefit. First and most important, is the concept of **Virgin Lines**. What most traders fail to do, because it is a laborious process, is to remove retracement lines from a chart once they are penetrated. Often times, traders leave these retracements on the chart, and the traders will continue to utilize the retracements as support/resistance once the retracement has already been violated and the market has started to create its inverse range. This is incorrect thinking because the market is continuously making new ranges that create new retracements. For example, a positive range that has a retracement leads to a negative range that has its own retracements, and on and on it continues until discreet highs/lows are breached based on Price Theory. In order to illustrate how we have to think, let us look at Figure 7.9.

Figure 7.9: Retracement Removal

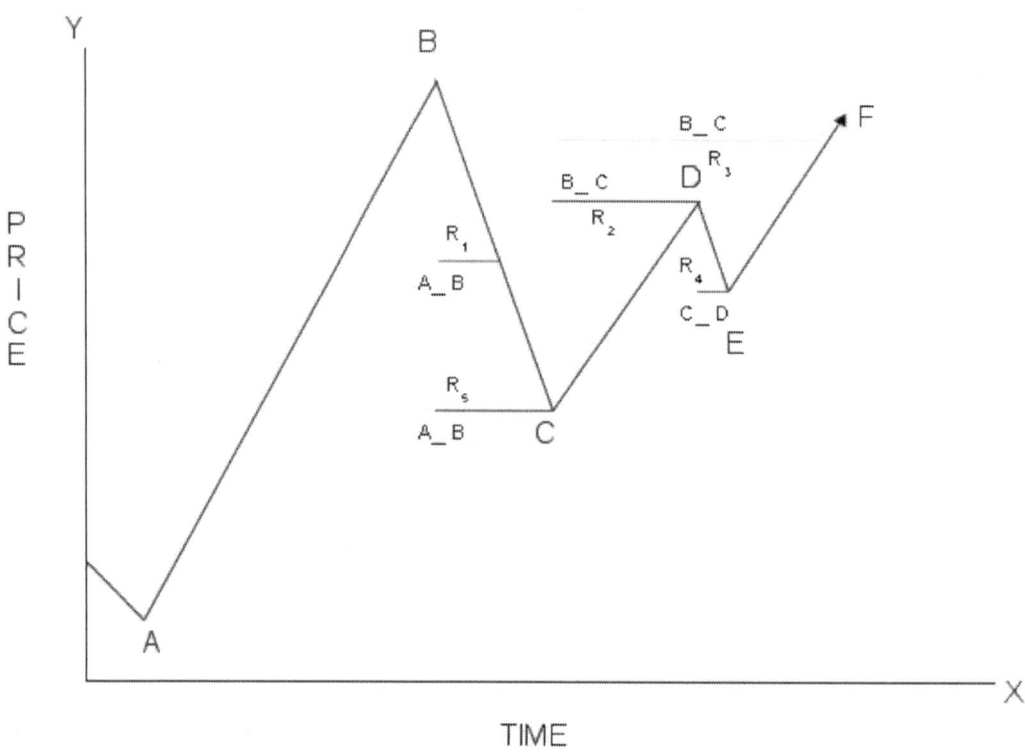

In Figure 7.9, we have the range A → B, which has a retracement range B → C, which is the reciprocal range. On the way to point C, the market blows through the first four retracements to find support at R_5. Let us call R_5 a 61.8%R. However, we observe that on the way to R_5, R_1 is taken out. As such, the trader needs to remove R_1 from the chart because it is now longer valid. It has been "penetrated." However, in the range C → D we observe a high at point D, which is a retracement of the B → C range. Let us say that R_2 our retracement of the B → C range, is a 75%R of B → C, but we observe that the price value of R_2 (point D) is equal to the price value of R_1 from our A → B range. This is irrelevant. R_1 is removed from the chart when the market penetrates the price level of D while creating the new B → C range. Finally, we see our market continue upward to the point F where R_3 equals the 87.5% retracement of B → C. Now, the question is, "Will we make a new high or a new low?" This example does not answer that question, but I merely state it to emphasize how are thinking needs to shift.

This discussion of virgin lines brings up another important topic if we were to simply ask, "When can we say a retracement line is penetrated?" In order to discuss this answer, we need to talk about the world tolerance. Unfortunately, tolerance is not exact, but as the range increases so does the tolerance given to each retracement before they are deemed as being penetrated. In addition, we have tolerances on both sides of a retracement. Sometimes we can fall short of reaching the retracement, and other times we can penetrate it by a tick or two and find support. However, the market is not random, and when we get to our discussion of mathematical cluster averages, we will learn how to find more exact support levels that are clustering near the retracement line. For now, we can become **a reaction trader**, which means that we can wait for a retracement level (or a mathematical support/resistance level) to hold, and then, if our stop-loss risk management rules allow, we can take a position in the market. Later, we will become **anticipatory traders,** when we introduce time, whereby we can use time to filter our trades in order to help us determine whether or not the mathematical support/resistance that the market approaches will hold. As such, as our skill evolves, we learn to anticipate that the market will reach a predefined inflection point, which is undeniably, extremely profitable because of the absolute conviction one can have in the market's follow through.

The last concept of this retracement chapter deals with an introduction of the trend. In a way, this is also an introduction to anticipatory trades as well. <u>When a trader is confident of the trend, a trader can purchase all of the retracement levels</u> (if we are dealing with an uptrend) as the market corrects back through down the primary range. We know from Price Theory that as long as our low/100%R (again in an uptrend) is not exceeded, our objective would be for the market to attain a new high outside of the given, primary range. Therefore, <u>all of the retracements have the same objective</u> if they hold, which is based on our conclusion of what the current trend is. Our task will be to balance our risk when purchasing all of the retracement levels because we could end up with a large position that has a very large risk of loss if our trend analysis is wrong. However, if our trend analysis is right, we can anticipate that one of the retracement levels from the 12.5%R to the 100%R may hold, which leads to a break of the 0%R, but as we have also learned, the 100%R, which is where our stop-losses would be place, may also require a tolerance, which will be discussed in Chapter 8. This, too is anticipatory, but it is much less powerful then Time Symmetry. However, it can be quite profitable if we are sure of the trend.

In summary, retracements are our first building blocks of understanding the true structure of the market that avails itself through a given range. Retracements are quantifiable, and when coupled with Price Theory, they can lead to a trading strategy in and of themselves. However, we have to properly make sure we are working with the right primary and secondary retracements at all times, which comes from our correct analysis of the discreet highs/lows discovery process discussed in the last chapter. As usual, I have also shifted the trader's thinking by introducing the concept of penetrated retracements, and how they can be removed from the chart as the market moves forward in time, which is tedious and necessary. Understanding retracements, and how they are designed to work, will be necessary as we build forward through price structure, but essentially, we have now properly covered the basic structure of the market itself. We now have to learn to recognize price patterns in the market movements itself in order to have further clarity on price objectives and price pattern objectives.

Chapter 8

Swings, Projections, Double Tops and Double Bottoms

Thus far, we have used Price theory to understand if a market is going to make a new high or a new low outside of a range based on analyzing what happens at various retracement levels. This chapter will serve to help us calculate where we can expect the market can go once we break out of any given primary range. In addition, we will discuss what it means in the market with respect to trend when the market breaks a given primary range, and in order to do so, I will introduce the concept of **Price Pattern Objectives**, which are calculations derived from the price action process that generates price patterns. After retracements, projections will be our second quantifiable mathematical support/resistance calculation, and I will describe different projection levels for different price patterns.

At this point, I must make it clear to the reader that Price Pattern Objectives are NOT the same as Price Objectives; projections are not the same as Price Objectives as well. As we can recall, Price Objectives are linked to what the market must adhere to based on Price Theory whereas Price Pattern Objectives/Projections help us decide where to possibly take profit, where to possibly to expect support/resistance, and where to possibly create cluster/averages. Therefore, we only have the *possibility* of what can occur at a given price level based on Price Pattern Objectives instead of what must happen based on Price Theory. In order to define a price pattern objective, we can say that it is a possible area of mathematical support or resistance that can serve as a market inflection point. To begin, I will make reference to the Figure that was introduced to us in Chapter 6, which is redefined as Figure 8.1 below.

Figure 8.1: Price Theory and Price Objectives

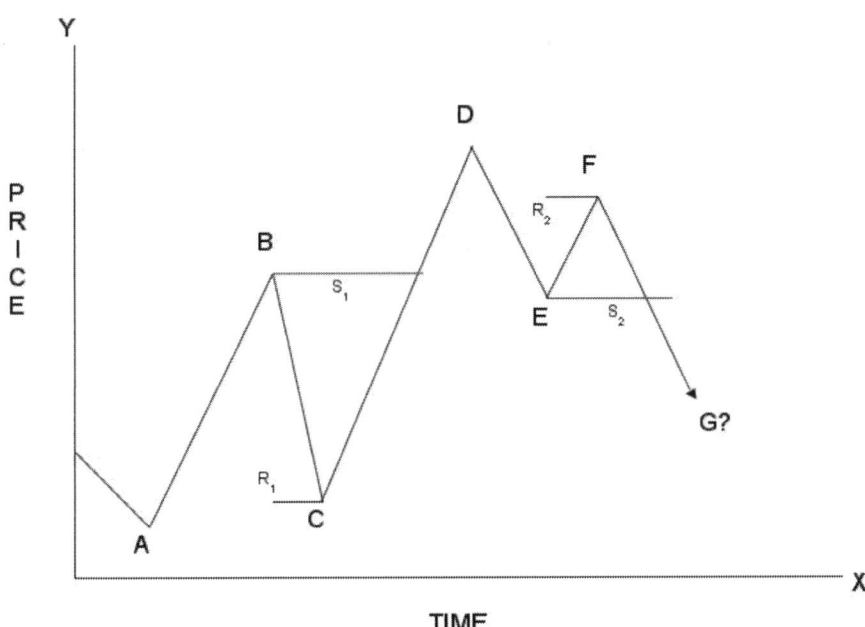

123

In Figure 8.1, we again have our range, A → B, which has a retracement down to point C. Now, we can again use Price Theory in order to tell us our target is new highs above point B. A break of point B erases our A→ B range, and we can define point B as our **Primary Swing Point**, S_1. Our primary swing point is the value at which a primary range is invalidated after a given retracement. The primary swing changes a secondary range/retracement range into a new primary range by being the first hint at a change in trend if the swing that is activated by a breach of the primary swing point meets the criterion of being a **Qualified Swing** as we will discuss later on in this chapter. We can see this type of secondary range/retracement range becoming a new primary range when the trend changes from being up after activating S_1 to being down once S_2 is activated. This is important and confusing for the reader to understand at this point, and to elaborate, I must say that the range D → E begins its life as a secondary range/retracement range of the primary, POSITIVE, range A → D. However, once point E is invalidated, we see that all points lower than E extend a primary, NEGATIVE range with point D being the base point of the range.

Using our first primary swing point in Figure 8.1, S_1, I can introduce **Swing Notation** in order to build off range notation. Swing notation is a three-part notation defined as either: **primary swings** or **additive swings**. Therefore, our base Swing Notation is represented as: $S_{p/a} : (T_A, P_A)$ → (T_B, P_B) → (T_C, P_C). As part of the notation, we see that we have two ranges. The first range A → B we will call our base range, and our second range B → C we will call our retracement range (or secondary range) as we have already discussed in Chapter 6. However, we must make sure our retracement range is a valid retracement of our base range. In addition, swing notation can be written in shorthand in the form as A → B → C, which some traders may have heard as an "ABC" swing or an "ABC correction." Both wordings can be used to define one of these corrective swings as well.

Our primary swing point can now be clarified based on these new definitions. The primary swing point is the point that causes our base range to be invalidated on a break to a new high/low where our terminal point of our base range is exceeded. In this case, point B. When the base range is exceeded, we know that discreet replacement occurs, and we are now building a new base range. If our primary swing point has been activated, we can now build additive swings off the new discreet that would form once point B is exceeded. However, let us go back to our primary swing point in order to understand what it means when we have a swing activate.

When we have a swing activate, the market is now extending its base range, and often times in bull markets when a market is extending a base range, it is moving into new areas of pricing. Therefore, they may not be retracements or mathematical clusters at these unknown, un-probed price levels. Therefore, we have to realize that whenever a swing activates, that swing has a corresponding range called a **Projection Range**, which begins at the terminal point (not the base point) of our Swing Notation. In the Figure 8.1 example, this Projection Range is added to point C for determining future, relevant price levels.

Essentially, the Projection Range is a pre-calculated range that is built off point C. The projection range is predefined by mathematical calculations, and we will either add or subtract price off our terminal point C in order to define possible terminal points for continued price action based of our Projection Range calculations. The basis for the mathematical calculation will be taking ratios of our base range, and adding/subtracting that to our terminal point in order to define our possible Projection Range values. (Note: we will have more than one possible terminal point for our Projection Ranges).

In order to define the calculation for our Projection Ranges, we will introduce **Projection Notation**. Projection Notation is defined as the equation: $P_{PN(A, B, C)} = (P_B - P_A) * P_N + P_C$ where P_N is a **Projection Percentage**, and A, B, C is our Swing. For our Projection Percentages, we will use the following values: 61.8%P, 100%P, 127.2%P, 161.8%P, 200%P, and 261.8%P. Once calculated, these derived numbers will be known as our **Projection Levels**. Also, we can use Range Notation in order to predefine our possible Projection Range if the terminal point of the Projection Range is equal to one of our calculated Projection Levels based on Projection Notation. We are only allowed to calculate these Projection Ranges once our swing activates by breaking any valid swing point be it primary or secondary.

In a way, these multiple ranges that are added to our terminal point of the retracement range can be used to anticipate where to take profits, or where to anticipate mathematical support/resistance will occur for possible market inflection points. Let us now look at Figure 8.2 in order to visualize our Projection Ranges/Levels, which will move us toward a discussion of the relevance of our projection levels.

Figure 8.2: Projection Levels

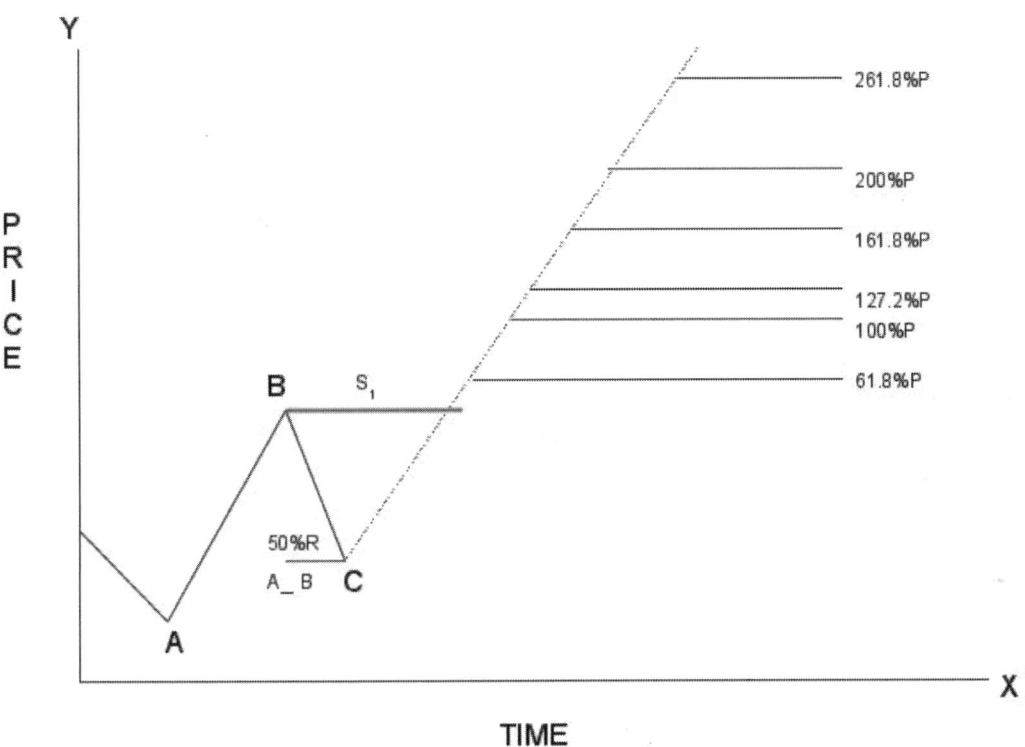

In Figure 8.2, we have a chart illustrating our possible Projection Levels that can be calculated when our swing activates. Visually, we can see the Projection Range that is generated once the swing activates. I ask the reader to please refer back to this chart as we define each of the projection percentages that yield these projection levels. Further, just like with retracements, each one of these projection percentages has their own set of characteristics that we must keep in mind in order to understand the full market structure. Also notable, just as we saw with retracements, the concept of projections is not new. In fact, it too is so common that it is usually built-in to most trading software applications as a Projection Tool. However, the knowledge that we can discuss regarding the relevance of each level requires a mental shift. Further, the way to use and understand what happens at this projection levels is part of understanding price structure. Therefore, just as we had the concept of "Virgin Retracement Lines," we also have the concept of "Virgin Protection Lines." Virgin Projection Lines are also removed from our chart once the market has violated/penetrated the given projection level.

61.8%P

This is probably the most well known of all the projections because it is built-in to most charting software packages as a predefined number in the settings of that software's projection tool. However, its use as a projection that leads to a market inflection point requires a discussion because this projection percentage is seldom helpful. However, by knowing when to focus on this projection level, we can then define the power of this projection percentage.

The reason that this projection percentage is seldom used is because this is the only projection percentage that is less than 1.00. Hence, the calculated projection level that is added to the terminal point is less than the size of the primary range, which can now be equated to a **wave** (waves will be studied further in Chapter 12). Because this percentage is less than 100%, the 61.8%P should be mostly ignored due to its small value *because it tends to appear below the swing point that makes it valid in the first place*. However, there are times when the 61.8%P can be extremely valuable as it was with calling the March 2009 low. Thus, the two criterions listed below are extremely important with respect to this projection percentage:

(A) Shallow Retracement Projections
(B) Elliott Wave Fifth Wave Calculations

Shallow retracements, as we can recall from the last Chapter, are retracements less than a 50%R, and that means that we have activated a swing that has a large base range with a small retracement range. Because the base range is large, the 61.8%P is useful in determining a shallow projection point that becomes valid because the market will tend to have a deeper retracement at some point. Thus, the 61.8%P becomes a market inflection point that keys the trader in to the possibility that if this level holds, the subsequent retracement of the expanded base range may no longer be shallow. Although this is a concise summary of criterion (A), this circuitous logic is immense, and I must follow this through with a figurative example.

Figure 8.3: 61.8%P Coupled With Deep Retracement

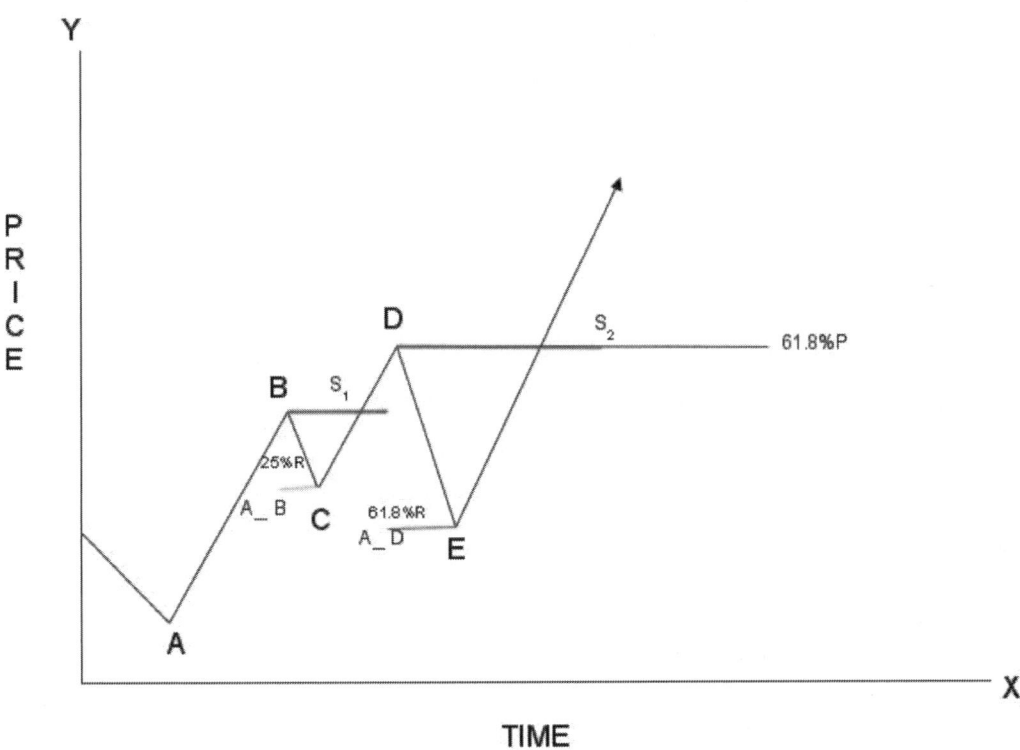

As the reader can visualize in Figure 8.3, we have the initial A → B → C primary swing that is based off of a 25%R of the A → B range. Because this is a shallow retracement projection, we see that the 61.8%P calls the market inflection point defined as point D. However, because the 61.8%P projection level held the market, we can be clued into on the future of the subsequent retracement. As we can see in the chart, this time, the market has a deep retracement to the 61.8%R of the A → D range, which is the only base range that is valid once point B was exceeded. Thus, once point E is reached at the 61.8%R, we can acquiesce to Price Theory in order to anticipate new highs over Point D, which may now target projection levels higher than the 61.8%P.

This knowledge has priceless value to the trader, and what is more, when we see a strong rally with a shallow retracement, we are further enforced on the logic as to whether or not the low formed as point A is a true low in the market. As such, this type of momentum based rally in the market coupled with understanding and visualizing our range expansion is useful in defining the possibilities of when a deeper retracement will start to form. As an aside, it will be quite interesting to see if the current market rally off the March 2009 low, which had a shallow retracement to implement the swing, will have a subsequent deep retracement before fulfilling its Price Theory objective of new highs over the November 2007 high.

As to Elliot Wave-based criteria (B), we will discuss this more in depth later, but it is just something to be made aware of at this time. In essence, it is based on a range expansion that yields a shallow retracement after a deep retracement; the inverse of the visualization of Figure 8.3

100%P

This is the most important of all the Projection Percentages. Like the 38.2%R and the 61.8%R, markets will typically encounter some type of support or resistance when reaching a 100%P. This could yield either a temporary pullback or a true market inflection point, which is why we need to focus on the price action when the market reaches this predefined projection level.

This level is also the Price Pattern Objective for every and any swing. This means that the 100%P can be thought of as a potential target once the swing activates, but only time will prove if this is a terminal point for a given market because it is NOT a Price Objective based on price Theory. As such, this Projection Level is a good area to consider taking partial profits or total profits, but it may not be a good level to reverse unless we are anticipating that we are in an A → B → C corrective swing as the next paragraph will discuss.

Just like the 61.8%P, there are inferences we can make by observing the markets reaction to this projection level. Primarily, we have to understand that this level can be the conclusion of a corrective swing. Again, this knowledge is relevant to Elliot Wave Theory, and it will be elaborated on in Chapter 12 as well, but for now, I simply ask the reader to keep in mind that if a trader observes that the 50%R held the market, which led to the swing activation, then, there is a higher probability that the 100%P will be a true market inflection point. Hence, these A → B → C swings are quite powerful because they can foreshadow that the market is now ready to adhere to its primary, underlying trend, which will be the inverse of the direction of this swing! As such, we can surmise that the market's reaction to the 100%P as the Price Pattern Objective can give us a clue as to if we are witnessing a true, new trend change, or if we are simply finishing a correction inside of the previous trend, which also yields a conclusion.

Should a 100%P level be breached immediately without much price action occurring at this projection level, then, we can determine that the change in trend indicated by the swing is legitimate. Therefore, the 100%P level can be thought of as the last line of defense for a market's prior trend while simultaneously serving as the possible inflection point to resume the trend.

127.2%P

This is the least known of all the projection levels by the masses, but it is extremely relevant. It has acute power in predicting where a double bottom or a double top will find major support or resistance once fulfilling the Price Pattern Objective of the Double Top/Bottom, as we will discuss later in this chapter. Moreover, there is a certain type of double top/bottom called an inconspicuous double top/bottom, which tends to foreshadow a 127.2%P for calling the end of that price pattern just like in an A → B → C correction. As such, we must remember that no matter the time frame, the 127.2%P has strength when we are looking at these types of patterns, and although the reader's vocabulary and acumen may not be ready for this figurative example, it simply belongs in this discussion regarding the 127.2%P.

Figure 8.4: 100%P & 127.2%P

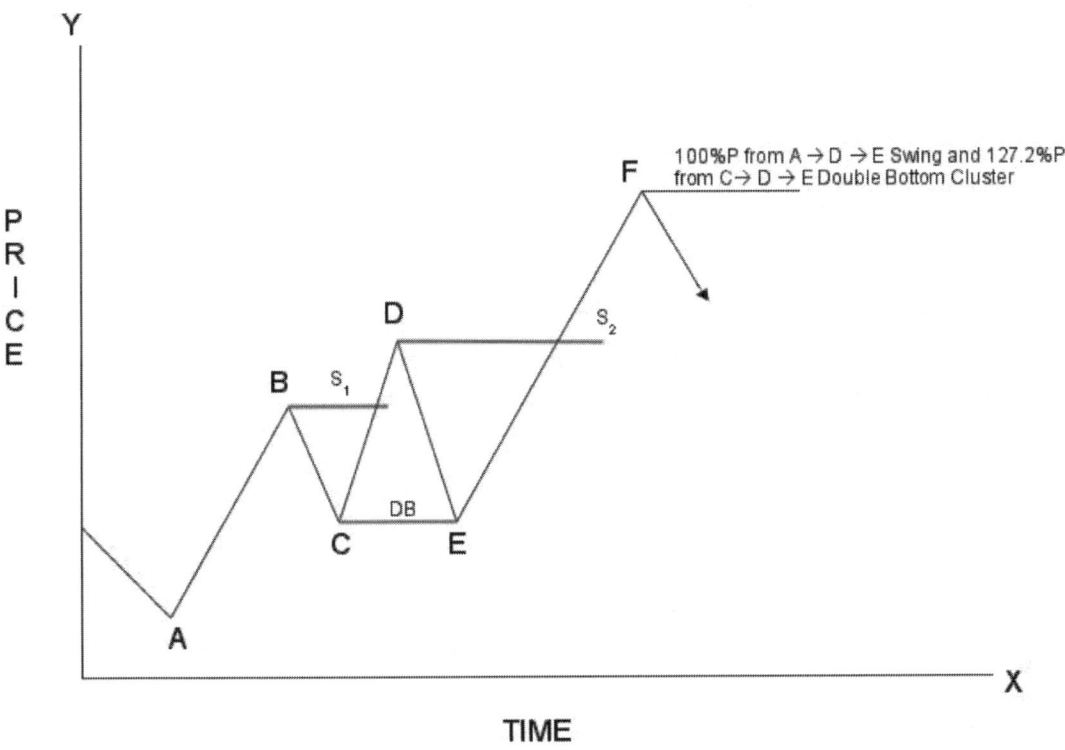

In Figure 8.4, the reader can visualize an inconspicuous double bottom that is formed at a primary, secondary range's terminal point. Further, the reader can visualize a larger swing shown as the A → D → E swing. This is not the primary swing on the chart, but it is very important to see that the 100%P of that **additive swing** and the 127.2%P of the double bottom shown as C → D → E are equal in terms of their relevant projection price pattern objective. In other words, one can say that the price pattern objective for the additive swing and for the inconspicuous double bottom were mathematically equal, and as such, the market may have found a terminal market inflection point, which means that a new downtrend can be started based on the down arrow shown off of point F.

I should mention that the 127.2%P is still relevant for our a standard swing as a projection percentage, and because of how little it is known to the masses, it can be quite powerful for calling market moves. Therefore, it should also be watched for like any other projection percentage, and if we are in a bigger trend type of trading day, a market can often find resistance at its 100%P during the lunch hour, which may confuse people by thinking that we have seen the end of the trend move as discussed when we talked about the 100%P. However, after lunch, it is quite common for the market to resume its original trend, and the 127.2%P ends up being the high for the day based on a larger swing pattern that was activated in the morning. Hence, this level can be quite useful for daytraders.

161.8%P, 200%P, and 261.8%P & New Price Territory

The last three Projection Levels have the most relevance during fast moving markets, markets that have continuous shallow retracements, or markets that have reached new all-time highs (or lows, but lows are much more rare). During high volatility, these Projection Levels will serve as the only remaining calculation areas of mathematical support/resistance, especially, when we are dealing with a market that has reached new all-time highs. Obviously, when we reach a new all-time high, we have no retracements on the chart from a prior range, and when that occurs, we will only have a few structural components left in order to define market inflection points. Basically, we only have projections and time cycles/repetitions when markets are in new price territory.

When a market reaches new price territory, we have to think of the market like a baby taking its first steps or like the mars rover moving forward for the first time. When new price territory is obtained by a trading instrument, the market needs to understand how price action feels about this new territory, and it can only get that feeling by discovering higher prices and retracing micro-ranges within those higher prices. Therefore, in new price territory, the underlying trading instrument is quite literally creating a new backbone to its Marketome when it is dealing with new all-time highs (or lows). Therefore, us market participants are crucial in the formation of this new structure at these new levels.

It is amazing how people have remained in the dark about this concept on why stocks tend to bubble once hitting new all-time highs. Quite simply, it is because there is not a lot of mathematical resistance left on the chart; mostly, it is just support. Therefore, we can have confidence in the fact that a stock that has finally broken out to the upside will want to continue to probe higher price levels that it has never reached before. This probing part of the price discovery process is very important for the reader to understand. It is necessary that the reader get this concept because the imagination must visualize that there is something *behind* the chart itself; something hidden and intangible. But as time moves forward and as this new price area is sufficiently probed, we can understand that the Marketome reaches a point of fulfillment, which brings back the rational components of *Time and Price Symmetry*. However, at these new price areas, every buyer and seller is contributing to the future movements of the stock based on the present moment price discovery process! Hence, the validity of waiting for a stock to reach one of these larger projection percentages because they are the only levels remaining on the chart until enough time has passed to create new discreet highs/lows that can yield Price Structure components.

As a corollary to understanding what happens when markets are in new price territory, when we are dealing with Time, it is irrelevant if we are at a new all-time high or not because the time cycle/repetition will kick in regardless of the underlying price level. In essence, the time cycle/repetition that is awaiting the stock will be more powerful then anything else when a stock is in new territory because that time cycle/repetition is also one of the few underlying structural components that exist within the nature of the market itself. Unlike price, we can see that this time component does not need to be probed. This time component is already established before we venture into this new price territory. *This time component does not care about price.*

However, we must also be aware of these Projection Levels when we are working with mathematical cluster averages, but we must also be aware that these Projection Levels may NOT be the current Price Pattern Objective. That is because we undoubtedly have created additive swings or new, qualified swings that are serving as the Price Pattern Objective (the 100%P). Therefore, we can use these higher Projection Levels of our first swing in order to determine possible mathematical clusters at our new Price Pattern Objective. As an example of this, if the reader was to go back to the Figure 10.3 example but forget the existing numbers, the reader can visualize that the A → B → C primary swing and the A → D → E additive swing may have aligned Price Pattern Objectives. For instance, the A → B → C 161.8%P may be the same as the A → D → E 100%P, which forms our mathematical cluster.

Qualified Swings

Now that we have our understanding of what a swing looks like along with the price projections that it provides, we can now introduce a swing's relevance to the trend. As a pure textbook definition, a **qualified swing** that leads to a trend change must be a swing that meets the following two criterions:

(A) The retracement range of the swing is 50% or greater
(B) The time between the base range's discreet base point (Point A of an A → B → C swing) to the terminal point of the retracement range (Point C) is at least 30 minutes. Meaning $T_C - T_A \geq 30$.

Once these two criteria are met and the swing activates, we can say the trend has changed either to being up or to being down. (I will illustrate the power of a qualified swing in the next chapter via several examples.) In addition, I ask the reader to notice that for the first time, I am introducing time as a filter to our thinking with relation to a price structure component. However, we also need to point out that sometimes condition (A) does not have to be met for a swing to be a qualified swing that changes the trend. In fast moving markets, when we have shallow retracements that meet criteria (B) we can see the trend change by the strength of the underlying market, and being able to rely on subconscious thought processes for the recognition of the trend change is of extreme importance that cannot be quantified.

As part of the discussion of Qualified Swings, I need to elaborate on criteria (B). Obviously, (B) is in reference to day trading, which is unarguably a subset of the overall market. However, the 30-minute rule is not equitable to 30-bars as was the discreet filtering shown in Chapter 6. As such, when we get to the trend, we will introduce the basic trend chart, which is a 60-minute chart (hourly chart), and in that discussion I will assert that the true trend changes when we have a 15-bar swing on a 60-minute chart.

Trading Swings & Additive Swings

Naturally, swing trading can be difficult on us as traders because of the market's inability to trend, and over the years, this trending nature has been in decline since the advent of computerized trading. However, there is an anticipation factor that we can start to discuss with respect to swings. Unknowingly, the reader has already been taught this anticipation factor by understanding the concept of Price Theory. Price Theory is telling us to anticipate the activation of a given swing if a given retracement holds the market (i.e. if a high/low is validly defended.) Therefore, the discussion that focused on using retracements of a range as areas to go long or to go short inside of that range holds validity here, but without time or without proper trend identification, this type of mentality is a way in which we can get in trouble by forecasting/anticipating. Thus, the trader must be aware of the evolving nature of understanding all of the facets of *Time and Price Symmetry* in order to become true anticipatory traders.

On the other hand, trading swings has a definitive set of rules for us as traders, which means that there is no ambiguity as to whether a trader should trade swings or not. Let me be clear, trading swings is the most profitable way of trading as long as they are qualified swings. However, as a corollary, if they are to be traded, then, EVERY swing must be taken regardless of the frequency. As such, a market will always have an applicable swing unless it is at new all-time highs or lows, which means we can setup orders to execute upon the breach of a swing point – long or short beforehand. In essence, if we are longer term/momentum traders, we will have ample time to set stop-based order entries based on outstanding swing points.

Now, we can define a **swing trader**, and all *Time and Price Symmetry* traders are swing traders to some degree because when all else fails, we have to remember to take every qualified swing in order to get us back in touch with the underlying trend. Yes, swing trading, as time can be our most important ally when we hit confusion. Thus, a swing trader is a person who goes long or goes short in the market upon the activation of a Qualified Swing. Often times, we can have a long or a short qualified swing existing at the same time depending on the time and the market's location in relevant ranges.

As foreshadowed in the last paragraph, the way in which a swing trader can enter the market is to place a stop-loss order one-tick higher or lower than current swing point, which is the terminal point for our base range. Unfortunately, for most swing traders, the market does not always follow-through in a clean way that allows us to mentally relax or be confident of the trade. If one was to go back and analyze commodity charts from the 70s and the 80s, one will get an angry reminiscence of how easy swing trading was before the advent of technology. In fact, W.D. Gann's entire theory was based upon "Gann Swings."

However, just as swing trades have predefined entry criteria, swing traders also must utilize the rules for placing protective stops. Just like every swing trade must be taken if one is to be a swing trader, then, every stop-loss rule must be adhered to. Therefore, a **swing stop-loss** must be placed one tick higher/lower than the terminal point of the retracement range of a swing, which would be one tick lower/higher of point C of an A → B → C swing. Obviously, if it is a long swing, we go one tick lower than Point C, and if it is a short swing, we place our stop-loss one tick higher than our terminal Point C. Let us revisit a Figure from earlier that is now shown as Figure 8.5. This Figure is helpful to the reader by allowing him or her to visually understand this concept.

Figure 8.5: Deep Retracements and Three Higher Bottoms / Triple Swings

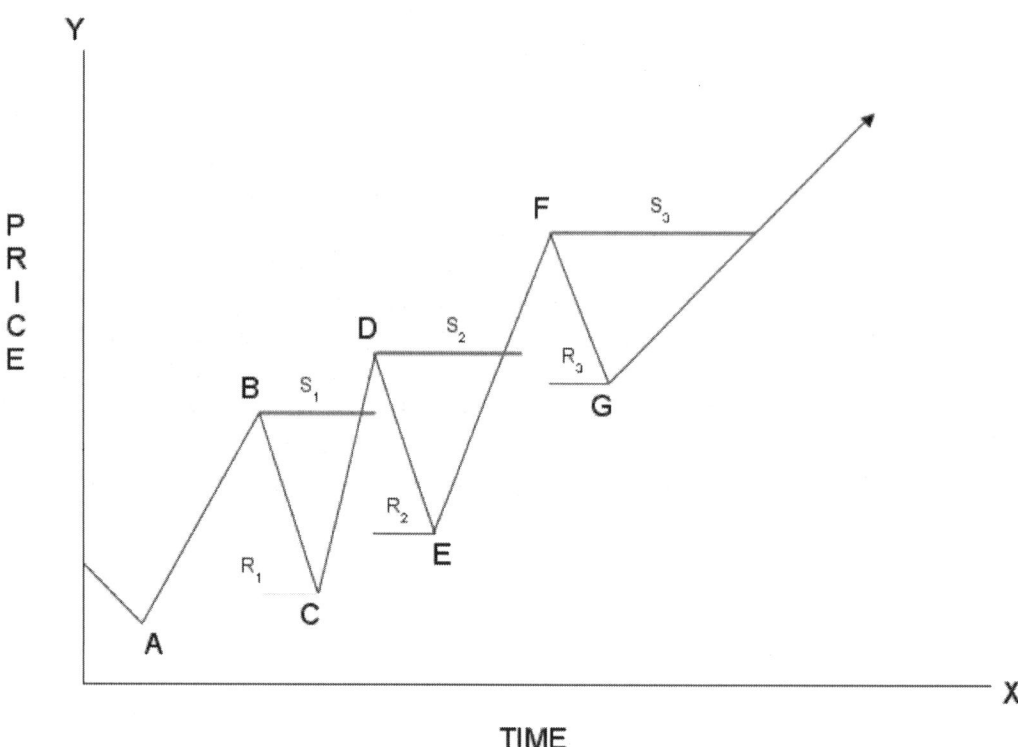

In Figure 8.5, we have three swings, S_1, S_2, and S_3 with corresponding swing points, B, D, and F. Our first swing is a primary swing and can be notated as S_P: $(T_A, P_A) \rightarrow (T_B, P_B) \rightarrow (T_C, P_C)$. In our Figure, we see that the market takes out our swing point for this swing, B, and a swing trader would go long the market at a break of B with a corresponding stop-loss one tick lower than point C, which is the terminal point of the swing. However, after our swing activates, we see that our example market swings right back, which challenges the conviction of the swing trader. This is common for the market because the market will want to shake as many traders as it can out of the market. However, we now form a second swing, which would activate at a break of point D. This swing would be an additive swing since we already had a swing activate, which should have gotten us into the market in the first place. We can write this swing as $S_A : (T_A, P_A) \rightarrow (T_D, P_D) \rightarrow (T_E, P_E)$. Here, even though I have used the generic term "additive" to describe these secondary swings, the trader can decide to use the "additive" swing to add to his or her position on the activation of this second swing, which means the trader would add to his position on a breach of point D. In general, a good filter to determine if we should add to a swing is based on our secondary retracement, which is R_2 in Figure 8.5. If R_2 is greater than a 50%R of our new base range, A $\rightarrow$ D, then we can add to our position on a break of point D, and also, move our stop-loss to a tick lower than our new terminal point, E. ***We would move our stop on both positions.*** However, in our example market of Figure 8.5, once S_2 activates, the market swings back down into our range by having a third retracement, R_3. Visually, we see that R_3 is a shallow retracement of the A $\rightarrow$ F range, but technically, we do have a new additive swing: $S_A : (T_A, P_A) \rightarrow (T_F, P_F) \rightarrow (T_G, P_G)$, but this may not be a qualified swing based on the retracement! Even so, it may not be qualified because it has a shallow retracement, the third swing is still additive once it activates at a breach of point F. However, because this swing has a shallow retracement, the trader has to decide two things:

(1) Do I add to my position on this third additive swing?
(2) Do I move my stop-loss to the new terminal point, G?

Sadly, there is no right answer, but in general, you must adhere to your risk management rules. Remember, money/risk management supercedes any trading strategy. Furthermore, I believe that with the market's continual loss of trending, that a swing trader must give swings as much room as possible to work in order to handle the subsequent retracement ranges that follow after the initial swing has activated. Therefore, the bigger the stop that you can afford, the better the probability for the trade, which is why a lot of swing traders actually place smaller positions at the break of the swing point because they often require large stop values. Thus, a good concept to remember about any additive swing is that it should also be a qualified swing. Graphically, we can now understand how to trade swings and how to build into a position, which is a useful concept for Investors as well as traders. Now, we have to get back to the actuality of the market, which requires us to acknowledge the stop-seeking tendency of the market, and in order to destroy any notion that swings are an easy strategy; I will introduce Figure 8.6 in order to describe a swing failure.

Figure 8.6: Swing Failure and Swing Retests

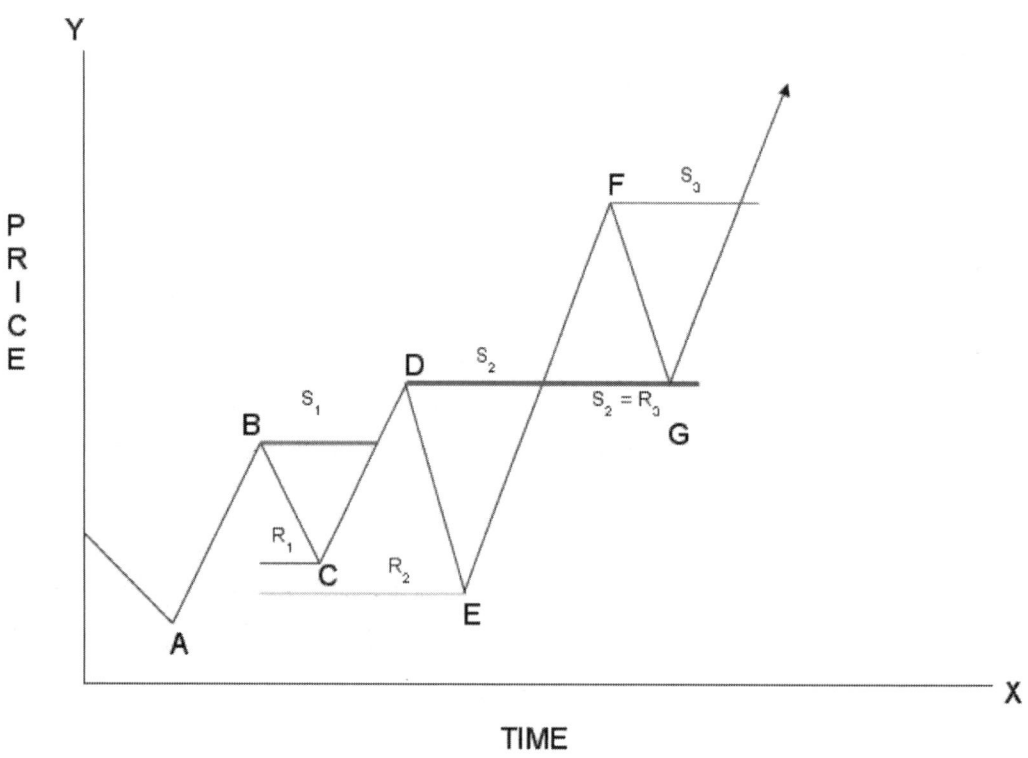

Just as swing traders have their convictions tested by stops, they will also have their convictions tested by failed swings. Now, I must differentiate between swings. Sometimes, there are swings that do not seem to follow-through quickly. This is not a failure. Remember, if you take the swing, you must put the stop where it is supposed to go. Only when that stop is activated, does the swing become a failed swing. Therefore, in order to be successful, a swing trader has to remember to keep trading swings, which can cause multiple reversals as times and ranges get bigger/wider. Bear in mind, swings will become the basis for the trend, and at some point, the market *will* trend. These are the examples that I have tried to instill via Figure 8.6.

In Figure 8.6, we have the swing $S_P : (T_A, P_A) \rightarrow (T_B, P_B) \rightarrow (T_C, P_C)$ that activates at S_1, which is a break of point B. In fact, this happens in our Figure, but immediately after, the market reversed to take all stops out at point C. We notice that point E does not take out our discreet A, which is in our base range, and therefore, because A is still valid, our negative range (retracement range) D → E is a deep retracement shown as R_2 of our new base range A → D. This forms a new primary swing: $S_P (T_A, P_A) \rightarrow (T_D, P_D) \rightarrow (T_E, P_E)$, which activates at S_2 or a break of point D. This is the second qualified swing that forms and executes on the chart. However, this time, the market does not take out our stops placed one tick lower than point E. No, what we see is that the market follows through to a new high, and now, the market has a shallow retracement. But, there is something interesting about that shallow retracement, and something that is more than interesting, something extraordinarily important.

134

Swing Point Retests

In Figure 8.6, I ask the reader to see that the shallow retracement that happens based on the A → F Range to point R_3 is equal to our swing activation point for the A → D → E swing. This is not random, and this is extremely powerful as a trade entry mechanism because not only do we have a swing retest point serve as a mathematical support number, but often, we will have a corresponding retracement make that mathematical cluster reinforced. Therefore, whenever a swing activates, the trader must draw horizontal lines from our swing points to have memory to see where swings have activated in the past (the color-coding of these swings also helps us to remember the underlying trend). Furthermore, these swing points do not expire in any given way, and these swing points can be useful years later on a daily chart. As a fictitious example, if there was a stock that broke over its 2001 high in 2003, when the market came back down in 2008, the 2001 high may have served as a support that called those stocks low in 2008/2009 crash. That is how powerful swing retests can be. Therefore, it is important to label the swing points on our chart as these horizontal lines because unlike the concept of "Virgin lines" with retracements or with projections, swing points can be utilized for trading opportunities in the future. Again, we can look at our A → D → E swing in Figure 11. After reaching an arbitrary new high after S_2 activates, the market comes back down to point G. Point G is obviously the same primary retracement of A → F, and it is also the secondary retracement of E → F. More important though is that it was also our previous swing point, which was point D. Therefore, this price action can properly define a **swing retest.**

Swing retests are important because they allow swing traders to re-enter the market if they missed the initial swing entry, but more likely, when a market comes back down to retest a swing point, the market is trying to take out swing traders who got into the swing properly and have moved their stops to break-even. By retesting the swing point, the market is trying to take out traders who placed their stops at their entry. (In future editions of this book, we will look at several examples of the power of swing retests for trade inceptions.)

With the prior discussion of a swing retest, we have now covered all of the technical nature regarding swings. It is also important to mention that this type of swing trading can be called *Gann Swings*, because W.D. Gann observed the power that time plays in the role of adequate swing trades, and since we are always in a mindset to discuss Price in Time with relation to the market, I must give Gann credit for this observation. As we move forward in this text, we will discuss more tendencies such as swing retests, but the knowledge of the proper implementation of swings is enough to build a very powerful trading strategy. Especially for investors who are using bigger swings on a daily bar chart. In essence, a fundamental fund can add in swings as technical criteria, and undoubtedly, their performance would increase 10-fold.

Double Bottoms and Double Tops

The importance of double bottoms ("DB") and double tops ("DT") is so extreme that I could write a whole book of examples and a whole book of explanations on DBs or DTs. However, upon inspection, these chart patterns are glorified swings with their own price pattern objectives and their own relevant price projections. The problem with double bottoms and double tops is the tolerance level that is given between two tops or two bottoms. Granted, that tolerance level is hard to quantify, but it pails in comparison to how profitable and important these price structure components are. Therefore, I must yield to the most obvious double top of all time that was completely ignored by nearly every market participant I have ever heard speak regarding this time period. Of course, the example I am speaking of is the S&P 500 Index's double top between 2000 and 2007.

To begin this example, I must again reiterate to the reader that, as always, we have to remember that every concept of this book works in any time frame, which means we are constantly looking at the same price patterns in ratio to expanding time periods. This is a hard concept to grasp with out the visualization of a chart in multiple time frames. To many, the 2008 crash was one of the hardest markets to trade in our lifetime. However, that is simply because the masses did not have the knowledge of double tops along with knowing their relevant Price Pattern Objectives, which I argue is *my own* defined assertion and more powerful then the basic definition of a double top. So, in order to understand the power of my assertion, let us talk through the real-life example that most people just lived through.

The S&P 500 index made a high in March of 2000. It then came down to a low in October of 2002 (this is coincidentally an inconspicuous double bottom with the low in July of 2002, but let us stay with our double top example in respect to 2008). At the time when the October of 2002 occurred, we know that we are essentially in a very wide range that can be linked from the 1987 low to the 2000 high. We can also choose to link the terminal low of the S&P going back over 100 years to the 2000 high as well. In either case, we can invoke Klatch's Price Theory in order to tell us that the market has failed to take out a new low, and therefore, it must take out a new high over the March of 2000 high. (In order to discuss this Range-low when talking about a long time frame in regards to an index, we must realize that the lowest low would basically be 0 because we are looking at the lowest low in the market to the highest high, but we may choose to look at a secondary low such as the one in 1987. Essentially, because the lowest low of an index would in effect be zero, we have intrinsically stated a possible proof as to why the market will trend higher. The market cannot go below zero!)

Anyway, after making the October 2002 low, the market staged a five-year rally to the high in November of 2007, which completed the Price Theory price objective of exceeding the March 2000 high. I ask the reader to pause and think about the power of Klatch's Price Theory for a moment… Moving on, the important observation is that the November of 2007 high did not take out the previous high by a big margin, and in fact, the November 2007 high did not exceed 2% of the previous high in March of 2000. The market then began a move lower after making the November 2007 high, and once a bigger picture swing occurred on the daily chart to the downside, the market indicated the trend has turned down. Once a double top has been made and confirmed by a qualified downswing, the trader can ascertain a higher probability in the efficacy of the double top being real because In effect, the market has just created and confirmed a 7-year double top by generating the relevant downswing!

Now, here is where the magic happens, and here is where my knowledge surpassed my mentors. If we go back to Price Theory, we recall that if we fail to make a new high, we must make a new low. In this case, though, we did make a new high, which fulfilled the price objective discussed in the prior paragraph. In fact, when we broke the 2000 high, the market activated a new swing trade that was just over 20 years in the making (hint: Time Structure repetition cycle: Oct/Nov 1987 to Nov 2007). Using what we now know about swings, once the market activated this 20-year swing, the respective stops had to be placed below the 2002 low, which we know is the terminal point of the retracement range of the swing. As such, not only is the activation of the longer-term swing that occurs in November of 2007 result in a swing failure, but due to the price proximity that existed between the two highs, we have formed a double top. What do we know about swing failures and double tops? Essentially those two price structure components have *the same Price Pattern Objective*! (Note: swing failures are not always equal to double tops/bottoms.) Furthermore, with respect to double tops/bottoms, I ask the reader to notice that I am using price pattern objectives instead of price objectives because we do have failed double tops and failed double bottoms in the market, which means these patterns are not constrained purely by Klatch's Price Theory *only* when the secondary top/bottom has exceeded the first. Thus, I can now fill in the blank for my mentor who failed to see the light with respect to Double Tops and Double Bottoms, and I will define their price pattern objectives as:

(1) The price pattern objective of a double top is to take out the low between the two tops.

(2) The price pattern objective of a double bottom is to take out the high between the two bottoms.

Simple enough, right? Now, getting back to our example of the 2008/2009 crash, the magnitude of the crash was remarkably easy to define simply by knowing the knowledge of the Price Pattern Objectives for DBs and DTs. Concisely, the price pattern objective for the 7-year double top was simply to take out the 2002 low (in regards to the S&P500 Cash Index). Again, as we will learn in later discussion regarding confirmation signals of Double Bottoms and Double Tops, the downswing that occurred in early 2008 after the larger 2007 swing activated on the daily chart, gave us the all clear signal that this was a valid double top! It was an all clear signal to reverse because this double top (just like a swing failure) had a goal to take out the stops placed under the October of 2002 low.

Again, I must ask the reader to pause and just think about this for a second. How many PhDs, market wizards, hedge fund managers, technical analysts, and people who are supposed to be the best traders in the world appeared on CNBC during the crash making all kinds of nonsensical predictions about various support levels, theories, fundamental research, historical comparisons, and on and on and on. They did this nonsensical dance because the truth is, the only thing that really happened in 2008 is that we had a single double top that was fulfilling its Price Pattern Objective! A four year old who knows what a double top is would have beaten any PhD on CNBC in 2008. Guaranteed.

Now, things are not always sunny, and even in our 2008 crash example, we can visualize a major issue with Double Bottoms and Double Tops. Sometimes, they take out a new high or low, which generates a swing. As such, how do we decide when a double top/double bottom is valid? Unfortunately, we do not have a definitive checklist because often, the ranges that lead to double tops/bottoms have already fulfilled their objective based on Price Theory, and as we now know, Price Pattern Objectives are not conclusive. That being said, we have three sets of criteria in order to *help us* define a trading edge with respect to understanding the validity that a double top/double bottom will reach its price pattern objective. These three criteria are:

(1) A swing forms in the opposite direction. For our 2008 crash example, once we formed our double top in November of 2007, the market generated a downswing in early 2008 on the daily bar chart, which acted as our first confirmation of the double top's authenticity as has been discussed. Again, this concept can be transmuted to intra-day trading by observing when a Qualified Swing forms after our relevant top/bottom.

(2) The 38.2% retracement of the range that is created from the low/high in the double top/bottom to the secondary low/high has been breached by a certain tolerance. Since we have discussed the fact that markets will tend to bounce off the 38.2% retracement for some type of inverse retracement, we can use the knowledge of the 38.2% retracement breach to give us favorable reward to risk. Essentially, our reward is 61.8% or more of the remaining range and our stop is 38.2% of that range.

(3) Third, we can use time cycles/repetitions in order to give us a better idea as to if this double top/bottom will hold.

At this point, we can discuss (1) and (2). We will get to (3) in Chapter 20. Quantitatively, we can actually define strict trade-logic for our entry criteria in regards to (1) and (2). I will use Figure 8.7 to describe these two entry methods visually, and I will also discuss the price pattern objectives and the corresponding stop placement rules for DBs and DTs.

Figure 8.7: Quantitative Double Top Entries

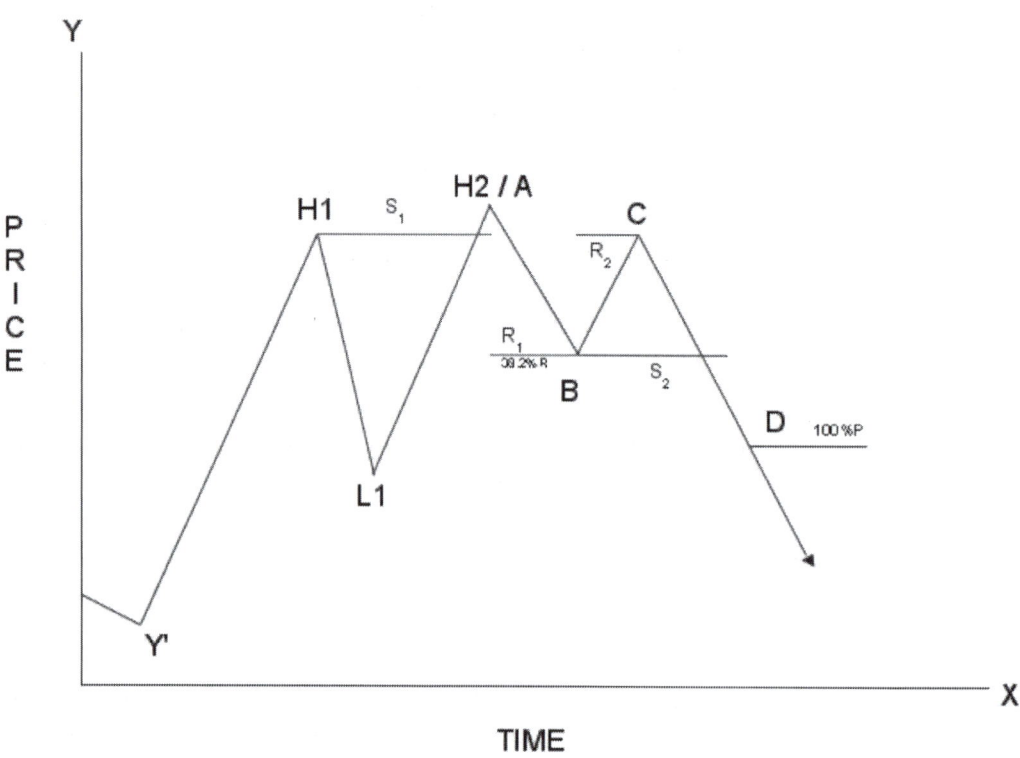

In Figure 8.7, we see a pattern similar to the 7-year double top in the S&P 500 Cash Index. We have a high, H_1, followed by a low, L_1, and finally, a second high, H_2. Here, $H_2 > H_1$, and a swing is generated at the break of S_1, which we know as our primary swing point. However, H_2 is barely greater than H_1, and for the sake of argument, let us assume that the second high falls into our tolerance to be classified as a Double Top. What we see happen is that the market comes down to retrace the $L_1 \rightarrow H_2$ range, which is our secondary range / our retracement range. This retracement, R_1, we will define as a 38.2%R of the retracement range. This is very important to understand. We are using the low between the two tops, we are not looking at the retracement for our primary range, which is $Y' \rightarrow H_2$. As such, we are singling out the secondary 38.2%R not the primary retetracement's 38.2%R, and this clarifies criteria (2).

After finding support at this retracement, R_1, the market starts to move higher, but it fails to take out a new high above H_2. Therefore, it must make a new low by Price Theory. Now, we have an A → B → C swing form that gets triggered at a break of point B, which is also a primary swing point on the downside (the primary swing of our negative range). Now, as we know, swings DO NOT give us price objectives, but just like DBs/DTs they do give us Price Pattern Objectives. As such, when we have an existing double top/bottom, we can relinquish the swing's Price Pattern Objectives/Projections because the double top in Figure 8.7 is much more powerful than the swing. In essence, we can rank the double top's importance higher than downswing because the Double Top is adhering to Price Theory, which means it has a price objective whereas the swing only has a price pattern objective. As such, the double top invalidates the 100%P of the swing, but that 100%P is not completely meaningless because it could be a level of mathematical support that leads to another retracement of the negative range that is being continuously generated by the market's further action to the downside.

Since we relinquish the swing's Price pattern Objectives to that of the commanding Double Top, we let the Price Pattern Objective for the Double Top be activated, and coincidentally the Price Pattern Objectives for double tops are equal to Price Theory Price Objectives if the secondary top is lower than the first top. However, for this example this is not true. In any event, the price pattern objective for the double top now becomes a new low below L_1. We can further conclude that the swing is our entry by criteria (1), but we are using the DT objective in order to maximize profit. In addition, this example is a dual extrapolation of criterion (2) because our swing and our 38.2%R breach occur at the same point, which is actually common! As discussed, we essentially have a 1.5:1 reward to risk ratio at this price level, and we may even have much more than that depending on how far the market follows through below L1. This means we have a trading edge, and I have alluded to an edge many times, but it should now be defined.

A **trading edge** is a price/time structured pattern or repetition that gives us higher odds of a favorable outcome (profit) then a potential loss; this can either be derived from favorable reward/risk scenarios or from knowing the percentage probability that a price pattern/time window has for a follow-through. Concurrently, a trading edge can be thought of as knowing the future profit potential of a scenario, which is in effect a contradiction to the *Efficient Market Hypothesis* as well. We will now conclude all of our discussions by discussing proper implementations of DBs/DTs.

Stop Placements, Profit Tendencies, Inconspicuous DBs/DTs, and DB/DT Failures

As we know, markets like to seek stops in order to take most traders out of the market, which is a proverbial mind-screw. As such, proper stop placement is crucial in giving DB/DTs room to work. Going back to our Figure 8.7 example, when we entered that Double Top trade by a swing, we chose to adhere to our Price Pattern Objective of the DT instead of the swing's. As such, we must do the same thing with our stop loss; we have to relinquish the stop loss to that of the DT instead of the stop loss of the swing because the DT is more powerful than our swing, and in essence, we can say the double top has *taken-over* our swing trade. Therefore, we can define stops for DBs/DTs as follows:

A **double top stop-loss** is placed a tick *or two* higher than the greater of the two tops.
A **double bottom stop-loss** is placed a tick *or two* lower than the lesser of the two bottoms.

Talking about stops means that of course we can have failed DBs/DTs, which we have already discussed because of defining our objectives in terms of the price pattern, which does not have to conform to Price Theory when a secondary top exceeds the first or when a secondary bottom exceeds the first. However, when dealing with double tops, this is irrelevant. The fact is that when a double top/bottom trades fail, we have to realize what they become, and what most people do not realize is that when a DB or a DT fail, *the stop-loss to exit the failed DB/DT is actually placed at the new entry for a primary swing point*. As such, a failed DB/DT leads to a very powerful swing in the reverse direction, which often times, has a much higher probability of following through because the market has had prior difficulty going above/below that given price level of the DT/DB. When we discuss market tendencies, we will observe that the more times a given high/low is challenged, the less likely it is to hold; thus, the break to a new high may have more momentum. In fact, as we will discuss later, we can sometimes get triple, quadruple, pentacle DBs/DTs, which are even more powerful swings. Therefore, stops on DB/DT trades should often be placed not only to exit the current position at a loss, but to reverse the position in the direction of the break, which often times can quickly recover any loss that has occurred. Again, I must reiterate what I said about swing trading: If you are a swing trader, you must take all the swings for them to be profitable including DB/DT failures.

In order to emphasize this reversal-type trading with a real-life example, I ask the reader to look at Oracle Corporation's Stock Price between the end of 2011 and the middle of 2012 (ticker: ORCL). What the reader would find is that there was a perfect DB that occurred in May of 2012, with a previous bottom that was achieved in December of 2011. However, since we have now moved forward in time, we can observe from the chart that the near-perfect double bottom was real and it lead to a profitable upward move that reached the Price Pattern Objective quickly. What is more, without any knowledge of time, this is an example whereby if Oracle's stock price would have exceeded the December 2011 low, which is essentially the same as the May 2012 low, then, the market participant should have recognized the Double Bottom failure and, unequivocally, the market participant should have gotten short! Hence, the stop placement would have been equal to a swing reversal had the Double Bottom pattern not followed through.

Since our discussion has now focused on stop placement with respect to DBs/DTs, we must also talk about a subject known as **Inconspicuous** double bottoms/double tops. These patterns also form due to the stop-seeking tendency of the markets, but these patterns actually occur in reference to the stop placement of swings, and in Figure 10.3, we saw an example of an inconspicuous double bottom.

As we know, stops for swings are placed at the terminal point of the retracement range of the swing, but as we discussed, swings are only indications of true changes in trend. Sometimes, they reach a projection level and reverse quickly. When this happens, we know that the market loves to go target stops in order to get people out of the market. As such, it is quite common for the market to go and take out the stops that exist near the terminal point of the swing. When this happens, the terminal point is often taken out by a very small value, and we can usually define this value based on other retracements, micro swing projections, or time windows, which are forthcoming. However, the *terminal point of the swing is a very powerful number in the market*, and this area can actually lead to inconspicuous DTs/DBs, which are **intra-range DBs/DTs**. The definition between an intra-range DB/DT and an inconspicuous DB/DT is the same. As such, we must be aware of these inconspicuous DBs/DTs because as we know the market loves to seek out stops of swing traders, and then, reverse back in the direction of the original swing. I cannot quantify how many times that I have seen this happen in order to test the conviction of the trader by dealing with the market's continual mind-screwing nature. However, being aware of this stop seeking nature can be used to our benefit, and even more important, we see that if we take a trade based on an inconspicuous DB/DT, we can now foretell the price theory price objective of reaching new highs (for a db) or new lows (for a DB), which would also be considered primary swing points. (As a word of note to the reader, I am aware of the repetitive manner in which I am stating things throughout this text. It is done with a purpose, and that purpose is to show that the structure of the market is continuously interwoven between various price patterns, and by realizing that an intra-range DB/DT foretells a primary, qualified swing activation is an amazing trading edge because you enter a swing trade before the swing activates, which means your stop-loss will be much lower. Further, should that stop-loss activate, you have a clear signal that the trend has changed, and you are now taking the inverted swing!)

As discussed with Figure 8.4, we saw that the 127.2%P is a powerful projection when we are discussing DBs/DTs. This projection level is extremely important, and it is even more likely on intra-range DBs/DTs to lead to an inflection point. Therefore, since we have discussed favorable reward/risk ratios that exist when we talk about DB/DT entry criteria, we are almost getting 2:1 reward to risk at this projection level. Just like any other projection, we use the base range to calculate the value of the 127.2%P, and we add that to the terminal range/ retracement range of the DB/DT *even if* the terminal range has exceeded the base range. Unfortunately, this too is a repetitive discussion but I had to introduce a simplistic Figure 8.4 earlier in order to build the mindset necessary to comprehend what is shown in Figure

8.8, and Figure 8.8 will be a summary to for us to visualize almost all the concepts in this chapter, and we will use this Figure to finish our discussion of this section of the chapter.

Figure 8.8: Swings, Projections, and Inconspicuous DBs

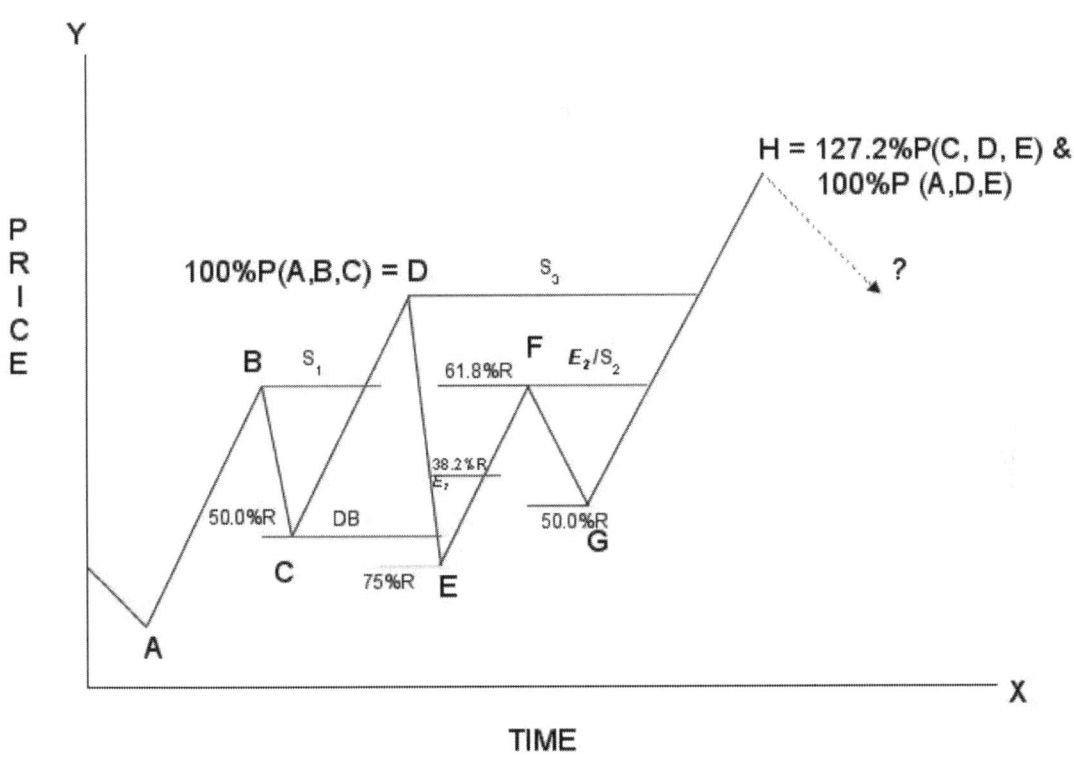

We begin this example with a swing, $S_P:(T_A, P_A) \rightarrow (T_B, P_B) \rightarrow (T_C, P_C)$, which reaches its price pattern objective of a 100%P at point D. At point D, the trader may decide to exit the trade, maintain the trade, move the stop to break-even on the trade, or exit part of the trade. However, let us assume that we got out just shy of point D for a profit. After which, we see in our Figure that the market snaps back to take out our terminal point C from the previous, primary, qualified swing. Furthermore, we see that this new low formed at point E is only a tick or so lower than point C, and point C is also a 75%R of the A → D primary range. As such, it creates a new primary swing, $S_P:(T_A, P_A) \rightarrow (T_D, P_D) \rightarrow (T_E, P_E)$, which remains the **primary trade** on the chart that has a primary swing point at point D. The Primary Trade is the trade that exists as a qualified swing that will get the trader back in tune with the primary trend.

Since point E is close to point C, we can say that this meets are tolerance level for an inconspicuous DB because C ≈ E. Therefore, we know that either we can enter the primary swing, which is awaiting activation upon a breach of point D, early by our knowledge of intra-range DBs by entering the trade at the break of the 38.2%R of the D → E primary <u>negative</u> range (this is a primary negative range because the second low exceeded the first low, otherwise it would be a secondary negative range), or we can look for a smaller swing to form inside of the D → E range after recognizing the formation of the inconspicuous DB. Let us discuss the 38.2%R breach first.

141

In Figure 8.8, we see that the 38.2%R breach is labeled as a point E_1 on the D → E primary negative range. We see that this has the most advantageous entry point because it requires the smallest stop loss, which would be placed lower than point E. However, since point E would also be a primary, qualified downswing, point E also serves as a reversal point. (Of note: when we get to Time Structure, we will be able to enter an intra-range DB with an even more advantageous reward to risk scenario.)

The second option, which is also shown in Figure 8.8 is that we do generate a swing, E → F → G. Thus, S_2 could be our second way of trading the inconspicuous DB by getting long at a break of point F, which is our **intra-range swing point**. An intra-range swing can be a micro swing as well, but they have separate definitions because an intra-range swing is a micro-swing that is generated after an intra-range DB/DT is formed. Thus, the intra-range swing is more valid than a generic micro swing, but it too must adhere to the micro swing definition as set forth in Chapter 11. Furthermore, if the trader fails to recognize the inconspicuous DB or the intra-range swing, the trader can still take the primary swing that occurs upon a break of our ever-present, primary swing trade existing at point D, which is still holding onto Price Theory by realizing that the 75%R of the A → D range failed to take out a new low, thus, the target to take out point D holds to Price Theory, and the reader can now properly see that all of the components of price structure are coming together!

On the other hand, if we did enter our inconspicuous DB, we can add to our position when our primary swing activates because the inconspicuous DB and our new primary swing A → D → E has the same exact stop loss value! We can then see that A → D → E is an additive, primary swing if we have successfully entered the inconspicuous DB via the 38.2%R breach rule or the intra-range swing point rule. As the setups unfolds in Figure 8.8, which occurs as time moves forward, we observe that our market reaches point H, which is a cluster of the $P_{100\%(A,D,E)}$ and the $P_{127.2\%(C,D,E)}$; both our swing projection and our inconspicuous DB projection are occurring at nearly the same value, which yields a possible inflection point at point H. Again, this is similar to Figure 8.4, and now, we can conclude the discussion regarding Figure 8.8, because now, the trader must get back into analytical mode, and how does the trader do this? Simply by becoming aware of the present moment in order to avail the trader's mind to the next Moment of Recognition/market inflection point that will allow us to use *Time and Price Symmetry* components that justify making a change to our trade position. Therefore, we have to use patience in order to see what the market decides to do next.

In summary, I have done my best to verbally and to visually define the two major price patterns that govern trend. These alone are enough to make a very profitable trader simply by knowing price pattern objectives for these setups. The power of recognizing DB/DTs cannot be stressed enough, which is why I walked the reader through the laborious example of the 2008/2009 crash along with the laborious Figure 13 example. With all of this being said, I am sure that the average reader has now reached a level of skepticism with the ease of the underlying price structure that governs the market, and the market is governed in this way, simply, because it has to. Unfortunately, this skepticism is real, and it is palpable. Therefore, the only way to overcome it is to allow the subconscious mind to witness thousands of hours of examples whereby the market adheres to these simple price patterns, which are simply expansions on Klatch's Price Theory. In fact, I too had this level of disbelief when I learned about swings myself, but when I learned about double tops/bottoms, I was not aware of their corresponding price pattern objectives. Thus, since I had the same feelings, it is okay that you are probably thinking, "It cannot be this easy. This is only basic mathematics!" Well, I am sorry to disappoint you, but it is this easy. It is basic mathematics. It does not require thousands of lines of code to understand and quantify. However, it does require the trader to garner enough visual heuristics in their mind as proof of these patterns, and once that level of insight has been achieved, this knowledge will feel like a veil has been lifted from your eyes by being able to look at any chart and see the swings, double bottoms, double tops, and even the inconspicuous double bottoms/tops that have always been there. In a way, the visual recognition of these charts will allow your mind to adjust to the enlightenment process that this book is attempting to do by slightly shifting the mentality of the reader to rid his or her mind of the preconceived belief in the difficulty of trading. Hence, before reading on, I encourage the reader to pull up every and any stock chart that is available to him or her, and go through and see the swings; see the DBs/DTS, and see Price Theory in action. It is right there in front of your eyes, and you never even realized it (at least until now). Once the reader has done this exercise, we can move forward, and we can now take a break from price structure. In fact, the reader should now have enough wherewithals for me to discuss the power of the trend.

Chapter 9

The Trend (is your Friend)

The power of the trend must not be understated, and trend analysis cannot be taken lightly. The knowledge of what the trend is will be sufficient trade logic itself in order to become a profitable market participant regardless of having any underlying knowledge of *Time and Price Symmetry*. This conclusion is why I have also directed investors to study this chapter after finishing Chapter 2 because it is pure and simple common sense that if you know what the trend is, then, you should never fight the trend, and this chapter will focus on qualitative and quantitative approaches to determining what the trend is in any given present moment in various different time frames.

Contrarily, the problem with trend analysis is actually summarized in the last sentence. The problem is Quantitative Synchronicity, which means that trend defining is an arduous process because, in the markets, there are multiple trends coexisting across multiple time frames and across multiple different market sectors. Thus, this chapter will allow the market participant to look for and discuss definable criteria in order to elevate the market participant's knowledge of the trend, which is almost as powerful as Time Structure. Thankfully, Klatch's Price Theory serves as the basic heuristic for trend analysis by knowing what the market's overall price objective is in the longest time frame.

That being said, if the reader has jumped to this chapter after Chapter 2, I will focus on the qualitative natures of trend analysis first. As such, I want to make it clear that the qualitative tendencies that are listed herein will be focused on stock indices themselves, which will act as a smoothing process to understanding the trend across multiple different market sectors. These qualitative discussions will not yield proper analysis in relation to interest rates, commodities, or currencies because these instruments revolve around different fundamental rules based on valuation or supply/demand (for technicians, I also must state that Klatch's Price Theory does not hold true for currencies because one currency is the inverse of the other). With that disclaimer, the quantitative technical parameters that I will discuss in this Chapter will hold true for any and every market instruments. Comparatively since this book is technically oriented, the quantitative criterion discussed in this chapter is definitive for all trading instruments because this criterion allows the trader to properly define the trend for any and every market in any and every time frame because as we are learning, "The Market is not Random."

I also feel that it is important to mention that the trend defining is somewhat equitable to Time Structure because if you know what the trend is, it is just like knowing when something is going to occur. That means that the underlying price of the instrument or price structure itself becomes irrelevant. For example, if you know that the trend for a given market up, then, going long (buying the market) should be done without any regard to price just as if you knew the market would make a high at 10:02am, you would reverse short. Hence, the trend is of extreme importance, but of course, it is not more important then time because in order to define the trend, we have to rely on price patterns (quantitative) or fundamental analytical techniques (qualitative). However, time can also clue us in to future trend changes, which will be discussed in Time Structure. Let me be clear on that subject here though. Time can be used to define a market inflection point, but it will take price structure to confirm that the trend has indeed changed. Thankfully, time can also clue us in as to when this will occur even before price action confirms the trend change. This all gets confusing to the general reader at this point in the book, but by the end of this book, most of the quantitative and qualitative discussions in this Chapter become meaningless because it is much easier to know the time that the trend will change then it is to apply rational thought to the market. Still though, the trend is of extreme power for traders and investors, and because of how esoteric Time Structure is, trend defining must be discussed

Trend Perceptions

As traders, many of us have been disillusioned with the thought of "buy low, sell high," and it too, is something that can link aback to Modern Portfolio Theory's idiocy. The "buy low, sell high" axiom is counter-productive the law of attraction thinking. Therefore, the mind must mentally shift to an accurate thought that says, "buy high, sell higher," and as we will see, that statement alone defines quantitative trend analysis because, if the reader has already understood how swing trades activate, which for an uptrend, occurs at the breach of a previous high, we can see how having a "buy high, sell higher" attitude aligns to defining what an uptrend is. (We will quantify this "buy high, sell higher" level of thinking via price patterns in the quantitative section of this chapter.)

Another area of trend discussion is in the relevance of countertrend trading, which is sometimes referred to as contrarian trading/investing. Undoubtedly, this type of trading can be extremely profitable, but people never take time to stop and think about their implementation of contrarian trading/investing, and I must change and define **contrarian thinking** for readers of this text. To me, contrarian thinking is simply using *Time and Price Symmetry* in longer-term time intervals that allow us to define a ***major*** market inflection point in time and in price. However, for the masses, contrarian thinking tends to be defined by human thought. The masses define contrarian thinking by a feeling; an emotion, and as stated, the market is 0% emotional. So, "What is this emotional, contrarian thinking?" Quite simply, it is having the *perception* that a price of an asset is too high or too low, which makes the market participant decide that he wants to be a contrarian, and by doing so, he is, by definition, countertrend trading. He is, "bucking the trend." That is what contrarians due, but that is ***not*** what time and price contrarians do. No, we always stay with the trend except when we have major *Time and Price Symmetry* coming into play, and furthermore, we as readers of this book, know that we cannot buck the trend until Price Theory has satisfied Price Objectives. (Remember, everything ties together no matter the strategy.) We have to remember that no traders and no investors are better than the trend, and like Lucifer, counter-trend trading is destined to lose even with *Time and Price Symmetry*. In the *Introduction* of this book, I defined that this book will allow a person to define time and price windows, which could serve as major highs or major lows. However, until a trader becomes a master of time, we have to rely on the currently proved trend (defined by price structure), and we must be careful in acting prematurely until we have a major confirmation that the trend has changed. Therefore, as a word of caution, there is no point to ever being a contrarian thinker (as I define it) until your trading has reached a level of mastery, and even then, be careful because once you start to hone your *Time and Price Symmetry* mindset, your confidence will become an irrational entity. As such, remember, trading in time and in price is way ahead of the curve, and therefore, you can afford to take small nibbles at time/price windows that the contrarian thinking believes will yield a market inflection point. However, never forget the importance of waiting for the confirmation of a change in trend. Remember, mass-market psychology is powerful, and there is no reason to "buck the trend" except to fulfill an emotional or gambling necessity, (I argue that the emotion becomes pride as the acumen of the *Time and Price Symmetry* trader increases.) If the reader avails the mind to this emotion, which I will call fear, then, the trader can overcome that emotion. Thus, in order to elaborate on the importance of this discussion, I wish to summarize a story from Jesse Livermore's pseudo-biography known as "Reminiscence of a Stock Operator," which was written by Edwin Lefevre. This story is the famous story of *The Turkey*.

Trading on Advice

How many of you reading this book has ever been given a stock tip from a friend or colleague? *The Turkey* was a man in a position of prominence, who had many friends and colleagues offering him stock advice. Consistently, he would listen to their advice, and he would buy stocks on their recommendation. However, when these same people told him to get out of the position, he would not listen, and it baffled his friends and his colleagues. In fact, it even pushed some of his friends to stop giving him advice because they were scared of his losses and not their own! However, *The Turkey*, was a smart man, and even without my Price Theory, he knew the purpose of the underlying trend. Alas, *The Turkey* found himself in a despairing situation because he kept getting the advice that he never even asked for, but *The Turkey* became observant of his friends. He observed that the advice givers with the greatest longevity were the people that would tell him to get out of his positions at a small loss because *they* had fear that *their* recommendation would yield a larger loss for him, which could cause the stock recommender to lose *The Turkey's* friendship. Moreover, these same friends would take a small loss in their own accounts as a testament to the confidence that their original idea was wrong. All of this was idiotic to *The Turkey,* and this caused great fear on behalf of his friends because when they told him to buy, he would buy, but when they told him to sell, he would not sell despite themselves selling in their own account! This made his friends panic because *The Turkey* was a powerful man! However, they didn't realize that *The Turkey* didn't care what he bought. He knew that the market trend was up. Therefore, he never cared about the analysis that his friends provided to him in the first place.

Simply, *The Turkey* knew the trend. He knew the trend was up, and that whatever he was buying did not matter. His friends told him when to get in, but he would never listen as to when to get out. Over time, the assets of *The Turkey* increased regardless of what they were because he knew of the underlying bull market. This is a true story, and it indicates the importance of trend analysis along with taking stock recommendations/tips from other people in our lives.

Do not trade off someone else doing the analysis you should be doing unless you are like *The Turkey,* and you know the trend. Although *The Turkey* listened to the idea and bought into it, he used his own analysis to hold onto the position, and more important, he knew when to get out. He used ***his own*** analysis on when to get out, which is the key to the story. In a way, the only reason *The Turkey* bought into these positions in the first place is that he knew that his trading size could benefit his friends, which meant he understood the purpose of the market, which has been eradicated in today's day and age. Therefore, remember the old adage that "the worst vice is advice," and always define and decide your own trades. Therefore, I ask the reader to use the example of *The Turkey* in order to never underestimate the power of the underlying trend. Thus, if we can now define our trends, and we can talk about the different methods we have available to us to define trend analysis.

Trend Definition

The definition of an **uptrend** is a market that is making higher highs and higher lows *that are recurrent, additive, qualified swing setups*.

The definition of a **downtrend** is a market that is making lower lows and lower highs *that are recurrent, additive, qualified swing setups*.

Although the definitions of both types of trends are similar, the characteristics of an uptrend and a downtrend are quite different. More important than that, many people become biased into having a proclivity towards bull or bear market scenarios, which is a painful ego-demon that must be conquered; immediately. Hence, this internal human failure is what we define as an **inherent trend bias**, which is a self-fulfilling failure mechanism that exists within the person's subconscious. As such, inherent trend bias can inhibit proper trading in whatever opposite bias you hold, and as such, it serves as another mental awareness issue that is raised for us traders. As an aside, the currency markets provide a quick fix to people who can never overcome their inherent trend bias because of the inverse relationship apparent in those markets. For example, if someone has a proclivity to bear markets, and the euro is in a bear market relative to the US dollar, then, the person should trade the EUR/USD pair. However, inherent trend bias is so hard to overcome that I need to reflect on another old time story, which holds relevance.

In order to provide the reader, with probably the most famous example of inherent trend bias, I will discuss the history of the famous trader, Richard Dennis, who is commonly known for his "turtle traders" of the 1980s. His trend bias led to great success for him in one type of market but not another. When his "turtle traders" were given a methodology that was based on channel-type breakouts (Donchian breakouts), they were able to correctly find profits. However, when the downtrend arose, it ended up killing many of the trader's portfolios, and it caused Richard Dennis to stop actively managing money! Therefore, we must remember that trend bias (either inherent or based on a quantitative trading system) will kill a trader's career because at some point, the trader will be consistently trading counter-trend, which greatly limits profit potential in order to pay for past mistakes.

Now, I must state a personal assumption that we, as traders, will favor downtrends over time because a downtrend yields higher volatility. However, for the investor reading this book, they too will experience a trend bias towards an uptrend, which are categorized by slowly rising prices. In general, markets rise slower than they correct is true, but what people do not realize is that markets can go up a hell of a lot more than they go down. Remember, a stock can only go to 0 in a downtrend, but a stock can go to infinity in an uptrend. More relevant to this discussion is that the trend bias that is built into the trading mind can be conditioned. If we remain humble, we can find benefits from either side of the trend coin. Therefore, in low volatility, we can find ourselves catching up on sleep or physical exercise. We can find ourselves increasing our leverage without taking on large risk, and we can find an approach that will work regardless of trend. However, if one does change his or her trading parameters, which would be in terms of money/risk management, then, we have to remember to change back. For example, if the trader finds justifiable reasons to increase leverage in an uptrend, the trader we must remember that when a downtrend emerges, the leverage must once again decrease. Thus, by comparing leverage and risk management criteria as we talked about in Chapter 4 with our two trading examples related to compounding of profits and contracting on losses, we can have equal profit opportunities in both types of trending markets. As such, these statements should be remembered because the acknowledgment of how to trade in different market trends is how we can best prevent inherent trend bias from forming in the first place.

Qualitative Trend Analysis

The qualitative areas I wish to discuss regarding trends are: VIX, Interest Rates/Yield Curve, and Job Growth/Unemployment Rates. These are the most relevant fundamental news bulletins, which consistently yield market reactions. Fundamentally, I also acknowledge that the political and world marketplaces are extremely complex. Moreover, there exists human intervention, which contains emotion. Therefore, like the KISS example in Chapter 5, we must understand that our brains are limited to only so much comprehension of the fundamental shifts occurring all over the world, and it is the role of the doctoral economic humans to worry/care about what each of these components mean in analyzing the overall fundamental view of the world. Therefore, we as investors/traders must deal with acknowledging how all of these fundamental components affect the level of fear in the market. Fear is what causes reaction; if you increase fear, you increase downward momentum; if you decrease fear, you increase upward momentum. Thus, fear is the driver of fundamental news, and fear is what we can use in order to look qualitatively at fundamental clues that reveal the underlying fear-induced trend. Now some, may think this is difficult, but thankfully, we market participants can quantify fear!

The level of fear is determined by the amount of people who "buy insurance" on their portfolio in the form of options. The **Volatility Index ("VIX")** is a technical indicator of measuring fear in a given market. Although it is technical, an investor should first turn to the VIX to get a clue about the trend. A low VIX environment, which will be categorized as a VIX < 20 for the S&P Index, is a clue that we have a stable market with a probable uptrend, but if we are in a high VIX environment, which is defined as the VIX > 20 for the S&P Index, we find a clue to a potential downtrend. Now, this is not a perfect indicator, and what is important is to determine the trend of the VIX. For example, if a VIX goes from 18 to 21, this is indicative of a new downtrend that may be in progress because it is a show of increasing fear. However, if we show a VIX that goes from 24 to 21, well we are seeing a decrease of fear even though the VIX is still over 20. So, the question is, "How can we use the 20 number to qualitatively define trend?" Well, we cannot. However, what we can do is we can say that when the VIX is low, and when the VIX is staying low, we can be confident in a continued up trend. Contrarily, we cannot say the same thing about when the VIX is high because markets can also rise during a high VIX environment, but eventually, the VIX will breach 20 and as it continues lower, we can become more comforted in a prevailing uptrend.

A high VIX environment is also opportune times to engage in *trading campaigns* because there are more opportunities existing throughout the day for larger price ranges in the underlying asset. The other problem about volatility is that it can come and go as a quietly as a "thief in the night." It can appear out of nowhere at any moment. When that occurs, markets do correct because of the nature of markets to half deep retracements of initial market moves, which we will talk about in later chapters regarding the market's tendency to back-and-fill. Moreover, a spike in the VIX does not always mean the end of one trend and the start of another, and we will look at time cycles in the second section of this book for more understanding of this. Because of the inconclusive nature of the VIX at any given present moment, we can use the VIX as a good starting place to clue us in on the amount of stress we will deal with as investors or the amount of elation we will receive as traders. Aside from the VIX, we have other logical macro-economic views to further our comprehension of the trend.

The interest rates that are controlled by the Federal Reserve are often misunderstood with respect to their impact on the market. For example, when interest rates are being reduced, people think that this is a good thing for the market because it will spur spending. Economically, we could discuss the impact on the interest rate with respect to the wealth effect, investing, saving, etc., but that is not our job. Instead, we care about logic when we approach a qualitative ethereal argument for defining trend. Thus, if interest rates are going down, it means there is a problem in the economy, and the economy needs a push. *Hence, a decline in interest rates by the Federal Reserve is an indication of a downtrend*. On the other hand, interest rates that are moving higher are clues to a healthy market that is strong enough in order to handle higher costs for borrowing. Thus, *a period of increasing interest rates are clues to an uptrend*. The problem with higher rates is that there is an asymptotical level that once hit, will cause the market to stop moving higher; instantly. In fact, that level is very powerful, and if unsafely hit, there is an immediate crash/downtrend market inflection point. Therefore, interest rate setting by the Federal Reserve is a fine art, and Former Fed Chairman Alan Greenspan, a man of very few but important words, knew the exact level that led to the bursting of the stock market bubble in 2000. In fact, he knew the exact level to place interest rates/fed funds rates in order stop the insanity of that bubble immediately because the markets was getting out of control. It is my decision that Former Fed Chairman Greenspan did this because had prices continued to increase, it could have led to a 30-40 year recession instead of a 2-year one. However, in a way, I can only hypothesize about former Fed Chairman Greenspan's reason for setting interest rates at the level to stop the bubble. My guess is that mass-market psychology and spending became destructive to borrowing, and he was trying to prevent the housing crisis of 2008 in advance in order to slow down over leveraging by banks and individuals, who were not used to having money. Unfortunately, the issue with his strategy was September 11, 2001. Because of that day, interest rates were forced to contract dramatically in order to influence mass-market psychology, and essentially, so the market would not fail. However, by this further reduction of interest rates, it allowed the Nuevo-rich to continue their lifestyle, which is what I believe Fed Chairman Greenspan was trying to avoid in the first place. The expedited contraction of interest rates allowed the uneducated wealth to use risky new products in order to continue expanding their lifestyle, and had the markets not needed to be jumped in an expedited way by September 11, 2001, I believe we may have prevented the 2008/2009 crash.

In a way, September 11, 2001, terrorist attacks really ruined the intentions of the Federal Reserve, but even so, we can still see that the immediate cut in interest rates that preceded the attacks was a clue to the downtrend that the market would continue in for the next 13 months until it reached the October 2002 low. The only reason I point to September 11, 2001 is that whenever we deal with qualitative economic models, we are dealing with unknown variables. This is unfortunate, and I am not a qualitative theorist or a qualitative modeler, but by using *Time and Price Symmetry*, the September 11, 2001 terrorist attacks were foretold by the market changing its trend to unequivocally being down before those attacks. Therefore, the Federal Reserve could have plied the market place with more money **before** the terrorist attacks by listening to the market structure forecasting future doom, and I do not mean to say this lightly, but it is possible to use *Time and Price Symmetry* to "see" future tragedies. In fact, I will have a discussion of this in Chapter 16 with respect to Orange Juice.

Obviously, discussions of interest rates must lead to the bond yield curve. The size of the bond market cannot be neglected, and bond traders have a tremendous impact on the stock market. There is an old trading adage that presidents even joke about that says, "Bonds happy, stocks happy." This quote exists for a reason; it is true. Therefore, a normal interest rate curve, which is where the interest rates go up with the maturity of the underlying bonds, is what makes the bond market happy. The problem is the monolithic size of the bond market, and the fact that it tends to move like a turtle. It takes a large amount of time to inflect the yield curve of bonds. Therefore, the fluctuations between a normal curve and an inverted yield curve are more important for qualitative trend recognition. Following that logic, I will assert that inverted yield curves are indications of impending stock market trend changes. This will be a change from bearish to bullish because as we will learn in Time Cycle Analysis, bear markets are shorter in time duration just like inverted yield curves. Thus, keep in your head that bond traders want to stay happy, and they stay happy with normal yield curves. However, just as an inverted yield curve makes us cognizant of the end of a bear market, a normal yield curve is also an indication of a bull market. In fact, both yield curves are indications of bull markets, but one (the inverted) is indicating the end of a bear market whereas the latter is referring to the continued momentum of the current bull market. Therein draws the conclusion of determining when the bond market indicates the end of a bull market. The disturbances that cause the yield curve to go from normal to inverted are clues to a forthcoming bear market/down trend. If a gun were put to my head, I would assert that a flat yield curve is indicative of a forthcoming downtrend in the market. However, this is far from an exact conclusion, and a flat yield curves exist for a tremendously short amount of time. That is why we have to understand what a flat yield curve is. It is simply a scenario where there is mutual, consistent demand in longer-term bonds and there is an oversupply of shorter-term bonds that cause this scenario. We can marry that to the logic that if there is more demand in longer-term bonds and excess supply of shorter-term bonds then we are seeing people's fear increase in the short term by seeking comfort in the long term. Again, the underlying emotion of fear is prevalent in this type of qualitative analysis, which is what I believe is the fundamental driver of qualitative analysis.

So far, we have logically looked at how fear can be discerned from the VIX, and we have discussed how fear can be interpreted by the interest rate decisions of the Federal Reserve. In turn, those decisions are digested by the conglomeration of traders in the bond markets. However, what about every other factor in the economy and most prevalent in today's day and age is the government's excess spending and ever-increasing debt. Granted, I can also argue that budget surpluses/deficits should be considered an extrapolation of Keynesian theory, but the bond traders already take care of the government's idiotic spending for us. Therefore, we can read the fear of government deficits by analyzing the supply/demand in the bond market, and there is no greater example then what happened in August of 2011. Thankfully, the bond traders can clue us in on these market calamities, and in a way, our work is done for us by the bond traders. Is it any wonder that after the market's collapse in August of 2011 that Federal Reserve Chairman Bernanke instituted "Operation Twist," which was a direct manipulation of the bond market? No, of course not, and therefore, do not worry about the government's idiotic spending unless you are a conspiracy theorist and believe in the termination of the dollar, as I do. But, there is one more piece of the puzzle that matters greatly to investors and qualitative analysis, and that is the trend derived from the job market/unemployment rate. This will be our last qualitative discussion regarding trend, and since we are in the qualitative realm, we have to factor in the unquantifiable political decision making process that influences jobs in the economy.

Thankfully, political decision making does ultimately play out in terms of job growth and the unemployment rate. In fact, it is my belief that all administrations can see all of their decisions culminates into these two numbers. For example, if the current administration's policies are good, we should see this reflected in higher job growth, which is also a function of more demand for American goods. We can observe that these two areas can effectively surmise all actions of our government with respect to the economy. Because of this, the market reacts to and becomes hypersensitive to shifts in the trends of any of these three government metrics. The problem is that they are all lagging indicators of the market's trend just like the yield curve of bonds or the interest rates stipulated by the Federal Reserve. Since they are lagging indicators, the market tends to make significant highs or lows before the trend in employment or job growths changes in a definable way. If you do not believe me, the March 2009 low is a fantastic example.

Unfortunately, the time of the lag cannot be measured, and all analysis that I have performed in my own quantitative outlook of job growth/unemployment rate has yielded random results with very wide standard deviations. However, that does not mean that profit cannot be made by using this knowledge. For example, President Bill Clinton had a major focus on investments in order to spur job growth. During his presidency, the U.S. created a record of 24mm jobs, and the market staged one of the largest rallies of all time. As such, 7 years of investing was profitable as Clinton unwound the Reagan-Bush economic policies that were inhibiting job growth due to lack of investment.

Traditionally, we can work on concluding job growth and the unemployment rate by equating the underlying trend of job growth/unemployment rate with the market's trend. If job growth is up, the market will usually yield an uptrend. Conversely, if the unemployment rate's trend is down, the market should be in an uptrend. Coupling these two areas with the VIX, the Federal Reserve, and the bond market, will provide investors with confidence that they are in a period of stock growth across the board even without any type of quantitative components. Therefore, these market conditions are the periods that I discussed in Chapter 2 for when an investor needs to find solid performing companies that have increasing revenue growth. During these time periods, we will have the conditions necessary on getting to our 1000%+ returns as investors. Further, we can now discuss the lifecycle of stocks that was mentioned in Chapter 2 because, if a stock begins to break-out of its rational market capitalization-based share price range during one of these uptrend periods and *if that stock has not bubbled once already,* we will find that during an uptrend, we will observe that individual stocks will experience a common lifestyle. However, things are different with commodities, and the discussion of commodity-based lifecycles will proceed this stock lifecycle discussion. Therefore, the discussion of the life cycle of a commodity we be our link to talking about the technical/quantitative characteristics of defining the trend, and for investors, this book is terminated after the individual market lifecycle discussion forthwith.

Individual Market Lifecycles

As we discussed in the previous chapter and as I have alluded to in this chapter, we are aware that a Qualified Swing is a necessity of understanding the underlying trend. By definition, an upswing is a period of higher highs and higher lows just like an uptrend, and during an uptrend, we have continuous swings that occur as new highs are breached. More often than not, these highs become primary swing points, which also serve as a reminder for the investor/trader to get back with the trend because if every swing is taken, it is impossible to not be with the trend. (In the second edition of this book, I will more adequately be able to illustrate this concept to the reader). However, the most important observation that required me to reintroduce swings is to discuss that at a major low, a swing MUST form based on Price Theory. Amazingly, the first swing off a major low could lead to a multi-year trade! In fact, the first swing off a low could be the lowest low that stock will have for the remainder of our lives. Swings are that powerful, and as I alluded to, we can discuss and visualize characteristics of uptrends and of downtrends for different types of markets. As an aside, characteristics of trades for forex markets are irrelevant because forex is traded as a currency pair (i.e. EUR/USD). As such, if one currency is in an uptrend, the other is in a downtrend, as discussed with respect to trend bias.

In general, an uptrend will consist of steadily increasing prices with daily and weekly closes near the top of their respective ranges. For stocks, an uptrend will eventually go parabolic (known as a "bubble") where rationality of price valuation becomes irrelevant, as was discussed in Chapter 2. After bubbling, the stock will come back to earth and find a new trading range for the remainder of its lifespan until the "Rule of Alternation" (Chapter 16) kicks in. However, it is very rare for a stock to experience two bubbles in its lifecycle. A good example of a stock that has seen two bubbles is of course Apple Inc. However, the two bubbles in Apple's stock price were separated by over 20 years, and this second bubble only occurred because of the way in which the company revived itself. Apple 20 years ago was not what Apple is today, which is very important to realize. In a way, they are two separate companies, and that is why most stocks will only ever see one bubble in their lifecycles. On the other hand, uptrends in commodities will have parabolic bubbles multiple times in their respective lifecycles, and these moves seem to be correlated in a decennial nature. This is logical because you can expect that supply/demand for a given commodity will be stressed at 1 time or another every 10 years or so. Even in the Bible, this commodity lifecycle is referenced with respect to every seventh year, and of course, W.D. Gann's exploration of the decennial cycle will require much analysis in our later discussions of time. He, too, knew about these gaps in time that lead to large commodity-based moves.

Thankfully, downtrends for all financial investments (again, except forex) have similar characteristics. Downtrends happen fast, and they complete much faster than uptrends. For instance, an average downtrend in the market itself is around 1.5 years whereas an average uptrend is over 6 years. In addition, a downswing always occurs before any major crash in the market. In fact, we can look back at any DOW chart of any of the historic crashes, and we will see a swing form to the downside before any big move. Let us visualize up and down trends/market lifecycles by looking at Figures 9.1 and 9.2.

Figure 9.1: Stock Lifecycle

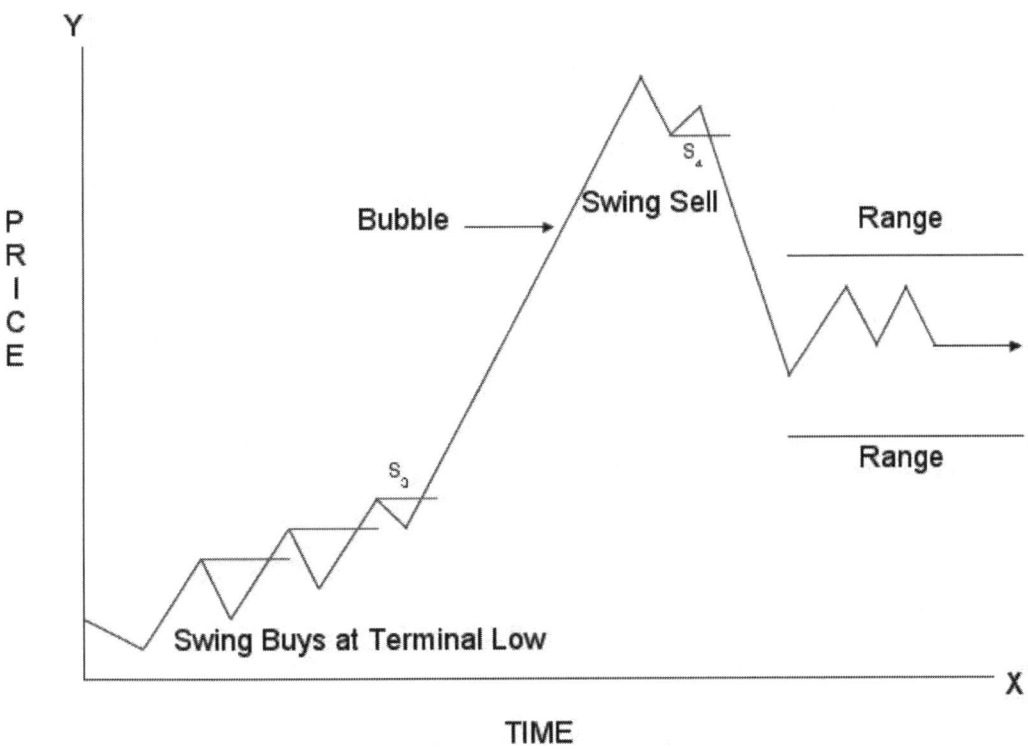

In Figure 9.1, we can see an example of a stock lifecycle. In the Figure, we see a move off some low that generates a swing up. Then, at some point, we will have our bubble that crashes hard, and then, the stock finds a comfortable trading range. As a write this book, there are two very relevant stock charts to look at with respect to this exact lifecycle chart: Netflix and Research in Motion. Both stocks had swing breakouts, then bubbles, and ultimately, they came back to earth to find their trading range. As such, it is unlikely for a company like Netflix that it will ever bubble again, and as an aside, unless Research in Motion finds some newfound success, it will either be acquired or go bankrupt. In fact, the reason I bring up Research in Motion is that after a stock bubbles, there does exist the finality perspective that the stock will cease to exist, which is an important emphasis to make with respect to individual stock prices. Even more important is to realize that a stock may artificially bubble because of an acquisition that is forthcoming. These price spikes are not true bubbles, and they are limited by the acquisition price. Therefore, do not be tricked into thinking that a gigantic up move in an underlying stock is always associated with a bubble, and unfortunately, the only way to determine if this is a true bubble or an acquiring-based bubble is to check the fundamental news for the stock.

Figure 9.2: Commodity Life Cycle

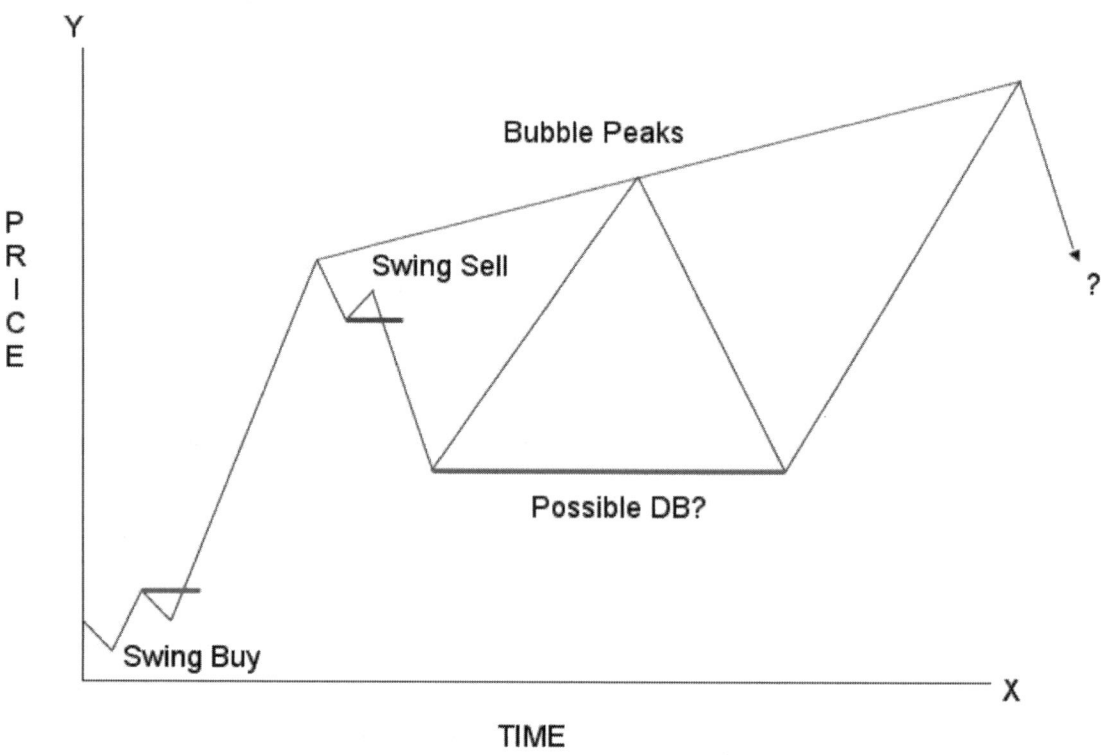

In Figure 9.2, we see a similar lifecycle with respect to a commodity, but we notice that there are multiple bubbles in this commodity. As mentioned, this is the difference between the two, and the logic is quite easy to follow. Because of inflation, commodities will increase in price over time, and as such, when demand becomes high, their goal will be to achieve a new all-time high. Now, what may not be easily definable is if that new high is a true new high or an inflation-adjusted new high, but for our concern that type of thought is irrelevant. Further, I must refer to Klatch's Price Theory.

Now that we can visualize the difference between stock and commodity lifecycles, one may ask me the question, "Well, based on your Price Theory, shouldn't all stocks have an objective to take out new highs just like commodities?" Quite simply, the answer to that question is undoubtedly yes, unless the stock was to be acquired or to go bankrupt. However, the momentum that fuels stock bubbles is enormous, but with respect to commodities, that momentum does not need to exist because of how the futures market is oriented. As such, unless there was to be another fundamental factor such as a hot new product, then, the stock will stick to an ever-increasing range, and eventually, at some point, it will make a new high. However, that new high may not be made in a bubbling nature. No, that new high may be achieved by gyrating slowly higher.

These lifecycles shown in Figure 9.1 and Figure 9.2 are very important for investors to understand in order to believe in the profit potential of their investments in stocks or in commodities. Determining a stock that has yet to bubble should become part of your investment selection criteria. Obviously, if a stock has already bubbled once, the probability of another bubble is infinitesimal. Only by investing in a stock that has the potential to still bubble will the fundamental investor be able to achieve multiple factors of return based on the current valuation. Therefore, only bubbles give validation to the statement, "$1,000 invested 10 years ago would be worth $100,000 today." Thus, having the underlying believe in the Price Theory objective that is to achieve new highs bridges the gap between fundamental trend analysis and technical trend analysis, and we can now complete the trend picture by discussing the quantitative criteria of trend indications.

Quantitative Trend Analysis

Quantitatively, determining the trend relies on Price Theory. We know that at a terminal high or low a swing must form because if we have failed to take out a new high/low of a given range, then we must take out the low/high of that range. For example, an uptrend inception occurs when the market finally reaches a point where it fails to make a new low, and then, that low is tested. However, when that low is tested, we are now aware of two things that will happen. Either we will have a deep retracement of that range, or we may take out that low by a few ticks, which results in a double bottom forming. Thankfully, even if the double bottom is the resultant formation at a terminal low that is lower than a prior low, we know that a swing must eventually form. Essentially, we are saying that a swing becomes the true criteria for quantitatively defining trend. Thus, when a market truly fails to move lower or higher, we have Price Structure components that tell us that the trend has changed.

That being said, with the reader's knowledge at this stage of the text, there is no definable way to know if a terminal high/low is the final high/low. As such, we are forced to wait for the swing to form. I must be clear; we cannot use trend analysis for determining the validity of a newly formed discreet. No, the only way to quantify the power of the discreet is by using a combination of Price Structure and Time Structure. In fact, once we have formed the full Marketome, we can define discreet points that have the potential to hold the given market for years if not forever. Hence, that application becomes the ultimate goal of trading and the ultimate goal of *Time and Price Symmetry*. Therefore, the purpose of understanding price action at a discreet is to define the trend in price structure analysis that tells us what the trend is! As such, the only definitive conclusion we can make is that a qualified swing determines the trend when it is activated by the primary swing point be exceeded. Thus, quantitative trend analysis rests in swings. The problem with this conclusion is that we can have a conflicting swing on a daily chart, 60-minute chart, 5-minute chart, or our 1-minute chart. Again, here we must too invoke the reality of the third-dimension's hard multiplicative understanding factor defined as Quantitative Synchronicity.

Thankfully and logically, even without a full understanding of Quantitative Synchronicity, we can rely on time as a qualifier for our primary trend, which is much easier because it is part of the two-dimensional market representation instead of the three-dimensional understanding derived from Quantitative Synchronicity. In fact, there is one easy answer to ensure high probability trend trading – just trade when all the swings agree in every time period. Now, please understand that I am not being facetious. I am fully aware that these trading times are rarities, and daytraders cannot afford to wait for these perfect scenarios. Therefore, we must understand the concept of what the market is doing by generating swings in various time frames. Conveniently, this must happen in succession because the fact is that when the overall trend of an underlying asset begins to change, the trend will turn up on the 1-minute chart first. Then, the 5-minute chart, then the 60-minute chart... etc. As times goes forward from a discreet low/high it will be the market's job to continue forming new, longer, qualified swings that each has primary swing points based on relevant retracements. Thus, the trouble comes in when the trend starts to change on the shorter term charts while still being conflicting with the longer-term swings. As such, I must state that stock traders can easily conquer this issue by choosing a different stock to trade. However, index traders and commodity traders are not that lucky because we are specialists in one market. So, the only answer to conquer this trouble for us is to differentiate between primary and secondary swings.

Now that the reader should understand that quantitatively we are looking to swings in order to define our trend, we have to be aware of relevant *Time and Price Symmetry* that exist in order to make us think in terms of counter-trend trading, which as I have already discussed, is a losing battle. In fact, as the last paragraph foreshadowed, it is an agonizing process to the trading mentality when we are faced with a 60-minute chart with a currently activated downswing versus a 1-minute chart showing us a new, qualified upswing (or vise versa.) The fact is that we, as time and price traders, need to be aware of all the inflection points that exist in time and in price, and we need to determine if we have profits to justify reversing at these inflection points. As such, another way to acknowledge the trend when we are faced with this conflicting swings is to look directly at our trade results. *The trend will become apparent if we start taking trades at counter-trend inflection points that keep failing.* Furthermore, the trader does not have to feel pressured to take the newly formed swings, and the trader must remember that the trend will avail itself by further price movement (further, agreeing swings) as time goes by. With this level of knowledge to help us, we can now properly define time frames.

Let me begin by quantitatively defining the time frames that we will use in order to yield relevant swings for our trend analysis. These charts/time frames are: daily, 60-minute (30-minute), 5-minute, and 1-minute. Each of these charts would be for the same asset/index, but they reflect all of the price action in a given interval. The reason that these different time frames are important is that we need to highlight the primary trend based on Price Pattern Objectives. The **primary trend** is whatever the direction of the active swing is on the 60-minute chart *until* the 100% projection of the 60-minute swing is reached. The last part of that definition is extremely important because it has been my observation that a primary swing, which will be defined in a minute, has a necessity to fulfill its price pattern objective. In fact, I would dare say that there is over a 90% probability that this price pattern objective be fulfilled. Therefore, if a counter-trend swing forms before this 100% projection is reached, the trader can achieve some type of edge in determining that this shorter-term swing is countertrend and thus, should be ignored.

Now, I will define the 60-minute chart of a continuous trading instrument (30-minute chart for a real time hours trading instrument) is the **primary chart**, and **primary swings** will form on this chart with a minimum of *15 bars* between the discreet low/high to the secondary high/low. For clarification to the reader, for instruments that trade in real time hours ("RTH") only, the primary chart would be a *30-minute chart and the primary swing on that chart would still have a minimum of 15 bars* between the discreet low/high and the secondary low/high for defining the swings. Defining the primary chart, primary swing, and the primary trend is necessary in order to understand what the underlying Price Pattern Objective may be for a given instrument. In addition, the primary chart is usually where we can see our primary retracements easier because we have a better macro-view on the "oldest" discreet high/low that the market has been moving away from. Furthermore by keeping our eye on the primary chart, we can see the power of the underlying trend, and by focusing on the primary chart and the primary trend, we can be aware of the fact that we may be trading countertrend. All of this being said, that does not mean the market cannot have a reversal day/countertrend day! In fact, we may see our 1-minute and 5-minute charts give us agreement on swings, and that is indicative that the market is going to *correct to some primary retracement value on the primary chart*. Therefore, we can use the knowledge of the primary trend to target these larger/longer primary retracements, and we can have some level of confidence that the primary swing that has yet to reach its price pattern objective will not have its stops taken out. Therefore, we can actually define possible retracements for our corrections by observing where swing traders have their protective stops. In a way, we can use the knowledge of that stop location to be aware of inconspicuous double bottoms/tops or to look at retracements higher than those levels that will hold our market to reverse back to the primary trend. This is a very important concept, and I encourage the reader to review this paragraph over and over in order to understand how the market likes to have corrections, but ultimately, the market will revert to the primary chart's price pattern objective; especially, if there is a primary chart price pattern objective that is yet to be fulfilled based on the primary swing.

Our daily chart is also important with respect to the primary trend, and it requires some further discussion as well in order to be aligned with conventional market analysis. In fact, W.D. Gann used a concept that has become a common word of market pundits: Dow Theory. It's actually funny, but most people who use the term "Dow Theory" have no clue what it really means! Dow Theory is simply the recognition of a swing trade on the daily chart that is a primary swing that is properly defined from our primary-chart (the 60-minute for Continues / 30-minute for RTH). Therefore, let's describe exactly how Dow Theory can be interrelated to the primary-chart. Dow Theory is simply a 3-day (3 bar) chart pattern where the second day is a retracement of the first day, and the third day is a swing that breaks the second day's low/high (sometimes if the second day is a rare, inside day (as we will discuss later) the first day's low/high is actually the target on the third day after making the relevant retracement). Since the Dow Theory is just a larger chart view, we must realize that when Dow Theory kicks-in, we are simply observing that the market fails to take out a new high/low, and a swing forms to confirm that direction by taking out the primary swing point, which could be the high/low of the first or second day. However, because we are being spread across multiple days, and because we know that it takes about 15-30 hours to fulfill a primary swing to define the primary trend, we realize the recognition that Dow Theory is aligned to our primary-chart swing. Dow Theory is another way in which I can conclude to the reader that the primary trend is available and definable in the primary-chart's relevant time frame. Quantitatively, there is no need for further clarification of defining the trend because swings tell us the trend. Rising prices mean newer highs, which mean an uptrend. Declining prices means lower lows, which means a downtrend. Thus, it is a logical conclusion that swings define for us, which makes it quantifiable and somewhat easy.

In summary, this concludes our first discussion of the trend and how to analyze it qualitatively and quantitatively using price structure. In our discussion of Time Structure, we will be able to analyze the trend in time as well by determining longer-term trends that give us clues to future price movement. The most important concepts from this chapter are that we can look to the logical economic data that tells us about the health of the economy, which yields the health of the market. Furthermore, we have discussed the power of the primary swings with respect to the primary chart, which yields our primary trend. More important, we have discussed the life cycles of stocks and commodities, which are important for investors to know with respect to targeting an investment that allows for the desired multiplier effect. Using the quantitative knowledge of swings with the power of acknowledging the eventual bubble in a stock we can allow our mind's to be cognizant of the possibility of larger percentage returns, and in our discussion of time structure, we can add in another component for the investor, which is determining the length of time of bull/bear markets along with when we can expect terminal dates for the end of each of those cycles! By using Time Structure, we can target certain, underlying market scenarios that allow higher confidence in pursuing long or short investments.

Chapter 10

Trendlines, Fans, and Triangles

Trendlines are an often-used phrase by the masses, and I would assume that they are the second most technical reference that most people are aware of after moving averages. However, the way 99.99% of people draw trendlines is wrong! **Trendlines fall into four categories: rising tops, rising bottoms, declining bottoms, and declining tops.** The normal convention that most people tend to use when drawing trendlines is to draw rising bottoms lines and declining tops lines, but these lines rarely work! On the other hand, rising tops lines and declining bottoms lines can hold a market forever as has can be seen on the logarithmic corn chart over the past three decades, which has held a rising tops line. As daytraders, we have to be aware that properly drawn trend lines can be important, and that they can hold a market many times in a day. In order to better represent these trendlines, let us turn to graphical representations shown in Figure 10.1 and Figure 10.2.

Figure 10.1: Incorrect Trendlines (Rising Bottoms / Declining Tops)

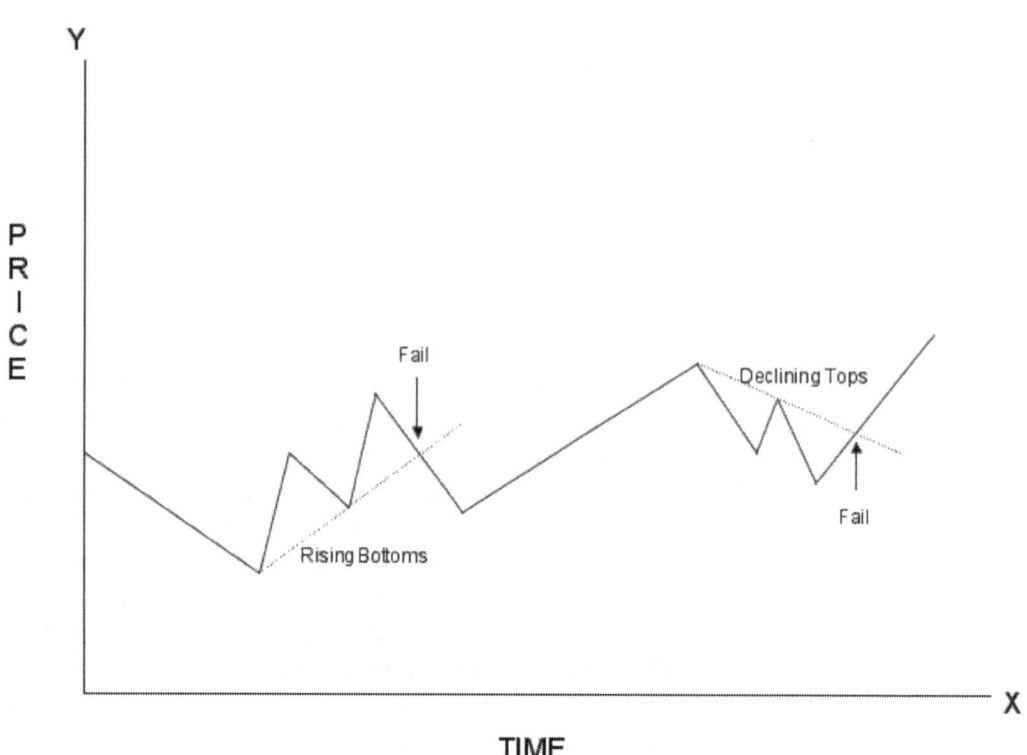

158

Figure 10.2: Correct Trendlines (Rising Tops / Declining Bottoms)

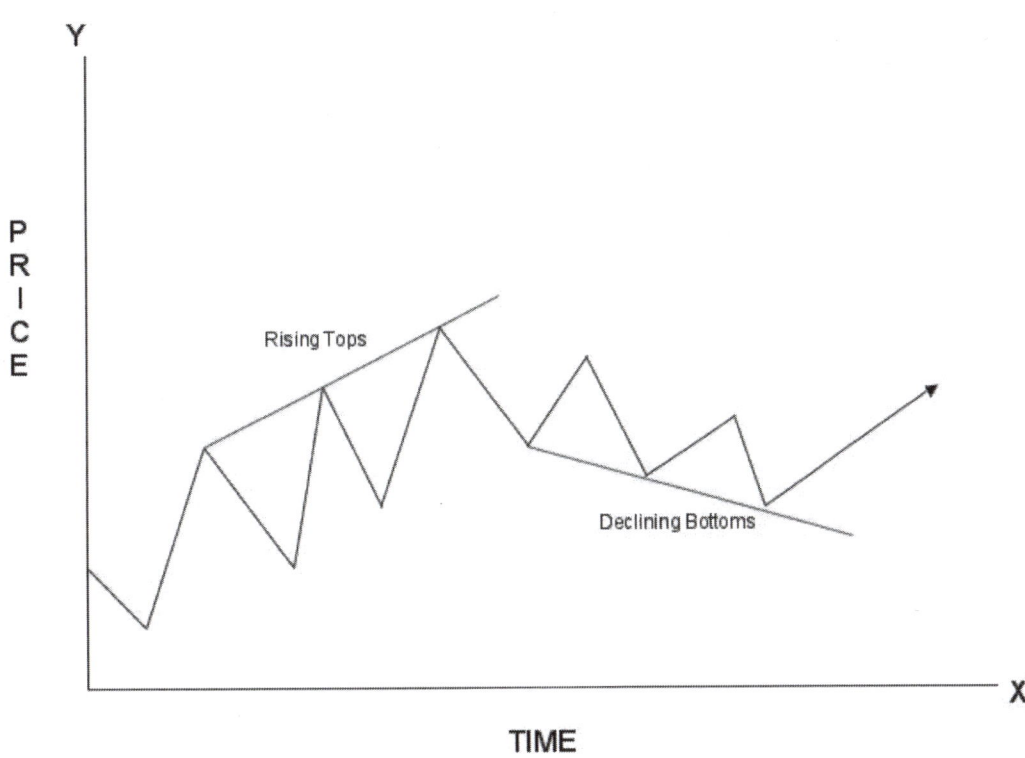

Figures 10.1 and 10.2 show **incorrect trendlines** (rising bottoms / declining tops – Figure 10.1) and **correct trendlines** (rising tops / declining bottoms – Figure 10.2). It is essential to draw these lines correctly because future chart patterns that I will discuss will rely on correctly drawn trendlines. Again, I hope the reader is seeing that a light shift in mentality provides tremendous results; here, we are just inverting the way in which people tend to define trendlines.

That being said let us marvel at the beauty of the market structure by the price and time definition that defines what a trendline is in the first place. Now, I ask the question of the reader, "If you look at Figure 10.2, which uses correct trendlines, what exactly are linking the two points that yield the correct trendlines?" Basically, the question becomes, "Why are these the correct trendlines?" It should be an obvious recognition now that we have shifted our mentality to correctly drawn trendlines. Quite simply, *correct trendlines link swing points!* These lines are predicting future possible discreet high/lows, which will serve as future possible qualified swing points! The market structure becomes more aligned by shifting to rising tops and declining bottoms lines by our discussion of swings that are derived from Price Theory. The market structure is availing itself right in front of our eyes, and most people are not even aware of it. As we can see, everything becomes interconnected. Ranges have retracements, which yield swings and swing points., and swing points become linkable via correct trendlines.

Now, as for a real-life example of correctly drawn trendlines, I wish to speak about something that has been recurrent in the news for the past several years, which is the European debt crisis. Obviously, the

...lead to a surge in volatility for the soverign debt markets linked to various European countries. One of the debt markets, Spain, had a perfectly drawn rising tops line between 2010, 2011, 2011, an 2012. This rising tops line held four times, and twice in 2011. Hence, the first two tag points, i.e. the high in 2010 and the high in 2011, have continued to hold the yield on Spain's government debt. What is more, the yield curve for bonds is inverted to the price, so in terms of the actual pricing of Spain's bonds, this became a declining bottoms line that has also held twice after the first two tag points were established, which generated the line in the first place. Hence, the power of properly drawn rising tops/declining bottoms line is paramount because when a trader notices that they are holding, they will continue to hold, and as is the case in this example with Spain, we see that it is an extremely simple mental exercise in order to simply understand that the 2012 high (essentially, the high of the year), was simply forecasted from a basic, properly drawn, trendline. What is more, this is not a rarity! No, on one minute charts, on daily charts, on yearly charts, and in almost every market these lines have extreme power, which makes them very relevant, and I have already spoke towards the power of these lines with the corn chart when we discussed commodity-based life cycles!. However, one of the biggest challenges with drawing proper trendlines is software packages themselves, which requires a discussion.

Let me clarify, one of the biggest problems with trendlines is that when they are drawn on a longer-term chart, and then, the user adjusts to a shorter-term chart, the trendlines may not link the correct points. Therefore, we need to make sure we are using charting software that allows us to define values off the trendline in terms of the future price/time window predicted by the line itself. (This is also important for mathematical clusters as will be discussed in Chapter 14.) Therefore, I encourage the reader to use a charting software program called Qcharts, which is owned by Interactive Data Corporation; the same people who own eSignal. Qcharts has a few major attributes for us time and price traders, and these attributes are very important. They are:

– Any retracement, projection, or trendline that is drawn in one time frame will appear accurately drawn in another time frame as we change the chart's time frame
– Any trendline drawn on a base chart will accurately calculate when switching to a logarithmic chart, which is very important for longer-term trendlines
– The cursor will adequately show future values of trendlines by placing the cursor on top of the line, which will be useful for cluster averages

The importance of the future existence of the Qcharts Software to me cannot be stressed enough, and I will be in major trouble as a trader if it no longer exists after my incarceration.

Unfortunately, the discussion on trendlines is this simple. We just needed to acknowledge the correct way to draw them, and we needed to observe the interrelationship of the trendline to swing points. However, we also must be aware that trendlines, like retracements, do have some degree of tolerance that we have to give them with respect to being penetrated or missed, and we have to understand that this tolerance increases with time or with price. As such, when they are missed, we can learn that there may be a cluster of trendlines, which is something known as a Fan.

Trendline Fans

I do not want to confuse the reader to by my discussion of Trendline Fans with the discussion of W.D. Gann's square of nine fans. The square of nine does not have relevance in this book, but I must be clear that many of the references to Gann may confuse an educated reader who is also aware of symmetrical time squares that Gann observed by creating fans. For us, Fans occur from multiple lows/highs and then, a peak high/low. The peak high or low is the terminal point for our trendline. In Figure 10.3, we can visualize what a fan looks like.

Figure 10.3: Trendline Fan

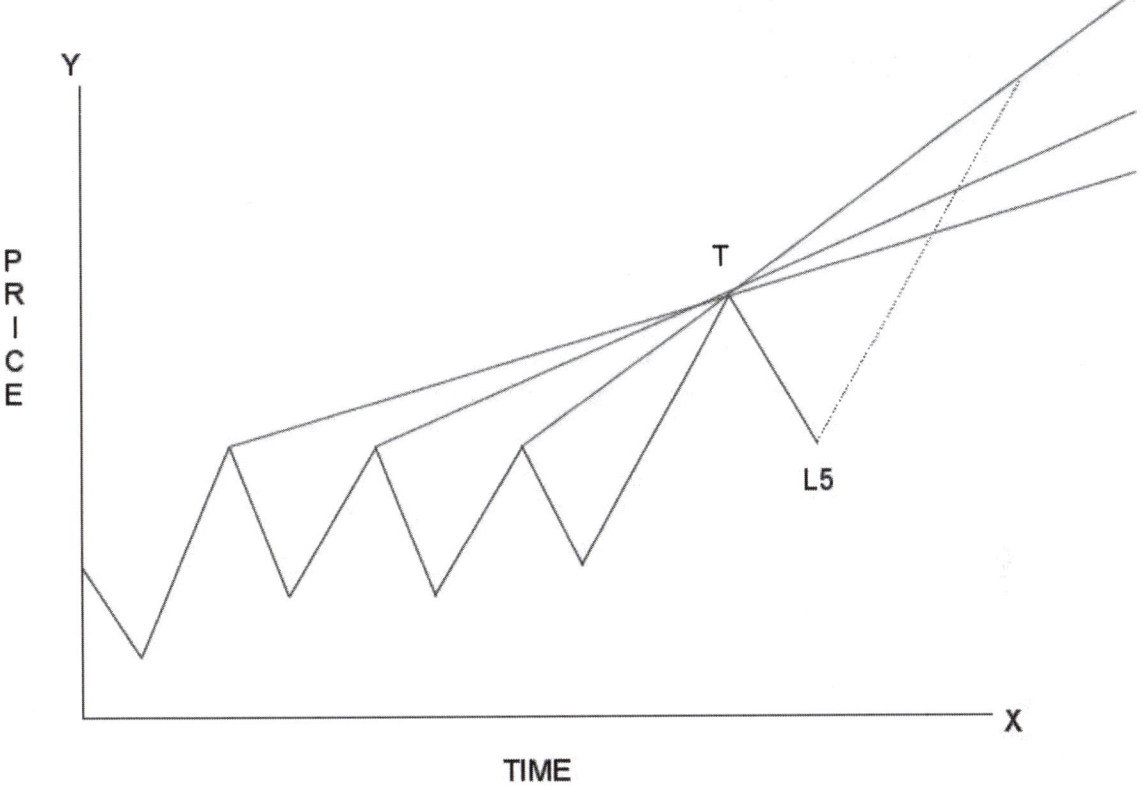

In Figure 10.3, 2e see a series of highs that act as our base/beginning point for our trendline, but all of these trend lines have the same terminal point, T, which is indicated in the chart. Notice that all of these lines are independent trendlines of each other, but we see the reason for calling these fans by looking at the fan that is formed by linking the terminal points together at point T. In effect, these lines will all serve as possible resistance points, and concurrently, the value of these lines **could** be averaged together! Figure 10.3 is an example of a rising tops fan, and of course, declining bottoms can have a fan as well. The importance of correctly drawn trendlines and fans cannot be understated enough, and their power is extreme on longer-term charts such as daily, weekly, and monthly charts. In fact, it is not possible to draw fans with incorrect trendlines. Further, in order to emphasize the power of trendline fans, if we go back to the reference of Corn from earlier, over the last 3 decades, the corn market has had three, large, bubble-like moves, which we learned is possible with commodities. A fan was created using the highs from the 70s, 80s, and 90s. Sure enough, the high in Corn in the 2000s and now in the 2010s was predicted by these fans. Remember, markets are not random, and there is always a reason behind every high or low.

Triangles

There are two types of triangles in the market: expanding triangles and contracting triangles. These triangles can exist in any time frame. Expanding triangles follow our correct trendlines by being formed from rising tops lines and declining bottoms lines, which looks like a less than sign ("<"). Expanding triangles are a swing trader's nightmare because every time a swing activates, the market drops back down into the range, and tends to take out the stop for the swing because of the expanding declining bottoms line. With expanding triangles, the market can do this over and over again. Figure 10.4 is an example of an expanding triangle.

Figure 10.4: Expanding Triangle

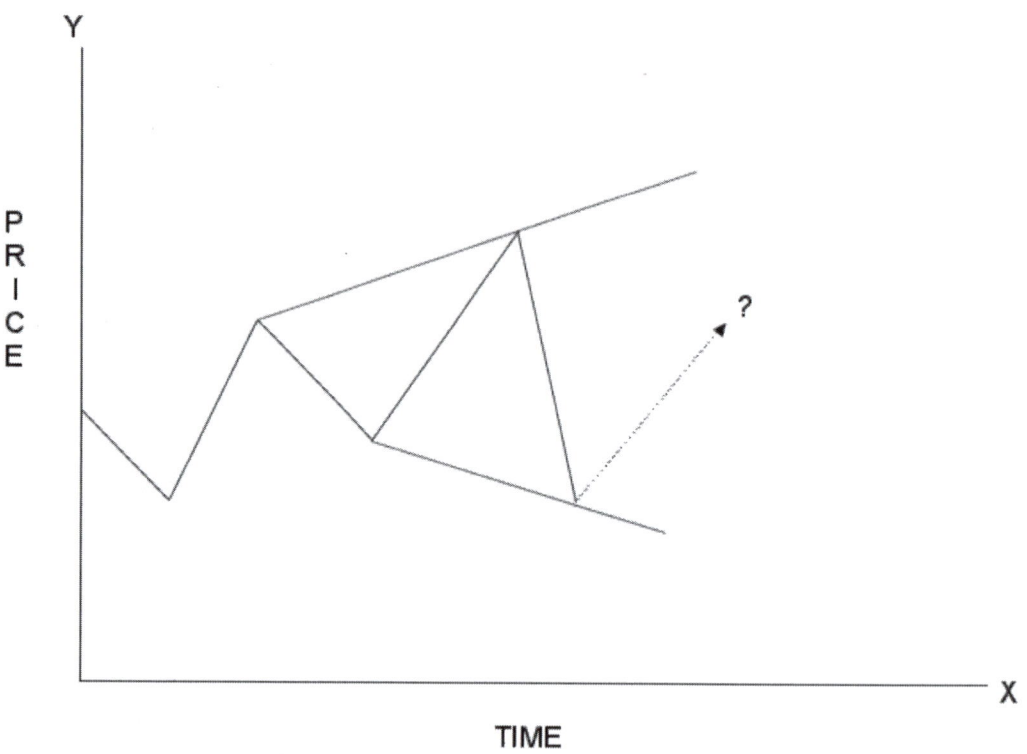

Thankfully, expanding triangles are quite rare compared to contracting triangles and a good edge for understanding when the probability of expanding triangle formations will occur is by simply understanding that they occur in market conditions of low volatility.

Moving to Contracting Triangles, Contracting triangles have characteristics of deep range retracements (75%R+), which was mentioned in Chapter 7. Contracting triangles look more like a greater than sign (">"). Moreover, contracting triangles are drawn by the combination of the two incorrect trendlines: rising bottoms and declining tops. Since these are the "incorrect" trendlines, we can observe that based on the triangle's visual representation, one of these trendlines MUST break because as time moves forward, the triangle must come to a terminal point. As mentioned in Chapter 6, these types of triangles actually challenge Price Theory because we are creating ranges inside of ranges, which means we are also generating retracements inside of retracements. Let us look at Figure 10.5 in order to discuss some more important things to be aware of regarding contracting triangles.

Figure 10.5: Contracting Triangle

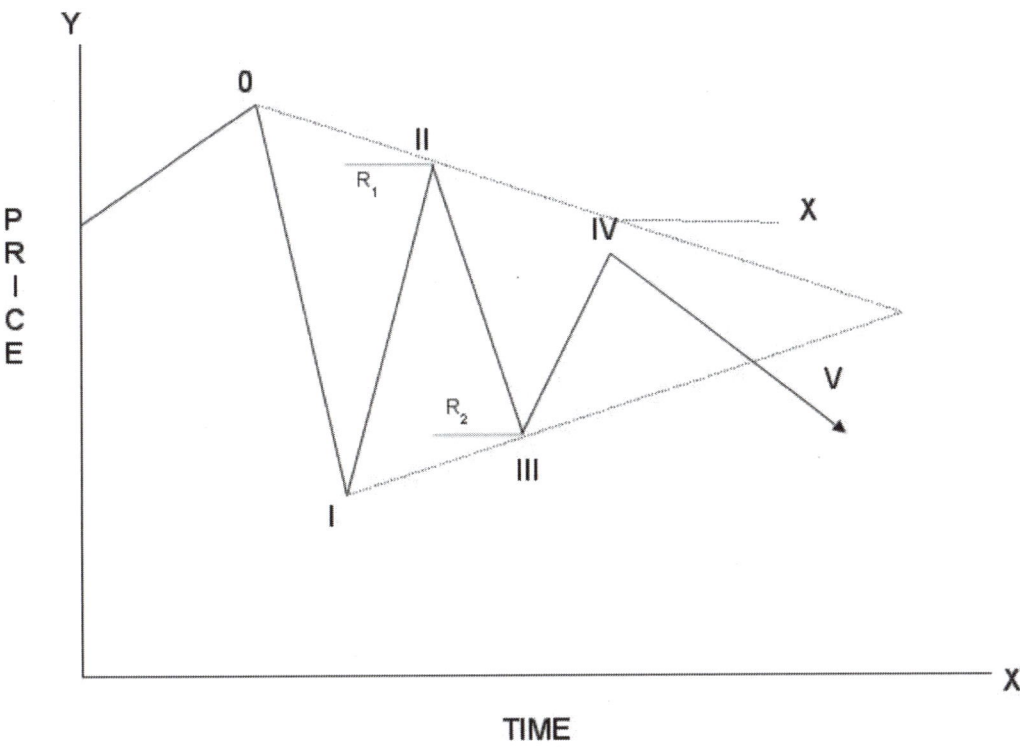

The first thing we notice about a contracting triangle is that the triangle represented in Figure 10.5 is created with dashed lines, which is how we would represent incorrectly drawn trendlines on our chart. The dashed line makes our subconscious remember that these lines will eventually fail. As such, the failure of these lines is related to the eventually adherence that the market must have because of Price Theory, and we can use Figure 10.5 in order to illustrate that fact.

In Figure 10.5, we can visualize that we first have the range 0 → I that has a retracement, R_1, which is point II. This foretells a break of point I by failing to take out a new high over 0. However, we come down to point III, which is a retracement of the I → II range. This foretells a break of II due to the failure to take out a new low below I. Again, we fail this Price Theory Price Objective at point IV. This is where we can now discuss the retracement tendency of contracting triangles along with forecasting the eventual triangle break!

It is my assertion that contracting triangles form due to the market's tendency to find support or resistance at 61.8%R of given ranges. That is why typical retracements that lead to contracting triangles are usually in the 75%R range. In Figure 10.5, R_1 and R_2 could be equal to 75%R of their respective ranges. These triangles form to take the 61.8%R traders out of the market! As such, we can use the first two intra-range retracements as to a clue about how the market is creating a triangle that will tell us what the trend will be. The trend will avail itself by the direction of the triangle break, and we can look to our knowledge of the primary trend from the last chapter in forecasting the direction of the triangle break. In fact, we can take comfort that there is some edge to define by knowing contracting triangles. Either contracting triangles will get us back to the primary trend, or a contracting triangle can be indicative of a trend change, which leads to further observations regarding the tendencies of contracting triangles.

The next two tendencies are illustrated in Figure 10.5 where we have five waves represented in roman numerals that make up the triangle. This labeling is common (and will be elaborated on in Chapter 16), but what is more common is the failure of the terminal point, of the last wave before the triangle breaks, to properly complete the triangle. In order to elaborate visually, we can see that point IV in Figure 10.5 is where the triangle would need to reach the value marked as X in order to properly construct the contracting triangle. Essentially, what we see at point IV is that the market has failed to tag the declining tops line, and when this happens, we can observe that the tendency will be to break the triangle. Therefore, once this starts to happen, wave V will finally satisfy Price Theory Price Objectives, which concludes our discussion on the observations of contracting triangles.

The last type of triangle that needs to be discussed is simply an extrapolation of a contracting triangle, and these types of triangles are known as wedges. A **wedge** is simply a triangle that is made by the market having many retests of tops or bottoms. Essentially, the top or bottom part of the wedge can be made up of double top/bottoms formation, and because we know that when a double bottom/top breaks, we get a powerful swing, we can similarly say that a wedge becomes a powerful market feature because its failure tends to lead to massive market moves due to the contraction of price that occurs inside of the wedge coupled with the break to new highs/lows based on a swing. Thus, the wedge becomes a massive swing in the market. For our example, we will focus on an inclining wedge, as can be scene in Figure 10.6. An inclining wedge has the same highs with subsequent rising bottoms. A declining wedge has the same lows with declining tops.

Figure 10.6: Inclining Wedge

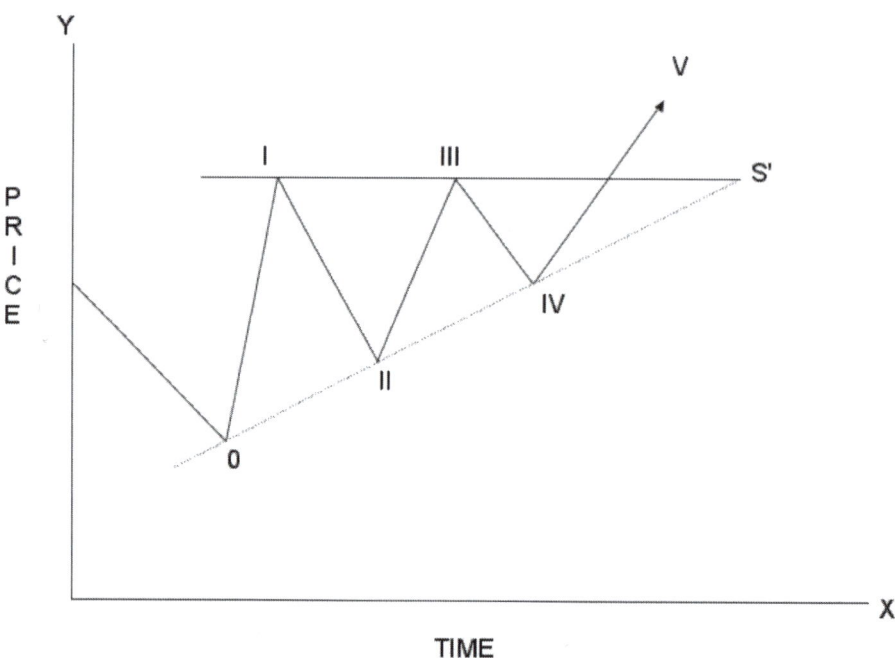

Figure 10.6 shows a five-wave triangle that is an inclining wedge. However, the tendency to have more than five waves with multiple tests of a swing point/price value as shown as point S in Figure 10.6 is quite common. It is also common that the wave that occurs before the wedge breaks (and thus, activates a swing) fails to fully complete as we observe in this illustration by point IV. This too is related to our Figure 10.5 example from earlier.

Parallel Trendlines

The last and most difficult to quantify subject in this chapter is that of parallel trendlines, which are sometimes referred to as **Channels** in conventional technical analysis. A **parallel trendline** can be borne from either a correctly drawn or an incorrectly drawn trendline, which falls in the four category types that we started this chapter off with. The reason for this is that an incorrect trendline that has its married parallel line drawn will yield a correct trendline; i.e. a rising bottoms line (incorrect) yields a rising tops line (correct). The way that we draw a parallel line comes from linking two price points, and then, cloning that line by placing it at the high/low between the two lows/high that generated the first one. Again, as an example, if we use a correct rising tops line between two highs, we would generate the incorrect rising bottoms line that has the same slope as the rising tops line and we would place this line at the low between the two tops. We can also look to Figure 10.7 for a visual example.

Figure 10.7: Rising Tops / Rising Bottoms Parallel Trendline

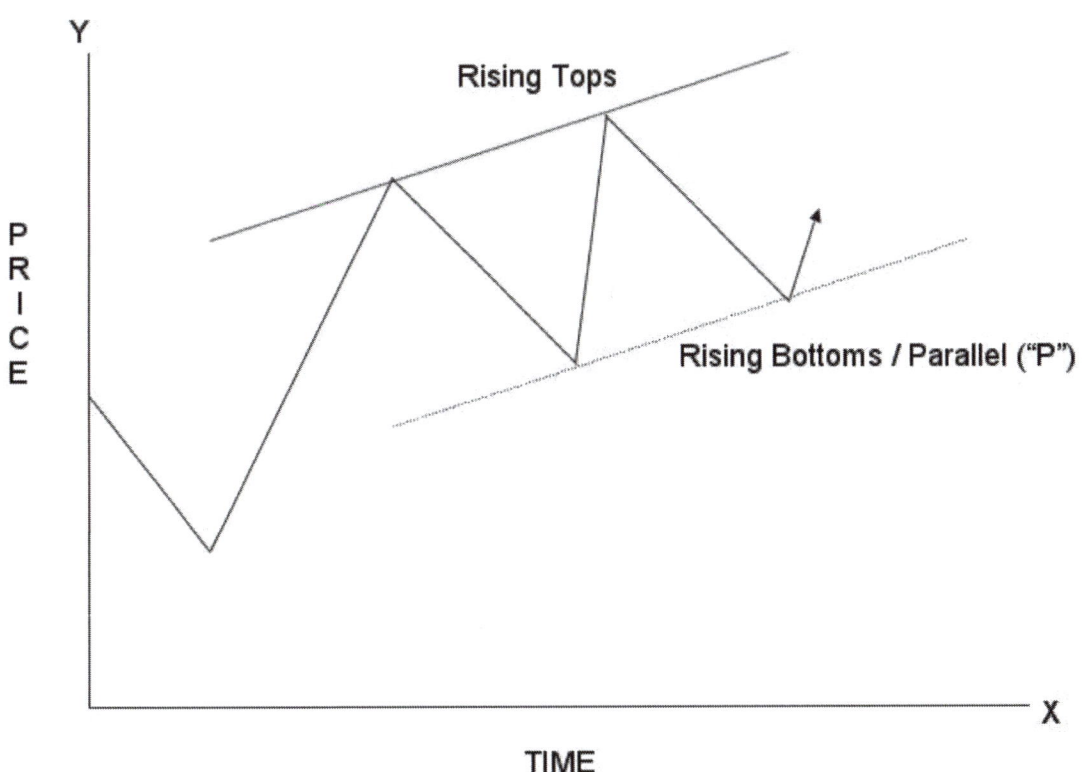

In this example, we have a rising tops trendline that connects points A & C. Once point C forms, we can now clone that line to form the dashed, rising bottoms parallel line. The use of this parallel line comes in as a possible area for market support. In my experience, when a market makes a high or a low that is not easily quantifiable based on mathematical support/resistance calculations, the high/low is typically created by one of these obscure parallel trendlines. As a word of caution, I encourage the trader to not be carried away with trendlines because they may ruin the visualization of a chart. Further, the more powerful a base trend line; the more powerful its reciprocal parallel.

Head and Shoulders Trendlines

There is one last topic that needs discussion with respect to trendlines, and they are called Head and Shoulders Trendlines. The head and shoulders pattern is a common pattern that most market technicians speak about, and it will be discussed in depth in Chapter 12. However, the importance of these patterns is that we may have trendlines that link the various shoulders, which can sometimes be used for trading references. In order to understand this, I will pre-introduce the chart that will be referenced in Chapter 12. Let us turn to Figure 10.8.

Figure 10.8: Head and Shoulders Projections

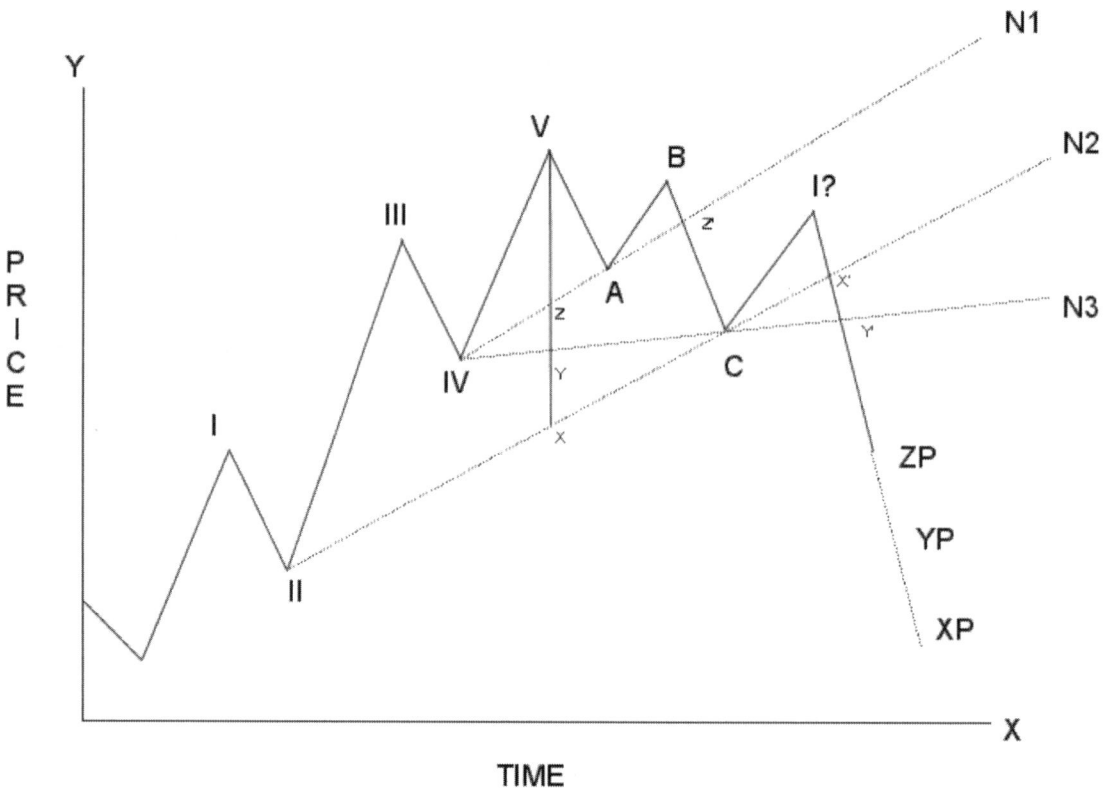

In Figure 10.8, we can see that there are three trendlines for this normal Head and Shoulders

166

pattern, and they are displayed as N1, N2, and N3. Traditionally, the concept of these trendlines is to enter trades upon a break of any one of these lines. For instance, since this is a normal head and shoulders pattern, meaning not an inverted head and shoulders patter, we would go short at a break of N1, N2, or N3. However, it is rare but possible that every so often, the market tends to use these trendlines as support. If that were to happen, we would be going long at a successful test of N1, N2, or N3, and we would be targeting new highs over the "head" based on Price Theory. Again, these are rarities, but sometimes, these trendlines can be used to find perfect mathematical clusters in order to confirm the non=randomness of the market.

In summary, I have presented another mental shift in order to properly observe the market structure through appropriately drawn trendlines that are built off swing points. More important, by drawing the trendlines in the proper way, we learn of the possibility to create fans, which cannot occur with incorrectly drawn trendlines. From there, we discussed the possible market triangles, which can be analyzed for warning / tendencies, and lastly, we talked about the concept of parallel lines. The importance of understanding trendlines will be apparent in the next Chapter where we will discuss relevant patterns and price pattern objectives that may rely on trendlines in order to be found/quantified.

Chapter 11

Common Patterns

At this point, we have covered enough of price structure in order to complete the basic market picture that is related to swings and ranges, which means that we have enough knowledge to deepen our understanding of *how* the market generates its secondary highs or lows, which leads to the violation of range breaks. As such, this chapter will focus on common patterns that emerge from already discussed patterns, which will allow us to find more specific price pattern objectives for intra-range price action. Furthermore, we will begin to clarify higher probability price confirmations and their associated price pattern objectives in order to give us definable trading edges when we are within a given range.

The focus of this chapter will be on micro-patterns, which will be defined by time, and therefore, this chapter is of most relevance to daytraders because micro-patterns tend to exist more often in shorter time frames. As an aside, it is very hard to properly describe these patterns for longer time frames, but they do exist in the same way; price may become wider and our bar counting may be done similar to the 180-bar rule discussed in Chapter 6. Thus, this chapter forces me to look at the shorter-time period patterns, but the reader should keep in mind that like with everything else in this book, the patterns will work the same way as you apply them to longer-term charts. However, because of the necessity to discuss these patterns in terms of shorter-time windows, I will be speaking as such along with supplying chart illustrations that reflect this dialogue. As an aside for the longer-term trader or fund manager, in the next chapter when we discuss the longer-term corrective market phases, which yield their own analytical/technical characteristics, which becomes more powerful in quantifying major market inflection points.

In order to stay aligned with the structure of this book, I will begin by discussing the refinements of predicting whether a given *retracement* will hold, which leads to a new high or low outside of a given range based on Price Theory. The first way that we can refine our trade decisions regarding the purchase or sale of a given retracement will be a discussion on **micro double tops/bottoms** that occur at a given retracement value inside of a given range. Since any double bottom/top that has less than 30 minutes between the two tops/bottoms is in effect deemed **micro**, we will be focusing on all such double bottoms/double tops that are less than 30 minutes but greater than 8 minutes. (Again, if we were to extrapolate this to a longer-term time-frame chart such as the 60-minutes, we would observe that a micro-double bottom on that chart by less than eight bars is actually a true double bottom since it would be wider than our 30-minute criteria by default; i.e. an 8-bar double bottom on a 60-minute chart is equal to 480-minutes hence why the discussion of micro patterns is less relevant to the longer-term trader.) In order to properly visualize what an 8-minute double bottom/top would look like, I will now draw a bar chart instead of a line chart as shown in Figure 11.1.

Figure 11.1: Micro Double Bottom

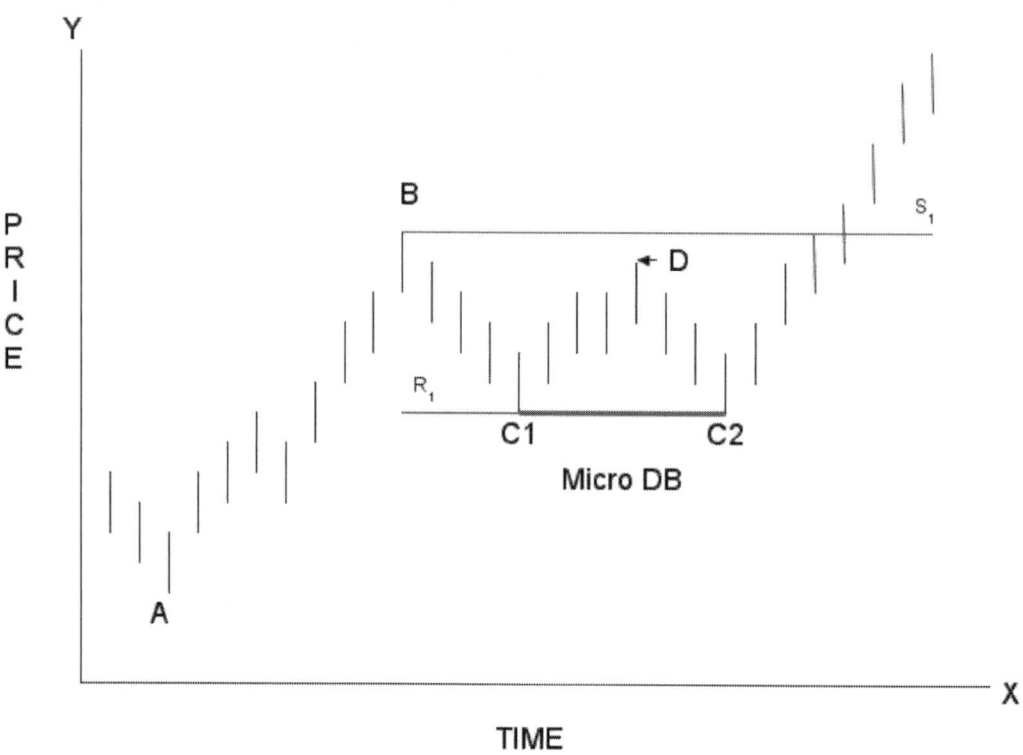

In Figure 11.1, we have a range A → B with a given retracement, R_1. Here, we observe an 8 minute double bottom that occurs at the R_1 value whereby $C_1 = C_2$. In this case, the market is giving us more information regarding the price discovery process that the market engages in as it moves throughout the day. The difference between a normal double bottom/top and a micro lies in the trade entry. In our longer term double bottoms/double tops, I mentioned two types of trade entries that give us favorable risk/reward based on price patterns: swings and 38.2%R beaches. However, in micro patterns, the value of a 38.2%R may be too minimal in order to distinguish from normal market noise, which is the markets tendency to back and fill. In addition, a micro double bottom will have a micro-swing, but it may not even be visible outside of a tick chart! Therefore, we must wait for a break of the high between the two lows (for a double bottom) in order to enter our trade. Later, we can use time to enter these trades even sooner when we get to Time Structure.

In Figure 11.1, a break of point D would be our trade entry criteria with price objectives above point B (due to Price Theory) and stop losses one tick lower than the retracement of $C_1 = C_2$. Notice that C_1 may not be exactly equal to C_2 just as in our larger double bottoms/tops, but we must allow for the double bottom to occur within the tolerance of the retracement as we discussed in Chapter 7.

Our discussion of micro-double tops/bottoms leads into a discussion of **micro-swings** as our next retracement qualifier. The problem with trading micro-swings whereby the time between the base swing-point and the terminal swing-point is less than 30 minutes is that the placement of a stop loss at the terminal point for the swing has a lower probability since it is not a true swing. Again, general market noise could lead to this swing's stop-loss being triggered since it is not reinforced by time or primary ranges. Therefore, our stop on the micro-swing has to be placed at the retracement low, which is the low of the retracement range (for going long a retracement). If the reader is astute, he or she should recognize that these patterns are the same as buying the retracement itself in some ways because we are placing a stop as if we bought the retracement itself. However, even though our entry may be less favorable than directly buying the retracement, we are gaining a much better win-rate by letting the price discovery process of the market show us price patterns that fortify our confidence. Therefore, instead of thinking of these patterns as being delayed from directly buying the retracement, I encourage the reader to think of these patterns as being early entry criteria for primary swings! Let us now move a more complicated micro-example of micro-swings.

Figure 11.2: Micro Swings

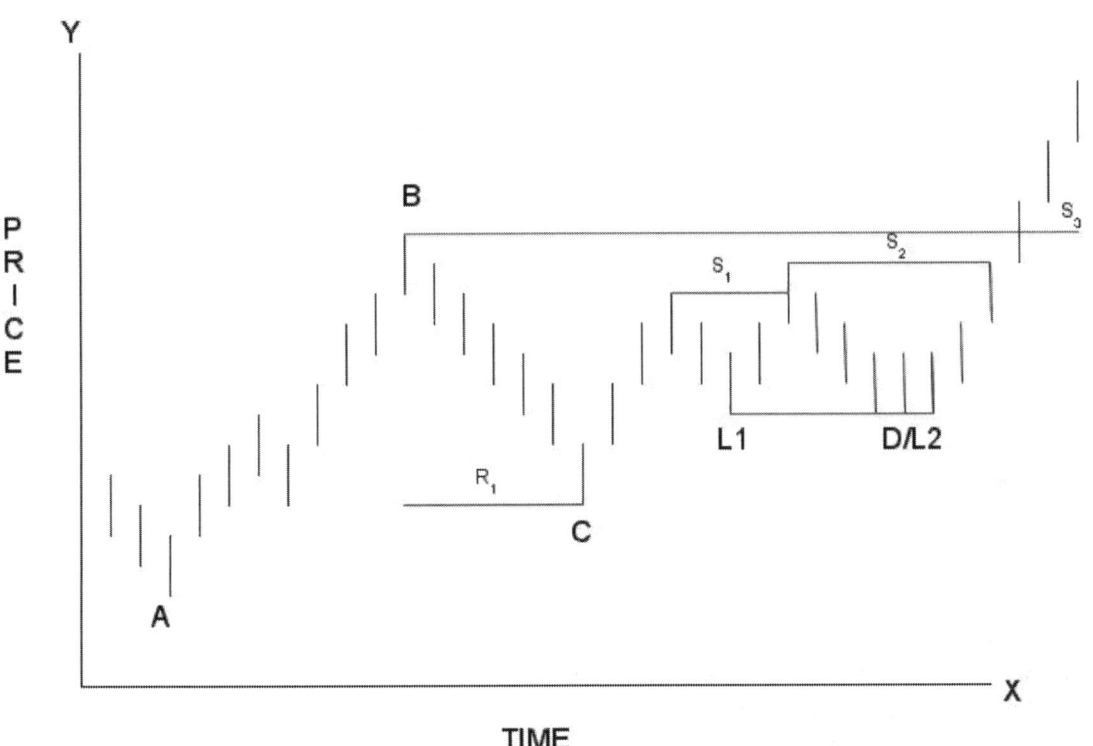

In Figure 11.2, we have an example using a bar chart that shows a market that creates an A → B range, and then, a retracement occurs to point C, which is a retracement value of R_1. As we learned, a qualified swing would now exist if the time between points A & C was greater than 30 minutes and the value of R_1 was greater or equal to 50%. This qualified swing would be triggered at a breach of point B as indicated by S_3. However, we can observe clearly defined micro-swings that occur before triggering S_3.

The first micro-swing has a base point C and a terminal point L_1. As a trader, we may decide to buy this swing at the trigger point shown as S_1 with our anticipation based on Price Theory of new highs over point B. However, because this is not a qualified swing, there is a lower probability of success, and we need to use a wider stop, which would go under the retracement low. An illustration of this is shown in Figure 24 where S_1 is triggered, and a new low is formed at point D. We can visualize that since D is lower than L_1, if our stop-loss would have been placed at one tick lower than L_1, we would have a losing trade. Nevertheless, by placing our stop-loss below the retracement, we see that we would prevent our trade from becoming a loser. As such, our true stop-loss would be placed under point C, which would be our stop-loss for either buying the retracement, entering a micro-DB/DT, or buying a micro-swing. As a note of confirmation, we have to acknowledge that by putting our stop-loss for the trade in the identical place had we just bought the retracement itself that we are actually using the micro-swing as another part of price structure to confirm the break to new highs based on Price Theory occurring inside the range, which eventually leads to new highs outside the range. Of course, this is not a coincidence, and if we decided to take a trade at S_2 instead of at S_1, our stop-loss would still be lower than point C with Price Objectives higher than point B and possible price pattern objectives derived from the larger, qualified swing A □ B □ C. Therefore, by trading the micro-swing, we have increased our reward to risk ratio by anticipating the qualified swing's activation! Our stop would be in the same place as the qualified swing, but we are entering earlier due to more knowledge availed through the price discovery process. It is important to further clarify that without time, these two micro patterns of double tops/bottoms or swings are ways of purchasing retracement levels with higher probabilities of success then we had previously.

Three Drives Patterns

The most important topic in this chapter is the theory of a pattern associated with the phrases "three drives to a top," "three drives to a bottom," or "three peaks and a domed house." Contrary to the micro patterns discussed thus far, 2-drives patterns can occur in any time frame to be useful. So, longer-term traders should pay attention to this section. In order to understand how powerful three drives patterns can be, I yield to an example whereby, a three drives pattern can appear intra-day in a span of 10 minutes or they can appear over many months as in the weekly three drives pattern formed in late 2009 by on the DJIA. (By the way, this 3-drives pattern was the instigator of the first major sell off from the March 2009 low, an as such, the 3-drives pattern is the first piece of Price Structure that becomes relevant after all the other concepts discussed thus far.)

The formation of a 3-drives pattern begins with properly drawn trendlines, which means we are once again back to the beauty of the market structure by acknowledging that those lines were simply swing points. Thus, three drives to a top links three tops by a rising tops line, and a three drives to a bottom links three bottoms by a declining bottoms line. Now, we can define price pattern objectives for 3-drives patterns, which are very important because the masses that recognize these patterns, as "three peaks and a domed house" usually never understand the proper price pattern objective for these patterns. Now, we can define these price pattern objectives for 3-drives patterns:

(A) *The price pattern objective for a 3-drives to a top is the lowest low between the three tops.*

(B) *The price pattern objective for a 3-drives to a bottom is the highest high between the three bottoms.*

Understanding the true price pattern objective for these patterns is crucial because, one of the most notable things about 3-drives patterns is that their price pattern objective often leads to inconspicuous double bottoms/tops at the price of the given objective. Furthermore, it is common for this price pattern objective to be exceeded by one or two ticks, and then, activate the double top/bottom that leads to an expansion of the base range. Thus, the market structure is such that these 3-drive patterns form in order to mind screw swing trades who added to positions on the last three swings. Remember, the market's goal is to always take as many people out of the market as possible. In fact, it is so common for the market to make a double bottom/top at the fulfillment of the price pattern objective of either of the two three drives patterns that I feel I must illustrate it to the reader, which I have done in Figure 11.3 below.

Figure 11.3: 3-Drives to a Top + Double Bottom

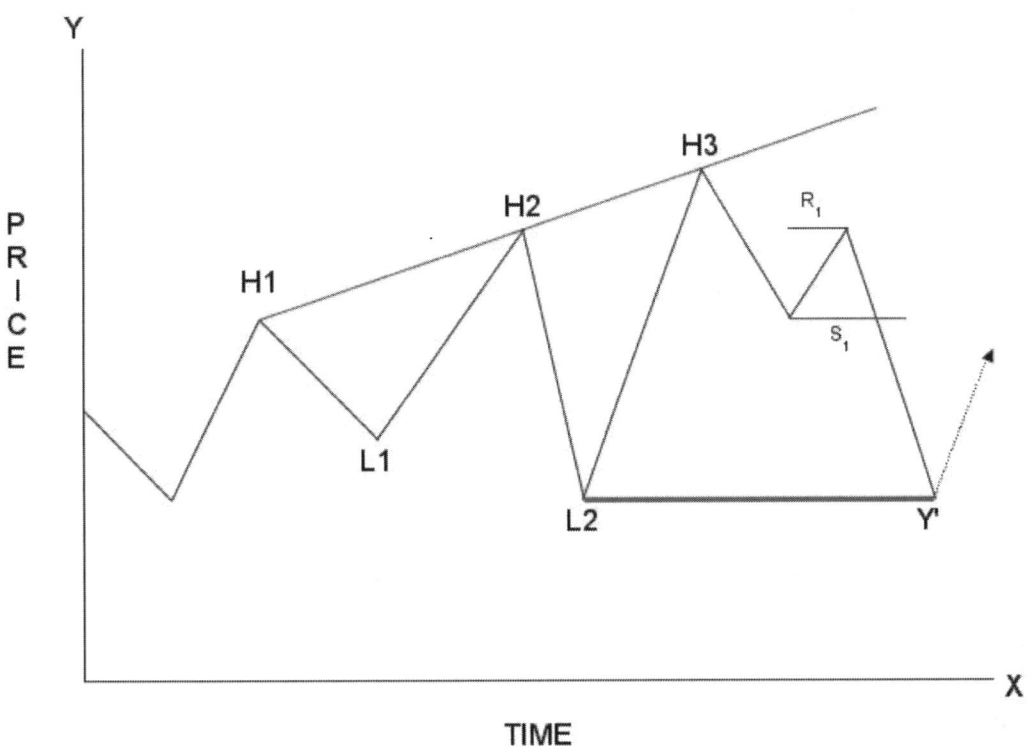

In Figure 11.3, I am essentially illustrating a noiseless graph as an extrapolation of the DJIA from late 2009 to early 2010, which is a three-drives to a top pattern. Here, we see a rising tops line linking the three highs with the price pattern objective of the lowest low between the tops. In this case, that low is L2. We then see the price pattern objective attained by reaching point y'. If we correlate this to the DJIA chart, we can see that the three-drives pattern reached the L_1 value, which yielded a double bottom in real-life in early 2010. Therefore, this 3-drives pattern and the associated inconspicuous DB was the extent of the mind-power needed in order to understand that once the 3-drives pattern was fulfilled, the market's double bottom goal (and the Price Theory Price Objective's goal) was to reach new highs.

Like with everything in the markets, we cannot always be sure a three drives pattern will hold, and we need to understand that a three drives pattern that fails is essentially a break of a rising tops line or a declining bottoms line. However, (and as we will see in our later discussions regarding repetitive tops/bottoms) we need to understand that when these patterns break, they tend to yield large, dynamic moves in the direction of the break. I believe this is because of the amount of disbelief the market has in a failed three-drives pattern, which causes a momentum rush once mass-market psychology catches on. Regardless, our only concern is that when we see a three-drives patter break, we must be cognizant that we are seeing an indication of the trend, which was similar to our discussion of an expanding triangle. Further, we can look to the real world for an example of a three-drives failure, and that example existed when Tesoro's (TSO) stock price had a 3 drives pattern that failed in the third quarter of 2012. However, that failure was not random, because the market is not random. Thus, that failure was easily scene as an inconspicuous double bottom at one of the lows of the three-drives pattern, but not the lowest low, which would have made the pattern complete. Therefore, we can see the power of the double bottom that occurred in TSO's stock chart, and we can see the power of Price Theory when new highs were obtained higher than the three-drive's patterns high.

Moving on, it is important to discuss tolerance and fast-moving markets when we talk about 3-drives patterns. Just like all patterns, as time gets wider, the width of tolerance given to a rising tops/bottoms line must be expanded, as is the case in the late 2009 3-drives pattern I referenced in the DJIA. Therefore, as market technicians, we sometimes have to look outside of the technical realm and use visual inspection in order to ascertain the relevance pattern of the pattern, and sometimes, we have to do this by moving to a logarithmic scale. Unfortunately, <u>this requires a qualitative eye that recognizes the underlying quantitative nature</u>. That last statement is very important, and I ask the reader to understand that although the market is not random, it is far from perfect. In a way, the reason I have chosen to become an index trader is that the index has effectively smoothed out the price patterns of the 30 or 500 underlying stocks that comprise the index, which creates a more technical picture. On the other hand, if we are to move out of the retrospection sphere of thought, we need to move to fast-paced markets, which also require a discussion.

Contrarily to tolerance, in a fast-paced market that is making very quick highs (or more often due to underlying market structure, very quick lows) we will often see a 3-drives pattern emerge quickly, which yields a market inflection point. This point may emerge purely out of the time and price relationship derived from a rising tops/declining bottoms line that is simply a quick heuristic since our mathematical support/resistance calculations may be time consuming or even nonexistent under high volatility. Therefore, we must always be cognizant of 3-drives patterns more than any other trendline reference due to the high-level of probability associated with the pattern itself. This is the main topic for this chapter.

In summary, this chapter has allowed the trader to refine Price Theory once again. It is allowing the trader to see how the underlying price structure that exists in every time frame can be used as a basis for predicting retracement holds or price objectives to be met by looking at intra-range Price Theory working through micro-double bottoms/tops or micro-swings. More important, we have also discussed the power of the three drives pattern in short time frames as well as in bigger pictures along with the tendency for the price pattern objectives to align with longer term double bottoms/tops. Next, we will take our knowledge of the bar chart into the realm of analyzing an entire range's move, which we will discuss as wave tendencies.

Chapter 12

Wave Analysis and Corrective Phases

In this Chapter, we will explain how to analyze movements of price and time as a singular entity that will be defined as a wave. Therefore, a wave will be noted in the same notation as a Range. However, a wave may be made up of more than one range (or, it may be the large expansion of our base range), which is why traditional Elliott Wave Theory eventually fails, but that does not mean that it isn't useful for qualitative inspection, which conforms to quantitative patterns (again, as discussed towards the end of the last chapter).

In essence, conventional Elliott Wave Theory is based on a 5-3-5 principle, which simply means five waves up, a three-wave correction, and another five waves up. The problem is that people can always find these patterns in a subjective way after the fact, which is useless for real-world application. In addition, Elliott Wave analysis is just as useful on the short side as it is on the long side, but there exists a duality between long and short waves. Therefore, in order to be useful, we need to use our learning of Price Structure in order to be aware of possible projections that result for Elliott Wave patterns. This awareness helps us to trade in the present moment. Once more, we will need a slight mentality shift from the masses in order to classify the usefulness of Elliott Wave Theory for powerful projections and powerful corrective phases. The usefulness of understanding wave analysis emerges from unconventional projections or realizations of the Price Objectives that are relevant at the end of market corrections.

Five Wave Analyses

Let us start by looking at a five wave up move using conventional Elliott Wave theory that is refined by our new knowledge of Price Structure. We will examine this pattern in any time frame, but of note, the longer in time that we go, the easier it may be to visualize the waves themselves.

Using our qualified swing principle, we can group the first three waves of a five-wave pattern. This is because we have our initial-wave (base range), our retracement wave (retracement/secondary range), and our projection wave (projection range). The first way in which Elliott Wave theory can be useful is if we ascertain that our third wave should be bigger than our first wave. Therefore, the 100%P for the qualified swing should no longer be our price pattern objective if we submit to Elliott Wave Principles. Not only can we expect this wave to be larger in price, but also, it should be longer in time, and it is quite common for the 161.8%P to be the terminal point for our third wave before we begin to form Wave 4. Thankfully, the formations of the first three waves do not require any type of different analysis than we have already talked about aside from the acknowledgment of a larger Wave 3. However, Wave 4 that is derived from an Elliott Wave standpoint can give us edge evidence about terminal points of the entire five-wave scenario. We will now discuss those observations because they are important in understanding an edge, and do not worry, after this forthcoming discussion; I will go through examples to clarify this language for the reader.

The first observation of Wave 4 is that it may bring us to a new low that is lower than the discreet low of the base range, Wave 1. If this occurs, our wave analysis is incorrect, and our Waves 1-3 were simply a deep A-B-C correction of a previously existing range! Therefore, we can invert our logic to analyze five waves in the opposite direction because Wave 4 may be Wave 3 for the inverted five-wave. The next two observations of a wave 4 speak in terms of Wave 4s that are truly Wave 4s, and therefore, they remain valid.

Thus, the second observation of Wave 4 is if we have a true Wave 4. This means that Wave 4 does not go higher than Wave 3's high, we do not go lower than Wave 2's terminal point (where stops are from the qualified swing), and we actually have a perfect measured move down as Wave 4 which is equal to the same price/time distance as Wave 2. In essence, Wave 4 = Wave 2, which would be a perfect measured move in price and time.

The third observation of Wave 4 relies in the question of whether or not two different things happen. First, does Wave 4 go lower than the terminal point of Wave 2? The second question is does Wave 3 have a shallow, quick retracement and then, take out the discreet high formed by Wave 3 as a fake-out Wave 5? Essentially, once taking out the Wave 3 high, there may be minimal follow-through, and we can observe that Wave 4 is still gyrating through these price levels instead of yielding to the inception of a new Wave 5. In this scenario, the gyrations of Wave 4 can be quantified as something called an Irregular Flat.

We can now discuss our possible fourth wave projections by discussing flats. A **running flat** (as I will define it) is a complicated Wave 4 that in some ways mimics a triangle. A Wave 4 that is classified as a running flat is when the time of Wave 4 exceeds the time for Wave 2, **and** has yet to take out a new high over Wave 3 or a new low under Wave 2. We can see this example in Figure 12.1. (Note: For wave retracements on charts, we will use Roman Numerals paced at the END of the wave, and I will now use Roman Numerals in our discussion of Waves.)

Figure 12.1: Regular Flat

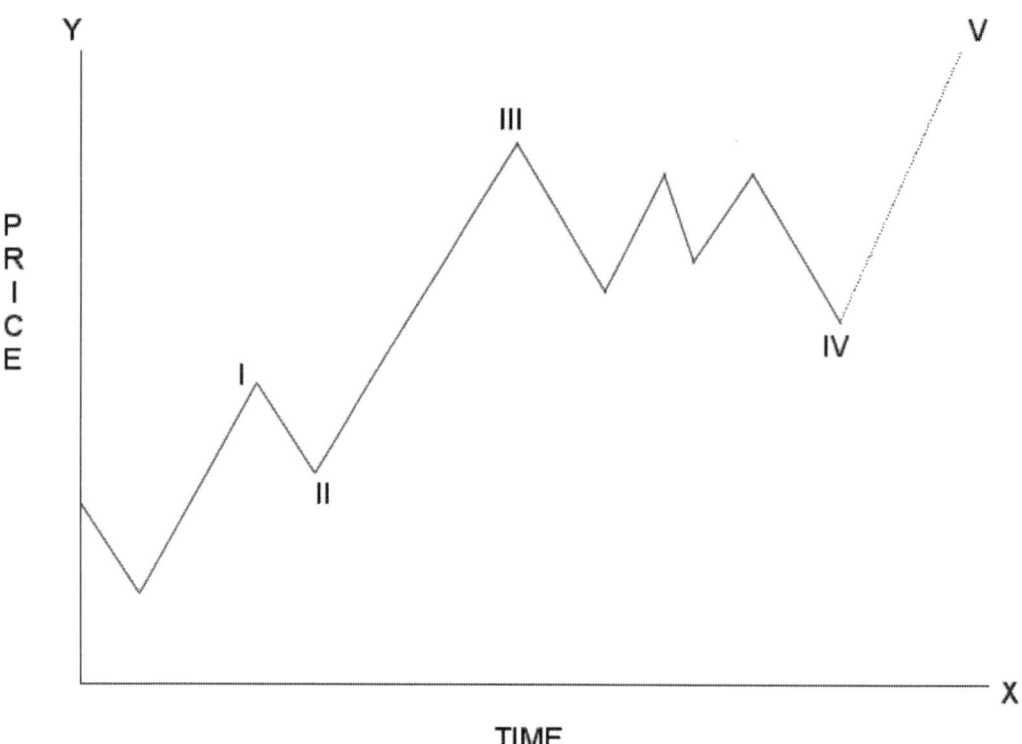

In Figure 12.1, the reader can see that we have a clean Wave I, II, and III, and I have decided to omit the swing point, which occurs on the break of Wave I. Then, we see our running flat Wave IV, which is indeed longer in time than Wave II, and most important, it does not take out Wave II's low or Wave III's high. Therefore, we have a seemingly normal approach to the first four waves, and once we have determined Wave IV is complete, we can be assured of the fact that Wave V should take us higher than Wave III.

The next type of flat is an irregular flat, and there are two-types of irregular flats; one with a price projection and one without. In order to define an **irregular flat**, we can say that an irregular flat is an irregular Wave IV whereby either Wave III's high is exceeded, Wave II's low is exceeded, or in rare cases, both are exceeded. One of the goals of an irregular flat is to trap swing-traders by taking out the Wave III high, which fools traders into thinking Wave IV is complete and they are in Wave V. Another way to screw with swing traders is to have Wave IV go all the way down in take out stops that should exist right below Wave II, which was our primary retracement range. (Again, I am speaking in terms of a five-wave up-move for these examples, and these examples would apply equally to the downside. However, since market's have tendencies to move higher, it is more beneficial to speak in up-terms.) Moving on, let us discuss and examine an irregular flat with price projections first.

This type of irregular flat has a shallow wave down after Wave III ends, and then, breaks to a new high over Wave III with immediate fallback into the range established by the original Wave III. We can then measure the price distance that wave IV exceeded Wave III and we can subtract that low from the first move down that started Wave IV in the first place. If we have a more complex Wave IV that actually targets stops under Wave II, then we can also use this measured distance and subtract it from Wave II's terminal point as another projection to determine a value for Wave IV. Should this happen, we can say that Wave IV may have also become a larger Wave II, with a deep retracement of the expanded Wave I. (I say this last statement to emphasize that waves can expand forward and backwards in time.) Now, let us examine these two types of projection calculations visually using Figure 12.2.

Figure 12.2: Irregular Flat

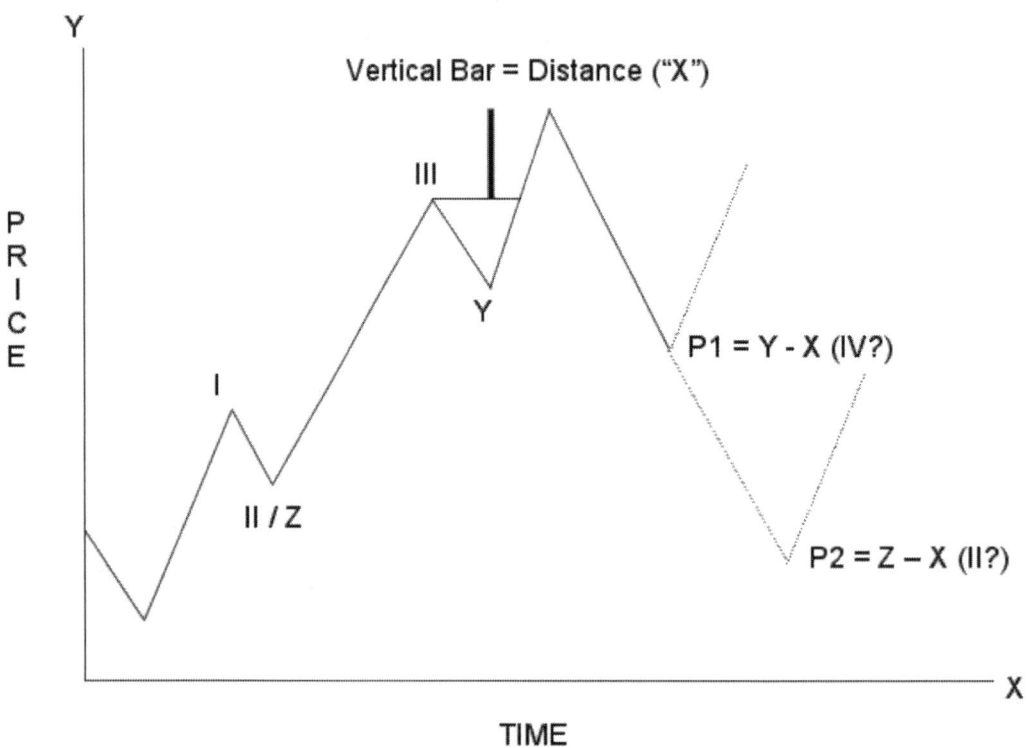

In Figure 12.2, we have an irregular flat formation that generates a distance, "X", by breaking higher than Wave III. This distance is subtracted from Y to get our first projection for the irregular flat Wave IV, which is labeled as P_1. When the market reaches P_1, we will look to see if P_1 has any other items clustering with it such as shorter projections or even a primary retracement from the expanded base range of Wave I through Wave III+X. Then, we can see if the price discovery process at P_1 causes the market to reverse to the upside, which would indicate the end of Wave IV, and the beginning of Wave V, which has a Price Objective based on Price Theory to go higher than Wave III+X.

The second projection shown in Figure 12.2 occurs by subtracting the distance, that Wave III was exceeded, again defined as X, from the point marked as Z, which was the primary retracement range that led to the swing above Wave I's high. This is shown in Figure 12.2 as the point labeled P_2. In some respect, this scenario becomes very powerful because of Price Theory. Should Wave I's initial low not be exceeded, we have indeed created the deep retracement of the Wave I-III+X, and we now have a Price Objective higher than Wave III+X. However, should Wave I's low be exceeded, all of the Elliott Wave logic falls apart. However, let's assume that does not happen, and we can see that our irregular flat/complex Wave IV may have indeed become our new Wave II, which is also indicated in Figure 12.2. Therein lies that problem with a complex irregular flat because we do not know if this P2 is actually the terminal point of Wave II and the Waves I-III+X were just a large Wave I. Not only is this the problem with Wave analysis but it is the problem of all Elliott Wave Theory, because we can simply find ourselves in the inception of a wider and wider five wave patterns as the market moves higher.

The next type of irregular flat is one that does not exceed Wave III, but it forms a deep retracement move that takes out the stops placed under the terminal point of Wave II. This type of wave generates a unique value that may serve as mathematical support or resistance that clusters with other mathematical support or resistance numbers to form a strong mathematical cluster. Further, this value is similar to our last example, but now, we measure the distance that our Wave II stop is exceeded instead. Once measured, we can add that value to the high of Wave III in order to produce a possible, shallow fifth wave projection. Let us look to Figure 12.3 as an example of this irregular flat.

Figure 12.3: Irregular Flat Fifth Wave

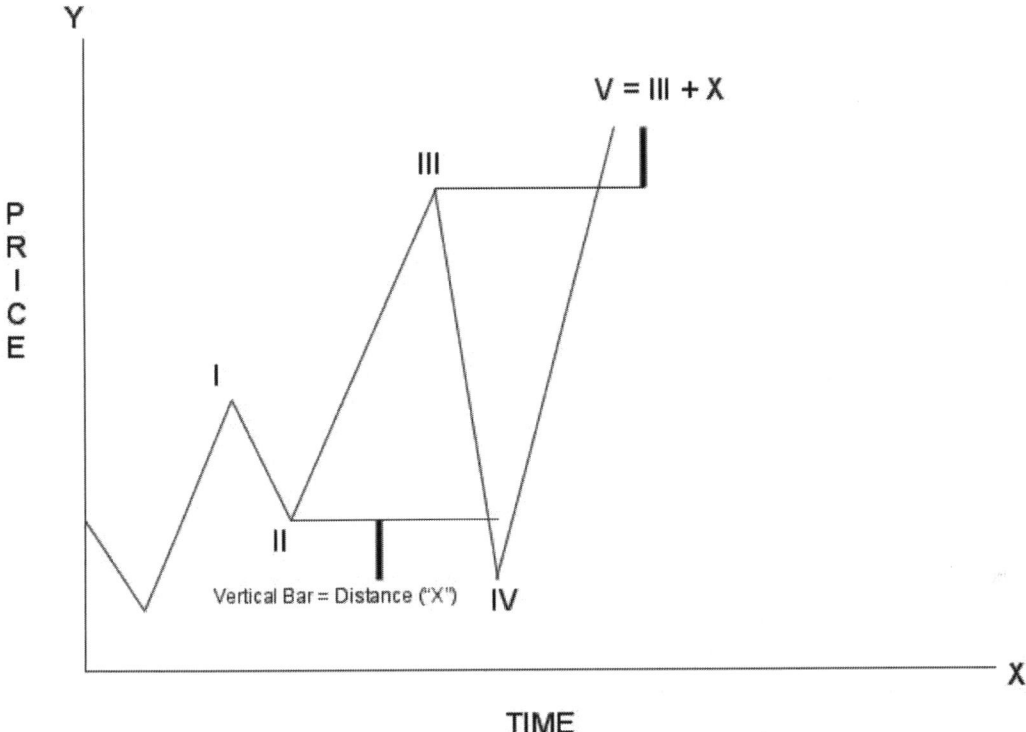

In this example, we can define our distance "X" by the amount our Wave II was exceeded, and we can add this to our Wave III high in order to get our first, fifth wave projection, which opens up the discussion of possible five-wave terminal points. Again, this would be considered a shallow Wave V because it did not exceed Wave III by a lot, but I must ask the reader, "What else could we have?" Well, the answer is simple. We could say that Wave I-III is actually a Wave I, and that Wave IV is a deep retracement of that range, which means it is actually a Wave II. This would mean that Wave V's high is really the 100%P of the Wave I-III → Wave IV → Wave V projection. However, this brings up something very important. If Wave V's 100% projection is exceeded, as we know should be the case in a standard Wave III, we then get confirmation that the Wave logic has expanded. Basically, we can conclude that our initial wave analysis was wrong, and our new wave analysis is forthcoming once we visualize that Wave III has exceeded the 100%P of Wave I-III → Wave IV → Wave V. Thankfully, we are done with the circuitous wave logic, and we can discuss the most important things to be mindful of with respect to wave analysis, which are the powerful fifth wave projections that were foreshadowed in our Chapter 8 discussion of the 61.8%P. In fact, the next three fifth wave projections are much more common and straight-forward.

The first way that we can use wave analysis in order to quickly benefit us is to define our Wave V as being equal to Wave I. Therefore, the Wave V terminal point (for an uptrend) is the Wave I price distance added to Wave IV's low. This is more typical of a five-wave pattern, and now we can discuss the typical five-wave pattern, which is a small Wave I, a large Wave III, and small Wave V. However, even though this first projection is simple, it is hard to draw correctly on the chart with the projection tool because the projection tool's secondary anchor point for this measured move is placed at the base of Wave IV, which may appear as an incorrect drawing to our mind, but it is not.

The second major projection for Wave V is the distance from the discreet low of Wave I to the distance of the discreet high of Wave III. This distance is multiplied by 61.8%, and then, this distance is added to the terminal point of Wave IV. We would call this the additive distance of Waves I-III times 61.8% added to Wave IV. Out of everything in Elliott Wave Theory, this is the most important. This is a calculation that is often useful and often neglected by the masses. Therefore, in longer-term charts, this Wave V calculation has a tremendous amount of power in calling market inflection points. Do not forget about it. Ever.

The last fifth wave projection comes form the fifth wave itself using the terminal point of Wave IV. In a way, the reader can think of this as a micro-swing even though when we use Elliott Wave it is often done on a longer-term analysis. Basically, I say this because once Wave IV terminates, we can have a move up, a retracement of that move, and then, a swing activation that adds a Wave V projection into our equations. Essentially, this becomes an A → B → C swing with its own price projection, which is a perfect lead-in to our three-wave analysis discussing ABC Corrections.

Three Wave Analyses

In Elliott Wave Theory, the three-wave pattern that is produced after a five-wave pattern completes is known as a corrective pattern with a 100%P as the primary target (occasionally the 127.2%/161.8%P comes into play). We have already discussed this in Figure 6 early on, and the power of recognizing an ABC correction is extreme because we know that once it completes, the market will have a Price Objective to reach new high/lows outside of its base range, which could be a substantially large move. Thankfully, we can now use Elliott Wave Theory in order to predict this three-wave pattern *if we have a fifth wave projection holding the market.* We can therefore garner an edge by anticipating this setup if we see Wave V holding to any of the values discussed at the end of the last section. However, this corrective three-wave pattern has tendencies, which allow us to build our trading edges. The most important thing to realize, after we become aware that we *might* be in a three-wave correction, is that this correction has a price pattern objective to take out stops placed at the terminal point of Wave IV, and rarely, Wave II. It is also possible that Wave II and Wave IV were previously formed as A → B → C corrective swings in building the currently terminated five-wave pattern.

In terms of nomenclature, when we discuss the three-wave corrective pattern, we will not use roman numerals and we will label these as A, B, and C waves. Now, as we turn to Figure 12.4, w can see the 5-3 pattern where we use the letters A, B, and C to define the corrective waves. As an aside, the terminal point of the corrective ABC wave is where Elliott Wave Theory starts to lose validity in my mind.

Figure 12.4: 5-3-5 Elliott Wave

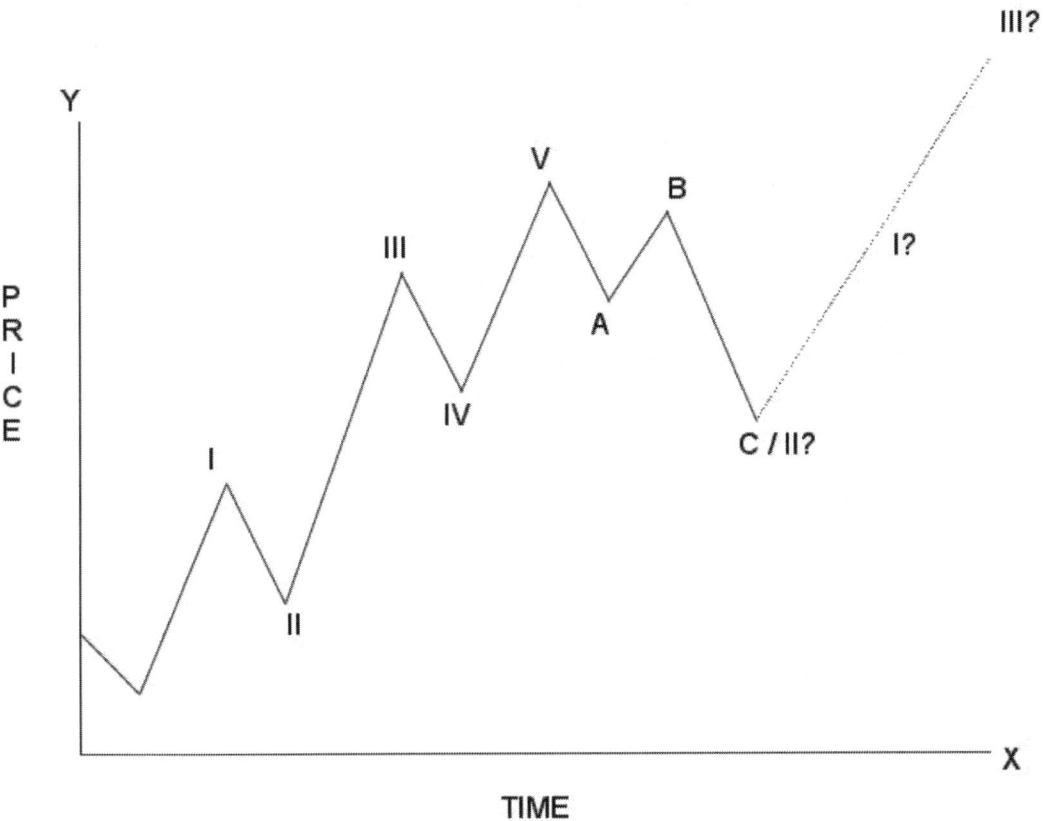

In Figure 12.4, we see the scenario that I foreshadowed earlier. We see that we have a finished five-wave pattern, which has a nice ABC correction, but what we don't realize is that the entire five-wave up pattern is just a Wave I, and this ABC correction was a Wave II! However, Elliott Wave Theory does tell us to expect that after an ABC correction completes that we can expect another five-wave pattern! You see dear reader, it becomes nonsensical and useless at some point because we can keep morphing and elongating waves, but thankfully, if we recall the concept of range replacement and secondary/retracement range replacement, we can allow our minds to focus on the true five-wave patterns and the true three-wave corrections in order to give us an edge, but ultimately, that edge is already linked back to Klatch's Price Theory. Lastly, I must mention that In Figure 12.4, I have illustrated this mental struggle by the question marks indicated as I?, II?, and III?

Head and Shoulders Corrections

In our discussion of trendlines in Chapter 10, I glossed over the Head and Shoulders pattern in order to indicate that the neckline of the Head and Shoulders pattern can be used either to buy/sell a bounce off that trendline or to go short/long on a break of that trendlines. The latter is much more common, and this section will focus on these neckline breaks. Moreover, Head and Shoulders patterns are commonly talked about, but more often than not, the masses draw them with error. Again, a slight shift to a primary focus on time is necessary in predicting the validity of the Head and Shoulders pattern in order to yield a potential, mathematical, market inflection point. The trick is easy and simple: the neckline of the Head and Shoulders pattern must be equal in time with regards to the midpoint, i.e. the left shoulder is equal to the right shoulder in terms of time ($T_1 = T_2$). That's it. That's the edge. That's the tweak.

Thus, if the condition imposed by Time is NOT met, then a trader should just stick to conventional price projections in order to determine the price pattern objective defined by the relevant swing. Because the swing will occur anyway, we have to keep the nature of a swing in mind with respect to our trading so that we are not too inundated with multiple Head and Shoulders patters. However, if Head and Shoulder patterns are properly quantified, they can give us a very powerful price entry point, which precedes the activation of the swing. Because of how much we can reduce our risk on these types of trades, it requires going through a lengthy example. Therefore, let us look to Figure 12.5 in order to properly define Head and Shoulders projections, but more important, Head and Shoulders entries. Figure 12.5 will focus on a short-sided correction, which is the easier vantage point in order to qualitatively "see" a Head and Shoulders chart formation. As such, do not forget that they exist as "inverted head and shoulders patterns" as well.

Figure 12.5: Head and Shoulders Projections

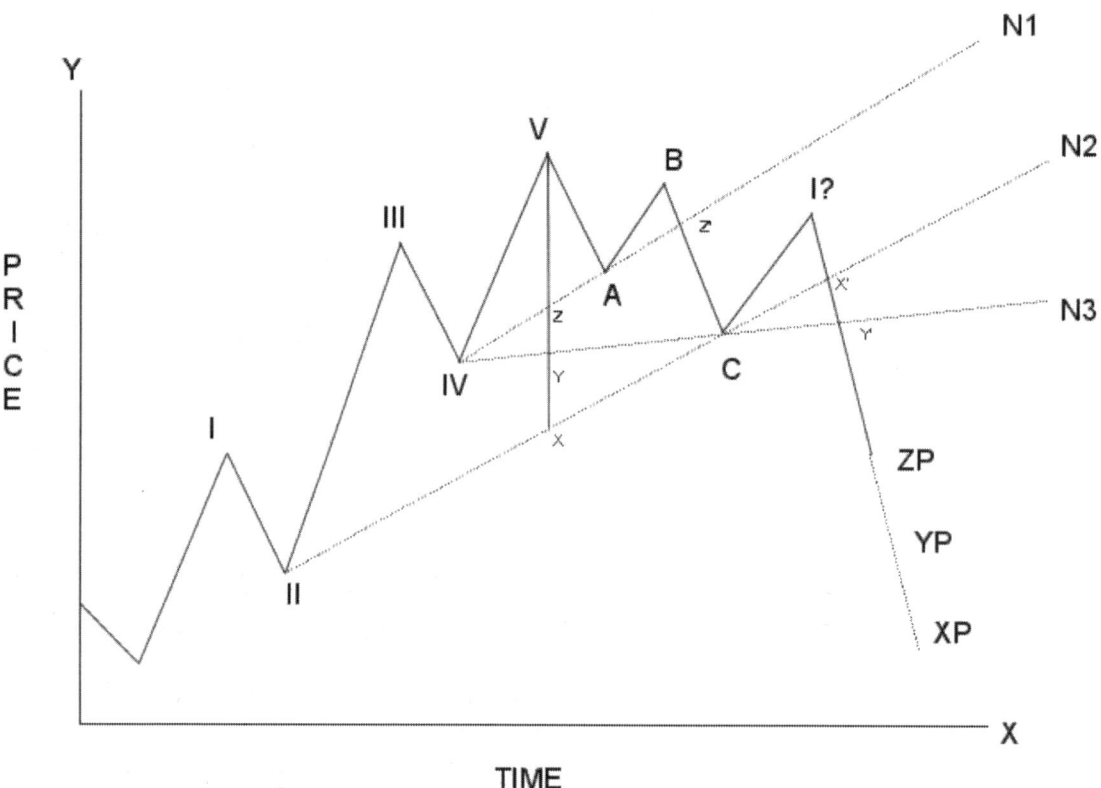

In Figure 12.5, I have drawn three Head and Shoulders Necklines with 3 corresponding Projections. The necklines are indicated as N_1, N_2, and N_3. The projections are indicated as ZP, YP, and XP, and the corresponding entry points for those projections are shown as Z', X', and Y'. Now, without time, the traditional head and shoulders technique would look at the two shoulders that are equivalent in price, this is indicated with Neckline N_3, and the first obvious thing about this neckline is that the entry point for the short, Y', has the worst possible entry compared to either Z' or X'. This is because in necklines N_1 and N_2 are drawn between shoulders that have an *approximately* equal amount of time on both sides of the head, shown as point V.

In order to further clarify, a standard Head and Shoulders drawer would incorrectly define the left shoulder by the low of Wave IV to the correction low at point C. Here, we use this dotted line as N_3, and we can easily see that T_1 (the time distance from the low of Wave IV to the time distance of Wave V) is much less than to T_2 (the time distance from the time at Wave V to the time distance at point C.) Since a standard Head and Shoulder's drawer does not factor in time (only price), we, as *Time and Price Symmetry* traders, gain an edge. We can see our edge graphically because the entry point for this incorrect head and shoulders is shown as point Y', which again, is significantly lower then the entry point that we get by using time. So, let us look at this entry points using time by looking at the chart in order to define two necklines N_1 and N_2.

If we factor time in, we can draw two different necklines where T_1 is approximately equal to T_2. The first, N_1, is when T_1 = Wave V – Wave IV (in terms of time) and T_2 = Point A – Wave V. This gives us an entry at Z', which is much more advantageous than Y'; thereby, giving us better reward to risk. The second correctly drawn neckline using time is shown in the graph where T_1 = Wave V – Wave II and T_2 = C – Wave V, which yields an entry at X' by the line N_2. However, this neckline is not as perfect, but still, when we factor in time, we have a more advantageous entry point than using price itself. However, in order to supply the mathematics to define the calculations for the projections, I will use the perfectly drawn neckline indicated by the line segment N_1 in order to illustrate to the reader the two ways to draw Head and Shoulders projections. There is a quick way, and of course, there is a complex mathematical way. Let us go through this simple mathematical way in order to appease the more technically inclined.

To begin the example, we know that the basic equation for a line is Y=MX+B, where M = the slope. For us, that means that Price = M*Time + B, but for the sake of simplicity sake, we do not need the B since we are looking for a point between two points, which are used to define the slope. Thus, we can now begin defining equations using Figure 12.5 and Neckline N_1.

First, we define M, and we define M as a delta in price divided by a delta in time. Using our example this would be M = $(P_A - P_{IV}) / (T_A - T_{IV})$, which yields the equation Price = $((P_A - P_{IV}) / (T_A - T_{IV}))$ * Time. Now, we can set Time = Time at Point V or T_V. Thus, our line equation is solved, and we can set this Price equal to the price at point Z, and we can have a cleaner solution that looks like this: $P_Z = T_V*((P_A - P_{IV}) / (T_A - T_{IV}))$. So, now all we have to do is find our price projection, which is simple, and is summarized by (A) and (B) below.

(A) The price projection for a normal head and shoulders pattern is: $P_{NH\&S} = P_V - 2P_Z$
(B) The price projection for an inverted head and shoulders pattern is: $P_{IH\&S} = P_V + 2P_Z$

Note: for equation (A) and (B), the mathematics are defined by the point definitions shown in Figure 30, and the only definitive math that we can say without using more variables is that P_V is equal to the price at the head/discreet high/low of the largest range.

In order to finish our visual example in Figure 30, we can see that Z_P, Y_P, and X_P are shown, which would be indicative of calculating these values for the given points. Of interest is that with our two time-based projections, Z_P and X_P, we see that Z_P has the lowest amount of risk and X_P has the largest reward, and that Y_P is distinctively worse than when defining necklines with time. Now, with the math finished, we can now look at the quick way of determining a Head and Shoulders Projection, but in order to do so, we again need a visual, clean example as shown in Figure 12.6.

Figure 12.6: Head and Shoulders Quick Method

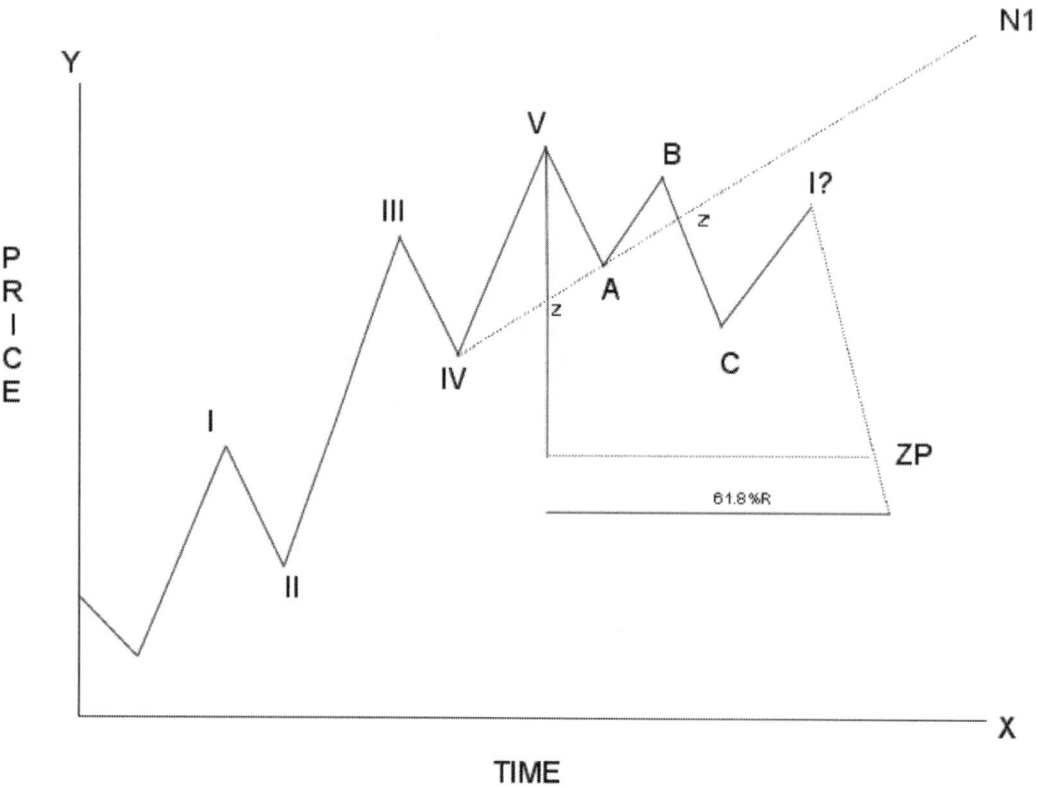

In Figure 12.6, we now see a cleaner chart with only our N_1 neckline, which has $T_1 \approx T_2$. Now, the simplest way to find the Head and Shoulders projections is to use the drawing tool of our chart and draw a line from Point V, straight down to the intersection point of N_1. In Figure 12.6 this is shown as the straight black line. Now, what we can do is clone this line and place it at the bottom/terminal point of the black line. Since this is a regular head and shoulders, we will use red in order to indicate a short position, and if it were an inverted head and shoulders, we would show this as a green cloned line. As we can see in Figure 12.6, the bottom of the red line is our price projection based on the Head and Shoulders pattern. If we draw a horizontal line over, we can see where the market would reach that point or where it can possibly exceed that point. This point is labeled as ZP, and the reason the quick way is more useful for a Head and Shoulders pattern is because more often then not, we will be close to a given, primary retracement, which will act as a mathematical cluster. Again, this is shown as the red, solid line in the chart which is a primary 61.8%R of the I → V range.

Lastly with respect to Head and Shoulders corrections, I want to point out a real chart pattern that existed where $T_1 \approx T_2$, and that was during the 2011 correction, which was the biggest correction (price-wise) since the 2009 bear market low was put in. If you look at the head and shoulders pattern, we can see that the head and shoulders pattern activated upon a breach of the head and shoulders trendline way before the swing activated to the downside. Again, these are not charts that are 10 or 20 years old where we are looking back at these patterns. No, just like the 2012 double top in the Dow Jones Industrial Average, which foreshadowed a down move during the early summer of 2012, we see that these patterns are existing today, at the present moment, in the market.

In summary, we have borrowed what is necessary from Elliott Wave Theory in this chapter in order to match our price-structured components. We also looked at the extrapolation that negates the usefulness of Elliott Wave by the never-ending growth/observation of more and more waves. That being said, we can find useful knowledge in understanding little known projections based on these waves along with understanding the large edge we gain in correctly defining a corrective A → B → C swing that emerges counter-trend. However, the knowledge of the underlying trend (and eventually time cycles/repetitions) is what provides us with large profit potential from understanding corrective waves. These corrective waves can also be defined through Head and Shoulders patterns, which are common in the market, but yet again, we have had to allude to the power of time in making sure our neckline/price projections hold greater reward/risk criterion. Thus, everything we are now learning about Price Structure is simply building upon the structural components of swings and retracements, which ultimately, drive price action itself. As the reader can easily see, time is slowly creeping into even the price structure components at an ever-increasing rate, and eventually, price becomes unnecessary!

Chapter 13

Mathematical Clusters

Mathematical clusters have been creeping there way into the discussion since the beginning of Price Structure, and now, we can formally introduce the power of mathematical clusters because we have all of the relevant price components necessary in order to complete this discussion. Most important, with *mathematical clusters also referred to as cluster averages*, we will have enough mathematical calculations in order to quantify every high or low in every market, which proves the non-randomness of the market.

The concept of clusters is quite simple, but like everything else, their importance is immense. For example, the cluster that called the bear market low of the 2008-2009 stock market crash in the S&P futures was 666.79, and the actual low was 666.75, which is the nearest tick. Moreover, the mathematical support/resistance equations that have thus far been given are derived from the continuous nature of the market. However, in further chapters, we will find other components that can be factored into our mathematical cluster averages, but these components are derived from human intervention in the markets based on our inability to trade on a 24-hour basis. For example, we humans are what make the markets open and close at certain times, and the values that the markets open or close at can be used in calculating cluster averages, but these are values that exist because of man's intervention instead of from the continuous trading that the markets gleam from divinity. Therefore, the structural components to the market are now completed for the reader at this stage of this text, and the rest of price structure will be focused on technical indicators, market tendencies, **synthetic price points**, and other market objectives. A synthetic price point is a price structure component that is created because of humankind's market interference. In later chapters, we will see these components, but for now, I ask the reader to be cognizant of these components because they are valid in cluster calculations. The primary synthetic price points that are useful for clusters are: previous day closes, previous day highs/lows, re-tests of pop-bars (Chapter 15), or mass-market psychology price points like a 200-Day Moving Average.

Cluster Issues

There are two major issues with clusters. One, it is easy to incorrectly calculate a cluster due to missing one or two numbers in the cluster's calculation. Two, the usefulness of a cluster relies on the trader being able to have the cluster calculated in advance, which unfortunately, can sometimes be a laborious process in order to define all parts of the cluster. For instance, we may have a primary and a secondary retracement close to each other, but then, we may also have a 100%P of an ABC correction. However, the hurried trader may forget to see the 127.2%P from the inconspicuous double top that formed at the ABC correction's swing point or the trader may forget to see the declining bottoms trendline value that is also nearby. See, this is where issues come in for traders who are not serious and focused on the present moment, and one of the great things about *Time and Price Symmetry* is that it is an interactive process throughout the trading day. The trader will always be moving retracements, calculating projections, and manually finding clusters throughout the trading day. Further, there is Quantitative Synchronicity with clusters as well because a trader may need to look at other technical price structure components that exist on the longer-term charts and not on his or her 1-minute chart. In fact, at major market inflection points, like the March 2009 low, it is not uncommon to have a cluster of 10 or so numbers with everything from primary retracements to micro swing projections factoring in.

Primary Clusters

The most important type of cluster is a **primary cluster**. As the name implies, a primary cluster occurs around a primary retracement if it is a cluster average defined by a market that is making a retracement. However, if a market is breaking out to new highs (or new lows), the primary cluster would be calculated at the longest, qualified swing's 100%P that is still remaining on the chart. Further, there should be caution at this projection-based primary clusters because as we know, projections are not guaranteed market inflection point, so, these are often clusters to use for reducing of one's position size. In general, when we talk of primary clusters, we will be talking about primary clusters occurring at primary retracements.

As mentioned in Chapter 6, primary retracements often have the tendency to be missed on the upside or downside, which becomes frustrating to traders that are trying to buy/sell the retracement exactly. This tendency of being missed occurs from the trader not being cognizant to the primary cluster, which is more powerful than the primary retracement itself. Thus, the cluster makes even the minor corrective phase projection or the minor secondary retracements valid. Often, a cluster will also have multiple projections resulting from intra-range double tops/bottoms that have could with the higher projection values (200%P/261.8%P) for swings that occur from initial swings and additive swings. Remember, we talked earlier about how these little known projections can still have validity with clusters. Thus, the conclusion is that major and minor numbers do not hold more weight in the averaging of the values for the cluster average. However, it should be cautioned not to make something out of nothing. Secondary retracements must be drawn from prior primary retracement points. Swings need to be understood. Double bottoms/tops (even intra-range/inconspicuous) must meet time requirements, etc.

A tendency of primary clusters is also to have primary retracements and secondary retracements that create a type of retracement range on the upside or downside of the primary retracement. As such, when we look at cluster averages, we have to define the min of the cluster and the max of the cluster along with the cluster average. The min-cluster is the smallest number that is factored into the cluster average, and the max-cluster is the largest number that is factored into the cluster average.

Cluster Calculations & Cluster Range

In order to accurately understand and accurately calculate clusters, we need to look at the values within the cluster. With every cluster, there exists three components, the min of the cluster, the max of the cluster, and the average of the cluster. Obviously, the average of the cluster is the most important, and a **cluster average** is simply all the price components of a given cluster added together and divided by the total number of values used. However, the min of the cluster and the max of the cluster are very important, and the min and the max values are used in creating the **cluster-range**.

The purpose to knowing the three components of the cluster is extreme because they are all used together in understanding trade implementation. Therefore, we have to realize that although the cluster average has the highest probability for calling the **exact** high/low, the high/low can occur at any value that makes up the cluster-range, which could be the min or the max.

As an example, let us use a market that is moving lower off a given high, which means that we are going to be looking for a primary retracement to hold, which would lead to new highs based on Price Theory. This type of example is shown in Figure 13.1.

Figure 13.1: Two Number Cluster

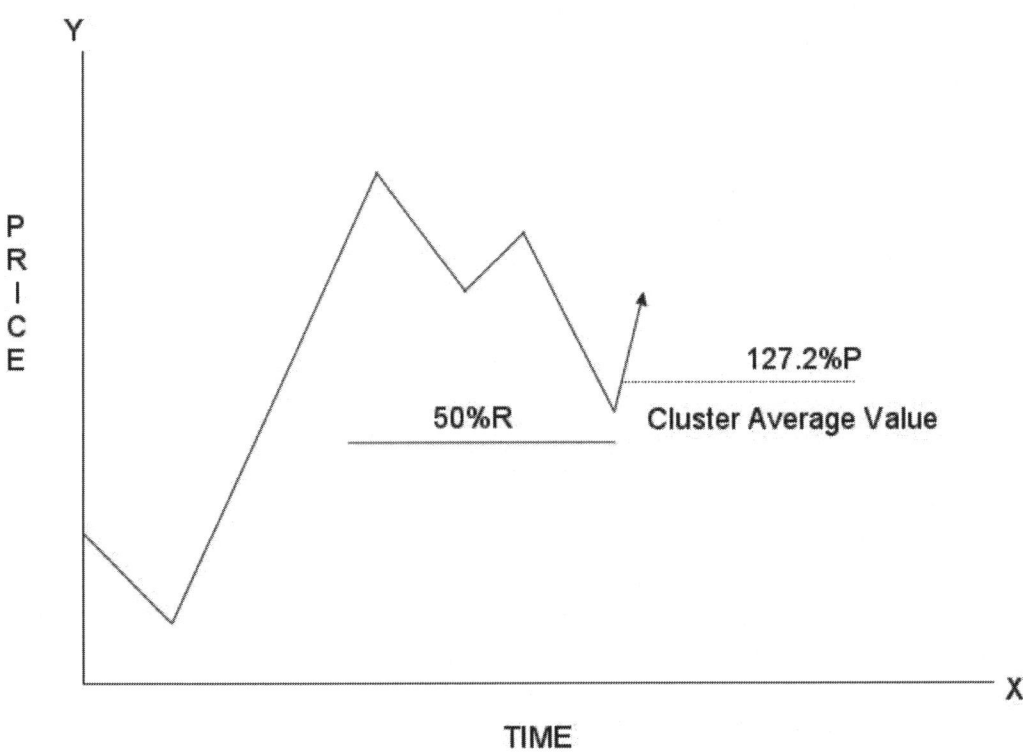

In Figure 13.1, we see a market that is moving lower, and we see that as it moves lower, there is a 127.2%P and a 50%R, which is a 50% primary retracement. As we see in the example, the 127.2%P would be the min of the cluster average, which may sound inaccurate to some because the 127.2%P is undoubtedly the higher value. Therefore, the **min value of a cluster** can now be defined as the first point where the market touches the cluster-range, and the **max value of a cluster** can now be defined as the last point that causes the cluster-range to hold. Thus, the min-value is the 127.2%P, and the max value is the 50%R. Now, these two values create our cluster average if we add the value of the 127.2%P + the value of the 50%R together and divide by 2. This gives us the cluster-average, and if we look to Figure 13.1, we can see that the market does indeed exceed the min value of the cluster, find support at or near the cluster average, which becomes the market inflection point, and the market starts to move higher.

Since this might be confusing, let us put some numbers in to make Figure 13.1 seem more palatable. Let us define our cluster range as 999.75 to 1001.25 on the S&P Futures. Using Figure 13.1, we can say that 1001.25 is the min value of the cluster because it is the first number the market will reach as it moves lower (again, the opposite logic would exist if we were looking for a short.) Now, we can also say that 999.75 is the max value of the cluster because it is the last value that tells us if the market holds the cluster or not. Next, if we plug these two numbers into a calculator, we find that they average out to 1000.50, which becomes the highest probability number that will be hit. This is what indeed happens in the Figure 13.1 example, but we must now talk about cluster trading implementation.

How to Trade Clusters

I want to continue with the numeric values assigned to Figure 13.1 in order to discuss how one is to trade clusters using the min value of the cluster, the cluster average, and the max value of the cluster. Again, these numbers were defined as 1001.25, 1000.50, and 999.75 collectively for the S&P Futures whereby we have a market moving lower and we are looking for a market inflection point to place a long trade.

There are a few different approaches to trading clusters, and they are known as "buy/sell the min value of the cluster," "buy/sell the rounded cluster average," or "buy/sell the cluster after the market adheres to it." These trade options are easy to understand. If we are buying or selling the min value of the cluster, we would put a limit order to place a trade right at the value of the min. Using our numbers, this would be the same as saying put a buy limit order in at 1001.25. Next, if we are buying or selling the cluster average, we would calculate the average, and then, we would round up a tick. Using our numbers, this would be the same as saying put a buy limit order in at 1000.75 (for the S&P Futures one tick would be 0.25). Third, if we were waiting to see a reaction to the market, one of the best things is to see if the market moves significantly off the cluster average, and if it does, the market's tendency will be to come down and retest the min value of the cluster or the cluster average itself. Regardless, we would err on the side of caution and we would buy 1001.25. So, what would happen is that we would wait for the market to tag our cluster, if the max value of the cluster holds, we would wait to see the market moving higher, and if it does, we can try to get in later at 1001.25, which as we know, could lead to a missed trade.

This third example raises something very important about the stop-loss criteria of clusters. I say that the cluster holds until the max value of the cluster is exceeded. Again, for our Figure 31 example this would be the 50%R defined as the number 999.75. As such, we need to understand that if the market breaks lower than our max value of the cluster, the cluster has failed us, and unfortunately, there is no magic formula for defining the tolerance of the cluster. Therefore, I say either the cluster holds or it doesn't, and with that line of thought, a stop loss should be placed at 999.50 for any trade gone long at within the cluster from 999.75 to 1001.25.

Cluster Tolerance

Another form of cluster tolerance, which is not in respect to stop-loss management, has to deal with the range of number used in order to create the cluster in the first place. Unfortunately, there is no magic formula for this either, but in general, we would be using our relative price chart for finding clusters. For example, if we are using a 60-minute chart, we may be looking at numbers that are within 1% of each other, but if we are looking at a 1-minute chart, we may be looking at numbers within 0.1% of each other. However, what is nice about *Time and Price Symmetry* is that if the trader has properly created his or her secondary retracements and if the trader has properly removed penetrated retracements, then, the clusters should be easy to spot with a qualitative eye. Again, it is my eternal hope that this book unleashes a new realm of market study, which can help us find more defined criteria for this figure, but for now, I must say that we must adhere to our human intuition.

Micro Patterns and Micro Clusters

Another form of clusters are those clusters that appear because of an analysis of micro swings, micro double bottoms/double tops, or retests of pop-bars, which will be discussed in Chapter 15. This chapter needs a short discussion on micro patterns and micro clusters because they are extremely important if a trader is to ensure being filled on a new position at a terminal high/low. For example, as we will learn in Chapter 15, the market will have a tendency to back-and-fill in order to allow traders who missed entry at the terminal point a second chance to get in at a less favorable price. So far, we have defined this as a deep retracement, but what is possible under high volatility conditions is that we do not form a qualified swing in order to move off an important high/low. Therefore, we have to be cognizant of the tight price range that may be forming, and we have to be aware of the micro swing, which may lead to the price correction. That micro-swing can couple with a micro-retracement (for lack of a better word), which will couple with the market tendencies we will discuss in Chapter 15. However, in general, we are only focused on these micro-clusters during high volatility scenarios, which are determined with a qualitative eye, and the reason they are only valid during those scenarios is that we physically lack the amount of time necessary in order to ensure the cluster's validity during high volatility.

In summary and as concluded in the previous paragraph, the actual cluster calculation is easy, but it is tedious. Often, when we review our trading day, we see that we may have missed a few numbers in our cluster average, which would have explained the exact market inflection point, but this is irrelevant because the point is that with the knowledge of clusters, there no longer exist any market instrument whose highs or lows cannot be quantified because every high/low will exist within some type of cluster-range. It is this reason and this reason alone that Price Structure can be equated to science because we can always find a definitive calculation that provides the value for any given high or low for any given trading instrument. Nevertheless, it may be from human error that we miss this value during a trading day. That is the unfortunate reality that we must learn to live with as traders, but at this point in the text, I can unequivocally say that, indeed, "The Market is not Random."

Chapter 14

Technical Indicators

As I alluded to in the early part of this text, when most people think of a technical indicator, they often reference moving averages, which are simply derivatives of price and time. Unfortunately, technical indicators are often called self-fulfilling prophecies due to the mass-market psychology gravitating towards a certain common number that is yielded from a technical indicator. Because of this influential effect of mass-market psychology to affect the market at values yielded from popular indicators, we, as *Time and Price Symmetry Traders,* must be aware of these numbers, and we must factor them into our trading decisions on some level. Therefore, there are a few indicators that I will discuss in this Chapter that are somewhat relevant to trading, but more often than not, they are meaningless in the larger picture of things.

In this Chapter, there are three technical indications that we will discuss, and these three technical indications will be slightly shifted by my personal observation of their usefulness. As always, we must remember that slight changes to our mentality can provide significant edges to us who do not conform to the market norm. I will discuss the indicators in rank based on their level of importance to us as *Time and Price Symmetry Traders.*

Volume

Some may argue that Volume is not a technical indicator, and in fact, volume is a derived component from the market itself like price and time. However, for the most part, volume is irrelevant. It has nothing to do with price or time except for telling us how many people are buying/selling at a given time and price. The major problem with volume (especially for continuous/futures traders) is that the U.S. market open causes tremendous volume surges that would eradicate any intrinsic volume analysis. Basically, to model a trade after volume for continuous traders, they would need a model that exist before 930am ET and after 1630 ET, but once volume does normalize after market opens/closes, it can provide us with two important clues.

First, at major highs/lows, which occur at *Time and Price Symmetry* inflection points, volume is typically anemic. Yes! Most traders are not buying/selling at the terminal/discreet highs/lows because there may be some level of fear, whereas, us, *Time and Price Symmetry* traders, are patiently waiting for the markets to enter these exact ranges in price and in time for us to place our trades (i.e. clusters). Instead, the market participants who are not as educated as we are tend to wait for confirmations of true highs or lows, and these confirmations can come from their own technical indicators, or possibly, their own analysis of swings. Further, even when markets make large exhaustion bars (as we will discuss in Chapter 15), the high/low of the exhaustion bar itself usually has the least amount of volume inside of the bar. Using a tick chart, we can go and see that exhaustion bars of high volume contain most of the volume within the mid-point of the bar, and frequently, the lowest volume is at the extreme. Thus, the first major edge we can gain by studying volume is that we can have confidence in our *Time and Price Symmetry* market inflection point if we observe low volume at that value (or range of values). To further clarify, we can rationalize that the absolute high or low is only discovered and anticipated by very few traders (us), and as the market participants become aware of the validity of that high/low we will have a herd mentality pushing the market in the favorable that is successfully defending the high/low for us.

The second thing that volume analysis can be useful for is swing trading. Since swing traders are waiting for relevant highs or lows to be breached, we can gauge that the chance for that swing's validity increases if we see an increase of volume on the swing's activation and after the swing's activation.

Initially, the volume spike at the swing activation is important, but because volume in inconclusive, we can run into quite a conundrum by focusing on the initial volume spike. Therefore, we have to focus on the subsequent minutes (or bars) after the market has activated a swing, and if there is still more volume coming into the market then there was *before* the swing activated, we could be more confident in higher/lower price follow-through. Essentially, we are glancing at the average volume before the swing, and we are observing if there is an increase in volume at the swing's activation. If there is, we can gain confidence by seeing that the average volume after the swing's activation is greater than the volume before the swing's activation.

Since our first observation of volume tells us most relevant highs or lows occur at low volume, we can have greater confidence in our swing trade by having a favorable surge of volume, which is an indirect but important conclusion. Using our understanding of how volume happens at terminal points, we can conclude that high volume on swings means that the breached high is not the absolute high, and we should see further, favorable price action.

The last cautionary use of volume must be done because it holds validity for Penny Stocks, Over The Counter Stocks ("OTC"), and/or Pink Sheets. Now, I must unequivocally state that I do not advocate trading these types of instruments because they are high-risk, often fraudulent, and irrelevant. However, because *Time and Price Symmetry* is the inherent market structure, the Marketome, that must exist, then, I must acquiesce by stating that *Time and Price Symmetry* must work for these trading instruments as well. Therefore, when the trader observes swing patterns building, (and it should be quite obvious that one would never short penny stocks) the trader should look towards volume in order to define the validity of the swing. Hence, I am saying that if one was to circle the penny stock scene, the trader should enter up trending penny stocks ***only if*** the swing activations are accompanied by outsized volume. That said, other than these observations, volume is meaningless except for larger traders who actually affect the market itself.

Moving Averages

For our purposes, we will ignore moving average on short-term charts. They do not belong there, and they only make things more crowded. Furthermore, the reason they do not belong there is because they are self-fulfilling prophecies only on longer-term charts. Therefore, we will only use moving averages on longer-term charts such as the daily, the weekly, or the monthly charts. Further, we will only look at simple moving averages not weighted or exponential moving averages. The primary two moving averages we will look at are the 50-day and 200-day moving average. I will also add the 65-day moving average into our chart for one reason and one reason alone: the fact that the Wall St. Journal uses it on their charts, which makes it a self-fulfilling prophecy as well. In fact, all three of these moving averages, are relevant only because of mass-market psychology. However, so that the reader of this book gets his or her money's worth, I will throw in another moving average that is based on *Time and Price Symmetry* analysis. That moving average is the 86-day moving average.

The derivation of the 86-day moving average can come from two calculations. First, it is loosely based on Fibonacci because $50*1.618 \approx 81$ (not 86). The second calculation, which is where it is truly yielded, comes from a circuitous calculation that is based on a time component that we will get into later. For now, that time cycle is known as the 8.6 Year Global Economic Business Cycle. In order to define the moving average calculation quickly, the 8.6 year cycle gives us 4x2.15 windows of time. We can take $50x=86$ and $200y=86$, which yields $x=1.72$, $y=0.43$, and $x+y = 2.15$. However, I state this intrinsic derivation for the reader to prove the validity of underlying market themes that exist under our very eyes, but this book is not about proofs. It is about using what works, and the 86-day moving average works very well, but if the reader is still skeptical, then use the 81-day moving average derived from Fibonacci.

Getting back to the discussion of moving averages, we are focusing on the mass-market psychology in order to utilize the 50/65/86/200 day moving averages as potential areas of support or resistance. We can also look for bullish/bearish crosses. The **bullish cross** is when the 50-day crosses on top of the 200-day, and the **bearish cross** (or death cross) occurs when the 50-day crosses below the 200-day. Major market participants actually use these crosses in determining trend, but it is insane how much of lagging indicator the moving average cross can be! The lagging natures of the moving averages themselves are why they can become of little use to trading in Time and in Price. Therefore, we will not rely on moving averages for our trend analysis as discussed in Chapter 9, but we will use the three moving averages discussed in this Chapter to help us define potential mathematical support/resistance, which can become useful intra-day or when calculating cluster averages. In a way, I consider moving averages a synthetic component rather than a price and time technical component because even though the average itself is technical, the market reaction is synthetic. Interestingly, it has always been my observation that the more powerful moving averages (the 50 and the 200) are often missed by some degree or exceeded by some degree just like primary retracements. Therefore, it is the cluster average that leads to the true price definition of the relevant high/low that the market uses as its true inflection point. Unfortunately, there is nothing else to say with respect to moving averages in my opinions. Sure, they can be useful as a quick heuristic on defining trend, but they are so intrinsically lagged that the trading edge disappears unless the market instrument is trading at or near one of these moving averages.

Self-Fulfilling Prophecies

Often times, one may hear that the problem with technical analysis is that some of the technical indicators can become self-fulfilling prophecies, and I have also referred to this as mass-market psychology. To me, both of those terms are equal with respect to derived technical analysis instead of intrinsic technical analysis, which I define as *Time and Price Symmetry*. Essentially a self-fulfilling prophecy or mass-market psychology means that because of how widespread the technical indicator is it tends to work with no relevant basis. So, the question becomes, "What does no relevant basis mean?" Well, it means that sometimes they work and sometimes they do not. Sometimes the technical indicator is bangin' on all cylinders for the market participants following it, but on the next day, it leads to total collapse. Hence, the definition of no relevant basis is that, in my opinion, derived technical indicators cannot be used in any time frame or on any instrument on any given day, week, month, year etc. Therefore, we understand how powerful *Time and Price Symmetry* is because it is not a self-fulfilling prophecy. No, it is an inherent market structure, the Marketome, that is fulfilled based on outstanding Price Objectives or Price Pattern Objectives.

Therefore, *Time and Price Symmetry* always has relevant basis because of its underlying components and my own Price Theory. At the beginning of my career, my skepticism was as big as anyone's with regard to Technical Analysis, and that skepticism was why I did not follow the market herd in treating Technical Analysis as god. No, I decided to spend my life finding and defining the precise reasons of "why" that is built into the market because my skepticism in traditional technical analysis forced me to look *inside the market;* it forced me to look at the derivatives of the market, which are Price and Time, instead of the various technical indicators that have cropped up over the years.
Simultaneously, just as I touched upon the self-fulfilling prophecy knowledge with respect to the 50 and 200-day moving average, we cannot ignore these self-fulfilling prophecies either. Therefore, by only using mass-market defined technical indicators when they couple with *Time and Price Symmetry,* we gain an edge because we are coupling their usage with the Marketome. Thus, the fact is that self-fulfilling prophecies must be formulated into our overall trading plan, but *they can never be the basis for our trading*.

Relative Strength Index: RSI

For us, Time and Price traders, RSI will be our most important technical indicator because it has existed for a very long time, and it proves useful in helping define highs/lows when time is not availing itself to us in some way. Aside from moving averages, this will be the only technical indicator usable on our charts, and the way to use this technical indicator is quite complex. As such, I encourage the reader to re-read this section many times in order to comfortably understand the gist of what I am saying.

To begin, we have to make a slight perception shift in order to make RSI usable for us. Therefore, although the mass-market psychology uses 9-period or 13-period smoothing criteria in defining RSI values, we will use a 5-period RSI to make RSI useful for us. Basically, I am saying that they are wrong, and I am right. This is not an egotistical statement because the knowledge of correct RSI is critical to helping us when Time cannot. Moreover, it helps us when we are researching longer-term position base trades, and I see this knowledge as critical if one is able to manage billions of dollars.

In fact, in order to emphasize how important RSI is, in my trading setup, I dedicate one entire monitor to RSI itself. On that monitor, I have the RSI values showing for one instrument, but in different time frames. On that monitor, I am not looking at the price/time chart, I have shrunk the chart to only show the RSI indicator. On that monitor, I have six RSI values for one instrument, but the time frames for the six RSI values that help us are: 5-minute, 10-minute, 30-minute, 60-minute, 120-minute, and 360-minute. These would be for the S&P E-Mini Continuous Contract, and if we were working in RTH, we would disregard the 360-minute and use a 180-minute or 240-minute. The other values would stay the same.

The way RSI can be analyzed is very complex, and sometimes the analysis is conflicting in different time frames. The least complex way to approach using RSI is to use it when the indicator is at its extremes. RSI is derived from a calculation that produces a range of values from 0-100. We will care about values of our RSI that are over 70 or under 30. Next, we will look at our six RSI charts in order to see if we are at these values in just one time frame or in all time-frames. This analysis of RSI at its extremes is our first discussion point for RSI.

The simplest use of RSI is for daytrading, which finds its basis in the shorter time periods (5, 10, or 30). As a daytrader, when RSI appears at its extremes, we have two possibilities. First, the extremes can be used for filtering highs or lows based on time and price window calculations. If the short-term RSI is at an extreme high (> 70), we can assume that a high is near. The question becomes, "Will this RSI derived high be a major high, or just a slight inflection point that the market will bounce off?" (An example of this would be a 38.2%R sitting as market resistance when the shorter term RSIs are sitting above 70. In this scenario, the trader can have greater confidence in selling the 38.2%R, but it remains ambiguous on whether the 38.2%R will hold or if it will break. Further, if all three of the short-term RSIs trend to the extremes when the market approaches the 38.2%R, we get even further clarification as will be discussed in the next paragraph.) The second possibility with RSI for daytraders is when we are using RSI as high/low filters, we can observe the level that the short-term RSI reaches in counter-trend corrections. That statement is not clear, so please allow me to walk through an example. Let us say we have our 5-period RSI indicating that earlier in the morning, the market found a high when the 5-period RSI was at 82. The market then sold off 4 S&P points, and the 5-period RSI was sitting around 45 after that four point decline. Later in the day, we can look to see if the 5-period RSI is again over 80, and if we have a *Time and Price Symmetry* inflection point that is indicating a short-term inflection point that is counter-trend, we can be more confident of taking the counter-trend trade, again for four points. However, instead of targeting four points, we can also use RSI as well. We can hold onto our short position until the 5-period RSI again gets below 50. Thus, we can look for repetitions in the market's movements based on RSI in order to determine how long we should hold onto the trade based on the indicator instead of on price or on time. Conversely, this would apply to a short-term low in day trading as well with extremes below 30. (In Time

Structure, we can see that targeting the 4-point move that occurred earlier with RSI is the better way to go because there are things known as measured moves, which require tremendous discussion.)

The second major thing that we can use RSI for, when it is at the extremes, is to observe that once one of these shorter-term RSIs reaches an extreme and stays there, we can watch the other RSIs gradually reach the same extremes. When RSIs gravitate towards an extreme in any time frame, we have a trend indication. It is common for RSI calculations, in all time frames, to be in the 70-90 range while the market is moving higher, and this is where convergence/divergence comes from, which will be discussed in the next paragraph. However, continuing on and of note to the trader, when all of the RSIs are in their positive extremes, we are no longer looking for a high. No, we are looking for a trend to continue, and if anything, we will see the shorter-term RSI values drop to their midpoints while the longer-term RSI values stay above 70. Thus, we would be using the shorter-term time period RSI values in order to give us indications that allow us to resume going long with the trend (again the opposite would be true for downtrends and RSI at the minimums). In a way, this is part of Quantitative Synchronicity as well because we may be short-term traders that are using the longer-term time chart's RSI values in order to trade in the short term. As a result, we are using the longer-term time chart's RSI values (the 180/360 period RSIs) to tell us the overall trend, and we are using the shorter-term time chart's RSI values (the 5/10 period RSIs) to show us when we should buy a given *Time and Price Window* that would get us back to the trend. By doing so, we gain a tremendous edge because we have *Time and Price Symmetry,* we have the RSI values, and we have the trend all working together. ***This conclusive edge is why RSI is important.*** Moving on, historically these inherent movements and understandings of RSI can be defined as convergence and divergence, which is a harder, more esoteric concept for the reader to grasp without real-life examples, but nevertheless, convergence and divergence must be discussed.

For uptrends, positive convergence is when all RSI levels in all time frames converge to the upper level of the extremes while the underlying market continuous to move higher, as discussed in last paragraph's example. However, in a bull market scenario, we can also see positive divergence, which means that the RSI values are actually decreasing while the market continues higher. This means that the RSI is diverging from the market's upward movement. Further, if all the RSI values diverge towards the 40-60 range without the market moving higher, it is an indication of the end of the Bull Run because the Bull Run has ran out of strength. Thus, we have positive divergence, telling us that although price is moving only slightly higher than its range, a top is about to form. On the contrary, even if the market continues higher while the RSIs converge to the low ends of the extremes (< 30), then we have a clue to a very strong market that has further upside potential. These last three thoughts are important and hard to understand, but essentially, a market that has stayed flat or drifted slightly lower while the RSI extremes become less than 30, implies that the large up move is just pausing. Therefore, this pausing nature indicates that the RSIs are cooling off while the market is not decreasing. Hence, the market may be range bound. Again, if the RSI values all reach the opposite extreme (< 30 for a bull market), we can use this knowledge to be aware of furthered upward momentum in the bull run. Again, for bear markets, the analysis would be reversed. We would have negative convergence and negative divergence in bear market scenarios.

Although the previous two RSI discussions focused on daytrading or momentum trading, the longer-term RSI (60, 120, and 360) are useful for major corrective clues, while simultaneously, giving us clues to a continued directional move. Therefore, just as we have swings in our market itself, we can have swings in the RSI indicator itself. For example, the trader can ask him or herself, "Is the indicator making lower tops and lower bottoms, which would indicate a downtrend in the indicator?" This can clue us in to a potential market high that is forthcoming. Unfortunately, in the shorter time frames, the RSI creates too many conflicting swings to be useful (especially, since we are using a 5-period RSI). However, swings on the RSI in longer time frames can actually be factored into Trend Analysis from Chapter 9. We can look at RSI rolling over in these long time frames to make us aware that we are possibly at the start of a new downtrend (vise versa for uptrend), and as we know from the last paragraph, this scenario would be defined as positive divergence.

Another issue to know about longer-term charts/longer-term trading using RSI numbers is that like we observed in our first example, we have to determine if the longer term RSI values find "support" at the same values as before, which can clue us in on market pivot points connected to RSI value retests. In order to elaborate, let us say that we are in a long-term bull market. We observe that the 360-minute RSI ran from 40 to 90 over a period of 3 months. Then, a correction begins, but this time we would wait and see the 360-minute RSI return to that same 40-level before looking for a *Time and Price Window* that would get us back on the long side of the market. At that level, we can almost think that the indicator itself has found support/made a double bottom! In that case, we can use the prior RSI values in determining the end of the corrective phase. Furthermore, investors can use this type of technical analysis on their core positions. Although this book is not a book on trading strategies per say, I would make a point here to say that investors that are savvy enough in order to know how to use option-writing against underlying positions to squeeze more profit out of their holdings, can use RSI analysis in order to properly time their option-writing activities. In the longer-term, RSI that has generated a downswing may be a prudent indication that all investments in general are heading for a corrective downtrend, and the Investor can use this knowledge to profit on writing options to protect the underlying positions in the downtrend, which would be my tactic on managing a multi-billion dollar portfolio.

The conflicting duality of RSI analysis is common with technical indicators, and the laborious, complex discussion that RSI required is why I simply do not like going outside of *Time and Price Symmetry* often. The fact is, with RSI or with any technical indicator, many traders can see things differently. However, with *Time and Price Symmetry* that is not possible unless one is confused of the underlying market trend. Therefore, I must state in this chapter summary that just as we had inherent trend bias, there is something known as inherent indicator bias, which can be tremendously harmful. Thus, I want to draw a clear distinction between *Time and Price Symmetry* and technical analysis. *Time and Price Symmetry* is a quantified, unequivocal underlying market structure that exists, whereas **technical analysis** is defined as a *lagging* interpretation of mathematically defined perception. In fact, there are hundreds if not thousands of technical indicators that sometimes work and sometimes do not. They are not objective, and they are not useful at all times like *Time and Price Symmetry*. Hence, I ask the reader to please keep in mind that this book is about teaching the market structure, which is inherently derived from the laws that govern the market's movement, and it is my assertion that unless one's trading strategy is based off time and price action, that strategy has a finite lifecycle. For that reason, as we move to the end of our discussion on Price Structure, I highly recommend that the trader acknowledge time and price as the root; the inception of the analysis, and as such, time and price must be the sole focus that begins any interpretive analysis. Hence in closing, I cannot stress this enough: traders should use extreme caution when looking at technical indicators when trying to define the trend or their own trades because understanding the trend based off of price structure is much more important than any indicator, and it is essential for the trader's ego to not be influenced in the wrong direction by inherent indicator bias. That bias will lead to losses.

Chapter 15

Tape Reading

The last two chapters of price structure speak to the "intrinsically learned knowledge base" that a trader will procure through thousands of hours of market observation. This knowledge will eventually lead to a sixth-sense-like premonition that is based on the mind's subconscious recognition of patterns in price and in time. In a way, you can think of the speed that the mind avails itself to the Moment of Recognition as a Moore's Law type of growth pattern that allows the mind to continue to get faster and faster through the strengthening of the axioms and neurons in the brain. However, we as humans each have a certain level of aptitude that can usually be defined by a combination of the Wonderlich test or the Raven's test, which are both useful, common I.Q.-like tests that quantify our thinking speed and our pattern recognition abilities. In addition, because we are humans, there is an eventual limit (unlike Moore's Law) on how fast we can attain the awareness to recognize the moments of recognition, but thankfully, being as fast as a half a second or one second does not make much of a difference. In order to equate this back to Moore's law, in general, the comparison between a 3 GHz or 4 GHz processor does not make much of a difference in average, everyday use. Therefore, it is my assertion that any person possessing adequate intelligence can learn an adequate speed of Moment of Recognition awareness, but it is also my assertion that the ability to become present moment-oriented requires a unique intellect. Thankfully, the mass-market psychology is made up of "masters of the universe" as the Wall St. Journal calls them, but most of these "masters of the universe" people are lazy money managers. Therefore, the markets give us and them a gift, and the markets have a general tendency to back-and-fill (a.k.a. Deep retracements) at major highs or lows, so even if one is extremely slow, that trader will often (not always) get a second chance to get back in to the market, which will only be at a slightly less favorable price.

In this Chapter, we will focus on tape reading skills, which is similar to Japanese Candlestick analysis that the technical community is often familiarized. However, for us *Time and Price Symmetry* Traders, we will be using bar charts instead of candlesticks, and a **bar** is made up of the open/high/low/close ("OHLC") for a given time period. In addition, these tape-reading patterns exist for all time periods of bars from the 1-minute to the daily to the monthly, but for continuous/24-hour trading markets, I do have to mention that low volume time frames often lead to minimal follow-through. Thus, the purpose of this chapter will be to further avail the trader's mind to chart patterns and bar patterns that will lead the mind's eye to focus on these patterns, while simultaneously providing us with another trading edge by knowing more about the market's underlying objectives based on studying bar charts. These edges are extremely important, and between this chapter and the next chapter, these edges will be discussed in a list from most important to least important.

Inside Bar

The concept of an inside bar will be first introduced here, but it will be elaborated on in the next Chapter since this Chapter and the next are somewhat conjoined. Moreover, this is the most important piece of conjoined information that exists between this chapter and the last chapter, and if a person learns anything from this book, this should be ranked right at the top next to swings.

The concept of an inside bar is based on the knowledge that *every bar in every time frame has an objective to take out the high or low of the previous bar*. Therefore, the formation of an **inside bar**, which does not take out the previous bar's high or low, is rare. However, the percentage probability of this occurrence increases as the time-period for the bar increases, but nevertheless, it is a powerful concept in tape reading as well because, although it is not equitable to a true price objective, it is my assertion that in any time frame, the price pattern objective for a bar is the highest probability price pattern objective. Therefore, its importance is immense, and it allows us to garner a true trading edge.

An example of such an edge occurs when we are approaching market inflection points. Therefore, the knowledge of the market's tendency (or the price pattern objective for the bar) is to take out the high/low of the previous bar becomes useful to us because that knowledge tells us that the market's reversal off an inflection point, which was defined in time and in price, allows us to enter trades sooner. Thus, as reactionary traders, this knowledge allows us to enter trades sooner because if we see the market reverse off a *Time and Price Window*, we can use the knowledge of a bar's price pattern objective in order to assume that the next bar will take out the high or low of the previous bar with a high probability. In essence, we can be more confident in the inflection point holding because we know that the market will have a lower tendency to take out the inflection point, and instead, the market will continue in the reversal direction by taking out subsequent highs/lows of subsequent bars! However, if we are to miss one of these opportune entries, we do not have to worry because, often, the market will give us another opportunity, which is the lead in to the next topic in tape reading.

Back-and-Fill Tendency

As mentioned many times, markets like to back-and-fill, and the concept of a back-and-fill is the market having a deep retracement of an important low. Now, as a word of caution, this deep retracement at terminal highs/lows is more frequently seen in an intraday time-period instead of on a daily or weekly bar chart. Therefore, I would like to redefine the concept of a **back-and-fill tendency** as a market that has a deep retracement of a tight range with respect to price at a terminal high/low. Thus, the concept of back-and-fill is more observable through intraday tape reading than it is on longer-term charts. Let us look at Figure 15.1 in order to visualize and discuss the back-and-fill tendency.

Figure 15.1: Back-and-Fill

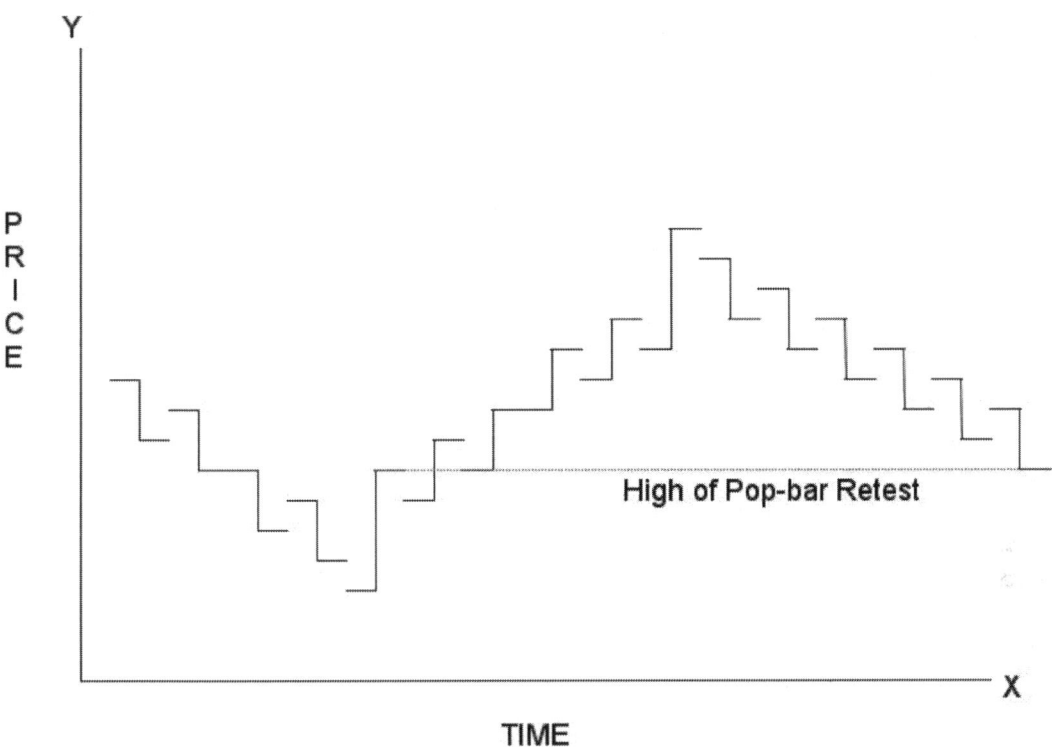

When the market forms a low off a market inflection point that we have predefined in price and in time, there is usually a pop bar off that calculated low. Thus, the back-and-fill tape-reading tendency is that <u>the market will re-test the high of the pop-bar that made the low</u>. Of course, the opposite is true for highs, and if anything, since highs are made in low volatility situations, the back-and-fill tendency has a higher probability at market highs than at market lows. However, in Figure 15.1, we can visualize this occurrence for a low. In Figure 15.1, we see that the market makes a low, and it has a pop-bar off that low. Then, we see that the next bar fulfills the inside bar rule, by taking out the high of the pop bar, and we see that the market continues up for a significant amount of time. However, at some point, we know that if this is a true change in trend we will have either a swing or a double bottom. Therefore, if we remember the back-and-fill tendency, we can focus on the retracement values along with the high of the pop-bar. As we see in Figure 15.1, the market does come lower, and the green line signifies the retest of the high bar, which satisfies the back-and-fill condition of the market.

This is a very useful principle if our Moment of Recognition is slow in recognizing a *Time and Price Window* that effectively called the market inflection point. Due to the back-and-fill tendency, the high of the low-bar can be used as an entry price via a limit order if our stop-loss criteria are sufficiently met for placing a stop below that low. However, it is often that the high of the pop-bar will be tested (again for lows), but that does not guarantee a fill. Furthermore, there may be a micro-cluster average between a micro-swing and a retracement that could be interfering with that pop-bar's high/low retest. Therefore, we can add the high/low of a pop-bar into our cluster average pricing as well in order to ensure that we are filled on our trade orders. Of final note regarding back-and-fill tendencies, I must say that the larger the market, the greater the back-and-fill tendency, which is why the S&P Futures are an ideal trading instrument because the size of the market that is summarized within that one contract is an ideal candidate for the back-and-fill nature in that market.

Repetitive Tops/Bottoms

Earlier, we discussed triangles that are formed as wedges. In that discussion, I mentioned that the wedge pattern is borne from retests of the same high or low over and over again. Therefore, in this section, I will expand our knowledge of what occurs when markets retest the same value more than twice, and this will be defined as Repetitive Tops ("RTs") and Repetitive Bottoms ("RBs"). A **Repetitive Top** is simply a high that is formed by retesting the same high more than two times, and a **Repetitive Bottom** is simply a low that is formed by retesting the low more than two times. These formations are sometimes referred to as triple tops/bottoms, quadruple tops/bottoms, etc...

Like DTs/DBs, RTs/RBs have their own unique price pattern objectives, which I argue are still based on Price Theory. The price pattern objectives for these patterns are defined as follows:

(A) The price pattern objective for a repetitive top is the low between the last two tops
(B) The price pattern objective for a repetitive bottom is the high between the last two bottoms

Now, in order to elaborate on these repetitive tops and repetitive bottom price pattern objectives, we need to use an example. Therefore, let us look to Figure 15.2 for an example of a triple top or a triple, repetitive top.

Figure 15.2: Triple Top / Triple Repetitive Top

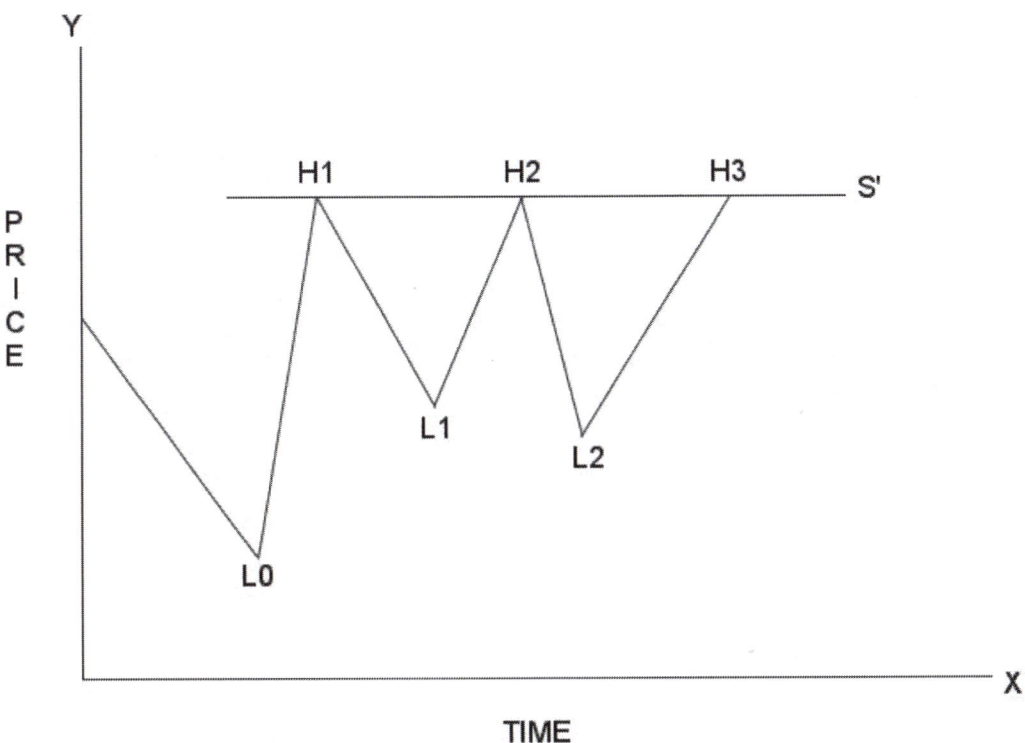

In Figure 15.2, we see the triple top. Because it is a triple, we will reference the last two tops for our price projections or for our price pattern objectives. Although not seen in this chart, the price projection should the market follow through to new highs over H3, we would base our swing projection based on the following swing criteria: $L_0 \rightarrow H_2 \rightarrow L_2$. As you can see, if we had a swing activate by a break of H_3 we would use L_2 as the retracement value for the swing parameters, because it is the last low between the last two tops. Similarly, if H_2 and H_3 ended up resulting in a triple top, the objective would be to take out the low between the last two tops, which is L_2. As you can see, the price pattern objectives is essentially filtered based on time by referencing the last two patterns that occurred in time. As mentioned and now emphasized, multiple retests of the same (does not have to be exact) high/low that produce RT/RBs do actually change price pattern objectives for swing trades or double bottom/double top trades. Therefore, we have to think of the last two tops/bottoms as if it was a double top/bottom, and even if there was 5 or more retests of the same value, we would only focus on the last two. Again, this was clarified visually in Figure 15.2.

The unfortunate thing about RTs/RBs is that the 38.2% entry criteria that we used with DBs/DTs is no longer applicable for RTs/RBs because the probability that they will fail is high. However, qualified swings are still applicable. For example using Figure 15.2, if we formed a qualified swing down after reaching H3, we could have confidence that the price pattern objective for the RT will be fulfilled. In general, though, unless we have a qualified swing form, we cannot simply decide to gamble on taking a trade based on an RT/RB unless we have time kicking for us, which will be discussed in Time Structure.

Therefore, <u>the only way that we can say that an RT/RB is real or not is when its price pattern objective is fulfilled.</u> However, even though this does not give us a trade inception based on the RT/RB, we can use our qualitative eye in order to understand what is going on in a market, and we can use the knowledge of these patterns forming and holding to make us aware of large price moves, which will be explained in a real-world example momentarily.

Before getting to the unique market scenarios that RTs/RBs foreshadow, I must mention that it is much more common to see RTs/RBs form in "micro time frames," which means that we may see RTs/RBs occur within minutes of each other at a mathematical cluster or at some given retracement. When this happens, the qualified swing entry is thrown out the window and we can actually trade off the price pattern objective of the RT/RB! In order to give an example of this, let us turn to 15.3, which is a modified example of Figure 11.2.

Figure 15.3: Micro Swings & Repetitive Bottom

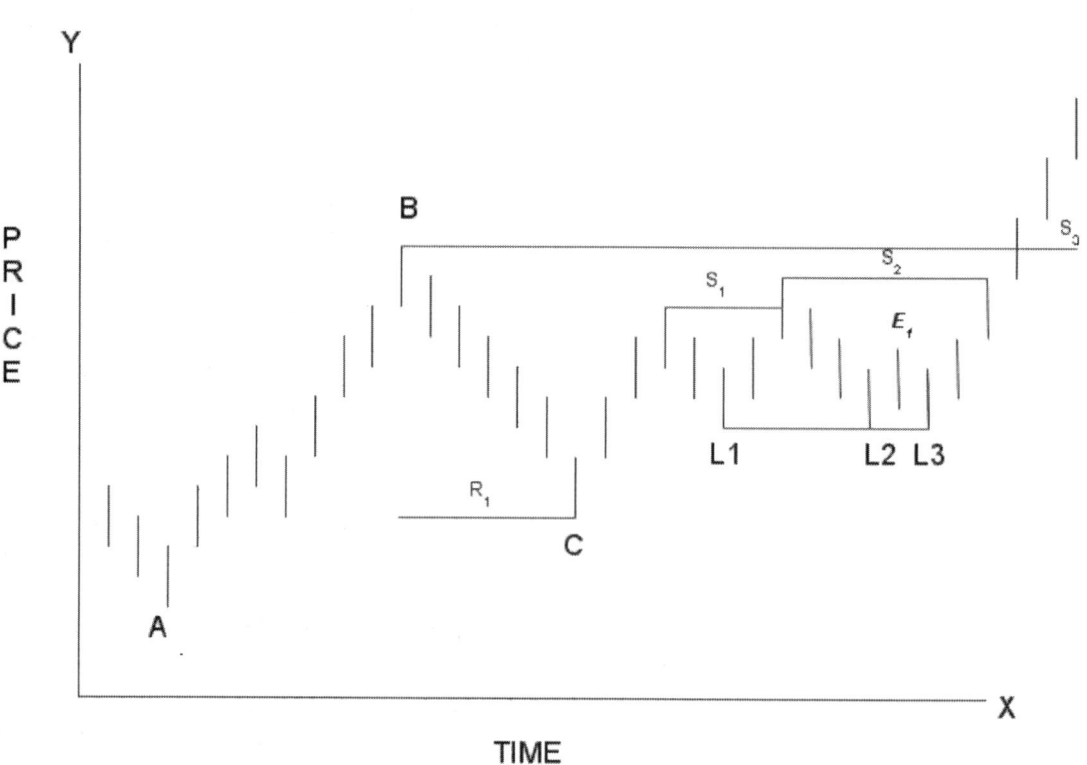

If the reader can recall, in Figure 11.2, we showed micro swings that were allowing us to enter our market. However, what we can see here is that we have a micro repetitive bottom form, which is indicated in Figure 15.3 as L1, L2, and L3. What is interesting about this example is that the typical trader would see this chart pattern, and the typical trader may decide to enter this trade based on a break of S2, which is the micro-swing and which is the highest high between the three bottoms of L1, L2, and L3. However, with our recent knowledge of how to trade an RB, we know that we are using time in order to define the price pattern objective along with *what confirms if this is a true* **RT** *or* **RB**. Therefore, our entry price would

204

actually be at E_1, which is the high between the last two bottoms, L_2 and L_3. This is not an obvious conclusion, so I emphasize this point to the reader. Additionally, we see that by trading at E_1, we get a better entry price than S_2.

Next, I must differentiate between the two types of repetitive tops/bottoms, which are important for tape reading. The first type of RT/RB is an RT/RB that occurs near our discreet high/low of a given range. Traditionally, we would see this RT/RB form at a qualified swing point where the market keeps retesting a break to new highs/lows and only exceeding each break by a tick or so (if at all). This becomes very annoying to us traders, but thankfully, this is the lower probability scenario that leads to RTs/RBs. The second scenario, which is more likely to avail RTs/RBs, is when we are retesting mathematical resistance (for RTs) or support (for RBs), which could be at an intra-range retracement or a mathematical cluster. At these points, we know that our skill as *Time and Price Symmetry* traders is superior to the average market participant so if we have a powerful cluster, we can have greater confidence that the cluster will hold even though we are seeing the market make a repetitive top/bottom at that cluster value. Again, this is annoying, but the formation of an RT/RB that holds is extremely valid. Now, I can discuss the real world example, which occurred on the flash crash day in May of 2010. On that day, an inconspicuous triple top formed in the S&P futures market between the overnight session and the mid-morning session. This triple top foreshadowed a powerful move down, but obviously, the trader would have no idea of the power at that time. However, when the trader sees a RT/RB hold a market, the power of these patterns cannot be understated, and again, the trader only knew that this RT/RB was valid either by a qualified swing or by seeing if the price pattern objective of the RT/RB was met. Therefore, we have to recognize all tops/bottoms that are formed in a complex way by multiple retests because they may lead to massive potential follow-through. Again, this is also true for DBs/DTs that turn into inconspicuous RTs/RBs, which was the case as well on the flash crash day. On that day, a trader who observed the RT fulfill its price pattern objective, and then, got short on a qualified swing, would have been holding a short position as the flash crash occurred. (I see this to emphasize the power of trading with the trend.)

Moving on, the reason I discuss RTs/RBs in this section is that their formation is derived from a trader's qualitative eye observing the tape. Thus, in order to elaborate, let us discuss what is actually happening when the market retests the same high/low multiple times based on the tape. By reading the tape, I believe there are two scenarios that reveal RTs/RBs. The first scenarios is simply a market that is building up to have a giant move by either (a) breaking the RT/RB or (b) adhering to it. I believe criterion (b) is important to discuss because when an RT/RB is proven valid, we see gigantic market moves. For example, we already discussed the importance of these patterns on the day of the flash crash. However, they can be just as important on the daily chart (remember the third-dimension of the Marketome, Quantitative Synchronicity, is always in play just like time and just like price!). In 2012, we saw a very lazy summer trading session, but when the market was quiet during late August and early September of 2012, what we saw form was a triple bottom on the S&P Cash Index. Once that triple bottom (or RB) was confirmed by a break of the high between the bottoms, we saw the market have a giant up move, which lead to new all-time highs! That is the importance of valid RT/RB, and in essence, in either case (a) or (b) defined above, the RT/RB foreshadows the fact that the market will have a large move. I believe the first reason for this to happen is because of the underlying Marketome, and if we are disciples of Price Theory, we know that either the price objective of new highs/lows outside of the given range will be reached, or we know that the price objective of taking out the last low/high of the price pattern objective of the RT/RB will be fulfilled. Concurrently, since these patterns have a high probability of failure, which is why we wait for their price pattern objectives to be fulfilled in order to tell us if they were real or not, is because the second way in which RT/RBs can form is **synthetic** or man-made. Thus, it is my assertion that an RT/RB can be synthetically formed because of a large volume buyer/seller at some specific price level, which may or may not be the swing point/range expansion point. However, since we know that the market will eventually adhere to time and to price, which means that if this formation is not valid (meaning it is synthetically created because of one (or more) parties market participation), then, the RT/RB formation will ultimately break, which means Price Theory will eventually hold. In effect, if we know that the market will eventually break based on other Price Objectives, then, we can confidently say that the RT/RB is synthetic. Thereby this allows us to further stipulate that this large volume buyer/seller will eventually get satiated so that the market can achieve its underlying price objectives. *Therefore, we know that the more the market retests a given price level, the higher the probability the market will break through that price level.* In effect, if a price objective exists, the value of the retested value becomes irrelevant just like the lifespan of our large volume buyer/seller. Lastly, there is an important tape-reading component that we must talk about when we are dealing with synthetic RTs/RBs, and that will be discussed in the next section.

Synthetic RT/RB Reversals

Logically, if we are dealing with a large volume seller that creates a synthetic RT, we know that there was probably a reason that person was selling in the first place. This means that when the RT breaks, we need to be aware of any potential, powerful, primary retracements or any potential, powerful mathematical clusters that may exist slightly higher than the RT or RB itself. This is very important because what happens more often than not (since we know RTs/RBs are highly unlikely) is that the RT/RB breaks, and then, there is an immediate reversal. In essence, the break of the RT/RB allows the market to tag the cluster average or the primary retracement just hanging above the market, and then, reverse off that value. Let us look at an example of this in Figure 15.4.

Figure 15.4: Synthetic Reversal

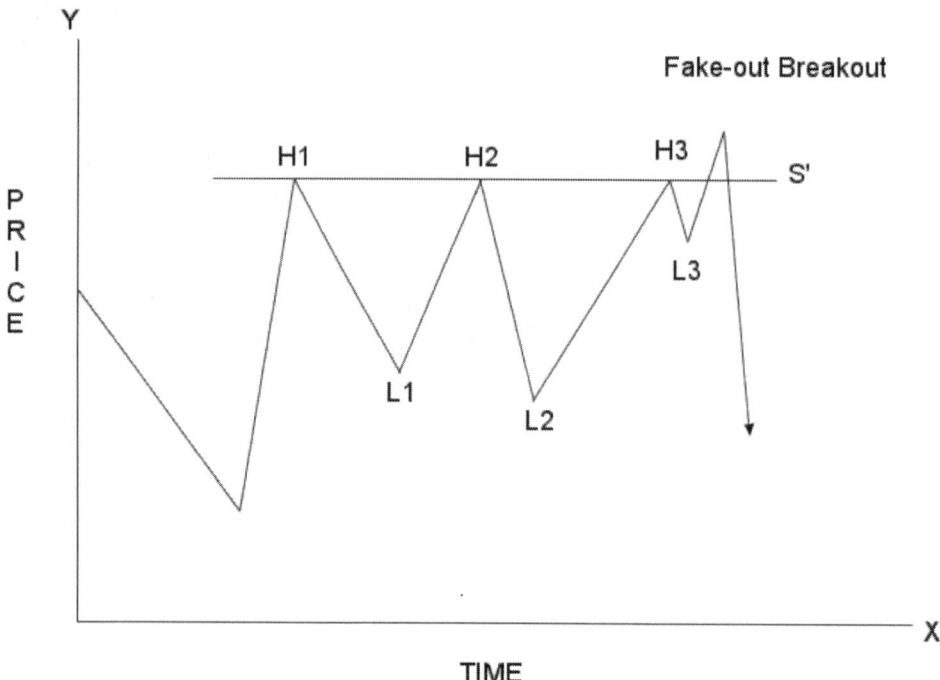

In Figure 15.4, we see the market exceed H3 that we looked at earlier, and what happens is that the market goes slightly higher by breaking the triple top/RT, and then, the market immediately reverses. What is important is that for this immediate reversal to happen, we must be trading in the present moment. We must know and we must predefine any important number that may exist just outside of the RT/RB, and we must be aware that that number may serve as a market inflection point. We need to know this for the simple fact that the break of an RT/RB usually leads to a powerful swing just like a break of a DB/DT leads to a powerful swing. Therefore, we gain an edge by knowing that if there exists a *Time and Price Symmetry* level that is just outside of an RT/RB, then, we know that we may be near a market inflection point, and in Time Structure, we will be able to use time in order to act as another filter for an RB/RT.

Price Spikes / Exhaustion Bars

The next discussion deals with markets that are influenced by fundamental news, which are called Price Spikes or Exhaustion Bars. Exhaustion bars and price spikes are major clues to a trend change, but what is not obvious is that exhaustion bars and price spikes can call trend changes in both directions. A price spike is indicative of a further move in the direction of a spike, and an exhaustion bar is indicative of the end of a market move. For example, when most traders see a large spike in the market, the mass-market psychology is usually focusing on the direction of the spike instead of looking at what happens after the spike. Thus, the majority of market participants believe that when a price spike occurs in the market, the market will continue to move further in the direction of the spike bar. However, the opposite is usually true, which is why I name these price spikes as exhaustion bars! An **exhaustion bar** is a bar that means that all buyers/sellers have been fulfilled on whatever their underlying objectives were (including Price Objectives from Klatch's Price Theory), which means that this surge of volume is indicating a major indication of the end of a market move. Amazingly, if we can see that the high of the exhaustion bar (for an upward surge) or the low of the exhaustion bar (for a downward surge) occur at a mathematical cluster, we get further confirmation that the cluster was tagged, and the market can now reverse. Therefore, when we see these large spikes/exhaustion bars occur with time symmetry, it is a slam-dunk trade. The only thing we have to wait for is the retest of the exhaustion bar's high/low, which is where the indicative nature of the exhaustion bar gains its true validity.

As such, it is common that after an exhaustion bar occurs, the market will stay inside of that bar for a significant amount of time because the market is trying to decide if that exhaustion bar was the end of the move or if that exhaustion bar is going to be exceeded. Therefore, we know that from Price Theory the market will have to either retest the high/low of the exhaustion bar or have a deep retracement. For example, if we are dealing with an upward price spike, it is entirely possible to see a double top at that high, which turns the price spike into an exhaustion bar. However, the much more common route is to see a swing form in the opposite direction of the price spike, which means we need an example to clear this logic up. Let us look to Figure 15.5.

Figure 15.5: Exhaustion Bars

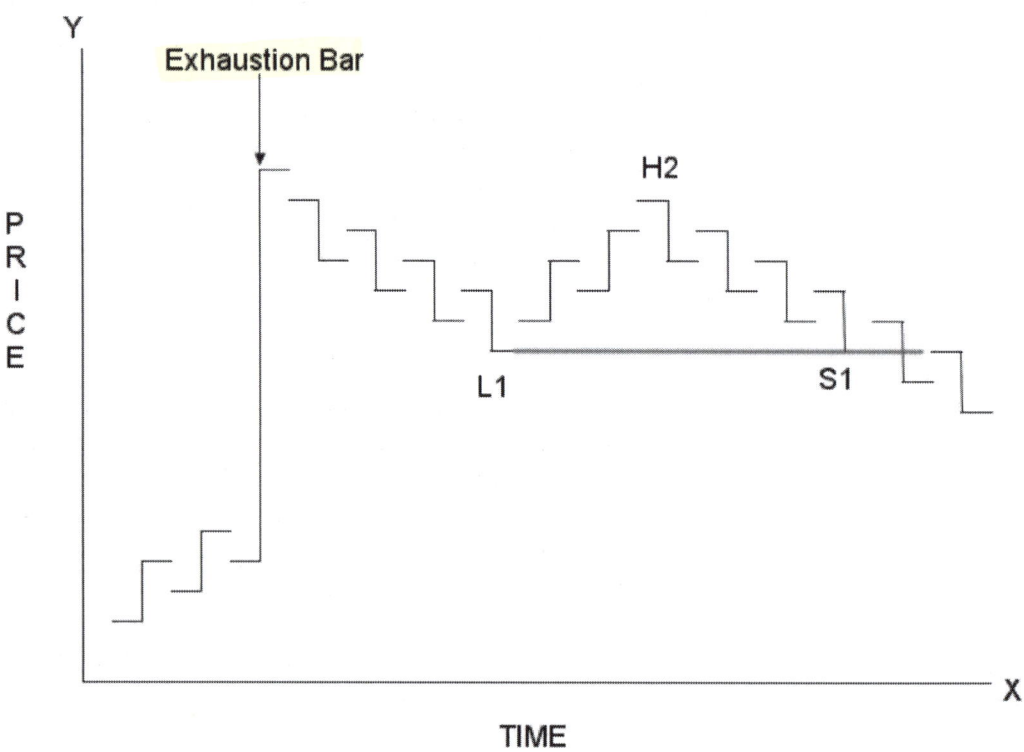

In Figure 15.5, we see the price spike, which is indicated with the arrow calling it an exhaustion bar. Again, it is only an exhaustion bar if the bar is not exceeded. If it is exceeded, it remains a price spike. However, since I have asserted the tape-reading tendency is for the market to form a swing in the inverse direction of the price spike, then, that is what is shown in Figure 15.5. In Figure 15.5, we see that the market comes down to L_1, it rallies up to a secondary high at H_2 (obviously, H_1 is the high of the exhaustion bar), and then, we see a swing activate at a break of L_1, which is indicated by the horizontal red line defined as S_1. This swing tells us that the market has reached its objectives, and is ready to correct.

The power of exhaustion bars cannot be understated. They are very typical on holidays or low volume trading days. They are very typical of major highs and major lows, and they are very annoying because for us *Time and Price Symmetry traders,* we tend to become perfectionists, which means that if we are not filled on an order at placed at the very high/low of the exhaustion bar, we may miss out on our trade entry. That is how powerful clusters can be with respect to exhaustion bars, and I remind the trader to remember risk/money management rules, which would allow a trader to still get in on the inverse swing after the exhaustion bar forms.

Price Spikes Becoming Exhaustion Bars through Quantitative Synchronicity

The hardest concept to understand with respect to price spikes/exhaustion bars is the interrelationship of price spikes and exhaustion bars that exist because of Quantitative Synchronicity.

Although this is a hard concept to understand, it is easy to discuss. Essentially, all I am saying is that if you have a price spike up on a one minute chart, and if the market tends to continue up for several hours, well then, on the 120-minute chart there may be a price spike that has combined that entire up move into one, 120-minute bar. Therefore, we can see that on the 1-minute chart, we have a price spike with continued upward movement, but on the 120-minute chart, we see that this price spike has become an exhaustion bar. Therefore, the same theory that held on the 1-minute chart can hold on the 120-minute chart. For example, if we see that the market does not exceed the price spike on the 120-minute chart, well, we can now begin looking for a retest of that high on the 120-minute chart or we can look for a swing to form on the 120-minute chart. Again, this becomes the reason why Quantitative Synchronicity is what makes *Time and Price Symmetry* a very hard tool to master because we have to constantly be observant of all of these events in every time frame simultaneously. Lastly, although this was an example for an upward spike, obviously, the same discussion holds true of a downward price spike/exhaustion bar.

The Doji

The last topic of discussion in tape reading is the recognition of a common candlestick known as a Doji, which is a powerful indication of a major high/low if the subsequent bar, after a Doji bar forms, is a big reversal bar, which is different than a price spike bar because this big reversal bar occurs after a major high/low has been tagged, and again, this major high/low that formed the Doji bar will always be some type of cluster average. Therefore, unlike a price spike/exhaustion bar, the Doji pattern that we will focus on results from the bar after the Doji and this two-bar pattern also has Quantitative Synchronicity. Moreover, Doji bars are more powerful as we go out longer in time, which means that if we see a Doji bar form on the daily chart, we have to be aware that the market may have reached a market inflection point, and obviously, we would obtain greater conviction if we had *Time and Price Symmetry* at the high/low on the day the market created the Doji bar.

The importance from the Doji bar pattern itself is not the Doji bar because the Doji bar is the bar that is indicative of a reversal. **The Doji** is a bar that tends to form on low volume (as we discussed in Chapter 14 when markets reach terminal points), and it is a bar that closes at the midpoint of the bar. Furthermore, the Doji bar is not usually large in range size relative to the other bars. However, it is the bar after the Doji that makes the magic happens, and this two-bar pattern yields an important tape-reading concept. As such, these common two-bar patterns that start with a Doji followed by a large range bar yield something known as **morning star / evening star** patterns, and they are very powerful. Moving forward, I want to go through two examples of these bars for the reader. The first example will be textual, and then I will introduce a visual example.

Let us say the market is near a high based on *Time and Price Symmetry*. At the day the high occurs, the market opens at some value, declines in the morning to find support, and then, the market rallies and forms a high at our *Time and Price Symmetry* level, which is higher than our open. From that high, the market reverses and closes approximately at the same value that it opened at, and our daily-bar does not look very important. However, what happened to form that bar is very important, and by closing off the high, we have a clue as to the next day's follow-through. The next day, after we observe a Doji bar, we can watch the market follow-through to the downside because we have found a major high based on *Time and Price Symmetry*. The two-bar pattern that is formed is now an evening star, and this often a clue to the validity of the high. As such, we can expect the market to have a subsequent deep retracement of the large down day, and then, form a large swing down in day 4 or 5 after the Doji, which, as we learned with Dow Theory, is a big indication of a top. This is the example that I want to highlight via Figure 15.6.

Figure 15.6: The Doji & an Evening Star

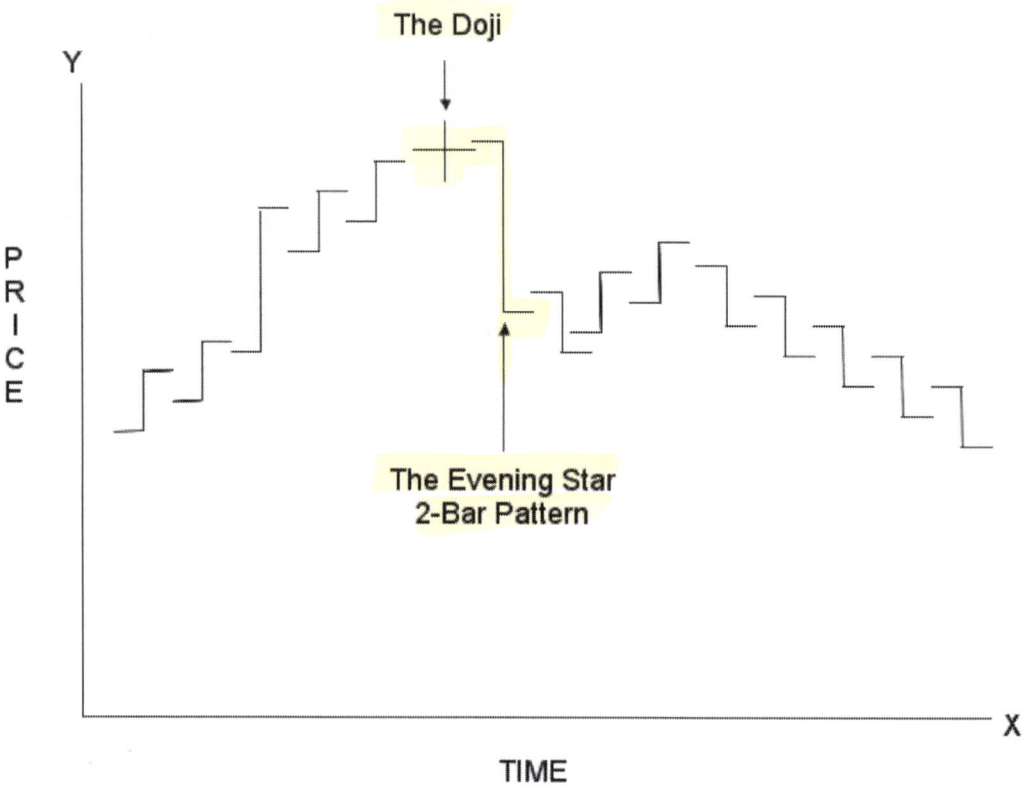

In Figure 15.6, we see that we have a market that is moving higher, and then, we see at the high, the market has created a Doji bar. Again, the Doji bar is a bar with a short range that opens/closes around the same value. After the Doji, we see that the market has a large down move, which created the Evening Star. Now, all we would need to see is a swing form, which would confirm that the trend has indeed changed.

The reason I asked the reader to look at Figure 15.6 is because I am only showing "bars" on this chart, and we have no idea what the time frame of those bars are. Therefore, I must make it clear that although I said that Doji bar-based patterns are more powerful on longer-term charts, that does not mean they are to be ever ignored in daytrading because in daytrading, Doji bars are also very powerful indication of intra-day tops/bottoms. In fact, the pattern would be the same, and the theory in what must follow in the subsequent bars would be the same as well. As such, Doji bars that yield morning star/evening star patterns are high probability indications, and if they occur at *Time and Price Symmetry* level, we can have greater confidence that our calculation is validated by the market's reaction.

In summary, tape reading is a methodology that allows us to get more information about how the market is forming its highs and its lows. Again, it is more of an acquired recognition that your mind will have from getting your 10,000 hours of market observation, which means that tape reading comes from your intrinsically learned knowledge base. These skills will allow the Moment of Recognition to become faster, which means that the subconscious mind does the thinking. For instance, that thinking may be along the lines of, "Wait, I've seen this happen before." Again, it is not the conscious mind thinking this because then the reaction may be too delayed. No, it is the subconscious mind, which has that thought, and it is the subconscious mind that allows the trade inception to be based on historical recognition. Because of this internal knowledge, there are thousands if not millions of different ways that market rotates through *Time and Price Windows*, but thankfully, our job is to become cognizant of how the market reacts off a given *Time and Price Window* instead of understanding every tick of the tape. Therefore, the market ultimately derives down to *me and Price Symmetry* that leads to the trading decision and not the tape reading itself. Thus, we can conclude that tape reading adds credence to *Time and Price Symmetry,* which helps us in validating new trades.

Lastly, although I pointed out a few of the most powerful bar patterns in this chapter, by no means is this chapter complete, but it is not our job as *Time and Price Symmetry* traders to become pattern recognition/tape-reading machines. If that was a goal, a computer could just as easily do our job, and after 7 years of automated trade testing, I have learned that a computer cannot replace me (yet). Thus, it is my belief that this is because it is the human trader's job to not only understand *Time and Price Symmetry*, but also, to understand the flow of the market itself as it rotates through its price discovery process, which allows the **qualitative eye** to be reminded of the underlying market trend and terminal market inflection points, which a computer does not have.

Chapter 16

Market Tendencies

This Chapter builds on the last chapter because part of the intrinsically learned knowledge base is that if a trader chooses to specialize in one market, then, that one market will have its own tendencies, which I argue are different from tape reading patterns. Thus, we can now move on to the last chapter in Price Structure, which deals with these market tendencies.

Just like reading the tape, understanding market tendencies is one of the most important reasons that a trader needs to accumulate thousands of hours of observation. Moreover, understanding <u>one market's</u> tendencies is why I stated, in the beginning of this book, that it is my belief that a trader's job is to specialize in one market in order to become "one" with all of the underlying tendencies of that market, which ultimately yields more trading edges. Therefore, since I have decided to specialize in the S&P 500 E-Mini Futures Contract over the last 7 years of my career, the tendencies discussed herein are most relevant to indices or commodities, which are also continuous / 24-hour trading markets. Because these markets are continuous, the tendencies that I have observed from trading the S&P are reciprocated in these markets to some degree. On the other hand, every stock, every future, or every commodity (note, options do not have tendencies aside from bid/ask market manipulation spreads) may or may not have these tendencies, and since individual stocks have their own underlying tape reading patterns, stocks are more prone to reacting on those tape reading patterns due to the market makers that exist inside of a given stock, which is often outside of time/price structure. By no means is this a contradiction to *Time and Price Symmetry*. No, I am simply stating that during an average trading day, the movements of a given stock may be based on the market maker's order book, but as technology progresses, it is my belief that the market maker's influence on a given stock will continue to diminish as it has over the past decade. Therefore, we can remember my original definition in Chapter 1 that sta5ed that appropriate liquidity is necessary for *Time and Price Symmetry*. Moreover, it is my belief that the terminal, market inflection points, of any trading instrument (including market maker manipulated stocks) will ultimately succumb to *Time and Price Symmetry*.

Thus, market tendencies fulfill the last piece of the price structure puzzle by allowing the trader to put all of the market's movements together in order to define every part of the reason "why." Therefore, these tendencies will (literally) fill the gap of defining the very last numbers that exist in price that can be factored into our trade decisions or our cluster averages in order for us to define all relative support/resistance that comes from price action itself. To begin, our discussion of market tendencies will start with pure price components that exist on the chart itself, and from there, we will look at more esoteric theories that will serve as a lead in to time structure.

Inside Day Rule

As I alluded to in the last chapter with inside bars, a market has a tendency to take out the previous bar's high or low. This knowledge yields primary validity on daily bar charts because it allows us to target a previous day's high or low during the trading day. I ask the readers to prove it to themselves by looking at a daily bar chart of any instrument. Upon inspection, you should find that ~95% of all of the bars should have taken out the previous day's high or low, which basically means we see around 10-20 inside days in a given year. They are rare, and the edge we derive from the "Inside Day Rule" is extreme when we are trading intra-day.

Often, with continuous trading instruments (like the S&P Futures), the previous day's high or low is actually taken out quickly when the market reopens in the overnight session. However, when this does not happen, we can discuss how we can utilize this edge for our profit. As a quick example, I would like to refer back to the Doji bar from the last Chapter. When the Doji bar is formed, we can use the inside day rule to understand that a morning star/evening star pattern is forming before the end of the next day actually closes. Since a Doji is typically a small range bar, we know that once the market takes out the low of the Doji (if the Doji was made *at the high of* on an up move), then, we may be able to get short by believing that the market will close at or near its high/low of the day. Next, let me explain with an illustration using swings, which can prove the efficacy and the power of this of this ***rule***.

Let us say that we have a down day in the market (S&P E-Mini Futures), and we fail to take out the low of the previous day on the overnight trading action. Instead, we form an up swing at some point overnight, which obviously yields price pattern objectives / projections levels. However, by using the previous day's high as the target for the swing trade, we can ignore all counter-trend trades that go against the swing. This is the power of the inside day rule. If the previous day's low was not taken out, and the market has continued to move higher ever since, then, we are now targeting the high of the previous day, which means that we can relax and stay comfortably with the trend formed by the upswings. Further, since we know that a qualified swing is the primary factor in determining the trend at the present moment, the previous day's mentality, which is leading us towards an trend bias to the downside can be ignored.

However, for this example, this type of reversal move after a big down day is rare. What is more likely is that on big down days, the market will form one of these upswings, which end up being just a corrective ABC type of move, and as soon as a qualified down swing emerges, we can reverse back to the downside with this new, qualified swing. Again, we could ignore the projection levels and retracements, and we can target the previous day's low instead! Therefore, the power of swing trading combined with the knowledge of the inside day rule is extreme because it allows us to not be mind-screwed by countertrend indications throughout the trading day.

Another possibility after a large day in the market, is that we actually DO form an inside day, which becomes a market tendency in and of itself (again we are talking about daily bars with the inside ***DAY*** rule). As such, we can continue the inside day rule to the next day (T+2) so that the original day's high/low (T_0) would still be a target based on the inside day rule. In effect, Day 0's inside day rule's price pattern objective has yet to be completed. Again, I call this a price pattern objective because an inside day rule is not a 100% rule.

Many times, the *Inside Day Rule* can help us outside of swing trading as well, if we are being more aggressive on our trading. As a market oscillates throughout a given day, it will eventually approach a previous day's high or low because of the inside day rule. Because of this tendency, we can hold onto our trades until the previous high or low is breached, but even more important, ***when we get closer to a previous day's high/low, we can actually have a trade inception that is based on this rule.*** This trade inception can be done by buying the shallow retracements on pullbacks until the market has reached its inside day rule objective. In essence, we are simply placing trades at a given retracement because of our belief that we will be taking out the high/low of the previous day, which will yield a quick profit. The inside day rule is simply pure power in the market. It really is a trading strategy in and of its own, and it is probably at the very top of the list of powerful trading edges in this book right after time repetitions.

Moving on, as a word of caution, you can fall in love with the inside day rule, and it can bite you in the ass. I say this because the reader should also be aware that true double tops/bottoms or deep retracements are very likely after major market inflection points are reached. As such, we must be cautious of the possibility that the market is trying to suck people in to take out the prior day's high/low only to fail them. Therefore, we have to recognize this failure via either a double top/bottom or a deep retracement, and by that recognition, we gain a significant edge by targeting the reciprocal low/high on the given day. (This sounds confusing but it is not.)

The last discussion of the *Inside Day Rule* has to deal with Quantitative Synchronicity. In order to understand the underlying market objectives in every time frame, we have to realize that part of that understanding is based on the logical conclusion that each bar has an objective to take out the previous bar. Further, I assert that the longer the bar is in time, the higher the probability that the current bar will take out the previous bar's high/low. As an example, let us say that we are looking at a yearly bar chart, which means that one bar represents one entire year of a trading instrument's trade history. For the sake of argument, let us say that in 2009 the DOW had a range from 6000 to 9000 points. Therefore, in 2010, the market still must adhere to the *Inside Day Rule* (even though it is now technically an *Inside Year Rule*). What this means is that the tendency to take out the previous bar's (in this case previous year's) becomes almost a 99% certainty. In fact, I do not believe any trading year in the DOW has had an inside year. Thus, we start to recognize the relevance of Quantitative Synchronicity.

Although this last example was based on a yearly bar, we have to understand that the converse is true. If one was to create a tick chart, one would be able to see that on a second-by-second basis (as long as it is a fast moving market), the market's necessity to take out the previous few second's bar is palpable, and in essence, the market is making micro-swings on a 20-30 second basis at all times. However, we cannot measure these minute details nor can we effectively trade off them, but the justification of understanding this principle holds relevance. Therefore, we need to understand that the one minute bar has an inside day rule-like objective; as does the 5-minute bar, the 10-minute bar, the 30-minute bar, the 60-minute bar, the 240-minute bar, the daily bar, the monthly bar, the yearly bar, and the decennial bar. (Of note, for continuous contracts, the longer-term bar charts between 30-minutes and the daily bar will have many inside bars because of the lack of market movement in the initial overnight session. I state this range as 30-minutes through daily because we must remember that this entire concept is called *The Inside Day Rule* to begin with, which means that once we get into the daily timeframe, the normalization process resumes of fulfilling these price pattern objectives.) Apropos, we now see the relevance of Quantitative Synchronicity because we have to align our mind to understanding that every bar in every period has a price pattern objective to take out the previous bar's high or low, which makes the Quantitative Synchronicity dimension defined as market depth hard to grasp. Therefore, we must understand this objective and we must be ale to meld the entire market picture inside of our heads for whatever relevant time frame we are trading. Hence, the trader's initial ease of understanding the *Inside Day Rule* is obviously simple and palpable, but the simultaneously comprehension becomes difficulty because of the mind's inability to easily align these trading objectives into one summation that yields the true market picture.

Lastly, I must state that these concepts and specifically the altruistic stated definition of the pure *Inside Day Rule* is so powerful that I keep a daily bar-chart open on one of my six trading monitors at all times just to remind me of this rule. As a day trader/momentum trader, that chart is extremely important because that chart is my heuristic that tells me if the previous day's high/low has been exceeded or not. Thus, if the inside day rule's price pattern objective has yet to be fulfilled, I can ignore almost all mathematical clusters/retracement/projections as long as I understand what the trend is in the present moment. Therefore, this concept is one of the biggest edges in trading, and it is why I focus on the previous day's high/low as a primary trade objective throughout the overnight session or the morning session before I do anything else.

Key Reversal Days

The last bar-related pattern that we will discuss, which ties the last Chapter and this Chapter together, is the tendency for a major high or a major low to be made by a *Key Reversal Day*. A **key reversal up day** calls a high, and it occurs when a market takes out the low and the high of the previous day in that order. In addition, for a key reversal up day, the market must close higher than the previous day's high. A **key reversal down day** occurs when the high and the low of a previous day is taken out in that order, and the market closes lower than the previous day's low. In a way, these days are like extreme inside day rule patterns because the take out both the high and the low of the previous day. At major highs/lows (especially in stocks), key reversal days are major trading edges, and they are most helpful in giving our qualitative eye a quick heuristic to defining discreet highs/lows in a longer-term basis. Because this language is somewhat confusing, let us look to Figure 16.1 for an example of key reversal days.

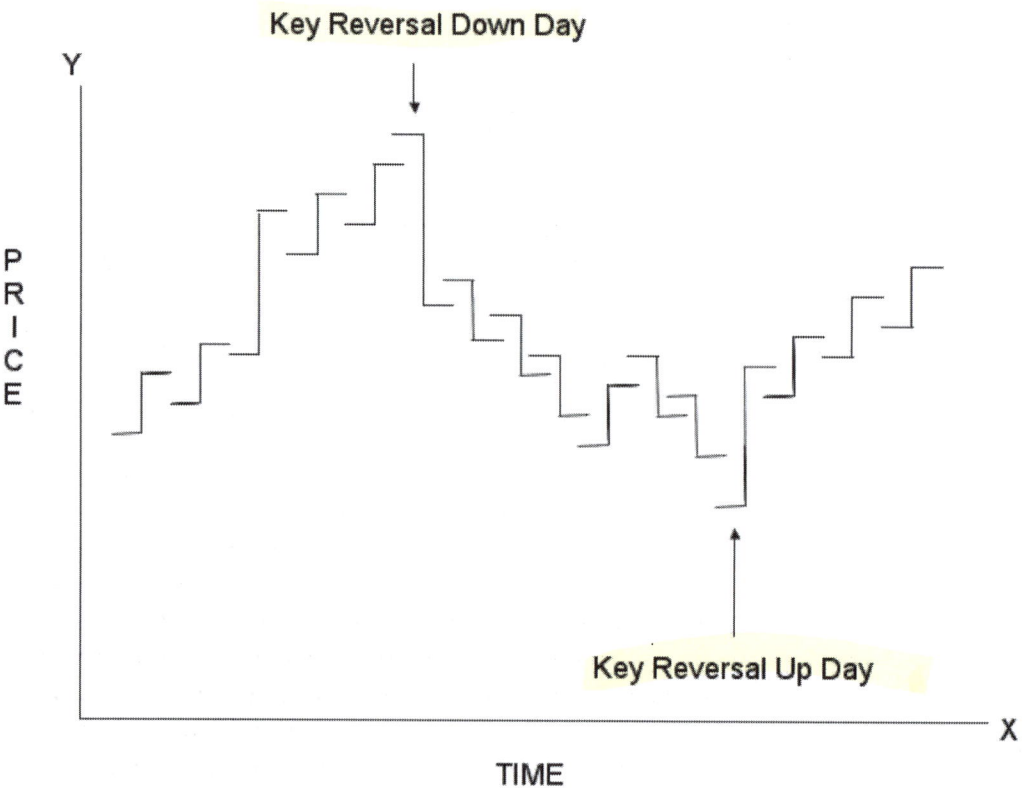

Figure 16.1: Key Reversal Down and then Key Reversal Up Day

As we can see in Figure 16.1, we have a market that moves higher, and then, a Key Reversal Down Day forms. Further, if this key reversal down day was formed with time symmetry or at a price cluster, we can have greater conviction in this Key Reversal Down Day leading to continued, downward momentum. Moving forward, we see that the market does gyrate lower, and ultimately, the market finds support again, which causes a Key Reversal Up Day to form. The only point that I wish to make here, which will be further emphasized towards the end of Time Structure, is that when the Key Reversal Up Day forms, we have to remember Klatch's Price Theory. We have to remember that based off Price Theory the market's new price objective should be to take out new highs of the previous range, and more often than not, if we are dealing with an up trending stock or market, that target will be new yearly highs. A good example of this is the 2012 Dow Jones Index, which had a double top that led to a nice down move, which had ended with a key reversal up day. Then, four months after that key reversal up day, the market broke to new yearly highs because the overall price objective from March 2009 is still valid, which is foreshadowing new highs over the 2007 high.

Lastly, there are also tendencies to *key reversal days* as well. First, due to the large range that is created on these days, there is a higher probability of an inside day after, and this knowledge actually helps our probability awareness of the *inside day rule*. Second, the subsequent days after a big key reversal day tend to have a deep retracement of the *key reversal day's* range. This makes sense because we now know that the market likes to have deep retracements at major highs or major lows because of the market's tendency to *back-and-fill*. Therefore, we also know that the deep retracement is foreshadowing a large swing, which is necessary to turn the trend down based on Dow Theory. More often than not, the high/low of the bar that is made by the *key reversal day* is typically used as the swing point. When the Key Reversal Day's high/low is breached, we then get confirmation that the trend has indeed changed, and that the market has made a significant high/low. Again, this pattern is almost identical to our discussion on *Dow Theory* from Chapter 9.

Triple Swings

At significant highs/lows (even intra-day), we know that the market will have to generate a swing at some point based on Price Theory, and that swing will change the trend. In addition, we know that the market will do whatever it can in order to test the conviction of traders, which means it will try to shake the weakest traders out of the market. Therefore, the market has a tendency to generate triple swings before makings its thrust move, which I will define as a dynamic market. A **dynamic market** is a market that has an extreme tendency to trend in the direction of the swings that foretold the trend chance, and a dynamic market is also characterized by shallow, primary retracements. Further, a **triple swing** is defined as the third swing that is activated after three higher highs and three higher bottoms for an upswing, or three lower lows and three lower highs for a downswing.

Essentially, what we are saying is that after three higher bottoms or three lower tops that have been formed as qualified swings, the third swing tends to foreshadow a market of strong momentum that we can expect to see only shallow retracements. We can say that he market is ready to have a dynamic move. Further, the strength of the market when it has gone *dynamic* is a scenario that tells us to ***not trade counter-trend***, and a **dynamic market,** which is defined as a market that is trending with very shallow retracements, tells us to just hold on to our trend trade/swing trade. In fact, adding to positions at each qualified swing is an opportunity for the trader to load-up on more and more positions with the trend, and for targeting massive position trades for investors, this is the ideal scenario, which also avails itself in every time frame. This is important for investors because the daily bar chart also tends to have dynamic moves after having longer-term swings that are easily viewable on the daily chart.

Another common tendency of a market, when it is trying to successfully defend a high or low, comes from the continuous charts. On a continuous chart, it is common for a market to take out the previous day's high/low based on the *inside day rule*, and then, start to reverse overnight. While reversing overnight, the continuous market may be generating longer-term qualified swings, and by the time the market opens based on real time hours, we can already be in a dynamic market, which is inverted from the prior day. In major bull markets, this is a common tendency because in major bull markets, the market will occasionally have large down days that find support at primary clusters, and ultimately, the market then yields to the Price Theory Price Objective of reaching a **new** high outside of the range, which makes sense because again, prices can always go up but they can only go down to 0.

The last relevant discussion about triple swings that lead to dynamic market moves is the tendencies of the retracements in defining the triple swings. The textbook example of the market to defend a high/low is to have two deep retracements, which are often times equal (we learned about this tendency when discussing retracement memory of the 75%R/78.6%R). If they are not equal, then it is common that they become shallower with each subsequent swing, which makes sense (and is clarified in our discussion of measured moves in Time Structure.) In order to elaborate further on this concept, it would not be common to see a 61.8%R and then a 75%R. No, we would expect a 75%R and then a 61.8%R, which indicates shallower retracements. However, the more interesting observation is that the absolute value of the price distance of each retracement can be equal. For example, if a 2.75 point movement down, after an upswing was activated, yielded a 75% retracement, well then, after the market holds that retracement, and breaks to new highs, again, a 2.75 point movement down could be expected, but this time, that 2.75 point down move would be found at the 61.8%R because the size of the range expanded after the previous range broke to a new high. Thus, after two deep retracements, the ideal, textbook, scenario is for the third retracement to be shallow, but it does not have to be. Therefore, the only remaining requisite for triple swings is that the third retracement has not breached the prior stop loss points (terminal points of the retracement ranges) for the previous two, qualified swings because we are observing that, in essence, all of those swings are still valid, and in play.

Real-Time-Hours ("RTH") Charting versus Continuous Charting

Throughout this book, I have referred to the duality between trading market instruments that trade in real time hours (which apply mostly to stocks) versus continuous hours (which apply mostly to Futures/Forex). For index traders, this is one of the hardest things that we have to deal with because we have to be aware of the real-time-hours chart and the continuous futures chart, which makes Quantitative Synchronicity even more complex (I ask the reader to now picture two cubes in his or her head instead of just one cube as stated in Chapter 6). Hence, because of this complexity, this section will be talked about with pure reference to the S&P 500 E-Mini Futures ("ES") Contract.

In the ES, the RTH chart opens at 9:15am ET and it closes at 4:15pm ET, and these charts sometimes have different highs or lows because they are not reflecting highs or lows that are made during the overnight/continuous session. Therefore, the values of the retracements, swing points, and projections can be vastly different between the continuous chart and the RTH chart. Therefore, ES traders need to be aware of these mathematical support/resistance numbers that exist in both charts, and also, we can add these types of numbers into cluster averages and cluster ranges as well even through the RTH chart is not being over laid on the continuous chart. To paint a clearer picture, a quick example between the duality of the two charts may be that on the continuous chart, we have a 75%R, but on the RTH chart, that same retracement is a 61.8%R because the primary range has different highs/lows for its discreets.

In order to emphasize the importance of the RTH chart, in my trading setup, I have one of my six monitors dedicated to the RTH market only, which provides me with the swings, the retracements, and the projections for the RTH market. This is necessary because these values are important. As we are aware, there is a large ETF market for the S&P 500, and because the ETF stocks do not trade 24 hours, the *Time and Price Symmetry* components for those ETFs are valid. Thankfully, they are summed up for us on the RTH chart of the ES contract. For example, I can look at these numbers as the market makes its movements and I can see if the market adheres to the RTH chart values versus the Continuous chart values. Although there is not much more to say regarding RTH vs Continuous charts, the importance is extreme. Novice traders love to trade the 61.8%R on the ETF chart, which is an example of why the 61.8%R is more valid with stocks, and since those traders are usually focused on the RTH chart for trading, it is common to see a 61.8%R hold on the RTH chart. However, if someone is purely using the continuous chart for his trading, he or she may be confused as to a seemingly random market inflection point because that market inflection point may have come from the RTH chart and not the continuous chart. In order to elaborate, let us finish this discussion logically.

When someone is trading an index via a futures contract or an ETF, we have to remember what the index derives its values from underlying stocks, which do not trade continuous. Therefore, major stock components of an index have their own *Time and Price Symmetry* Structure, which is yielding trades intrinsically in that stock. In fact, every one of these stocks have *Time and Price Symmetry,* and all of these stocks have swings, retracements, etc. that become normalized through the index. Thus, because indexes ultimately derive their values from these stocks, the normalized RTH movement of the index is quite powerful, and I would argue that the RTH retracements/projections do have some higher-degree of probability than continuous chart data. However, as we will learn in the next session with Time Structure, Time will be a good normalizing factor because Time that was applicable on the continuous chart is just as applicable on the RTH, but not vise versa. Therefore, a continuous chart trader, who has a good concept of Time Structure, may ignore the RTH chart's Price Structure components.

The last part of this discussion is not focused on the S&P 500 Futures contract, and this final discussion talks about the pre-market and post-market sessions that stocks trade in, which hold extreme validity for some unknown reason. Unrecognized by most traders, the fact that stocks create chart patterns in their extended hours trading sessions is a very important piece of knowledge. However, extended hours trading sessions for stock traders may function as a double-edged sword. During these times, volume can be anemic, which means that there can be irrational ticks. These irrational ticks need to be filtered out in order to properly draw retracements, projections, etc. However, that does not mean that the extended hours trading sessions of stocks is not important. No, it is very important because more often than not, the extended hours trading sessions lead to relevant discreet highs/lows, which become Price Theory Price Objectives for the formation of swings or more commonly double tops/bottoms. In fact, I believe it is a pure tendency for a market to retest the extended hours discreets in order to satisfy Price Theory, which ultimately yields a higher probability DB/DT or RB/RTs. Lastly, like our discussion of triple swings, day-traders that are looking at stocks can see swings forming in the per-market extended hours session that provide continued follow-through at the open.

Range Ranking

Thus far, I have often times mentioned the term "Primary Range," but it has not been defined. Likewise, in Chapter 6, I introduced the concept of Discreet Highs/Lows, and I gave a determination heuristic of the "180-Bar Rule" in order to isolate Discreets. However, this is inaccurate determinism, and the concept of the Primary Range coupled with true discreets can can now be discussed.

First, the reader must understand that discreet highs/lows exist in two levels depending on Quantitative Synchronicity. In a way, I classify that there are two types of Discreets even though the term Discreet is somewhat absolute in and of itself. First, Primary Discreets exist based on the Daily-Bar Chart, and simultaneously, there are Secondary Discreets based on shorter term Bar Charts, which are ALL Valid for the Primary Ranges. Therefore, we now have three classifications of highs and lows: Primary Discreets, Secondary Discreets, and Secondary Highs/Lows. Primary Ranges exist off both types of Discreets, but not off any Secondaries. The Secondary ranges become additive/retracement, etc. type of ranges, but now we must understand why this is imporant, which means we can discuss Range Ranking and the Primary Cluster.

Range Ranking is a method of giving preferential weighting to different range retracements. For example, a Primary Range built off two Primary Discreets should be more powerful then a Primary Range built off Secondary Discreets, but is this true? Alas, I do not know, but what is imporant here is "The Concept, not the mathematics," as Einsten once said. That said, we can definitely understand that the largest price distance between Primary Discreets shouldgive us the highest mathematical attraction, and some day, I believe we may be able to factor a probabilistic/expected value-like weighting into the cluster calculation. Alas, we are relegated to leave this topic open for future philosophic/mathematical discussion in future editions of this book. Nevertheless, we can definitely instill and understand that a market will give preferential treatment to primary ranges over secondary ranges, but the pure quantitative definition of those said ranges is more of an observational tendency that comes from a trader's intrinsic knowledge base - the subconcious mind.

Thankfully, this conversation is not useless for practicality purposes, and we can now understand a concept that I will define as The Primary Cluster. Likewise, Primary Clusters tend to exist in two forms via Quantitative Synchronicity - longer-term charts and shorter-term charts, but for our purpose the Primary Cluster is defined based on the trading time we are using for a trading strategy. (I.E. A Day-trader would use the Primary Cluste ron his 1-minute chart, a Momentum Trader would use the 15/30/60, etc.) But, where does the Primary Cluster gain practical purposes? Simple, it is simply the FIRST magnetizing area that we will target for a market inflection point. The Primary Cluster is defined as the projection values that emerge from our first counter-trend Qualified Swing that forms against our current tradable Primary Range coupled with the Primary Retracement of that range. Simply put, this ABC corrective swing's projections gives us the first cluster averages possible in order for us to reverse back to the trend. The Primary Cluster is the strongest possible cluster because we know that once we hold retracement support, Price Theory tells us to target Range Expansion, which makes the Primary Cluster immensely practical/profitable.

Earnings Reports / Fundamental News

To continue the discussion of RTH versus Continuous charting, the emphasis of this section will be on the fundamental news that affects stocks, indices, or commodity futures. As *Time and Price Symmetry* *Traders*, we must be aware of fundamental news at all times, and our awareness must be focused on the time of that news instead of on the news itself. These times are easily found on many Internet sites or in your Monday Wall St. Journal or your weekend copy of Barron's. However, in order to elaborate on this section, I will provide the reader with a story of mine that occurred in a discussion I had about the validity of technical analysis. The discussion was on Orange Juice Futures.

After a friend's wedding, I was discussing *Time and Price Symmetry* with a potential investor. I explained to him what a double bottom was, and that the market had price objectives that would be met when a double bottom avails itself. Our discussion was on a long-term double bottom in Orange Juice Futures, which he knew a lot about. His inquisition was that the double bottom meant that I was essentially saying, "Oranges would be blighted out in a deep freeze in the coming winter, which would drive up prices." I found this interesting because he was using a price structure pattern to forecast fundamental news that would affect Oranges. He asserted that my take on the market could not be possible because I was predicting the weather months in advance! Thankfully, we had a logical conversation, and my rebuttal was simply that "I don't know what will happen to oranges, but I do know the price is going up if the double bottom is real." However, this conversation is extremely relevant because of the claim towards divinity that I believe is availed through the *Time and Price Symmetry* as the underlying Marketome because as the reader is now learning, "The Market is not Random," and because of this we often see the market reverse at *Time and Price Windows* before any fundamental news impacts the market. In fact, utilizing *Time and Price Symmetry*, we will often find that markets tell us what way the news will cause a reaction, which could have happened many hours beforehand! However, because of the volatility that emerges through news, we have to realize that fundamental news is a necessary evil that we have to deal with as technical traders.

In most trading instruments, news occurs before markets open and after markets close; especially, with earnings reports. In regards to stock traders, I must make the shorter-term stock traders aware that they risk stop-loss execution because of the volatility that can exist in extended hours trading. On the other hand, Futures traders that are dealing with large markets can usually rest comfortably in the normalization that occurs. As for longer-term investors, earnings news should be ignored because the investor's trades are derived from the longer-term charts to begin with. Therefore, daily fluctuations should be ignored for the most part, unless a stock is close to its stop-loss exit point. If that happens, investors must be aware that stop-losses can be executed due to the irrational price action that exists after news.

Another problem that many new traders face is the inherent, human, gambling tendencies that are activated under the volatility that comes from news. Because of our human nature, we have to be aware of this need for "trading excitement." This need can lead to irrational decisions because of the profit potential that exists from large moves in stocks that occur when reporting fundamental news. In fact, many traders tend to use short-term options to purely gamble on earnings reports, which is idiotic! As I stated in the introductory chapters, the market is not a gambling machine, but it can be made into one. Buying options or placing huge bets in front of fundamental news is foolish, and futures traders must also be cognizant of the inherent human condition to not be over-trading going into important announcements; especially, Federal Reserve announcements. Like everything else in this book, when we approach a fundamental event, we have to remain in the present moment, we have to keep our qualitative eye in check, and we have to adhere to risk management and money management in order to prevent us from treating the market as a casino.

For Futures traders that are trading specific commodities or normalized indices, we also have to be aware of the time that news is occurring, which often aligns itself at the top and bottom of the hour, as we will discuss in Time Structure, which is why this section is a good lead in for Time Structure. During these fundamental news-based time periods, we will learn in our future discussions of Time that markets have tendencies to reverse at specific time windows, and when news happens, volatility immediately increases in the markets. *When volatility increases, we have to be aware that micro-swings or micro-double tops/bottoms can occur, and they become more powerful.* In a way, under high volatility, a micro-swing or a micro DB/DT have as much power as a true, qualified swing or a true 30-minute DB/DT. For example, a micro-double top that occurs after a Federal Reserve announcement can indicate a major high, and the market can have a massive sell off into the close. As such, I encourage newer traders to exit positions during major news announcements until volatility normalizes, and the trader can trade confidently. For more advance traders, fundamental news can be immensely profitable if we are able to live in the present moment in order to effectively utilize *Time and Price Symmetry*, but in general, we have no reason to gamble on news. It's not worth it.

Gaps, Previous Day Closes, Chart Fills, and Islands

The last area of concern for RTH charting versus continuous charting is the discussion of gaps. A gap occurs on a chart due to the continuous movements on the 24-hour chart. Therefore, when the RTH chart opens at a specific time, there can be a gap between the previous day's close and the previous day's opening that comes from the continuous movement of the market. These gaps can be positive or negative.

The market will have a tendency to fill this gap so that the underlying cash index has a continuously filled chart on the daily bar chart graph. Often, when we discuss gaps, we hear phrases such as "fading the open" or "buying the dip." These phrases come from the market's gap-filling tendencies, and fading the open is a short whereas buying the dip is a long. However, we can apply a mentality shift in this discussion as well because the market can fill a gap in one of two ways. First, the most obvious way to fill a gap is just to retrace to the previous day's close, which ensures continuous price movement on the RTH chart. However, *the only requisite the market needs in order to fill a gap is to fill the gap to the previous day's high or low*. This is the second way that markets can fill a gap, and because we have to think differently in order to define this method of gap filling, it is another edge that we get by mentally shifting the requisite for a gap fill. In a way, this is also an extrapolation of the *inside day rule* because we are linking the RTH chart to the continuous chart. As such, we can use either the previous RTH chart's high or low as price targets or cluster calculations, and we can do the same with the RTH chart's previous day close depending on how far away these values are to be effective in our mathematical support/resistance calculations.

The last discussion regarding chart fills is when the markets make an **island** based on the RTH chart. An island occurs between two ranges, and it is a three-day pattern. In order to visualize an island, I will reference Figure 16.2.

Figure 16.2: Island Gap on Real-Time-Hours Chart

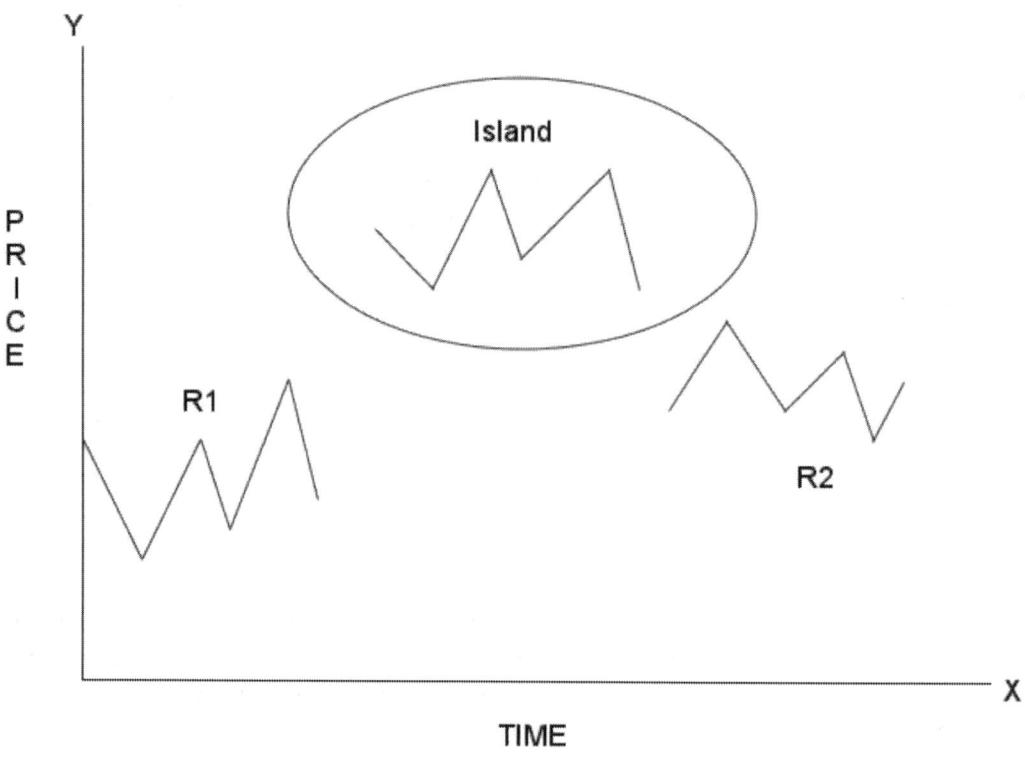

An island occurs often times after a major news announcement in a given market, and they are more typically seen in stocks. An island occurs when a gap is not filled either by testing the previous day's high or low or by testing the previous day's close, which you can see in Figure 16.2. You see that the island existed outside of the normal range, and it only existed there for one day. Islands are very rare, but they are extremely important in calling the end of market moves (a.k.a. major tops or bottoms). They are powerful because when a market creates an island, which may be the only day that that market ever has where prices are traded at those values. Therefore, the prices that exist during an island may never exist again! Again, islands can occur at highs or at lows.

Closing Tendencies

As an introduction to bull and bear market cycles, which is further elaborated on in Time structure, we can discuss the ways markets tend to close on bullish up days/weeks/months versus bearish down days/weeks/months. In bull markets, markets tend to close very close to the high or low of the given daily/weekly/monthly bar. For example, in the S&P 500 E-Mini Futures, it is quite common to see the market close within 5 points of the high for the day and week on a Friday in a bull market. In the last trading hour or day during a bull market scenario, the market will also tend to exert its most strength, and it is a good rule to not use the last hour or day of a given period to trade counter-trend. Because of knowing the markets tendency to close at the high of a given time period in bullish scenarios, we have defined an edge based on closing tendencies in bull markets, which is often helpful to option traders.

On the other hand, bear markets do not tend to close in the same way. In a bear market, we often see the end of a given daily/weekly/monthly bar yield to some type of correction move. Commonly, this tendency is referred to as "short covering." However, the term short covering is irrelevant, and on big down days, markets may also use the last hour of the day to sell off into the close. Further, when a market does have a larger down day and closes near its low, then, we know from the inside day rule that when the continuous market reopens, the tendency will be to immediately target the previous day's low, which makes daytrading objectives harder because the inside day rule has already been met. In a way, I feel that there are conflicting messages with bear markets, which do not garner true trading edges, and because of these conflicting statements, there is really no definable edge in a down market based on the closing tendency; we can see corrections into the close or we can see a close near the low of the day. I believe this edge is mitigated because of the amount of volatility that exists in bearish markets.

Bifurcated Markets

In order to further clarify the closing tendencies of markets, we need to acknowledge the disparity that exists under bifurcated market scenarios. **Bifurcated markets** occur when one index is trading positive and another is trading negative on a given day. For example, the DOW is down, but the NASDAQ is up. These conditions make closing tendencies difficult to quantify, but more important, when dealing with bifurcated markets, we have to be aware that swing trading can be useless. Even if you are a specialized trader in one index, when dealing with bifurcated markets, it is often useful to analyze both markets simultaneously in order to determine if the swings in play for each market are inverse of each other. This is a tell for us traders, and tells us to not expect large follow-through for a given market while the markets are bifurcated. Therefore, bifurcated markets should be treated with a certain level of skepticism or reduced trading size.

I must make it clear to the reader that someone who specializes in one market should not trade based off of another market, but when bifurcation exists, it is necessary to look to another market to determine what is going on that could impact his or her market specialty. However, if a trader focuses too much on two markets, the level of conviction will decrease due to uncertainty, and also, the Moment of Recognition will become delayed due the time requirement of dual analysis. As such, bifurcation is useful in telling a short-term trader to focus on smaller profits until qualified swings form in both markets that are in agreement, which means a trend is about to emerge. In essence, qualified swings are the true criterion that serve to tell us the underlying trend in both markets, and when all markets have agreeable swings, then, there is no longer a reason to have a lack of conviction.

The Rule of Alternation

Although this subject was not mentioned in Chapter 9 in our discussion of the trend, I believe that the Rule of Alternation, which I quantify as a market tendency is very relevant because it helps us to define stocks that may or may not trend. However, this is more about a money management technique then it is about being a trend qualifier, and I will use this section in order to elaborate on the usefulness of this rule, which will conclude our discussion of Price Structure. This tendency is useful for an investor more than a trader, but a short-term trader can use this knowledge in order to define if a given stock will be in a trending mode or in a range mode. In addition, traders that focus on the medium-term period (momentum traders) can benefit from the rule of alternation in order to define instruments that will have a higher probability to trend.

The Rule of Alternation is simple, and it is defined as a market tendency because some stocks will always trend. It simply states that a market that trends higher in one bull market will tend to stay range bound in the next bull market. There is no bearish knowledge to gain from "The Rule of Alternation."

In order to further elaborate, we can look at the bull market of the late 90s. Obviously, technology was the leader and commodities were laggards. However, in the 2002-2007 bull market, technology lagged and commodities surged. Now, in the 2009-present bull market, we are seeing technology surging once again after staying range bound during 2002-2007. With these examples, I have only focused on two industries, but the reader should get the point.

Therefore, this tendency is critical in my mind for portfolio selection and for investment choices that will be deemed as multi-year holdings, and the knowledge of this rule is literally priceless for asset allocation because it can be used in order for a portfolio manager to make sure money is not being wasted by being placed in non-trending instruments / industries. Once again, just knowing about "The Rule of Alternation" is a slight mental shift that has the potential to yield incredible results for money managers, who use it as part of their stock selection criteria. In effect, "The Rule of Alternation" should be the number one heuristic for a portfolio manager because it will lead to the definition of stocks that have the potential for momentum that may last for several years.

In summary, all tendencies are just that. They are observations of possible ways that markets work, and they are not set in stone principles that markets have to adhere too. Even "The Rule of Alternation" is not a true rule, and that is why I have listed it with tendencies because, of course, a stock can perform in one bull market and also in another if revenue continues to grow. Furthermore, inside days are rare, but they happen. Non-gap fills are rare, but they do happen. And triple swings may turn into quad swings or penta-swings before having large, dynamic moves. As such, we must remember that tendencies are observations that are based on our intrinsically learned knowledge base that is created by our subconscious mind's absorption of witnessing thousands of hours of market movements. Therefore, we have to remember that tendencies are trading edges that can be used successfully when coupled with true price structure components, but more important, the application of knowing when to look to a given market's tendency occurs by understanding when the tendency would have relevance outside of Price Theory in order to successfully define the applicability of the tendency in the present moment.

TIME STRUCTURE

Chapter 17

Time Structure

As we learned with Price Structure, the underlying market structure that exists as Price Theory, retracements, and swings has to exist because that is how markets generate recorded prices in order to generate the actual chart patterns. However, Time Structure is not easily recognized and is not easily defined by a quick glance at a price chart. For example, one can easily pick up a newspaper, flip to a stock chart, and be able to see Price Structure, but with time, that ability is lost because measuring and observing time is very exact. Although it is not science, Time Structure does require precise measurement, which is hard to do without appropriate, specific charting tools. Furthermore, I find it hilarious that time has always been staring us in the face, but not many people even discuss it. For example, how often do you hear pundits on CNBC talking about time? Because time is not easily understood or recognized by the masses, it gives *Time and Price Symmetry Traders* a massive edge, which makes our trading abilities superior to the masses. Unfortunately, that edge is not definite, and the truth is that, when we observe Time Structure, nothing is certain or definite.

When a trader deals with Time Structure, the critical thought must be, "Is this working or isn't it?" That is the thought that allows the trader to build an edge by using time, and it must be the question that is continually asked during a trading day (for a daytrader) or on every given week (as a longer-term trader). Therefore, when we deal with Time Structure, the reality is that every trader may pick and choose certain elements of time for their analysis, and this decision making process can come from the trader's own analytical observations of how time has worked for him or her. Hence, the question, "Is this working or isn't it?" This is where the correlation to art becomes palpable because anyone can look at a painting and anyone can see something different. That is true for time, and that makes time non-computational and non-quantifiable (to some degree).

Thankfully, we are not left alone to wonder about time, and thankfully, this book will teach you the core of Time Structure that can be used by the trader in order for the trader to start Trading in Time, which is the title of Chapter 20. However, because of the uncertain application of Time Structure in regards to trading, the trader must be aware of the ego more than anything else because a trader may fall in love with a certain component of Time Structure that, all of a sudden, just stops working, which should prompt the question, "Is this working or isn't it?" Therefore, the ego must be held back in order for the ego to stay present moment-oriented, which means the trader must keep asking, "Is this working or isn't it?" Furthermore, the ego must now be trained to become aware of Time Structure, and thankfully, that is the easy part, and that is the purpose of these chapters on Time. Hence, the key training for the ego will be in the belief in understanding the simplicity of time because time is derived and defined quite easily, and time is partitioned into two quadrants that the ego must be made aware of: (1) repetition of time or (2) the cycles of time. Both of those quadrants are necessary in order for a trader to predetermine a *Time and Price Symmetry* market inflection point, which can now be defined in time as well as in price. Thus, we can now define Time Structure, and **Time Structure** will be defined as *repetitions of time or inherent cycles of time, which occur in a methodical way in order to provide the trader with a window of time that the market may utilize for making an inflection point.*

What is time?

Now, in order to begin the discussion of time, we have to understand what time really is. For the purposes of this book, **Time** is a movement from the past through the present into the future, but that is how we, as humans see it. Moreover, time is a measurement. It tells us quantified intervals: minutes, hours, days, etc. These measurements are based on astrological cycles, and humanity has found isotopes that decay at certain rates equal to certain time valuations that have been previously defined by man. More interesting, is that time is also related to light, and this is where I will shed the first inclination of shifting the conventional thought on time regarding the future to the reader.

If you are to imagine a star that is multiple light years away, the point in time that we receive the light from that star is our present, but that light is coming from that star's past. However, if you were to imagine a midway point between Earth and that other star, you would, in effect, be seeing the future before Earth, but that future is still the past to the star. As such, the point in time where we observe the past on Earth has a simultaneous position in space where we are viewing Earth's future, but all of these viewpoints ultimately culminate at the same present moment when the speed of light is removed from the equation. As such, we have to keep in mind that time is, in many ways, fiction. Time is something that we, as human beings, have defined, but if we are to believe that the markets are not random nor efficient, we must realize that the efficiency exists at some price level based on our knowledge of Price Theory. Furthermore, Price Theory does not tell us the efficient price; just the direction of the *probable* efficient price. Therefore, the viewing of time with respect to trading can be viewed just like the fictional star example because if we were to live in the present at the midway point from Earth to the star, we know that Time's objective is to get that light to Earth, which means we know the future beforehand by observing the present. However, we also can see the past by acknowledging that it exists at the star itself. Therefore, we must realize that time equates to that coexistence in all three domains of time (the past, the present, and the future) by telling us, as traders, that the current price and the efficient price are irrelevant while, at the same time, maintaining extreme relevancy. That may be circuitous and hard to grasp, so I will deduce that last sentence.

The price that our market reaches its efficient price at is an unknown, but the Price Objective that was a certainty from Price Theory told us that a future price is the present moment's Price Objective. Thus, Price Theory tells us that the future and the present are coexisting, and that the market's objective is the Price Objective. However, Price Theory fails to tell us the exact price where the market will inflect because that exact price is defined from Price Pattern Objectives and Cluster Averages. Therefore, we cannot rely on a solid theory like Price Theory in order to define a market inflection point because as we know, Price Pattern Objectives and cluster-averages do not have to obey any given "law." Therefore, time enters into the equation instead of Price Pattern Objectives and Cluster Averages. Time can be used to tell us the exact time in the future where the market will inflect ***AFTER PRICE THEORY*** has been fulfilled, which means that in the present, we know the Price Objective based on Price Theory and we know the future possible time(s) for market inflection points. Therefore, we can simultaneously know the price by knowing the exact time of the market inflection point(s), and as the reader should be able to put together, we have a relationship between Time and Price that is linked by one component to the other. Thus, we now have a second criterion for quantitatively defining market inflection points, which defines *Time and Price Symmetry*. Furthermore, time is more powerful than price because the predefined Time(s) can be utilized for a trade regardless of the market inflection point's price! That being said, there is a word of caution about abandoning oneself completely to time, which means that Price Structure must be learned and it must not be forgotten.

In order to elaborate, I must quote Gann. Gann used to say that "Time is twice as important as price," but I humbly disagree. I believe that if one can master time, price can be irrelevant because with Time and Time only, we can trade with ultimate conviction, and as foreshadowed in the *Introduction* of this book, that conviction can lead to an irrational, delusional belief in one's trading abilities. For me, that level of conviction led to a federal arrest! Hence, the disclaimer of caution to remain humble and in the present moment. Quite simply, the reality we must face with time is that it is illusory; it is man made, and we have to realize that. Time is an illusion to humanity, and because of this, we know that it is inherently flawed, which means that the markets build in a failsafe for us with respect to time, which I defined as Price Structure! For this reason, Price Structure can never be completely ignored because time is inherently flawed, which means that Time can serve as our Price qualifier, and Price can serve as our Time qualifier.

Shifting to Time-Oriented Thinking

With the conclusion of the last section, we have to realize that in order to become traders in time as well as in price; we have to shift our thinking to using Time Structure before Price Structure. Because time is superior to price (even though it is illusory), we now have to *start thinking that time is our primary trade criterion but time criterion must be backed up by price criterion*. In essence, one serves as testimony to the other, and we are choosing to use price in order to validate Time because Time is more powerful, which should be the logical conclusion with respect to a trading strategy. Simply, it makes sense to use the more powerful component first, right? Conversely, if we decide to completely ignore price, we face a very hard, human, stumbling block by learning to trade in time without price. As a result, time-oriented thinking must never forget price, and I will explain why this is so.

When we use Price Structure to place our trades, we can visually see that the market is hitting an area of mathematical support/resistance, and we can visually see that the market is moving off that value. Further, we can see Price Structure by observing double tops/bottoms, swings, etc. Therefore, we can "see" Price Structure, but we cannot "see" Time Structure. In fact, we have to learn to trust time, which is a scary thought. In essence, what I am saying is that if we decide to neglect Price Structure completely, we could trade without a price chart. Hell, we can even turn our computer monitors off in order to trade. Then, instead of looking at price, we can look at a clock, and when the time on that clock hits a predefined time window, (let us say 2 minutes after the hour), we have to click the buy/sell button on our brokerage screen. At that moment, we are literally abandoning ourselves to time and to the present moment, and we are learning to trust time even though we may not see it. Now, this may be an extreme example, and I do not advocate trying this example in real life, but the emphasis should be quite clear to the reader. Time becomes the one and only trading decider, but we, as humans, do not contain the ability within ourselves to make it the only decider. Thus, we can use Price Structure to observe that if the market has reached a level that makes sense for a reversal in terms of time and in terms of price, we can reverse. Therefore, we will be able to say that our trading has shifted to being **time-oriented** versus **price-oriented**, but we also have to understand that time-oriented thinking requires a price-oriented back up. I believe these definitions can be self-defined by the reader.

Now, as we have to learn to trade in time first, we have to learn how time avails itself for our purposes through Time Repetitions or Time Cycles, which are the purposes of the next two chapters, but at the same time, we cannot forget about Price Structure, which is the purpose of Chapter 20. And Chapter 20 brings everything together. In that chapter, we will finally be able to reach the entire conclusion for this book by saying that if we have a time window open for us as the market reaches a Price Structure-defined market inflection point; we fulfill the non-randomness of the market. Thus, Time and Price create symmetry at that point, and we fulfill the objectives of this book.

Price Theory and Time Structure

In order to complete our understanding of defining Time Structure, I feel that an elaboration must be done by extrapolating Price Theory's Price Objectives. In fact, we have to realize that Price Objectives based on Klatch's Price Theory are exactly the same as knowing the future in advance. For instance, a retracement range of a low to high base range has an objective to take out the high, but it does not tell us when. As such, when we have a base range, a retracement range, and an observed inflection point, which tells us to target a break of the base range, we are seeing the past (base range), present (inflection point of retracement range), and future (Price Objective) simultaneously! In a way, this is how I believe that God sees time. He does not see time going from moment to moment, but He sees the past, present, and future simultaneously. He knows what we are going to do tomorrow because He already sees tomorrow. As such, we can extrapolate this analogy to complete the parallel between the importance of time and the unimportance of time. A Price Objective is void of time because that Price Objective is inevitable; it exists simultaneously in the present and in the future. As such, this is why time may not always be a factor at discreet highs or discreet lows, but simultaneously, it will guide us in defining the most relevant market inflection point after Price Objectives have been met.

Now, you may be thinking that I am trying to make my own Price Theory more important than time, but that is not so. No, I am redefining the introduction of Time Structure here in order to allude to God along with understanding the proper way in order to invoke the Law of Attraction. It is our job as traders to be focused on the present moment, by surrendering ourselves to the present moment. However, when we are surrendering ourselves to the present moment, we have to automatically understand and see in our mind's eye the fulfillment of the underlying Price Objective. In essence, we have to visualize the market completing its Price Objective before it happens, but we cannot fall in love with that Price Objective. We must visualize it because we must visualize the profit potential that it holds, but we must be aware of the fact that Time Structure will avail itself in order to clue us in on the future, and that thought path is undoubtedly difficult to achieve. However, I feel that is the burden of the cross that we must strive for as traders.

Because of how difficult that present moment and future moment thinking are to achieve simultaneously in one's mine, I must say that for many traders (especially those with higher intellects), being able to let go of normal convention, and believe in something that is not palpable is very hard. However, being able to define market inflection points in terms of time is the most powerful trading edge that exists, which makes it worth the risk to understand. As I said, if one achieves a complete understanding of time, price becomes irrelevant. It also makes price structure irrelevant. In fact, the only reason we discussed price structure in this book is to observe the certainty that price structure will give us when time is used in order to correctly call a market inflection point. However, I have also stated that Time is not 100%, and it is not 100% because I cannot define it as 100%. It is 100% accurate to God, but it is not 100% accurate to me because my brain and my intellect are limited, and the higher intellect trader must remember this corollary. You are not God. You are only elevating yourself to His thinking at several times throughout the day, week, or month. You are not elevating yourself to every time window because it is not humanly possible, and part of writing this book is the hope that future generations will use computers to quantify and define time in order to completely remove Price from the equation. Further, being able to remove one's self from conventional analysis, and to believe in an ethereal application that has minimal analytical components is quite difficult, and it is quite difficult because Time is a human creation, and the way God sees Time is best described by C.S. Lewis in *Mere Christianity*. He can already see the Time windows in advance because he sees all time at the same time.

Now, getting back to real, scientific applications of time, I must say that these chapters serve as a way to obliterate as much of the *hocus pocus* of Time Structure, by giving the reader quantified tools to begin his or her own interpretation on how to use time for her or her trading benefit. I will also discuss my own observations, and as always, I encourage the reader to review some of W.D. Gann's own analysis in regards to time, which will mostly be summed up in these next, three chapters.

The Time and Trend Debate

Although I stated that there is an illusory effect to Time, which meant that Time could fail us, we have to be aware that time can fail us by tricking us in to counter-trend trading. As traders, we can be inundated with trade ideas because of Time Windows that get opened and closed throughout the day, but just because they are opening and closing, doesn't mean that we need to take every trade. In fact, we need to use time to get us back into trading with the trend in the first place, which will be clarified in the next chapter. Therefore, the qualitative eye argument of knowing the trend along with the longer-term Price Objectives is necessary in order to use Time Windows that get us back with the trend, and unarguably, time can cripple us just as much as it can help us. I believe that this is also because time can sometimes be quantified, which gives us a time window to focus on, but we have to be cognizant and aware that the market does NOT have to react at that quantified time window, which does make price structure useful as well (again, all of the Price Structure learning was not done in vain). Therefore, every quantitative tool that the trader employs with defining time windows is not absolute; because ***with time, nothing is certain or definite*** (to us humans). In fact, every trader may pick and choose certain elements of time in their own analysis because they have found a repetition or a cycle that has proven useful for them. That middle ground of using time to help us is necessary, and the choice is to use that knowledge with the underlying trend and with Price Structure. In fact, this is the entire basis of these chapters on Time Structure because in no way am I stating that a trader can have the mental ability to trade solely in time, and that means that above all, the trend still reigns as supreme.

Time for our Purposes

My discussion on time, for the reader, will be focused on the usefulness that I have found by trading in time with Price Structure. However, by no means is this a complete and an absolute set of Time Structure components. Therefore, these chapters will be focused on daytrading and position-trading/investing, and I encourage every trader to use and understand time in their own, different way. ***We are only using time for the purpose to help us and not hurt us!*** Thankfully, it can serve as an immense help, and it serves as this help because it was built in to the X-axis on a price chart. It has always been there, and it will always be there. Thus, because of the simple fact that time is a component to the market's structure, there is a level of certainty that the trader can attain by being able to use time in trading, and once that level of certainty is achieved for the trader by understanding time, insane profit and accuracy can result. However, the truth will lie in the ability of the trader to trust in time, and to trust in that trader's intrinsically observed knowledge base that has witnessed how time has been a predictive factor in the past.

When time and price meet in *Time and Price Symmetry*, the trader can have 100% conviction of the market's inflection point, which justifies immense leverage in order to seek returns in the 1000%+ range even on a daily basis! When market inflection points become coupled with Time Structure, which is also in agreement with the trend, we have extreme certainty in our trades. Above all else, that is the end goal of trading. Therefore, as foreshadowed in my *Introduction*, this can also cause the trader to become too confident, and the trader's conviction will cause the trader to lose concept of risk/money management. Also because of extreme conviction, the trader may decide to place fully levered positions, which the trader's psyche cannot properly handle due to the underlying fluctuations to the Profit and Loss in the trader's account. Since conviction based on time can lead to position sizes that are not normal for the trader, the trader may begin to make irrational decisions that are different from prior trades. These irrational decisions can be classified as: unjustifiably moving the stop to break-even due to the fear of the position size, placing a stop too tight because of the fear of loss, taking partial profits off the position in order to feel more calm/peaceful, and most importantly, becoming too hopeful in forecasting how much money the trader will make on the given trade, which means the trader stops the analytical process of defining new market inflection points; the trader may miss a reversal opportunity due to the bias derived from having too large of a position. Hence, the trader loses his present moment thinking, and he becomes money-oriented and he starts to trade on the emotions of "hope" and "fear." As the famous old saying goes, "A hoping trader is already a dead trader."

Time, a Personal Perspective

In my personal trading, the irrational decision making process in the prior paragraph summarized all of my biggest problems with my ego's confidence with respect to trading. Because I was able to define market inflection points so well, I often levered up too quickly, and once I was fully employing margin/being fully leveraged, I would stop the analytical process. Quintessentially, I would put all my hopes and dreams into this one trade, and I would not reverse at another market inflection point. In fact, I would rely on the market's underlying trend and the ability of the market to trend in order to justify my mentality shift to being in an observed perspective instead of remaining in a connected, analytical way to the market. Although this is the correct approach if one is to trade on a multi-day basis, it is not possible to trade with the trend every hour of the day as a daytrader. Sure, at the end of the day, the overall trend should avail itself, but as we know, the intraday market has several movements up and down, which means that the overall trend becomes irrelevant the more you zoom in on your trading time period. Therefore, I have defined one of my primary failures because I was trading as a momentum trader in a day-trading time period. Had I given the positions a smaller size, which would justify a larger stop, my underlying trade decision would have been right, but my ego had me believing that I could effectively navigate every Time Window, which is idiotic. As stated, that thought path is the same as elevating oneself to God, and we all know what happened when Lucifer tried to do that.

Therefore, my primary failure was that after taking a loss, I would abandon myself to high leverage and to the underlying trend, without respect for the current trend in the current time period I was working with. Therefore, I feel that my primary failure came from unjustified leverage due to the certainty that I viewed from **Time Structure**, and I ended up breaking my risk management rules as defined in my "Trading Size Calculation" spreadsheet (*See Resources: Interval Trading Size Calculations*). My ego became too satiated in the ability of recognizing the primary high or low for a given trading day, and my ego forced me to constantly fall in love with my trend-oriented position when I was not trading with a trend-oriented mindset. Nor was I trading in a trend-oriented time frame. Thus, because of the large trading size I employed, I ended up being fearful of being stopped or missing profits, and I just let the trade go while I sat back and watched. I took myself out of the analytical mode, and I became aligned with my hopes and dreams for this one trade. I do not think this was because of laziness or fear, but it was because I was burned out. By the time I grasped these concepts, I could only execute for a few short hours per day, which is equitable to any type of athlete. As such, I now realize that aggressive daytrading is unsustainable at the highest level of trading, and that is why my mentor took 19 years before doing a trading campaign. He had 19 years to psyche himself up in order to conquer the mental difficulty of working 14 hour days using *Time and Price Symmetry,* which again, is an interactive process. Further, even my mentor did not trade like this for longer than 2 months. I also believe that because of the CFTC's investigation of me, I worked myself like this for 16 months straight, and that led to irrationality, which culminated in criminality with the objective to keep fighting every day. Physically and mentally, I was not performing at my peak as a star athlete. I was not even taking care of my physical and mental health. As such, I feel that I need to make reference to the doctoral comparison from the *Perception* section of this book, I must ask the reader this question in order to emphasize my mentality at my arrest, "Would you let a surgeon operate on you if you knew that he spent the past 16 months performing surgery 14 hours per day, 6 days a week, with no breaks?" No, you wouldn't because the rational thought was that he cannot keep that pace going. At some point, the surgeon would make a mistake, and you did not want the surgeon to make that mistake on you! Therefore, the obsession of being ***too good*** at trading along with pressure becomes a trader's worst flaw because of pride!

Furthermore, since I have also stated in the *Perception* section of this book that I do not equate a "good trader" to profit, I must further explain that it is my belief that being a good trader ***does not*** lie in the analytical process of making trading decisions based purely on *Time and Price Symmetry,* which is undoubtedly counter-intuitive to the reader. For me, being a good trader knows when to trade on every single market inflection point defined in price and in time versus when to know to abandon one's self to the trend and to keep using *Time and Price Symmetry* in order to get back to the trend. These two separate approaches need to exist as possibilities for all times for the trader. And understanding when to trade in each approach is where I feel the essence of being a good trader lies. This differentiating mindset should also couple with having a favorable reward/risk ratio, the ability to stay in the market for most of the day, and most important, a good trader has the ability to adhere to his or her risk/money management rules. In effect, it is a summation of all these concepts in this book that makes the trader adequate, but it is knowing when to use these concepts that makes the trader "good."

On the other hand, being a good analyst is different from being a good trader, and I define a good analyst as a person who has the ability to determine the underlying trend, and also, to determine *time and price windows* that lead to market inflection points on a consistent basis. A good trader *may* also be a good analyst, but as we can see in my earlier discussion about the irrelevance of performance numbers based on leverage, which is in the *resources* section of this book, a good trader does not have to be a good analyst if their trading strategy has favorable win rates and reward/risk ratios. Therefore, my failure as a trader broke most of these rules because of my analytical certainty of *Time and Price Symmetry,* and *the* main reason behind my failure is that although I was often correct in my analysis, I never allowed myself opportunities to be wrong, and since I now realize that I am human, I must be aware of the fact that Time Structure requires the understanding that sometimes Time Structure stops working. Thus, I must be aware that part of trading, as a human, is the fact that my trades and your trades can be wrong, which is perfectly okay.

Now, as I move towards concluding this text, I feel that the awareness level that the reader should have at this point in my writing with respect to *Time and Price Symmetry* will be forever ingrained into the reader's thought process whenever he or she is to approach the market. I find this knowledge similar to a person who is studying for the LSAT exam in order to be accepted into law school. It has been proven, through neuroscience that the brain's logical reasoning processes actually change just by studying for the LSAT exam itself! I find that astonishing, and I find it amazing how simple it may be to change the conventional pattern recognition/logical-reasoning that exists within ourselves. Therefore, I expect that this book will be able to do the same thing for a person, who was ignorant about Price Structure and Time structure, and I say this because even the governmental authorities use price and time. However, they use it unconsciously, and to elaborate on this example, I must ask the reader, "Did you know that the SEC mandates that exchanges fill orders in a method known as Price-Time Priority?" I bet you did not, and I bet the SEC did not even realize the power of their mandate, and interestingly enough, that Price-Time Priority exchange requirement is what is getting the exchanges into trouble because they are violating the rules of Price and Time for High Frequency Traders. To me, the reality that this rule violation is leading to illicit/illegal gains makes sense because people should not screw with the Price/Time relationship, which serves as the market structure.

Concluding Remarks on Time Structure

Thankfully, learning the two disciplines that Time Structure analysis falls into is much easier and much shorter than learning price structure. Unfortunately, the application of time is infinitely harder. As such, a definitive learning curve begins with the trader observing time windows for price pattern confirmations. From there, the trader's application of time will only progress forward to a deeper understanding of the flow of time, which sometimes is derived from a sixth sense-type of recognition that our subconscious is recognizing due to past experience. Once the trader has reached this level of holistic oneness with the market, price becomes irrelevant due to the predictive certainty that time affords. Until the trader reaches this level of analytical conditioning, time can be useful in other ways, and as already discussed I believe that the best way that time helps a new trader is by forcing the trader to use his or her mental energy at specific time windows, which will also slow down one's trading. (Overtrading is a common problem for new traders.)

Lastly, in order to understand the edge that time gives us by what I am putting forth in this book, we have to observe how the masses incorrectly try to use time in their trading, and I can assure the reader that the methods defined in this book are the correct thought paths that the masses should understand in order to further the study of Time Structure because understanding time is the hardest task that a trader can partake in, but it is the most rewarding. Therefore, most people, who do not realize the ethereal nature of time, try to quantify time, which does not work, and the first tendency that most people have with time is to measure the amount of time between two points, and then, they try to extrapolate that time into the future. This simply does not work, and it is a lucky occurrence when it does. Measuring time is **not** the same thing as defining repetitions of time, and as we will discuss, these measurements are defined as measured moves, which do hold validity in some rare scenarios.

The second way that the masses tend to use time incorrectly is that they take a time measurement, and then, they multiply it by some arbitrary value (this multiplication factor can often come from Fibonacci numbers). Again, since this is based on some type of measurement, the multiplication by some arbitrary number is also irrelevant, and I must be clear that repetitions of time are NOT the same as measurements. As such, the mental shift of understanding the true way in which time works becomes quite easy, but the application never is. With that, let us finally understand how powerful of an ally time can be, and let us see that "The Market is Not Random."

Chapter 18

Repetitions of Time

The first and most important way for us to understand how time can become a deciding factor for future trades is to be aware of the concept that a market inflection point that occurred at some point in the past will occur again at some point in the future at that same time, and that defines a **Time Repetition**. Furthermore, in order to understand the phrase "at that same time," which I used in the definition, we need to understand that time repeats itself, and in effect we are looking for an echo of the past that will present itself again in the future, and we are patiently and we are humbly awaiting that future echo time-period in the present moment. Summarily, we can think of it as simple as this: time repeats itself. In order to further elaborate on the concept, you can think of this as the market celebrating its birthday in every time frame, or again, alternatively, you can see this in the market's memory of prior events that have happened at some time in the past.

For trading purposes, time repetitions are used primarily for short term and medium term analysis because they provide us with an extreme trading edge, but that does not mean that we cannot use time repetitions for longer-term trades as well. Thus, in Chapter 20, we will discuss how to use repetitions of time in defining higher probability outcomes for trade decisions, which can be amplified into every time frame using Quantitative Synchronicity. However, in order to understand how powerful trading can become by making one's self aware of a forthcoming repetition-based time window, we have to understand that the mentality of the time-based trader is completely different. By understanding "when" something is going to happen, we can truly learn to anticipate trades instead of reacting to the market for defining our trades, which was introduced in the last chapter with respect to the hyperbole-based example of trading by a clock.

Now, the reader has to understand that Time Repetitions exist in all time frames, which can be: hourly, daily, weekly, monthly, yearly, decennial, and as we are able to view more historic data at some point in the future, we will also be able to look centennially. What we look for and what we record on our chart is easiest to explain in hourly and monthly examples, and since Time Repetitions provide such a strong edge to daytrading, it makes sense that we must elaborate on these time frames. In addition, these are the two most useful time frames for us to use repetitions of time, and it is important for us to adequately discuss hourly repetitions and monthly repetitions laboriously.

In order to begin the explanation of time repetitions, we need to use examples. I will focus on the S&P 500 E-Mini Futures Contract because it is a continuous chart, which means we have more data inputs for analyzing time on an hourly basis, which will be our first example. Then, I will walk the reader through a second example of monthly repetitions in order to emphasize time's importance for longer-term traders/investors.

Daytrading with Time

To begin our daytrading example, let us once again turn to our phantom trader, Jim, and Jim begins his trading day at 8am ET using the S&P 500 E-Mini. At the beginning of Jim's trading day, he begins by looking at the overnight session in order to find market inflection points; some of these inflection points can be discreets, some can be qualified swing points, and some of these inflection points could have occurred intra-range (these distinctions are important for clarification later in this Chapter). As Jim goes back to review the overnight session, which opened at 6pm ET (1800 hours), he starts to record the times that the market made highs or lows overnight. For our example, let us say that he records these times as follows: 1802, 1929, 2201, 0001, 0114, 0302, 0315, 0401, 0515, 0630, 0701, and 0732. This is what will become the basic time listing, which can be broken into a time histogram. A **Time Listing** (or "time list") is a recording of times that the market has made a pivot point defined by price structure (of note, when create a time list, we will use military time for notation, and we will always assume we are using Eastern Time). Purely by looking at these numbers, I hope that the reader is able to become aware of some type of recognition to an underlying repetition existing within those numbers. However, if we were to list the numbers like this, we would not see the pattern easily, and it only takes a slight perception shift to understand the way in which we can see the pattern. Thus, let us follow Jim's process when he starts trading shortly after 8am.

Since Jim is an active daytrader, he wants to make time useful to himself on an hourly basis so he can adequately profit from as many waves as possible during his trading day. As such, Jim simply creates a time histogram of the minutes that caused prior highs and lows, and he decided to not include the hours because he is working on an hourly repetition basis, which will be elaborated on shortly. Further, we can now state the definition of a **Time Histogram** as a grouping of times that appear close together, which are segregated based on that closeness. For every time frame and regardless of the fact we are using repetitions or cycles (Chapter 19), we will always align time into a combined histogram of both repetitions and cycles, but at this point, we do not need to be concerned with cycles because they are irrelevant on an intraday/daytrading basis. Therefore, let us now look at Jim's constructed time histogram from his basic time listing that he uses for daytrading. His time list appears as follows once he truncates for his repetition relevancy, which for a daytrader, would mean minutes hold validity:

$$2, 1, 1, 2, 1, 1$$
$$14, 15, 15$$
$$29, 30, 32$$

The first thing that should be easily recognizable is that in order to generate the histogram, Jim dropped the "hour" requirement from the histogram, and he has decided to just list the minutes. Jim did this because he is not looking at trading on a daily basis; he is looking to trade on an hourly basis. Thus, he is focused on the market's hourly birthday, and therefore, only the minutes hold relevance. However, since this is somewhat confusing, let me introduce another definition that will be extrapolated on in Chapter 20. If we were to assume that Jim was not a daytrader and that Jim was only trading once per day, he could look at exact times of the past day's discreet highs/lows, which would make a daily cycle relevant. In that instance, the hour and the minute become useful because, if the discreet highs/lows of the previous day(s) were at 0701, Jim would put more focus on today's 0701, which makes Quantitative Synchronicity a hard echelon of understanding to grasp within Time Structure, because concurrently, even within Jim's daytrading, if 0701 was a discreet low from yesterday, it becomes a Focal Time Point for today, which can be profitable for daytrading. If that is the case, we can observe how the hourly component and the minute component can line up through Quantitative Synchronicity regardless of whether Jim was daytrader or a momentum trader, and the third-dimension of the Marketome is the difference between the great trader and the best trader. Again, in Chapter 20, we will discuss additive understandings like this, which fall under the realm of the qualitative eye. That being said, I make the reader aware of this observation at this point as a basic introduction to Focal Time Points because we must now discuss and talk about weighted times, which are different but related to Focal Time Points; both of which are highly useful for Jim's present daytrading.

A **weighted time** is a time repetition that appears multiple times within the time list, which is also observed and accentuated once divided into the relevant sections of the time histogram. Ergo, we can say that the weighted time value is more important in the presently defined trading time period. However, for now, let us just observe that a weighted time is like the mathematical definition of mode with respect to a list of numbers, and each time histogram segregated section will have a different mode based on the original time list. With that laborious, confusing allusion to Quantitative Synchronicity, we can now understand Jim's histogram in order to understand how he makes time repetitions relevant for his daytrading, which begins shortly after the 8am hour. For this example, I ask the reader to refer to Figure 18.1. (Of note, in the chart there are four letters after the labeled times. These letters, B, S, F, R refer to the following: Buy, Sell, Flat, and Reverse.)

Figure 18.1: Jim's Trading

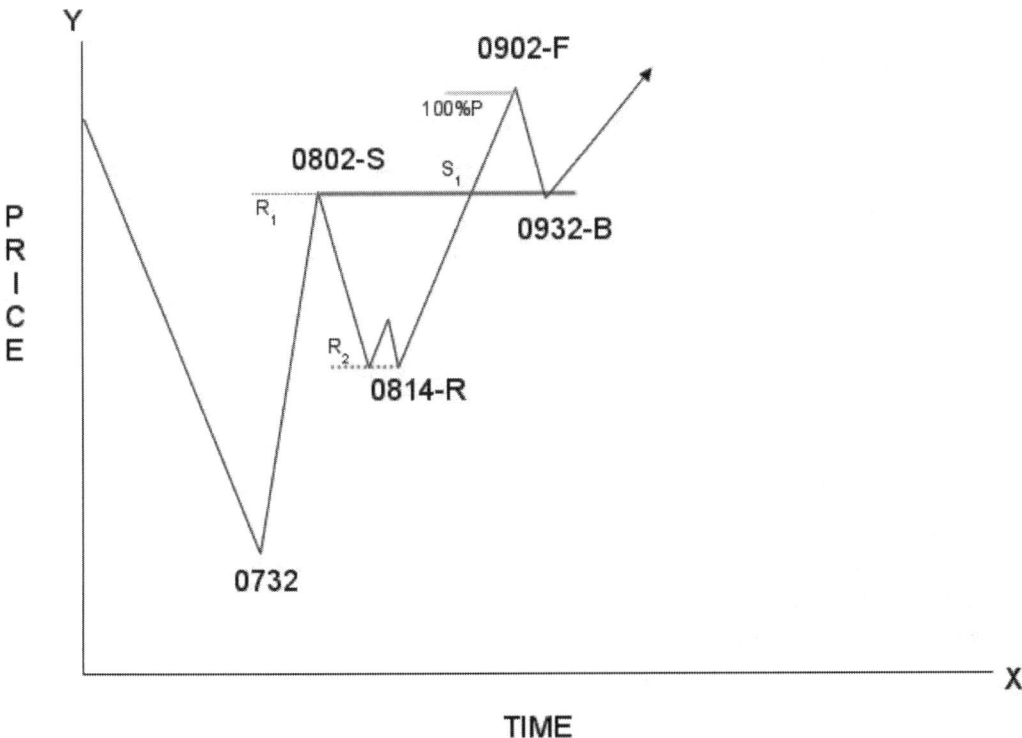

If we look back to the histogram, the second most obvious thing should be that we clearly see three different segmented groups that make up the Time Histogram, and these groupings become the basis for formulating Time Windows, which will be defined properly in Chapter 20. Further, the third observation from the histogram is that we see that two out of the three Time Windows are referring to the top and the bottom of the hour. The top and the bottom of the hour observation is extremely important, and witnessing this recurrence at the top and the bottom of the hour day in and day out is the leading observation to uncovering time repetitions in the first place. Essentially, what we are saying is that at the **top and bottom of the hour**, the market tends to reverse. This is so common of an occurrence that in the quantitative analysis that I had performed using an automated trading model, if one neglects fundamental news from the equation, a trading strategy of reversing a position after a high or low is made at the top or bottom of the hour is a profitable strategy in and of itself! In fact, it is so important that before moving on, I even encourage the reader to go look at a 1-minute bar chart of any, liquid trading instrument. As such, I encourage you to do this type of analysis for yourself in order to be placed in a state of awe about the reality of these, simple, basic time repetitions that are staring you in the face. As an aside, what I have found as even more amazing is that whenever I tell a trader about this top and bottom of the hour Time Window, 99 out of 100 times, that trader was never even aware of the fact that time mattered except for knowing that the market opened at 930am ET and that the market closed at 4pm ET!

Getting back to Jim's histogram, let us now understand how Jim uses these three time segments from the Time Histogram in order to help his trading after 8am. By 8am (0800), Jim has created his time histogram, and since he has a top of the hour Time Window, he immediately starts looking for a high/low shortly after or even at 8am. For our purposes, 2 minutes later, he does indeed observe a high at 0802, which is at a primary retracement from a previous negative range, which means that the market was continuing lower over night, and that it is now moving back up (retracing) that negative range. Therefore, Jim is invoking Price Theory in order to anticipate a new low of that negative range, and because of the *Time and Price Symmetry* that exists at 0802, he sells short at this point of *Time and Price Symmetry* because he has an opened Time Window and because he has a primary Price Structure component. Therefore, because of the time repetition, he has greater conviction in the efficacy of taking this trade. Now, Jim can comfortably leave his stop-loss at a break to new highs above the 0802 high. This last sentence alone requires more elaboration as well because let us assume that the 0802 high leads to a retracement that is deep enough to qualify the 0802 high as a primary swing point. Well, if we just used Price Structure, we know that if we were to be stopped on this short position, then, we should be reversing long after the 802am high is exceeded because it is a swing. However, with Time Windows, we no longer have to trade with blind faith in Price Structure. We no longer have to reverse on that 0802 high-breach/swing-activation because we know that Jim can simply wait until 14 or 15 minutes after the hour, which is his second Time Window, in order to see if a new trade inception is justifiable. However, let us assume that Jim's short is favorably following through to the downside after he sold the primary retracement, and he has observed that the market has now created a decent retracement range of the up-move that terminated at 0802.

Moving on, at 0814, Jim sees that the market has made a micro double bottom off a primary retracement from the positive range that terminated at 0802. Therefore, using Time Symmetry, Jim reverses long at 0814, and he uses Price Theory in order to target new highs over the 0802 high. He holds onto his trade, and he is now waiting for the bottom of the hour, which is his next Time Window within his segmented Time Histogram. He is focusing on this next Time Window in order to see if he should reverse again. This time, however, he does not see a reversal trade avail itself, and it looks like the positive reversal trend has emerged after the negative overnight trend. Jim comes to this conclusion based on knowing that quantitative trend identification is based on the activation of the primary swing point that occurred once the 0802 high was breached. Jim has placed his stop at break-even, and he was able to use Time in order to predict the break of the range. He is now patiently waiting for the swing's price pattern objective to take some profit, or he is waiting until a new time window opens, or he has decided to just hold this one position for the rest of the trading day because he believes the market will continue to trend, and he will only be out of the market if another qualified swing forms against him or if he is stopped out at break-even. I supply all of these scenarios because we must realize how a trader can use all of the concepts in this book at one time. *Essentially, the true purpose of trading is always to make profits with the trend, and once a trader has a profitable position placed with a stop at break even, that trade has already been deemed a winner. Thus, the trader can relax and let go to the trend, but as a word of caution, this type of thinking is not present moment oriented. As such, if the trader is to take himself out analytical mode, the trader must realize that greater potential for failure.*

Now, let us continue forward through Jim's trading day, and let us assume that Jim is a competent *Time and Price Symmetry* Trader, which means that he wants to make as much profit as possible by trading every market wave (I.e. he is not just letting go to the trend). Therefore, since Jim's bottom of the hour

Time Window did not avail any new trades and he is still long, he is now waiting for his next Time Window to open up again. As such, Jim is now waiting until 1 or 2 minutes after the hour to find a reversal. This time, at 0902, Jim does see a 100%P of the qualified swing appearing around this value, and he is using his knowledge of the 1,2 minutes after the hour time repetition in order to exit his position. He does not want to trade counter-trend because he realizes that the qualified swing changed the trend up. Therefore, he exits his position just shy of the 100%P, and he waits for his next time window to emerge. This time, at 14,15 minutes after the hour, he doesn't see much of an opportunity that would give him favorable reward/risk so he waits again until the next time repetition at the bottom of the hour. At the bottom of the hour, we know that the US Markets open, and that causes massive volume that usually has massive initial volatility. Therefore, Jim waited for the market noise to quiet down, and now Jim is watching the market pullback at the open, but at 0932, he observes the market retests the primary swing point from the high at 0802. Here, Jim gets long at 0932, and once again, he is targeting new highs over the 100%P using Price Theory (since the 100%P high has expanded the base range), which called the high at 0902. Now, when Jim takes his 0932 trade, he updates his histogram with the new highs and lows that were made in the past 90 minutes of trading, and his updated histogram looks like this:

        2, 1, 1, 2, 1, 1, 2, 2
        14, 15, 15, 14
        29, 30, 32, 32

    As an aside, as I stated earlier in Price Structure, *Time and Price Symmetry*-based trading is not a boring, dull process. It is an interactive process that requires continuous chart updating, and just as one would constantly be drawing retracements/projections and removing penetrated lines, one would also be continuously updating the time-based histogram. Therefore, the histogram will continue to get updates throughout the day so that Jim gains confidence in time repetitions that enable him to take further trades. Amazingly, it is that simple.

    In order to continue the discussion on time repetitions, we have to be aware of all the **Price Structure Components** in order to properly build our histogram in the first place. Price Structure Components are defined as any high/low that is quantifiable based on Price Structure, and in our later discussions of time shift, understanding price structure components will be very necessary. This term was mentioned in Chapter 6 in order to make the reader aware of these components, but it is worth defining here because it is how we define our time values for creating our time lists. Using the Figure 35.2 example, we can see that retracements, projections, and swing retests are being used as the price structure components that have called the inflection points for Jim's updated histogram. However, the more important observation is that these are the price structure components that supported and added conviction to his time-oriented trading approach. Thus, we can say that we focused on Time Structure first, and we were helped with Price Structure Components. Again, I must emphasize that when we record times into a list, we are trying to rely on the underlying Price Structure Components in order to indicate to us what the relevant time repetition recordings should be based on the past. Therefore, we again see that our analysis of Price Structure has not been in vain because we need to know Price Structure in order to find our time repetitions. What is more, there are times when Time does not help us in defining these market inflection points, and at those times, all we have is Price Structure. Therefore, every single component of Price Structure is usable in defining times that are relevant for generating our time lists even if these highs/lows are simply discreets, but we know that "The Market is not Random" and that we will always have a way to quantify a relevant high or low that leads to a range expansion of our base range due to Price Theory. As such, the application of Price Theory is a confirmation of the components that are utilized for defining time repetitions. That being said, we have to be careful to not be inundated with too many time windows. Therefore, a good rule of thumb is that under conditions of low volatility, we should not see more than two relevant highs/lows per hour. During volatility, we can ignore this rule, and we can utilize any major high/low that has been defined by a Price Structure Component.

Obviously (and as mentioned already) one of the major problems with time repetitions is that a new time window can be generated at random throughout the day, but the randomness of a new time window makes it applicable for further inspection. Let us continue along the example with Jim because only by walking through the real world do we understand the power of Time Structure. For Jim, it is now lunchtime. Jim observes that after the 932 low that he bought, the market has continued to make highs/lows at relevant Price Structure components, and those highs/lows occurred at the following times: 1002, 1040, 1101, 1141, 1202, and 1214. Jim has been consistently updating his histogram, and after 1215, his histogram now looks like this:

        2, 1, 1, 2, 1, 1, 2, 2, 2, 1, 2
        14, 15, 15, 14, 14
        29, 30, 32, 32
        40, 41

Here, we see that previous time windows are still holding based on our earlier repetitions, but now we see that the new time window in the 40-41 range has been generated due to market inflection points availing themselves at that point during the day. As such, Jim now has four time windows in order to use throughout the remaining time of his trading day. What is interesting is that we now see the level of competence and concentration that is required to use *Time and Price Symmetry,* and I believe that this laborious example emphasizes that fact. Therefore, I feel that a reiteration of the fact that time can be our "friend" is necessary because, due to the immense amount of mental concentration required of traders, time becomes our friend via this time windows segregated by the time histogram! The time windows availing themselves through the histogram allow us to focus our mental energy at these specific times for trading, and it allows us to remain in an analytical role instead of a trading role for most of the day. In fact, based on Jim's current histogram, there are only 8 minutes out of the hour where we have to shift our conscious mind into the present moment unconscious awareness state. However, sometimes, the most relevant thing about knowing Time Structure is that it tells us when we can go and use the bathroom, which is a common trading problem that most trader's don't discuss for obvious reasons!

Trend & Time

So far, I have alluded to the fact that time repetitions are powerful because they help us to get on the right side of the trend, by ignoring underlying price and just reversing at a relevant time window from our time repetition-based time list that generated our time histogram. Therefore, since we have confidence that the market will make an inflection point at a specific time, we can remain in an analytic mode that allows us to quantify the trend. With this line of thought, we can use more brain power in order to not focus on the next trade until we are sure of the trend. Thus, once the present moment (again defined by the trader's time frame) trend is understood, we can use time repetitions in order to wait to reenter the market with the trend.

In Chapter 9, we discussed the quantitative and qualitative nature of trend definition, but we have to understand how Time Repetitions help us to trade with the trend. If we are aware that the market is in an uptrend, for example, we know that we should be getting long the market. However, because of our egotism, we decide that we want to try to trade countertrend at every relevant *Time and Price Symmetry* market inflection point (again, my certainty in these inflection points made me ignore risk/money management, which led to disaster). However, undoubtedly, being a reversal trader in the present moment is the ultimate objective to profit maximization, but since we must deal with human frailty, we must realize that trading at every inflection point can only be done for a certain amount of time. Again, this example has correlation between trading and sports. That being said, although ever movement of any market in any time frame can now be quantified based on the techniques of this book, we simply need to realize how mentally exhausting this continuous, interactive trading process can become. Therefore, sometimes we have to *let go to the trend*, and the best way to do that is to wait until we have a clear picture on the underlying trend. Then, at that point, we can simply focus on *Time and Price Symmetry* that is favorable to the trend. In fact, in our example with Jim, he did just that. Furthermore, I encourage the eager trader that wants to trade more often to realize that he or she can simply take profits at counter-trend market inflection points instead of reversing at every inflection point. By doing this combined approach, we know that we have a greater chance of continuous profits with the trend, and even if we make a mistake by taking a portion of our profits to soon, we are still making money. Therefore, unknowingly, we are allowing our subconscious mind to invoke the Law of Attraction. Ergo, the conclusion must be that time is our ally, and it helps us get back to the trend just as much as time can help us quantify every market movement, which is unnecessary for success because *we are already trading at significant edges over all the other market participants in the first place!*

We also know that time repetitions will allow us to focus at certain time intervals, and we know that time can increase our probability of trade success when properly coupled with Price Theory in understanding underlying Price Objectives for the market. More important, we can also rest comfortably in the knowledge that Time repetitions do exist, they do work, and they are extreme trading edges. Now, as we expound to our monthly analysis of time, we need to talk about the unfortunate realities of time repetitions that can really screw us up.

First, simply knowing a future time window does *not* mean the market will react, which is what price structured components can help us with, and again, we observed this in our Jim example when he decided in order to simply take profits at 0902. Second, as we go longer in time, we have a wider tolerance just as we had in price structure. In our daily example, we saw in Jim's histogram that 1 and 2 minutes after the hour were important, which could also mean that 0 and 3 minutes after the hour are also important, but because 0 and 3 minutes after the hour are not yet added to time list, we must be aware that the true inflection point has an immeasurable, higher probability at the already recorded times. However, we can take this example and apply it to a longer-term investor, and we can say that on a monthly chart, 1 or 2 could refer to the days of the month, which also means that the 31st of the prior month or the 3rd of the current month could be valid time windows. This could cause tremendous inaccuracy because of the possibility that the market may move a tremendous amount on any given trading day! As such, the obvious conclusion is to focus on the exact time repetition for our trading decision couple that with the trend analysis, and simultaneously make sure that we take the trade at the first sign of an inflection point based off Price Structure Components, because as we learned with *the turkey,* as long a we know the trend, we will be safe. Thus, the obviousness of the time-oriented conclusion is elaborated by saying that it is most important to make time repetitions useful for our benefit instead of using them to our detriment, which I define as trade prevention. Although it is always a safer bet to make sure "all your ducks are in a row," it is also limiting if we are going to wait for the all-in moment. Since trading is often equated to Poker, I must ask the reader, "Would you *always* wait to play until you had a royal flush or four aces with a king in your hand?" No, you would not wait for those statistical outliers, because you would miss too many opportunities. Again, *Time and Price Symmetry* provides an extreme edge to trading. When everything becomes aligned, we are not saying we have a 52% probability of success, we are saying we have a 99.99% of success. However, just like any good casino, the house knows that if the customer derived a methodology that was only consistent at a rate of 52% probability, the house would go bankrupt. Hence, *Time and Price Symmetry* can beat the house quite easily even with using just one component from this book, which is why almost every thing listed in Price Structure and Time Structure can almost exist as their own trading strategies!

Time Repetition Expansion and Replacement

Repetition replacement, which is defined by its name, is useful in order to prevent us from getting too elaborate in our time analysis. We must remember that Time Structure is our friend, and that it is not difficult, which I emphasized in the last section. In fact, we have to realize that it is our inherent, human condition that tells us that using time cannot be this simple, and trust me, it really is this simple. Therefore, we need to use repetition replacement in order to replace as many times as possible from our histogram so that time windows that are opened in the present moment are the most useful/correct time windows that we need to use. Hence, we are saying that we need to minimize as many time windows as possible by replacing them with the most valid time windows that exist in the current, present moment. Unfortunately in order to define the process of repetition replacement, we need to walk through every time period, which means that I have to walk the reader through another laborious example in order to properly explain repetition replacement in every time frame. This will illustrate the usefulness of repetition replacement, and to begin, let us start with a daytrading outlook because that is the shortest time interval.

As we saw with Jim, in order to begin a trading day as a daytrader, we know that since we may not have a lengthy list of times, we cannot yet construct a time histogram. As such, we turn to our first heuristic of time repetitions, and we start our day by look to the top and the bottom of the hour in order to find our initial time repetitions, which become the basis for constructing the time listing. Further, regardless of the constructed histogram, *top and the bottom of the hour time cycles are always in play and they are always valid regardless of whether or not they have appeared in our histogram already.* Therefore, it is undoubtedly unlikely that we do not have top and bottom of the hour time windows defined already, and if we utilize a continuous chart such as the S&P Futures, by the time we start trading at 3am or even 9am, we should have many market inflection points defined with their relevant times listed on the chart. I must make mention that labeling your chart with times will be expounded upon in the *Reflections* section of this book because it is very important, but for now, I ask the reader to please understand that the recording/labeling of time must be done accurately and precisely. Being off by even one minute could be disastrous. Therefore, when we record the time of a market inflection point, we record the time of **the last print of price**. The last print of price is simply the last time the market touched the value of the market inflection point (i.e. the reader should think of a micro double bottom/top and in that instance, the time value of the second bottom/top is the recorded value of the inflection point). Further, if the reader again looks at Jim's example in Figure 18.1, the reader would see that the micro double bottom at 0814 was the recorded price on the chart.

Moving on, as the day progresses, the market will be oscillating through the price discovery process in order to expand price structure components (i.e. making wider/longer ranges/swings, bigger retracements, etc.). However, even on an intraday basis, it is then important to label the time for the low of the day and the high of the day (the primary discreet points if you will), but instead of using our 1-minute chart to label the high and the low of the day, we can label these times on our 10-minute chart in order to keep the data from being to overabundant on one chart. In essence, when we are in a daytrader mode, the previous day's histogram becomes irrelevant, but the previous day's high/low time repetitions are relevant, which was also observed in our example of Jim when we mentioned the 0701 previous day low inflection point. Further, by looking at the 10-minute chart, we can also see the discreet/terminal points easier, which is important for Price Theory. Conclusively, as we move to our next trading day, we are using repetition replacement in order to replace all of our previous times on our intraday histogram with our new times for the current day, while simultaneously focusing on the weighted-times of the prior day's high or low, which we still have recorded and not replaced on our 10-minute chart. Thus, the intraday chart is labeled in minutes, but the 10-minute chart is labeled in hours and minutes.

At this point, we come to the true reality of Quantitative Synchronicity, and we start to visualize

Quantitative Synchronicity in our minds because we are looking to the 1-minute chart's histogram, and we are synchronizing our minds to be aware of the 10-minute chart's relevance because on the 10-minute chart, the time repetition at <u>the same hour</u> ***or*** <u>at the same minute</u> holds relevance, which means that just like Price Structure, every time can keep expanding and expanding and expanding into more and more time periods each with their own, applicable time windows!

Continuing on, let us move from a daytrading mode to a momentum trading mode, which means we make on average 2 trades a day. Therefore, we are moving and ignoring the time listing derived from our 1-minute chart because we no longer need to trade on the hour. Therefore, we move to the 10-minute chart that has our larger discreet highs/lows labeled by the larger ranges, and typically, these highs and lows are derived from the previous day's high and low or major secondary retracements.

Now, on the 10-minute chart, we should have listed the hours and the minutes, which is the same format that we had as a daytrader. Therefore, we can create a time list on the 10-minute chart that looks at the last 12 trading days, which we will define as T-12. T-12 means that we are looking at today's date (T) and we are looking at the last 12 trading days. In general, there should be around 36 values on this histogram, and this histogram is annoying to construct on a daily basis, but alas, it must be done. Further, we must now introduce the 60-minute chart, and on the 60-minute chart, we are labeling times as well. However, on this chart we can now drop the minutes from the time list altogether, and on the 60-minute chart we can now label the hours, which gives us an hourly histogram.

At this point, we see that the 1-minute chart starts to become phased out completely unless we were trying to better time our momentum trades, but for a momentum trader, our major concern is the 10-minute chart and the 60-minute chart histograms. Essentially, repetition replacement is being used to zoom us out in order to focus on relevant Time Windows for our trading goals. I correlate this to the word "zoom" because each bar contains data within. In fact, if one were to think of it like a microscope, it makes sense because on the outside, we may see a piece of onion, but as we zoom in, we see individual cells. If we were to zoom even farther, we would see inside the cells, and we can go on and on and on until we are at the atomic level. Similarly, if we start with a 60-minute bar, we know that if we zoom in, we see six 10-minute bars, and if we zoom in again, we see ten 1-minute bars.

Now, for the momentum trader we need redefine the criteria for the 60-minute histogram, and thankfully, this too is the same T-12 concept. Therefore, we do have an intersection between the 10-minute histograms and the 60-minute histograms, which can help us. Thus, at this point, we are now done with the shorter-term repetitions, and we can now focus on repetition replacement for portfolio construction; i.e. for investors.

Repetition Replacement for Portfolio Management

As we move out of weekly and into monthly repetitions, things will change again because we are no longer looking at the hours within the week, but we are now focusing on days. Again, our starting point for our time list come from Price Structure Components, but now, we are looking at inflection points in our daily bar chart. As such, we are looking at months as a whole, and by doing so, our first starting points are to look at the previous month's major high(s) and low(s), major swing point(s), and major terminal point(s), and we record these days of the month. Thus, this is where time repetition analysis gets tricky (as if it were not already), and in order to properly explain, I must use an in depth example which will properly convey the usefulness of monthly time repetitions.

When we are looking to use Time Repetitions for portfolio construction, we must be aware that there are three histograms that provide our data, and this is true if we are looking at bull/bear market terminal points or just monthly inflection points. These three histograms come from the following criteria: Monthly, Yearly, and Decennially. However, these three time periods will yield days that intersect with each other, which is okay! In fact, these intersections lead to weighted times, which add strength to the repetition. Therefore, we have to understand that when are working at this combined, zoomed out level, we must use our qualitative eye along with Price Theory in order to understand how often we should reverse. For example, a person may decide to reverse 4 times per month based on the Time Windows generated from the three intersecting Time Histograms. Or, if the person knows that the trend is up and the trading instrument has a Price Objective based on Price Theory, the trader may use these intersecting Time Histograms to enter a long trade that he/she will hold in the portfolio until Price Objectives are reached. With that being said, let us define how to construct this intersecting time histogram, which is based on the three time histograms.

First, when we look at a month itself, we take the current month, and we go back 12 months. For instance, if we took April of 2012, we would record dates within April of 2012, and we would go abck and record inflection dates every month until April of 2011. Further, we would also go back and look at Every April for the last 12 years. This means we would use April of 2012 all the way back to April of 2001. Lastly, we would look back decennially, and we would look at the last four (T-4) Aprils; if they exist. For example, we would look at April 2012, April 2002, April 1992, April 1982, and April 1972.

Next, once we have these three histograms, *we leave them separate,* but we also construct our intersecting histogram. This is done for a very obvious reason. First, we may find that every single date is possible for an inflection point in April, which obviously does us no good at all. However, this is where the concept of weighted-times hold relevance, and we can also introduce a more important concept, which is similar to a skew in probabilistic terms. Hence, we come to the topic of weighted repetitions and phased repetitions. Thankfully, these are easy to define. A **weighted repetition** is simply the idea of focusing on the last 4 months across our three histograms (well 2 histograms considering the decennial histogram is most likely not relevant) for currently emphasized Time Repetitions along with observing any phased repetitions that may hold cyclic relevance, which will be discussed in Chapter 19.

Now, a **phased repetition** is a time repetition that exists on monthly/yearly charts where we could find a valid repetition that phases in and out in some kind of pattern. For example, on February 2nd we see a high, on April 2nd we see a high, and then on June 2nd we see a low, which means that if our current month was August, the second day of the month hold more relevance based on the concept of phased repetitions. For the non-pattern recognition reader, we are simply observing a tendency that the market is holding its repetition on the second day of the month, but on every other month. However, by no means does a phased repetition guarantee that August 2nd, will lead to a market inflection point, but we can garner increased conviction if we see a Price Structure Component coming into play because remember, on these longer term charts, we only have primary components listed, which in and of themselves are given much more weight regardless of time.

Along with phased repetitions, we also must be cognizant of continued repetitions. A **continued repetition** is a repetition that appears at least twice in a row within the past *four* months that is expected to emerge *one* more time. (A continued repetition is only valid for three times in a row, but that is simply because our intersected histogram takes over.) For an example of a continued repetition, let us say, that we are again in April of 2012, and we have observed that on the 9th day of February, there was an inflection point and in the 10th day of March there was an inflection point. Well, we can also look at the 9th and the 10th day of April for a possible inflection point as well. However, what is not clear with a continued repetition and what is important about a continued repetition is that if we saw January 9th and February 9th emerge as inflection points, but this time, March 9/10th was meaningless, well we can still look at April 9th for an inflection point. I believe the reason this is valid is that the market is celebrating its quarter-year anniversary, which was also a tendency that Gann observed because it may be linked to seasonality, which will be discussed in the next chapter. The last item that we have to mention in part of this informational overloading discussion is in regards to the decennial times list that produces a time histogram that intersects the nearer term time histograms.

The decennial times list is helpful only occasionally when we are speaking in terms of days, but its true power is observable if we are to focus on the month itself. And unarguably, a month is a hell of a big time window to be wrong about, but that does not diminish its relevancy for portfolio management / trillion dollar money management implementations. Furthermore, because most trading software cannot even go back for 40+ years, we are intrinsically limited based on data. (As an aside, I had the 10 year charts going back to 1890 on the Dow prior to my arrest, and I hope I can still get access to them.) Therefore, we must understand this data limitation, but thankfully, major crash points in history tend to circulate within our culture, and when we are dealing with the decennial cycle, we have to realize that not only are we giving it a 1 month tolerance, but we are giving it a two month tolerance on each side of a crash-like event. Thus, the **decennial cycle tolerance** is defined as a 4-month window of time that exists as crash echoes, and we only look for those crash echoes within the last 4 decades. Again, this may seem like a lot of time, but if you consider that we are looking at a 120-month period when we look at the total decennial cycle (10 years * 12 months/year = 120 months) well, then we are talking about an accuracy rating of 4/120 (3.33%), which is pretty darn good. However, it is only pretty darn good if we are focusing on super long-term trades (I.e. investments), but this relevancy also exists for finding be bull/bear market terminal points. Thus, we can rely on a real-life example already alluded to. Using the decennial cycle, we observe that the 1987 high holds relevance for the next four decades, and we would be looking at a tolerance of +/- 2 months, which means that in 1997/2007/2017/2027 we can focus on August through December for major inflection points, and if one was to indeed look at 1997 and 2007, we would find very surprising conclusions. Most notable is that the 2007 high was only 1 month off from our prediction!

Ergo, defining bull market highs and bear market lows is also an important discussion, and some day, we may even have centennial analysis, which is why I want my darn Dow Charts back. As such, we are coming up on some major volatility echoes that will be interesting to watch between 1918 and 1934.

Lastly, I must state that the power of this longer-term analysis is truly priceless, and I fully believe that people like Warren Buffett are aware of these repetitions. In fact, bull/bear market inflection points are so important that I believe I can run a Hedge Fund of Funds that invests purely based on my quantitative and qualitative ability to understanding these forthcoming market periods. Because of this importance, in the next Chapter, we will discuss inherent properties in bull/bear markets that are more cyclically relevant compared to repetitions, because defining the terminal dates of these market conditions based on time repetitions is quite difficult and requires a large tolerance.

Discreet Points versus Terminal Inflection Points

So far, we have learned about time histograms, and about the complexity that is involved in defining them. However, we can choose to make the complexity of histogram construction easy or hard on ourselves based on how many dates we want to factor in to each segmented part of the histogram. Further, we know through Price Theory / Price Structure that we will also be able to define highs or lows based on those components, and Time is just an added bonus. Therefore, we have to expand the thought on time in order to talk about where/when time windows can kick-in, and when they do, these time windows must be recorded like everything else. This concept is important for daytrading just as much as it is for looking at monthly inflection dates.

The emphasis here is that, *the market does not have to utilize a time window at its terminal high or terminal low (i.e. the discreets)*. A time window defined either through repetitions or cycles can be utilized at the discreet high and low of a given day, week, year, etc., but it can also be utilized at the terminal point for a swing, which we know is a retracement. For example, in 2011, our discreet high occurred on April 27, 2011, but we had our deep retracement of that high/the terminal points of our swing occur in Mid-July of 2011. Even though this high was not the high of the year and it is intra-range, which does not mean that a defined time repetition is not relevant. In fact, in most cases we will see time repetitions become most useful intra-range.

Therefore, the conclusion is that one of the most useful ways to use time is not at absolute highs or lows! True, time repetitions are most powerful when they avail time windows at discreet highs or lows, but the knowledge of Price Theory coupled with time repetitions is much more powerful put together than that knowledge itself. The reason behind that statement is that if we are intra-range, we know the market's objective will be discreet replacement by breaching the high/low of a given range. As such, when we use a time repetition in order to place a trade intra-range, it is easier for us to define reward / risk. For example, let us say the market has a positive range of 100 → 110 with a 38.2%R at 106.18. If we have a time repetition clicking in (i.e. April 27th in 2011), which means we reach 106.18 on June 27th (only an example), then we have greater confidence of buying that retracement, and if we see a swing develop from that value (intra-range), we gain a high probability of knowledge that *Time and Price Symmetry* has occurred, which justifies a positive range break.

Measured Moves

In price structure, we alluded to the diagonal line that creates a range (i.e. links two discreets). If we think of what this diagonal line means in terms of the range, we can easily understand that it is measuring the movement of price over a given time, which yields a line with some type of linear line with a slope defined in price and in time, which is essentially, a range. However, now that we are looking for repetitions of time, we can look at these measured move lines in order to predict time and price. In the beginning of this Chapter, I asked the reader to NOT measure time in defining repetitions, and this discussion of measured moves may seem contrary to that statement. However, I assure you it is not.

Measured moves exist in two ways, which I will define here: **measured retracements** and **measured swings**. A measured retracement is a measured move line that exists as a predictor of corrective sizes during a countertrend move. A measured retracement is the ***only*** time that measuring time in order to predict future movements in price and time is valid. As an example, let us say, we have a market going higher; first it pulls back to a 61.8% retracement in "X" minutes. Then, it breaches the discreet high, and continues moving higher. When it reaches a new market inflection point, which yields a retracement, we can look to have the same amount of price distance occur in the same amount of time. What is more, since our range is now wider, our price distance may place us down at the 50%R instead of the 61.8%R, which may be an equal sized move from the previous retracement that now exists due to the wider range. At the same time, it is perfectly fine to look at the time of the first retracement to be equal to the time of the second retracement. Often, when these times and prices are of equal size, these are high probability trades. At the same time, if the market is moving lower over a larger amount of time in our second retracement move, we can see that *time is indicating a larger correction*. If a given, market correction is of a greater time then a prior one, we can often see larger movements in price. Let me be clear, a measured retracement does ***not*** have to have the same time measurement as it does price in order to be useful, and the last section of this explanation of measured moves will focus on how time repetitions factor into our analysis.

The second way, in which we can talk about measured moves, is by defining measured swings. A measured swing is simply the movement that occurs off a retracement, which yields a new, larger range. It makes sense in using "swing" in this nomenclature because the calculation of projection levels is actually similar to a measured move. For example, a 100%P is equal to the measured move of the base range (in regards to price but not time). Arguably, one can say that a measured swing is also a measured retracement of some reciprocal range that may exist in the opposite direction, and I would concur. However, as we know, as time or price gets larger/longer, we start yielding higher tolerances, which may make the analysis irrelevant for an accurate predictor.

I must be clear, a measured move is ***different*** then a pure time measurement, and I will now explain how we can use measured moves that are measured swings or measured retracements with time repetitions, which is why I decided to not discuss measured moves as price structure components. The true usefulness of a measured moves line whether it is a retracement or a swing is to predict price, and then, utilize time repetitions in order to define time windows that are in alignment with the measured move in price. Notice that we are not using the time value derived from the measured move, simply the price, and the logic behind this is simple. If we had a measured move occur off a prior retracement, which then found a terminal point at a 100%P, the times for the inflection point at the retracement and the inflection point at the 100%P have already been recorded in our time histogram and segmented into Time Windows. Thus, *the repetitive nature of the times is more important then measuring the amount of time the move occurred*, and that statement is a very powerful distinction I have to make to the reader. Therefore, the measured move line is important in time repetitions if properly applied, and the proper application of measured moves is visualized similar to a trendline fan in Price Structure. Since this is somewhat confusing, let us elaborate on our triple swing example, by adding measured move price projections, which can be seen in Figure 18.2.

Figure 18.2: Measured Moves

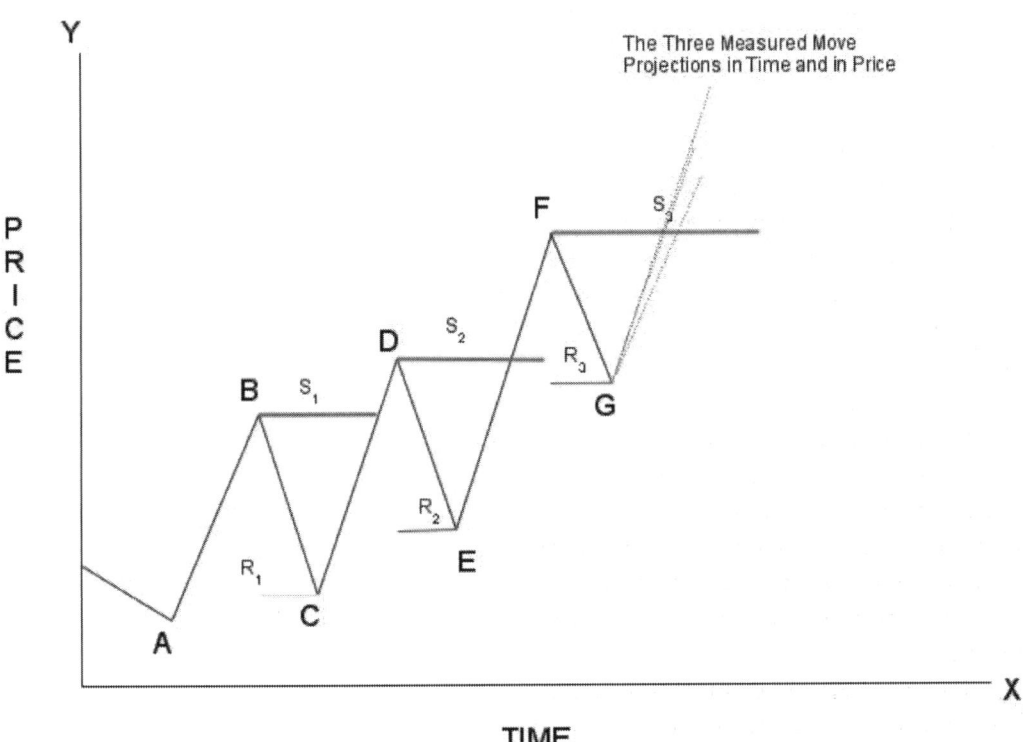

In order to illustrate this concept to the reader, I must use an example market, which can be seen in Figure 18.2. In figure 18.2, we see that we have a low at point A. From that low, the market has made three moves up: A → B, C → D, E → F. Now, two of these three moves had the same price distance off a given retracement because the inflection point at point D would be a 100%P to the astute reader.

However, the third movement was a bit steeper in price, but not by much. Nevertheless, all three moves occurred in approximately the same amount of time, which is difficult to discern from the chart in Figure 38. Now, this third move is important because we must understand that if the third move has moved higher in price distance (Delta-P), but lesser in time, then time is indicating further movement in price, which is obvious if one understands that the market is waiting for a Time Repetition to avail itself.

However, now that we have three different measured moves, we can now do something different than simply making a projection of price on the third swing. What we can do is we can clone the range lines that made the three up moves overnight, and we can paste those three range lines at the third higher bottom. Since this is an up move, when we clone these range lines, we ill market them as green. Concurrently, if we were using measured move lines for downside projections, we would make them red. If we do indeed copy these three ranges, we will see that we are now projecting three new terminal points in both price *AND* time, which again, is why I waited until now to discuss measured moves. What is more, because we have three new terminal points, we must realize that these terminal points may cluster with other mathematical support/resistance calculations, which means that measured moves are relevant for cluster averaging. However, they *ALSO* may be clustering with Time Windows themselves, and as such, we can observe if these projected times are clustering with any of our open Time Windows in our histogram!

Unfortunately, this is hard to do with our Figure 18.2 example, and all I am asking the reader to understand is that these measured move lines are giving us time and price projections that when coupled with outstanding mathematical clusters or outstanding time windows, we gain supreme market edges.

Measured Moves in RSI

In our discussion of the technical indicator RSI within Price Structure, I mentioned that RSI can also be useful for measured moves. I stated that we would be looking for measured moves within the indicator itself in order to determine when a market has retraced a sufficient amount in order for the RSI to indicate a potential high/low that will be forthcoming in order for the trader to resume the trend. What becomes more interesting is that we can also measure time based on RSI when we do this type of analysis. Therefore, since the reader now understands that a measured move is simply a line segment that represents a range in terms of time and in terms of price, I can further elaborate the fact that we can draw a similar conclusion by the RSI indicator itself. There is not much more to be said, but so the reader understands measured moves, let us go through an example scenario.

In a bull market scenario, we know that the most typical case will be positive convergence, which means all of the RSI numbers will be converging higher in every time frame, while the market itself continues higher. However, at some point, the RSI values on the shorter-term time frames will need to pause in order to give the market some time for the rally to continue. Therefore, what we can do is measure previous corrections within the current rally itself that are still visible on the RSI. (Sometimes for the shorter-term RSI periods, we may have to scroll back in time in order to find the appropriate RSI-based correction.) Now, what becomes interesting is that we can draw a line segment from the peak in the RSI to the trough in the RSI, and then, we can copy this line segment to our latest peak in the RSI, and what this gives us is a measured move in the indicator itself. Therein we find the relevance of this measured move-like analysis to RSI. With the RSI measured move, we now get to add in time to the indicator as well as the previous low value in the indicator as a potential spot to look for a low. The edge that time gives us is significant because that end time given by the measured move line tells us that the "time" for this current correction was the same "time" as the last correction based on the RSI. Again, this is not an obvious piece of information for the reader to be aware of, which is why I feel it is necessary to mention it here. Obviously, the inverse of these would work for bear market scenarios as well, but for bear market scenarios, I must caution that more often then not, the value of the RSI is more valid than the time based on the measured move, which makes sense because bear markets tend to move faster than bull markets.

Bull / Bear Market Repetitions

The second way that I want to address measuring the length of time is to understand how bull/bear market characteristics can be utilized for our benefit, and this last section of repetitions will be a lead in to our next Chapter. Although we touched on repetitions in dates regarding bull and bear markets in our prior example of constructing monthly histograms, we also need to discuss an interesting parallel in time repetition regarding bull and bear markets themselves. Earlier, we mentioned that the terminal dates for bull/bear markets are useful to us yearly and decennially. For example, as mentioned once already in this text, March 6, 2012 has now become an extremely important day for time repetition-based theory, because this date is the terminal, bear market low of the 2007-2009 bear market. As such, the terminal dates of bull/bear markets reveal a unique time that stays relevant for four decades decennially and most likely four centennial anniversaries as well. The reason I choose this bear market example because it is easier to describe this nature with a bear market example because they are faster (shorter in time). Thus we get to understand the other relevance for bear market/bull market terminal points, and they are classified as time shift dates. Although this will be our first introduction to time shift**,** which will be expanded upon in the next chapter, these bull/bear market terminal dates are interrelated with cycles as well. However, I mention it now because we are looking to repetitions within bull/bear market cycles, and the cyclic tendency of Bull/Bear markets will be discussed in the next chapter.

Now, before we move on though, I must present a fictitious example to the reader using the dot-com bear market. Let us say that from our relevant 2000 high, we observe two major lows that occur in March and September of 2001, and our terminal low of the bear market occurs in October of 2002, which are all true so far. (Conversely, we can do the same for the bull market of 2002-2007 by looking at the relevant, major highs and the terminal high, which occurred in November of 2007.) What is important is the major inflection dates that occurred on a yearly basis during bull/bear markets; meaning it is irrelevant if we are looking at highs (bull market) or lows (bear market). To see the repetitions that are useful from looking inside of the markets, we need to invoke time repetitions and the Rule of Alternation, which may get a little complex to the reader. In order to understand the cyclical repetitions, we need to actually use measured move lines from *any* major inflection point. So, using our 2000-2002 bear market, we would measure the time from the terminal 2000 high, and we would measure the time to the three terminal lows in the bear market. From there, we would take these measured moves, and we would place them at the terminal point of the next bull market, which would be the 2007 high. Now, we would ignore the price distance of the measured moves, *and we would be looking at the measured times* that have been shifted to the next bull market. This is another way of measuring time for usefulness, but the interesting revelation will occur to the reader when this analysis is combined with repetitions derived from the yearly and decennial repetitions. *What these measured times based off of measured move lines become is estimations of understanding the length of time of a bear market or a bull market, and when combined with repetitions from the longer-term cycles, we can get high probability date ranges that couple with major price clusters.*

In order to become even more helpful, we can use these cyclic repetitions in stocks as well by coupling filtering investment decisions, by using the Rule of Alternation. Unfortunately, on many stocks, we do not have much historic data, but as the future expands, we will have more. As such, in order to provide the reader an example, we can use The Rule of Alternation in order to determine where stocks will find *time and price windows* that lead to inflection points during their next bull market rally. We can use the same analysis from the last paragraph by measuring the times of the last rally that the given stock had, which The Rule of Alternation tells us to look back two bull markets, and then, we can go and measure the time of their rallies from that bull market in order to predict future turn dates. In essence, we can use these measured times in order to determine the length of the current stock's bull market! As I introduced earlier, The Rule of Alternation is mostly valid through the stock market, and not the indices themselves. This tendency is why that statement is true.

In summary, many of these discussions on time have been lengthy because it is hard to quantify the ethereal nature of how to use time, and I have needed to use laborious examples in order to attempt to convey the theory and the power of time to the reader. This approach also requires a method of recording things properly so that our time lists are relevant in creating our time histograms depending on the time frame we are trading in. However, the best way to learn time is not by the words of this book. No, the best way to learn is to look at charts, and honestly, I ask the reader to focus on an index chart first because the normalization that occurs by using an index smoothes out the time repetitions, which is why I am an index trader myself. However, that does not limit time to indices and let me be clear, everything from knowing that markets make inflection points at tops and bottoms of the hour to understanding repetitions on yearly/decennially bases are all extremely powerful edges in trading. The understanding and the comprehension gained by the subconscious mind's observance of Time Structure to call a valid market inflection point, will lead to a level of trading conviction that I believe cannot be effaced nor rivaled by *ANY OTHER WAY*. Knowing the precise date and time of a movement not only yields the justification for the implementation of massive leverage, but also, the ability to reverse with the proper trend when trend analysis has been accurately done. Thus, Time Repetitions are much more important than anything else in Time Structure, and as we move to Chapter 20, I will be able to further elaborate to the reader on how Time can be used in order to shift the trader's mentality to being an anticipatory trader, which will occur once all of Price Structure and Time Structure (hence, *Time and Price Symmetry*) is understood by the trader's subconscious.

Chapter 19

Time Cycles

Time Cycles are segregated into two classifications: synthetic or inherent, which are basically, God-made/astrologically-aligned Time Cycles. A **Synthetic Time Cycle** is a Time Cycle that was created by man through some arbitrary mathematical formulae. Moreover, Time Cycles should be treated with a certain level of caution and skepticism, and the trader can easily become inundated with too much information by not keeping things simple. Remember, it is not possible for us to become masters of Time Structure, but it is possible for us to become masters of Price Structure. Therefore, whenever we implement any Time Structure component, we must make sure that it is done simplistically and with the purpose to help us. What is more, I must add a corollary to that statement, which is that Time Structures must help us quickly and efficiently, due to the fleeting nature of Time Windows. Nevertheless, Time Cycles (just like Time Repetitions) can be extremely powerful when Price Structure and Time Cycles show synchrony.

However, because of the unquantifiable naturalism of Time Cycles, many topics in this chapter will undoubtedly fall under the heading of Skepticism 101. As such, if you do not believe in Time Cycles, then do not read this chapter. However, the proof that the market has adhered to Time Cycles is listed herein, and you will be shocked and awed at the simplicity of the market once a Time Cycle is validated. Truly, a validated Time Cycle is like falling upon a hidden tomb full of gems because, if one has the conviction that a given Time Cycle will work, then the trader has found something priceless. Literally, uncovering a valid Time Cycle has the potential to be worth trillions of dollars if one had the ability to implement such a large trade at a predefined, time-based inflection point, by trading in the derivatives market.

In W.D. Gann's research, he did not have access to computers nor did he have easy access to historic data, but his observations with time cycles are now easily validated and made relevant. It is a pity that Gann is not alive in this age because his analytical mind would be able to yield such profound revelations for trading that we would spend the next hundred years analyzing, and I can only hope that what I have done in this book can spawn a similar type of research. Thankfully, most of what we mentioned in the last chapter is relevant for Time Cycles as well (i.e. time listing dates, time histograms, etc.). Further, Time Cycles have the potential to be just as powerful as Time Repetitions, but unlike repetitions, knowing *how* to use Time Cycles is much harder, because it requires the qualitative eye / a belief in an intangible. Therefore, part of this Chapter's purpose will be to focus the trader's thought energy on a deeper comprehension of understanding major market inflection points. However, unlike Price Structure Components and unlike Time Repetitions, these inflection points are not easily viewable on the chart, and they often require a predetermined calculation-like approach in order to be useful.

Another issue with Time Cycles is that there are hundreds of synthetic Time Cycles that people have attempted to idiotically define by curve fitting. However, because most people are not geniuses and because most people are egotistical, most people who derive and populate an idiotic Time Cycle-based assertion, will have the trouble of refusing to accept the finite lifecycle of their Time Cycle. Hence, very few Synthetic Time Cycles have longevity. Therefore, because of the idiocy of the common man, I will stick to Time Cycles that I have validated as being real, and not only real, but still in existence today. What is more, I believe that the synthetic Time Cycles I am listing herein still tie back to some divinely inspired concept. Earlier, this was already mentioned when I discussed the fact that the 8.6 Year Economic Cycle was aligned with Bull/Bear market terminal points. As such, it is my belief that these are synthetic Time Cycles that will exist in perpetuity, and because of how hard it is to validate one of these synthetic Time Cycles, I will be focusing on only three synthetic Time Cycles that I have found to be extremely useful.

Additionally, because of the error of the common man, I doubt I will ever expand my Time Cycle analysis wider than these three man-made / synthetic time cycles because when coupled with Time Repetitions, there will always be enough Time Windows in order to validate trading edges, because again, with *Time and Price Symmetry,* we are trading at 99.99% accuracy when everything is aligned, and we only need to trade at 33% accuracy (with 2/1 reward to risk), to be profitable. Thus, the three synthetic Time Cycles that I will discuss are: The 8.6 Year Global Economic Confidence Model, Terry Laundry's T-Theory, and The Bradley Cycle. Lying between the realm of man and God, we also will further analyze Holidays and Bull/Bear Market Cycles, which will lead us to the Nobel-like assertion of this book, and from there, I will discuss the predestined Time Cycles that are divinely derived. These cycles will be defined as: The 400 Year Master Human Cycle, Seasonality, Half-Seasons, Moon Cycles, and Mercury Retrograde.

In order to begin the proper implementation of Time Cycles, I need elaborate on the concept of Time Shift. Obviously, shifting time is only relevant to synthetic cycles because the predestined cycles cannot have an inherent shift unless the Earth was shifted off its axis in some way.

Time Shift

Sometimes, the cycles that we humans develop become seemingly irrelevant after a period of time. Sometimes they work, and sometimes they don't. In a way, I believe the cessation of a given synthetic Time Cycle is derived from the "irrational exuberance" or the "black swan" that exists in the market, which is essentially derived from human fear (meaning emotion). Moreover, sometimes other cycles/repetitions can conflict with each other, which also cause a base cycle to seemingly provide inaccurate analysis. Therefore, when a given cycle fails us that does not mean it is now invalidated. It could just mean that the trader has not applied the concept of Time Shift! **Time Shift** is defined as a way to recalculate a Time Cycle based on major market inflection points, and one can think of this shift like a Doppler effect. In addition, a **Major Market Inflection Point** is defined as the terminal point of any bull/bear market cycle.

Because we need to understand the time location of these Major Market Inflection Points, we observe that the said inflection point becomes the place where we shift our Time Cycle. Thus, we can easily say that in order to properly implement Time Shift, we are shifting a Time Cycle's beginning date to the terminal point of each Major Market Inflection Point. Simultaneously, this yields the obvious logic that our Time Cycle has now been shifted because of these new terminal dates, and the reason it needs to be shifted is something that I believe ties back to humanity's imperfection. I say this because the major market inflection points occur under the most duress/fear and that emotion screws with the divine plan.

Implementing Time Shift is quite easy if using a spreadsheet type program, like Excel. In fact, in the *Resources* section of this book, I have a quick example of how you can construct this simple spreadsheet, and all we have to do is take a cycle calculation and Time Shift its start date to the Major Market Inflection Date. Once done, the spreadsheet should auto populate and give us the new Time Cycle prediction dates. The reason I talk about spreadsheets is that they are very helpful for doing calculations of dates, which is hard by hand. For example, we can put in our terminal date, multiply that date by some factor, and the Spreadsheet will yield for us the new date. It can also tell us the day of the week the shifted date occurs on in order to determine if the market will actually be open or not on that date. In order to elaborate on the power of Time Shift, I will look at the first synthetic Time Cycle.

8.6 Year Global Economic Confidence Model

Before getting to the intricacies inside of this cycle, we will first conclude Time Shift with an example using this cycle. The 8.6 Year Global Economic Confidence Model (or "The 8.6 Year Cycle") is useful if we divide it into 4x2.15 year cycles, which is not obvious. However, that is why we have to study and interpret these synthetic cycles. Now, if we look and if we conclude that this cycle failed us in calling the March 6, 2009 low, we must realize that its failure is not permanent. Therefore, by applying the concept of Time Shift, we can shift the start date of the 8.6 Year Cycle to that Major Market Inflection Point terminal date. Once we apply Time Shift, we can shift our 4x2.15 dates out, and we will see that our first shifted date is 4/30/2011. Yep, that's it. This is the date that called the 2011 market high! And this is the power of Time Shift applied to a valid Time Cycle!

Now that the reader should understand the power of Time Cycles and the power of Time Shift, we can discuss the 8.6 Year Cycle in more detail. If we decide to do a back test-like study of this Time Cycle, we would find inconsistencies without the concept of Time Shift. However, with the understanding that this cycle has four quadrants and with the understanding that this Time Cycle needs Time Shift, we can find that over the last four decades, this cycle has been extremely useful not only in measuring highs to highs, lows to lows, but lows to highs. This last sentence is a little confusing, and I ask the reader to think of this as a sinusoidal graph as we move through the next few examples.

The next major component that we look for in a synthetic Time Cycle is standard deviation. As mentioned in Time Repetitions, we can sometimes get very high tolerances depending on what type of repetition we are focusing on. However, for a portfolio manager / trillion-dollar fund of funds manager (like I hope to be someday), this cycle provides us with four inflection points over a given decade, and I do not believe that is too much. In fact, I believe it is the perfect amount of dates for us to truly analyze what the market will do on those dates, but what really makes this Time Cycle beautiful is that even as we saw thus far in the example of Time Shift, this cycle tends to be exact like it was in 2011. Thus, the reason this Time Cycle is being discussed in this book is because once Time Shift is correctly applied, this Time Cycle has minimum deviation, but the difficulty with this Time Cycle is because the trader must understand how this cycle must be used by comprehending that it is a sinusoidal Time Cycle, we must realize that this sinusoidal graph contains peaks and troughs, by definition. Therefore, the definition of this Time Cycle must now be expanded in order to understand that this Time Cycle, when properly shifted to a Major Market Inflection Point, is useful for calling lows or highs based on the sinusoidal tendency. Thus, when this Time Cycle is shifted to a Major Market Inflection Point that is a high, this Time Cycle would be placed into our spreadsheet in order to define Time Cycle inflection points that would be 2.15 years from peak to trough, 4.30 years from peak to peak, 6.45 years from peak to trough, and 8.6 years from peak to peak. Conversely, we also must understand that when the 8.6 Year Cycle is Time Shifted to a Major Market Inflection Point that is a low, we find the opposite sinusoidal wave (the cosine wave if you will). In fact, this is exactly what we saw in the Time Shift example presented earlier in this section because we saw that when we shifted this Time Cycle to a Major Market Inflection Point that was a low (March 6, 200), we saw that the sinusoidal wave predicted a high on April 30, 2011, which was the accurate assumption. Conversely, this logic is not over yet because as soon was this Time Shifted Time Cycle was recalculated, we now understand that June 23, 2013 can be predicted in advance for a potential low!

Before moving on, this Time Cycle was introduced first to the reader for many reasons. First, it is not obvious that this Time Cycle should be split into four quadrants even when the person who defined this cycle did so as a sinusoidal curve. Second, this Time Cycle needs time shift, and again, I hypothesize that this is done for two reasons (a) it is synthetic and (b) human emotion. Third, we had to understand that this cycle could be simultaneously shifted to market highs as well as market lows to create overlapping predicted inflection point data. Thus, the reader must comprehend that Time Cycle use is not easy, and it takes a truly educated mind to sit down in order to understand. However, unlike Time Repetitions, once the trader has confidence in his Time Cycle understanding, the rewards are extreme, but let us discuss the challenging nature that we face with this Synthetic Time Cycle.

Where time cycle analysis gets challenging is when we start to create Intrinsic Overlap. **Intrinsic Overlap** is defined as a Time Cycle that has been shifted to two or more Major Market Inflection Points that overlap the Time Cycle itself. For example, if we were looking at a Time Cycle that occurs once a decade, we would have no intrinsic overlap. However, with the 8.6 Year Cycle, since we partition it into 4x2.15 quadrants, we understand that there is Intrinsic Overlap because Major Market Inflection Points occur in less than 8.6 Years. Therefore, let us discuss the implementation of a Time Cycle at prior bear/bull market lows/highs.

Here, is where the trader can start getting conflicting dates for market inflection points (note: Time Cycle inflection points do *not* have to call Major Market Inflection Points, as can be seen with the 2011 high already discussed). Now, in order to further elaborate, we can pick the November 2007 high and we can simultaneously pick the March 2009 low. If we apply Time Shift to both of those dates, we can picture the 8.6 Year Cycle overlap. What is more, we must understand that this overlap is an overlap of a sine and a cosine wave. Therefore, we have to invoke Quantitative Synchronicity as well, and this starts to get extremely difficult if we were to undergo the arduous mathematical task of calculating the overlap points/merger points Time Cycle, and I do not encourage the reader to get that intense. No, what I encourage the reader to do is simply to understand that if we add 6.45 years to the November 2007 high, we would be predicting a low around April of 2014. Similarly, if we add 4.3 years to the March 2009 low, we would also be predicting a low (as mentioned) in June of 2013. Thus we can easily picture this overlap, which leads to one last insight regarding The 8.6 Year Cycle, and this insight applies to all Time Shift-based Time Cycles.

Since we are using this Time Cycle to not only predict market inflection points but to also predict if these market inflection points are going to be highs or lows, we need to observe what happens when we have Intrinsic Overlap. Because of intrinsic overlap, we get a Time Cycle Window, which is of immense size, and a Time Cycle Window is different from a Time Window, which will finally be defined in the last chapter. Thus, because we must be aware that this Time Cycle Window is open for a long period of time, we can now define a **Time Cycle Window** as a defined interval of time probability (inflection point probabilities) whereby we can find a market inflection point between the open and close times of the window, but simultaneously, we must understand that the probability for the market inflection point in severely increased at the extremes (the window open/close date). In essence, the Time Cycle Window is a synthetic chart that cannot be quantified, and the Time Cycle Window accounts for the Intrinsic Overlap of two conflicting dates of a merged Time Cycle. Let us look at Figure 19.1 as an example of what this chart could look like.

Figure 19.1: Time Cycle Window Probability Curve

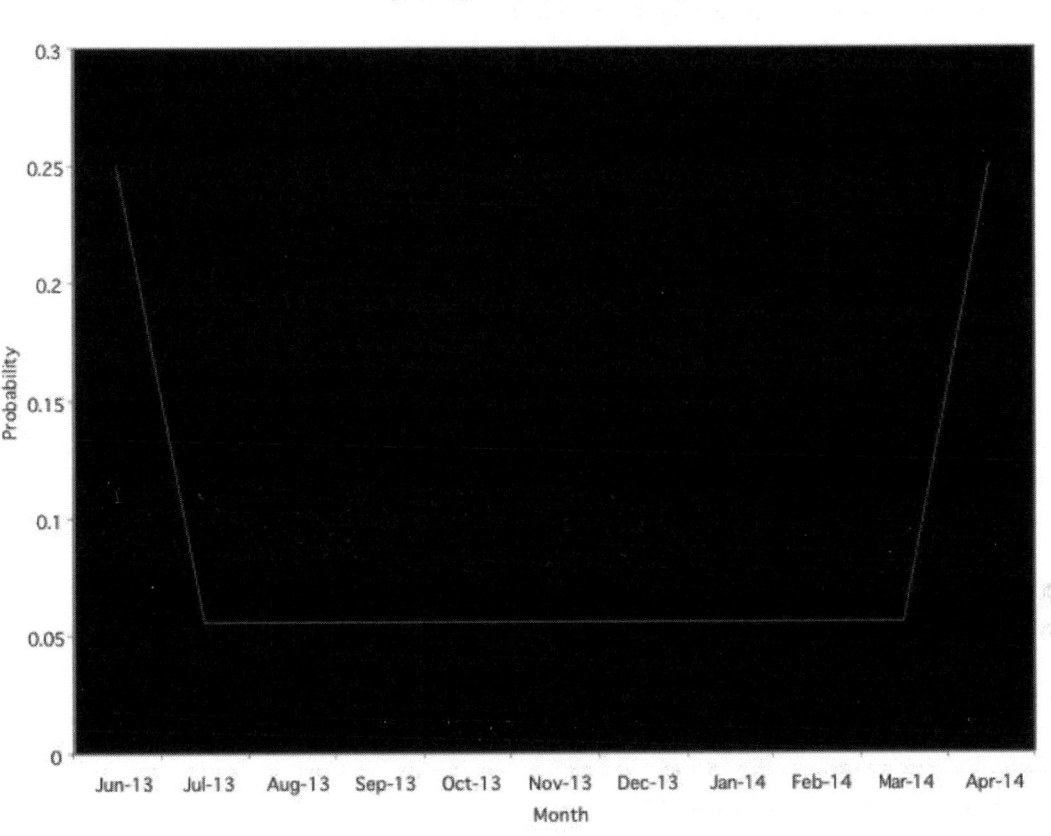

Terry Laundry's T-Theory

The second Synthetic Time Cycle that I will discuss was created by a historic, risk-averse money manager named Terry Laundry. The relevance of discussing this Time Cycle is done in order to illustrate another clandestine concept about Time Cycles, and that clandestine concept is that, again, the Time Cycle needs interpretation in order to be useful, which is obvious because it is Synthetic.

As we saw in the 8.6 Year Cycle, we had to understand that The 8.6 Year Synthetic Time Cycle was useful if defined into four quadrants, and also the 8.6 Year Cycle had to be recalculated based on Major Market Inflection Points. Contrarily, this Synthetic Time Cycle requires a synthetic technical indicator in order to be useful. However, the reason this Time Cycle is mentioned is because, although Mr. Laundry's concept of equal timing is nothing new, the application of equal timing to a synthetic technical indicator coupled with a Time cycle is very obtrusive. Thus, let us understand this concept of Time Cycles and Time Repetitions based off a synthetic technical indicator, by using Mr. Laundry's T-Theory. What is more, the reason I am using this Synthetic Time Cycle as a demonstration to the reader is because, quite simply, this Synthetic Time Cycle known as T-Theory has worked for decades, which means that Mr. Laundry has a 30 year track record that is phenomenal. I ask the reader to pause at that last statement in order to understand something amazing about a Synthetic Time Cycle, and that revelation should be that one could create an entire money management career just off one Synthetic Time Cycle, which is what Mr. Laundry has done. Hence, the power of Time Cycles with respect to money management.

Now, I do not claim to be a master of Mr. Laundry's Time Cycle, but it is my understanding that T-Theory is implemented by measuring the time of an indicator from peak to trough, and then, using that same time to define a future time window. It is a useful analysis, that has proven extremely successful aside from the 2007-2010 trading environment, and due to its failure during that time frame, it emphasizes the fact that time cycles sometimes cease to work. However, that does not mean they cease to work forever, and that, too, is why I have selected this cycle for relevant discussion to the reader.

In order to visualize T-Theory, we have to picture a T. Then, we have to picture that the left side of the T is time, and it predicts the right side of the T, which is also Time, and the reader should hopefully understand that this concept is very similar to a Head and Shoulders Pattern that is in the process of forming the right shoulder (i.e. we have the left part of the T (the left shoulder) and we have the mid-point of the T (the head), and we are predicting how long it will take the right shoulder by supposition). Thus, if we were to describe this with verbiage, the first step in applying T-Theory is to the synthetic technical indicator that Mr. Laundry uses, measure the time it took for that indicator to go from its peak to a current trough, and then, superimposing that same time back onto the indicator chart itself, which calculates our Time Cycle market inflection point. What is more, this concept is similar to a measured move in RSI, which I also discussed in the last Chapter.

Now, there are two more hidden understands that the reader must have about T-Theory. First, if the indicator is making continued lows, we simply recalculate the time that is used for defining the right side of the T, and second, T-Theory can be applied in EVERY time frame. Again, as part of proving that "The Market is not Random," we have to remain focused on theories that work in every time frame and for every trading instrument. Thus, because T-Theory can be implemented in various time frames, I like it. As an aside, T-Theory can also be used to calculate the time for up moves, but it is my understanding that Mr. Laundry is fully aware that the market has a Price Objective to observe new highs. Thus, he is only using his T-Theory in order to understand the length of market pullbacks, which means that once his right T has been fulfilled, he will start to reenter the market, by purchasing stocks. This is further evidenced by the fact that Mr. Laundry tends to be a long-term holder of stocks instead of an active trader or a holder of short positions. Quite simply, he has found a trading edge that tells him, approximately, how long a market correction will last, and then, he can get back in at a preferable price. This is not rocket science, and a trading edge does not have to be extreme (as we used the 8.6 Year Cycle to demonstrate) in order to have efficacy in trading results.

Now that we have an understanding of how T-Theory works and how Mr. Laundry applies it, we need to discuss the fact that we are working with a synthetic technical indicator. Hence, we need to understand that this T is NOT applied to the chart itself, which means it is not linking terminal, discreet highs/lows that occur on the chart. This also means that we are not working with the pure derivatives of price and time, which may seem somewhat contradictory to the reader. In fact, the T is used on the advance/decline line of a given market index. Essentially, we are measuring the time the advance/decline line has moved up/down to predict future inflection points, i.e. the peak to trough or trough to peak. From there, we can extrapolate this time outward in order to define an inflection date, which is done *vis a vis* Time Shift. Unfortunately, this inflection date may be a price inflection date ***or it may be the indicator's inflection date***. As such, T-Theory is not always useful for predicting the exact date. Instead, it is useful for making us aware to a possible, market inflection point, and when we cluster these data points with other time and price components, we can yield a profitable analytical technique in refining our inflection dates. For large investors, this is very important because those investors can use options/futures to start "purchasing insurance" for market retracements/corrections.

The Bradley Cycle

The Bradley cycle brings up further clarification of the subject in T-Theory of predicting how cycles can be useful for predicting market moves instead of predicting the terminal dates for discreet highs/lows. This is a very important characteristic of the Bradley Cycle because using the dates that are predicted as highs/lows by the Cycle itself, we can find that these dates tend to correspond with changes to the VIX. Again, this observation is not obvious, and this observation requires the trader to go and do his or her own analysis in order to understand the validity of this Synthetic Time Cycle.

Now, in order to understand how the Bradley Cycle can help us, we can refer back to our earlier discussion of a trading campaign. Because a Bradley Cycle high correlates to a low in volatility, we can wait until the Bradley Cycle has peaked in order to define trading campaign start points. What is also inferable from the Bradley Cycle (but less accurate than calling a change in VIX), a Bradley Cycle high predicts a VIX low because a Bradley Cycle high (based on its definition) is predicting a market high, and as we know, as markets decline, the VIX goes up.

Looking at a chart of the 2005-2012 Bradley Cycle and the VIX, one can easily picture all of the high volatility periods foreshadowed by the Bradley Cycle highs. This knowledge is easily hidden to the masses without some type of ethereal analysis that I have been able to accomplish. In a way, volatility is manifested inside of the Bradley Cycle. Therefore, we have to remember that finding a trading edge usually requires a slight mentality shift that allows the market participant to be playing at a level higher than most other market participants. By coupling the Bradley Cycle with Volatility, we can find that trading edge, and one can look to the Bradley Cycle to attempting *trading campaigns* or purchasing puts options as portfolio insurance.

Bull / Bear Market Cycles & Fundamental Investor Cyclic Approach

Although I have cautioned the reader about measuring time regarding one's approach to Time Structure-like analysis, the reader does need to be made aware that measuring time does have usefulness in understanding the bigger picture, which means that time measurements can help us in determining future market inflection points. Thus, we can expand the definition of measured moves from the last chapter, and the reader needs to understand that for Bull/Bear Market cyclic turn dates (i.e. Major Market Inflection Points); we uncover a true trading edge. Therefore, we need to understand that the true edge of measured moves (in Time) come from the quantitative and qualitative thought summations that helps us to determining Bull/Bear Market Cycles, which is literally priceless for longer term investors. Thus, we need to elaborate on qualitative concepts as well in this discussion because there are also overall economic objectives that must be considered for longer-term cyclic approaches, and obviously, these objectives are different but similarly derived from the two classifications of market types (i.e. bull/bear markets). By doing this cumulative analysis, we will finally reach the ultimate conclusion of my thesis-like assertions in this book by coming up with an overall view of market purpose, central bank purpose, and inflation purpose that gets rolled into Price Theory and a new Theory, which will be defined momentarily. *As such, this section of the book may contain one of the most powerful conclusions ever stated in regards to the Financial Markets*. In fact, even with my disproof of *The Efficient Market Hypothesis* in Chapter 21 of this book, the analytically and fundamentally derived conclusions that I set forth within this section of this book are conclusions that I believe will carry extreme, logical relevance for comprehending *any* market's objective. What is more, the reason these conclusions are defined towards the end of this text is that I had to create new terminology in order for the reader to comprehend these conclusions. Ergo, my full market hypothesis conclusion can now be defined as Klatch's Marketome Theory (or "Klatch's Inflation Theory"), and once defined, I believe that Klatch's Marketome Theory has the potential to shift all market participants' thinking with respect to all trade implementation types be it daytrading, momentum trading, investing, portfolio management, or even entire country analysis.

Klatch's Marketome Theory states: *commodities <u>and</u> market indices will always return to some type of bull market because, after a true low has been formed, the market will have a Price Objective to make a new high outside of a given range, which for a commodity or for an index, would be a new all-time high.* Therefore, this Price Objective would exist even if it were derived from a multi-year/multi-decade range. Further, this is the importance of Klatch's Price Theory, and this is my (future) Nobel Prize winning conclusion: *"The fundamental investor can always take on a cyclic approach to the market whereby the underlying objectives of all the fundamental investments will have Price Objectives to attain new highs, which is why investors, as a whole, stand to always make profit from the market if they understand that these Price Objectives are the goal for their investments. What is more, because markets reach all time highs on a fractional second basis, markets will always be pulling back inside of a given range no matter how big or how small it is with respect to time <u>and</u> with respect to price. Thus, we prove that markets controlled/monitored/regulated by central banks will always have the Price Objectives of new highs, unless the system were to fail"* And the reason for this is concluded in one word, "Inflation." Once inflation is understood as the goal of central banks, we can understand that, *with inflation, markets will always move higher*, which properly defines a possible, circuitous proof for Klatch's Price Theory, which concurrently proves that "The Market is not Random." Thus, we also find the opposing reason as to why deflation is disastrous for the central banks and for the markets because deflation raises the *potential* possibility of producing an overall market with a Price Objective derived from Price Theory of $0.00 (or even less than $0.00)! However, there is a corollary to this discussion that must be addressed.

The corollary to Klatch's Marketome Theory must redefine what an index is, which adheres to Klatch's Marketome Theory by taking out a new high. Obviously, the best way to do so is to define a market capitalization weighting to the given components of an index, which is also valid should one create a new index in the future or should one of the current indices cease to exist. Hence, in order for Klatch's Marketome Theory to hold true for all indices, we must redefine an **Index** as: "Either a non-trading market instrument shown as a summarized constructed value that is continuously recalculated throughout a trading day (the S&P 500 Cash Index is an example of this non-trading instrument) or an index is a trading market instrument that fluctuates in price throughout the trading day (Exchange Traded Funds and Index Futures are examples of these trading instruments). Further, the index is composed of underlying market instruments that, when combined, total a minimum outstanding market capitalization value of 1% of the GDP of the country, whose stocks represent a majority of the index based on capitalization weighting coupled with the criteria that the index must be composed of at least five market instruments." Unarguably, this 1% figure is arbitrary, but the general idea of redefining an Index is that it must be large enough whereby enough of the underlying market instruments have Klatch's Price Theory Price Objectives to attain new highs versus those that may reach zero, which makes correlated logical sense to the corollary because once a market instrument, in the index, reaches zero its market capitalization reaches zero, which means it no longer has any input on the Price Objective of the index itself!

Fundamentally speaking, Klatch's Marketome Theory and coupled corollary make logical sense because Klatch's Marketome Theory coupled with the redefined index will hold true for the qualitative objectives / arguments used by central bankers. Thus, we find the qualitative validation in the fact that it is *the job of all central banks around the word in order to continue price inflation*, which is why deflation avoidance is critical to the fiat money system. In essence, a deflation scenario could lead to a Price Objective less than zero for an index, which would make the system fail should a major index, like the S&P 500 have all 500 of its stocks targeted at zero. Concurrently, it is the job of the central bankers to prevent defilation wile ensuring that the inflation rate must be contained at less than 10% per annum in order for the human psyche in order to palpably handle price increases in a methodic way. Hence, it makes sense why all markets are simply boiled down to humanity perception, and that perception of the average work must not feel slighted by quickly increasing market prices. Ergo, we must reach the conclusion that *the purpose of the dollar, as a financial instrument, is to continue its depreciation*. Thus, we find the truth behind economic policy, which is *human ego maintenance*. Moreover, GDP growth itself is not an actual measure of output growth in a given country. No, it is the measure of the increase of dollars processed, and under a system that has goals of continued inflation, we realize that GDP growth is most likely stationary. Thus, we must understand the inflationary objective of central banks, which is to continue the production of upward numbers that make the individual man feel good, but ultimately, this positive performance is irrelevant once converted to nominal/inflationary dollars. However, the human psyche is inclined to think that if things are increasing at a logical rate, everything is okay in the world, which causes the individual to feel good about spending and more importantly, to feel good about obtaining credit. For example, if a person believed the economy was contracting, they would not be inclined to take on debt. Thus, we find the real game of the market because, what is not apparent to the common citizen, is that this increase in the economy is ultimately synthetic (i.e. through man), which is why the Chairmen of the Federal Reserve have cared so much about economic confidence models. *Thus, it is my belief that people like Mr. Bernanke, Alan Greenspan, and ECB President, Mario Draghi, understand that inflation is necessary so that markets can reach new all-time highs, which causes a positive, emotional stimulus with respect to the masses that encourages more spending of more dollars that become inflated by the central banks that are derived from increasing bond sales on behalf of governments*. Only under that normal flow of economic *law* can the fiat currency survive, but at the end of the day, that survival is based off the creation of more money out of thin air. Thus, the target for governments is to keep constantly printing more money in order to keep inflating the economy, which yields growth of economic indicators as well as correlating to new all-time market highs. Once this understanding is achieved, we find that the conclusion is ultimately attained, but thankfully, since the reader now knows of Klatch's Marketome Theory and Klatch's Price Theory, he or she can profit from this knowledge; just like central bankers! Hence, we can conclude that Klatch's Marketome Theory only fails under *continual* deflation, which is something I believe that the central bankers know and understand but never, ever, speak about, because of the need to contain mass market psychology/monetary-illusion. Now, I must state that I do not believe these assertions are anything new with respect to monetary policy, but when one applies my thoughts to the market, by using Price Theory Price Objectives for Indices, we uncover the reality that the market cannot be random since we can theoretically know that the market has a need to attain new highs.

Furthermore, I can expand my assertions regarding deflation by comparing it to bear market scenarios. Thus, the original assertion is expanded to say that, "*Bear markets cannot exist in perpetuity, like bull markets can, because, for that recurrent situation to manifest itself through Price Theory, we would echo the previous assertion that the recurrent bear market would continue to breach discreet lows, which would trigger swing projections that would approach zero or even less than 0 based on Price Pattern Objectives*." Therefore, the markets themselves cannot be in a recurrent bear market, and the probability that a market will have a new bear market before achieving the Price Objective of new highs outside of the base range, is infinitesimally low *if not impossible*. For example, if the market were to breach the March 2009 low, before reaching a new high over the November 2007 high, the swing projection calculation would yield values less than zero on the charts. On the other hand, we can look to individual stocks as a basis for uncovering these bear market life cycles. Of course, many individual stocks have reached bankruptcy/hit zero on their charts. Although this may be fine for a stock, indices are different, which is why Klatch's Marketome Theory is defined for the indices. As such, I further define the fact that since bull markets are categorized with low volatility, that the bull market cycles are longer in time due to consistent price action. Therefore we can now say that *the termination of a bull market will only occur once Klatch's Price Theory's Price Objectives have been satisfied, which means that once the indication of a bull market has occurred, we can remain in a long position until a new high is reached.* Only then, can we start to be concerned for a new bear market, which is possibly the largest trading edge ever defined. Therefore, as I write this paragraph (4-14-12), the real life example is that we are currently in a new bull market that will not end until a new high is achieved, which is currently the November, 2007, high in the S&P. (Of note, I am stating that his new high objective should be in terms of notional dollars, and this concept is expanded upon in the *Reflections* section of this book.)

Summarily, we can now come to the root definition of what exists in the market place, and we can find that *there is a codependent causation that has a singular deterministic goal.* Hence, we have the fundamental (economical) need for inflation coupled with a theory, my Price Theory that must be satisfied to the upside at all times. With the market's goal being recurrent new highs, we find the disparity that exist between the two causal singularities, which prompts the question, "Is it Klatch's Price Theory's eventuality that leads to the market's objective of higher prices, or is it the human being's free will at play through the summary factors of the central bankers?" I do not know which is why these concepts are defined as Theories and not as Laws.

Conversely, we now have a quantifiable way in order to determine when to look for a new bear market, which is the key for fundamental investors because a bear market is the major source of drawdown for mutual funds, brokerages, and investors. Thus, using the concepts in this book, I can now state that for our definition, a **bear market** is simply a *market that is existing once a retracement greater than 25% of the range created by the last bear market's terminal point to the currently ending bull market's terminal point has been breached.* Conversely, we can now define a **bull market** as a *market that has inflected upward with Price Objectives that adhere to Klatch's Price theory after a bear market has been established.* For example, if we look at the 2002-2007 markets, we can say that a new bear market cannot form or be characterized until the Price Objective of the 2002 low is achieved, which is to take out the notional value of the 2007 high. Simultaneously, once the 2007 high is breached, we can begin the search for a new bear market, by observing if the market that exists after the 2007 high is breached has a retracement of 25% or more of the 2002 low to the 2007 high range. Hence, we understand that in 2008, it was now possible to start looking for a new bear market, and in fact, we had the indication of the new bear market once the 25% retracement level was breached from the 2002 low to the 2007 high, and this understanding will simultaneously define for us the fact that a new bull market scenario can only occur when we can say, conclusively, that the market is now targeting new all-time highs. As another example, we can look at today's market (the 2009 bull market), and once the trader believed that the March 2009 low was real, the longer-term trader/investor can now simply hold long positions until a new high is obtained based on Price Theory. Thus, we can rest confidently in our long market positions until Klatch's Price Theory is satisfied! Once satisfied, we can start the bear market observance again, but one must be aware that immediate reversals, as was seen in 2007, are unusual. Hence, once Price Objectives of bull markets can be reached, the market participant can hold onto long positions until the markets have *retraced 25% from the 2009 low to whatever high is reached higher than the 2007 high, which becomes a portfolio management strategy in and of itself.* This strategy is not obvious, and its power is paramount, so this concept must also be elaborated on.

As we saw in 2011, the market had a very large down move that started in August. In fact, this move was so large that if you measured a retracement from the March 2009 to the April 2011 high, we would see that the market did retrace more than 25% of the range from the bear market low. However, *we cannot look for a new bear market inception because Price Theory Price Objectives have yet to be reached,* and this statement yields the definition of **Price Theory Overriding** for portfolio managers, investors, mutual fund managers, etc., because the Bull Market Price Objective overrides until it has been satisfied. Thus, although that down move was large in 2011, it was not possible for a new bear market to exist yet because new all-time high Price Objectives were still withstanding, which contradicts my definition of when a market participant can look for a new bear market. Further, the only way to contradict this condition is if the market was to take out the 2009 low before taking out the 2007 high, and should that happen, we again find ourselves in a discussion regarding Price Pattern Objectives less than 0 for the overall market, which is indicative of the fiat money system's imminent collapse. This last piece of market understanding is critical for an investor who is determining if he or she should sell immediately once Price Theory's Price Objectives or fulfilled, or if he or she should hold onto their position for further gain because we only have two decisions for the mutual fund manager, fund of funds manager, or other long-term investor. The strategy is either (a) sell as soon as Price Objectives are reached, or (b) sell as soon as a new high is reached AND a the 25% retracement is breached from the range created by the last bear market's terminal low to the *current* bull market's high. Personally, I believe option B is much more effective because if one were to look back before 1999, we would see that the markets gradually moved higher without large bear markets as we have seen in the last two decades. Therefore, we must assume that these last two decades have been outliers, and at some point, the market will continue upward for a long period of time. Ergo, only by holding onto a position for that extended amount of time as subsequent highs are being made, can the longer-term investor make sufficient profits.

Moving on, we can finally discuss the Time Cycle tendencies of bull/bear markets. First, since market highs tend to occur under low volatility, we can further define the bear market starting point by looking for **Complex Tops**, which can be characterized as deep retracements, double/repetitive tops, rising tops lines/3-drives patterns, etc. The power of understanding this knowledge is that by using Price Theory, we can wait until the underlying objective is reached before we have to mentally exert ourselves in determining a cluster average in price and in time that yields a Major Market Inflection Point that is a high, which *could* indicate a new bear market. In order to use real-life as validation, if a mutual fund manager or a stock investor were to liquidate all of their underlying holdings at the exact moment the market that Price Structure Component appeared (the double top) from the 2000 high to the November of 2007 high, then, that investor would have been completely protected against the 2007-2009 bear market. However, I think this immediate reversal of an index is rare, but at the same time, it does not diminish the power of *Time and Price Symmetry* because even at all-time highs, we know the market is not random. Hence, we understand why this becomes the most powerful portion of this book because what is more, we can use Time Structure and cyclic understanding in order to measure the time of previous bull markets, which will give us the longevity of your average bull market, and how do we do this? Easily, if we go back to the first paragraph of this section, we can say that we can define bull market terminal dates by the use of measured moves (in time) from the last bull markets! However, as a corollary, since we have now stated the market's purpose is somewhat related to inflation, we must understand that those measured moves lines are only applicable for time, which is why I waited until this portion of the book to discuss the true assertions of this book.

Thus, we reach the corresponding conclusion that makes measured moves indicative of further price action if we incorporate the understanding of the true Time Cycles inherent to bull/bear markets. Thus, measured move lines measured from Major Market Inflection Points alert us to the fact that if markets have moved more in terms of price but less in terms of time, we have future, further price action! In other words, since the 2002 to 2007 bull market was approximately 5 years and moved approximately 800 points on the S&P index, well we can then observe the current bull market, and if the current bull market has moved more than 800 points before 5 years, which I expect to happen later this year (again I am writing this on 4/14/12) then, we can be assured that we will be moving much more than just 800 points because we are only 3 years into the current bull market (plus, an 800 point move off of the 2009 low does NOT fulfill Price Theory's Price Objectives). For what it's worth, let us also bring Time Repetitions into this example because the reader of this book should now be aware that all of these subjects are interrelated. Thus, we can also observe that it was the decennial time repetition that called the 2007 high. This Time Repetition was simply an echo from the 1987 stock market crash within a probability of 98.33% or 236/240 (remember +/- 2 months around a Major Market Inflection Point spanned over 2 decades is where the calculation comes from). Therefore, we see extreme overlap of Price Structure with Time Cycles and with Time Repetitions for Major Market Inflection Points because we have a Price Structure Component (the double top), we have Klatch's Price Theory telling us that we can only look for the end of the bull market once the previous bull market's high was exceeded, we have the approximate length of time for our bull market (as measured by measured move lines related to Time Cycles), and we have the decennial Time Repetition calling a 4 months window of time with a 98.33% certainty. With that verbiage and that powerful discussion now out of the way, the reader should be left in a state of awe about the power of *Time and Price Symmetry,* and all that remains is how to understand these concepts deeper. Thus, in order to conclude this discussion of Bull/Bear Market Time Cycles, let us discuss their cyclic tendencies in detail.

Typically, we can observe that a bull market lasts for approximately 5-7 years after a given bear market low has been found. Once we get confirmation of the start of the bull market by a qualified swing on the weekly chart, we can rest comfortably until Price Objectives are reached. Conversely, we observe that bear markets happen under higher volatility, and because of this larger range of price action, we observe that bear markets run from 1.25-3 years on average, and this conclusion is an inverse conclusion to the measured move time-based predictor of further price action whereby with this scenario we can see that the further price corresponds to a *shorter* duration of time. What is more, if one studies all available market it data, we must realize that it is almost a nonexistent probability that a bear market will be over in less than 1.25 years, which was a crucial peace of cyclic understanding that told the world that the market was going to head lower after the late December rally of 2008, which faked a lot of people back into the market thinking that the bear market was over (including myself). Further, it is an interesting conclusion to see that the additive range of a bull/bear market cycle is in the 6.25-10 year range, whose average is approximately 8.25 years, which is close to our 8.6 Year Global Economic Confidence Model. In a way, defining a bear market low is much easier because the low is typically sharp, retested, and then, a clear cut swing will form. Thus, we realize that bull markets have Complex Tops and bear markets have simple bottoms, and I believe this is because under higher volatility, the market tends to adhere to price structure components rather then the trend. For instance, if a bull market, one can stay long with the trend and simply make money, but with bear markets, one must be able to capitalize on all the volatility moves up or down. Therefore, we get quick, clean Price Pattern Affirmations at bear market lows, and a **Price Pattern Affirmation** can simply be defined as *Time and Price Symmetry* because we have Time reinforcing Price. What is more, it is a typical tendency of a major bear market low to experience a longer-term (multi-month) swing that has a 61.8%R. Categorically, every bear market low except for the current 2009 low has had these deep retracements. Because we did not observe ANY deep retracement of the 2009 low, we have to analyze what changed like any good financial scientist, and what changed was governmental manipulation. For the first time ever, the Federal Reserve engaged in their Permanent Open Market Operations that drove prices higher, faster, which caused the deep retracement tendency to fail, but by no means did *Time and Price Symmetry* fail because a shallow swing did form 6 months after the low.

The last way that we can talk about time in relationship to bull/bear markets is to observe that years ending in 5 (1985, 1995, 2005, etc.) tend to have large up moves over the past 130 years. Due to this observed tendency, we can estimate the times, on a yearly basis, when we need to start to recognize the possibility of a new bear market inception, which corresponds to a bull market Major Market Inflection Point. Since years ending in 5 are up-years and the fact that we know that bear markets last for 1.5~3 years on average, we can conclude that the years preceding years ending in 5, which are years ending in 3 □ 4, are low probability time windows for observing bull market highs, and we define this as **Five Year Bull Market Terminal Predictor**! Therefore, we can estimate that bear market starting points can occur towards the last part of years ending in 5 through the following decade that has years ending in 2! Simultaneously, we can also understand that bear market terminal points have a higher probability in occurring between years 2 □ 4 and 8 □ 9 as well, which we define as the **Five Year Bear Market**

Terminal Predictor! This is powerful for investors to realize because it shows how we can use a simple Time Cycle observation in order to derive many conclusions. Granted, this is far from a perfect analysis, and it is a cyclic tendency, but if one understood this tendency, we get another qualifier for our 2009 low by the dates given from the Five Year Bear Market Terminal Predictor. As an aside, if a trader cannot grasp this concept, you are probably not smart enough to be involved in the financial markets because although this concept is not apparent, it must take an analytical mind to grasp.

Lastly, we can finally move on, but what will be interesting to observe with this tendency and all of the other descriptions/observations of bull/bear markets is the possibility of when our current bull market terminal point will emerge. Since we started our new bull market in March of 2009 and we have learned about the 8.6 Year Cycle, we can see that the calculation for a given high occurs in the second half of 2015. However, from Klatch's Price Theory, we know that we will not observe this bull market's terminal point until we have breached the November 2007 high, which means this (the 2009 bull market) can be one of the largest bull markets in history, if not thee largest!

Holidays

As a bridge between synthetic Time Cycles and God, we find inherent tendencies of Holiday dates. I have labeled Holidays as a bridge because one can be inclined to believe that the dates chosen were not of man-made origin. Take Christmas for example, we are told that this is Christ's birthday, but if one looks at the original construction of the roman calendar, that is not true. However, it may have been God's Will that allowed December 25th to become Christ's date of celebration, and I hope that logic makes some sense to the reader because you can also say that it was God's Will that allowed the founding fathers of America to pick July 4th, or, July 4th could have been a synthetic creation of man, but nevertheless, July 4th is a Holiday and July 4th yields cyclic tendencies. Although holidays are in front of everyone's face, the average trader never gives them any thought, and like everything else in this book, a slight shift in perception leads to profound results. Unfortunately, I did not think of this on my own. No, W.D. Gann was the first person to write about Holiday Time Cycles, and his observations hold extreme relevance today.

What Gann noticed was that the commodity markets made important highs/lows around or on a holiday, and as I discussed about the concept of an "island" in Price Structure along with the "volume" discussion in Price Structure that stated that inflection points tended to happen on low volume, holiday tendencies are likewise related, because of minimal market participation. In order to discuss this relevancy, we need to understand that markets are always moving 24 hours per day, but due to our human necessity in order to define market-closing dates in order to live our lives, we have to keep in mind that holidays are like any other day. As such, markets that are open on Holidays (especially commodity/futures markets), have a tendency to use minimal market participation as a time to mind screw the mass-market participants by making important highs/lows, while people are spending time with their families. How much crueler can the market get than this tendency! Really!

Anyway, all this means is that a trader must create his or her own holidays because Holidays are extremely important for market inflection points, which means that trade implementations can be placed with the least amount of risk, and unfortunately, another tendency is that markets do not tend to Back and Fill as much on Holiday-based inflection points. Further, if the reader does not believe me about Holiday inflection points, you need to go and pull up a futures chart because a regular cash index chart will not show the true inflection points (of note: if someone is a stock trader and they are recording time repetitions, he/she may choose to also see if the index that stock is listed in had an inflection point based on the futures during the holiday). As a real-life example of the power of Holidays, I ask the reader to do a quick visualization by looking at the Thanksgiving holiday in the U.S. One can easily see major highs/lows occurring during that week in late November due to the cyclical holiday tendency. More important of an example is if we look at the July 4, 2010, low in the S&P Futures. The low of the year occurred on July 4th

at a major Price Cluster (a 38.2%R and a 61.8%R)!

The last observation of the cyclical holiday tendencies is that we need to be aware when markets are close to major highs/lows when going into any holiday. If we are in the middle of the range, holidays become less important, but if we are at new highs or new lows, we need to get back to work on holidays; pure and simple.

The 400-Year Humanity Cycle

There is a little known belief that as we recognize that "there is nothing new under the sun," humanity may be adhering to a major cycle of 400 years. Using the Internet, the reader can find his or her own research regarding the esoteric nature of thoughts regarding this 400-year cycle, but this 400-year cycle is our first understanding with respect to divinity and Time Cycles, and I will not be preaching divinity in these next few pages. However, I have no other basis for this validity.

Moving on, we obviously cannot wait 400 years for this cycle to be useful. Thus, for our purposes, we need to split the 400-year cycle into an 80-year cycle, a 40-year cycle, a 20-year cycle, and a 10-year cycle, which is our decennial cycle, and as the reader should now realize the Time Repetition definition of the decennially-derived Time Histogram is interrelated with this 400-Year Humanity Time Cycle, because as discussed, that Time Repetition looks back 40 years. Because of these observations, we can give importance to these four time windows given by our 400-year cycle.

What we need to be able to do is to keep the concept of Time Shift in mind because of how disparate this Time Cycle is. Therefore, the implementation of this Time Cycle is truly on the Decennial Time Repetition, but nevertheless, let us discusses it again. For example, I ask the reader to look back at any of the past four decades that are derived from the 400-year cycle. From there, we need to visually inspect our current market's chart patterns in order to determine if we can find a linear relationship between the current year's chart pattern and another year's chart pattern. For example, we would look at our current 2012 chart, and we can compare it to any of the years inside of the 2000s, 1990s, 1970s, and 1930s. We can observe that some part of our chart may be found between the years inside of these decades as well, which means that the first half of 2012 could look like the second half of 1974 (purely an arbitrary example). As such, we derive forty possible chart examples that may be mirroring our current market, but because of how superfluous forty charts can be, the only true edge we gain from this cycle isif we find a historic chart in any of those decades that perfectly aligns to the current market, and in fact, for the 2010/2011 markets this did exist, but I encourage the reader to find it! This is necessary research on a quarterly basis because we can often find that previous chart patterns (even 80-year-old ones as was the case in 2010) can lead to exact replica of Major Market Inflection Points!

Seasons and Half-Seasons

One of the prominent discoveries that Gann had in his observation of time is to observe the 13-week seasonality tendencies and the 6.5-week seasonality tendencies that exist in the markets. These yield eight days per year that we can use to look for market inflection points, and obviously, these cycles are based astrologically. Thus, like Holidays, we only need to be aware of these seasonality turn dates when markets are near the highs/lows of a given range, because we can often observe that these turn dates occur exactly at discreets, which as we will learn in the next chapter, is unusual about Time Structure. However, this analyst is also simplistic, and it too can be used an analyzed a quarter at a time. What is more, these days are straightforward, but the reader must remember that as we approach leap years, the true date of the season can be shifted by 1 day, which becomes reset on the leap year itself. Thus, if you find the market inflecting on September 22nd instead of September 21st, it could be that you forgot about the leap year calculation, and obviously, being off by one day can lead to a major difference.

The last two cycles that I wish to discuss to the reader are purely astrologically linked, and if you do not believe that astrology influences the market, please skip to the next chapter. Hence, these cycles are more about predicting the manner in which the market trades during these Time Cycles instead of actual market inflection. As such, it is useful to keep these cycles in mind instead of allowing them to dictate trades because our next cycle often foreshadows an increase in volatility, which is useful for trading campaigns.

Mercury Retrograde

When Mercury is in retrograde with respect to Earth, the markets tend to become range bound with no large trends emerging, but concurrently, these markets due tend to yield consistent range expansions, which hinder swing traders. What is more, these ranges sometimes look like large expanding triangles with false breakouts and high volatility. Thus, when Mercury is in Retrograde with Earth, we find that these are good periods in order for the trader to focus on a trading campaign because once volatility emerges through the VIX, we can expect volatility to continue until Mercury is no longer Retrograde.

Another interesting observation of Mercury Retrograde is in terms of Time Windows. If the reader can recall, we saw in the last chapter a Time Window chart of probabilities for when cycles overlapped. Thus, there was an opening and a closing date for that overlap, which yielded higher probabilities, but that same approach is not relevant for this Time Cycle because this Time Cycle is about finding tendencies within the markets price discovery process itself. Thus, the exact beginning and end dates for the Time Window defined by this Time Cycle is not relevant for finding Major Market Inflection Points. Lastly, there is one more tendency associated with this Time Cycle, and that tendency is that markets will make major highs or lows before or after Mercury Retrograde because once Mercury has moved out of retrograde, the market will have an objective to retest the values that existed before entering retrograde. Thus, the entire Mercury Retrograde range is often reexamined again.

Moon Cycles

Our only concern with moon cycles is dates of new moon and full moon occurrences. These dates sometimes yield large volatility that comes one day and is gone the next. It is often a time that people can be faked-out by a spike in the VIX, and it is often a time when longer-term swing trades fail. Therefore, we have to be cautious of these dates because if we see a swing activate under high volatility, we may have found a new Major Market Inflection Date. Hence, these Time Cycle dates are useful for Major Market Inflection Dates as well, and what is more, is that we can observe the market's tendency to actually make Key Reversal Days if we are near the high and low of the range. This is valuable knowledge, and it is useful in predicting higher probabilities of Key Reversal Days or Major Market Inflection Points existing at trend qualifying criteria.

In summary, we have discussed a tremendous amount of data in this chapter, and with these discussions, Time Structure is essentially complete. The next task is to show how we can combine Time Structure with Price Structure in order to add trade-qualifying criteria. Furthermore, this Chapter stated my overall market view, which was defined as Klatch's Marketome Theory. Hence, the trader is now encouraged to begin his or her own quantitative analysis of *Time and Price Symmetry* before moving to the last chapter of the book, because that last Chapter is the *reason d'etre* of understanding Time and Price together. Lastly, there is probably some cynical thought in the readers mind that I am proving the non-randomness to the market by coming up with dates and prices that can be used for every cent and for every minute, and undoubtedly, there is truth to that statement. However, if that were true, we could not find trading edges, and as such, the reader must be made aware that every concept in this book can potentially be its own trading strategy. Thus, what we are trying to do is find increasing symmetry across all price components and all time components, and if we couple that with the qualitative eye necessary for Quantitative Synchronicity, we find price clusters and time windows that stand out. Hence, at the end of the day, the true purpose to all of this writing is to get the trader to understand the trend and the current Price Objectives based on Klatch's Price Theory, and therefore, I must state that with the knowledge of Time Cycles, the reader has everything needed to become the best trader of all time.

Chapter 20

Trading in Time

The beauty about time is that it allows us to anticipate trades instead of reacting to what is happening in the market, which has already been discussed in terms of anticipatory traders versus reactionary traders. What is more, time tells us when the Moment of Recognition *may* occur, which allows us to focus our mental energy at certain periods of time, and I ask the reader to think about how powerful of an ally Time Structure can become if we are successful in analyzing it. Therefore, throughout this book, I have stated the power of Time Structure many times in order to emphasize its importance with respect to trading. However, time needs to be coupled with price, due to the illusory nature that one gets with time, and I define this illusory nature as a human shortcoming; not a market failure. At the same time, when we define mathematical price clusters and Time Windows in successful ways, we have fully proven the title of this book by realizing that every major high/low of every instrument that trades in every time frame can be quantified in terms of price and in terms of time. Thus, the only question that we, as traders, need to define is how to profit from this knowledge, which is always the difficult part. Therefore, in order to explain profit attainment of trading in time, which is essentially defined as *Time and Price Symmetry*, I will use the real example of the March 2009 bear market low, because one can define an infinite amount of *profitable* trading implementations if one were confident in the legitimacy of using *Time and Price Symmetry* just to calculate one Major Market Inflection Point.

As stated within Price Structure's chapters, the S&P E-Mini Futures defined a mathematical support cluster at 666.79, which called the bear market low in 2009. However, that was not the only price cluster that existed, which was lower than the 2002 low, and again, the reason we were waiting for the 2002 low to be breached was based on the Price Pattern Objective of the double top, or the Price Objective based on Price Theory if we converted the 2007 to a real value (which is discussed in the *Reflections* section of this book). However, the reality is that there were many price clusters existing lower than the October 2002 low, and we did not know which one would hold the market. Therefore, if the trader were trading off price alone, he/she would be taking trades at each price cluster, with the hopes that it would hold the market. Hence, we find the key word that must be banished from the trader's mind: ***hope***. Hope is the enemy of a trader, and once one starts to *hope* for an outcome, he or she is no longer in the present moment. However, this begs the question, "How do we remove hope?" Well, it is quite simple and quite obvious, at this point, and all we have to do is learn to trade in time as well as in price, which is the goal of this chapter and the logical conclusion of this book.

Continuing on with the 2009 example, once the market breached the 2002 low, we can go back and do the analysis, which would prove to the reader that there were four cluster averages existing between 600 and 800 in the S&P Futures, and there were a myriad of clusters below 600, which was indicative to the fact that the 600 level was most likely to hold, but that observation comes from the qualitative eye; not time and not price. Regardless, in order to refresh the reader's memory, we can find a cluster based on the 127.2% double top projection coupled with all of the higher level projections from the gamut of swings that existed on the daily charts coupled with ***retracements that went all the way back to the early 1900s***! (Yes, the lows set 100 year ago were necessary in order to find the true mathematical cluster that defined the S&P Cash Index low!) Therefore, the reader must make sure that all of these Price Structure Components were correctly found and correctly calculated in order to yield the four major price clusters between 800 and 600, which were all powerful enough in order to call the bear market low. However, without Time Structure, the trader could only buy each cluster, and again, have *hope* for his or her trade. Now, this is not a bad thing in and of itself because, if the trader knew that the Price Objective is new highs over the 2007 high, then, taking small losses by a failed cluster average is not a big deal. Obviously even a 10-point move up from a given low paid for all of these possible, failed trades. However, we must not allow for any error at all in this book because if we do, we cannot prove the non-randomness of the market. Thus, let us introduce the concept of Trading in Time with daily, Quantitative Synchronicity during March of 2009.

If one has followed Time Structure thus far, I have no doubt that he or she should have no trouble constructing the Time Histogram for 2009. In that Time Histogram, we were able to find an explicit Time Window, which was derived from many Time List intersections, and this Time Window was somewhat large in size. However, our Time Windows became more important than Price because of the observation of the cyclic tendency/weighted times therein. Hence, the major Time Histogram yielded a subsection that had specific date ranges necessary for observing this low. These date ranges were: March 5 □ 12, and there were more repetitions around the 9th day of March then any other value, which will be defined as mode momentarily. Therefore, once these dates were properly defined, all the trader had to do was to buy each of the mathematical price clusters that the market "discovered" during that opened Time Window. Luckily, there was only one, and it was tagged almost immediately!

Thus, once we observed that one of the price clusters was tagged during this Time Window, all that we needed to do was wait for the primary trend to change, on the 60-minute chart, in order to confirm the validity of this low. What is more, because this bear market came to fruition from a double top pattern, once the October 2002 low was exceeded, the Price Theory Price Objective was complete, which alerted the trader to be open minded to the fact that the market's price discovery process was approaching completion. Hence, we find that the Time Window defined in early March coupled with a primary price cluster, and we had *Time and Price Symmetry*. Therefore, the only remaining component that was needed in order to define a new bull market that had Price Objectives higher than the 2007 was to wait for the trend to change on the weekly chart, which occurred when we the market executed a swing above the July 2009 high, which was large enough in order to qualify as a retracement that allowed for a projection. (Remember, a 25% retracement is the shallow possible retracement that allows for swing projections, and if one were to get anal with me regarding the qualified swing concept, I must refer back to the definition that a qualified swing only needs 15 bars on at the 60-minute chart – not the daily or weekly chart – in order to change the primary trend. What is more, if one goes and looks for this qualified swing, he or she will see that on the following Monday and on the following Tuesday after the bear market low was put in on Friday, the market had two qualifying swings; both with higher bottoms and higher highs!) Regardless, I still like to look for the daily swing, and when the July 2009 high was breached, we were able to finally take comfort in the reality that a new Bull Market had arrived. Therefore, the trader was able to acquiesce to Bull Market cyclical tendencies that are always coupled to my Price Theory. By doing so, the trader was now clued in on the future of the market that foretold that the markets were now targeting highs over the 2007 high, and that our expected time period in order to do this was sometime before the middle of 2014, which is derived from previous measured times of bull markets. However, we also know by this point in this book that the sooner Klatch's Price Theory Price Objectives are fulfilled; the higher we can expect the market to go based on the cyclical nature of bull markets (again, remember, measuring time is seldom useful *unless* we are dealing with Bull/Bear markets themselves). Hence, we can end this real example by observing pure *Time and Price Symmetry* that is now speaking in terms of quantitative definitions of time and of price along with the qualitative eye analysis that tells us, logically, what the market is planning to do. Therefore, when all the concepts in this book are pooled together, the extreme recognition of the underlying Marketome becomes apparent, and the market matrix becomes decoded.

Before moving on, the reason I have decided to focus on this macro view is because this last bear market is widely known to the masses, and moreover, I am trying to appeal to all market participants. Therefore, this example of the macro view to trading is only one aspect of trading in time and in price, but for portfolio managers, it is the most important. In fact, this analysis is lengthy and hard for most people to do, but a portfolio manager can have these clusters and these dates calculated for an entire decade within an 8-hour workday if he or she was astute enough in understanding my words. However, therein lays the rub, and the rub is that as daytraders, we are doing this analysis every single hour of a trading day; not once per decade, and this analysis becomes tediously tiresome. For me, this analysis led to obsession and burnout, which cost me the life I expected to have. That being said, if getting rich was easy, everyone would be rich, and performing this type of quantitative and qualitative reasoning is where the interactive process becomes palpable as technical trading disciples of *Time and Price Symmetry*. The trader's ability to commit to the present moment needs of *Time and Price Symmetry* will afford the trader riches unimaginable, but in order to reach that level, there must be a sacrifice. Further, that sacrifice is what separates the boys from the men, and that is what separates the best traders from the mutual fund manager. However, with that corollary, almost everything in this book can stand in and of itself as a trading edge in every time frame and on every trading instrument, but if a trader's goals were to assure 0% losses, this type of conjoined analysis is what is necessary in the present moment. Hence, because we are human, that reality is not possible unless the trader is successful in driving all of these techniques into the subconscious because our conscious minds cannot compute these concepts fast enough, nor, can these concepts be purely defined for a computer because they require qualitative observations along with Klatch's Price Theory and Klatch's Marketome Theory.

Henceforward, I will be doing my best to find the simplest ways that we can combine time and price together in order to achieve a realistic level of efficiency that allows the trader to consistently use Price Structure and Time Structure throughout the trading day. Thus, this chapter will make the reader aware of the variety of methodologies that one can use time for with respect to trade confirmation/trade validity/price pattern affirmations. However, it will ***always*** be the trader's goal in order to understand as much as possible at every given present moment because defining price clusters and time windows even on an intraday basis is where we can recognize the potential for enormous profit possibilities, with almost no risk, which only become constrained by the market size that the trader is dealing with.

Therefore, this chapter will clearly state the most profitable trading edges that can be defined as *Time and Price Symmetry* by matching Time Repetitions and Time Cycles to all of the Price Structure Components. Once combined, the reader will finally be aware of the power of *Time and Price Symmetry,* and the conveyance of knowledge will be completed from me to the trader. At that time, the only remaining question will be the trader's willingness to sacrifice his or her life in order to attain the intrinsically learned knowledge base that will allow the subconscious mind to recognize *Time and Price Symmetry* fast enough in order to be used on an hourly basis. Or, will the trader succumb to the pressure, which means that the trader needs to accept the reality that they cannot execute on an hourly basis? If so, then I encourage the trader to accept this form of market humility, by accepting that you are too feeble minded in order to achieve this success on an hourly basis. It is not a slight, but it is simply a truthful conclusion that the trader must ask him or herself. Nevertheless, do not fret because, remember, *Time and Price Symmetry* can be executed in any time frame, and I encourage people to accept their limitations, which will allow them to work in the trading mindset defined by their inherent brilliance. Hence, you can admit your weakness and play to your strength because just think about how profitable the knowledge is if one were to just get long in July of 2009 targeting new highs over 2007! Therefore, do not feel bad if you cannot remain focused in the present moment because for you, your present moment focus may be a daily focus, which is just fine. However, regardless of what your trading aptitude is, the trader must always remain focused on the underlying Price Objectives of the market as a whole, while simultaneously, adhering to money management and risk management self-defined concepts. Lastly, it is my belief that with the conclusion of this chapter I will have conveyed to the reader the true Marketome, which means there will no longer be an outstanding question of humanity as to whether the markets are random or not. Hence, all that has to be done is to understand Quantitative Synchronicity applied to all these concepts in order to remove the last portion of mental-fog, but until the trader attains that holistic oneness, we must rely on the pure, irrefutable edges that are done as Price Pattern Affirmations in this chapter, which will work in any market, on any instrument, and in any time period. Thereby, the reader will reach my level of understanding, which avails the conclusion and the reality that the market, is indeed, not random.

Time Windows

Time Windows are the most important topic of discussion for trading in time, and I have needed to use this definition throughout the book without properly defining it beforehand, which may seem idiotic to some readers. However, I believe that the concept of a Time Window had to be placed into the subconscious mind in order for me to adequately define it for the reader. Basically, what I am saying is that I wanted the reader to come up with his or her own vision of how a Time Window works before I was to introduce a mathematical simplification, and I did this because the understanding is more important than the definition. With that said, we now need to understand Time Windows properly, and by doing so, we will realize how they are similar to mathematical clusters like those that we discussed in Price Structure.

In order to understand the importance of a Time Window, I have had to convey to the reader the ways in which time avails itself for our use through repetitions and through cycles. Thus, **Time Windows** are time/date ranges that are segregated from our Time Histogram by **both** time repetitions and time cycles, and we can now expand our definition of a Time Listing by including all Time Repetitions and Time Cycles that are used to create our Time Histogram. Further, Time Windows exist in order to allow the trader or the investor to anticipate market inflection points *based on Time*. Therefore, since Time Windows also include Time Cycle dates/times, we have to understand the power of the additive time(s), which creates a full/complete cluster of Time represented in just one Time Window. Hence, Time Windows are essentially time clusters based on the two parts of Time Structure delineated as Time Repetitions and Time Cycles. Thus, we now see the full picture, and we can now understand the full terminology with respect to time. Therefore, we understand that a Time Window is a predetermined time frame that allows us to look for a market inflection point. Furthermore, we have to understand that these Time Windows can be defined intra-day by looking at repetitions that exist as minutes, or they can be defined on yearly basis by looking at yearly repetitions, yearly cycles, the 8.6 year cycles four 2.15 year quadrants, etc. Remember, every concept in this book can expand into every time frame and for every instrument. However, unlike Price Clusters, Time Windows are **not** an average of a given time segregated histogram. In fact, that is why I choose to call these Time Windows instead of time clusters. Further, the last part that the reader must understand about the Time Window is the concept of weighted-times that may exist within the Time Window's time listing. Thus, we can now understand the range of times that yield a market inflection point, and we can understand the focal point to focus on. Let us go through an example.

For our purposes, I will walk the reader through a daily example and a yearly example that are useful in generating our Time Window. Let us assume we have some time repetitions that are occurring at the bottom of the hour in the S&P Futures for our daily example. This yields a time histogram segment that looks like this, when put in ascending order: 28,28,29,30,30,32,32,32,32,33. Again, a time histogram segment is a grouping of times that appear close together. For this example, let us say that this time histogram is grouped by using the "bottom of the hour" trading reference. Thus, going into the last hour of trading, we would use this Time Window in order to focus on the 28-33 minute time window in order to look for a market inflection point, and it is very important for the reader to understand that this Time Window must be defined in advance, which creates the trading edge. Moreover, if the market is approaching a Price Cluster, we see the combined bipartite symmetry of Time and of Price. However, the reader must not forget about weighted-times because the given Time Window also shows us that the market has made more inflection points at 32 minutes passed the hour then any other time in the Time Histogram Segment / Time Window. Because of this weighting, we now can mathematically define and conclude Time Windows by stating **Time Window Notation** as TW = T_{min} → T_{max}; T_{mode} – Thus, we can finally define a **Time Window** mathematically as well by saying that it is equal to the min to max of a given time histogram that was segregated from the total Time Listing. In addition, the definition must include the weighted times within the segregated column from the Time Histogram, which can be equated to the mathematical definition known as a **mode.** Thus, the mode of a Time Window is the most repeated times within the Time Window. Now, let us conclude this hourly example.

For the hourly example of a Time Window, our notation looks like: TW = 28 → 33; 32. Using words, we can say that this means we are looking for a Time Window between 28 and 33 minutes after the hour, and we are focusing on 32 minutes after the hour for our highest degree of certainty, *which I cannot adequately equate to probability*. (As an aside, the diminutive definition differences between Time Windows, Time Ranges, Time Lists, and Time Histograms done throughout this book are mostly interchangeable. However, the true understanding of Time comes from the ability to define Time Windows, which are represented via Time Window Notation, and again, I apologize to the reader for these circular definitions because of how complex these concepts become.)

Now, let us expand our explanation of Time Window Notation by looking at a yearly, fictitious example. Let's say we use the 8.6 year cycle to derive the low of 10/11/17 by linking the March 9, 2009 low and adding 8.6 years, and then, we use the 8.6 year cycle in order to get the date of 10/10/17 by using the April 30, 2011 high and adding 6.45 years in order to define a low. Now, the trader/investor has to go and observe other October dates of importance, and the trader will need to observe October turn dates that are repetitions through the yearly repetitions, the decennial repetitions, and the 400-year cycle. We end up with four dates after these repetitions, 8, 8, 11, 15, 17. From there, we look at the prior months inside the given year using T-12, and we find that we have relevant highs/lows for the last 12 months on dates within that window of 10, 11, 11, and 14. Now, we construct our Time Range as: 8, 8, 10, 10, 11, 11, 11, 11, 15, 17. We would define two separate time histograms from this Time Range in order to define two Time Windows. The Time Windows expressed as Time Window Notation are: (a) TW = 8 → 11; 11 and (b) TW = 15 → 17; N/A. This means that we our defining one of our Time Windows to have a 3 day window with an emphasis on the 11th day of the month, and obviously, we can filter out the weekend days as well. We also have another Time Window around the 15th and the 17th of the month to look at if we our time window defined as (a) expires. However, should either date coincided with the market being at the high or low of a given range, we can find the relevant Price Clusters in the longer-term basis that will allow us to define our market inflection point in price and in time! (As an aside, it will be exciting to see if the 8.6 year cycle becomes validated on 10/10/17 or 10/11/17 through a relevant bear market low that shares time symmetry with the 1987 low because of the intrinsic overlap!)

Focal Time Points & Time Symmetry Itself

In finding Time's usefulness, we now must summarize and focus on how to make it clearer because, as of now, we have an intersection of Time Listings from Time Repetitions and from Time Cycles that form our total Time Range. From there, we segregate the Time Range into various Time Histograms, and we construct the Time Window based on this data whereby the repetitive dates or the intersected dates are useful in finding our mode. This usefulness was also equated to a weighted-time as was introduced at the onset of Time Structure. However, something is missing from the Time Window that requires the qualitative eye. Therefore, we must expand our quantitative mind into a logical, humanistic approach that will rely on our subconscious servomechanisms in order to create points that give us a "feeling" of *when* the market will inflect, and one could even say this is a "sixth sense" approach. However, I would not acquiesce to that conclusion. No, I would say it in the subconscious mind recognizing the upcoming market inflection point, and it is sharing that information to us via a "feeling." Thus, we must continue our understanding of Time Structure by realizing that sometimes our "gut feeling" is actually justified, and we can find that "gut feeling" by this discussion of Focal Time Points. A **Focal Time Point** is a labeled time on a chart that we are giving a higher reference too based on observation not repetition (the qualitative eye) and *the forthcoming discussions about trading in time will be an elaboration of Focal Time Points*, which is not an obvious conclusion until one observes the Figures illustrated to the reader in this chapter. For this reason, a Focal Time Point becomes the second basis of combining Price Structure with Time Structure, and the Focal Time Points are helpful when we are looking at Price Structure Components.

Thus, the trader's ability to focus on the true Focal Time Points reveals to the trader the internal belief that the market will avail to our subconscious a regularity that occurs by the *active* observation and by the active understanding of Time Structure patterns. Further, the most important Price Structure pattern is the range itself derived from Klatch's Price Theory, and when that combines with Time Structure patterns, we sometimes get this "gut feeling," which an finally be described as Time Symmetry. Therefore, **Time Symmetry** is now defined as the minds' conscious and subconscious recognition of repeated patterns that hold quantitative and qualitative relevance within the fabric of the market's time itself. For example, we can observe that if the low of the range occurred at 10 minutes after the hour, the market will have a proclivity to create subsequent lows at 10 minutes after the hour, which is a Focal Time Point that is observed with our qualitative eye. In fact, all of the trading in time concepts in this chapter are based on Focal Time Points rather than the Time Histogram, but both are of equal importance. What is more, we can also equate Focal Time Points to Time Repetitions if we were to observe that the market has a repetitive Time Window at 10 minutes after the hour as shown in our Time Window definition. In effect, we are observing the market's tendency to create symmetry that exists within our human minds as well as within the market itself, and we can combine these qualitative time "feelings" with Time Windows defined from repetitions and cycles in order for us to have the full belief in true Time Symmetry. Therefore, we get to the crux of the problem with Time because we are now defining Focal Time Points based on historic, mental feedback along with historic market feedback (repetitions of the past), future calculations (cyclic futures), and human observation/intuition (the present moment). However, do not be despaired because this observation/intuition is teachable, which is why *Time and Price Symmetry* requires 10,000+ hours of observation because, just like Bayes' Theorem quantified the hunch, we can use our hunch to quantify Time.

Time = Terminal Price or Time = Retracement or Time = Volatility-Move

Because of how time acts like a muscle memory in the market, we may have a time anniversary/repetition or time cycle that occurs after the terminal high/low is made in the markets. As such, if we use a swing as an example, the time window that is in play could be useful in order to call the higher bottom or the lower top, which is essentially the deep retracement move. In addition, we may see a volatility spike that avails itself at a time window, but the market may have already started to make its move. As such, time becomes more like an interpretive art to the avid watcher because we can look at how time windows can clue us into the future direction of price action just as Leonardo DaVinci was trying to clue us into his beliefs through his painting of The Last Supper. Thus, the reader should not be under the belief that Time is interpretive, and the purpose of this chapter is to avail the reader's mind to Focal Time Points that occur *with* Price Structure Components, and again, all of the Figures in this Chapter are useful for observing this concept. As such, we must remember that Time-based market inflection points do not need to occur at discreets, but they can occur at any point, which means all the trader has to do is observe an inflection point in a smaller time frame during the Time Window.

In order to emphasize a real-life example of where Time requires interpretation is in a way that is not obvious in 2011, and I use the word "interpretation" in order to describe this example because one must interpret the market and not the Time Window. The reason for this is simple, and that simplicity exists because of the fact that the Time Window has been defined by the market already. However, what is not clear is that the Time Window is actually in play. Let us get to the example to clarify.

As we know, the 8.6 year cycle provided a specific component that was factored into the Time Window that precisely called the market's April 30, 2011 high. However, the Bradley Cycle provided us with the time window for our end of July high, which resulted in a deep retracement of the April high. This time window opened in late July not at our terminal high, but instead, it opened at our finishing move of our retracement. Moreover, the large spike moves that occurred afterward triggered our price awareness as to how the time window was in play. We already touched on this volatility/muscle memory by observing the market's memory of March 6, 2009 by the large down day that orchestrated on March 6, 2012, and therein lies the realization that Time Windows always require market-based interpretation.

Paired Index Time Structure

One of the hardest parts about Time Structure is that, occasionally, another market's underlying Time Repetition or Time Cycle could have an influence on the market we are trading. However, throughout this book, I have cautioned the reader against using another market in order to trade against your major focus area. For example, I have cautioned against using the Dow in order to trade against the NASDAQ. However, I need to bring the reader's mind to the logical conclusion that some markets do have impacts on others, and I believe this is for two reasons: (A) shared components and (B) human tendencies. Thus, we find a correlation between markets, and not just markets, but entire countries, which should also be obvious. This concept is now defined as Paired Index Time Structure, which builds on top of our last section. **Paired Index Time Structure** is the interpretive observation that another market is adhering to our primary market's Time Window in a manner whereby *the other market is inflecting at a new discreet, which tells us that our market has also reached an inflection point that is not as obvious to the trader as is occurring in the other market.* In order to elaborate on this concept, I will go through to real examples for the reader, and our first example will be correlated with the introduction of this chapter by continuing with the March 2009 bear market low.

So far, we know that the S&P 500 Futures achieved *Time and Price Symmetry* in March of 2009 based on Time Windows and a mathematical support cluster. However, what we did not see is a clear indication of Klatch's Price Theory at the low, which meant that we were waiting for the confirmation of the swing in order to invoke Klatch's Marketome Theory that told us to expect new highs over the last bull market's high. However, if one were to pull up the chart of the New York Stock Exchange ("NYSE") composite index, one would find that the low in March 2009 on the NSYE was a perfect Double Bottom! Therefore, since we had *Time and Price Symmetry* in the NYSE, we can understand and we can apply this knowledge to our primary trading market, the S&P. So, the question the reader asks is, "How?" Simple. All that is required is to realize that the NYSE must first adhere to Klatch's Price Theory, which states that the Price Objective is now to take out new highs! Hence, the NYSE was able to simultaneously invoke Klatch's Marketome theory instantly because Klatch's Price Theory and Klatch's Marketome Theory had the same objective. On the other hand, if we only focused on the S&P we had to wait for another five months before understanding that Klatch's Marketome Theory is in play because Klatch's Price Theory is in play! Therefore, we need to be aware of the power of paired indices if we are index traders, and if we are not index traders, then we have to be aware of something else. If our trading instrument is listed *in* an index (for example, Apple is listed in the NASDAQ Composite and the NASDAQ 100), well, it is a good idea to see if either of those composite indices are adhering to cleaner *Time and Price Symmetry*. Now, the word "cleaner" can be somewhat circumspect because it is inferring an element of randomness, which I do not mean to infer. However, what I am inferring is that the composite market (being a composite) is summing together all Price Objectives and all Price Pattern Objectives along with all Time Windows into a composite as well! This means that we may be able to invoke Klatch's Price Theory or Klatch's Marketome Theory earlier in order to understand if our trading instrument is also going to acquiesce to these *Time and Price Symmetry* turns due to mass-market influence. With the longer-term example finished, I want to get to a more recent non-obvious example, which is quite illustrative of the paired index concept, and in order to do this illustration, let us look at 2012's market.

In March and April of 2012, the DOW and the S&P found relevant tops that led to a 1000-point decline in the DOW. On the S&P 500 Cash Chart (not the Futures chart), there was a perfect three drives to a top pattern that occurred in late march/early April. This led to an initial sell off, but then, the S&P rallied to an 87.5% retracement, and Klatch's Price Theory kicked in, which made the low of that range the intended target, which happened to be breached towards the end of May. The date of this 87.5% retracement was within the April 30th Time Window that was a repetition from the year prior's 8.6 Year Time Cycle (cyclic echoes will be defined in this chapter as well). Moreover, April 30th corresponds to a half-season tendency, which afforded even more Time Symmetry with the April 30th one year repetition from the year earlier. Now, I ask the reader to please notice that, in the last section, I stated that "Time = Retracement," which means that, when the Time Window kicked-in, the S&P was not at a new high, but the DOW was; or was it? In fact, although the DOW achieved its Price Theory Price Objective of new highs, this new high was infinitesimal, and in fact, the DOW ended up with an absolutely stunning example of a perfect double top that had Time Symmetry! Hence, we uncover the paired index time structure because what becomes hard is the fact that Price Theory failed in the S&P Index, because it was targeting new highs, but instead, we must observe that Price Theory succeeded in the DOW. Thus, we can find the benefit of Time Structure similar to the NYSE example from earlier because this time, the DOW was the foreshadower of a massive sell off in order to target new lows, and if one were to realize this because of Time Symmetry, the trader would be able to ascertain that the 87.5%R was real, which meant Price Theory was predicting a swing that would take out the low, which again, occurred in May of 2012!

There is only one last thing that must be mentioned with respect to this section and that is currency. In the currency markets, by their definition, we must realize that we are trading a "pair." As such, I caution a Forex trader to not think that the other side of the trade is the same as a paired index, because, in theory, the values should be equal. What is more, I do not feel that currencies share time symmetry, and when they do, I classify that as illusory.

Date Oriented Time and Price Symmetry

Part of trading in time is to also look for certain price levels that may have importance based on the time when those price levels were initially formed. These are quite simple to see, and we already lightly touched on this earlier in Chapter 18. However, it must be emphasized further with regards to trading in time because there is an additive probability that gets applied to these price levels.

The price levels that are achieved as the high and low of a given month or the high and low of a given year are very important. Monthly, these time levels tend to only be relevant by looking back to the high or low of the previous month. However, on yearly charts, the high and low of a prior year can be utilized as far back as possible unless those highs and lows have been penetrated already. This penetration rule also applies monthly. For example, if we look back to the previous month, and if we have already taken the previous month's high out, then it is irrelevant. Furthermore, these high or lows based on monthly or yearly high/lows are areas that retracements can be drawn from, which can add into our cluster calculations. To sum up this section, I must state that if one can find a time and price window based on a previous month or a previous year (multiple years) whereby that price and time window is hit on either the same day (for month) or on the exact same date, then, we reach a high probability time window that can be traded with extreme confidence.

What an astute reader of this book should know be asking is, "Why does the market target these monthly/yearly dates?" Well, this too is easily answerable, and the answer is The Inside Bar Rule. Even though we may be looking at highs/lows from month to month or year to year, we must remember that these are still "bars." It doesn't matter if these are 1 minute bars or 1 year bars, and once the trader realizes that the market has an objective to take out its previous bar, we find the reason that the market targets these values. However, all I am trying to get across to the reader is that the dates of the prior month or the prior years high hold more weight if they appear within our Time Window, but again, I do not believe I can correlate this observation with any type of strict probability.

Cyclic Echoes & Phasing

In our paired index time structure examples, we touched on the fact that the April 30, 2012 high that coupled with a perfect double top in the Dow was a Time Repetition of the high of 2011. What is more, using the last section I noted that the date of that 2011 high was very much valid in 2012 because it had more weight within our Time Window. However, what we are also observing is 2012 is that, although the 2012 high is a Time Repetition, the Time Repetition was caused by a Time cycle, and this interrelation is defined as Cyclic Echoes. Thus, a **Cyclic Echo** is a Time Repetition that is borne from a Time Cycle. Furthermore, that assertion should make obvious, logical sense because, if a Time Cycle causes a market inflection point, then, Time Repetitions should have that Time Cycle's inflection point recorded within the Time Histogram.

Now, there is something that is unique to Cyclic Echoes that are on a longer-term chart, and I must outline this unique concept as a bridge between Cyclic Echoes and phased repetition. If one were to recall he Rule of Alternation, we must understand that, in a way, the Rule of Alternation is phasing certain industries in and out, which means that it, essentially, is a Time Cycle that manifests itself through the fabric of time. As I mentioned already, we know that in the bull market of 2002-2007, we saw that oil went higher and that oil stocks/commodity stocks went higher. Now though, we are in a new bull market where these stocks have little relevance; in fact, they will stay range bound until the next bear market completes, unless of course, there is massive inflation. Sure, one can take hypothetical guesses that this is occurring because of all the "fracking" of "oil shale" that is going to lead to massive United States output, which will drive down prices, or one can see that the peak oil theory was wrong. Obviously, the fundamental excuses for why this is occurring are numerous, but by simply utilizing the concepts in this book, we can see the technical nature of "Why." We can see the rule of alternation foreshadowing the movement of these oil stocks to stay range bound; we can see that oil's impact on the stock market is minimized for this bull market; we can see that time cycles gave us the first clue as to major inflection points; and, we can see that time repetitions are causing cyclic echoes to emerge into our trading. Remember, everything in this book is interconnected, and the ethereal practice of incorporating everything that I have written thus far truly requires monumental intelligence aptitudes in order to properly weave the fabric of the markets; the truth of what is really happening and why. Hence, we must realize that the Rule of Alternation contains a vast Time List that becomes phased back in as echoes when the market starts to rally, and this is the takeaway form this entire paragraph. Therefore, let me illustrate this concept as a fictitious example.

Let us suppose that we are currently in a very strong bull market, but on a percentage basis, we see that other industries, like technology, have gone up much higher than the oil industry. Further, let us say that this bull market terminates in October of 2017. After October of 2017, we see a bear market form, which interestingly enough, has a low form in March of 2019 as a decennial Time Repetition. However, for this "new" bull market, we can now believe that the oil stocks/commodity stocks are back in play. Therefore, we can look at the dates that were relevant for these stocks during the last bull market they participated in which would have been the 2002 to 2007 bull market, and we can "phase" these dates back in as part of our Time Cycle turn dates! What is more, we can get a second listing of dates by using the concept of Time Shift. In essence, we would be overlaying the inflection point data from the 2002-2007 bull market to the start date of the new 2019-bull market in order to measure the days from the bull market start to the inflection point. Contrary to what the reader may be thinking at this present moment, if this is done correctly, you should only see about two dates per year per stock that are ascertained from this analysis; not 20 or 30. Now, dear reader, you get to the extent of my Marketome analysis because, what should be apparent is that these two derivations are esoteric, unobvious, and seemingly random, but I assure you, they are not. In fact, if you do not believe me, please go and look up a chart of Apple Stock's last bull market run, and then, overlay that chart using Time Shift, and also, pick out the Major Market Inflection Points based on the exact day, month, year, which must be overlaid as well. Once done, you will be shocked, amazed, flabbergasted, and speechless.

The last thing that must be mentioned about finding cycles based on repetitions is regarding the concept of Phased Repetitions, which were discussed in the last chapter. When we observe a repetition that starts to act like a Cycle (I.e. every other month the market is making a high on the 2nd day of the month instead of doing it every month), we can start to find patterns within that repetition by thinking it is a cycle in and of itself. However, it is more elaborate than that conclusion because it is not a cycle, and we have to realize that <u>the phased repetition is actually a weak repetition</u>. In fact, had I not mentioned this to the reader, I believe that the reader would have thought that this type of phasing in and out was a strong indication of the phased repetition's validity. No, it is the exact obvious. As such, the observation is two-fold. First, if we have seen two repetitions that have a cyclic basis (as in appearing every other month), we can say that we still have a repetition, but it too is not easily labeled in our Time Window. However, that repetition is intrinsically weaker because it is not occurring regularly. As such, we make an observation that the cyclic tendency of the repetition *can phase out completely* after occurring two or three times. Therefore, in a way, a Time Repetitions that is phasing in and out should be thought of like an incorrectly drawn trendline, because as I stated with respect to incorrectly drawn trendlines, they have a tendency to break after the third touch of the line, and I encourage the time-based trader to realize the frailty of trying to find patterns within cycles/repetitions because by my definition explained herein, the mathematical mind excursion that has the purpose to replicate my work by attempting to find patterns within repetitions is a failing objective because those patterns within the repetitions are a signal that the relevant time repetition is about to be phased out, which is why the PhD-like market insight is doomed to fail, because they never take into account the need for the Qualitative Eye. (Even so, these phased repetitions are still quantitatively valid within a Time Window notation.)

Thus, we come to the root of why the educated masses fail in their understanding of Time Symmetry because they cannot believe it is this simple. Therefore, the reader should know that the underlying, ulterior motive the market has is to *always* engage in the continual purpose of mind-screwing the higher intellect, who feels superior to the market, and I enjoy this market objective because it is a beautiful thing that I contain within my brain, which is that I can look at a chart and see every pattern in its true simplicity. Therefore, the market has a human like characteristic in my eyes of being a true ironist in and of itself, and if you don't believe me, take a look at the beautiful double bottom in the 10-year treasury, then the beautiful double top, and then the beautiful double bottom that occurred in 2012. It was all so breathtakingly easy, but how many people appear on TV squawking about fundamentals and the fed and all that other bullcrap. Hence, although I am somewhat slighting myself by stating that I know how easy the market is to the uneducated, the reality is that if we were to look back on most of the successful traders that lived before the advent of computers, the person would find that the best traders were the ones who never even went to high school. The best traders, before computers, were the ones that were just thrown into the market pits, which allowed them to build their intrinsic knowledge base, which ultimately, coupled with their "gut feeling" as to the "when" in the question, "When is it time to get in/out?" See, the uneducated trader back then did not care why the market did this as do today's money managers. No, the uneducated trader cared about making money, and nothing else. Hence, they did not question the simplicity, and they just observed it unconsciously, which allowed them to accept it for what it was worth. Ergo, we realize the truth of the market, which is that the market is made for simplicity because nature's mathematics are simple, and in fact, everything becomes simple, in hindsight, once it is adequately laid out to the masses, which was the purpose of me writing this book. Thus, the uneducated traders of yesteryear were not tainted by the educated mass's conclusions on idiotic market theories/economic theories/portfolio theories, and the like. Therefore, I humbly ask the higher intellects to be aware of the fact that we, as humans, are trying to make this trading experience more complicated than it needs to be because we are becoming prideful and God-like by creating our own formulae that makes no sense. But, the truth is we must acknowledge and fight the erroneous assertion in our mind that is saying that, "Time Structure cannot be this simple!"

Moving on, in order to conclude this discussion on Phased Repetitions, we must draw a difference between phased repetitions that are skipping certain intervals (i.e. every other month or every third month) versus Time Repetitions that are occurring every month. As the reader needs to understand, these are two separate scenarios, and repetitions that occur every month or even every hour can lead to intrinsic conclusions in and of themselves as we discussed already in our discussion of using time in order to indicate trend changes. Ergo, we must now take this a step farther by using all of the esoteric concepts about time before we can move onto discussing Price Pattern Components that can be reinforced with Time Structure in order to arrive at pure *Time and Price Symmetry*.

Inflecting Time / Patterned Time & Time Trending

As a segue into this discussion, I ask the reader to recall all of the theory (quantitatively and qualitatively) that was discussed in Chapter 9 regarding the understanding of the underlying market trend. In Chapter 9, I stated that the trend relies on the use of the Price Structure Component that I defined as "swings" in order to define trend quantitatively because, by pure observation, for a trend to be up, price action must move higher (again, simplicity in market logic is all that is required). However, before this uptrend is defined by the market's price discovery process, we can often see that Time itself can lead us to conclude that the underlying market's trend has changed before price has, which makes this one of the most powerful concepts of this entire book while simultaneously being one of the hardest concepts for the reader to grasp because this is not obvious nor is this simple. Therefore, for those PhD inclined minds, I am appealing to your ego after deflating it so harshly in the last section. That being said, as with everything else, it only requires a simple mental shift in our awareness in order to yield extreme profit through an extreme trading edge. Thus, we arrive at a new definition that I will call Time Window Inflections. A Time Window Inflection is something that occurs within the Time Window itself, but it must be coupled with Price Structure, which makes this section of the book an excellent bridge between esoteric time concepts and Price Pattern Affirmations / reinforcements. Thus, we can define a **Time Window Inflection** as a change in the pattern of a Time Repetition from calling a high to a low or vice versa. Further, a Time Window Inflection can be used in order to define **Patterned Time**, and Patterned Time is defined as a listing of Time Window Inflections that correspond to conclusions of the next Time Window Inflection. Consequently, we get a very hard circuitous definition to understand, and I will do my best in order to convey this subject to the reader. But before I do, we need to understand how to label time in order to pattern time, which should make simplistic sense. What is more, thankfully, this too is easy, and our labeling refers back to our discussion that stated that Time does not have to occur at discreets, but it may occur at other terminal points that are not as obvious. Hence, we can now define four letters needed in order to label time patterns that allow us to view Patterned Time. This labeling system is also easy, and it is shown as; 'H' means High. 'L' means Low. 'D' means Discreet. 'S' means Secondary. Therefore, we have four combinations of these definitions that are used for listing our Patterned Time. Concurrently, these four letter derived definitions must be placed together in order to define composite terms from this simplistic 2x2 matrix. These composite terms are: HD, HS, LD, and LS. With that nomenclature defined, let us begin with a simple example in order to emphasize Time Window Inflections coupled with an example of Patterned Time. This is shown in Figure 20.1.

Figure 20.1: Time Window Inflections

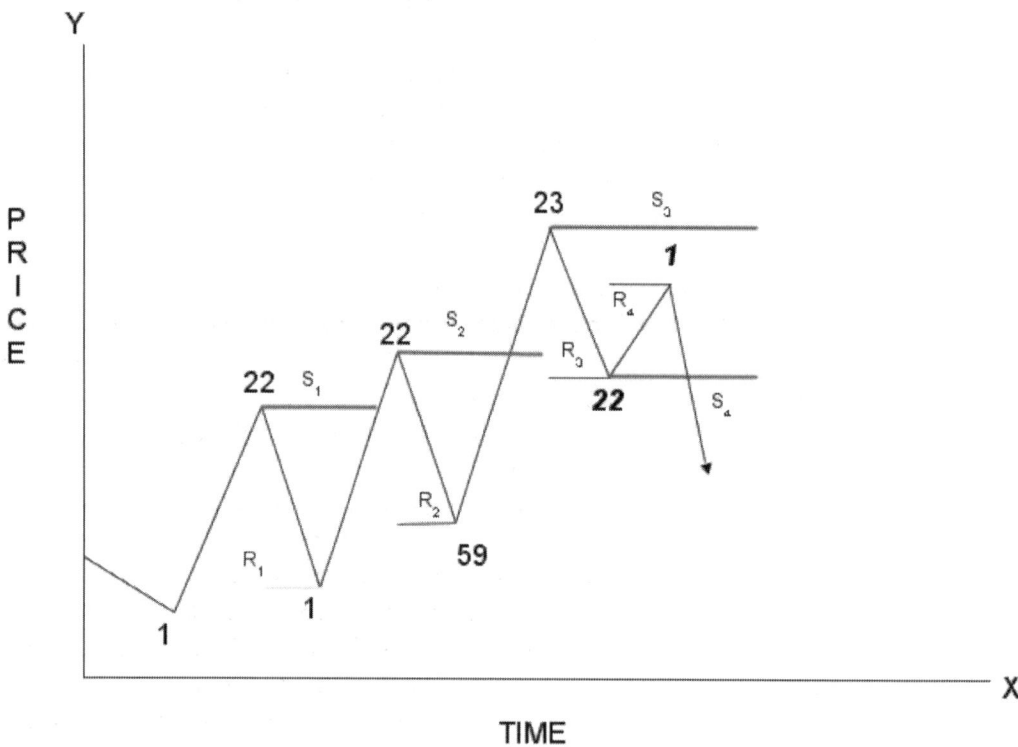

Let us assume that we have a market making highs on an hourly basis, which we see as three higher swings in Figure 20.1. We observe that we have had discreet highs occurring at 22 or 23 minutes after the hour for the last three hours, which means we have TW = 22 → 23; 22. However, in our fourth hour observation, we observe that our Time Window is in play, but it **did not** occur at the high. Instead, it occurred at the retracement low, and we can say that this Time Window has now "inflected." However, the Time Window definition itself has not changed, and it would still appear as TW = 22 → 23; 22. Thus, we get no information about future patterns within the Time Window without using the Patterned Time combinations. (This is done on purpose because Patterned Times require a lot of mental energy, and if we are trading intraday, we do not have the luxury to engage in this analysis.) However, before getting farther, let us continue with this new example in order for the reader to understand this concept. Therefore, we can now visualize and summarize what we observed in order to see the Time Window Inflection.

We have had three highs at 22, 22, 23, and then, we have a retracement low at 22, which is adequately shown in Figure 20.1. The retracement low is defined as a 38.2%R at R_3. Therefore, because our Time Window has inflected from calling highs to calling a low, we can now be skeptical of the trend, and we can redefine our Time Window by a Patterned Time List. A **Patterned Time List** is defined as a listing of times that contain an intrinsic pattern that can be useful in understanding future locations for market inflections. Therefore, our Patterned Time List would look like this: HD, HD, HD, LS. Hence, we see the inflection from calling a high to calling a low (or a retracement) using the *same* Time Window. Therefore, this changes our perspective on the future, and this can clue us in on a Price Theory failure, which is what indeed does happen in this example. Thus, we can observe that after we saw this low form at 22 minutes after our fourth hour, we would be blindly targeting new highs outside of the range using Price Theory only, and this leads to the incredible power of *Time and Price Symmetry,* when properly implemented. What is more, I believe this observation also falls under Quantitative Synchronicity, because it is something that the mind must synchronize in order to get a subconscious intuitive recognition that something has "changed" in the market. Thus, even before a swing generates, our mind must subconsciously avail to us this "change," which means that we should be wary of this Price Objective based on this Time Window Inflection. In fact, what will now happen is that we must focus on our next Time Window (if it exists), and we must observe the reality that our next Time Window may be calling a lower top, which indicates that the LS at 22 minutes after (our inflected time point) becomes the market's Price Objective based on Price Theory! Remember, Price Theory will never fail us, but we must live in the present moment in order to shift the markets' current Price Objective.

For the sake of argument, let us say that this is what happens, as we can see in Figure 20.1, and that for this market, we now see that the market has simply made a deep retracement of the third HD at time 23 minutes after hour three. Thus, if we were to assume that another Time Window exist, again as it does in Figure 20.1, such that TW = 59 → 1; 1 with a corresponding Patterned Time List defined as LS, LS, LS, we can assume, but not be confident, that we may have an HS (or HD) form. (As an aside, I say 'or HD' in parenthesis in that last sentence because it is more likely that since the LS came from an HD that the HD would replace the LS in the other Patterned Time List, which would make the original Price Objective hold true as well.) Moving on, again, for sake of argument, let us say that this does indeed happen, which means that the retracement low, the LS, failed to take out a new high, and our other Time Window called a lower top at 1 minute after the hour, which now allows the market to have a Price Theory Price Objective in order to take out the low that occurred as the LD, which is also a swing labeled S_4. When this happens, we can see that we had two Time Windows inflect, and we can also see that the Time Window Inflection clued us in to the fact that the market was getting ready to change its trend, before it generated a swing to do so! Therein lays the amazing conclusive importance of this concept because Time is calling a market trend change *before* a qualified swing forms and/or executes, and what is more, this often happens on monthly charts, which means that this concept is one of the most extreme edges that exists. Hence, we reach a priceless esoteric conclusion from Time Window Inflections and Patterned Time Lists by Figure 20.1 because before Price Structure/Price Theory activated, we were able to observe that the Patterned Time inside of Time Window one allowed us to recognize an upcoming Patterned Time in Time Window 2. Therefore, we can conclude our usage of Figure 36.0 by observing that the HS called by our second window was simply a deep retracement defined as R_4, which means that we are now going to target a new low, which adheres and activates quantitative trend change criterion. (As an aside, if we notice a Time Window Inflection, it is helpful to label these times the same way, but to make them italicized for us to be made aware that something is changing within the Marketome itself. This italicizing is done in Figure 36.0 as well.)

As stated, on our monthly charts, this is extremely powerful, and because of how much present moment awareness we need as a daytrader, finding Patterned Time is sometimes counterproductive because it takes qualitative brainpower that may not be available to us since we are focusing on the market. In fact, this is why I am repeating myself in this paragraph, because I must emphasize the mental exercises that are requires this to be successful. Hence, we find that Time Window Inflections and Patterned Time Lists become more powerful trading edges as we go out longer in time, and this "power" is human derived and not market derived. For example, if our monthly chart has a Time Window defined as TW = 1 → 3;

2, which have all been lows, and then, we see a high on the 2nd day of the month, we can infer that the trend may be ready to change to the upside, and that will be confirmed with qualified swings! Hence, Time Window Inflections are very powerful tendencies of Time, and their importance cannot be understated.

The last thing that must be discussed before moving on is Patterned Time itself because it is broken down into two areas of study. First, we can find Time Windows that are conjoined, which we saw in our Figure 20.1 example. However, this is a rarity, and I call this a rarity because we used one Time Window's Patterned Time List in order to call a pattern time in another Time Window that was conjoined, but in the real world, this is minimally observed. Therefore, it is much more common that we will be focusing on a Time Window's Patterned Time List itself in order to observe changing changes in Patterned Time within that Patterned Time List. Again, let us acquiesce to an example.

Suppose that we have a given Time Window that generates the following Patterned Time List on a monthly chart: HD, HD, LD, LD, HD, HD. What is our next conclusion from the Patterned Time List? Well, it is easy; we can observe that at our next Time Window reoccurrence, we should be targeting a low of some type instead of a High. However, this low does not have to be a discreet in order for this Time Window to have an inflection. Hence, we can understand that using Time Window Inflections along with understanding the Patterned Time observed in the Patterned Time List, we find that the inflection is simply telling us to look for the opposite regardless of discreet/secondary. However, it is useful for us to list these discreet/secondary values in the Time List because they are useful in understanding if we are seeing one last conclusive inflection from Time Window Inflection, which is that we may go from a Discreet Time Window to a Secondary Time Window, which is defined in and of itself.

To conclude, let us use a real-life example that I was able to get my hands on, which is the Dow Jones Utility Index from March to September of 2012. In this Index, we can generate our Time Window, which shows us that, towards the beginning of the month, we have a market inflection point. What is more, some of these market inflection points are discreets and some are secondary. Some are highs and some are lows, and if we were to write the Patterned Time List for this Time Window, we find: HD, HD, L**S**, LS, H**S**, LS, LS. Thus, we need a highly pattern recognizing mind in order to understand what this Patterned Time List is indicating for the inflection point predicted for the first week in October. Hence, we must look at the inflections within the Patterned Time List. First, we observe that the market has gone from Discreets to Secondary, and that pattern has not changed. What is more we observe that we have two highs, two lows, and one high, and now, two lows. Hence, we can make a reasonable assumption that the next inflection point will be a high, and most likely, it will be a secondary high. However, we do not know explicitly what this will be, but it does help us massively in understanding the indices Price Theory Price Objectives should that high form the next time this Time Window is open. That being said, we can now get out of the qualitative realm of Time Structure, and finally bring Price Structure and Time Structure together in *Time and Price Symmetry* for the explicit Price Structure Components defined in this book.

Retracements

These next set of topics that will conclude Time Structure are based on true *Time and Price Symmetry*. Therefore, we can now observe that Price Structure Components can be fully *reinforced* by Time, which concludes the true Marketome. In order to stay aligned with the way I presented Price Structure to the reader, we will begin with how we can use time in order to confirm retracement holds. As always, these concepts will work as well on the intra-day chart for day-traders as they will on the daily chart for investors. In order to understand how time can work for our benefit with price structure components, all we need to do is have our Time Windows properly defined through histograms that we have summed into Time Windows on our charts, which have been labeled in Time Cluster Notation.

In order to provide a trader with confirmation of a retracement hold, ***all we need to do is observe a Time Window that occurs when our market enters a retracement / a retracement cluster.*** Since we know even micro-swings can provide price pattern objectives that couple with even small retracements, we can utilize time windows and price clusters with minimal inputs.

One of the most common things that we observe for retracement holds comes from our knowledge of Focal Time Points. For example, if our low of the day occurred at 22 minutes after the hour, we would continue to look for retracements holding at 22 minutes after the hour. (Conversely, we can use Focal Time Points in order to understand that a major price cluster that is calling a high at 22 minutes after the hour has more power, which has already been defined in Focal Time Points, but is repeated as an example here for the reader.)

Purchasing/selling retracements at time windows is the absolute best way to trade in time. If we can define a retracement price cluster that occurs at a valid time window, we can take a trade that targets new highs outside of the range based on Price Theory. Nearly all of my personal trading is focused on buying/selling retracement values/clusters, and this is the absolute best strategy in this book because it can always provide extremely favorable reward to risk trade setups when coupled with Price Theory. Moving on…

Double Tops / Double Bottoms

The reader may be shocked at the easiness of understanding time with these powerful price patterns, but please allow your mind to accept the reality of this easiness. The easiest way to determine if a Double Bottom/Double Top is *valid is if the time of the second high/low is equal to the first, or if the time for the second high/low is equal to the high/low between the two tops/bottoms*. Basically, we see that time gives us two inputs, which can be validated by one output. The first two inputs are the first high/low and then the low/high that leads to a retest of the original high/low. If the time of one of the first two is equal to the third, we have a high probability scenario for a true double top, and amazingly this is interrelated with Inflected Time, as we can observe in Figure 20.2.

Figure 20.2: Double Bottom/Top with Time

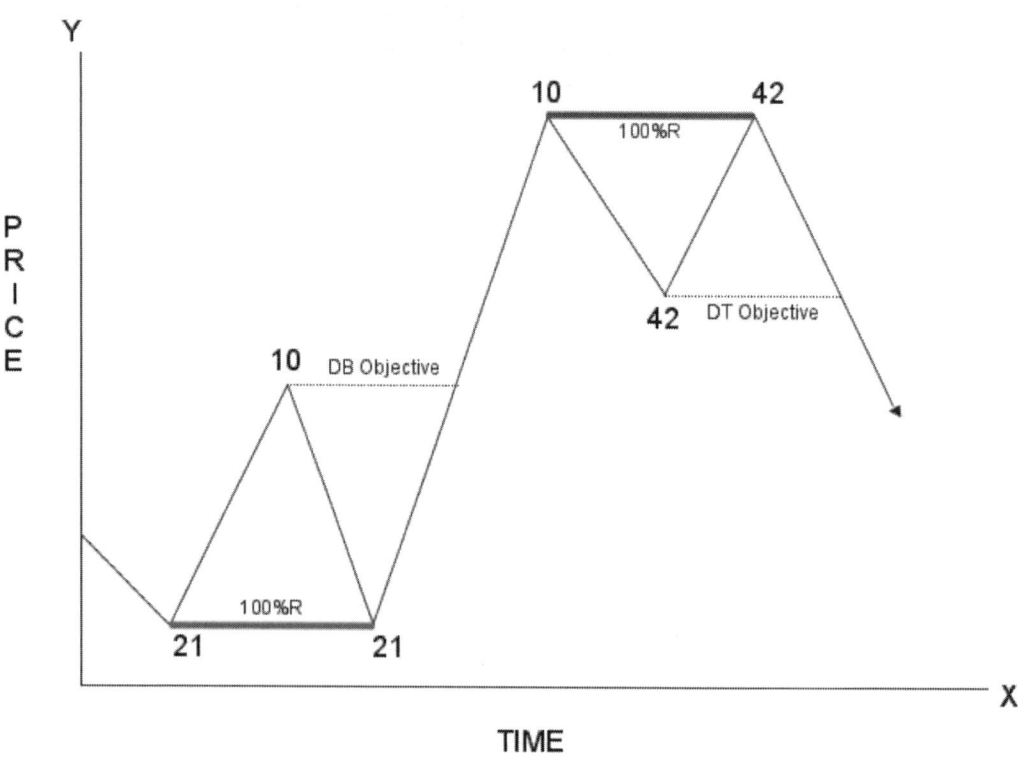

In Figure 20.2, we are again looking at the Double top/Double Bottom objective figure from earlier, but now, we are labeling the two ways that we can increase our probability for a true double top/double bottom. As such, this example in Figure 20.2 is shown with respect to intra-day traders who are using minutes to trade, but the same thing applies in any time frame (for example, these times can just as easily be dates, but obviously, there is not 42 days in a month).

This method of using time in order to predict large moves is amazing when we look at stocks as well as commodities. Remember, everything that applies in one time frame applies in another. So, if we are looking at stocks in regards to equity holdings in our portfolio, we may decide to look for positions that can be held for a year or so. In this case, we could look for double tops/bottoms occurring exactly one year apart on a yearly scale. For example, we have a perfect double top TO THE DAY in the stock FCX in December of 2009 to December of 2010, but we must remember that his is real-life example is counter-trend to the overall market's bull market (recall the story of *The Turkey*).

Repetitive Tops / Repetitive Bottoms & Clusters

In our discussion of tape reading, I had to discuss certain situations that are born from multiple retests of a given high or low. In that section, I stated that the probability of an RB/RT holding is very rare, and that the market's tendency is to satisfy Price Objectives based on Price Theory, which typically caused the RB/RT to fail. However, I also stated that an RB/RT that holds is an extremely powerful pattern to the market, which leads to massive follow-through as discussed on the day of the flash crash in May of 2010. Therefore, there are two ways that time can be used in order to assist us in using these price structure components.

First, since I stated that we can think of RB/RTs as just double tops/bottoms by focusing on the last two tops or bottoms, well, that logic does not apply the same way to time. Thus, I need to illustrate the difference with an easy example, and I do this via Figure 20.3.

Figure 20.3: Triple Top / Triple Repetitive Top With Time

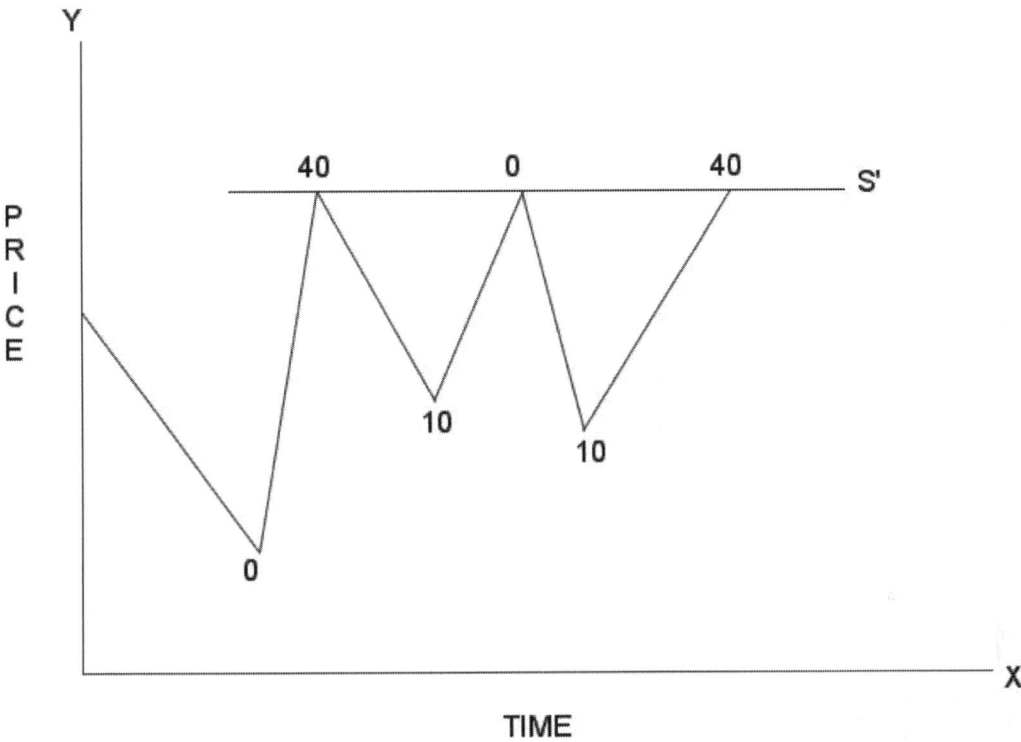

In Figure 20.3, the reader should see the triple top that we discussed in Price Structure, but we have now replaced the points with the time that the high/low was made. This is where the difference comes in. If we look at the repetitive triple top, we can see that the first top now has validity instead of just the last two. In Price Structure, we said that these last two tops are relevant in terms of swing projections if the top was to fail, or if it was to hold, we said that the last low between the last two tops was the price objective. That remains true, but what changes when we add in time is that we can now see that the time value that created the first top at 40 minutes after the hour is the same value that created the last top at 40 minutes after the hour. Thus, we have greater confidence that this triple top is real. Concurrently, if that third top occurred at 0 or 10 minutes after the hour, we would still have more confidence in the trade because that occurrence is still classified as a time repetition. I feel this is an important distinction that must be stated and understood by the trader, and I encourage the trader to reread this text if there is anything left missing.

 The second discussion regarding RB/RTs will also serve as an adequate discussion to mathematical clusters. I say this because mathematical clusters at retracements or at projections have already been covered by Time Structure thus far (and they are also vaguely mentioned in retracements), and I believe it is an obvious realization that has already been conferred to the reader that *the entire goal of Time and Price Symmetry is to have a market hit a cluster average at a time cycle or time repetition, which leads to a market inflection point.* Moving forward, if the reader can recall from our RB/RT discussion in Price Structure, I stated that it is often a tendency that a market that is retesting a high/low many times tends to break that price pattern, and then, reach a primary retracement or mathematical cluster, which causes an immediate reversal. Therefore, we can use time in order to help us with these reversals as well. As such, I have to refer to figure 20.4.

Figure 20.4: Cluster Time Reversal

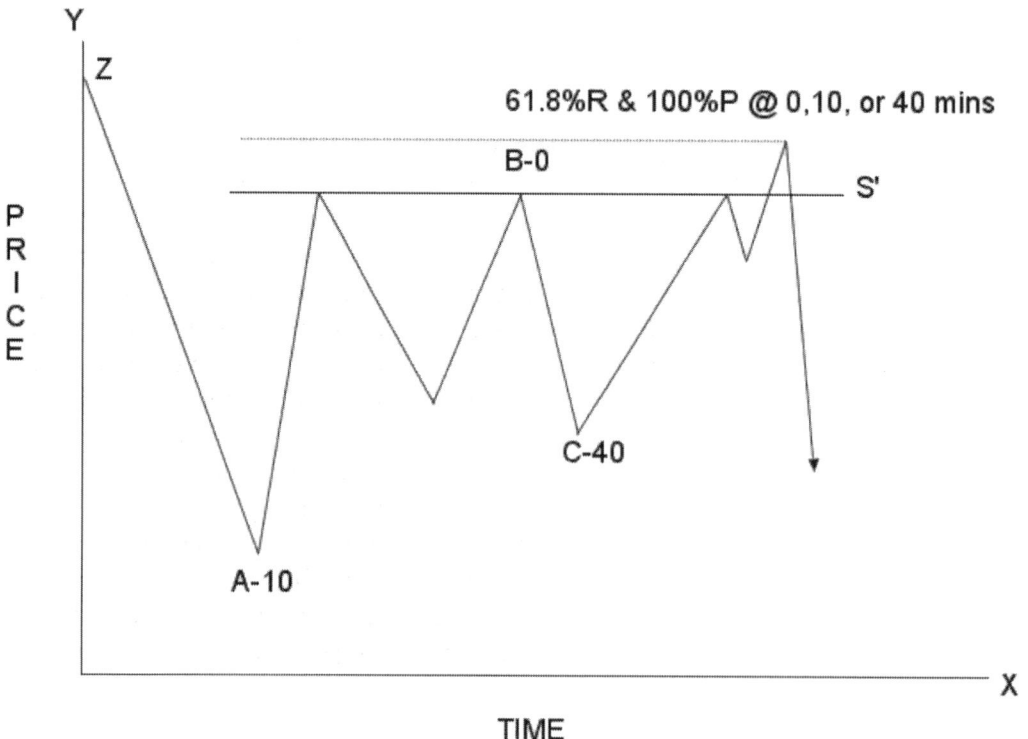

 In Figure 20.4, I ask the reader to understand that we have a range created as Z → A, but we do not see the terminal high at Z because we have to assume that time is infinite in order to generate this chart. Therefore, we see that we have a red, dotted line coming across the chart, which represents the 61.8%R of the Z → A negative range. However, what is most important is that we also see an Elliott Wave ABC correction, which is a swing indicated from the low at point A, to the second top (again we would ignore the first top if the second top holds as discussed in Price Structure), which becomes the high of the A → B range, and then we see that we use the low occurring after the second top for the projection.

That low is indicated at point C. However, not only are we suing ABC to indicate the corrective waves, but we are also recording time. We see that point A occurs at 10 minutes after the hour. Point B occurs at 0 minutes after the hour. Point C occurs at 40 minutes after the hour. Therefore, we have three potential time windows to look at for reversals.

I feel that this example is fantastic because it is a very common market scenario, especially in stocks that are priced under $10 that have very high volume. As such, the take away from this section, which leads into our next section, is that when the market "breaks" the triple top, we see that there is a mathematical cluster providing resistance. This cluster is made up of the 61.8%R of Z →A, and this cluster is made up of the 100%P of the ABC corrective swing. Therefore, if that cluster is hit at any of the three time windows, we have a tremendous edge. *This means that we are seeing Time and Price Symmetry in its full glory*, (which one should expect considering this is the last chapter) and when we couple that with our qualitative eye that tells us the market is ready to resume its downward trend. Further, we can use Price Theory in order to help us understand that the price objective is new lows below point A! Remember, we must keep everything in mind, and with everything in this book combined, we see the inherent market structure unraveled to our own eyes, which I hope instills a humbleness and an appreciation regarding the fact that the Marketome has existed and will always exist. Now, let us move on to swings themselves.

Swings

As the last section alluded to with respect to an ABC swing, we can now discuss swings, and the reason I mentioned double bottoms/tops, clusters, and repetitive tops/bottoms first was to illustrate something powerful for swing traders who know how to trade in time. In order to begin this discussion on swings, let us assume we are dealing with an upswing in order to illustrate the power of time in relation to swings. Here, I ask the reader to visualize that the *time* that the swing activates is actually at the same time as either the retracement hold or the swing point. So, dear reader, "What do you think will happen?" Well, based on our last discussion, when we observe this setup, we can infer that our swing is going to fail because we know from our last discussion that when this occurs we are observing a high probability for a true double top! In essence, the time symmetry inside of the building swing tells us to expect that the break is really a market inflection point and not a swing. As such, we can use time in order to filter out swings that may not work, and if we observe a swing that does activate where we have no time windows in play, we can have confidence to add to our position on the swing because we know that the market will continue to trend until we reach another cluster of *Time and Price Symmetry*. What is more, we can also bring in the concept of volume, and if we observe that volume is increasing as well as the lack of a Time Window, we find qualification criteria that adds probability to the swing's success. Let us look to Figure 20.5 in order to move forward on this example.

Figure 20.5: Time in Relation to Swings, Retracements, Focal Time Points

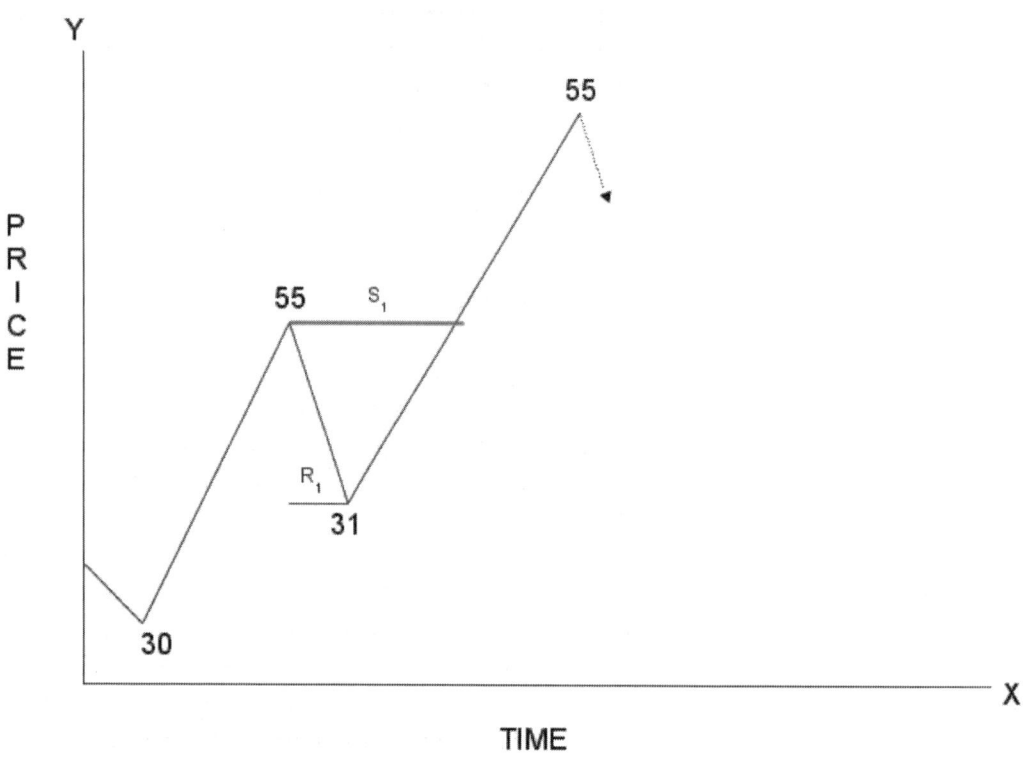

Conversely, we can look at Figure 20.5 in order to triunely elaborate on Focal Time Points, Retracement holds, and Swings in relation to time via this one chart. In the chart we see that our Focal Time is "30" minutes after the hour, because that is the low of the day. When we see this hold for our retracement value at 31 minutes after the hour, we have a high probability for a retracement hold because we have our Time Repetition. Since the only other important time is 55 minutes after the hour (at least as shown on the chart), we can observe that this swing does lead to a nice follow-through to new highs instead of double topping, which is expected. As such, we can be hypothetical and wait until 55 minutes after again comes around in order to see if we make another relevant high. Furthermore, if we were to observe the market have an inflection point that is a high at 30 minutes after the hour, we can say that Time is starting to indicate a trend change. This Figure can also tie into the observation about time occurring not at the terminal high/low of a move. In Figure 37, we see that the higher bottom at 31 minutes after has time symmetry with the terminal low 30 minutes after. Due to time symmetry at this value, we can observe the large follow-through off the same time window. Again, even though this is a simplistic intra-day example, this same logic can be applied in any and all time frames in the exact same way!

Lunchtime Swings

Of significant reference to day-traders, when we observe European Lunch Hours or when we observe American Lunch Hours, we have to be wary that the market could lack enough market participation to have sufficient follow-through to justify reward to risk ratios, which makes volume somewhat relevant. As such, lunchtime is an area to be avoided with swing trading, and highs/lows that are made during lunch hours are often retested, and if the time of those retests occur at time windows, we actually can quite often expect double tops/bottoms that have *time and price symmetry* coming out of lunch or even during lunch. These are great patterns to observe during lunch hours, but still, do not anticipate much in the way of follow-through. As an aside, obviously, if we are operating under high volatility, lunchtime becomes irrelevant.

Trendlines / Rising Tops / Declining Bottoms / 3-Drives Patterns

One of the most powerful ways to validate trendlines that act as market inflection points is when we have time windows that avail themselves at the touch of the trend lines. Since we are now using time in order to anticipate market inflection points, we can actually use the time and price value that a trend line provides to predict the price of our market when our next time window opens. Not only are previously existing time windows important, but what is quite common with trendline inflection points is that they will actually occur at the same time repetition. For example, we could have a major trend line in the daily chart of some instrument that keeps touching a trendline on the 12th day of the month. Every time the market approaches that trendline on the 12th day of the month, the trader can expect an inflection point to avail itself (if we assume these are correctly drawn trendlines). This logical application of *Time and Price Symmetry* is an incredibly powerful edge that exists, and it becomes most useful in a three-drives pattern.

In a three drives pattern, we know that we are using correct trendlines by default, and if we are daytraders, we can garner highly profitable trades from these recurring time repetitions. For example, if our first two tops, in a three-drives to a top pattern, occurred at 44 minutes after the hour, if we then, observe our third top at 44 minutes after the hour, we have a huge edge that has availed itself through *Time and Price symmetry*. This is a rather easy, explanatory example, which does not need further clarification via a Figure, because in fact, all of these application are easy enough for any 10 year old to grasp. Anyway…

Exhaustion Bars

What we learned earlier about exhaustion bars is that, when they occur, there is typically a low amount of volume at the extreme price level of the exhaustion bar because that inflection point is only known to us Price Structure learned traders. However, what we can now use time in order to do is tell us if that Exhaustion Bar's high/low will hold or not. If the reader recalls, the exhaustion bar's extreme price level is often a true market inflection point that yields a reversal, but in order for that to happen, we know that the extreme must be retested based on Price Theory. Therefore, we can use time in order to understand the validity of the extreme of the exhaustion bar.

This is quite simple to do, and again, it can be done in any time frame. For time to be useful with exhaustion bars, all we have to do is observe that if the time of the exhaustion bar occurred at a repetition or cycle (summed together in a Time Window), then the exhaustion bar is probably a legitimate reversal indication. However, if Time Structure is not giving us any feedback when the exhaustion bar occurs, that exhaustion bar will have a tendency to be exceeded, which will yield continued price movement in the direction of the exhaustion bar itself.

Fundamental News

Now, the reason I listed exhaustion bars and fundamental news next to each other is that they are often related. What is more, fundamental news typically occurs at the top and the bottom of the hour, which tells us that the exhaustion bar itself may be an inflection. This may seem counterintuitive, but actually, Fundamental News does yield to some type of instantaneous inflection point. However, because of the increase in volatility, we have to be aware that the next available Time Window, which may even be within our current time window (for example if it is only 4 minutes later), could possibly be another inflection point to reverse. Therefore, we find an edge by knowing the tendency to double reverse on fundamental news, and again, for the non-daytrader, this is mostly irrelevant. Thus, I again must state that since we are not gambling, and if you are not present moment-oriented, then, just ignore the darn news. It is not worth the risk, and unless there is some major disaster, the news schedule is published with plenty of advance notice. However, this leads into our final topic of discussion with respect to Time Structure and that is total commitment to this methodology, which makes the reality of a unforeseen "major disaster" irrelevant.

Presidential Cycles

When constructing this book, I was unsure about where to place the fact that markets exhibit cycles based on presidential terms. Part of me feels that it is a cycle that belongs next to the 8.6 year cycle, but then again, the Presidential market influence does not correlate with dates. Further, part of me feels that Presidential Cycles could possibly exist as a Time Repetition that factors in every four or eight years, but again, this is not consistent because every country has different election cycles. Third, I thought, well it may be the reality that because a President is chosen from the group collective that the choice of the President is inherently divine, but I could not be happy with that conclusion as well. Lastly, the effect of the Presidential cycle itself is similar to the tendency observed in Chapter 19 regarding inherent market conditions that tell us that every decennial cycle with a year ending in 5 has tended to be positive, but I was not happy including Presidential Cycles as part of that discussion as well. So, I am putting it here, almost at the end of our discussion on Time Structure, and now, I will discuss what the President's influence over a market is. For the sake of this discussion, I will be focusing on America.

In America, we have a four year cycle that is emergent from every president, and although I do not have the chart in front of me, a quick Google search should be able to illustrate this Time Cycle to the reader because this Time Cycle is formed by the cumulative analysis of overlapping a president's four years into one cycle. Upon that analysis, we find that there are peaks and there are troughs. We also find that we have consistent periods of unchcange, which are similar to Mercury Retrograde. Obviously, this tendency occurs within the six-month period before a new November election, and if one were to examine the 2012 election, it is easily recognizable if one were to look at the May to November period. During that period, the market basically stayed flat. What's more, the first full year of a president's term (the January after they are inaugurated, for President Obama this would be the year of 2010), we tend to see the cycle correlate to its strongest up moves.

In any event, the Presidential Cycle is palpable in the markets, but it is not a rule. It is merely a Cycle that must be understood, and it is my opinion that this cycle is helpful for investors that decide to Trade in Time. With that revelation, I hope the reader can accept that I have decided to paste this cycle here in order to be beneficial for actual trade implementations.

Unwavering Faith in *Time and Price Symmetry*

In the discussion of Fundamental News, I mentioned that we typically know the times that news will happen, and we only need to be worried about some disaster. However, because I must yield to divinity with respect to *Time and Price Symmetry* validation, I assert that even those disasters are predicted by *Time and Price Symmetry* inflection points, which is a frightening conclusion that one must come to because it reveals eschatological-like conclusions regarding divine providence and divine predestination. In fact, I didn't believe it myself, and it took almost three years of obsessive research in order to realize that, sure as crap, the market predicted the news before it happened through *Time and Price Symmetry* **always**. But the corollary is, that prediction only happened if *Time and Price Symmetry* is completely understood in the present moment.

Take for example 9/11. The indices gave swings down earlier in the week. Take for example the 1987 crash. The indices gave a swing down on the Friday beforehand. Take for example the small airplane that flew into a building in NYC a few years after 9/11, which caused a sizable crash and instantaneous rebound, which occurred based on Time Structure. In fact, the market gives us plenty of notice before this huge moves, and the only move that we didn't get a lot of notice on, which was the Flash Crash day of May 2010, still adhered to *Time and Price Symmetry,* because as already stated, the market had an inconspicuous repetitive top early in the AM Session, and the market had generated a swing down on the daily chart. Thus, we can conclude this book because not only is *Time and Price Symmetry* a proof to the non-randomness of the market, but it is akin to "The Bible Code." The reason I say this is because once the reader realizes the efficacy of *Time and Price Symmetry,* the reader will know the future of humanity, and once that reality hits, there will be a new guttural fear instilled in the trader because even though the markets may tell us the trend is down by Price Structure or Time Structure, we do not know just how far down we will go and we do not know how bad the catastrophe will be. Now, let us get to the real mind-blowing nature of *Time and Price Symmetry,* which is its application to realms outside of the market.

Obviously, this book was written in order to validate the Marketome that exists as time and as price. However, what is not obvious is that *Time and Price Symmetry* can be applied to any-type of chart. Let me explain. Take for example the chart of consumer confidence, which is produced by the University of Michigan. Obviously, this is not a trading instrument, but if one was to study a longer-term chart of consumer confidence, the patters of time and of price become apparent. In 2005 and 2006, the indicator itself had a double top. In 2008 and 2001, the indicator had a double bottom, and what is more astonishing, is that these price structure components fulfilled their Price Objectives even though this is not an indicator represented as Price! In order to personally reflect on this conclusion, I must talk about video games, which is also not obvious.

Since I was a lover of cars, I often played Gran Turismo Five with a "soaped-up" version of my own Ferrari that was sitting in my garage. However, there was one day where I decided to look up my historic time trials for my favorite course, and what I viewed left me awestruck. In my time trial chart, I observed that my times followed swings perfectly, which explained how sometimes my times became worse and sometimes better, but overall, the trend was to the downside, which meant I was improving. Now, I do not think that Sony has some type of market model that defines the computer-based competition cars that yields this result. No, I believe it is an inherent human condition that causes *Time and Price Symmetry,* or concurrently, it truly is a palpable oneness to God Himself living through us as the Holy Spirit. Hence, we find an astonishing reality that not only is Klatch's Price Theory applicable to the markets, but it is applicable to any type of scientific data that is represented as an X-Y line chart. As a corollary to that, I must say that the chart cannot be mathematically defined (as in $y=x^2$), and that the generation of the chart must be derived from people (a.k.a. mass-market psychology or an subconsciously executing methodology like driving a car in a video game). In order to emphasize this reality, I must state one more example, which is my own historic, money management track record that is attached in the

Appendices section. It too followed Price Theory Price Objectives, and that realization is absolutely ludicrous because that means that a manager's future performance is predetermined, and a Fund of Funds can use the monthly performance data to graph a chart of any hedge fund manager in order to graph swings, double tops, etc., that can be used for investments/redemptions just as if the Fund of Funds was trading oil contracts! (Again, this is one of the reasons I hope to run a massive Fund of Funds one day because it will require someone to have the same level of believability that I have in *Time and Price Symmetry* for this to be a profitable, money management, allocation methodology!)

Furthermore, on my own historic track record, one would find swings, double bottoms, and even a triple top, which lead to my arrest! Remember, repetitive tops are large indications of massive future moves, and in my case, that massive future movement was the destruction of my life! How scary is that realization? Hence, we find that it is truly astonishing that my 7-year trading history adhered to Price Structure even before I knew about Price Structure, and if one were to examine many performance charts of independent traders, you always find the same exact patterns within the equity curve. It is mind blowing, and if you do not believe me, grab an encyclopedia, and look up any relevant statistic, say, population growth/decline or tax rate expansion/contraction. Upon that analysis, you will find Time and Price coexisting based on *Time and Price Symmetry*, and that realization is, in my mind at least, equivalent to Fibonacci's recognition of his famed sequence. Thus, it is my intention to submit these two theorems and the forthcoming mathematical contradiction to the Royal Academy of Sciences in Stockholm, Sweden, because it is my belief that these concepts are Nobel prize worthy, and dear reader, please believe that this great experiment of the financial markets is not random. That being said, we can end this book on a lighter note...

Closing Thoughts on Time Structure

It is my unending hope that the reader of this book is able to understand these concepts displayed in this first edition of "The Market is not Random," and I say this because, admittedly, it is hard to learn the Marketome without seeing live trading charts. However, please believe that adding time to your trading arsenal really is quite simple because it is not hard to observe Time Repetitions, and it only takes a few hours of work every month in order to update intersecting Time Histograms from Time Cycles and from Time Repetitions. It is easy work for incredible reward if one is to let go to the present moment. Thus, it is only your mind and your human nature that leads to disbelief regarding the ease with which time can be implemented for our benefit. What is more, we, as highly educated humans, (which is who I expect will even make it this far in this text) fail to allow our ego to accept this simplicity of the true Marketome because of the preconceived notion that the market is so complex when the truth is: No, it really isn't. In fact, the market is not complex, but the psychological mind-screwing that is derived from market participation (i.e. trading) is extremely complex because understanding trade rules requires the individual to have the ability to turn these price and time patterns into profit. What is more, trading requires adherence to strict money management and risk management rules, which is very hard mentally, and again, I remind the reader how important these rules are by using me and my incarceration as a martyr-like metaphor. I have emphasized these concepts recurrently through every stage of this book in order try and drive the point home into your subconscious. Because of my incarceration and because of my obsession with defining what has never before been defined by man, I became disillusioned with validation, and because of that disillusion, the person who I was is truly dead, and I lost the person I loved the most. However, if that person did not die, I never would have written this book, which finished the validation process that I needed to prove what I already knew. Therefore, I see my incarceration as part of God's eschatological plan for me if it was my human purpose to define the true Marketome for my fellow humans. Thus, the sacrifice for humanity has already been made by my unsheathing of the true Marketome, and I mean no disrespect by this Jesus-like comparison because the harmonic relationships that I have defined can provide continuous, extreme edges to the trader if applied properly. However, in order to expand the Christianity metaphor, I can also say that the market participants need to learn to put their faith in this methodology, and they must do so by having "child-like faith." However, by no means am I delusional to the point that I believe these words (my words) will live forever, and as such, I must disagree with Woody Allen, who once said, "I don't want to achieve immortality through my work. I want to achieve immortality through not dying." Hence, I am not trying to attain eternal, human immortality by this work, but I am hoping to be remembered. What is more, because I have been forced to come to grips with the evil truth of society, I have no desire to live on this planet any longer than God has defined for me because there are many things I am angry at Him about, which I look forward to discussing with Him. Thus, I wish not to live forever, but I do wish that this book becomes my and my future family's legacy now that I have tarnished my name with acts that I believe were wrong, unethical, but never criminal. Hence, my drive by writing this book was to attain a reverence equitable to Gann himself, and not God. In fact, despite my anger with God, I hope that there is a hereafter because I cannot wait to sit down with Gann someday myself!

Nevertheless, let us return back to reality, and as I close this analytical portion of this book, I have to say that I believe that I have listed all possible price structures that exist based on how price moves, and I believe I have done the same for Time (aside from other time cycles that the reader may wish to investigate for his or her own trading application). Because I was able to list these Time Structure Components in relatively easy, succinct chapters, I believe that the reader should embrace this ease and understanding instead of fighting it. I ask the reader to go look at charts in order to find his or her own validity if the trader does not believe me, and it will be my goal in the second edition of this book to produce these type of charts. In addition, the belief in the simplicity of time is one of the reasons why our subconscious needs to observe thousands of hours of the market in order to properly accept that reality is much easier than we thought. Once that belief is attained, the only thing left is to specialize in a market, and then, execute your trading plan in order to reach whatever goals you set based on your risk management and money management declarations as part of your trading plan. Remember, Time and Price will always be there, and they will always be waiting. It is up to you to understand this relationship, and it is up to you to recognize the relative ease in implementing time and price for your own benefit.

Now that I have been able to sum up the thoughts on TIme and Price Symmetry, by providing consistent trading edges that are usable on every trading instrument in every time frame, I feel it is important to acquiesce to the reality of market implementation, which ultimately succumbs to risk/money management. Therefore, we must understand that there is an underlying need that we have as traders in order to selectively choose which trades to implement. Granted, these trades should always be with the trend, but in reality, we need a defense mechanism to ensure that we are always working in terms of proper risk management.

The word "objective" can mean to look at things for what they truly are, but I have also used the word to mean a goal that the market has outstanding. In my eyes, both definitions are correlated through Price Theory. Through Price Theory, we must understand that markets always have multiple Price Theory Price Objectives coexisting in every given moment, and what's more, we have to understand that each objective is somewhat sequential based on Quantitative Synchronicity. Thus, no matter what the trader may be focused on in terms of Time and Price Symmetry, the trader must never forget underlying Trade Theory, which puts reward to risk in a certain relationship for each trade.

That said, how do we use this knowledge of multiple objectives for our benefit? Well, first, we need to understand the time frame we are trading in, and the Price Objective for that time frame. From there, we need to take a trade using Time Windows and Price Clusters to get us inline with that Objective. However, IT DOES NOT MAKE SENSE TO REVERSE OR HEDGE until that Objective is reached. We must let go to the present moment, while simultaneously maintaining our awareness to the trade that we implemented. What's more, multiple Price Objectives may align in the same direction, and we can witness the market cascading through these objectives in a sequential manner.

Chapter 21

Klatch's Contradiction to the Efficient Market Hypothesis

By writing this book, I have intended to postulate three idioms that I feel are equitable to Nobel Laureate-like recognition, because each of these hypotheticals have the ability to change conventional financial theory. Let me summarize the first two theorems as a way to introducing the piece de resistance of this book. First, I discussed *Klatch's Price Theory*, which was a theory based on market ranges, which lead markets to break/expand those ranges for some unknown, unquantified reasons. Second, I stated *Klatch's Marketome Theory*, which was essentially the application of *Klatch's Price Theory* with respect to the purpose for an index (as I redefined) to always obtain new all-time highs, and should that goal not be reached, then, the markets would have the *potential* to fall apart through either deflation or through Price Pattern Objectives pointing to less than zero. However, this third theorem-like discussion, which I have yet to clarify to the reader, is a mathematical contradiction to the *Efficient Market Hypothesis (or efficient markets theory)*, which is why I see this Chapter as the piece de resistance of this entire book. Thus, my proposed solution in order to contradict the *Efficient Market Hypothesis* could stand alone as its own, valid conjecture that is separately eligible for Nobel status because I have, finally, conclusively determined that the need for traders exists in the market. This question has always existed, and many people feel that traders harm investors,. However, mathematically and conceptually, this person validates the reason for the trading profession, and I believe this mathematical contradiction sheds insight on why people like me *should* exist as a market participant. Now, I must apologize if I have offended anyone by equating my (somewhat) simplistic contradiction to Nobel Prize worthy edification, but I am hopeful that by making this claim, these contradictions and/or theorems can be validated and/or expanded by the caliber of people that cling to the Nobel society. In a way, I am posing the question and a possible mathematical solution to the Royal Academy of Sciences in Stockholm, Sweden. Therefore, I am acquiescing to *this market* in order to validate all of the discussions I have postulated thus far. What's more, by asking for this type of recognition, I am trying to invoke the Law of Attraction along with the biblical quotation that says, "We have not because we ask not." What is more, this third collegiate level assertion is something that I feel is more concrete because it has mathematical basis. In addition, I feel that if one were to evenly weigh the two theorems and this mathematical contradiction with other Nobel Laureate-types like Mr. Harry Markowitz, who defined the *Modern Portfolio Theory;* one would find that my three idioms would be just as ground breaking for the financial industry.

Again, I do not say these egotistical conclusions without relevance, and I must apologize for the lack of humility and humbleness, but I am angered by Mr. Markowitz's idiotic theory, which the financial community has embraced as being the de facto standard for money management. I say this because Mr. Markowitz's theory is completely illogical and against the purpose for the market investor, while being purposeful for the money manager. Thereby, I conclude that his theory only exists to keep mutual fund managers and the like gainfully employed while neglecting the best outcome for the client. In a way, I see that Mr. Markowitz's *Modern Portfolio Theory* is an illogical solution that is solvable if one were to invoke Nash's *Game Theory*, which would easily show that it is not the optimum solution for all parties! Thus, if a person can win a price, a Nobel Prize no less, for an idiotic theorem like *Modern Portfolio Theory,* then I have no qualms about my egotistical assertions that the two theorems listed thus far and this mathematical contradiction that is outlined in this concluding Chapter are qualified for a similar prize. In fact, I must make one last claim about the ignorance of *Modern Portfolio Theory,* and that claim is that I would equate *Modern Portfolio Theory* to a more elaborate scheme then I was ever charged with by the government. I say this because *Modern Portfolio Theory* is a scheme that allows Investment Advisors and mutual fund managers to stay gainfully employed while simultaneously preventing their investors from achieving the full gains derived from the "white swans," which means this "theory" has cost people more money then I ever have. That said, I am extremely fortunate to be given this gift of intelligence by God, which allowed me to formulate these theorems and this Contradiction, and to God, not man, do I remain humbled. Accordingly, my intelligence has now led me to find a method using defined terms in this book in order to contradict the *Efficient Market Hypothesis* through logic. Thus, let me begin the contradiction.

In order to dispute the *Efficient Market Hypothesis (or efficient markets theory)*, we need to prove that for any given point in time, there exists enough information that will conclude that at that point in time, we have two alternate prices that are more efficient. Hence, we have three prices coexisting and independent from one another: two efficient prices and one non-efficient price. A non-efficient price would indicate that at that moment in time, we would have two simultaneous efficient prices that tell us there is an underlying profit. As such, having three prices coexisting at the same point in time would disprove the efficiency of the market by mathematically concluding that the market cannot be efficient because the non-efficient price has some factor of discernible profit. In order to accomplish the contradiction, we need to use theorems from mathematics, economics, intrinsic market structure (defined within this text), and relativity. In addition, we need to discuss the actual concept of time, which has occurred at many points in this text as well.

For the non-mathematically inclined, I need to refer to Chapter 2 of this book. In Chapter 2, I discussed that when we use revenue in determining a market capitalization-based stock price, we may have two prices. We will have the current stock price that is based on the current revenue, but we may have a future stock price that is based on expected revenue growth, which created a price range based off these two revenue calculations. Therefore, the fundamental argument, which is quite simplistic compared to what lies ahead, is that there are always two simultaneously accurate prices in a stock price, unless revenue was to remain constant. Even then, (and I assert that constant revenue is not possible unless it is contractual) whenever a stock price is not equal to its market capitalization-based stock price, then, there must always exist a simultaneously linked stock price. Therefore, we can conclude that from a fundamental perspective there will always exist two possible stock prices based on current revenue or future revenue unless revenue was to remain constant and the value of the stock price was to remain constant as well.

Now that I have addressed a fundamental, logical reason for inefficiency, let us get to the math. In order to begin the mathematical contradiction, we will define that for our purpose, we need to use the set of positive, real numbers. We will define X_N to be price and Y_N to be time for $N \geq 0$. This will be represented in the X-Y coordinated pare as (X_N, Y_N), which is actually an inverted Cartesian plane.

Next, we will assert the definition of a subset of (X_N, Y_N) in 4 representative sets: (X_0, Y_0), (X_1, Y_1), (X_2, Y_2), and (X_3, Y_3). Along with this subset, we will still have variables for X_N, Y_N for all $N > 3$. In order to utilize market structure, we will set forth constants on our subset in order to define a Range. These constants are: $0 \leq X_0 < X_1 < X_3 < X_2$ and $0 \leq Y_0 < Y_1 < Y_2 < Y_3$. Now, I claim that for the *Efficient Market Hypothesis* to be valid, $X_N = X_2$ for all $Y_N > Y_2$ and $N > 2$. In order to remove range bias, we also constrain the values as follows: $|X_2 - X_0| = |X_1 - X_0|$. This last constraint simply means we have equality of the range, which could be stated as the 50% retracement.

Figure E.1: Efficient Market Hypothesis Visualization

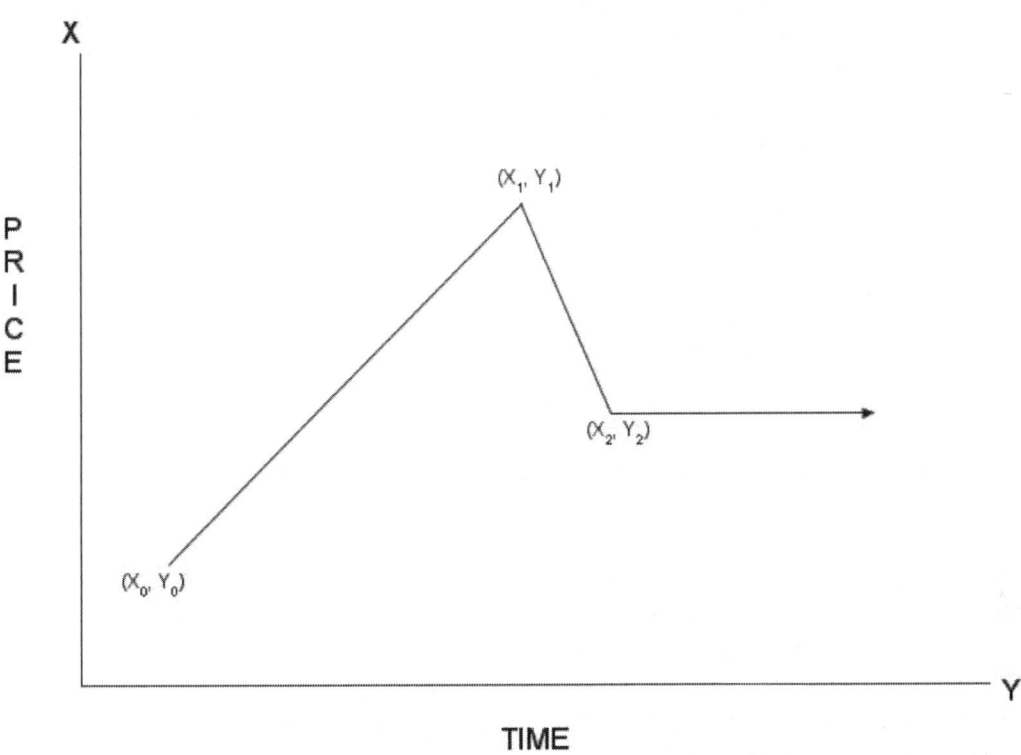

The graphical representation of this range with constraints is shown in Figure E.1. In this graph, we have a range that shows an infinitely continued price at the mid-point of the range as indicated by the arrow. In addition, we have used the defined (X_2, Y_2) point to visualize a point for $N > 2$.

In order to prove that $X_N = X_2$ for all $Y_N > Y_2$ and $N > 2$ must be true, we need to use the definition regarding the valuation of an asset at any given point in time, which is simply the last transacted price defined by a buyer and by a seller at some point in the *past*. Therefore, the only way to define the current price of an asset, in the present moment, is to utilize our knowledge of the current bidding price and the current asking price, which means that we can make a transaction occur in the present moment at either of those price levels. We will assume that we are a buyer for the sake of explanation, which means that our current price is the asking price at our current present moment of time, and we will see at the end of my contradiction that we will successfully cover the demand side (the bidding price) as well. However, in order to base the efficient valuation at the current time, we only have the last known exchange by a buyer and by a seller because we cannot guarantee a price match at the current Y_N (time) since bidding/asking prices may change. Hence, the last known price exchange *must* be (X_2, Y_2). The problem is that once that transaction is recorded, time has already shifted forward into a value such that $Y_N > Y_2$. This would be the present moment. Therefore, to assume efficiency for all $Y_N > Y_2$, we would need the current asking price for all $Y_N > Y_2$ to be $X_N = X_2$ for all $N > 2$. This is the hardest concept to grasp, but it is the basis for the start of contradiction.

To explain in a clearer manner, I am simply stating that the last known transaction was efficient at the time of that transaction, but we only have that transaction to base our valuation for the *current* present moment's efficiency because, as any trader can tell you, we cannot guarantee a price match at current bid/ask price. Therefore, we must have an infinite amount of supply at the asking price where the asking price is equal to the last known price. We can further conclude that, in the present moment of time, the *Efficient Market Hypothesis* states that the current efficient price at our present moment must be based on knowing the current price in the present moment, but we only have knowledge of this price if it is derived from *the last recorded price*! Thus, this last recorded price must rely on a historical price / the last transaction! As such, the asking price is the only way to find our current price in the present moment, and this is where we find our contradiction because we cannot guarantee a future transaction at any $Y_N > Y_2$. This means we have two contradictions in order to disprove the *Efficient Market Hypothesis*:

1. *Supply or Demand cannot be infinite from Economic Laws / Theories*
2. *Time may not be infinite based on Relativity.*

Now, I will use Klatch's Price Theory in order to define a point (X_N, Y_N) such that for any $Y_N > Y_2$ there also exists multiple possible values for price X_N at the same Y_N such that one X_N is greater or less than another X_N for the same point in time Y_N. This means we have two potential prices (the Price Objectives from Klatch's Price Theory) at one point in time, and in order to prove the contradiction, we have to prove that these prices exist simultaneously in time. In a way, I also see this as a possible intrinsic proof for my own theory, and this is why I chose a range in order to define the contradiction of the *Efficient Market Hypothesis*. However, my Price Theory is not needed in order to prove the contradiction, and I am only illustrating it with my contradiction in order to posit a possible, graphical explanation of how my own Price Theory could define the future profit.

In order to begin proving the existence of multiple prices coexisting at one time, we will be working with the same subset that we have already defined, and as we saw, this subset yielded a range where by all $X_N = X_2$ for $N > 2$. This meant that in our graph, we were printing continuous price at $X_N = X_2$, which was the 50% retracement of the range D: (X_0, Y_0) □ (X_1, Y_1). However, since supply cannot be infinite, we must prove that $X_N \neq X_2$ for some value of $N > 2$. As such, the opposite argument, which would prove the *Efficient Market Hypothesis*, would state that for all times, Y_N, we cannot have a conclusive basis for profit ("P"). As such, for *Efficient Market Hypothesis* validity, $P = 0$ for all (X_N, Y_N). Therein, the contradiction of the Efficient Market Hypothesis lies in proving $X_N \neq X_2$ for some value of $N > 2$, whereby $P \neq 0$.

In order to prove the invalidity, we can now utilize mathematics from our currently defined equations. Hence, $X_N - X_2 \neq 0$ for some value of $N > 2$, and since $P \neq 0$, we have $X_N - X_2 = P$. Since we are reliant on positive prices we can further state that $| X_N - X_2 | = P$ for some $N > 2$. Since we have already discussed that supply cannot be infinite, we know that for some X_N for $N > 2$ that $X_N \neq X_2$, which proves the validity of the already defined equation $| X_N - X_2 | = P$ at some value of $N > 2$. We know that at some Y_N for $N > 2$ we will have exhausted the supply at our asking price for using our valuation, which means that our historical price reference has now shifted. Now, we can remove the absolute value of our base equation in order to see that once supply is exhausted at some point in time Y_N at $N > 2$ we visualize that for our last historic price, we yield $X_2 = X_N +/- P$. Therefore, the efficient price(s) when supply is exhausted is "$X_N +/- P$". Now, if $P>0$ then $X_N > X_2-P$ which means that here we have disproved the *Efficient Market Hypothesis* because at some point in time, the present moment can no longer rely on the previously matched price, and that we have knowledge of multiple possible prices existing at some time Y_N for $N > 2$.

In order to assert the graphical illustration of how my own Price Theory can find our profit targets defined as Price Objectives, we can look to one of the +/- P equations. (Again, this is not necessary to prove the contradiction, but it is helpful in observing values of "P.") Let us choose $X_N = X_2 + P$ if $P>0$.

This means that no matter what the retracement of a range is, we have proof that the market will challenge a high based on the knowledge that for some value in time of Y_N for $N > 2$ we have the last known price X_2 at $N = 2$, but we also have the present moment price for $N > 2$ which has been defined as $X_2 +/- P$. This means that we can conclude that whatever the value is of the range, there are two simultaneous profit objects, which may occur inside the range, outside the range, or at the extremes of the range. The important proof is that we know that the market has a Price Objective at one of our defined points based on our knowledge of prices that are not efficient: "$X_2 + P$" or "$X_2 - P$." In a way, for $P > 0$, we have proven the profit potential for long trades and for $P < 0$ we have proven the profit potential for a short trade. We also have to rely on the fact that a buyer and a seller must be constrained by price as a subset of the real, positive numbers. As such, since $X_0 \neq X_1$ and $X_0 \neq X_2$ we can define three numbers that *may* exist as a simple illustration of the contradiction and the intrinsic proof of Klatch's Price Theory. We can set $X_0 = 0.01$, $X_1 = 0.03$, and $X_2 = 0.02$ if we use our new constrained set and P is set to either +/- 0.01. Since $P \neq 0$ we can conclude the visual representation in Figure E.2, which proves that for some Y_N when $N > 2$ the price of X_N may equal X_0 or X_1 when supply at X_2 is exhausted and the amount of profit is defined as the distance from the top/bottom of the range to the last known price, which satisfies Klatch's Price Theory as well.

Figure E.2: Visual Proof of Supply Exhaustion

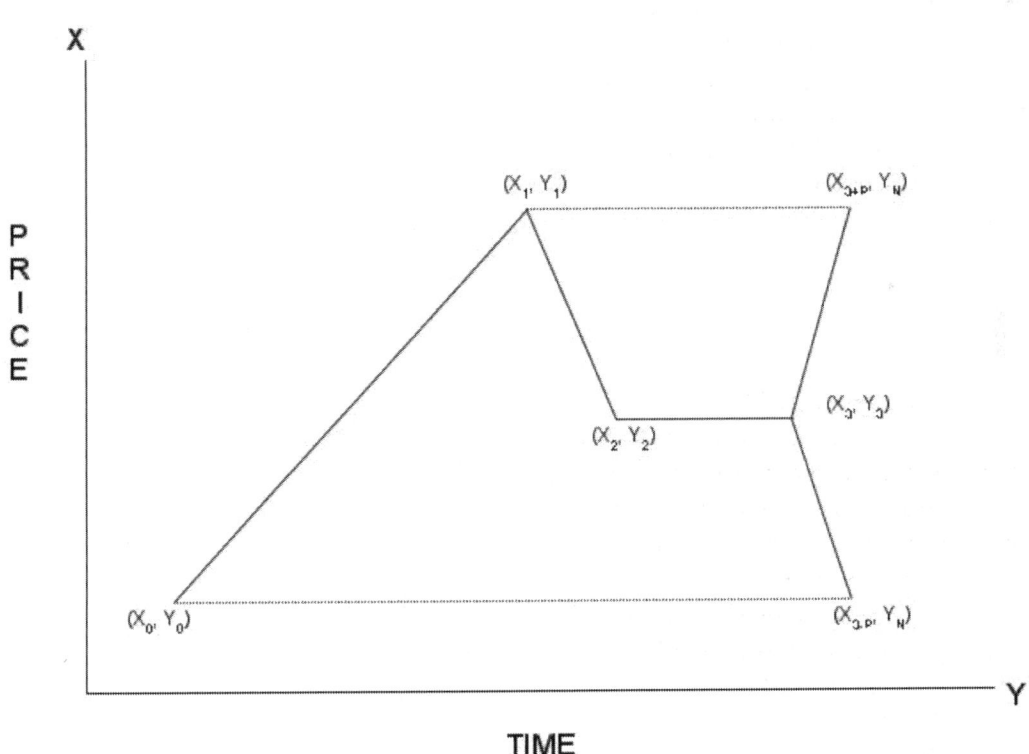

Therefore, I have concluded the contradiction fundamentally using logic, mathematically using supply/demand, and also visually via Klatch's Price Theory. Thus, I have proven multiple values of price at the same point in time since supply cannot be infinite, which occurs for P > 0. In addition, we can rationalize that demand cannot be infinite for our last known price, which means P < 1. Thus, the contradiction is complete for both sides of the required economic argument, and the *Efficient Market Hypothesis* is invalidated.

As a corollary, which is in regards to the second contradiction in regards to finite time, if we are also to believe that time is not infinite based on observations derived in the theory of Relativity, then, we would also be faced with a terminal point to disprove the *Efficient Market Hypothesis* as well because when time ends, then there can be no more asking/bidding price at that point in time. If that occurs, we are placed in the same graphical representation of what happens when supply/demand at a given price ceases to exist, and the proof of what happens, when time ends, is already intrinsically stated.

As I have stated through this contradiction, we have to understand that profit, "P," exists. Once we have proven its existence, I find that my contradiction is easily equated to Heisenberg's Uncertainty Principle in Quantum Mechanics. In order to visualize the correlation, we observe that once supply or demand approach an asymptotic limit, which creates our "P", we can visualize that "P" *can* exist in multiple places at one time, and by utilizing concepts I have stated in this book, we can see that "P" can exist at our Price Objective, our Price Pattern Objective, or at new Price Objectives that are created as time/ranges expand, and "P" is essentially determined by wherever the market wants it to be; we only need to prove that it exists in order to satisfy my contradiction, which makes "P" as elusive as an electron.

Furthermore, the purpose to disproving the *Efficient Market Hypothesis* is necessary to do for the trading vocation, and it is why I have thought about this contradiction for almost ten years. For the trading to logically exist, the trader cannot believe in the *Efficient Market Hypothesis* for, if the trader did, the trader would essentially be saying that he/she does not believe that he/she has a definable trading edge at any given moment in time, and if the markets were efficient there would be not justification for trading aside from investing and/or hedging. If the efficient market hypothesis held true, the trader is essentially resigning himself or herself to the logic that trading is a random, gamble. Thus, my whole book has been written to disprove that thought process, and I believe that if my contradiction is someday confirmed, people that participate in the trading vocation, can rest easy in the knowledge that markets are inefficient, which means that defined trading edges have validity. Thus, profit, "P," is possible, and *the reason to trade is justified*.

Afterward

I started this book by handwriting it in early January of 2012, and then, with the Warden's permission at Perry County Correctional Center, I was able to use a computer without Internet and without a good writing program for 18 hours per week in order to type this book. Along with my young age, I ask the reader to be reminded of the limitations that I had in order to properly construct this book. Once those two factors are placed together, I hope the reader will at least understand the level of commitment and the level of knowledge I had to the market, and I have done my best to put that same commitment into these writings. Furthermore, in order to write this book, I had no charts; I had no text books; and I had no internet! However, I did have a select few Wall St. Journals and a select few glimpses of CNBC. Thus, I wrote this book entirely from memory, and I created the 50+ charts in this book also from memory. That alone is an intense accomplishment, but I feel like this solitude from the markets and from the Internet was necessary in order for me to complete W.D. Gann's work. Like Gann in 1940, I was forced to rely on a minimal usage of technology, which allowed my mind to finish the comprehension I had from his work. Thus, I believe I have finished Gann's work by learning his work through technology, and because I believe I finished his work, I am confident of all of what I have stated therein. Thus, as I begun to type this book, I realized that my handwritten pages were more like notes instead of an accurate portrayal of the sophisticated analytical techniques divulged in these writings, and it required this isolation-like setting in order to understand those analytical techniques. What is more, I believed that this setting concluded my market-based education, and I have a sense of wonderment and a sense of understanding of why PhD programs require students to write a thesis because the thesis is necessary to prove one's understanding of a true subject mastery. Hence, as I stated in the *Introduction*, this is my thesis.

That said, some people, like my parents, may think the conviction of my assertions are delusional, but that type of thinking is pure naïveté once the reader attains the proper comprehension deduced from my words. When that happens, the market structure will be unveiled before the reader's eyes as if by magic. For me, I can remember when this happened to me; distinctly. It was early September of 2008, and at the end of one of the trading days, I moved my 1-Minute S&P Futures chart to the 46" television in my office. I remember staring at the chart, and just seeing every pattern and every reason pop out at me, and I believe that the visual cues that my brain was deriving came from the fact that my subconscious was able to see and recognize every twist and turn of the market. That feeling was and is truly indescribable. At that moment, I can distinctly remember the state of awe, and I can also remember that my then girlfriend, Amanda, was with me. As I was rambling on about retracements and double bottoms, she was giving me that look that said, "Can we just go to dinner now?" Hah. She had no idea what I was talking about, but if anyone could attest to that market-based awakening, it would be her. It was a magical moment, indeed.

Furthermore, if anyone tries to question the techniques in this book, then, I can rely on millions of market examples that I cannot state right now for the reasons listed in the first paragraph of this section. However, despite not having that plethora of data to back up my claims, I can point to some of the trades that I have listed herein such as the Oracle ("ORCL") double bottom between December 2011 and May 2012. Just knowing and recognizing that double bottom could have been a billion dollar trade if one was well capitalized. Or, I ask the reader to look at the perfect double top with Time Symmetry that occurred at the end of April 2012 in the DJIA. That trade alone was worth billions of dollars if one could implement it properly. Thus, do not doubt the power of the words within this book, and erasing that doubt in the minds of the masses was a driver in writing this book.

One of the other major reasons that I had to write this book was also to be able to properly define everything that I have learned in my financial career over the past 12 years. In doing so, I had to make the reader of this book become aligned to how my thinking is non-conventional in my belief of what is possible from the market. Not only do I hold this belief, but I have proven to myself several times in my career that 1000%+ returns are possible via a *trading campaign* in as little as 5-10 trading days while simultaneously acknowledging through this book that I have a logical concept of returns in the grandeur scheme of things. For example, I do not mean to say that $1mm is not a large sum of money, and if anything, my track record shown in the *Resources and Appendices* section of this book should help the reader realize how realistic my mentality is with respect to the value of money.

Writing this book has been much more than writing a technical, trading book. for me. Writing this book has been part of the psychological rehabilitation that I have deemed necessary as part of this incarceration process in order to define my rationale, and only by writing this book did I connect the missing synaptic gaps in my brain. Therefore, this book is literally a perspective on the oneness that I believe the best traders must maintain with respect to the market, and I believe that that oneness is culminated in the universal law of mathematics that one can argue governs nature and Creative-Evolution. Obviously, some part of this thinking has a basis in a theological perspective of humbleness that I believe is required to trade the markets for a lifetime, and above everything, I hope that, although I tried to minimize God-speak in this text, I believe God is very important in the life of a trader. Further, although I have no formal education in theology, religion, or psychology, my intelligence has been able to observe and find direct connections between God and man through the markets. I have tried to do the best I can to ply these beliefs to the reader without passing religious judgment, and I ask that the reader only take my side commentary as part of the full-circle perspective on life, which I now realize is required in order to properly execute a job for many years. Therefore, this journey of life is not just about money. No, it is about finding a way to have longevity in doing a job that you love along with being around the people you love. Hence, I must realize that a balanced life is necessary, and the thought of working 14 hours per day for the next 40 years will lead to irrationality. Unfortunately for me, that irrationality caused me to lose the person that I loved, but alas, at the end of it all, at least I know that I have a skill, a literal "trade" that cannot be taken away from me. Therefore, I hope I have done my best to show the humbleness that we must have to God and to the markets, while trying to illustrate to the reader the effects of a severe obsession with the market that can lead to destruction.

Now, in regards to my educated mind, this book has served as an outlet for me to explain what has happened in my life in order to reach the point of federal incarceration, and I find it interesting that this book contains my dual education mentalities of engineering and project management coming together in one document. The engineering component has manifested itself through the chapters that have dealt with *Time and Price Symmetry*. The project management component of my mentality has manifested itself in the first five chapters dealing with *perception,* which yielded an ethereal discussion regarding "Trading for Life," which outlined the evolving career mentality that one can have while dealing with the markets in order to find a purpose for continuous trading longevity. In addition, my project management mentality has been able to quantify the risks/problems in my own trading along with finding a solution to those risks, which is the role of any good project manager, and I have also looked at the problems that new fund seeders have. I have tried to explain what is required by the hedge fund seeders/incubators to yield a higher level of success (specifically, a high amount of initial capital coupled with complete monetary transparency between fund manager and fund seeder). What is more is that project manager mentality has been useful in the structure and outline of trading intervals within a *trading campaign,* and the project manager mentality has distilled ways to reach billionaire-status. Hence, I have quantified the markets and my trading plans aloud for the reader.

Now, this *Afterward* serves as a bridge between the past, the present, and the future. The past will be explained through looking back at the best money managers 25 years ago, and how their mentality provides even further conviction for everything I have stated here in. The present has been made fulfilled by writing all that I have learned at the time of my arrest, because in effect, at that day, a pause button was hit on my life. On that day, the present for me stopped, and my future will not resume until I am released. And, finally, the future will be discussed in my autobiography, which I call the future since it talks about the hopes and the dreams that I have for my life. Furthermore, I can state that the future is also referenced by the fact that the future is simply a cyclical tendency that is found within humanity, and my future is currently unknown. However, in my autobiography section of this book, I do have to describe what I have learned, which will affect my own future forever. I have to also understand that this book may be the culmination of my 12 years study of the markets, and maybe, this book is the end of my trading career. It could be a real possibility, and I do not mitigate the reality that I may die while being incarcerated.

Moving on, be it a twist of predestination via divinity or simply a coincidence, I came across a book in the prison library where I am typing this text, which was published in 1989; two years after the 1987 crash. The name of the book is "Market Wizards: Interviews with Top Traders" by Jack D. Schwager. Amazingly, this book is highly based on Futures and Derivatives! In fact, the "top traders" that Mr. Schwager discusses in the book all state/confirm many of the things I have written in this book, and these traders were doing this almost 25 years ago! Gann was doing this over 100 years ago! The point is: nothing has changed, and I also emphasize that the reason I wrote about examples from 2007 onward was because of the current audience relevance! Therefore, I am bridging the past to the futures through these traders as well, and as such, I will heavily borrow from Mr. Schwager's text many of the comments from some of the most well-known traders/money managers of all time in order to provide the reader of my text with even more, concrete validation regarding the three beliefs of this book by utilizing the very words of some of the top traders of all time. Here is an example of the traders listed in Mr. Schwager's book:

- Michael Marcus turned $30,000 into $80,000,000
- Ed Seykota earned 250,000% in 16 years
- Michael Steinhardt realized a 30% annualized return over 21 years
- Marty Schwartz took $40,000 and ran it up to $20mm with never more than 3% drawdown
- Paul Tudor Jones whose fund would've went to $17,482 from $1,000 invested in a four year period
- Bruce Kovner whose track record would've realized a $1,000,000 valuation after starting with $2,000 ten years earlier

In fact, in "Market Wizards," there are 16 traders that were interviewed for Mr. Schwager's book. Out of all of the interviews, one trader caught my eye more than any other, and he was a trader I had never heard about until a month ago. His name is Mark Weinstein. In Weinstein's interview, he stated he never had a down week, had a 99% accurate trade ratio, and the market was "so easy." In fact, Schwager was so amazed at these facts that he realized the skepticism that the reader may have, and Schwager went on to interject a two-page analysis in order to better explain these seemingly impossible results.

In that two-page clarification, Schwager states that Weinstein's trading is 100% technical, and the techniques used by Weinstein are: "Elliott Wave, **Gann** Analysis, **Fibonacci** numbers, and [most important] **cycles**." [P. 340-341] Out of all the traders in Schwager's book, none have come even close to the numbers that Weinstein portrayed in his interview, and once his analysis aligned with my book, I knew why his numbers were so good; he was trading in price and in time, which, as the reader should now know, is the fundamental basis that the market exists in. No other traders came out and said anything close to Weinstein's numbers, and no other traders mentioned Gann or Fibonacci with such emphasis either; hence, the correlation to this book.

In order to further validate my text, I will quote from a few of the "Market Wizards" interviewed in Schwager's book:

- "I remember all my losses. For example, I have had three losing days in the last two years. Out of the thousands of trades I made during that time, I had 17 losers, but 9 of them were because my quote machine was down, and when that happens I just get out of my position." - Mark Weinstein [Always get out of a position if you can't follow it or if it was an error.]

- "You have to learn how to lose; it is more important than learning how to win." - Mark Weinstein
- "Although viewing markets as **nonrandom** over the long run, I have long believed that very short-term market fluctuations (i.e., intra-day price movements) were largely random. Weinstein has shaken this belief." - Jack Schwager himself
- "I know floor traders that have made money for 20 straight years. You can't call that gambling." - Mark Weinstein
- "I was not using any type of rational judgment. I was being guided by my material desires." - Mark Weinstein [A discussion involving a trading goal to purchase a new home, which hinders trading. The old traders from the 30s, used to call this "don't trade for a fur coat."]
- "It was an **obsession**! I slept with it; I dreamt about it. Sometimes I would stay up all night thinking about what I would do the next day. If I didn't need sleep, I would have done it 24 hours a day." - Mark Weinstein [in reference to when he first entered the market.]
- "[The markets today are] the same as markets in the 19th century. The same things make markets go up and down." - James B. Rogers Jr.
- "Learn to take losses. The most important thing in making money is not letting your losses get out of hand. Also, don't increase your position size until you have doubled or tripled your capital. Most people make the mistake of increasing their bets as soon as they start making money. That is a quick way to get wiped out." - Marty Schwartz [this is related to my concept of intervals]
- "[Most traders who lose money] would rather lose money than admit they're wrong. What is the ultimate rationalization of a trader in a losing position? 'I'll get out when I'm even.' Why is getting out even so important? Because it protects **the ego.** I became a winning trader when I was able to say, 'To hell with my ego, making money is more important.'" - Marty Schwartz
- "I found a guy named Terry Laundry." - Marty Schwartz [in reference to the validity of the T-Theory going back nearly 25 years]
- "The conventional wisdom about how to make money in stocks is summarized by the semi-facetious advice: Buy Low sell high. David Ryan would disagree. His philosophy can be summarized as: Buy High Sell Higher." - Jack Schwager [echoing swing trading throughout this book]
- "**Diversification is a hedge for ignorance**. I think you are much better off owning a few stocks and knowing a great deal about them. By being very selective, you increase your chances of picking superior performers." - William O'Neil
- "Over the years I came to realize that the markets are inefficient." - Larry Hite
- "People don't change; that is why the whole game works. In 1637, tulips in Holland traded for 5,500 florins, and then crashed to 50, a 99% loss." - Larry Hite [in stating that large percentage returns or losses have always happened since the beginning of markets]
- "A lot of people would rather understand the market than make money." - Ed Seykota
- "Gut feel is important. If ignored, it may come out in subtle ways by coloring your logic. It can be dealt with through meditation and reflection to determine what's behind it. If it persists, then it might be a valuable **subconscious** analysis of some subtle information. Otherwise, it might be a dangerous sublimation of an inner desire for excitement and not reflect market conditions. Be sensitive to the subtle differences between 'intuition' and 'into wishing.'" - Ed Seykota
- "I feel success comes from my love for the markets. I am not a casual trader. It is my life. I have a passion for trading. It is not merely a hobby or even a career choice for me. There is

no question that this is what I am supposed to do with my life." - Ed Seykota
- "The key to long-term survival and prosperity has a lot to do with the money management techniques incorporated into the technical system. There are old traders and there are bold traders, but there are very few old, bold traders." - Ed Seykota
- "Don't focus on making money; focus on protecting what you have." - Paul Tudor Jones
- "The exact same thing happened in 1929, two days before the crash." - Paul Tudor Jones [reflecting on the parallels between the 1987 crash.]
- "I don't risk significant amounts of money in front of key reports, since that is gambling not trading." - Paul Tudor Jones
- "Trade small because that's when you are as bad as you are ever going to be. Learn from your mistakes. Don't be misled by the day-to-day fluctuations in your equity. Focus on whether what you are doing is right, not on the random nature of any single trade's outcome." - Richard Dennis
- "Trading decisions should be made as unemotionally as possible." - Richard Dennis
- "I've certainly done it – that is, made counter-trend initiations. However, as a rule of thumb, I don't think you should do it." - Richard Dennis
- "In the long run zero. Absolutely zero." - Richard Dennis [in reference to there being any luck in trading.]
- "A common mistake is to think of the market as a personal nemesis. The market, of course is totally impersonal; it doesn't care whether you make money or not. Whenever a trader says, 'I wish,' or 'I hope,' he is engaging in a destructive way of thinking because it takes attention away from the diagnostic process." - Bruce Kovner
- "Undertrade, Undertrade, Undertrade." - Bruce Kovner
- "We define the ranges we expect for each currency and what we will do if it breaks out of those ranges." - Bruce Kovener [essentially, swing trading.]
- "Bear markets have different characteristics than bull markets. Bear markets [have] very sharp down movements followed by quick retracements." - Bruce Kovner
- "Only to a limited extent [can trading skills be taught]. Over the years, I have tried to train perhaps thirty people, and only four or five of those have turned out to be good traders. [The other 25] are out of business, and it had nothing to do with intelligence." - Bruce Kovner
- "If trading is your life, it is a torturous kind of excitement [it is not fun]. But if you are **keeping your life in balance**, then it is fun. All of the successful traders I've seen that lasted in the business sooner or later got to that point. They have a balanced life; they have fun outside of trading. You can't sustain it if you don't have some other focus. Eventually, you wind up over-trading or getting excessively disturbed about temporary failures." - Michael Marcus
- "I think to be in the upper echelon of successful traders requires an innate skill, a gift. It's just like being a great violinist. But to be a competent trader and make money is a skill you can learn." - Michael Marcus
- "I was making 100 percent a year for years and years." - Michael Marcus
- "I think the secret is cutting down the number of trades you make. The best trades are the ones in which you have all three things going for you, fundamentals [revenue growth], technicals [Price Objectives from Price Theory], and market tone [trend]." - Michael Marcus

Amazingly, I have learned that Mr. Schwager has gone on to run a fund of hedge funds because he had access to many of the great hedge fund minds over the past several years. Now, in 2012, he has recently come out with a book entitled *Hedge Fund Wizards*. Apropos, I look forward to reading that book, but I feel that his first book is much more relevant to this text in proving that time and technology are irrelevant to trading. No, Schwager's text and the trader's comments therein serve as historic relevanc, which serves as testimony, in proving that the theories in this book existed back then and they exist today no matter how far technology or time has advanced.

As stated in the *Introduction,* for me, the pursuit of the knowledge that I have attained was the primary goal; money was always secondary. I needed to prove to myself that the market is not random in order to validate a trading methodology that can be used in any market, in any time frame, and in any stage of my life. This pursuit of knowledge cost me the life that I knew along with the family I expected to have. The attainment of what I have accomplished through my thousands of hours of study is a true mastery of one subject; the market. In a society that no longer cares about apprenticeships or masters of any given job because of the fact that people no longer work the same job for their entire lives; we have to remember that our human gifts are being eroded by the prevention of attaining mastership of one field of study. Therefore, people who commit to one job such as traders or doctors should be commended. The world must get back to being in a master/apprentice relationship if we are truly going to push to new limits with our humanity. Unfortunately, technology is now becoming a hindrance in my eyes. Instead of being able to remain focused on one specific task of tremendous importance, we are allowing our brains to constantly multitask, which is not what I believe our Creator had in store. Through creative-evolution, I can easily see that for the first time in humanity's history, we are moving towards a race-less society through the repopulating of mixed marriages, which is a great thing, but the question is, are we doing so while maintaining an emphasis on allowing the supreme genetic gifts of intelligence in order to be properly circulated throughout the gene pool? Unfortunately, I believe the opposite is happening because intelligent people choose to have only 1 or 2 children if any; in fact, I only want one or two myself, which arguably cheats humanity out of my additive intellectual genes, which adds to the debasing of intellectual evolution. Thus, I am part of the problem as well.

Unfortunately, instead of evolving to a new level of intellectual acuity that finally blurs the lines between race or color, we are simply mass producing lower intellects that are causing us to unsuccessfully balance the equation of resources. I mean no disrespect to anyone, but this is just my observation. More important, the tremendous amount of mental energy that I have used in order to construct this book would not have happened had I not been incarcerated. By being incarcerated, for the first time in my conscious life, I have been without the ever present computer or cell phone; In essence, I have been without interruption in order to let my intelligence manifest the thoughts and the ideas correlating the market as being nonrandom and a link to divinity. As such, it pains me every day that I am prevented from putting my mastership to work in order to make things right, but in some ways, I believe this phase of my life was somewhat necessary in order for me to recharge my mind and my body in order to adequately digest everything I have spent the last 12 years learning. Thus, this book, which I believe will serve as mandatory reading requirements for all traders in the future was only possible because of my incarceration, and that is the irony of life. Conclusively, now that this book has been written, when I get released from Federal prison, I will be able to logically and methodically trade the market for the first time since learning *Time and Price Symmetry,* and who knows (aside from God) what heights are in store for that proper implementation and execution.

Resources & Appendices

15 Interval Campaign at time of my Arrest Requires Brokerage with Low ES Margin Requirements

Interval #	Base Capital	Margin/Contract	Total Contracts	Goal Percent	ES Points Needed	Stop Loss %	Stop Loss (Points)	Capital Final
1	$22,000	$1,000	22	100%	20	80%	16	$44,000
2	$44,000	$1,000	44	100%	20	50%	10	$88,000
3	$88,000	$2,000	44	50%	20	33%	13	$132,000
4	$132,000	$2,000	66	50%	20	33%	13	$198,000
5	$198,000	$2,000	100	50%	20	33%	13	$297,000
6	$297,000	$2,000	150	50%	20	33%	13	$445,500
7	$445,500	$3,000	150	50%	30	33%	19	$668,250
8	$668,250	$3,000	224	50%	30	33%	19	$1,002,375
9	$1,002,375	$4,000	252	33%	27	25%	19	$1,333,159
10	$1,333,159	$4,000	334	33%	27	25%	19	$1,773,101
11	$1,773,101	$4,000	400	33%	30	25%	22	$2,358,225
12	$2,358,225	$5,896	400	33%	39	25%	29	$3,136,439
13	$3,136,439	$7,841	400	25%	40	20%	31	$3,920,548
14	$3,920,548	$9,801	400	25%	50	20%	39	$4,900,685
15	$4,900,685	$12,252	400	25%	62	20%	49	$6,125,857

Blue = Furthest Interval Reached in June of 2011
Intervals Get Easier Due to Size Constraints, Less Margin, and Larger Stop Allowances
Hardest Part of a Campaign is First 2 Intervals – I was Passed This Value!
$6.125mm would have made the TASK Investors and the Vigilant Investors whole

Days (est)	56.875
Months (est)	2.73

Two Month Campaign / Standard Margin for S&P E-Mini Futures Contract

Interval #	Base Capital	Margin/ Contract	Total Contracts	Goal Percent	ES Points Needed	Stop Loss %	Stop Loss (Points)	Capital Final
1	$15,000	$6,000	2	25%	38	66%	99	$18,750
2	$18,750	$6,000	2	25%	47	20%	37	$23,438
3	$23,438	$6,000	4	25%	30	20%	23	$29,297
4	$29,297	$6,000	4	25%	37	20%	29	$36,621
5	$36,621	$6,000	6	25%	31	20%	24	$45,776
6	$45,776	$6,000	8	25%	29	20%	22	$57,220
7	$57,220	$6,000	10	25%	29	20%	22	$71,526
8	$71,526	$6,000	12	25%	30	20%	23	$89,407
9	$89,407	$6,000	14	25%	32	20%	25	$111,759
10	$111,759	$6,000	18	25%	32	20%	24	$139,698
11	$139,698	$6,000	24	25%	30	20%	23	$174,623
12	$174,623	$6,000	30	25%	30	20%	23	$218,279
13	$218,279	$6,000	36	25%	31	20%	24	$272,848
14	$272,848	$6,000	46	25%	30	20%	23	$341,061
15	$341,061	$6,000	56	25%	31	20%	24	$426,326
16	$426,326	$6,000	72	25%	30	20%	23	$532,907
17	$532,907	$6,000	88	25%	31	20%	24	$666,134
18	$666,134	$6,000	112	25%	30	20%	23	$832,667
19	$832,667	$6,000	138	25%	31	20%	24	$1,040,834
20	$1,040,834	$6,000	174	25%	30	20%	23	$1,301,043
21	$1,301,043	$6,000	216	25%	31	20%	24	$1,626,303
22	$1,626,303	$6,000	272	25%	30	20%	23	$2,032,879
23	$2,032,879	$6,000	338	25%	31	20%	24	$2,541,099
24	$2,541,099	$6,353	400	25%	32	20%	25	$3,176,374
25	$3,176,374	$7,941	400	25%	40	20%	31	$3,970,467
26	$3,970,467	$9,926	400	25%	50	20%	39	$4,963,084
27	$4,963,084	$12,408	400	25%	63	20%	49	$6,203,855
28	$6,203,855	$15,510	400	25%	78	20%	62	$7,754,818
29	$7,754,818	$19,387	400	25%	97	20%	77	$9,693,523

* For Total Contracts, All Values Have Been Evenly Rounded, Which Violates Margin/Contract, but Intra-Day Margin Is 50% of Overnight Margin Anyway, So it Will not Effect Trading Ability or Trading Results

Days (est)   114.5
Mths (est)   5.496

Irrelevance of Performance #'s When Able to Employ Leverage

Account Size: $1,000,000.00

% Time in Market	% Trade Accuracy	Average Profit(Pts / trade)	Average Loss(Pts / trade)	Average Weekly Range	Expected Points	No Leverage ($60000/ contract)	$10,000 Margin (6:1)	$6000 Margin (10:1)	$1000 Margin (60:1)
75.00%	40.00%	3.0	1.5	40	9	0.75%	4.50%	7.50%	45.00%

Expected Points = (Expected Value of Profit – Expected Value of Loss) X Average Weekly Range X % of Time in Market
% Returns would be the percentage return per week

Interval Trading Size Calculation

Interval Value	% Return	% Drawdown	Profit Goal	Stop Loss	Current Profit/Loss	Risk Total	Remaining Profit	# of Trades	Stop (Pts)	Stop Amt / Trade	# Contracts	Points Remaining	Leverage/ Contract
$1,000,000.00	25.00%	20.00%	$250,000.00	$200,000.00	$0.00	$200,000.00	$250,000.00	10	1.25	$625.00	320	16	$3,125.00

Color Codes:
Blue: Refers to the Current Interval's Objectives and Trading Size
Gray: Refers to the Current Interval's Return/Drawdown and Leverage Requirements. Leverage Decreases if P/L Decreases
Green: Refers to Current P&L In Current Interval for Compounding on Profits / Contracting on Losses
Yellow: Refers to Trader Defined # of Trades Remaining and Value of Expected Stops before Exhausting Current Interval's Risk

Interval Trading Size Calculation

Interval Value	% Return	% Drawdown	Profit Goal	Stop Loss	Current Profit/Loss	Risk Total	Remaining Profit	# of Trades	Stop (Pts)	Stop Amt / Trade	# Contracts	Points Remaining	Leverage/ Contract
$1,000,000.00	25.00%	20.00%	$250,000.00	$200,000.00	$100,000.00	$300,000.00	$150,000.00	10	1.25	$625.00	480	7	$2,291.67

Color Codes:
Blue: Refers to the Current Interval's Objectives and Trading Size
Gray: Refers to the Current Interval's Return/Drawdown and Leverage Requirements. Leverage Decreases if P/L Decreases
Green: Refers to Current P&L In Current Interval for Compounding on Profits / Contracting on Losses
Yellow: Refers to Trader Defined # of Trades Remaining and Value of Expected Stops before Exhausting Current Interval's Risk

Interval Trading Size Calculation

Interval Value	% Return	% Drawdown	Profit Goal	Stop Loss	Current Profit/Loss	Risk Total	Remaining Profit	# of Trades	Stop (Pts)	Stop Amt / Trade	# Contracts	Points Remaining	Leverage/ Contract
$1,000,000.00	25.00%	20.00%	$250,000.00	$200,000.00	-$100,000.00	$100,000.00	$350,000.00	10	1.25	$625.00	160	44	$5,625.00

Color Codes:
Blue: Refers to the Current Interval's Objectives and Trading Size
Gray: Refers to the Current Interval's Return/Drawdown and Leverage Requirements. Leverage Decreases if P/L Decreases
Green: Refers to Current P&L In Current Interval for Compounding on Profits / Contracting on Losses
Yellow: Refers to Trader Defined # of Trades Remaining and Value of Expected Stops before Exhausting Current Interval's Risk

Time Cycle Shift

High / Low Beginning Date	Days/Year	Cycle Value	Shifted Terminal Date
Fri, Mar 6, 09	365.25	2.15	Sat, Apr 30, 11

* In displaying dates, it is useful to see the day of the week by formatting the cell
** Spreadsheets can simply take a date and add a value to it for a new date!
*** Terminal Date = High/Low date + Days per Year * Cycle Value

Appendix: How to Always Beat the Market

Let's face it, you bought this book for one reason, which was to learn how to always beat the market in order to make money. Therefore, if you are a casual investor/trader/money manager/etc. that picked up this book and that flipped to the last page, I am here to give you the simplest possible strategy that will always make you money and will beat every hedge fund, every mutual fund, and *almost* every trader over the long run by using Klatch's Price Theory and Klatch's Marketome Theory.

To begin, I am hopeful that you have read through the theories and that you understand that under inflationary monetary policy, markets have objectives to always make new all-time highs. If that's the case, then, going long an index ETF (unleveraged) will *always* yield price appreciation. That is where this "System" begins, and I hope to instill the ease of the markets if you remain disciplined.

Simply put, the easiest way to beat the market and almost every market participant is simply to buy an index-mirroring instrument every time that index has pulled back 4% from its latest all-time high. Then, after entering the position, you can set automatic orders to liquidate your positions every time that previous high was exceeded by 3%. This means that you are making a 7% gain on your funds, guaranteed!

Now, imagine this… imagine that the markets have become only mildly volatile, and have pulled back 4% (or more) and have rallied to new highs several times over the past 5 years. Let's assume this occurs four per year. If that's the case, then, in five year's, you've pocketed twenty, 7% chunks. If you've compounded that, well, then, you can do the math.

In closing, that's not all. If we take the market's absolute drawdown over the last fifty years, which of course is the 2008 crash (let's just say 60%). Well, that means that we can actually use some leverage in our calculations. You can use a combination of Ultra ETFs, options, futures, etc. that all have the objective of reaching new all-time highs, and as long as your stay long, you will never lose money. I do not think it is possible fo rme to explain it any simpler, and I ask you to always remember that "The Market is not Random."

Printed in Great Britain
by Amazon.co.uk, Ltd.,
Marston Gate.